THE LIFE AND DEATH OF
ANCIENT CITIES

THE LIFE
AND
DEATH
OF
ANCIENT CITIES

A NATURAL HISTORY

GREG WOOLF

OXFORD
UNIVERSITY PRESS

OXFORD
UNIVERSITY PRESS

Oxford University Press is a department of the University of Oxford. It furthers
the University's objective of excellence in research, scholarship, and education
by publishing worldwide. Oxford is a registered trade mark of Oxford University
Press in the UK and certain other countries.

Published in the United States of America by Oxford University Press
198 Madison Avenue, New York, NY 10016, United States of America.

Library of Congress Cataloging-in-Publication Data
Names: Woolf, Greg, author.
Title: The life and death of ancient cities : a natural history / Greg Woolf.
Description: First edition. | New York : Oxford University Press, [2020] |
Includes index. |
Identifiers: LCCN 2019042392 (print) | LCCN 2019042393 (ebook) |
ISBN 9780199946129 (hardback) | ISBN 9780190618568 (epub)
Subjects: LCSH: Cities and towns, Ancient—Mediterranean Region. |
Urbanization—Mediterranean Region—History—To 1500. |
Imperialism—Social aspects—Mediterranean Region—History—To 1500.
Classification: LCC HT114.W66 2020 (print) |
LCC HT114 (ebook) | DDC 307.760937—dc23
LC record available at https://lccn.loc.gov/2019042392
LC ebook record available at https://lccn.loc.gov/2019042393

1 3 5 7 9 8 6 4 2

Printed by LSC Communications, United States of America

For Maud and Ben,
with love, admiration, and gratitude

Contents

PART IV: DE-URBANIZATION

List of Illustrations

Figures

Maps

Preface

The ancient world is often celebrated for its cities. This book is not another celebration. Instead it tells the story of how late cities appeared in the ancient Mediterranean world, how small most of them were, and how precarious urban life remained throughout antiquity.

Ancient cities have become grandiose in our imagination. There are several reasons for this. We remain spellbound by the neoclassical monuments of modern metropoleis, many of them capitals of recent empires, like Paris and London, Washington and Berlin, St Petersburg, Madrid and Rio. The ancient world inspired those architectures but was built on a much smaller scale. Our habit of seeing the ancient world through the eyes of its most educated inhabitants, who for centuries were committed to an urban ideal, has not helped. The authors of Greek and Latin literatures were themselves ignorant of how their urban world had arisen, and they projected back into their past a world of grand cities that never really existed. Troy VII was a splendid fortress by the standards of the late Bronze Age, but it covered barely 20 hectares and probably had a population of 5,000 to 10,000 people. The Rome in which Virgil wrote the *Aeneid* covered nearly 1,800 hectares and had nearly 1,000,000 inhabitants. No wonder their accounts of early first millennium were so anachronistic.

Rome was exceptional. Research conducted over the last thirty years has made clear the tiny scale of most ancient cities. That research has brought together many disciplines. Archaeologists have laboured to date and map early settlements, often disentangling them from the accumulated matter of their successors, and locating them in broader settled landscapes and at the nodes of complicated networks of exchange and migration. Philologists have read ancient texts more and more closely, putting aside modern assumptions about their meaning, looking more closely at their rhetorical and political agenda. Historians have compared ancient Greek and Roman cities with those of other societies from the time before industrial revolutions and demographic transitions changed everything. Most recently historians have engaged with the life sciences, which have taught us so much in recent years about the human animal, about the primate bases of our social life, about ecology and climate. Our new understandings of antiquity depend on a collaboration between the humanities and social science and biology. This book is an attempt to show what that collaboration has achieved so far in relation to ancient cities.

This book begins broad and narrows down in focus. The first part looks at the prehistory of urban growth across the world and follows developments in one corner of it—the Ancient Near East—to the end of the Bronze Age. Mediterranean urbanism was an offshoot of those developments, and a late growth at that. The second part tracks the emergence and growth of urban networks around the Mediterranean Sea in the first half of the last millennium B.C.E. Some villages were replaced by tiny cities, and the landscapes and societies they organized became connected. The third part follows more brutal histories of connection, the rise of empires and with them the first really great cities of the region. A short fourth part sketches a kind of reversion, in which horizons narrowed and great cities shrank. But cities never disappeared completely, nor the ideas and technologies created in their construction. Those ideas, technologies, and often the actual physical remains of great cities would be recycled in Byzantium, in the Caliphate, and in tiny mediaeval capitals in the west like Aachen, providing material for a whole series of postclassical urbanisms, some of which would be exported to other continents.

The story of ancient Mediterranean urbanism is one episode among many that make up our species' urban adventure. Over the last six thousand years, humans have laboured to build cities right around the planet. Cities have been invented several times quite independently, and the results have been surprisingly similar. This is why the broader picture presented in the first part of this book is so important. The first chapters explore what we have in common as a species and argue that we are unusually—but not quite uniquely—well suited to city life. Some species of animal have evolved to make the most of urban life. Our species is preadapted to it; that is, there are some features of us, features that appeared for quite other reasons, that can be co-opted to make us urban animals. Only by understanding that can we understand the highs and lows of urbanism in the ancient Mediterranean world.

This story could have been told in a variety of ways, and I considered several alternatives before beginning work. One conventional technique is to build a narrative around a series of case studies, something like Knossos, Mycenae, Athens, Syracuse, and so on. *A History of Antiquity in a Hundred Cities* would have some attractions, bringing out the differences in architectures and planning, providing a scaffolding around which to retell accounts of foundations and sieges, fires and plagues, imperial rebuilding, and so on. But it would inevitably have directed attention to the largest, the most glamorous, and best documented examples—and therefore the most unusual and least typical of cities. A sequence of cases studies might also have obscured the passage of time. Many ancient cities were very ancient indeed. Athens has been continuously occupied for nearly four thousand years. Rome, Naples, Marseilles, and Alexandria are still great cities today, all well over two thousand years old. The history of Mediterranean urbanism is not a succession of cities, but a succession of urban worlds in each of which some of the same cities played key roles. Another approach would have begun from a series of types: the Greek City, the Etruscan City, the early Roman colony, and so on. There have been some successful books of this kind, including the Italian classic *Storia dell'Urbanistica*, but my attention is more sociological than architectural. Least attractive was the idea of simply retelling a familiar historical narrative, while emphasizing the presence of cities. Political history does not take centre place in this story. For much of the time considered there were no states, no governments, no politicians, and no citizens. Individuals will make the occasional appearance, but mostly this is the story of human communities, of the human animal and its companion species.

This book has an explicitly evolutionary agenda. I shall return to what I see as the advantages of this approach along the way, and I shall leave it to readers to decide at the end how useful the approach has turned out. But I should say at the start what I mean by this. Urbanism has recently become a central part of the experience of the human species, and cities have become one of our species' favoured niches. By recently I mean in the last 10,000 years—that is, for the greater part of the Holocene Period, which began with the latest retreat of the glaciers. Evolutionary theory offers a way to understand change as the result of selective pressure operating on a species, or part of one. Members of a species, and groups within in, vary in all sorts of ways, including how they live. Ways of life that resulted in populations multiplying were, under these selective pressures, likely to spread. As a shorthand we say these advantageous traits were selected *for*, but properly speaking less competitive traits were selected against. The central argument of the first part of this book is that our species has a number of traits that incidentally make us good at living in cities, and that city life has turned out to give those who pursue it an advantage over those who do not. The city-dwelling humans have, over the last millennia, squeezed out, dominated, and replaced many of the others.

This does not mean we have to live in cities. Evolutionists admit no design, no destiny, no fate. At present it looks as if our species has existed for around 300,000 years, and we have been building and inhabiting cities for maybe 3 per cent of that period. Even in the Holocene, most humans have not lived in cities. Yet in recent millennia living in cities has turned out to be a solution to a wide range of problems. Living together in one place has brought security, economies of scale, and new opportunities for specialization and accumulation. The world most readers live in, with its vast range of specialized manufactures, its amenities, its epic levels of connection, is unthinkable without cities. Living together in cities also has costs and brings new risks of its own. The argument of the remainder of this book is that the particular ecology of the Mediterranean Basin makes urbanism a more risky strategy there than in many other environments. The solution found (selected for) was that most cities had to remain small. Exceptions to that rule required exceptional support, and this almost always meant impe- rialism. When empires failed, the larger cities became more precarious and eventually shrank.

There are complications of course, many of them, but two I need to mention right now.

The first is that evolutionary change is rarely reversible. It is true that not all human societies have urbanized even today, and in this sense we can speak of different options that remain, and of paths not taken. But the changes generated by urbanization are so profound that they cannot easily be undone except in a catastrophic fashion. A simple example is demogra- phy. Urbanization allows populations to rise dramatically in size, but they cannot easily be dispersed back into the countryside, not just because the population levels are now higher than before urbanization took place, but also because the preurban countryside that sustained earlier modes of living is not there any more. Urbanization transforms all aspects of a society, all parts of a connected landscape. Even ancient urbanisms had the power to reduce forest cover and plant and animal biodiversity, to change the soils (pedology) and water supplies (hydrology) of a region. Cities are just the most visible sites of accumulation of new more complex social orders. This

nonreversibility is much more acute now than in the past, since the proportion of the population who live in modern cities is so much greater.

The second complication is that unlike most living species, humans consciously make plans and set about implementing them. For some historians
and archaeologists this used to be thought of as a good reason *not* to use
evolutionary theory for recent human experience. The idea was that if our
ancestors had responded to selective pressures with physiological changes,
more recently we responded with quicker technological or cultural changes.
Others framed this as cultural evolution taking over from biological evolution. If the climate was colder other animals might develop thicker hair
or change their body shape, but we would develop clothing, for example.
It is now clear that this idea is too simple, perhaps even the latest version
of the Romantic and Biblical idea that humans are in some fundamental
ways quite different to other animals. It is now clear that early humans'
relationship to technology is millions of years old. Our physical evolution
as a species is bound up with technological evolution, and human history is
entangled with a history of things. Besides this, we continue to adapt phys-
iologically to our environment. Most of the variations in skin colour, hair
type, and height and body shape between human populations today, at least
outside Africa, have appeared during the last 100,000 to 50,000 years as we
have expanded our range across the planet. There is evidence of adaption to
extreme environments among peoples as remote as the Inuit of the Arctic
and the inhabitants of the Tibetan plateau. Some adaptions, such as the ability to drink milk in adulthood, have spread in the few thousand years since
domestication. All this means that treating humans as if they are immune to
evolutionary pressures is a mistake.

Selective pressures operate on any feature of a population that influences
its ability to reproduce. That variation might be a matter of biology—the
shape of haemoglobin cells, for example—or it might be behavioural. Eating
meat, having large families, and building cities are all behavioural traits, and
selective pressures operate on all of them. It is true that some patterns of
behaviour are the result of deliberate plans. Some cities show a high degree
of planning. Others seems to have emerged organically as a product of many
convergent patterns of change. The selective pressures don't care whether
the variation was driven by genes or generals. Things that work survive
and spread, things that do not will fail. Evolution continues to explain the
differential success of various human traits, whether those of biological in
origin (like hair colour) or cultural (like the decision to live together in one

place). And selection is blind. No evolutionary forces directed humans into cities nor determined the path they would follow.

It is always tempting, when telling a story, to use hindsight and pick out the first appearance of this or that innovation that would later turn out to be important. I have tried to be a good evolutionist, to note the paths that led elsewhere or even nowhere, as well as those that led to urban foundations. I have tried too to remember that the explorers, traders, craftsmen, chieftains, navigators, generals, and kings had no more idea of where history was heading than we do today. Ancient Mediterranean urbanism emerged from their activities, but it was never planned. The Greeks sometimes imagined that we travel backwards into the future, watching the past recede but blind as to what lies ahead. This is a good image for the historian, and I have tried to keep it in mind.

Acknowledgements

I spent much of the nineties teaching at the University of Oxford, where I had done my first degree before moving to Cambridge for graduate study and a postdoc. Coming back felt strange in all sorts of ways, and among other things I discovered I was no longer the ancient historian who had left there. I was still fascinated by Greeks and Romans (especially the latter), but a range of different experiences had broadened my interests to include other cultures. My research had become more focused on archaeological material and that, together with some inspirational supervisors, had also led me to think in a broader, more comparative way about the past. So it was enormously good fortune to be back in Oxford just when the University launched a new degree in archaeology and anthropology, the first time either subject had been taught at the undergraduate level. The plan—a good one—was not to marry two half-degrees, but to encourage students to constantly make the connections for themselves in almost every paper. It succeeded fabulously. It was for that degree I started to lecture and teach comparative urbanism, to think about state-formation and imperialism in world perspective, and to try to marry an environmental perspective with an historical one. There is a sense in which this book grew out of those experiences. Many of the team involved in that project had a huge influence on my work. Those lucky enough to have known one of them, Andrew Sherratt, will catch glimpses of his jovial ghost between these pages. Intellectually curious, forever turning up new things to read and argue about, endlessly enthusiastic and enormously good fun, he is missed by many of us. This book would have been much better if I could have argued about it with him for a little longer.

The text itself has been written largely in the Institute of Classical Studies in the School of Advanced Study of the University of London. Directing the ICS has been a huge privilege. At the heart of all we do there is an extraordinary library, run by the University and the Hellenic and Roman Societies in partnership, provided not just with fantastic collections but also with a marvellous specialist staff. I owe it and them a great deal. Sections were also composed on research stays abroad, at the University of Carlos III and the library of the German Archaeological Institute of Madrid, in the École Normale Supérieure of the rue d'Ulm at Paris and at the Max Weber Kolleg of the University of Erfurt, where I have been fortunate to be an associate fellow. Jaime Alvar Esquerra was my host in Madrid, thanks to a Catedra de Excelencia funded by the Banco de Santander; Anca Dan and Stéphane Verger were my hosts for the LABEX TransferS fellowship in Paris; and Jörg Rüpke welcomed me on many occasions in Erfurt. I am very grateful to them all, and to many other colleagues during those stays. At Paris I had the chance to lecture on the theme of this book. Earlier versions were given at the British School at Rome, thanks to the kindness of then-director Christopher Smith, and at the University of São Paulo at the invitation of Carlos Machado and Norberto Guarinello. Ian Morris and Arjan Zuiderhoek read the whole text and improved it considerably with their comments. All mistakes and misconceptions remain my own.

Ideas are one thing. Creating a book out of them is another. Stefan Vranka at OUP New York helped me design the project and has been there at every stage. Only those lucky enough to have been edited by him will understand how great a contribution he makes when he adopts a book. Georgina Capel has been the best of agents. Thank you all.

PART
I

An Urban Animal

I

To the City

The Long View

We are embarked on an urban adventure.

Numbers fail to capture the enormity of change, but they are impressive all the same. As I write these words there are seven point seven billion of us on this planet.[1] One half of us already live in cities. By the end of this century, that figure will probably reach 75 per cent. Cities are growing so fast that it is difficult to keep count. One recent estimate lists nearly a thousand metropolitan areas that each have at least half a million inhabitants. The United Nations' latest survey of World Urbanization Prospects lists 33 megacities—cities with more than 10 million inhabitants each.[2]

What counts as a city? The answer (and the definitions used in those reports) varies from place to place. In Nicaragua a settlement with street lights and electricity is a city, even if it has only 1,000 inhabitants. Japan sets the threshold at 50,000. Some definitions stipulate that a city must have a continuous built-up area, that a certain proportion of its population must earn their living in ways other than farming, or that the settlement must have some formal legal existence or administrative function. And where does one city end and the next begin? Cities are merging into other cities on the Atlantic and Pacific seaboards of the United States, in the Dutch Randstad, and in the Greater Tokyo Area. Some geographers prefer to speak of metropolitan areas, their populations running up into the tens of millions.

Such giant cities did not exist in antiquity anywhere in the world. In fact until the eighteenth century even cities of a million people were rare. It is not easy to define a city in terms that will satisfy everyone even in relation to the preindustrial age. This question will crop up again in a few chapters in the context of the notion of an "urban revolution," but if might be useful to sketch a provisional definition now, so that the term "city" can be used clearly.

A city is one variety of nucleated settlement. For most of human history we have not settled in a permanent place for the simple reason that very few environments are rich enough in natural resources to support a population of fishers, gatherers, and hunters all the year round. Most preagricultural populations were mobile. The had temporary, seasonal settlements of course, and sometimes settlements where some of the population would live for long periods while others were off hunting. Comanche villages of the eighteenth and nineteenth centuries are a good example. The peoples who hunted mammoths in the last Pleistocene era built great structures from their bones which, if not settlements, were central places of a sort. This raises another complication: that we often write as if human landscapes were organized mainly around residences, but some places were important for other reasons such as hunting, burial, or worship. These places all feature in the lineage of cities, but are not cities themselves.

A city is more than a village. Most agriculturalists lived close to their crops. Because agriculture has often allowed populations to rise, these settlements often became quite large. Finding a way to distinguish a large village from a small city is genuinely difficult. Size does not work as a criterion. Many Neolithic villages were much larger than some later cities. It is difficult to imagine a village of 100,000 or a million people, and when we write of a "global village" we understand that this is a paradox, a hyperbolic claim that distance has been so collapsed by modern communications that we are all close neighbours. But even if we could agree on an upper limit in size for a village, it is less easy to set the minimum size for a city. Over the course of this book it will emerge that most of the cities of the Roman world had populations smaller than the village of Çatalhöyük did in seventh millennium B.C.E. Anatolia. Even bigger Neolithic villages are known from prehistoric Europe, like Talianki in the Ukraine that in the fourth millennium B.C.E. covered hundreds of hectares and may have had a population of 15,000. Size is not everything. We need other criteria of urbanism.

Cities are more complicated social worlds than villages.[3] If one of our early farmers were to walk through one of the world's first cities she or he would immediately notice that there were more *kinds* of buildings and more *kinds* of spaces than at home. Domestic architecture was more varied: some houses were bigger or more elaborate than others, meaning some families were richer or more powerful than others. Some stood out by their size, some by their design or decoration or the materials in which they were constructed. The details varied from one culture to another, but early cities all expressed the sense of a social world that advertised differences between urban residents. The same applied to their funerals and the mounds or monuments that marked the resting places of the privileged.

Most of the cities discussed in this book also had public buildings and religious precincts. Some had town halls, law courts, or palaces, often taller than other buildings, or else constructed on natural or artificial mounds so the population took them as landmarks as they moved around. One very common feature seems to have been the creation of large open spaces, passages, and views that displayed the city to the gaze of its inhabitants. Elaborate assembly spaces—landscaped valleys, circuses, great plazas—allowed immense crowds to participate whether in sacrifices, drama, performances, or debates. Teotihuacan had its great processional way, Greek cities their theatres, while the pyramids of the Aztecs and the Maya served the same function as the ziggurats of Mesopotamia, providing great platforms on which the crowds could watch their priests and rulers approach the gods. Early cities brought together the spatial and monumental complexity of megalithic ritual sites with the dense sedentary settlement of Neolithic villages. Cities were at once monumental *and* residential, sites of mundane sedentary life *and* sites of extraordinary political spectacle. The same kind of calendars that had once periodically assembled and then dispersed scattered rural populations to worship the gods now organized urban time, declaring holidays, carnival, Mardi Gras. Cities had become stages for performing a more complicated social order. Their spectacular monumentality advertised that new order as Civilization. Almost all urban societies had a concept like our concept of civilization, one that reflected their sense of superiority over other peoples.

Alongside these monuments most ancient cities had a range of other less flashy structures that are rarely found in cities. These included workshops, fuller's yards, warehouses, smithies, potteries and breweries, marketplaces and shops: together they reveal a more subtle transformation of society. The urban world was not only divided into rulers and ruled, but also by occupation; it included many varieties of craft-workers and service providers, all supported by the fruit of others' farming. Once permanent market structures appear, we may presume there is a population that buys food every day. That means they needed to earn money to do so. Bronze Age cities had no money and perhaps not much retail, but there was trade and exchange. The fundamental difference between a city and a village is that a city is based on a different kind of solidarity. Cities have that organic solidarity based on the cooperation of those with complementary skills. Villages have a mechanical solidarity based on cooperation between agriculturalists with similar values and similar skills. This is a little schematic of course, but brings out a fundamental point: urban life is based on social differentiation, on inequality, on a division of labour to the extent village life, even in quite large villages, is not.

It follows that cities are not just places: they are the most visible physical manifestations of deeper and wider changes in society. When archaeologists began to compile checklists of things that were typically urban, many related to this new level of specialization within society and to the new inequalities this included. Not only were there priests and generals and kings, but there were workers sustained by the rulers. Carving a seal stone of the kind known from early Mesopotamia or the Indus Valley took enormous amounts of skill and then enormous amounts of effort. Apprenticeship—the time to work on seals, food and accommodation while one did so, and the rare and exotic substances used—all depended on some kind of sponsor, whether a king or a patron or someone who seems to be a bit of both. We could say the same about the craftsmen who perfected the art of casting the great bronze vessels of the earliest Chinese cities. Other items on the lists included writing and monuments, fine art and literature, science and mathematics. These too depended on freeing some individuals from the need to work the fields. Underpinning all of this was inequality.[4]

If at first sight these early cities look like little islands of complexity in a sea of sameness, this is an illusion. Walk out of the fourth-millennium Mesopotamian city of Uruk and soon one was back in the flat fields where everyone was a farmer and most lived in tiny squat villages with no ziggurats and no mighty walls. Yet when a society has cities in it, everywhere else has changed too. The villages are no longer self-sufficient small worlds, but are parts of a more comprehensive social order. The farmers no longer grow crops only for themselves and their neighbours, but send some of it away. Some will also have to be soldiers now and again, fighting far from home. And their household gods are no longer the centre of the cosmos.

Cities are different from villages in another way too. They are more connected to wider worlds and distant places. The surpluses produced by villagers did not just sustain their urban rulers but were used by them as the base of vast webs of exchange. Later chapters will introduce the exchange networks that linked Bronze Age Mesopotamia to Afghanistan, northwest India, and Anatolia, and that connected Mexican Teotihuacan to the jungles of the Yucatan peninsular and the steppe of the American Southwest. The complex social web most densely woven in city centres stretches out across the countryside, linking one city to another and enmeshing everyone else within it. Cities were not only nodes in this network: they were also key components of the hardware through which information, as well as people and their possessions, were moved. Cities were hubs that accumulated all kinds of centrality—administrative, religious, economic.

The Mediterranean Story

Most of this book concerns a smaller portion of the urban planet, a world anchored on the coasts and islands of the Mediterranean Sea. The rise and fall of ancient urban systems was contained with the last millennium B.C.E. and the first C.E. But in order to understand the context within which those cities were created, it is necessary to take a detour through prehistory. Before doing so I offer this short summary of what will follow.

The Iron Age Mediterranean was explored, settled, and connected by Phoenicians, Greeks, Etruscans, and a few of their neighbours during the first centuries of the last millennium B.C.E. On their travels they found few cities and indeed there were almost none in the Mediterranean world around 1000 B.C.E. Over the next few centuries this changed. The world came to be bound together by ever denser networks of migration and exchange. Those dense webs of connections eventually stretched across the islanded Aegean from what is now Turkey to what is now Greece. Long sea routes connected Tyre (in the Levant) to the Straits of Gibraltar via Sicily and North Africa, Sardinia, Malta, and the Balearic Isles. These routes ramified—put out branches—and joined up. Where they crossed—at the nodes or vertices of these networks—some of the first Mediterranean urban settlements appeared. At first they were not very like the monumental cities of the Bronze Age Near East, but they helped anchor the emerging network and more traffic flowed across it. By the middle of the last millennium there were few places in the Mediterranean world more than a day's sail from a city. By 300 B.C.E. a few of the biggest cities had already won and lost micro-empires. Kingdoms and empires expanded over these urban networks, using their connections and depriving them of their autonomy. By the turn of the millennia the Roman Empire had engulfed all its predecessors, and was busy seeding cities in the wilds of woodland Europe, on the fringe of the deserts of Syria and Libya, on the upland plateaux of Asia Minor, and in the steep valleys of the Alps. Many of the sites they chose were failures, but enough succeeded to expand the system. Then—after a few centuries during which traffic between cities hummed back and forth from the Atlantic and the North Sea to the Persian Gulf and the Baltic—everything went into reverse. Most cities shrank. A few were abandoned altogether, or stopped being cities. In many places urban monuments were dismantled to make walls or houses. Gardens were planted in the vacant lots of contracting metropoleis. Continental trade networks that had once carried stone and grain and wine and oil for thousands of miles retracted back to the Mediterranean coastline. The greatest sea vessels were decommissioned. Mass movement of commodities reverted to a commerce in luxuries. Harbours silted up and were left undredged. All this began before Rome's western provinces were ceded to Germanic tribes, and long before Arab armies assassinated the Persian Empire and captured Syria and Egypt, Asia Minor and North Africa, Spain and Sicily in the first years of the eighth century C.E.

This spectacular story of the growth and withering away of ancient Mediterranean urbanism is often drowned out by the noise of the rise and fall of the Roman Empire. But this is different story, and its timing is different too. Cities began to grow and connect when Rome was just a cluster of villages. And at its height, in the second and third centuries C.E., the ancient urban system stretched far beyond the political limits of empire. Traders, missionaries, and diplomats travelled through the caravan cities of northern Syria and Iraq to connect with ancient Greek cities, by then lying in the heart of the Persian Empire, in Babylonia (now southern Iraq), and even Afghanistan. Others set sail down the Red Sea in search of the entrepôts of East Africa, southern India, and Sri Lanka, or traded down the Nile beyond Egypt to Nubia. Amber was brought from the Baltic and ivory from south of the Sahara long before Rome's imperial adventure got off the ground. Ancient historians and geographers like Herodotus, Strabo, Pliny, and Ptolemy knew there were yet even more distant cities, in central Asia and among the distant Silk People of China.

Even in the darkest period of economic and political collapse, the chain of urban societies that stretched across the Old World was never broken.[5] It already existed in the Bronze Age. The oldest cities on the planet were created in the fourth millennium B.C.E., first in Mesopotamia and Egypt and soon elsewhere in Eurasia. Mediterranean urbanism was a late out-growth of a much older tradition, and was always more dynamic in the east. Latest to appear—and first to fail—were the cities of the western and northern fringes of the Roman world. For most of the period described in this book the largest cities of the Near East were far bigger than those of the Mediterranean. After Rome, Baghdad would dwarf the remnant cities of the early mediaeval west.

An Urban Mirage

Yet open any book on the glory that was Greece or the splendour that was Rome and you will be told that the ancient world was "a world of cities." If you wander through any of today's great capitals, especially in Europe or the eastern seaboard of the United States, you will see endless visual references to classical urban architecture. Piazzas recall the Roman forums and neoclassical churches mimic ancient temples. Civic buildings built in the nineteenth century often have great pediments supported by columns and approaches by monumental staircases. The British Museum (see Figure 1) designed in 1823 and completed in 1852 is a case in point, and so is the Philadelphia Museum of Art (see Figure 2) chartered in 1876 and completed in 1928. As it happens the ancient world had no museums or city halls or banks in a modern sense, but the Victorians built them as if they were palaces and houses of the gods. The same was true around the world. The Capitol Building in Washington, DC corresponds to no ancient structure: Athenian assemblies met in the open air, and the Roman Senates in temples. Right up until the middle of the twentieth century, some of our greatest cities spoke almost uniquely in a classical dialect: their centres were dominated by massive structures, built in marble and travertine and granite, and they raised up their great facades before wide horizontal vistas. The National Gallery in London towers over Trafalgar Square with its stat-ues and lions and great basins. Not until the invention of skyscrapers and the mastery of steel, concrete, and glass did we learn to imagine great cities except as larger versions of classical ones.

The reasons for the dominance of classical urban style are well understood. The latest and most intense phase of our species' headlong rush to urbanism is only two or three centuries old. During that period European empires dominated the globe, and they did so spellbound by Roman antecedents.[6]

Figure 1 The British Museum in London
Federico Julien / Alamy Stock Photo

Figure 2 The Philadelphia Museum of Art
Phil Degginger / Alamy Stock Photo

The British built great Victorian cities in India and Australia. The young American Republic looked to Roman politics and Greek architecture. Across Europe the proceeds of nation-building and colonialism were lavished on the redevelopment of Berlin and Paris, Brussels and Madrid, erasing early modern and mediaeval cityscapes and replacing them with marble just as Augustus boasted he had done in Rome.

The truth is that ancient Mediterranean urbanism was far less grandiose than its modern imitations. The greatest Roman buildings hardly compared with the civic architecture of nineteenth-century industrial towns; the early modern architecture of London or Amsterdam is on a grander scale than that of most classical cities. Indeed it is possible to follow this trend back further. The most impressive ruins in Athens are Roman imperial structures, not those built by the classical democracy, even though Roman Athens was a rather dignified provincial city while the Athens of Pericles ruled an empire. Likewise, Rome of the emperors more or less obliterated the visible traces of the Republican city that had gone before, just as Napoleon III's architect Haussmann obliterated most of mediaeval Paris in the 1850s and 1860s.

There is no mystery about all this change in scale. Technological advances and economic growth explain why the biggest Roman structures dwarfed those of classical Greece, and also why neither could compete with the grand civic architecture of the industrial age or the monuments set up by European empires that straddled the globe. And besides, there were so many fewer people in those days. During the second century C.E. there were perhaps one billion people on earth, more likely rather fewer. If 75 per cent of us will soon live in cities, around the same proportion of them lived on the land, in villages, hamlets, or scattered farms. This is why ancient cities were—by modern standards—very small indeed. Even at the high point of classical urbanism, when there were maybe two thousand cities in the territory of the Roman Empire, around three-quarters of them had no more than five thousand inhabitants. Many of the inhabitants of classical cities were themselves farmers, working fields and orchards just beyond the city limits, or even gardens right in the centre of town.

For the longest time historians of classical antiquity have been spellbound by the grandiose rhetoric of ancient writers. Epic poetry, drama, and rhetoric took the centrality of the city for granted; *urbanitas* (literally "city-ness") is Latin for a certain kind of cultural sophistication, and the Greeks called their states *poleis,* which is the origin of our term "politics." When early Christian writers called the polytheists country folk (*pagani*) (hence our pagans), it was a dismissive label. As long as we knew antiquity mostly through literary creations composed by and for the wealthy, we accepted their valuation of city and country. The cult of ruins that emerged in the Renaissance, and the cities that formed staging posts on the Grand Tour, all encouraged the idea of antiquity as a world of monuments. But most ancient cities were not like Rome and Athens, and they were never as grand as they were imagined by Enlightenment scholars and Romantics. Only in the last few decades have archaeologists and historians come to realize just how small-scale classical cities really were.[7]

Besides, it suited the interests of many to build up the ancient and make it "classical." Long before the Grand Tour took young gentlemen to visit classical sites, they had been indoctrinated by the prejudices of a class for whom urban life was the same as civilized life. Their study, their mastery of obscure languages, and their experience of the wider world marked them out a members of a ruling élite. The common experience of antiquity (or rather its traces) bound the ruling classes together, made them feel themselves aesthetically and culturally superior to the rest. When Europeans acquired empires Rome provided a vocabulary, a set of visual symbols, and a bundle of slogans, quotations and half-memories out of which to fashion an imperial civilization. Classicism served fascist parties in the twentieth century. The stages on which the superiority of "Western Civilization" would be performed, in marches and parades, with spectacular monuments to victory and learning, had to be imperial cities.[8]

The word "civilization" was itself not coined until the end of the eighteenth century. It sums up the ideals of Enlightenment scholars, an account of the world they wanted to build and imagined they were rebuilding. "Civility" was an older term, describing the character of a citizen (rather than a peasant). During the colonization of the New World it was opposed to the barbarism of the indigenous peoples. Barbarian is another classical idea: first of all the Greeks' word for those who did not share their language and values, then a Roman term for peoples thought of as halfway between beasts and educated men. Look back down this genealogy and we can see how the ideas of urbanity, civilization, metropolitan sophistication, and the rest all became to be represented by classicizing idealizations of the city .[9]

It is an historical accident that Greek and Roman images of empire still lie at the heart of so many modern cities. Our species' urban adventure has many roots, in the valleys of Mexico and the jungles of the Yucatan, in the

Sahel region south of the Sahara and at Great Zimbabwe, as well as in the valleys of the Tigris and the Euphrates, the Yellow and Yangtze Rivers, and along the Nile. Perhaps by the end of the twenty-first century one or so of these other architectural idioms will have replaced the classical, suitably presented in the materials of the day.

This book offers a more sober account of the rise of cities around the ancient Mediterranean Sea. It is based less on the literature produced by those who ruled them, and more on their material remains and on the documents that record the everyday lives of those who lived in them. This book argues that the Mediterranean world was always better suited to life in villages than in great conurbations, and that building cities in this particular environment was a work of great effort. That effort did not end with their construction. Ancient Mediterranean cities were sustained only at phenomenal cost, and the great downsizing at the end of antiquity is less difficult to explain than the centuries in which just a few ancient cities sheltered tens of thousands, and a tiny number hundreds of thousands of souls. This story is based partly on archaeology, partly on traditional historical sources, but most of all on the new openness of today's researchers to the work of social scientists and life scientists. Human geography, demography, and environmental science have set the pace here for a re-evaluation of ancient urban civilization. That re-evaluation has only just begun, but the story is too exciting and the results too surprising to wait before writing this book.

Wrapped around that story, however, is another even bigger one. Our human urban history stretches back just a few millennia, quite close to the time at which some of us first began to farm the wilderness in which our more remote ancestors had foraged. Cities had no single starting point. Urbanism was invented again and again in Asia and Europe, in Africa, and in both the Americas. How did this come about? No dreams of urbanism accompanied the first humans to enter the Americas, who were hunters and fishers and foragers. The inescapable conclusion is that as a species we have some kind of urban potential, not a force driving us through history to a common urban destiny, but a kind of aptitude for urban life, a capacity to inhabit civic spaces—a tendency, given the right circumstances, to build up and live close. If we are indeed "urban apes," as the next chapter argues, then those who specialize in the ancient Mediterranean need to ask not *why* the city, but rather what took them so long. And it is from that direction I will be approaching the underurbanized and mostly rural world of classical antiquity.

2

Urban Apes

The Great Disconnect

If we could trace a family tree for all the world's cities back to one single moment of invention, we could begin our story from there. In reality urbanism had many origins. Cities have been invented again and again. They were created in the river valleys of Egypt and Mesopotamia and northern China, in the High Andes of the Inca, and on the Anatolian plateau by Hittites and their neighbours. The Maya built cities in what are now the forests of the Yucatan peninsula and traded with urban populations in southeast Mexico. There were cities in ancient Thailand, and cities south of the Sahara. There were cities in woodland America long before the arrival of Europeans, and perhaps even in the Amazon basin where in the last few years a new method of laser scanning called LIDAR) (Light Detection and Ranging) has revealed densely populated landscapes beneath the jungle. Of the inhabited continents only Australia has (so far) has produced no evidence for early urbanism.[1]

Multiple origins can mean only one thing. Somewhere in the complex matrix of what it means to be human there must be a propensity to build cities, or at least a talent or an aptitude for urban living. Not every human society builds cities, and not every person likes living in them. But as a species we have some kind of urban potential, a tendency or a capacity, when it suits, to go urban.

As well as asking which bits of being human transform so easily into being urban humans, we need to ask, Why now? Humans like us—anatomically modern members of the species *homo sapiens*—have been around for at least three hundred thousand years. Other early humans, with some of whom we shared the planet until just a few tens of thousands of years ago, were around even longer. Yet the entire history of cities begins only six thousand years ago. If we are naturally urban apes, what took us so long to get to the city? Urbanism is entirely contained within the most recent of geological eras—the Holocene—that warm period we are still in that began when the ice caps began once again to melt and the glaciers to retreat.[2]

The Holocene began around 12,000 years ago. By the time the first cities appear *homo sapiens sapiens* was settled on every continent except Antarctica, and there were probably no other species of early humans still alive.[3] Genetically speaking, the first city-dwellers were already in modern times, our genes overwhelmingly dominated by those of the latest population to leave Africa, with just tiny admixtures from other human species we had reconnected with along the way. Physically, they no longer all looked quite the same. Those who had settled in high latitudes were a little paler, making it a bit easier to metabolize vitamin D where the sun was less bright. Those living closer to the equator—especially in Africa, southern India, and most of Australia—were darker. People were generally taller where food was abundant, smaller where it was scarce. Some populations in extreme environments—living at high altitudes on the Tibetan plateau or in high latitudes around the Arctic Circle—had adapted in other ways. Tibetans deal better with low levels of atmospheric oxygen; the Inuit tolerate a diet high in the fatty acids contained in fish. Each time early humans colonized a new area the genes of the founding population—usually very small—were a slightly different mix to those settling other regions. That lead to the variations in blood groups, hair colour, and eye colour we still see from one part of the world to another. Yet just as today, all humans were essentially the same. No differences between cultures have ever been convincingly shown to reflect genetic differences.[4] Whatever urban aptitude we had in the early Holocene was common to all humanity.

Consider the first groups who moved into the Americas perhaps around 15,000 years ago from Beringia, a broad territory between Siberia and Alaska, flooded when the ice melted at the Pleistocene/Holocene transition. Genetically they were wholly modern, but culturally and technologically they were very different to us. They foraged and fished and hunted, but did not really farm, partly because except in the richest environments they had to keep moving to find food. They cannot have brought with them much more than a few small portable tools. Like all early humans they were knowledgeable about the species they hunted and the plants they ate; they were skilled manipulators of the material world able not just to modify objects into tools but also to construct tools made of several materials combined. Like all humans they had evolved a powerful social intelligence, and had a keen imagination. The first Americans were adaptable too. Their ancestors had survived both the Ice Age that created the land bridge from Asia to Alaska, and the warm periods that followed. As they spread south and east their descendants had had to learn to hunt and fish new species; to survive first in the sub-Arctic, then in the Great Plains; to colonize tropical jungles and the Altiplano of South America; and finally to use and domesticate a range of animals and plants. They were resourceful survivors, just as we are.

Urban life, however, was completely outside their experience and beyond their imagination. There had been no cities anywhere on the planet when their ancestors left Eurasia. The flooding of Beringia meant that they and their descendants had virtually no contact with non-American populations until the arrival of Europeans some five hundred years ago. Yet within a few thousand years of arriving in the continent early Americans had created a number of urban cultures, each one different from all the others in detail, yet all spookily similar to those being created around the same time by their fantastically distant cousins across Eurasia and North Africa. When conquistadores in Peru encountered the great Inca city of Cuzco they could immediately recognize temples and palaces, avenues and piazzas, great monuments and humble dwellings just like those they had known at home.[5]

The earliest of the New World cities was perhaps the city of Caral in the Peruvian coastal desert of the Supe Valley, a cluster of pyramids and public squares scattered over around 60 hectares. It was built in the third millennium B.C.E. about the same time as Old Kingdom Egypt flourished. Perhaps the most spectacular pre-Columbian city was Teotihuacan in the Valley of Mexico, which rose and fell in rough synchronization with the Roman Empire across the Atlantic Ocean. Teotihuacan was a vast planned city. Its boulevards were lined with thousands of buildings, and ceremonial routes connected great plazas to its enormous temples. Those temples bore great monumental sculptures and reliefs of marble and granite decorated with gold and jade and bright painted murals. At the height of its power Teotichuacan probably had over 100,000 inhabitants. Trade routes and imperialism connected it to every part of Central America. After its fall in the middle of the sixth century C.E. it was mythologized, imitated, and even excavated for treasure by later pre-Columbian civilizations. Among them were the Aztecs whose own capital city, Tenochtitlán, the city built over a lake that lies under modern Mexico City, was already nearly two hundred years old when it was sacked by the Spanish in 1521 (see Figure 3). It was a vast imperial capital with a population of probably more than 100,000.

To the south and east of the valley of Mexico was the broad territory inhabited by Mayan-speaking peoples, a territory that included the jungles of the Yucatan Peninsula, the highlands to their south, and stretched from the Atlantic to the Pacific. Mayan urbanism dates back to the middle of the last millennium B.C.E., perhaps even earlier. During the Classic Maya period (250–900 C.E.) some of the largest cities like Tikal and Calakmul had populations in the tens of thousands. This is another region where recent fieldwork is just beginning to reveal the density of urban networks. The decipherment of Mayan glyphs in the last decades of the twentieth century means it is now possible to write a history of city-states and their kings fighting to build and destroy alliances with all the energy and ferocity of their near contemporaries in classical Greece or pre-Imperial China.

Pre-Columbian urbanism was not confined to Mesoamerica. The great Andean empire of the Inca was ruled through a network of cities. The capital at Cuzco was connected to subordinate centres, royal estates, and castles by thousands of miles of roads. Meanwhile to the north, the mound-builders

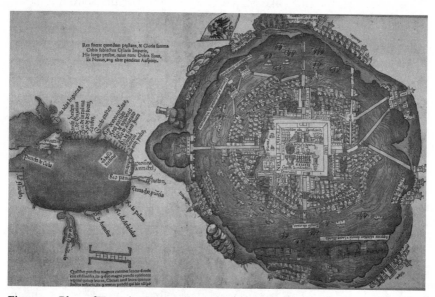

Figure 3 Plan of Tenochtitlán
Newberry Library, Chicago, Ayer 655.51.C8 1524b

(whose name for themselves we do not know) created Cahokia near today's US city of St. Louis, in Missouri.

Each of these urban traditions had its own peculiarities and style. Some societies invested much of their labour in creating one vast metropolis like Tenochtitlan or Cuzco. The Maya built many smaller centres, low-density cities in the midst of tropical forests, their pyramids and ball courts nested among the trees. Different as these were to each other, and to the urbanism of early modern Europe and Islamic North Africa, the first Europeans to arrive in the New World immediately recognized that these were real cities.

Those Europeans seeing American cities for the first time in the fifteenth and sixteenth cities can be set in a longer tradition of travels between urban clusters. Ibn Battuta, born in Morocco at the start of the fourteenth century, travelled widely through Iran, central Asia, and India, visited the Arabian peninsula and the Swahili coast, and on later voyages made his way to the cities of the Sahel in West Africa south of the Sahara. About a century before him the Venetian Marco Polo saw and described the cities of China and the Indian Ocean. The most famous novel of the Italian writer Italo Calvino, *Invisible Cities,* imagines Marco Polo describing his travels to the Mongol Emperor Kublai Khan by evoking more and more fabulous cities he has seen (or never seen).

Early modern travellers like Marco Polo and Ibn Battuta were not hacking their way through dense jungles looking for lost civilizations like the heroes of Victorian romances. They travelled along well-established trade routes that had connected the urban centres of the Old World, routes that went back to the Middle Ages and sometimes even earlier. Alexandrine merchants had traded with southern India in the time of Christ, riding the monsoon from the mouth of the Red Sea to Sri Lanka and Tamil Nadu. What we now call the Silk Road was really a complex of these routes, stretching some north, others south of the Himalayas linking the urban civilizations of China and her neighbours to central Asia, Iran, India, and ultimately the Mediterranean world. The Indian Ocean was connected by maritime trade routes first in the Roman period and then intensively in the Islamic Middle Ages.[6]

This reconnection was not a product of the European Age of Discovery. Vikings encountered indigenous peoples in Newfoundland and Greenland. The peoples of northern Australia were never completely cut off from South Asia: one set of connections is attested by the arrival of the dingo in probably two waves, both within the last 10,000 years. Some studies of domesticated plants from South America suggest some tenuous connections may have existed right across the Pacific Ocean well before the arrival of Christopher Columbus. It was in our nature to travel, and travellers on a globe will always eventually cross each other's paths.

The first travellers to record their experiences were often amazed at what they saw in foreign lands, but they were not amazed to find urban cultures. The city for them was absolutely normal. Another fourteenth-century traveller, Ibn Khaldun, elevated this to a general theory of history. He postulated that there was always a cyclical struggle between urban civilizations and the tribal populations that surrounded them. Each time an urban civilization fell to the barbarians, the conquerors themselves began to grow soft and less warlike, to enjoy the comforts and luxuries of the city, until they in turn were overtaken by new invasions of barbarians. That opposition had classical precedents. The Greek geographer Eratosthenes had proposed classifying peoples into those who lived by law and in cities and those who did not (the barbarians), and the historian Herodotus had had one Greek character tell a Persian Emperor that "soft lands breed soft people." Thucydides, pondering the early days of Greece, suggested that once upon a time everyone lived as barbarians did in his day. These writers shared an underlying assumption that urbanization was a sign of civilizational progress. Premodern travellers were not surprised to find that some distant peoples had been moving on parallel tracks to those at home.

The globalized culture of the modern world has its roots in journeys of discovery like these. There have always been a few intrepid adventurers. Visitors from India pop up in Greek histories from the middle of the last millennium B.C.E.[7] Roman merchants found their way to the court of the Han Emperor of China sometime in the second century C.E. Viking expeditions wove a loose network of connections from Newfoundland to Byzantium, through the Russian river systems as well as via the Atlantic and Mediterranean Seas. The Chinese fleets of Zheng He cruised the Indian Ocean in the fifteenth century. Almost no populations were wholly isolated from their neighbours.

Over the last five hundred years, the human family has been definitively reunited. Our Great Reconnect was driven by the thirst for riches—spice, gold, and other treasure—and by the hunt for land, manpower (mostly meaning slaves), and ultimately markets. It was made possible by advances in maritime technology funded by monarchies eager for those things. More formal imperial expeditions played a part too. Meeting up with distant relatives was incidental. But when the distant cousins met up again, they discovered how similar they were. During our long disconnect we had independently created similar architectures and sculptures, warfare and writing, priesthoods, monarchies, and nations. Time and again the city lay at the heart of them.

Apes on the Move

Chimpanzees do not build cities, nor do our other closest relatives among the great apes. What makes us different? Why are we the only urban apes?

One way to answer this question is to look at another respect in which early humans are different from the Great Apes. Chimpanzees, bonobos, gorillas, and orangutans today mostly occupy a rather narrow range of ecological niches. Once this was probably true of our own ancestors, but for at least the last two or three million years that has changed. We are descendants of a large family of mobile and versatile apes.

Traditionally prehistorians have thought in terms of distinct species—*homo habilis, homo ergaster, homo heidelbergenis*, and so on—and tried to spot the points at which different lineages diverged. The investigation of the human genome, the capacity to sequence DNA quickly and cheaply, and the ability to examine ancient (paleo-)DNA has shown that reality was much messier than this.[8] Ever since our ancestors separated from those of the chimpanzees—perhaps as long as thirteen million years ago—different human populations have expanded and contracted, drifted apart, run into their distant relatives again, lived near them, fought, and occasionally interbred. Most of this complicated story took place within Africa, or rather in a geographical region based on southern and eastern Africa but extending up the Nile and Jordan valley—part of the same great tectonic rift—to Georgia at the eastern end of the Black Sea. Roughly 1.8 million years ago, some early humans began to move out of this corridor until around 800,000 years ago they occupied all those parts of continental Europe and Asia south of the ice.

This epic story of human expansion took place against a background of constant climatic change. For the last two and a half million years—since the start of the Pleistocene Epoch—the earth's climate has been swaying back and forth between periods when the poles are covered in ice, and great deserts appear in the equatorial zones (ice ages), and periods when the

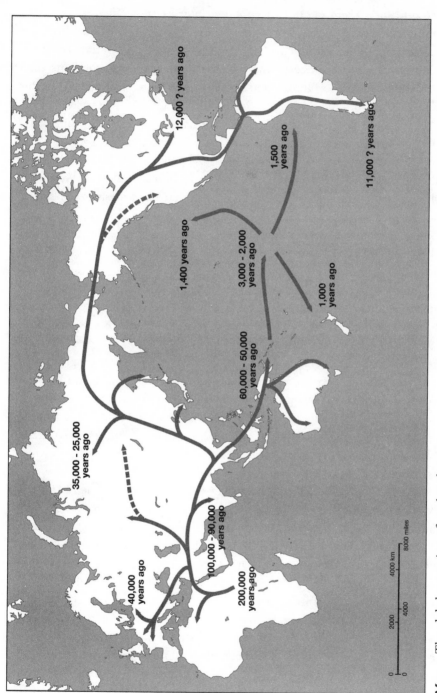

Map 1 The global expansion of modern humans

ice caps shrink and the deserts contract (interglacials). When water is tied up in ice caps, sea levels drop around the world, opening up land bridges and plains —like Beringia—that connect islands and continents. When temperatures rise, the oceans and islands reappear, while at the same time plants and animals recolonize land liberated from the retreating ice. For our remote ancestors and their close cousins this meant that the territory available for them and their food sources kept increasing and decreasing, connecting and fragmenting, changing in shape. During the interglacial periods new pastures and warmer temperatures drew prey species farther north and the predators who fed on them—humans included—followed. Whenever the icecaps expanded again we were all driven back to sheltered niches which prehistorians call *refugia*. Early humans responded to the alternation of cold periods and warm ones too, moving back and forth, but after a while they also began to adapt to the changing conditions, technologically and physically.

As recently as 40,000 years ago there were several kinds of early human species coexisting in Africa and Eurasia. Most of our own genome comes from a population we call *homo sapiens sapiens*—or anatomically modern humans—a group that originated maybe as long as 300,000 years ago and probably in East Africa. Most of us are descendants of a tiny subgroup that moved out from these core territories around 60,000 years ago. (All these dates are provisional as well as approximate, because research is moving so fast.) Part of that population headed first into Arabia and Asia, then along the coasts of India and what is now Indonesia into New Guinea and Australia. Slightly later a related group moved through the Near East and westwards into Europe.

As our ancestors expanded their range they encountered long-lost cousins. Some of us still carry traces in our DNA of other species of early human, among them Neanderthals and Denisovans. There were certainly other groups not yet identified and characterized who have left faint genetic traces in the genomes of modern populations. Only recently evidence was found of a now extinct population of dwarf hominins from Flores in Indonesia. Who knows which new cousins will appear next? Some kinds of early human were adapted to specific environments. One interpretation of Neanderthal physiognomy is that it was well adapted to the cold conditions of the ice ages and when those conditions disappeared, they went the same way as woolly mammoths. Other palaeontologists point out that Neanderthals lived for tens of thousands of years in the warm

Mediterranean lands and the Near East. The small size of the hominins of Flores might be explained by the fact that they seemed to have lived on just one island. Island dwarfism is a well-established phenomenon. Visit the archaeology museums of the Mediterranean islands and you can still see the bones of dwarf elephants and hippotamuses. Perhaps there was direct conflict between different groups of humans, or just competition for resources. Either way, something about our own ancestors gave them some sort of edge, a competitive advantage. They multiplied rapidly and expanded beyond the limits reached by other early humans. Among these new territories were the colder lands around the Arctic, the continental masses of Australia and the Americas, and in the last couple of thousand years the most remote islands of the Atlantic and the Pacific Oceans.

One of the most striking features of our species' great expansion during the late Pleistocene and the Holocene is the range of environments it mastered. Apes had expanded their range before. There was a great expansion in the Miocene Era (from about 23 to 5 million years ago) but this was in an age of relative stable climate and more uniform landscapes. The Pliocene and especially the Pleistocene brought change. Those grouped together as *homo erectus* left Africa in the middle of the Pleistocene and both their descendants and our ancestors had to cope with less stable environments. Despite this environmental stress, or perhaps partly because of it, they became highly mobile and highly adaptable in terms of their behaviour. For at least two million years humans have had big brains, walked on two legs, made tools, and used fire. Most made use of language more complex than those used by other primate societies today. Probably they were better at collaboration too, to judge by comparisons between human infants and the young of great apes. Our direct ancestors were even better than their cousins at expanding out into new habitats, at colonizing new niches, at discovering and making use of new resources, of altering their habits and bodies to thrive in new environments.[9]

No other early humans were as mobile as *homo sapiens*. Within just a few tens of thousands of years after they left the Rift Valley they appear across the entire Old World. They learned to cross open water, perhaps very early and certainly before they settled the Indonesian archipelago. They crossed to Australia, which they circled rapidly, avoiding the central desert. Those movements are now being reconstructed from ancient language families. Several successive populations occupied the frozen territories around the Arctic Circle where most foods they were used to were not available, and where they encountered extremes of cold and darkness no human population had ever tolerated before. Wherever they moved they had to learn how to eat new plants and hunt new species of animals, and they did so with such success that they transformed every environment they entered.

All species modify their environments, and even Great Apes have a history, one we are trying hard to reconstruct, although many of the scientific techniques that have illuminated our recent past work less well in the tropics. But there is a huge difference between the transformations undergone and engineered by the human animal over the last few million years, and the experience of the Great Apes in the same time.

Between ten and five thousand years ago human populations on every settled continent except Australia had begun to domesticate plants and animals and to settle together. A few thousand years later they began to build and construct states. Powered by agriculture, humans were able to reach the most remote islands of the Pacific, Atlantic, and Indian Oceans. Iceland and Madagascar were first settled in the ninth century C.E., New Zealand and Hawaii three hundred years later. For the last few hundred years our species has had a single global history once again. Like siblings separated at birth who meet again as adults, our strong family resemblances tell us something about who we fundamentally are. Our common ancestors were foragers and hunters. But we found that before we were reunited almost all of our kin had become farmers. Many had founded cities, created writing systems and states, built temples and palaces and roads and ports, and made statues of gods and men.

Accidentally Urban

Let us be clear: there was no plan, no road map to urbanism buried deep in our brains or written in our genes. Darwin taught us that variation in the present is the product of selective pressures in the past. Each generation is comprised of the children of those who were best suited to survive and reproduce in the immediate past. Evolution is never directed towards a particular goal. If we are urban apes it is not because we were ever *designed* to live in cities, but because changes that our species underwent in different and (obviously) nonurban conditions have made city life an increasingly viable and attractive option. We are accidentally urban.

Some people resist this idea very strongly. The association of urban life with a high culture of "civilized values" remains very strong in many traditions, not just those that look back to Aristotle and Plato. For those who see a great gulf separating humans from (other) animals, urban life seems to represent a pinnacle of achievement, the ultimate distancing of ourselves from the natural world. Again this is not confined to traditions that look back to the European Enlightenment which defined itself for good or bad against a state of nature. Perhaps the success of urban life has brought with it a host of convergent and mutually supporting ideologies in which city, civilization, humanity, and progress are intimately related. Those who belief in the literal truth of biblical scripture have their own arguments against evolutionary theory of all kinds. A strong sense of commitment to the values of today, whether religious or secular, coexists easily with ideas like manifest destiny, so that our collective urban journey seems purposeful. Some find it frightening to think that all our species has achieved, for good or ill, has come about by chance.

The idea that the natural world was formed by an accumulation of accidents also seems shocking to some. It is not just that many of us want the world to seem full of some larger meaning. It also often strikes us as very well put together. The sky is exactly the right shade of blue, the sound of wind in the trees so soothing, the movements of animals so graceful, and so on. These sentiments provide a romantic underpinning for conservation (and of course there are other, better arguments for preserving biodiversity). In an earlier age thinkers sought knowledge from either the Book of God of the Book of Nature. Both seem to tell us that the natural world into which we were born is intrinsically well designed and of value.

There are good reasons for humans to feel this way. A knowledge of the natural world was fairly essential to our ancestors: those insensitive to its changes would have been eliminated in the course of natural selection. Either they would have been less successful in using natural resources than their peers, or they would have been careless in doing so. The search for transcendent value too is a distinctive feature of our species. There is no sign of art or music or ritual among the Great Apes. We have developed a talent for finding and making patterns, and for attributing significance to them. Pattern-finding is fundamental to language and science. But the sense of wonder is something else. Even when we *know* that the shape or speed or appearance of a dolphin illustrates the power of selective evolutionary pressures, that graceful swimmers outcompete their graceless and clumsy siblings, that speed gives a predator a crucial advantage and so on, we still catch our breath at the beauty of its movement. We can enjoy our reactions, but they explain very little.

Evolutionary trajectories are the perfect example of this mirage. Sometimes a species seems—with hindsight—to have been evolving in a particular direction for a long period of time. Take the great cats.[10] Around 5 million years ago the common ancestors of the cheetahs and the pumas began to use one of two strategies to hunt prey. Early cheetahs relied on speed to chase down prey, while early pumas relied on strength to ambush it. Faster cheetahs succeeded better than slower ones, and more robust pumas outcompeted their less bulky brothers and sisters. The middle group—slow cheetahs or light pumas—were unsuccessful at either strategy, and as a result had fewer descendants. In this way the two lineages separated, and came to follow different evolutionary trajectories. The logic of previous adaptions made evolution in a particular direction more likely. Going back to being a slower cheetah or a weaker puma was never going to convey an advantage, so throwbacks (of which there must have been quite a few at first) had fewer descendants. Today the two species, or groups of species, seem perfectly suited to their very different ways of life. But of course there was no plan. What we are observing is path dependence, the phenomenon seen in many fields where the next step is shaped by the results of previous steps. Cheetahs became faster and faster because they were competing with each other. They were also locked in an evolutionary arms race with their main prey species, the antelopes, which were also getting faster and lighter. Pumas grew stockier and stronger for similar reasons. None of this was planned or designed and in the long term, there were costs. Cheetahs are the most fragile of the big cats and have to avoid conflict if at all possible. Perhaps as a result of the high-risk path they have taken, they nearly became extinct 12,000 years ago. Today's cheetahs are very inbred, have high infant mortality, and are very vulnerable to some diseases.

Humans too have followed certain evolutionary trajectories. Again there was no plan, no design, and again there have been costs. One key path followed by all the hominins over the last two and a half million years has been encephalization, the growth of our brains both in absolute terms and in relation to the rest of our bodies. "Hominins" is a term covering not only all the species called homo—including homo sapiens, Neanderthals, Denisovans, homo erectus, and the rest—during the last two and a half million years but also the Australopithecine species of Africa, from which they almost certainly evolved. Around the same time as archaic cheetahs embarked on a path leading to speed and fragility, our ancestors began to be selected for big brains. Plot the brain sizes of different kinds of hominins on a graph alongside the periods in which they flourished and the upward trend is really striking. Our mean brain size has nearly quadrupled in size over that period, from around 400 cubic centimeters to nearly 1,600 cubic centimeters.[11] But big brains come at a cost. The proteins they are made of demand a high intake of high-quality food, and almost certainly forced hominins to make meat a more central part of their diet. Other organs were reduced in size as our brains increased. We have shorter and less efficient guts than many mammals. Another set of costs is born by the parents of big-brained young. The bigger the head, the harder the birth, and so quite a bit of our development has to take place after we have been born. As a result human childhoods are longer than those of other apes. Our children are more dependent on their parents for longer, and mothers are more dependent on their kin as well. We have selected for life in families, and can survive only in social groups.

Sometimes in a romantic moment we imagine that our dependence on technology is a recent fad, that just a few centuries ago we lived close to nature. Not a bit of it. Technology has been central to human evolution for a very long time.[12] Our big-brained babies and dependent infants would slow down small groups that had to move about in search of food, so we have depended on devices like the baby sling for a long time. Many of the environments early humans settled are too cold to be endured without clothing; early *homo sapiens* certainly sewed clothes, and some Neanderthals probably used wrap-around hides. Investing in big brains has been made possible by our lack of investment in thick pelts, in sharp claws, in the speed of a cheetah or the strength of a puma. An adult human is no match for an adult chimpanzee in a fair fight. Instead early humans used tool kits of stone, bone, and wood. As we evolved the tools we made became more varied and specialized. At first these were found stones and sticks, lightly modified— several mammal and some bird species do the same—but we got better at choosing and at shaping them. Around 50,000 years ago we learned to make tools composed of more than one substance—a knife with a handle, a bow with a string, and so on.[13] The trajectory we followed—always by accident—made us more and more committed to the use of technology.

None of this has taken us away from nature, nor has our biological evolution slowed in recent millennia. Quite the reverse. Just think of the huge variation among modern human populations in height and hair types, or in skin colour and body shape. Skin colour variation is largely an adaption to the different amounts of ultraviolet light we are exposed to, depending on whether we live nearer the equator or nearer the poles. Darker skin protects us from burning and near the equator still allows enough UV to get through for the body for it to manufacture sufficient vitamin D from cholesterol. Nearer the poles the risk of burning is much reduced and darker skin hampers vitamin D production, which is why skin colours are often paler. These effects have occurred independently in the Americas, in Africa, and in the Indian Subcontinent, and reflect the potential of our genome to vary the amounts of pigmentation in the skin. Almost all of this has happened in the last 50,000 years. More recent is the development of a capacity to digest milk in adulthood, especially the milk of domesticated cattle. That genetic adaption is still very unevenly spread around the world—perhaps unsurprisingly, since cattle were first domesticated less than ten thousand years ago. Our diet and environment are still changing, quite fast in some respects. Further adaptions are inevitable. Evolution never stops.

None of these changes were designed to lead us towards urbanism, but city life builds naturally on some of them. To put it differently: we are *preadapted* to life in cities. The idea of preadaptation is that a trait developed in response to one set of selective pressures may later co-opted be to serve a new function, under different pressures. Feathers, for example, almost certainly developed to help dinosaurs control their body heat, but then turned out to be phenomenally useful when some lineages of dinosaurs entered on a trajectory that led to the evolution of birds. Preadapted does not mean preordained or destined. It simply means that when particular opportunities come along, a species may be in a good position to grasp them by virtue of features that have been selected for in other circumstances. Humans have not lived in cities for most of their 300,000-year history. But just by accident—happy or not—our species has urban potential.

What makes us so well adapted for urban life? For the moment let me pick out just three dimensions of human nature: how we eat, how we move, and how we get along.

Urban Appetites

As our brains got bigger so did our appetites, especially for protein. But we were not fussy. Our ancestors did not become omnivores in order to colonize new worlds, let alone to live in cities. But being flexible eaters meant that they were better adapted than our nearest living relatives to move out of their ecological comfort zone. Many species today are threatened by habitat loss, by the disappearance of particular places they live in, and by threats to the foods they depend on. Pandas will not survive without bamboo forests, orangutans too have become highly specialized eaters. We are not. Humans are more like rats in that we can survive on a variety of food sources, can swop between high-meat and low-meat diets, and can survive quite prolonged periods of hunger, depending on whatever a new environment had to offer. Rats and humans do very well in cities. That is a happy accident for each species.

Our ancestors probably became flexible eaters because the particular environments where they first developed the Rift Valley of East Africa and the Middle East were for a while relatively unpredictable in terms of what foods they produced.[14] Omnivory, or at least a tolerance of variations in food sources, was a trait which then gave early humans the capacity to expand beyond the environments in which they had evolved. We have a dentition that can deal with nuts, tubers, grains, and flesh (so long as it has rotted for a bit or been processed). Even better, we have learned to predigest outside the body many foodstuffs that we could not digest raw. We soak, dry, mash, ferment, and heat various vegetable and animal products until our puny digestive tracts can cope with them. Growing lactose tolerance shows that our guts, as well as our cooks, have been working on the problem too. Turning milk into cheese helps a little, but being able to produce the enzyme lactase into adulthood helps much more.

As *homo sapiens* spread out over the globe they used the skills they had developed for hunting wildebeest and gazelle to hunt down mammoths in northern Eurasia, giant wombats in Australia, bison in North America, giant birds in New Zealand, and sea mammals in the Arctic. The extinction of the megafauna—literally the big beasts—in the Pleistocene Era probably had complex causes. But archaeological evidence is accumulating to show that within a few millennia (and sometimes just a few centuries) of humans arriving in a new part of the globe there were regularly extinctions of the larger mammals and birds. This happened to the large marsupial mammals of Australia, to the giant birds of New Zealand and other islands, and to many populations in the Americas. The idea that our primitive ancestors lived in harmony with their environments is a myth. We have not changed that much.

The extinction of their main prey species did not slow down *homo sapiens*. Late Pleistocene populations on the move already had to cope with a range of new environments, and with the alternations of Ice Ages and interglacials. Adapting to new kinds of prey was no more difficult. Food waste on occupation sites dating from the late Pleistocene show that some human populations were already eating much smaller animals and taking greater trouble to catch them. Fishtraps, tiny delicate arrowheads, slender spears, and harpoons appear for the first time. Every time humans entered new lands there were episodes of bounty. Human populations rose, those of their larger prey collapsed, and successive generations returned to living on a wider and more varied diet. The first settlers of New Zealand probably numbered in their thousands, but within two centuries entire species of seals and Moas were gone. By the time Captain Cook arrived the local populations had already adapted to new food sources. On Madagascar human settlement—again beginning with a tiny number of settlers—was followed in a couple of hundred years by the disappearance of giant lemurs, elephant birds, pigmy hippopotamuses, and giant tortoises. In their place agricultural regimes of various kinds were introduced. By the very end of the Pleistocene we can see the first signs of a more intensive kind of foraging, which in some places would soon develop into full-blown farming. On most continents this appeared near the beginning of the Holocene, around 10,000 years B.C.E. We had begun the great leap down the food chain from a diet rich in meat to one based on vegetables.[15]

Farming could not return humans to the low-protein diet of their smaller brained ancestors. Our brains were still hungry for more. Early agriculturalists commonly relied on a small range of cultigens—wheat, maize, rice, yams, and so on—which were to varying degrees good sources of carbohydrates. These provided fuel for the body but were not enough on their own to grow and sustain big brains. Early farmers supplemented cultivated crops with gathered foodstuffs, especially pulses and nuts, fish and small game. Most cultivated crops were also available only at certain times of the year. But we learned to cope with this too. Some hunting populations who lived in the temperate zones had already learned to cope with seasonal fluctuations in food availability. Our species can cope with this in various ways. We have evolved the capacity to store food as body fat in times of plenty, to delay puberty in prolonged periods of scarcity, even to alter our fertility so that babies are born when they have the best chance of survival. A few present-day forager populations, such as the Inuit, have developed these capacities to a very marked extent. Settled agricultural populations had additional options. They could dig or build granaries, they learned to salt and dry meat and fish, to turn milk into cheese that lasted longer and was easier for many to eat, and to use domesticated animals as "walking refrigerators" that could be fed in times of plenty, and eaten in times of hunger.

All this prepared our species very well for eating in cities. Today's urban populations in the developed world tend to have the widest choice of foods. But this is a product of their relatively high purchasing power, and of the invention of refrigeration and cheap transportation. In the past urban food choices were much more restricted. The first urban populations depended disproportionately on grains in Mesopotamia, Egypt, and the Indus Valley, on rice in China and northeast India, and on maize in the New World. High-carbohydrate diets of this kind have their drawbacks. Third World urban populations today show us what they are. Many are malnourished as well as undernourished; levels of endemic disease and vulnerability to epidemics are high. Poor nutrition reduces fertility, reduces the proportion of pregnancies carried to term, and impacts on the health of those children who are born. Malnutrition in childhood has lifelong effects on health and strength. Resistance to disease is lowered. The first agriculturalists worked harder than their forager ancestors, and were less healthy.[16] When they moved into cities their workloads increased and their health got even worse. But evolution selects for survival, not comfort, and today humans can survive on surprisingly poor diets.

Urban Bodies

If we had the guts for urban life, we had urban legs and eyes as well.

Humans live pretty well out of doors, and for much of our history we wandered the wide-open spaces. Walking on two legs—bipedalism—probably began around six million years ago, as various groups of apes colonized the African savannahs that grew at the expense of forests in dry periods. Like all primates today, these apes were already relying more on vision and less on smell than many other mammals. Like monkeys, they had good binocular vision—meaning their two eyes were set side by side and could be focused on the same object, giving them a good sense of perspective and distance. With this came a capacity to navigate and move easily in complicated spaces. Any species of monkey or ape that spends much of its time in forest environments has to be very good at judging distance and height, otherwise it would find it difficult to move about safely and quickly. These features of our wider family were selected for a very long time ago, but they have proved to be consistently useful as our ancestors moved into other kinds of environments. They were useful when we became top predators, and even more useful when we developed projectile spears and bows and arrows, the use of which depends on excellent eyesight and the capacity to judge distance. Traits adapted for moving in trees turned out to be useful when exploring caverns or climbing ladders; once again, preadaption. Even today much of what we do—motorway driving for example, or playing golf or tennis—is completely dependent on being good at calculating how far away things are, how fast and in what direction they are moving, and how we can safely move in ways that do not intersect with their paths. Put simply, we are well adjusted to living fast in three dimensions.

Why does this matter for urbanism? One straightforward answer is that urbanism involves packing people closely together. When we first wandered we wandered in smallish bands, tens of people who sometimes came together into groups numbering a few hundred at most. Almost no environments are rich enough to support dense populations of foragers. Agriculture increases the carrying capacity of the land, and it also demands more labour than foraging. Villages concentrate populations. Ancient villages were often tiny, but some of the earliest, like Çatalhöyük in Turkey, had thousands of inhabitants. Perhaps as many as 8,000 lived densely packed together in houses built so close that access to some was across the rooftops of others. Many early cities were smaller, and some were quite low-density, vast sprawling areas of yards and gardens and compounds loosely connected by paths or even separated by patches of woodland or common ground. But often this was not feasible. No ancient cities approached the population densities of today's megacities, but some had population densities of 10,000 to 20,000 people per square kilometre. This was only possible by building up and building down, by packing homes close together. Modern cities can often spread horizontally, because transport systems allow people to live long distances from where they work or find food. Modern communications allow members of a team to work together almost as well remotely as when they are together. Early urbanism was more constrained. City-dwellers had to live close together, clustered around narrow lanes and tiny yards, in cellars and on rooftops. Life in some early villages must have required almost as much physical dexterity as life in the treetops. Humans were fortunately preadapted to inhabit complicated urban warrens, good at shaping and inhabiting small spaces, and physically and psychologically suited to those spaces being tightly packed and stacked on top of each other. Our bodies are well suited to navigating narrow and uneven passages; we can climb ladders, ramps, and narrow staircases; we often find high points and panoramas invigorating, and most of us do not suffer from crippling claustrophobia or vertigo. Even today we know, at some level, that we have reproduced versions of the habitats of our very remote ancestors. We talk of urban jungles, of concrete canyons, and spaces that are cavernous. We have built homes that fit our bodies as well as our clothes do.

Cities have become our nests. One influential study of social animals argues that for a species to get the full benefit of social living, it needs to build nests.[17] Animal species may be social to a greater or lesser degree. Sociality has evolved as a strategy among many species of birds and mammals, fish and insects, even reptiles. The most intensely social creatures are those varieties of insects—some species of ants, bees, and termites—that live in communities of tens or hundreds of thousands, dividing between their members the jobs of food gathering, defence, breeding, laying eggs, nursing the young, and so on. That level of cooperation and mutual dependence—sometimes termed "eusociality"—really only works when animals live in tightly packed multigenerational colonies. These colonies take many forms. Some species of eusocial shrimps live inside sponges, many insects build elaborate nests, termites create great towers, and many eusocial ant species and eusocial mole rats live in underground burrows.

Cities are not anthills—not quite—and our reproductive division of labour is less tightly defined than in strictly eusocial species. Humans can survive alone and in very small groups, in ways that social shrimps and termites cannot. But it is easy to see the advantages that urban nesting offers when there is a complex division of labour, as a means of protecting the vulnerable, and of allowing a colony to work together most effectively.

Urban Brains

Finally those big brains—for which we gave up our claws—learned to cook, and accepted the burden of looking after children that take nearly two decades to become independent of their parents.

Physical anthropologists have realized for a very long time that an increase in brain size has been one of the most consistent themes of human evolution. Specifically it is the neocortex, that grey matter outer portion of the brain, that is characteristic of mammals and makes up 76 per cent of the human brain, that expanded in volume. *Homo habilis*, who lived 2.5 million years ago, had a brain capacity of 650 cubic centimetres, half again as big as the brains of its Australopithecine ancestors and rivals. Brain size continued to grow. By 600,000 years ago the mean brain capacity of *homo erectus* was around 1200 cubic centimetres. *Homo sapiens* have a brain capacity of around 1500 cubic centimetres, Neanderthals only a little less.

It is easy to see how the physiological changes of cheetahs served a lifestyle based on predating fast prey, but what is so good about large brains? The question matters even more now that we appreciate the enormous costs of this evolutionary trajectory, especially the demand for high-quality nutrition, and the vulnerability of slow developing human young and their mothers. Growing big brains led us to carnivory and cooking, prompted our investment in technology, perhaps even drove us towards monogamy. Less than 3 per cent of mammal species show social monogamy, the formation of long-lasting pairs who live together and share the task of raising their young, but one in four species of primates practice it. Big brains run in the primate family, but why did humans take this to such an extreme?

A number of ideas have been suggested—that we needed bigger brains to make better tools or to develop language, for instance—but archaeological research has shown the chronology of these innovations simply does not work. Big brains came first; more complex tools and linguistic ability followed. By far the most plausible explanation today is what is called the social brain hypothesis.[18] The idea is that our larger brains evolved to allow us to maintain more and more complex social relations with a larger and larger group of others. Large group size, the hypothesis posits, is the evolutionary gain for which big brains were selected. Other benefits and consequences were incidental.

Of course plenty of other animals, some with much smaller brains, live in large groups: shoals of fish, swarms of locusts, and herds of wildebeest, for example. But primate groups are organized in a different way to theirs. All primate societies are held together by a web of one-to-one relationships, meaning that each member potentially has some sort of relationship with every other. Moreover, these relationships change over the relatively long lives of the members as new pair bonds are formed, as authority is challenged, lost, or reaffirmed, and as individuals die and younger ones take their places in the social web. Managing these relationships takes primates a lot more work than bees undertake in their simpler eusocial universes, where a drone is a drone is a drone. Each member of a primate society has to create, and then maintain a social map. Updating it requires observational and interpretative work by every individual, and the neocortex is where this work is done. The most compelling evidence in support of this is the demonstration that if we compared primate species today we find a very strong correlation between the size of the neocortex and the size of the typical social group. About the same time cheetahs invested in speed, we invested in a complicated social life.—hence our big brains. The smaller the brain capacity of a primate, the smaller the social group it typically lives in. Apply this relation to fossil hominin skulls and we find that over the last three million years the number of individuals in the predicted group rises from 60 odd individuals to around 150. Whether or not that number stands up to analysis—a lot depends on what we mean by a relationship—there is no doubt that our social capacity is far greater than that of most of our near relatives.

Most primate groups have what is termed a fission–fusion social structure.[19] There is a larger society—the size of which varies from species to species between say 50 and 150 individuals—but at any one time that larger society tends to be divided up into smaller groups. How these groups combine and redivide depends a little on where food resources are to be found, and a little on the security of the groups. Primates are not the only social animals to display this sort of social structure: similar things have been observed with herds of elephants and pods of dolphins. In the case of some species the smaller groups are pretty stable; society then becomes a sort of federation of families, or pods. In chimpanzee and human society the smaller groups are not stable in membership. This makes our kind of sociality astonishingly flexible, but it takes a lot more work. Primates spend a lot of time engaged in social grooming: it has even been suggested that human language developed as an extension of that activity. Human social intelligence is far superior to that of even the largest brained of our primate cousins. We can cooperate in large groups to do quite complicated tasks such as planning and organizing a hunt, building a house, or playing football. It is easier enough to teach a chimpanzee to play a game with a ball, but unimaginable that a group of chimpanzees could learn to play team sports.

There are other exclusively human dimensions of social life. As a species we have a special talent for friendship.[20] Perhaps this originated in the usefulness of being able to recruit members of other groups in times of expansion and exploration. One of the costs of migration to a social animal is that it has the potential to fragment kin networks: that cost can limit the willingness of individuals or small groups to move far from their kin. *Homo sapiens* seems to have been better than other early humans at overcoming these costs, partly by being better at maintaining connections over a distance, and partly by being good at making new friends in new places.

Our social world is not limited to kith and kin, to friends and relatives. We have also recruited members of other species. Many species live in symbiotic relationships with others—pilot fish and sharks, oxpeckers and elephants, to name just two examples—but the connections established tens of thousands of years ago between humans and dogs are rather different. Those connections depend on co-opting the social capacities of both species. There is more to it than that, of course. Genetically dogs have few differences from wolves, but they have been bred or at least selected for their social capacity. How this process began is very mysterious. Domestication is a uniquely human trait and so there are few analogies to help us out, but perhaps abandoned or captured wolf cubs were raised in human families, and certainly there would have been selection in favour of those that formed strong social bonds with humans and against those that were more aggressive or independent. The process would be repeated later with other social mammals: sheep and goats, cattle and horses, and so on. Perhaps we should simply say that humans were preadapted to domesticate, meaning that one unexpected side effect of our species' investment in sociality was the capacity to socialize members of other social species.

The original team of apes and wolves was a winning combination. Dogs' sharp olfactory senses and physical robustness complemented our developing weaknesses in both areas. No other species of apes or early humans domesticated dogs, but *homo sapiens* probably did it several times during our expansion around the globe. Dogs are not only social like us but also mobile, creatures willing to sacrifice territoriality to their membership of a wider social group. They accompanied the first humans into the New World and later crossed from Eurasia into Australia and Africa. Dogs accompanied us on all our great explorations to the most remote Pacific and Atlantic islands, and then to both polar ice caps. Dogs even preceded us into space. At first they helped us hunt by day and guard our temporary nests during the nighttime when our primate eyes were so much feebler than theirs. Later, when we had domesticated other species, they helped tame and control them, and protect our flocks from other predators. Now they mostly provide companionship, a fundamental human need that also derives from our increased sociality.

Our social talent was not limited to recruiting strangers and forming alliances with other animal species. *Homo sapiens* was probably the first kind of human to establish social relations with invisible entities—with ancestors, ghosts, spirits, and gods. Reconstructing the thought worlds of earlier kinds of humans is not easy. Symbolism and ornament certainly antedates our species, and there is fierce debate about the ritual and aesthetic capacities of Neanderthals. Cases have been made for song and dance, burial and decoration among late Neanderthals. But when it comes to *homo sapiens* there is absolutely no doubt that they conducted rituals wherever they went. Rock art and cave paintings from southern Africa to Australia depict humans and animals. Gods and ancestors were part of the social world: they had desires and needs, and formed friendships and enmities with particular individuals. Ancestors were already the kin of living members of the group. Worshipping them extended the power of kinship groups into the afterlife.

One last category needs to be added to kin, kin-shipped friends, animals, ancestors, and gods if we want a complete account of the social world of early humans. That is possessions. At first sight the idea that some inanimate objects might be social beings seems very strange. But think about the way we talk about objects that are important to us. We sometimes say we are attached to an object, perhaps something given to us by a close friend, or inherited from a parent. We feel comfortable surrounded by "our" things. We miss familiar objects. When we move to new places there are often some things we take with us to make us feel "at home." Possessions—things that possess us as much as we possess them—are not simply property. A coin in your pocket may be your property if its only value to you is whether you are willing to exchange it for something else. But a clock inherited from a deceased relative means more than a physically identical manufactured object. This habit of investing a bit of ourselves in certain objects, and in feeling that some objects have a bit of someone else in them, is a human universal. Our social world has become entangled with the world of objects that surrounds it.[21] And the process of making, sharing, giving, and receiving possessions is almost always heavily freighted with social significance.

The social worlds of human beings are very unusual. No other species has created anything like them. Our social universes were to begin with largely portable so that we could move alongside friends as well as relatives, accompanied by our animals, and carrying a few precious possessions. But our distinctive brand of sociality cried out to settle down. Once we were settled we could built houses for the gods and cities for the dead. Our wide and complicated social worlds could live in rough proximity. Our possessions could become grander and larger. Even while we wandered around wider territories throughout the year there were places we came back to repeatedly, so-called super-sites visited each year, or the caves where wall paintings passed on religious messages from one generation to another. But villages and cities would allow us to express and develop our complicated social world much more fully. Here too we were preadapted for social life.

Our social brain evolved to suit the needs of various early human species that lived and moved in large groups. We were selected for big brain size as part of embarking on an evolutionary trajectory in which we invested in sociality rather than speed or strength. As early humans dispersed and wandered farther and farther afield they found many new uses for their big social brains. But it was when that species began to settle that their big brains really came into their own. Living densely packed in villages like Çatalhöyük or in early cities like Uruk takes serious social work. It is more difficult to scatter when tensions arise, and very costly to engage in the kind of violence and warfare some chimpanzee bands practice today to preserve a social hierarchy and keep control of territory. Our nests are created and sustained by negotiation, not by genetic programming. Our intense sociality and the big expensive cumbersome brains that make it possible really opened up the world of cities. Big social brains preadapted us to become urban apes.

3

Settling Down

Into the Holocene

Around 12,000 years ago the glaciers began their last—or rather their latest—retreat. The deserts and the ice caps contracted once again. The water released flooded territories like Beringia that had once connected Alaska to Asia, and the great plain of Doggerland, beneath what is now the North Sea. New islands appeared, isolating populations that began their own distinct evolutionary journeys. Meanwhile animal and plant species that had survived the glacial period in *refugia* began to expand their ranges once again, recolonizing lands revealed by the retreating ice. Global temperatures rose rapidly between 13,000 and 10,000 years ago (although nowhere near as rapidly as they have over the last century). The world entered the current interglacial—the Holocene, the warm period that we still enjoy today.

All this had happened many times before. But this time it was different, and it was our species that made the difference. Some scientists have even proposed that the Holocene be renamed the Anthropocene, the age in which humans have fundamentally altered the planet. To tell the truth, we had already started work on this well before the ice began to melt. During the long two-and-a-half million year Pleistocene period, humans of different kinds had often experienced the alternations of glacials and interglacials. Their geographical ranges had expanded and contracted like that of other large mammals. But in the meantime, what it meant to be human had been changing fast in Africa. During the last glacial period *homo sapiens* had moved out of the Rift Valley and colonized most of the Old World. At the start of the Holocene they entered the Americas. Only the most remote islands and the ice continent of Antarctica now had no human populations.

From Foragers to Farmers

At the start of the Holocene all humans were foragers.[1] That loose term embraces many different combinations of fishing, hunting, and gathering edible plants, and in a sense it could describe the way all species of early humans and most apes found their food. But the foragers of the late Pleistocene were something new. They were skilled and knowledgeable exploiters of their environments. They made and used high-tech equipment from stone and wood, from hides and bone, from vegetable pastes and fibres. They worked together in teams as no other species had ever done before. Lions hunt in prides, but they do not sit down first and plan ambushes. Early foragers could shift from one food resource to another with a facility that few species of mammals today possess. They leapt from ecological niche to niche. Many forager populations were already selecting plants with such care that they were on a trajectory that would make them into farmers. Once the ice began to melt, all this became much easier. The climatic improvement at the start of the Holocene unleashed the potential of anatomically modern humans.

The lives of our earliest *homo sapiens* ancestors have left few traces: they travelled light around and between their territories. They had few possessions and made few permanent marks on the landscape. But we can tell a good deal about how they lived from the lifestyles of their nearest modern counterparts. Most prehistoric foragers probably lived in smallish communities of just a few dozen individuals at most. Some bands were even smaller, just large family groups roaming the less hospitable landscapes. Every so often they would meet up with other bands to take part in shared rituals, to find mates, and perhaps to trade stories and a few rare, and easily portable, objects. In most respects they formed typical primate fission–fusion societies.

Every so often freak conditions of survival have preserved some of their tools, or the remains of some of their meals. So we know they had learned to fish and hunt with nets and harpoons, could set traps for small mammals and birds, and gathered many different sorts of fruits and nuts and vegetables. Fishing and hunting probably made up a more important part of the diet of those who lived in the colder regions far from the equator. Vegetable resources were more important where it was warm. It was especially in these warmer zones that forager bands moved around larger territories each year, following seasonal food sources just as many chimpanzee bands do today. These were not random searches but were based on a good knowledge of what was edible and what was not, and when each fruit ripened. Forest-dwelling populations today have a compendious knowledge of the local flora, and rich vocabularies to describe plants and trees, vocabularies which we have mostly lost. Despite this skilled knowledge, the carrying capacity of most territories was low. It is a fundamental rule of ecology that top predators are always thin on the ground.[2] If human populations were to multiply and flourish in places where they could not rely on fish and meat, a greater part of their diet would have to be fruits and vegetables. And so our ancestors expanded the range of plants they could eat.

Some potential foods were barely digestible. So they learned to mash them and soak them and cook them. Back in our African cradle it was meat-eating that had powered the steady increase in the size of their brains. Now we were sleep-walking down the food chain to compete with the plant-eating animals we had once hunted. During the early Holocene the proportion of vegetables in human diets rose and rose, until in early states meat eating was often the prerogative of gods and heroes. Only in recent times has meat become once again a major part of our diets, and then only in the developed world. Democratic carnivory may turn out to be a short-lived experiment, as our numbers grow and grow. If we want to remain numerous, we may have to become herbivores.

Early in the Holocene numerous human populations, widely separated in space and experimenting with different cultigens, became farmers. In retrospect, the logic of cultivation seems obvious: what can be gathered from the wild is always less that what could be harvested. Cut down the wildwood, pluck out the weeds, plant only what humans can eat, and breed newer and more productive strains of those crops. Soon the same land will support bigger populations than ever before. Yet there was almost certainly no sudden moment or revelation. Instead, humans learned by trial and error how to transform their environments into ones that would produce more of the plants that were useful to them. That learning process began before farming proper.

Foraging can have as heavy an impact on ecosystems as hunting. Even during the late Pleistocene many humans had been environmentally interventionist in all sorts of ways. Hunters selected their kill by age and sex, gatherers chose some plants rather than others, some populations probably even burned areas of the bush to allow preferred species to grow. When reindeer and caribou colonized the tundra some humans followed them, and came to shape their lives around the rhythms of the herds, and then shaped the age profile of the herds in turn. That way of life continued for millennia before reindeer were properly domesticated. Wild sheep too show traces of human intervention long before they were fully domesticated. At the largest scale there is nothing unusual about this. Predator species always shape their prey, and the natural world has never been a stable equilibrium system. And as always in evolution, our success came at the expense of others. If there was a difference it was that our very varied diets and our ingenuity in making use of new food sources meant that human populations were not limited by feedback effects of the kind that limit most predator populations. With highly specialized predators—like wolves or cheetahs—the size of the predator population is limited by the size of the populations of their normal prey. Eat too many deer and the wolves go hungry, and their population drops. The first human settlers of New Zealand or North America seem to have gorged on the prey species they found there, but once the megafauna were gone or drastically reduced in numbers, human populations did not collapse. They moved on to other foods.

Early in the Holocene a one thousand-year-long cold snap, known as the Younger Dryas, may have provided the stimulus for one of the first inventions of agriculture. It happened in the Near East. From preserved plant and animal remains it is possible to reconstruct changes in the environment of a broad sweep of territory between the Mediterranean and the desert interior, from the modern borders of Egypt through Israel and Jordan to northern Syria. Largely arid today, between 13,000 and 8500 B.C.E. this was a landscape of open woodland bordering on upland steppe. As it gradually dried out its inhabitants—known today as the Natufians—transformed themselves from hunters of gazelle and gatherers of wild plants, to first mobile and then sedentary foragers. Only a few environments have ever been rich enough to sustain large populations of foragers who do not move about. For a while the Near East was one of them. Studies of Natufian skeletal remains show that once they settled down they began to eat more carbohydrates than did earlier populations. But when the climate shifted, sedentary foraging no longer produced as much food. Most likely it was the drying up of a once rich environment that nudged the Natufians into actually farming the grasses they had previously gathered. They could never have done this without the big brains and technical dexterity that *homo sapiens* alone of human species possessed. They observed and learned how germination worked in the wild, and how plants that were no use to them—weeds—could crowd out their food sources if they were not removed. They adapted tools to help them clear land, to plant seeds, and to reduce the biodiversity of their fields. They organized themselves to work together, as they had worked together as hunters and as foragers. Other species faced with environmental degradation might have retreated to better territory, or simply collapsed in number. Our ancestors could do better than that. They stayed and farmed.

The Natufian invention of agriculture is a very local story. Agriculture was invented many times around the globe, in radically different ecologies. Each local story must have been different, but there is a general pattern. Moves from intensive foraging to planting and farming took independently on at least a dozen occasions (that we know about so far). The first domestications took place in the Middle East 10,000 years ago (wheat and barley) and in Mesoamerica (pepo squash). Around 8,000 years ago millets, rice, and foxnut were domesticated in China, and arrowroot and perhaps manioc in different parts of South America. Around 7,000 years ago domestications of yams, bananas, and taro took place in New Guinea, of maize in Mesoamerica, and perhaps potatoes in the Andes. Between 6,000 and 4,000 B.C.E. there were domestications of millet and pulses in North India; of squash and sunflowers in the eastern United States; of chilli peppers, cotton, sweet potatoes, yams, and quinoa in South America. African domestications are at the moment least well known, but sorghum was grown by 2000 B.C.E., millet by 1000 B.C.E., and rice around the turn of the millennia.[3] Some of these dates are more provisional than others. Research is moving fast in this field and some questions, such as when collection of wild rice became rice cultivation, are controversial. That said, the big picture is clear.

One proof that agriculture was invented again and again is that most early farmers began with different sets of crops. Each crop had different needs and each cultigen had to be processed in different ways: this means that the basic skills of agriculture are not that transferable. Watching the sowing and harvesting of grain does not help much if you want to grow rice. Each invention of farming started from scratch. Other domestications followed as more and more vegetables and fruit crops, and later plants from which textiles could be woven, were tamed.

At a second stage there were exchanges of plants and seeds, some over enormous distances. Bananas are native to Southeast Asia and were first domesticated in Papua around 7,000 years ago; by 5,000 years ago they had not only spread as far as India, where they appear on Indus Valley sites, but also into East Africa. Between 5000 and 1000 B.C.E. varieties of maize—first domesticated in Mesoamerica—spread north to the Great Lakes region and south into tropical South America. Creating varieties of maize that could thrive in such a wide range of temperatures and altitudes and soils must have taken enormous and skilled work. The number of basic cultigens we rely on today remains very small, but they have now been bred into a bewildering number of varieties.[4]

Meanwhile, humans were also becoming closer and closer to some of their prey species. Sheep, pigs, cattle, and goats were all domesticated on the mountain fringes of the Fertile Crescent between 11,000 and 9,000 B.C.E.; pigs in China around 8000 B.C.E.; cattle in northern India around 5000 B.C.E. By 4000 B.C.E. donkeys, horses, camels, alpacas and llamas, guinea pigs, chickens, and ducks had joined them. Reindeer were probably not domesticated until the last millennium B.C.E. New lifestyles emerged, based on cohabitation between humans and a small range of domesticated animal species.

The term "domestication" conventionally describes how wild plants and animals are changed in human hands. Wolves became dogs, grasses grains, and so on. But in the process humans changed, too. We too were in some senses domesticated, as we built a common home for ourselves and our chosen companion species. But it was our species that took the initiative. None of these symbioses could have emerged without being planned by human minds and engineered by the tools humans made. We did not stand still while nature changed around us. Sheep lost their huge horns when humans took control of their breeding, and males became less aggressive. Humans developed a tolerance for lactose as they tamed wild cattle. Our new high-carbohydrate diet changed the shapes of our bodies and the workings of our brains, even as we changed the size and shape of the animals we most relied on. Domestication created multispecies societies, societies managed by their human members. Almost all of the animal species recruited to these multi-species societies were originally herd animals. Dogs, sheep, cattle, horses, and pigs are all in some sense social animals: it was their sociality that humans co-opted, asserting dominance over the herds or packs, and suppressing the dominant individuals in each. Dogs and humans have coevolved so success-fully that we are adept at reading each other's moods and intentions. We have become a single herd.

Ecologically minded historians now think of these processes as bringing about new biological complexes within which the lives of humans and their domesticates became more and more closely involved. These new complexes were not limited to animals and plants. A closer connection with former prey species brought some unexpected passengers, not all of them benign. Measles is so closely related to the cattle disease Rinderpest that it almost certainly developed in the context of cattle domestication. Many of the diseases that still affect us today are zoonotic, diseases that pass from one species to another. Salmonella and flu pass from domesticated fowl to humans. Some other diseases probably come from undomesticated animals. The most likely origin of HIV is in a similar condition endemic to some populations of African monkeys. And many human and animal pathogens are new, results of random mutations that gave them an evolutionary advantage at our expense. There are also companion species we never sought to domesticate, like rats. There is even a species of lice that has specialized to survive in human clothing. Around the globe a range of different multispecies societies emerged during the Holocene, each one comprising humans, their main animal domesticates, and the pests and pathogens they harboured.

When distinct multispecies societies encountered each other, the results could be explosive. Perhaps the best illustration of this is what happened when Europe and the New World were brought dramatically back into contact by the voyages of the navigators of the fifteenth and sixteenth centuries. It was not just long-separated humans that came into contact, but entire biota.[5] The encounter has been termed the Columbian Exchange, but that sounds a little benign. Most populations have some degree of immunity or resistance to pathogens with whom they have cohabited for a long time. The encounter with an unfamiliar disease pool is much more threatening. New World societies collapsed as much under the pressure of Old World diseases like smallpox, measles, and whooping cough as in the face of guns and iron technology. Other aspects of the exchange also led to rapid competition between native and entrant species. Horses and new grasses transformed life on the Great Plains and the Pampas long before European settlers arrived in force. Only a little later, the arrival of New World crops like potatoes and maize transformed Old World societies. Once sugar cane began to be cultivated on a grand scale and sugar exported to Europe, the effects on the diet (and dentition) of European populations was dramatic.[6] Coffee and chocolate soon followed, while some American societies crumbled on exposure to distilled alcohols made from Old World grains. We are still living with the consequences of these exchanges today.

This had, of course, happened many times already. Three million years ago the continents of South and North America were connected by tectonic movements. The animal and plant populations of the two regions had developed quite separately for more than 60 million years. Once connected species moved north and south across what we know as the Isthmus of Panama, the result was the massive disruption of both ecosystems. This event is known as the Great American Interchange. Opposums and porcupines came north, but mostly it was the fauna of the north, especially mammals, that crowded out their southern competitors.

Humans were not involved in the Great American Interchange, but they played a major role in the transformation of Australian fauna. The first settlers, arriving around 50,000 years ago, are probably implicated in the extinction of that continent's megafauna. Tens of thousands of years later, new arrivals brought dogs from South Asia; dingoes established themselves as top predators across the continent, crowding out native predators and having a dramatic impact on native prey species. The impact of animals brought by settlers of European origin from the late eighteenth century has been even more dramatic: cattle, sheep, camels, rabbits, and various species of rats and mice are among the more intrusive. European imperialism is only the latest phase in the spread of multispecies societies. Around 5000 B.C.E., once dairy farming was established in the Near East, cattle pastoralism began to spread all the way down eastern Africa to the Cape: in the process, the new complex of humans and cattle squeezed out a whole series of local ecosystems and foraging practices.

All around the globe biological complexes of this sort expanded at the expense of the more diverse landscapes through which foragers had once wandered. The shrinking wilderness is very obvious to us today, but it began to shrink millennia ago with the extinctions of large mammals and birds in the late Pleistocene. New landscapes emerged, characterized by fewer plant species and fewer predators. The useful crowded out the useless as well as the threatening. Around the world the first cities would be built in cultivated landscapes of this sort. The earliest literatures and oral poems imagine a time when great heroes—Gilgamesh, Theseus, Herakles, Meleager—fought off giant lions and bulls and boars to protect bread-eating mortals and their rich fields. In reality, the top predators were already on the way out, deprived of their habitats and their prey even when they were not hunted for sport. Anthropogenic habitat loss meant that other species disappeared even if they neither competed with humans nor were hunted by them. These changes unfolded in the forests of Amazonia and New Guinea, in the deserts of Mesoamerica and the Near East, in the High Andes and along the river valleys of China. The only common factor was our species—omnivorous and hungry, good at working together in large bands, clever with our hands, problem-solvers and problem-creators.

Not every human population opted for farming right away. But between 10,000 and 5000 B.C.E. farming spread through Eurasia, Africa, and the Americas in fits and starts, through a combination of migration, imitation, and exchange. Farming was not always adopted for the same reasons. Once adopted, however, if was difficult to reverse. The trend towards a farmed planet was cumulative.

We are beginning to map these processes with animal and plant genetics, and the distribution of world languages.[7] Differences between the DNA of forager populations and that of the farmers who replaced them in many regions suggest that foragers were often swamped by incomers or outbred by them. Foragers were pushed to the environmental margins, to swamps and mountains and the deep forest. Every so often a biological complex reached the limits of the territory that could support it. A long frontier between farmers and foragers existed for millennia in Scandinavia. Successive settlers of the lands around the Arctic have had to rely on fishing and hunting to an extent that has been rare for millennia. When New Zealand was first settled by Polynesians they found their tropical cultigens would flourish on the North Island, but not in the harsher temperate landscapes of the South Island. In those conditions farmers might revert to foraging. Yet the overall trend was inescapable. By 3000 B.C.E. farming communities were to be found across Eurasia, India, Africa, and the Americas wherever possible. Foraging was restricted to the densest tropical forests, to desert regions, and to the Arctic. The first Pacific mariners were farmers; so were the first settlers on the North Atlantic islands and probably Madagascar. In the five centuries since the Columbian Exchange our various farming regimes have joined up, so that most local agricultural societies can deploy a rich combination of domesticated crops and animals. The global ecosystem has shifted gear, even if it has not stabilized.

These changes are irreversible. Biodiversity plummets wherever farming takes hold. Most predator species—along with many others that could not be domesticated but simply competed for the same niches as humans and their animals—have either been deliberately eradicated or else have suffered irreparable habitat loss, as farmland expands at the expense of other ecologies. Meanwhile, the populations of humans and domesticated animals grew and grew. By some estimates there are now 1.5 billion cattle, 1 billion pigs, and 1 billion sheep sharing the planet with 7.6 billion humans. Our multispecies society has gone global. Going back is not an option. Populations that have mushroomed in size thanks to farming could never be sustained in the same territories by foraging. The wilderness is gone forever.[8]

Staying Put

Farming did not just change the way we ate. It changed everything. For a start, we settled down.

Sedentism—living in the same place all the year round—was already practiced by a few foragers. The Natufians were once such a group until the woodlands dried up and they were driven to become farmers. Another place where sedentary foraging was possible was in the Pacific Northwest, where some of the earliest humans in the Americas lived well on a mixture of shellfish, marine fish, and sea mammals. When great migrations of salmon began, around 6500 B.C.E., they provided such a rich resource that local populations were able to catch enough to store as a food source throughout the year. If you lived in the right place then rivers or the sea might bring you so much food that you did not have to move to look for it. But most foragers moved around their territories throughout the year, using up one local resource after another. During the preceding glacial period some hunters travelled even greater distances, following the annual migrations of reindeer and mammoth. Hunters and foragers alike had temporary camps—nests if you like—and some members of their bands moved longer distances than others. Quite likely there were often camps where the old and the very young spent much of their time, while their more mobile relatives ranged more widely. It has been suggested that one reason *homo sapiens* became much more long-lived than other early human and primate species is that older women in particular became valued for the role they played in childcare, allowing parents to spend more time away from the camp or at least from looking after the young. Long childhoods demand more adult care, and older members of families could provide it. We should imagine late Pleistocene and early Holocene foragers as living lives part on the move, part at rest. Foraging is not as time-intensive an activity as farming. Even those who had to move about most—because they lived in less hospitable environments—spent only a few hours a day gathering food.[9] In later periods many nomads had winter camps, and travelled most in the summer months. That could have been true in some prehistoric environments. Settling down would not be a sudden change for many, but something they got used to over time, some more completely than others.

Once a group began to farm, however, its members were tied to their fields as never before. Labour was required throughout the year. First the land had to be cleared of brush and stones, or clearings made in the forest. Then the soil had to be turned or hoed before seeds were pressed into the ground, or rows of maize laid out, or forests had to be cleared, and so on. Some crops needed to be watered. There was always weeding to be done, and the rising crop had to be defended from animals and birds and even sometimes from human enemies. This was all very hard work, especially in the millennia before animal traction was available. Growing seasons meant there was almost always a rush at the harvest—in which everyone, young and old, men and women, participated—to gather everything in when it was ripe and to process and store it before it perished. During quiet periods other tasks needed to be done. There was the making and repairing of tools, fencing and ditching, the weaving of wicker baskets and the construction of other containers out of wood, textiles, and eventually pottery. The earliest farming was really more like gardening than modern agriculture. Until there was animal labour it was very labour-intensive, and the whole family took part.

Settling down had other consequences, ones that were unplanned and unexpected. Land that is farmed supports more people per acre or hectare than land that is foraged, and for farmers manpower is a key resource. Populations rose as a consequence. Meanwhile, health declined. The diets of early farmers were less varied than those of foragers. As carbohydrates became a bigger and bigger part of their diets the risk of malnutrition grew, and in many communities people were short as a result. Permanent settlements were also dirtier places than the temporary camps of foragers, who left their waste behind them when they moved on. Endemic diseases multiplied as parasites learned to jump between domesticated species and humans, and also between humans who lived much more densely packed than ever before. Farmers were also more liable to face years of hunger when their key food crops failed; they were less able to diversify their diet or simply move. Humans were better able to survive this sort of pressure than many species, but bad years exacted a price in reduced fertility, in the early deaths of the weaker members of farming communities, and in fewer live births. Cemeteries began to be laid out around the villages.

Settling down also allowed humans to accumulate possessions, those special objects that are some ways an extension of ourselves.[10] The *homo sapiens* groups that colonized the planet during the late Pleistocene and early Holocene carried with them weapons and tools, axes, bows and arrows, spears, nets and harpoons, and also needles and clothes and ornaments made of shells. Some had portable images carved from stone and mammoth ivory, which took hundreds of hours to make. But in general they travelled light, as they had to. Once they settled down the range of possessions increased enormously. They built elaborate homes and filled them with tools, ornaments, and containers. Furniture appears, made of wood in most cases, but in near-treeless environments like the Orkneys it is made of stone. Pottery had been used by some sedentary foragers. It came into its own in agricultural settlements to store food, to cook in, for use in milking and in processing food, and even for use at communal meals. Families personalized their living spaces. At least some objects and images served as mementoes, messages from one generation to another, props for religious rituals, and carriers of personal and social memories.

The archaeology of agricultural communities is completely different to that of foragers. Foragers have left traces of only a few shelters, some scattered burials and the remains of the tools they made and the animals they butchered and ate. Only in exceptional cases, as when they made tents from mammoth tusks or amassed great middens of food waste, does a little more survive. But for most forager populations we have to reconstruct their lives from the most slender of traces. Farmers created a more durable world, one which archaeologists find easier to explore than the human worlds that preceded it.

Once again it is the Near East that provides the best documentation. As settled foragers, the Natufians lived in small settlements of perhaps 100 to 200 people, living in a cluster of semisubterranean houses marked out with stones supporting conical thatched roofs. This is perhaps one of the simplest kinds of housing that can be created. But as farming spread far and wide across the Natufian territory and into adjacent areas including southern Anatolia, Cyprus, and the Zagros Mountains that now lie between Iraq and Iran, larger and larger sites appeared. The prepottery Neolithic

A settlement built at Jericho around 9,400 B.C.E. consisted of around seventy houses packed into an area of 2 to 3 hectares.

Between 8500 and 6500 B.C.E. a range of sites appear, the smaller ones around 2 hectares in size, the larger around 12 ha. Most spectacular of all is Çatalhöyük in Turkey, which covered an area of 14 hectares in the period between 7400 and 6000 B.C.E. Estimates of its population range from 3,500 to 8,000 people and it probably varied over its long life. The houses of these new, larger villages were still very small by modern standards, but they were much more complex than those of the first Natufian settlements. They had multiple rooms and were built on more than one floor level. Distinct spaces were allocated to different activities. Their walls were made of mud, often supported by a wooden frame or resting on stone foundations, and some were covered in plaster and decorated. Each house had a hearth and storage pits. Burials have been found beneath the floors, and offerings at doors.[11] There is little sign of public spaces, no town walls, no civic halls, and no grander houses for chieftains or village magistrates. Each house was a place of ritual as well as a place of work and a home. Some were treated with great care, carefully rebuilt generation after generation. And they were full of possessions. Wall paintings at Çatalhöyük depicted animal and human figures, and there were stone figurines, pots with human faces on them, animal skulls, and tiny deposits of rare stones.

Forager bands were so small that every member knew everybody else. Early agricultural villages quickly crossed the threshold beyond which a community based on personal relations of this kind was possible. The limits for a face-to-face society remains set by our big social brains at around 150 people.[12] That sort of size continues to define the smallest military units, the size of clubs and active social networks, and so on. Tensions and conflicts in larger social worlds can no longer be dealt with so easily in traditional primate fashion by displays of dominance and subservience or by spending time apart. Fission–fusion societies—the primate standard—work far better for mobile than for sedentary populations. Farmers had to stick together, or at least stay in the same place, and so they had to get along. If there was a quarrel around the time of the harvest it was not possible to split up into separate bands and ignore each other. There were quarrels, of course, but the costs of not resolving them were now higher. Agriculture imposed a discipline of sorts.

It is difficult to reconstruct the exact stages by which a more complicated social order began to emerge, one that was more disciplined and no longer based on a dense web of personal relationships constantly being renegotiated. The household was now an economic unit. Villages consisted of households that worked together. Personal bonds articulated each household, and connected key figures in each household with each other.

This new kind of social order had to extend further in time as well. A way of life that depends on foraging is in some ways lived in the present. Food is gathered as soon as it becomes available. Little can be stored or carried, so it is consumed rapidly. Long-range planning is not really needed, so long as there is a shared knowledge of where to forage at which times of year. Even then there is the need for some social discipline. Ethnographers who have worked with the small number of forager societies that exist today suggest there are often very severe sanctions against antisocial individuals or freeloaders. But farming involves thinking about time in a different way. Farmers in effect bank labour in the present in the expectation of being able to withdraw food in the future. When they do acquire food they need to preserve and store as much as they can, and some seed needs to be put aside to be planted to ensure a crop next year. That requires some calculation, and some rationing of their resources between harvests, some collective commitment to the community. A disgruntled farmer cannot wander off without leaving behind a valuable investment in labour. Nor can reduced cooperation be tolerated in farming communities. Common fields, a shared village, established means of dealing with water rights and waste, and so on all require consistent collaboration. At some times of the year—when tree crops ripen, for example—there is no time for renegotiation of the division of labour. Being social became more important than ever before.

This was not a sudden revolution, any more than farming was. Thinking back on the mammoth hunters of Ice Age northern Europe or the great salmon harvest of the Pacific Northwest, it is clear that humans had long had the ability to work together when necessary. But farmers had to do this more of the time. Settling down was the first of successive surrenders of personal freedom that have characterized the last ten thousand years of human history. We work longer and harder, we live among strangers, and we submit to the discipline of others.

There were great potentials too in the new social order. Some of the most spectacular of prehistoric monuments were built by early farmers. The great megalithic tombs of Atlantic Europe, built in a range of styles from northern Spain to Brittany, Britain and Ireland, and southern Scandinavia belong to this period. Stone Age farmers also built Stonehenge and the other great earthworks of Wessex, raised the Moai on Easter Island, and created the mounds of the Mississippi. Some of these were temples, but many were burial sites that express the new long-sightedness of human societies, societies that now thought about a deep past and a far future as well as from one season to another. Was there some connection between a tacit understanding of generation following generation, the placing of the dead in the ground, and the annual replanting of seeds? Archaeologists have long puzzled over the connection between agriculture and monumentality.[13] Did agricultural societies simply have more labour available to realize these projects? Did monumental tombs serve as claims to land? Or were they simply a manifestation of the greater organizational potential of less egalitarian societies? Did the new ranked social order build simply because they could?

One tantalizing clue is offered by the discovery that there were indeed a few forager societies that built monuments. Not very far from Çatalhöyük, but a few millennia earlier, is the site of Göbekli Tepe, a cluster of buildings constructed across 8 hectares of a hilltop in southern Turkey.[14] Only a few kilometres from the site is the region where wild einkorn was first planted. Wild sheep would be first corralled there just a few thousand years later. But the animal bones from the site show that its builders were not farmers. They ate gazelle and red deer, wild sheep, wild boar, ducks, geese, and cranes. The buildings they constructed might be the earliest temples in the world.

Even before humans settled down into permanent settlements their lives revolved around fixed places in the landscape. Nothing illustrates this better than the nonportable art created by prehistoric foragers. On the sides of the huge monoliths from Göbekli Tepe were carved images of all sorts of wild animals: foxes and vultures, snakes, lions, and scorpions. Some of these stones weighed up to 10 metric tonnes. Monumental art came in many media. A 5-metre-high wooden statue from Shigir in western Siberia was carved from an ancient larch tree around 11,000 years ago. It was covered in strange signs that sometimes look like runes, sometimes like human faces. The top of the idol is carved into a human head. Even earlier are the paintings of animals and occasionally humans made in the pitch-black cave systems eroded by water under the mountains of northern Spain and southern France, at Altamira, Chauvet, Lascaux, and other sites. Most of these images are dated to betweeen 20,000 and 15000 years ago, but some are probably much earlier. Some of the earliest rock art of southern Australia may be as much as 40,000 years old, and some from the northern territory is certainly over 20,000 years old. The attachment to particular places—an attachment formed by art, ritual, and perhaps storytelling too—must have made the move to sedentary life all the easier.

A World of Villages

No doubt many early experiments in farming failed. Domesticated species were not adequate, the environment was not propitious, and societies failed to stick together long enough to make it work. Yet as the Holocene progressed more and more experiments were successful, and around the world cultivated fields and plots and gardens were carved out of the wilderness. It used to be common to write about *the* agricultural revolution, as if a world of foragers changed suddenly into a world of farmers. In reality it was more complicated. Different groups of foragers approached farming by various routes. All they had in common were those social and cognitive capacities that had evolved for other purposes. Mostly these changes happened sooner in those warmer regions where plant resources had always been a bigger part of foragers' diets: in Mesopotamia and Mesoamerica, Egypt and northern China. But in the last few decades other early experiments in domestication have been revealed in forests and high plateaux.

Most farmers lived in villages of one sort of another, but they were not all alike. Some—like Jericho and Çatalhöyük—were relatively large with populations in the thousands, but most were much smaller. Some comprised a few immense longhouses, others a ragged clutter of round huts; some were built out of mudbrick and others of stone, yet others of timber and earth, or wood and wicker. They were built on the windy cliff tops of Skara Brae, on the parched hilltops of the Aegean, in clearings in the forests of Amazonia and Papua New Guinea. Yet the villages of early farmers had some distant family resemblance. Almost all the buildings in them were houses, inhabited by humans or animals or quite often both together. People slept, worked, and prayed in the same spaces. Trackways were small, dirty, and often crowded, convenient paths winding between gardens, yards, and huts. When they could, people worked outdoors because artificial light was scarce. Children were everywhere, both because there were many more children relative to adults than today and because in a world without schools or nurseries and in which women worked (at least) as hard as men, there was nowhere else for children to be. As soon as they were old enough they would take their turn weeding the gardens, and looking after the smaller domestic animals and their own smaller brothers and sisters.

Communal parties happened when food was plentiful. Every society that has learned how to grow carbohydrates discovers, sooner or later, how to ferment them.[15] Residues of a drink made of fermented fruit and rice have been found in Neolithic China, beer appears on cuneiform tablets from Mesopotamia, a number of pre-Columbian societies made sweet wines from fruit, and *tiswin* was brewed from maize. Agricultural communities have synchronized cycles of work and relaxation. Communal life led to shared fortune and misfortune, shared poverty alternating with shared plenty. If we were to wander around one of their villages we would not see many differences between the inhabitants apart from those deriving from age or sex. If some families were more successful, had a few more possessions or livestock or simply carried more weight in discussions, this was generally a temporary state of affairs. Leaders probably mostly emerged through good fortune or ability, not a reflection of differences of class or birth. Within a given region every village was pretty much the same as its neighbours. Up until six thousand years ago, most societies were pretty egalitarian.

Eventually some villages began to regularly produce more food than they needed for themselves. Differences in wealth began to appear, and so did trade. Animal domestication and the use of their secondary products changed life in other ways.[16] Woollier sheep were bred along with stronger cattle, horses, and donkeys. Old World farmers began to use carts and ploughs, which allowed them to extend the range of their cultivation. It also made it possible for some people to farm much more land than others. Textiles were at first produced at a household scale, but during the Bronze Age much larger productions emerged, aimed at producing goods that could be traded.

Burial grounds tell a similar story. Very few forager burials have been found, although probably Neanderthals and certainly our immediate ancestors buried their dead. But there were so few of them, and they possessed so little, that their graves are rarely found. Burial archaeology really comes into its own with farming societies. In southern Scandinavia some burial mounds echo the architecture of the houses of the living. Very occasionally we suspect we are looking at the family tomb of a powerful clan, just because such effort has been expended on the tomb, and sometimes some signs of ritual surround it. But it is only in the Bronze and Iron Ages that really rich individual burials appear, for women and children as well as male warriors. By then society had been replaced with a new social order with ranks, classes, and hereditary distinctions. Kings and cities were just around the corner.

4
Uruk

Gilgamesh the King

The world's first urban society is described in the world's oldest narrative poem, the *Epic of Gilgamesh*.[1] This is how it begins.

> He who saw the Deep, the country's foundation
>> who] knew ... , was wise in all matters!
> [Gilgamesh, who] saw the Deep, the country's foundation
>> [who] knew ... , was wise in all matters!
> [He] ... everywhere ...
>> and [learnt] of everything the sum of wisdom.
> He saw what was secret, discovered what was hidden,
>> he brought back a tale of before the Deluge.
> He came a far road, was weary, found peace,
>> and set all his labours on a tablet of stone.
> He built the rampart of Uruk-the-Sheepfold,
>> of holy Eanna, the sacred storehouse.
> See its wall like a strand of wool,
>> view its parapet that none could copy!
> Take the stairway of a bygone era
>> draw near to Eanna, seat of Ishtar the goddess,
> that no later king could ever copy!
> Climb Uruk's wall and walk back and forth!
>> Survey its foundations, examine the brickwork!
> Were its bricks not fired in an oven?
>> Did the Seven Sages not lay its foundations?
> [A square mile is] city, [a square mile] date grove, a square mile is
>> clay pit, half a square mile the temple of Ishtar:
> [three square miles] and a half is Uruk's expanse.

> *The Epic of Gilgamesh* Tablet I lines 18–24 (trans. George)

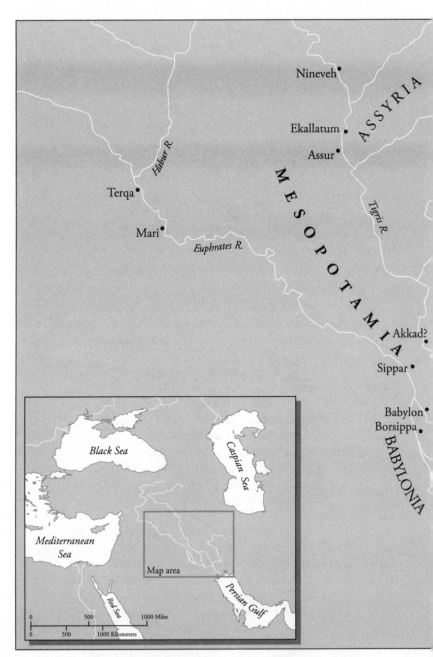

Map 2 Mesopotamia from the fourth to the last millennium B.C.E.

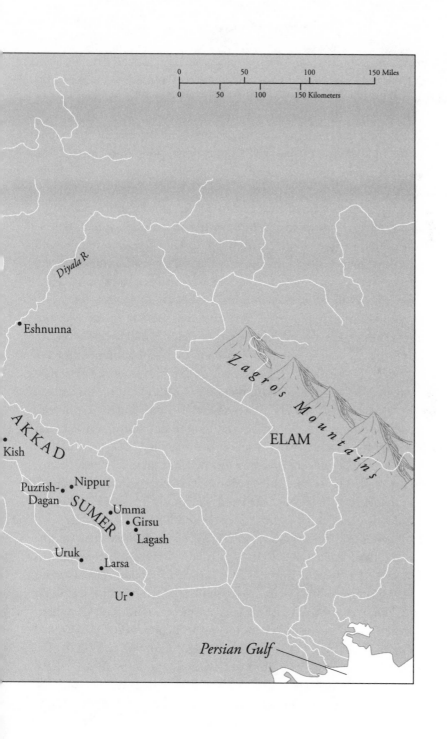

0   50   100   150 Miles

0   50   100   150 Kilometers

Diyala R.

•Eshnunna

Zagros Mountains

ELAM

AKKAD

•Kish

Puzrish-• •Nippur
Dagan SUMER

•Umma
•Girsu
•Lagash

Uruk•
•Larsa

Ur•

Persian Gulf

Gilgamesh, king of Uruk, was two parts god, one part man. He was tall, magnificent, terrible, a handsome hero and the son of a goddess. He defended his city and built it new ramparts, but he was also feared by his own people. The story opens with him striding around Uruk like a wild bull terrorizing the city folk, intimidating the young men and keeping all the young women for himself. The people seek help from the gods who create a rival to Gilgamesh, a wild man named Enkidu who eats grasses with the gazelle and jostles with the other animals at the water hole. Stories about Enkidu reach the city and Gilgamesh sets out to catch him. Enkidu is tamed by sending a woman to sleep with him until the animals, who smell her on him, will no long come close. Heartbroken, Enkidu agrees to return with her to the city. Once in Uruk, Enkidu becomes Gilgamesh's companion and together they set out on a great series of adventures. They travel to the great Cedar Forest and kill the giant who guards it. Then the goddess Ishtar falls in love with Gilgamesh. He rejects her, knowing the fate of her previous mortal lovers once she had become bored of them. A divine bull is sent to punish him, but he and Enkidu kill it. Enkidu dies—a punishment for the lack of respect the two heroes have shown to the gods—and Gilgamesh is stricken with grief at his loss and possessed by a horror of death. Guided by his divine patron, the sun god Shamash, he goes on a long quest to seek immortality, and he meets Uta-Napishti, the lone survivor of a flood with which the gods had once tried to eliminate mankind. Gilgamesh learns secrets from him that no other man has learned, but these do not include a remedy for death. He returns from his journey a wiser man, a great king, a builder, a shepherd of his people. He reigns gloriously but in the end passes away. On his death he rules in the Underworld.

The earliest stories about Gilgamesh, King of Uruk, were first written down in the third millennium B.C.E. in a language we call Sumerian. It is related to no other known language. We know little about the Sumerians before they sprang into history in the second half of the fourth millennium B.C.E. and founded the world's first urban civilization in what is now southern Iraq.[2] They invented a writing system too, using a complicated script called cuneiform, made by pressing patterns of wedges into clay tablets, like the one depicted in Figure 4.[3] The story of Gilgamesh has to be reconstructed today from hundreds of baked clay tablets, many of them damaged, hence the gaps at the start of the extract quoted at the beginning of the chapter. Quite possibly there was a real Gilgamesh in one of the Sumerian city-states, as his name appears in king lists that predate the epic, but all of his story is myth.

The cities of the land of Sumer rose and fell over the fourth and third millennia B.C.E., but the *Epic of Gilgamesh* became a classic. During the early second millennium, in the Old Babylonian period, it was translated into Akkadian, then the language of diplomacy across Palestine and Syria, Mesopotamia, and even Anatolia, in what is now central Turkey. Clay writing tablets with parts of *Gilgamesh* have been found from all over this region. Fragments of an early second-millennium version of the epic have been recovered from Hattusa, the capital of the Hittite Empire in central Anatolia. Translations into Hittite and Hurrian also existed. The longest continuous version that has survived is what Assyrologists call the Standard Version, an Akkadian edition compiled between the thirteenth century and eleventh centuries B.C.E. For centuries the Standard Version was the centrepiece of the scribal curriculum. More than seventy copies of *Gilgamesh* have survived from the last millennium B.C.E., including more than thirty from the

Figure 4 A Clay Writing Tablet from Uruk

libraries of Nineveh, the vast capital of Assurbanipal II, who ruled the Neo-Assyrian Empire from 668 until 627 B.C.E.

Assurbanipal was one of the greatest of Assyrian emperors. During his long reign he inflicted defeats on Egypt, on Babylon, and on Elam. His death marked the beginning of the empire's collapse. Nineveh itself was sacked in 612 B.C.E., incidentally preserving the contents of her libraries, baked and sealed for posterity in the ruin. Three years later the Assyrian Empire itself fell to a coalition of her many enemies and former subjects. The Achaemenid Persian Empire, which expanded into the power vacuum that followed, made little use either of Akkadian or cuneiform writing. Instead the Persians invented a new script to inscribe their own language (Old Persian) into the living rock, made some use of Elamite, and for everyday purposes preferred the Aramaic language, a language on the rise even before the fall of Assyria and spoken over a vast range of the Ancient Near East. Like Hebrew, to which it was closely related (and like Greek, Latin, and Arabic), Aramaic was usually written in ink, on parchment or papyrus, in a version of the original alphabetic script invented in northwest Syria a few hundred years before. Persian archives written in Aramaic are known from Egypt to Afghanistan and from many places in between. The combination of a change in language with a change in the media used for writing was a death blow for ancient Mesopotamian literatures.[4] A few temple communities in Babylonia continued to read and copy out the *Epic of Gilgamesh* as late as the second century B.C.E., by which time Alexander the Great's conquest of the Persian Empire had ushered in yet another language change. From the third century B.C.E., Greek was the new lingua franca from Italy to the Hindu Kush, at least for public and official writing. Dialects of Aramaic remained widely spoken in the Near East and spawned new Christian literatures in late antiquity. But *Gilgamesh* was long forgotten.

The King and the City

The Epic of Gilgamesh is not just the world's oldest poem. It is a classic, in the sense that it remained central to the literature and though of a whole series of cultures across the Near East over millennia. We can account for its significance in several ways. Some of its themes are universal. We still agonize that even the greatest human life is limited in span; we mourn and rage against the loss of our loved ones; and like Gilgamesh we still want to know about our origins and the meaning of things. One title for the epic was *He Who Saw the Deep*. Gilgamesh goes on a quest for meaning. His failure to find acceptable answers is our failure too. His fortitude in the face of that failure is true heroism. Like so many epic poems, the particular story speaks to our wider experience.

But there is another themes of the epic that is close to the subject of this book: the life of humans in cities. For *Gilgamesh* is about civilization and wilderness, about war and peace, and about a world of cities.

Civilization and wilderness stand vividly opposed in the first tablet of the epic. Gilgamesh is *both* the protector of the city who built its rampart, *and also* the wild bull terrorizing the citizenry. Then the civilized life of brick-built Uruk is opposed to the steppe where Enkidu lives like an animal with the animals. Woman tames Enkidu, and Enkidu tames Gilgamesh. The opposition between the domesticated world of the farmer and the surrounding wilderness recurs in many literatures, but here we read it expressed in poetry for the first time. Even the written poem, ordered by line and tablet and copied out again and again over the generations, seems like a domestication of wild impulsive speech and song. When the gods complain to the chief god Anu about Gilgamesh's behaviour they say, "A savage wild bull you have bred in Uruk-the-Sheepfold." The city, with its gardens, its date grove, and temples, is compared to the enclosure built to protect domestic livestock, but there is a wild animal inside the pen, Gilgamesh the King! His path in the story will lead him from uncontrolled violence to assuming the role of a culture hero, a civilizing force.

> Gilagamesh the tall, magnificent and terrible
> who opened passes in the mountains,
> who dug wells on the slope of the uplands,
> and crossed the ocean, the wide sea to the sunrise
> who scoured the world ever searching for life,
> and reached through sheer force Uta-napishti the Distant:
> who restored the cult-places destroyed by the Deluge,
> and set in place for the people the rites of the cosmos.

The Epic of Gilgamesh Tablet 1 lines 37–44 (trans. George)

Male heroism in the epic is bound up with the city, with sieges and attacks and sacks and bold defences, and with a restoration of order. The two most ancient story cycles in the Greek world—the siege of Troy and

Seven Against Thebes—also revolved around these themes. Epic began as a song about the civilizing process, and these epics have at their heart the precarious achievement of the city and its farmers, besieged on one side by the wilderness and its monstrous beast and on the other by immortal gods whose passing whims condemn whole human generations to misery.

Centre stage in all the Gilgamesh stories is Uruk. The Standard Version was composed at the beginning of the Near Eastern Iron Age, around the time Troy fell and Mycenae was abandoned. But five poems remain from the earliest Sumerian versions of the story and from these we can tell that the city was from the start central to the tale of Gilgamesh (Bilgames in Sumerian). One poem describes a war between two neighbouring cities, Kish and Uruk, each of which has its own king or champion, Akka in Kish and Bilgames in Uruk. Uruk has great ramparts, Akka's army lays siege to it, and after an exchange of embassies Enkidu sallies forth and battle is fought before the walls. Only a glimpse is given of the society of Uruk, but Bilgames addresses both a council of Elders and also the young men of the city, who seem to make up its warriors. From administrative records we hear of an assembly called a *puhrum* in Sumerian cities, which some scholars have compared to primitive democracy. Other Sumerian poems about Bilgames mention priests and priestesses, a royal minstrel, craftsmen and merchants. Uruk itself is dimly visible, a city of wider and narrow streets, with the palace and the temple of Eanna the only prominent structures within it. This is essentially the same image of the city that appears in the later Middle Babylonian and Neo-Assyrian period versions. (Indeed it is more or less the same image we gain of Troy from reading the *Iliad*.) Later versions of *Gilgamesh* add more detail. The Uruk of the Standard Version has walls made of fired brick; it possessed a great temple and precincts laid out for the gods, and the walls also enclosed gardens for the production of dates. Around the city are the orchards and grain fields, beyond them the ranges where flocks graze and around that the wild steppe, where Enkidu appears.

Beyond that familiar landscape lay mythologized lands to which Gilgamesh and Enkidu travel and where they encounter strange creatures. There was the Cedar Mountain, home of the giant Humbaba, protected by strange magic. There were the terrifying scorpion men who guarded the mountains where the sun rose and set. Far to the east was the sea which Gilgamesh had to cross to reach the island home of Uta-naphisti. We can try to put these places on a map if we choose—Lebanon for the Cedar

Mountain? the Persian Gulf for the eastern ocean?—but perhaps it makes better sense to say that once any people begin to think of the world as centred on civilization and cultivated fields they will always come to imagine its limits in terms evoked by the mediaeval cartographer's note "Here be dragons."

The centrality of the city in the *Epic of Gilgamesh* goes a long way toward explaining why it became so important in Mesopotamian culture. City-states of the kind that appeared in Sumer around 3000 B.C.E. provided the enduring framework of social life in Mesopotamia for all the epic's long lifetime and long after it was forgotten. Meanwhile, empires rose and fell and Amorites and Kassites and other peoples invaded. Eventually there were cities of one kind of another in most of the places the epic was read: coastal cities like Byblos and Ugarit, followed in the Iron Age by Tyre and the other Phoenician centres; inland hill towns like Jerusalem and Amman; desert oases and caravanserais like Palmyra and Petra; and rich farming centres in the fertile river valleys of the Bekaa in Syria and the Tigris and Euphrates in Mesopotamia. Whatever the political regime, and whatever the basis of the local economy, the city remained the fundamental building block out of which Ancient Near Eastern civilizations were built. For their populations epic tales of cities in conflict never grew old, and the matter of how kings ought to behave never went away either. The *Epic of Gilgamesh* is one of the earliest examples of what is sometimes termed a "Mirror of Princes," a book that illustrates the conduct of both bad and good rulers, and makes clear the difference between them. Just as the story of Troy—first written down in archaic Greece—remained full of meaning in democratic Athens and Republican Rome and for Macedonian and Roman emperors, so the stories of Gilgamesh the King and the city of Uruk would always resonate in Mesopotamia.

The *Epic of Gilgamesh* gives us a precious glimpse of how the world's first urban civilization was imagined by its inhabitants. If it is a surprisingly familiar picture, then that is a sign of how influential Near Eastern ideas would be on later civilizations, even those that had forgotten that an *Epic of Gilgamesh* ever existed. Today Uruk has another resonance for Sumerologists and those interested in the origins of cities. For the shift from village life to urbanism in Mesopotamia has for long been known as "the Uruk phenomenon," and the period in which it occurred, roughly 4100–2900 B.C.E., is known as "the Uruk period."

The Uruk Phenomenon

"Mesopotamia" means the land between the rivers. The rivers in question are the Tigris and the Euphrates. The Euphrates flows from northeast Syria down to the Persian Gulf with the high Arabian desert on its right (southern) border. The Tigris runs to its north and east, fed by rivers coming down from the Anatolian plateau and the Zagros Mountains, which now lie along the frontier between Iraq and Iran. The Zagros is also the western limit of the Iranian plateau, rising up above the lowlands through which the two rivers flowed. The northern part of Mesopotamia came to be known as Assyria, a cooler land of low hills where farmers could depend on rainfall to water their fields. The southern part, where the rivers flowed more sluggishly and the summer sun baked the soil into hard mudflats, was Babylonia. Here agriculture depends on careful irrigation, but when well-watered the deep alluvium is very fertile. South of Babylon the land is so flat that even the slightest change of sea level turns marshes into farmland or back again. Only recently have archaeologists begun to reconstruct the Holocene history of this environment, and built up a picture of the shifting patterns of land, marsh, and sea. East of the Tigris other smaller rivers drained down to the gulf across what is now Khuzestan in southwest Iran. Their valleys and the surrounding uplands formed the land of Elam, closely connected to Sumer from the very beginning, and later named Susiana after its most important city, Susa. These landscapes formed the stage for some of the first experiments in city life.[5]

Mesopotamia is also the eastern half of what has long been called the Fertile Crescent, a great arc of land wrapped around the Arabian Desert. Its western half curls down from northern Syria through Lebanon and Israel, Palestine and Jordan to the borders of Egypt. It linked the world's two oldest urban civilizations, Egypt and Mesopotamia. It was also the main corridor through which domesticated species and technical innovations were exchanged, since direct routes across the desert were more or less impossible until the spread of domesticated camels in the early Iron Age. Even then it was often easier for caravans to move from city to city around the crescent. The term "Fertile Crescent" is a little misleading. While all these lands are more fertile—or easier to farm—than the interior of the Arabian Peninsula, they are not all alike, nor are they uniformly fertile. Many of its ancient societies flourished in areas where they could exploit contrasting ecologies, and some were only made fertile by human ingenuity. The Land of Sumer, where cities first appeared in the fourth millennium B.C.E., was framed by the desert and the mountains, the uplands of northern Mesopotamia and the marshes to the south. Applying irrigation to the rich alluvial deposits laid down by the two rivers, the Sumerians were able to make the most of the potentials of plant and animal species domesticated thousands of years before on the upland fringes of the Crescent. Once they were producing surpluses they were able to trade with neighbours in Assyria, Elam, and even Egypt and lands beyond the gulf. The world's first cities were built by the people who farmed those muddy fields, but it was their proximity to different ecologies that made the Sumerians rich.

It is not easy to trace the earliest stage of this process. Right now, of course, things are especially difficult, because Iraqi archaeologists and their overseas colleagues have for almost thirty years been working against a background of warfare and civil conflict. Almost every part of the region from the gulf to Kurdistan and now Syria has been ravaged by the conflict. Quite apart from that, the archaeology of the world's oldest urban civilizations is often obscured by the accumulated remains of later periods. Many of the most important archaeological sites take the form of great mounds—tells— in which Arab or Crusader remains stand on top of Byzantine, Roman, and later layers which themselves cover the remains of Iron Age, Bronze Age, and prehistoric settlements. Uruk itself is partly obscured by late first-millennium B.C.E. remains. Other problems are less obvious, but still important. We presume that before an urban network was consolidated there were many experiments in city-building, some of which must have failed, leaving few traces. We usually see only the remains of the success stories. Add to this the ever-shifting river courses of southern Mesopotamia and the rise and fall of the waters of the Gulf, which together erode deep channels through archaeological deposits or cover them in deep layers of mud. It is miraculous that so much has both survived and been recovered.

The first farming communities in Mesopotamia date to the eighth millennium B.C.E. Those farmers lived in tiny villages of mud brick houses and they did not use pottery. They had tools made of stone and of the volcanic glass obsidian; they grew barley and wheat and kept sheep and goats, but hunting also remained an important source of food for them. Those settlements are best known in north Mesopotamia, but by the seventh millennium are documented from the foot of the Anatolian plateau down to the Persian Gulf. Farming villages of up to ten houses remained the largest kind of settlement for around two thousand years. The population of each village was usually less than the Dunbar number, the supposed maximum number of individuals with which each of us can maintain individual social relations. These were small worlds indeed.

During the following millenia things did change, but mostly by small increments. A few more species were domesticated, some settlements and burials were sometimes a little richer, the scale of irrigation gradually increased. But in gross terms Mesopotamia remained fairly similar to all those other areas around the planet being farmed during the mid-Holocene. It was not until the middle of the fifth millennium—in the late Ubaid period—that new patterns began to emerge. Two stand out in particular. First there is a huge expansion of the geographical range of styles of man-made objects characteristic of southern Mesopotamia. Late Ubaid forms of pottery vessels and statuettes, tools and even architecture appear on sites up and down Mesopotamia and even in Syria. There is unambiguous evidence of the appearance of ranked societies such as rich burials alongside poor and larger houses alongside smaller ones, and a few settlements of 10 hectares where most covered no more than a hectare. Most significant is the appearance of the "public" buildings, larger and more complex than houses, apparently nonresidential, and some containing tokens and seal stones, presumably used to manage storage and exchange. How exactly the expansion of late Ubaid style, a growing agricultural surplus, and the appearance of social ranking appear together is unclear. Was some threshold crossed beyond which egalitarian communities were unsustainable? Did a gradually expanding set of connections suddenly gel? But the trajectory is very clear. These farming societies were heading toward greater complexity.

Those changes were just the start. Around 4000 B.C.E. cities suddenly appeared. The earliest known are Tell Brak in northeast Syria, and Uruk and Nippur in southern Iraq. During the early fourth millennium B.C.E., each covered an area of between 50 and 75 hectares. The largest of the Ubaid villages had only covered 10 hectares. In addition, the number of sites known increases four- or fivefold. Around Uruk and Tell Brak there were village-free areas of territory about 5 kilometres in radius. Beyond them the landscape suddenly filled up. Uruk—the modern site is called Warka—has been excavated off and on for more than a century. Much more recently excavations at Tell Brak in Syria suggest urbanism might even have been earlier than Uruk.[6] This is a real surprise, and not just because Brak was hardly known until recently. The ecology of the two regions is completely different; agriculture in northern Iraq depended on rainfall rather than on irrigation. So much for the old hypothesis of "hydraulic despotism," which suggested that the first states arose in order to organize common projects of irrigation! Yet it can hardly be coincidence that urbanism appears for the first time more or less simultaneously in two locations nearly 900 kilometers apart. The growing web of long-distance connections in which both sites were enmeshed seems all the more important.

By the end of the second half of the third millennium B.C.E., the city of Uruk covered 100 hectares and dominated the smaller settlements of the southern part of the land of Sumer. The city must have been a spectacular sight rising above the flat muddy fields, visible for miles and miles around. At the centre were two huge sacred precincts, each enclosing a series of temples raised up to heaven. The cities that appeared in the south of Mesopotamia began a tradition of building temples on great artificial platforms—ziggurats—which eventually gave rise to the story of the Tower of Babel. One of the ziggurats at Uruk supported the temple to the sky god Anu, known as the White Temple because it was white-washed so that it would shine brilliantly like a palace on an artificial mountain, high above the level of the city walls. The other sacred precinct was dedicated to Inanna, the Mesopotamian prototype of Aphrodite and Venus, that terrifying goddess of love who never forgave Gilgamesh for spurning her advances.

These temples were not just eye-catching; they were also at the centre of the economy.[7] One alabaster vase, a metre in height, is decorated with a series of reliefs that seem to show animals and grain and perhaps beer being brought in tribute to the god. Rare traces of statuary survive too, showing that the Sumerians had begun to create monumental art. We know a little of what this new urban world looked like from the images carved into cylinder seals (see Figure 5). Carved in hard stones like carnelian, they are beautiful objects and survive in their hundreds. The seals were cylindrical so that they could be rolled across a clay surface to authenticate or authorize a document. The number of seals show the importance that writing—another new invention of the Uruk period—had in organizing society. The first texts were much less ambitious than the *Epic of Gilgamesh*; they were primarily long lists of products and people. Probably stories about gods and heroes existed in oral form already, but it took a while to modify a technology designed for counting and recording objects and property into a medium that might immortalize poetry.

Figure 5 A Mesopotamian Cylinder Seal
Photo © RMN-Grand Palais (musée du Louvre) / Les frères Chuzeville

Underpinning the creation of temples and ziggurats and great walls enclosing settlements bigger than any that had existed before was a new way of organizing society. The Uruk phenomenon brought the city; it brought the state; it brought metallurgy; and it brought writing.[8] It also generated new styles of material culture too, which spread rapidly through Mesopotamia and Syria, with distant echoes even further afield. Most characteristic is a range of rather bland plain pottery vessels produced in huge quantities. When we think of mass-produced products today we generally think of the products of industrial and mechanical manufacture. The beveled-rim bowls, the nose-lug jars, and the rest of the Uruk repertoire were all handmade, perhaps for distributing rations to workers. So there were large numbers of craftsmen working together, almost certainly supported by the city or temple authorities, and those authorities played an active part in determining what they made. There were specialist potters, there were smiths, and there were textile workers and skilled craftsmen making cylinder seals. Full-time artisans have to be given rations of food. There must have been some systems of gathering food contributions from farmers, whether this was understood as rent, as tax, as tribute, or as gifts to the gods. Those economic exchanges needed to be organized. The authorities—king and priests and perhaps some people who claimed to fill both roles—coordinated all this in the name of the gods.

Mesopotamia is not only the world's first urban civilization. It is also the first world that speaks to us. The origins of writing go back to counting systems and tokens older than the Uruk period. Once societies settle down and need to think and plan in the medium term, they have to organize storage and begin to manage exchange. Routines of counting and remembering and passing on information become more important. If farmers had to think further ahead than foragers, city-dwellers lived even more enmeshed in the long term. They looked further back, creating the first king-lists. And they looked further forward, making laws that were intended to bind their distant descendants. Visitors to the Louvre Museum today marvel at a shiny black monolith more than two metres in height, on which are inscribed in cuneiform writing nearly 300 laws passed by the Babylonian king Hammurabi in the eighteenth century B.C.E. (see Figure 6). Inscribing those laws into volcanic diorite must have taken an enormous effort, a great monument to the king and the

Figure 6 The Law Code of Hammurabi
Photo © RMN-Grand Palais (musée du Louvre) / Franck Raux

durability of the code he laid down. It is so impressive in fact that it was stolen centuries later by a king of Elam and set up in Susa, where it was found at the beginning of the twentieth century. Many other copies existed on the clay tablets through which Mesopotamia was governed.

The Code of Hammurabi was not the earliest law code. Others are known from the end of the third millennium B.C.E., and there were probably earlier ones as well. The clay tablets of the Uruk period on which those beautiful seals were impressed were first written in what it called proto-cuneiform with the evolved writing system appearing only in the late Uruk period. One of the documents found from Uruk is a text known as *The Standard List of Professions*. More than a hundred Sumerian signs designate every possible occupation from gardeners and cooks, to craftsmen and shepherds, and priest and king—complexity, hierarchy, monarchy, redistribution, discipline, numeracy, and literacy.

That world is vividly illustrated by a beautiful wooden box called the Standard of Ur, now in the British Museum (see Figure 7). We do not know for sure what it was originally made for, but we know it was worth a great deal. It was found in one of the so-called royal tombs just outside the Mesopotamian

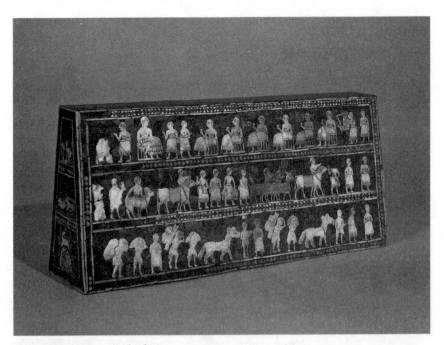

Figure 7 The Standard of Ur
© The Trustees of the British Museum

city of Ur, and it dates back to the middle of the third millennium B.C.E. Not only was it buried in the grave of someone very important, it was intricately decorated with material brought enormous distances. It is decorated with red limestone, with shell probably imported from the Persian Gulf, and with lapis lazuli that had been traded overland from what is now Afghanistan. Each long side is divided into three horizontal bands, one side showing military scenes, the other peaceful ones. The "war panel" shows donkeys pulling four-wheeled war carts and trampling enemies below them, soldiers marching in formation and in combat, and prisoners being handed over to a leader. On the other side a group of men sit at banquet, attended by musicians and serving women, while below them are depicted processions bringing animals and other goods—to be eaten or sacrificed, booty or simply tribute?

Nothing quite like the Standard of Ur has ever been found, but the rich imported materials it is made from, the bright colours, the banquet, and the scenes or war, were already part of an international currency of elite status that stretched well beyond the Fertile Crescent.

Why Uruk?

For all the attention that has been devoted to the Uruk phenomenon, there is still no consensus about why it happened.

It is clear enough, of course, that the potential for city-building had been growing for some time. Urbanization is expensive: it depends on marshalling reserves of labour and diverting agricultural surpluses, agricultural and demographic growth with necessary preconditions for urbanization. It has been estimated that the construction of the White Temple would have taken 1,500 labourers five years; getting these numbers right is very difficult, but the figure gives some idea of how many workers would have to be fed and housed by the labour of others. The population of lower Mesopotamia was already dense in the Ubaid period. Millennia of farming and domestication lay behind the agricultural systems that made Uruk possible. The fact that southern Mesopotamia—the "heartland of cities," as it has been called—was not far from the areas where its main crop species and farm animals were first domesticated gave it a head start. Underlying this was the urban aptitude of all modern humans. Put like this, we might almost ask why it took so long.

Thing are not quite so simple. It is true that city-building in Mesopotamia depended on prior social change, among them sedentarism, the spread of farming, successive domestications, and a range of technical innovations including pottery production, metallurgy, stone-cutting, and writing. Yet none of these were produced as a means to an urban end, any more than our dietary flexibility and social brains were. Urbanism was never in any place the result of a long-term plan. So it is pointless to ask questions such as why the builders of Çatalhöyük did not create the first cities in Anatolia, or why the descendants of the Natufians at the other end of the Fertile Crescent did not do likewise. Why should they have done so? In point of fact there have been many agricultural societies that never seem to have tried to create towns. For example, the core group of cultigens developed on the northern fringe of the Fertile Crescent did not just power the urban cultures of Mesopotamia and Egypt (many millennia after domestication, of course) but also the late prehistoric societies of Europe. Neolithic and Bronze Age populations farmed, grew, accepted new domesticates into their economies, built monuments, and probably went to war, but did not create cities or states. To their east and north the emergent pastoralist peoples of the Eurasian steppe also made different uses of the fruits of domestication. The story can be repeated around the world. Cities were not the inevitable sequel to agriculture. Farming was a necessary precursor of urban experiments, but not sufficient to stimulate them. This will be even clearer after the survey of early urbanisms in the next chapter.

Urbanization, when it does happen, is usually a rapid transformation. It is often violent, disruptive, dislocating. That is true even when the resources assembled to make it happen have been accumulating over a long period. Our difficulty in each case is in trying to understand the trigger, the specific circumstances in which "going urban" seemed something worth trying. One practical difficulty is a lack of information. Once the city and the state arrive there is suddenly an abundance of material remains. In most cases we soon have writing as well. This can drown out the slighter remains from preceding periods.

Occasionally external information helps. The Uruk phenomenon appears in a relatively warm period within the Holocene, and it is possible that it was preceded by rises in the sea level. Sea levels do not have to rise very far to flood much of the low-lying marshes at the head of the Persian Gulf. The fields of southern Mesopotamia are easy to irrigate but hard to drain. One possibility is that a prosperous society of farming villages was suddenly put under pressure, and this galvanized them into investing in

greater organization of a state. But that does not explain the near simultaneous growth at Brak in Syria, far from those ecological dynamics. Other
scenarios have been suggested. Maybe the rising population at the start of
the Uruk period was the result of migration, either from the desert or the
mountains. Did that tip the balance in favour of state-building and provide
the labour needed to build those first spectacular cities? Or did the slow
growth of population and production through the long Ubaid period cross
a tipping point, prompting a phase change, a dramatic shift from one kind
of system to another, whether we think of this as sudden expansion of connectivity across the region or the emergence of ranked societies? And if we
could work out the exact means by which the Uruk phenomenon came
about, how far would that answer be generalizable across all the early urban
cultures on the planet?

One influential answer is that creating cities might have been a good
answer to a range of different problems. In the jargon of his time, the archaeological theorist David Clarke put it like this:

> The process of urbanization was an equifinal solution to many different but
> related problems and stimuli connected with postglacial changes in ecology
> which affected different regions at different speeds and in different ways—in
> some areas not appearing at all, in others only very recently. Globally it would
> seem that the stimuli, pressures and courses towards urban systems were dif-
> ferent but analogous.[9]

Put simply, Clarke was suggesting that as the Holocene progressed more
and more situations arose in which it seemed a good idea to reorganize
society on different lines. This reorganization usually involved less equality, greater surplus production, and landscapes that contained one or more
densely populated urban hotspots. Clarke emphasized the early Holocene
context of these changes, and subsequent research has strengthened his case.
But there was more to it than the beneficial effects of a warmer climate.
Preurban landscapes around the world were littered with the building blocks
for urban projects. Whether it was big social brains, skills at making artefacts
from a range of materials, histories of domestication that now generated
big enough surpluses to support at least a few nonfarmers (whether priests,
craftsmen, or other kinds), populations grew large enough in places to supply the brute labour to build cities. None of this material was designed for
city-building, but it was ready if anyone was prepared to co-opt it.

For the moment we simply do not know enough about fifth- and fourth-
millennium Mesopotamia to be sure exactly which problems the new cities

and states were designed to solve. But since that solution involved writing, monumental architecture, and extraordinary images, we do have a very clear idea of what this early urban world was like. It was not entirely unlike the world imagined in the *Epic of Gilgamesh*.

Perhaps, too, origins matter less than we think. Evolutionary biologists are generally not too worried about the origin of each new trait that appears in a species, often as the result of a random mutation. What matters in evolutionary terms is whether or not a new trait conveys an advantage. If it does, it survives and is replicated; if not it perishes. It is perfectly possible that Uruk, Nippur, Brak, and other early Mesopotamian cities were created with one end in mind, but actually thrived because they worked well for other reasons. What matters is that urbanism conveyed some sort of advantage over other societies that stayed simple, and that those advantages were evident enough for others to try—some successfully, some less so—to imitate the Sumerians.

And we should remember too that some changes also become entrenched because they are in effect irreversible. Slower cheetahs will not evolve; whales will not return to the land. For human societies there are even more complications. Those who benefit from a change will often resist its reversal: Gilgamesh would never let his people leave the sheepfold, even if it was in their interests to do so. Domestication and social hierarchy are difficult—if not impossible—to reverse. And the entangled histories of technological change and human evolution mean that our things, too, prevent us turning back. Cities and all that go with them will not easily let us go. Looking back through the history of cities the Uruk phenomenon seems a momentous first step on a very long but inevitable journey. At the time it probably seemed nothing of the sort.

One sobering thought on which to end this chapter. If we rarely see clearly the moments at which cities emerge, we probably never see moments at which they are stillborn. Evolutionary biologists are aware that the only new traits they can follow in detail are those that gave rise to new species. Most mutations are disadvantageous or effectively neutral in survival terms. How many times around the world did groups of farmers begin to create a city only to have it fail? Was Uruk beginners' luck, or the fruits of long perseverance? On the ground it felt that the success of Gilgamesh and his real-life analogues was written in the stars. But the creation of the first cities may in reality have been a good deal more precarious.

5

First Cities

Where Cities Grew

Today it is easier to list places where there are *not* cities.[1] There are no cities in the deserts of the Gobi or the Sahara, and few in the rain forests of South America, Africa, and East Asia. Cities have only rarely been built more than 4,000 metres above sea level, although there are a few in the Andes and the Himalayas. Antarctica is the only continent without cities. There are hardly any cities in the high latitudes between 60 degrees and the North Pole. Outside these arguably extreme environments, cities are everywhere.

A few patterns are obvious. Cities are thinner on the ground and smaller where food is scarce—on the steppe, on the savannah, and in the taiga. The most densely urbanized regions are mostly coastal, and this is also where the largest cities are usually to be found. Then there is an element of inertia too, which means that some of the most successful cities today are former metropoles and provincial hubs of nineteenth- and early twentieth-century empires, cities like Mumbai, Cape Town, and Rio de Janeiro. Their days are numbered unless they can find new roles in new postimperial world orders.

New and unfamiliar names appear among the list of the world's fastest growing cities, reflecting the uneven growth of the world economy. Some of the largest cities have grown rapidly in chaotic and unplanned fashion. Since the Industrial Revolution, migration along new transport infrastructure has piled up vast populations. Chicago famously grew from less than 5,000 inhabitants to more than a million in the second half of the nineteenth century. Toronto had only slightly less dramatic growth in the late nineteenth and early twentieth centuries. The latest megacities are growing fast in West Africa and Northeast India, in parts of China, and along the western and eastern seaboards of the United States. Modern states are often more successful at planning or at least accommodating growth.

Ever since the days of Gilgamesh rulers and governments have tried to control urbanization, planting cities in new lands, amalgamating cities, even obliterating some or resettling entire subject populations in new lands to create dynastic and national capitals. Nineveh and Persepolis, Alexandria and Constantinople, Washington and Brasilia represent success stories of this kind. Governments have often gotten it wrong, of course.[2] Planned cities flourish only if natural resources and communications favour them, or if the power of great states can sustain them against the ecological odds. The jungle and the sand cover many imperial follies.

The Earliest Urban Experiments

If cities are almost everywhere today, the first urban systems were small and strange local experiments. The first we know of took place 6,000 years ago in the Fertile Crescent of the Middle East. They were built not on the mountain fringes where the earliest domestications had taken place millennia before, but in the river valleys of the Tigris and the Euphrates, on land that was already intensively farmed and, by prehistoric standards at least, densely populated.[3] By the end of the fourth millennium B.C.E., Uruk was just one of a dozen or more city-states in southern Babylonia, some less than twenty kilometres apart. Their rulers made war with each other, struggled for regional pre-eminence and territory. Farther north other clusters of cities appeared around Tell Brak, this time in a landscape where agriculture depended on rain, not on irrigation.

Those cities are the most visible traces of broader patterns of connection, patterns that involved seminomad pastoralists, a trade in wool, and the manufacturing of textiles. The sharp ecological frontiers in Mesopotamia between the river valleys and the steppe, and between lowlands and hills, provided plenty of incentives for exchange. More and more societies wanted wood and metals and grain and the secondary products of domesticated animals. During the Bronze Age a loose network of urban societies emerged between the Persian Gulf and the Syrian coast—"from the Lower to the Upper Sea," in the words of one third-millennium ruler. Over time these urban societies established connections to even more distant regions, among them Anatolia, Cyprus, and Egypt. Cedar wood was traded from Lebanon, chlorite stone bowls from Iran, and faience from Egypt along communication routes that carried more perishable items too, textiles, food, and even artistic motifs and religious practices.[4]

Urbanism had a second birth in the Nile Valley.[5] The first cities we know of there were smaller and less spectacular than those of Mesopotamia. By and large they used the same range of domesticated crops and animals, for these had spread all around southwest Asia millennia before, but the first Egyptian cities had no ziggurats bearing temples and no great walls. Some we know only from their cemeteries. The Nile has washed away the traces of many of the earlier settlements and later cities have eradicated the earliest levels on the small areas of land available for building. But excavations at Hierakonpolis, south of Luxor and north of Edfu, have revealed a Predynastic city from the middle of the fourth millennium B.C.E. that stretched nearly three kilometres along the Nile. Houses and graves, potteries and breweries have been found, but little monumental or religious building to compare with what would come after. The differences in scale and architecture from the cities of Mesopotamia, as well as the distinctive hieroglyphic script that appeared in Egypt soon after, show that the Nile Valley followed its own path towards urbanism. It would be imitated (and adapted) farther south in Nubia in modern Sudan, where pyramids and other urban features appeared at Kerma around 3000 B.C.E.

The ecology of Nile Valley urbanism was different too. As the Holocene warmed up, a vast landscape of lakes and savannah that once stretched across the whole of North Africa dried up to become today's Sahara Desert. One likely scenario for the appearance of population concentrations in the Nile Valley is the arrival of migrants fleeing the expanding Sahara. Populations grew denser and denser within the tighter constraints of the valley. Agriculture came to depend on cooperation in managing the flood waters and the alluvium they brought downstream. New pressures and new opportunities are a plausible context for the invention of other cities. Farther south at Nubian Kerma, connections continued with transhumant cattle-herders who swelled the urban population for a few months each year; at other times the first cities were more like the ceremonial centres of preurban societies.

The third area where cities appeared was the Indus Valley, a vast area that now straddles the borders of India and Pakistan.[6] Unlike Mesopotamia, where dozens of tiny cities were packed close together, or Egypt where the Nile Valley concentrated urban growth into one long corridor, the

Indus Valley (or Harappan) culture produced just five great cities, each hundreds of kilometres from its neighbours. They emerged around 2800 B.C.E. above a background noise of much smaller centres that had been multiplying for centuries. What sparked the sudden creation of just a few cities of 50 to 200 hectares in size? The two most impressive sites, Harappa (see Figure 8) and Mohenjo Daro, are vast complexes of walls, water tanks, and platforms.

Seal stones found there show connections with ancient Mesopotamia, and Indus sites are mentioned on cuneiform tablets found at Ur. There were also connections between the Indus Valley and Turkmenistan far to the north in the cities of Altyn-depe and Namazga-depe, which nestle between the Iranian plateau and the Karakum desert.[7] The architecture of the Indus Valley cities is unique, the Indus Valley script that appears on seals and a few objects has never been deciphered, and their social world remains mysterious. So is the gradual breakdown of Indus Valley urbanism during the early second millennium B.C.E.

Urbanism appeared for a fourth time in what is now northern China in the early second millennium B.C.E.[8] Early farming took many forms in

Figure 8 The City of Harappa in the Indus Valley
DEA / G. Nimatallah / Getty Images

eastern Eurasia, depending on rice cultivation and water plants in the southern more tropical zones around the Yangtze River and on millet in the central plain of northern China along the Yellow River. Some Neolithic villages were very small but a few were very large, and there has been inevitable debate about when large villages became small cities. In practice this has meant looking for the first signs of specialization and writing, the hallmarks of more complex societies. One area where cities certainly appeared early is the central Henan region of northern China, where the population and the number of sites began to increase rapidly from the late third millennium B.C.E. Early in the second millennium a 70-hectare site appeared at Erlitou, and a few centuries later major centres were created at Erligang and Zhengzhou. The largest sites of the Erlitou and Erligang cultures were not only large but also had monumental building, and large cast bronze vessels. Someone was managing to marshall the labour of skilled craftsmen, to obtain expensive raw materials, and to stage great ceremonies using the bronzes. Looking back from later periods it seems almost certain we are observing the emergence of powerful lineages dominating their neighbours through the monopoly of rituals. By the middle of the second millennium there is no doubt that these urban sites were the centres of states. The city of Anhang, built around 1200 B.C.E., is associated with major tombs and has traditionally been linked to the Shang dynasty mentioned in much later Chinese historical records.

Cities appeared in the Americas slightly later. Urbanism appeared in the early centuries C.E. in the highland Basin of Mexico, and at Monte Albán in the Valley of Oaxaca nearly 500 kilometres to the south.[9] In the basin of Mexico the number of small farming villages increased steadily over the last millennium B.C.E., until they could be found every 8 or 9 kilometres along the shoreline of a shallow lake. By the end of the millennium there were few larger villages of 40 hectares or more in size, and then the two largest of these, Cuicuilco and Teotihuacan, faced each other across the lake. At some point in the early centuries C.E. Teotihuacan mushroomed in size until its pyramids and plazas, its processional ways and temples covered around 20 square kilometres of territory. It seems Teotihuacan was created by scooping up almost half the population of the Basin of Mexico, leaving only tiny rural hamlets in the fields around it. By contrast with early Mesopotamia, we seem to see a civilization focused on a single massive city. Within Teotihuacan different ethnic groups lived in different residential quarters, and residential and public spaces were organized by a great grid plan of roads.

Monte Albán was smaller in scale and looked quite different. In effect it was a cluster of pyramids and tombs, a palace, a ball court, and a vast plaza, all built along a high ridge visible from most of the central valley. Unlike Teotihuacan it was surrounded by other major settlements and its own population was probably never more that 20,000. But the mass of statuary and reliefs shows it was at the centre of diplomatic and ritual exchanges that stretched far beyond the valley, to central Mexico and to the jungles and coasts of Guatemala, Belize, and El Salvador, where the lowland Maya were following their own path towards urbanism.[10]

The sixth canonical invention of urbanism happened far to the south on the coasts of northern Peru. Rich natural resources had made this an early area for agricultural intensification during the second millennium B.C.E. Great monuments were created there too, and some researchers regard these as the traces of cities. But the majority view is that these early complexes were great ceremonial centres, comparable to those built by other early agricultural societies, and that true urbanism began around the sixth or eighth century C.E. with the emergence of the states of Wari and Tiwanaku, predecessors of the great Inca Empire that confronted the conquistadores just a few centuries later.[11]

One possible addition to this list is the huge mound complex at Cahokia in today's US state of Illinois that flourished for a few hundred years around the twelfth and thirteenth centuries C.E. It included more than a hundred mounds, grouped in three adjacent conurbations (see Figure 9). The architecture descends from that of ceremonial mounds built for millennia across what is now the eastern United States, but the scale and concentration is unparalleled. Traces of horrific mass human sacrifices have also been found, and in many respects it looks more like a vast ceremonial complex than a city. But at its peak it had a population of around 40,000. It was abandoned just a few centuries before the arrival of Europeans.

It would not be possible to produce a final and complete catalogue of early urbanisms. Recent discoveries, like those in the Amazon Basin or at Tell Brak, have the potential to change the picture. Chronologies are always open to refinement, and there will probably always be cases where we wonder if we are looking at the remains of an early city, of a large village, or a ceremonial site. But what is not open to doubt is that urban civilizations emerged—independently of each other—on numerous occasions across the globe during the second half of the Holocene. Why this happened is one of the big questions of human history.

Figure 9 Monks Mound, Cahokia, Illinois
National Geographic Image Collection / Alamy Stock Photo

The beginnings of urban systems always lie at the very limits of our historical vision. It is not just that urbanism when it comes shines so brightly that it obscures the image of what went before, although that is often true. There is also a shift in the nature of the evidence. The appearance of cities almost always meant a vast multiplication of objects, even as their designs often became more and more standardized. Uruk illustrates this perfectly with the mass production of a small range of pottery vessels and the creation of seal stones that led to mechanical replication of the same images again and again. Failed urban experiments leave many fewer traces, so we are forced to study successes without knowing how common they were. There is a final complication. Most urban civilizations depended on some kind of record-keeping, and some of these notational systems eventually formed the basis for writing. Many ancient cities, put bluntly, speak to us. Their voices often drown out the silence of the villages. All the same we have to have some way of describing how cities began.

One conventional way of telling this story is to say that after the city appeared independently six or seven times, urbanism spread from those starting points to neighbouring peoples either through imitation or as a result of coercion.[12] These arguments have been strongly linked to the parallel but different question of state-formation. In this account those first urban civilizations have sometimes been called "primary" or "pristine," the remainder being secondary. One result is that attention has been focused on the primary or pristine cases, and other urbanisms have been neglected.

Older textbooks are littered with abandoned and contradictory general theories of the origins of cities and states. The state in this sense is both a socioevolutionary category (like band, tribe, chiefdom, or empire) and also shorthand for a particular set of political structures. States in that sense are characterized by institutions—citizenship, courts, magistrates, assemblies, councils, and so on—rather than the more personal power exercise by chieftain and their kin. States are for that reason usually thought of as more stable, and more likely to be organized by law. It is easy to see how this kind of political entity is easily associated to the physical community of the city, with its division of labour, its social hierarchy, and its emerging civic architecture. How cities and states are in fact related has been a matter of debate for decades. There definitely are some states that do not have cities in them or in which cities play a small part, such as the states set up by steppe nomads. Equally, there are a few urban systems that seem not to be part of a state of the kind we usually recognize. The Yoruba cities of late precolonial Nigeria seem ordered more by kinship and organized by chiefs, for example. It has also been suggested that there were cities in the early Mediterranean before there were states, and that will be discussed later. These are good counterexamples and remind us how diverse early cities were, and how many kinds of early states there have been. But it is easy too to see why some researchers tend to regard urban origins and state-formation as closely linked phenomena.[13] A common shorthand is to include both under the umbrella concept of increasing complexity, although like all umbrella concepts this one conceals quite a lot of tricky nuance, some of which I shall return to.

Early states, like early urbanism, have been explained in many ways, mostly on the grounds of what they might have been good for. States have been held to appear in areas where they were needed to coordinate the management of water or the control of people; they have been thought to appear where societies were richest, or alternatively, where economies were most precarious; they have demonstrated the power of cooperation or the effects of coercion; they owe their origin to war, or to law, or to religion, and so on. None of these lines of argument has really managed to explain their sheer diversity or the variety of urban forms associated with them.

It is striking how much energy has been expended on urban origins and how little on the spread of urbanism. A part of this is perhaps to be explained in terms of the confidence early twentieth-century archaeologists had in progress. Urbanization, state-formation, and growing complexity were all seen as indices of cultural development or civilizational progress. Why would a society not go urban as soon as it could? Were cities and states not obviously the future? More thoughtful writers, like V. Gordon Childe, saw history as an upward trend punctuated by periods of collapse or decline, but with each new peak higher than its predecessor and successive collapses less and less serious.[14] That perspective was not confined to archaeology, of course. Many others believed that human history was the history of progress that might be measured technologically, economically, and even spiritually, morally, or cognitively. Those who associated civilization and modernity and rationality with the rise of cities were predisposed to find the spread of cities pretty easy to understand. Who would turn their back on progress once they had it?

Another reason the spread of urbanism did not seem to need much explanation was that archaeologists for a long time tended to explain many things in terms of the diffusion of innovations: writing, the wheel, metallurgy, and so on seemed such obviously useful things that it was not surprising that once invented, their use spread outwards. When diffusionism was all the vogue, the spread of cities and states around the globe over the last six thousand years seemed easy to explain. The spread of ideas and innovations obviously has some part to play in all this. Domesticated species and crops spread rapidly within ecologies where they could be used. Technologies, like iron-working or the making of chariots, were also taken up quickly by society after society. Maybe it is not so obvious that institutions were so readily imitated and appropriated, and customized to local needs. Could kingship, taxation, or law courts have been spread by "contagion"? Might cities have been spread in the same sort of way? If so we would only need to understand why they were invented in the first place, and the rest of the narrative would take care of itself.

There are very good reasons to distrust this kind of thinking. Both diffusion and contagion are invoked much more rarely today in the explanation of cultural change. For a start, these approaches have almost nothing to say about cases of nonspread or slow spread. Why did Harappan cities not inspire imitations across the subcontinent? Why did Mediterranean urbanism not spread into woodland Europe before the end of the last millennium B.C.? They are also unforgivably vague about the means by which ideas are transmitted or borrowed, the social circumstances of these exchanges, the roles played by those involved, and how much adaption has to take place in the course of adoption. Most fundamentally, of all these ideas are profoundly at odds with what we know of evolution more generally. The spread of a species, or of a particular trait within a species, can rarely be understood just in terms of why it appeared in the first place. In genetics new traits often appear through random mutation, and most mutations are useless or even harmful to a species. Origins, the dictum goes, explain nothing. What matters is how useful new traits turn out to be, and what advantages they gives to those who carry them, over those who do not.

It follows that understanding why urbanism did (and sometime did not) spread means asking what competitive advantage urban societies enjoyed relative to their neighbours. Were urban societies better at supporting economic growth, either because they were more organized or simply had more labour at their disposal? Were states able to support the craftsmen and soldiers that would give them an edge over their neighbours in military conflicts, or the artists and priests who could create even more compelling collective rituals? Either way, what mattered was not why cities appeared but why, having appeared, they were so successful.

We might go further; indeed we must. In the long term, a successful new species often modifies its environment to make it more suitable to its needs. Did the first cities created a world better suited to urbanism? Here evolutionary theory reminds us that things can easily go wrong. A species may put such pressure on the environment it colonizes that it becomes less well suited to support it. Ruminants can overgraze grasslands until populations dwindle; predators or pathogens can be so efficient that they run out of prey or hosts. Population collapses are in fact quite common. Steady progress for a long time in the same direction is the oddity, and perhaps it only exists as a brave ideal or as a self-serving narrative like "the civilizing mission" that justified so many recent imperial ventures.

Inventions, Collapses, Reinventions

The main reason to distrust a simple model of urban diffusion is that it explains too little. Three problems in particular spring to mind. First, many early urban traditions collapsed after just a few hundred years: How could this happen if urbanism was so obviously an advance? Second, many of the neighbours of the world's first urban civilizations resisted their allure very successfully: urbanism was obviously not *that* contagious. Third, even when new urban cultures did emerge on the fringe of older ones (like Nubia beside Egypt, or the Maya close by Mexico), they often seem very unfaithful copies. I suggest that it does not make much sense to draw a sharp distinction between primary and secondary urban civilizations. We have been inventing urbanism over and over again for thousands of years, and almost every invention is in some sense a new original, and most are also unfaithful copies.

Consider the urban traditions that petered out. Maybe the most famous example is provided by the great cities of the Indus Valley which disappeared around 1900 B.C.E., not quite a millennium after they appeared. There was no cataclysm that we know of—although quite a few have been suggested—and most of the smaller settlements that had flourished before and between the big five cities carried on regardless. But the subcontinent remained without cities until around 700 B.C.E., and when cities did reappear in the Early Historic period (India's Iron Age) it was in quite a different region, the Gangetic Plain to the east. As far as we can tell the new cities, which were nowhere near as grandiose as Mohenjo Daro and Harappa and owed little or nothing to them in design, emerged out of a background of gradually growing populations living in larger and larger villages.

Collapse is not that unusual in prehistory.[15] The rapid disappearance of Cahokia provides one New World example. Much more famous is the shrivelling away of Mayan civilization in the jungles of Belize, Guatemala, and surrounding countries. The Maya had begun to build monuments not very long after other peoples in central America. Trade goods and some architectural forms—such as ball courts and small pyramids—show they were in touch with regions to their west and north. What the Maya created when they went urban was quite distinctive. Teotihuacan seems to have been built by compression, bringing the populations of many smaller centres together

into one place. By contrast, the Mayan cities that began to appear around
C.E. 200 were mostly low-density, planted in spaces won from tropical forest
rather than in arid highlands.[16] And where Teotihuacan and Monte Albán
seem in different ways to express centralizations of power and ceremony, the
Mayan urban world was chronically fragmented. For seven hundred years a
cluster of rival city-states ruled by aggressive dynasties—Tikal and Palenque
are the most famous—struggled for power and wealth. And then, in the
ninth century C.E., the cities collapsed, populations shrank, and monumental
building ceased. A variety of explanations have been proposed incorporating different mixtures of ecological and agricultural disasters, political
turmoil, social unrest, and disease (all the usual suspects). At the moment
there is no consensus. But whatever outside disaster or internal failures we
blame, the cities disappeared and were never rebuilt. The Maya themselves
are still there, for when the glyphs that decorated the royal monuments were
deciphered it was immediately clear that the city-builders spoke versions of
the same language as today's inhabitants. Somehow or other, their ancestors
had turned their backs on urbanism.

We could compare the similar debates that still take place over the end
of the Bronze Age civilizations of Crete and Aegean Greece near the end
of the second millennium B.C.E. Current explanations invoke migrations,
rebellions, volcanic eruptions, and the collapse of vital exchange networks.
There is not even agreement about how local the causes of collapse were,
since crises of one kind or another affected parts of Asia Minor and the
Near East and Egypt at the same time. Nor was this the first time. Urbanism
in the Fertile Crescent went into some sort of decline after the initial Uruk
expansions, and only began to grow again from around 2600 B.C.E. The
chronology is so uncertain that it is not possible to rule out global fluctuations (inevitably coupled today with notions of climate change), but it may
be that we are in fact seeing many crises at a much more local scale.

One possibility is that early urban systems and early states were simply
quite fragile. Individual cities were major projects, costly not only to build
but also to sustain. They depended on balancing acts that were at once ecological, political, economic, and even theological. So they broke easily. What
happens when a city breaks down? Large populations always depend on
food produced by others, and often on food that needs to be supplied from
outside the immediate vicinity. If food stopped arriving, or if they ran out
of water, or if the rivers failed to flood, or if sea levels rose, then urban populations simply had to disperse. Even today our cities are rarely so resilient

that populations can last for long without vital services. Villages are in many ways more self-sufficient because they mostly contain fewer mouths to feed, and because more of the inhabitants farm and store their own food. Often the population of early cities must have returned to the villages, while some cities became villages once again. During the early Middle Ages many former Roman cities were replanted with gardens. Marble monuments were melted down in lime kilns to provide fertilizer for the fields laid out within the ancient city limits. If you have any doubt about just how quickly the wilderness can reclaim the city then Google Pripyat, the city abandoned in 1986 after the world's worst peacetime nuclear disaster at Chernobyl Reactor 4.

What about resistance to the charms of urbanism? Urban literatures from Gilgamesh on have distinguished the city from its surrounding wilderness, sometimes interposing an intermediate space of cultivated lands. It is rare for those literatures to express a conscious rejection of the city that could be compared to Romantic celebrations of the natural world in the age of industrialization. Early texts were mostly produced in cities for city-dwellers and celebrated the city's potential.

On the other hand, there were many ancient peoples who knew cities very well—and often were involved in close relationships with them—yet do not seem to have attempted urban experiments of their own. Around the Fertile Crescent, Bronze Age cities appeared in southwest Iran and Syria in the third millennium but did not spread to Anatolia or the Aegean world until much later. Harappan civilization was well connected to its urbanized neighbours in Mesopotamia, Iran, and central Asia, but its scope remained contained within just one part of the subcontinent. Cahokia appeared and disappeared like a lonely supernova. It very definitely exercised an influence over surrounding regions, but it did not inspire imitations in them. Perhaps the rituals practiced there were simply too horrific.

Sometimes urban systems came up against a hard ecological frontier, such as the central zone of the Arabian Peninsula, the Western Desert in Egypt, or the dense jungles that fringed southern China. These were territories that were not only difficult to assimilate into urban landscapes, but also often produced things city-dwellers desired, so an eradication of the difference was unattractive.

But we cannot explain the limits of all early urban systems in this way. How should we explain the westward limits of urban civilizations in the Bronze Age? Regions such as southern Italy and Sardinia were in touch with the Levant during the second millennium. At the site of Pantalica in Sicily a hilltop structure resembles some from the Aegean world, and a Mycenaean painted vase has been recovered from a nearby tomb.[17] Sherds of Mycenaean pottery has been found all over southern Italy (admittedly in very small quantities), and a trade in copper stretched from Sardinia to Cyprus and beyond.[18] Means of transport clearly existed, and the rapidity with which the Phoenicians established connections between the Atlantic coast and the Near East in the early last millennium B.C.E. shows there were no hidden barriers. Yet the world of the palaces remained confined to Crete and southern and central Greece. We could ask the same questions about the North Aegean and the Balkans. One answer of course is to say there is nothing to explain. These are only failures of urbanism if we start from the assumption that cities, once invented, will always expand their reach, either because urban life has a remorseless expansionist logic of its own or because cities are so obviously a good idea. Perhaps not everyone thought so.

Perhaps for an urban experiment to have any chance of lasting long enough to leave traces that we can find, it had to have had some local roots. It is not certain whether or not the first Egyptian cities were created in the knowledge of what had been built in Assyria or southern Babylonia a few centuries before. There had been traffic around the Fertile Crescent for millennia, and Mesopotamian objects are found very early in Egyptian cities. But structurally, architecturally, socially, and religiously the world's first two urban civilizations were quite distinct. Likewise, the first cities of Nubia bore only a superficial resemblance to those of Egypt, and their economies were completely different. We could say the same if we compared the various urban civilizations of Mesoamerica from the High Andes to Illinois via the jungles of Belize and the Highlands of Mexico. The best we can say about pristine urban civilizations is that they—or their ruins—offered a set of models or resources for those who wanted to use them.

Some urban civilizations were self-conscious about their status as successors. The founders of cities in archaic Greece believed (some of them at least) that Homer's heroes had once inhabited cities a little like their own. Successive Mesopotamian civilizations found the *Epic of Gilgamesh* good to think with, as they recreated cities again and again. Several copies of the epic were found in the libraries of the Assyrian King Assurbanipal in his new creation of Nineveh. That royal city created in the seventh century B.C.E. covered more than 7 square kilometres and at its peak perhaps had between 100,000 and 150,000 inhabitants. It dwarfed Bronze Age Uruk, yet

Gilgamesh's city was in some sense an inspiration. Almost certainly the city-builders of the New World made similar use of their past. Olmec artefacts and customs dating to the late second and early last millennium B.C.E. were reused by many later peoples in Central America. Sometimes what look to us like continuous traditions are better understood as long sequences in which each urbanizing culture borrows from earlier ones and claims them as their ancestors. The archaeology of early Chinese urbanism is a good example. Looking back from today, or even from the historical records of the Han dynasty (roughly contemporary with the Roman Empire), it is tempting to organize earlier material around the standard narrative of successive early dynasties each of which (in some sense) ruled all China. But what the material record seems to show is several centres of early urbanism, some based on very different agricultural systems, that only became connected rather later.

As the millennia passed, urban experiments were attempted in more and more parts of the world. From time to time standardized forms became entrenched. For East Asia that meant something like a standardized model of the Chinese city as it was known in the Yellow River Valley under the Zhou dynasty: multiple appropriations and borrowings spread south, west, and east right up to the Japanese urbanism that appeared in the seventh century C.E., and that of the kingdoms of Korea a little earlier. New clusters of cities kept appearing, some in areas where urbanism had been tried before and then collapsed, like India or the Aegean world, sometimes in new territories. Cities spread (again) through the Mediterranean in the last millennium B.C.E., this time extending far farther than their Bronze Age predecessors, spilling over into southern Russia and the Atlantic seaboard. At the turn of the millennia, a long frontier between the urbanized societies of the Mediterranean and Black Sea and their nonurban neighbours in the continental interiors collapsed: cities were briefly scattered across temperate Europe south of the Rhine and the Danube rivers. That experiment lasted only a few centuries in most places, but the next expansion (that of the early Middle Ages) took cities to the Baltic.

Meanwhile, cities appeared in the Sahel, south of the Sahara.[19] One key area of urban growth in the last and first millennia was the Niger Valley, where a sequence of events not unlike those that had led to urbanism in the Nile Valley gave rise to Jenne-jeno, Timbuktu, and other centres.[20] Another cluster of cities formed around the shores of the Indian Ocean as that area became connected by trade in the first centuries C.E. Great Zimbabwe was built between the eleventh and fifteenth centuries C.E., Angkor in Cambodia between the ninth and fifteenth centuries. The expansion of Europe over the last five centuries spread some urban models—all those plazas and cathedrals in the Americas, all those Victorian town halls in India, South Africa, and Australia—but local forms were never extinguished. New urban experiments and new variations on urban themes continue today.

What does this complicated history of urbanism tell us about ourselves? That as a species we have an aptitude or even an inclination to build big urban nests? That in the special conditions of the current interglacial, the Holocene, when almost all of us live in societies sustained by farming, that aptitude has been expressed many times?[21] We have other aptitudes and capabilities too, some doubtless not yet realized. But during the last six thousand years cities have often turned out to offer some advantages, and so we have invented them often and lived in them more and more. From where we stand now our urban systems seem more resilient than those first Bronze Age experiments. But it is always risky for historians to take the present day as the benchmark, and recent experience should make us distrustful of narratives of progress. Perhaps we have not come so far as we hope.

What Were Early Cities Like?

Today's greatest cities have come to resemble each other closely. Their major architects are international figures, their builders have access to the same materials, and they have been designed to suit societies increasingly alike in their needs and ambitions. Each urban outpost of our global village reaches up to the sky with ever more precarious ziggurats of glass and steel, their gracile skeletons animated by fibre-optic nerves through which they talk to each other by day, and by night light up the sky. Beneath them vast artificial rivers discreetly supply water and remove waste, while cavernous metro stations link the scintillating business districts with the far-flung residential districts where those who work in them live. Our cities have a single economic logic. Shanghai and Johannesburg, New York and São Paulo seem like cousins, apart from their tiny historic centres that give them their originality.

Six thousand years ago the first cities were much less alike. Think of the palaces of Mycenaean Greece and the ball courts of Tikal, the ziggurats of

Uruk and the vast reservoirs and walls of Harappa. Even so, the earliest cities had some things in common.

Most were spectacular not in scale, but compared to what had gone before and in the impact they had on their residents and especially on visitors. They were not the first spectacular monuments to be built by human beings. It was foragers who created the great megaliths of Göbekli Tepe, farmers who built Stonehenge, and gardeners who set up the Moai, the great stone heads of Rapa Nui on Easter Island. It is not always easy to distinguish traces of great ceremonial centres like these from the remains of ancient and nearly forgotten urban experiments.

There are some major differences between the ceremonial centres of non-urban societies and those of cities. One is a matter of possession. Whoever organized the creation of great prehistoric megalithic projects—and someone must have done so, whether it was priests, chieftains, or charismatic individuals—they were built by entire peoples. There was no other way it could have been done, especially not in the case of those built by quite tiny island populations or foragers who gathered only periodically. These were community building projects so freighted with significance that the building projects themselves built communities.[22] Some ancient ceremonial complexes took generations to build. While they were under construction there were places where scattered populations gathered if only for a few weeks each year, contributing their labour before dispersing again.

Cities, by contrast, had permanent populations. Like sedentary village-dwellers they almost always lived in tight family units, fashioning small domestic worlds inside the larger urban ones. Formal legal title is less the issue than the way in which families dug in, forming cells within the urban fabric, cells that gave it strength.

The emergence of cities made a huge difference to those left outside the city walls. Sometimes, as in Teotichuacan and probably in some densely packed Nilotic societies, that might have been just half the population. More often rural populations outnumbered city-dwellers five or ten to one, because in most places it took five or ten peasants to create enough surplus food to feed one city-dweller. These new societies based everything on that new distinction—town and country—that was at first geographical and economic, but soon political and moral as well. The arrival of the city meant the arrival of the countryside. It might look at first sight rather like the more egalitarian agricultural world that had preceded it, but in reality it had been suddenly decentred, marginalized, and made peripheral. Living in a village means one thing in a world of villages, quite another in a world ordered by cities. Tribesmen become peasants and village-dwellers became less self-sufficient. When the land is owned by those who live at least part of the time in the city, farmers becomes tenants if they are not already slaves. Sometimes countryfolk would need to go to the city for justice, or to sell their produce or buy tools. Permanent markets never completely replaced periodic markets and travelling salesmen, but towns took over many functions and guarded them jealously. Peasants typically owed taxes or rent or labour or all of these to urban elites. Anglo Saxon peasants were subjected to the *trinoda necessitas*, the "three knotted obligation" to maintain bridges and roads, to build and maintain the fortified centres called *burghs* (in effect cities), and to serve in their lord's army. Around the globe the appearance of cities was almost always accompanied by obligations of this kind.

A moral barrier had been raised between city-dwellers and countryfolk. Time and time again we observe that dichotomy acquire a new edge: rustics, peasants, and *pagani* ranged against urbane, civilized, and *cittadini*. Metaphors drew on the language of agriculture and industry: city-dwellers were cultivated (like their fields) and refined (like precious metals). Country folk were savages (like beasts) and wild (like the forest margins). The city was placed at the centre of countless civilizing narratives. Societies that built megaliths had never been completely egalitarian. Some families and lineages were certainly grander than others. But now inequality was mapped out in space. Each *kind* of person had his or her place, and knew it.

6

Cities of Bronze

Connected Cities

Our species' story in the very long term is one of repeated separations and reconnections. Migration has been the main connector for most of history, but once we settled down we began to connect through exchanges of various kinds. Before urbanism much of what was exchanged was alive—domesticated animals, marriage partners, slaves. Early farming societies also went to great lengths to get materials for tools, obsidian from various Mediterranean islands, flints and greenstone from hundreds of miles across Europe, and so on. Jade and lapis lazuli, tin and gold, amber and ivory and coral: these were the earliest objects of long-distance trade. Urbanism brought about a huge change in the scale of what was exchanged, and its variety. Bronze Age states added a trade in manufactured goods, textiles, metalwork, luxury goods of all kinds, and carved gems. Eventually consumables travelled too: wine, spices and incense.[1] It is not an exaggeration to compare this proliferation of exchanges to modern globalizations.[2]

Systems of exchange grew in an unplanned, incremental fashion. We must imagine the early stages were opportunistic contacts. When these turned out to be profitable, the volume of goods expanded, and other products might be added to a cargo speculatively. Some traders and some trading centres grew rich. Among the first signs of contact between the urban civilizations of Mesopotamia and the horse-taming nomads of the Russian steppe are rich chieftains' graves in the Caucasus.[3] The rulers of Ugarit on the Syrian coast found they controlled a key hub between Egypt and Syria, the Near East, Cyprus, and the Aegean. There were other consequences of long-distance connections that can never have been expected.

Technologies moved. The use of cylinder seals and the potter's wheel are good examples. New ways of extracting metals from ores and then smelting, moulding, stretching, rolling, and hammering them spread across Bronze Age Eurasia. So did new domestications. The chicken, whose ancestors inhabited the forest of eastern Asia, eventually reached the Mediterranean in the last millennium B.C.E. The spread of bananas and of maize has already been mentioned.

Objects often travelled much farther than information about them. Ridiculous legends circulated about the origins of obscure materials. Gold was excavated in India by giant ants, Herodotus reported. Amber was either the remains of a shattered sea queen's palace, or else the tears of the daughters of the sun god. Pliny had heard that marble grew in the earth, so that quarries would eventually be replenished. Images too were subject to repeated reinterpretations en route.[4] Fabulous animals depicted on the earliest seal stones made in Babylonia made their way to northern India. Asian images of lions were eventually transmuted into Chinese dragons as copies of copies spread across central Asia and the steppe. One thing this tells us is that early Bronze Age Eurasia remained an archipelago of urban civilizations, increasingly well networked, yet each following their own path in almost complete ignorance of one other. Parallel urbanisms, then, each stretching their tendrils long distances, but each deeply rooted in their local soils.

A Bronze Age World-System

The Ancient Near East was not a world in itself, but words like "region" or "area" fail to express its sheer scale and complexity. By the fourth and third millennia B.C.E.—the Bronze Age—there were centres of power and urbanized core regions, and so there were also margins and economic peripheries. Typically, cores and their margins were closely related. Pastoralists provided wool, which was transformed into textiles in urban centres, which paid for the exchange in manufactures and sometimes grain.[5] Beyond these local exchange systems, most of them based on the ecological complementarities, there were now the longer "global" trade systems. To participate in the trade for luxuries, urban rulers needed some sort of stake: this they acquired by extracting more surplus from the peasants than they needed to maintain their own establishments, or by setting the terms of trade with the margins in such a way that cities benefit from "complementary" exchanges. This is what historians and archaeologists mean by the term "world-system."[6]

The Ancient Near East had a number of core regions, each with its own margins. The most important were those in southern Mesopotamia, Syria, and Egypt. At the centre of each were one or more great cities where wealth was accumulated and impressive monuments were constructed.[7] Alongside the pyramids of the Pharoahs, we may count the ziggurats of Babylonia—great artificial mountains crowned by temples—and also city walls like those that featured in the epic of Gilgamesh, and royal palaces.

Populations were higher in these cities, and some at least were crowded into urban agglomerations of several tens of thousands. Most lived in small and very basic houses. These have left only the most unsubstantial traces for archaeologists to find, and to be honest domestic housing has until recently never had the same attention as has been lavished on great monuments. But the accommodation created for the population that built the pyramids of Giza outside modern Cairo gives some idea. At any one time there were perhaps as many as twenty thousand workmen there, volunteers drawn from all over Egypt staying for a few months at a time. They lived in huge cramped barracks, sleeping in dormitories, and were fed on rations of bread and beer. Nearby a village provided for around five thousand families of permanent officials, craftsmen, and supervisors; they had slightly more comfortable lives, and their own graveyard. Maybe every great construction project for a temple or a palace created worker villages of this kind.

It was through the remains of those grandiose temples and palaces—the homes of gods and kings—and the rich tombs of the latter that the Bronze Age first came into view in modern times. Their décor often included great relief art and free-standing statues. Many were also covered in monumental inscriptions, for the Bronze Age is the first age of writing.[8] Hieroglyphic systems were created in Egypt and Anatolia and even in Crete, and cuneiform writing, designed to be impressed on clay, was carved into the hardest of stones for make royal stelai like that of Hammurabi.

Writing marks another major change in how we understand these societies as well as a change in how they worked. Most writing was not monumental, of course, but was scratched on broken pottery, painted on papyrus, or most commonly imprinted on clay tablets with wedge-shaped instruments which gave the script the modern name "cuneiform," from *cuneus*, the Latin word for "wedge." Cuneiform tablets are found across the Near East, recording a huge variety of languages. A few palaces also had great archives in them which revealed the working of the palace economies; copies of letters sent from one king to another or from kings to their governors; epic poetry and sacred poems; and decrees from which a political history can for the first time be reconstructed. A few archives have transformed our understanding of the Bronze Age. At Ebla a palace burned to the ground sometime in the middle of the third millennium B.C.E., preserving around 20,000 clay tablets which in the local language Eblaite and Sumerian give a snapshot of the culture and organization of a kingdom that once ruled much of what is now Syria. At Amarna in Egypt, the capital of the Pharaoh Akhenaten in the fourteenth century B.C.E., a great diplomatic archive was discovered written in the Akkadian language in the cuneiform script developed in Mesopotamia, which by that point had become an international language of diplomacy. They included letters to and about the rulers of Assyria and Babylonia; the smaller kingdoms of the Levant including the Canaanite cities Ugarit, Byblos, and Tyre; Damascus; and perhaps even the Hebrews of Jerusalem, to the Hittite Empire and their neighbours and rivals the Mitanni. and to the kings of Cyprus. Our knowledge of the political geography and history of the Hittite Empire in Anatolia—modern Turkey—derives almost entirely from 30,000 cuneiform tablets found in its capital Hattusa. They date a century or so later than the Armana letters, and some of the place names in the Hittite Far West are tantalizingly close to those known from Homeric epic.

Each of these urban centres was not only a political centre, it was an economic hub. Local roads brought tribute, produce for market, taxes, and labourers from the fields around. The same cities were also hubs for those longer-distance routes—some by land, some by river, and a few by sea, like those that connected Egypt and Cyprus with Lebanon, or the Persian Gulf with the Indus Valley. These routes carried trade goods and diplomatic gifts. As the urbanized cores of the Bronze Age grew, they began to depend more and more on long-distance trade to supply some commodities that were not exactly luxuries. The valleys of the Nile, the Tigris, and the Euphrates were fertile in food production, and that was the main reason that populations grew so much more densely there. It is unlikely that any early urban civilization could have grown for long unless it was in an area rich in food. But they were poor in some other essentials. Southern Mesopotamia, for instance, was poor in timber, which had to be brought down from the mountainous margins, from Lebanon and the Zagros Mountains. Mesopotamia was also terribly short of metals. Assyrian traders set up entrepôts in Anatolia, and they were evidently successful since quite often the first major local citadels were built where the Assyrians had settled.[9]

A Bronze Age world-system emerged from these dynamics. No single state or king designed it. It emerged from strategies of exchange that turned out to be successful, were then imitated, and eventually established a ramified network of connections; path dependence again. Thinking about the processes through which our planet became divided into the First, Second, and Third Worlds, the Global North and the Global South, the developed and the developing countries, gives us a way to think about how the Bronze Age world-system was built, despite the great differences in scales and technologies. Bronze Age rulers accumulated treasures by declaring monopolies, by controlling access to distant lands, and by keeping goldsmiths and stone carvers and other craftsmen in their employ. It took so long to make a beautiful object like the Standard of Ur, and it demanded materials so rare and difficult to obtain that only kings could fund it. Once treasures were made they might be displayed to command the admiration of the masses, as banners or in the form of elaborate jewelry or ceremonial clothing. Treasures might also be ostentatiously put out of use, as when pharaohs were buried with masses of furniture, weapons, and statues. All that hard-won treasure, all those objects on which skilled hands had laboured.

Not all exchange took the form of a trade in commodities: there were also diplomatic gifts. Some of the first royal letters in the world concern exchanges of cedar and precious metals between "brother monarchs" from Egypt and the Levant. These "brothers" almost never met, and knew very little of each other. Their letters were written and read out by scribes using languages that almost none of them spoke. But the prestige of trading with a great king at the end of the world was enough, and the power to display at home things that were almost legendary must have been extraordinary. It was an economy ruled by kings, not by markets.[10]

Early Experiments

The first cities appeared in the Ancient Near East around the middle of the fourth millennium B.C.E. For a while urbanism must have seemed very fragile, for they were not much imitated. The Uruk expansion, in which elements of southern Mesopotamian culture were taken up as far afield as Syria, faltered late in the fourth millennium B.C.E. Urbanism collapsed, most dramatically in the north where the village cultures that replaced it no longer used southern Mesopotamian styles of ceramic, built no monuments, and invested in no great works of art or writing. Something similar happened to the Indus Valley system. A dispassionate observer at the time might have concluded that urbanism was too complicated and precarious a way of life to survive, and that the well-established rhythms of agricultural villages—a way of life spreading very successfully across Europe in the same period—was more sustainable. Yet Syria followed a different path to the Indus valley and by the middle of the third millennium, cities had reappeared. Temples and palaces began to appear in just a few of the villages of the region, and around 2500 B.C.E. a great Royal Palace appeared at Ebla, an hour's drive from the mediaeval and modern city of Aleppo. Underpinning this growth was more control of metallurgy, better use of irrigation and hydraulic engineering, and the reappearance of cuneiform writing, this time to record a Semitic language.

Cities were back in Mesopotamia as well. The southernmost part was again divided into city-states. Ur and Uruk and Eridu and the others fought with each other over farmland, and probably water too. Something new was happening to the north. Around the middle of the third millennium a new state had emerged in Akkad, just south of modern Baghdad. Soon after 2350 B.C.E. Sargon of Akkad founded a new capital and began to extend his power much further afield. He claimed to have conquered all the territory between the Upper and the Lower Seas. For some this is the first empire in the world, and it certainly involved one people dominating several others. Sargon expanded his power to the Cedar Mountain of Lebanon, conquered Ebla and pressed on onto the Anatolian plateau. This was a new way of controlling access to the products of the margins. The history of the Ancient Near East would, from now on, be a story of empires as well as of cities.

Egyptians presented their history as a smoother series of transitions. It is true that the main lines of its peculiar social and economic structures were laid out at an early stage, but this royal ideology exaggerated continuity. From an Egyptian point of view Upper (southern) and Lower (northern) Egypt were normally united under the rule of a pharaoh, treated as a living god yet governing through a complex bureaucracy of royal officials, and with the support of a priesthood. In reality, Bronze Age Egypt experienced palace intrigues, struggles between rival elite groups, and tensions between central powers and overly mighty governors on the frontier just like any other early state. There were even periods of political fragmentation, and periods when parts of the Nile Valley were conquered and ruled by outsiders. The Old Kingdom—roughly equivalent to the third millennium B.C.E.—was a relatively stable period. The pharaohs invested heavily in building monuments. Royal pyramids were the greatest projects, inspiring tomb-building for courtiers, family members, and other powerful individuals. By the middle of the second millennium enormous temple complexes were being constructed, most spectacularly at Karnak. Some were physically connected to palaces, such as at Luxor, Memphis, and Medinet Habu, and around them towns grew up. Pharaohs toured other urban centres too, including Edfu, Abydos, Sais, and Elephantine, at the first cataract of the Nile. Like their brother-monarchs in Babylonia, Assyria, and among the Mitanni and the Hittites, Egyptian pharaohs went to great pains to acquire and control exotic materials. Royal expeditions and trade brought gold and ivory to Egypt, and there was trade with the rest of the Ancient Near East. And there were imperialist operations too. There are records of warfare in the Western Desert against Libyan nomads, and some sort of hegemony was asserted, from time to time, over Nubia to the south.

The Expansion of Multispecies Societies

The rise and fall of cities and empires is one of the traditional themes of the history of the Bronze Age Near East. These were, after all, the themes that interested the monument builders. Sargon of Akkad's boast, the decrees of Hittite emperors, and the bombast of the letters from Amarna all tell us about the importance of war, treasure, and building projects. Archaeologists have worked hard to rescue the rest of the population from the disinterest of their rulers. But from the fourth millennium on a vast wealth gap had opened up between rulers and the ruled, one that has left most of the population hardly visible. The power of Bronze Age rulers rested, at the most fundamental level, on their capacity to compel others to work for them in the fields, in the mines, and on their vast building sites. This was why they had worked so hard to perfect those earlier, shaky experiments in state-building. Urbanism came with a price tag, and that price tag was the impoverishment and subordination of most of the population. They were richer to be sure than their forager ancestors, by the measure of how much material they left behind, but early excavators were dazzled by rich tombs and monuments. It is the relative poverty of the commons that makes them so hard to see at this distance .

But urbanism rested on more profound changes yet, changes that take us back to humans' ever intensifying relationships with our companion species. The first domestications, aside from our partnership with dogs, were mostly aimed at providing ready sources of meat. Prey got scarcer. That was an old story going back to the impact of human expansion on the megafauna and the effects of climate change on hunters and hunted alike. But the shift to agriculture made things worse. For a start, more of us were sedentary and therefore could not follow those prey species that moved seasonally, in the way some earlier societies had built their way of life around the migrations of mammoths or reindeer. Farming also crowded out wildlife because it destroyed their habitats. Some animals were deliberately hunted down because of the damage they might do to crops. The growing size of sedentary human populations added to the pressures. These problems recurred all around the world wherever farming took off, and they continue to be reflected today in the plummeting biodiversity of the planet. The first object of domestication was to create accessible herds of prey animals, ideally rendered more docile and better suited to eat whatever food humans could spare them. Cattle, sheep, goats, pigs, and even horses were first of all sources of meat. It was a bonus that their carcasses also provided some other useful materials such as bone and hides.

Once we lived more closely with these animals, new options appeared. Prehistorians used to write about a Secondary Products Revolution, as if there was a single moment at which farming communities realized how much living animals could provide.[11] Living animals might provide wool, or be trained to pull a plough or a cart or carry loads; they could provide milk, which could be drunk by humans or easily converted into cheese, which was easier to digest as well as to store. It is now clearer that some farming communities were experimenting with these secondary products very early, perhaps even in the seventh millennium, to judge from some stress marks on cattle bones and the organic residues left in some of the earliest pottery. Over time these experiments, again repeated on many continents independently of each other and with different species, became more and more successful. By the fourth millennium multispecies societies were central to their economic life.[12] The chronological coincidence with urbanism is obvious, as are the links with expanding economies.

Cattle had already been bred for strength, and probably for good humour. Herd animals typically live in social groups, and their social instincts were co-optable to make them more docile and more biddable. Gelding or castration was another means of making male animals more manageable. Stronger, calmer beasts of burden made building, agriculture, and trade more feasible. It was during the Bronze Age that animals were first used to carry loads, drag ploughs, and pull carts. Until that point humans had no beasts of burden. Cattle, especially oxen, could do some of this work, but a crucial advance was the domestication of equids.[13]

Wild asses were first domesticated on the southern fringes of the Ancient Near East. DNA studies of donkey skeletons from early dynastic Egypt show that they are descended from wild Nubian and Somali populations. Donkeys rapidly spread through the Nile Valley and around the Fertile Crescent and appear in many representations from ancient Sumer. Horses were domesticated far to the north, on the Russian steppe between the southern limit of the forest and the Black Sea coast. At first they were probably most useful as a winter food supply, a useful prey species that could forage for food even in the snow. By the end of the fifth millennium some horses at least were being ridden, making it easier for pastoralists to keep control of their flocks on the steppe.[14]

Equids became central in the urbanizing societies of the Mesopotamian Bronze Age. Sumerian images and texts from Ebla show the use of domesticated asses, sometimes cross-bred with wild onagers, and a few images of horses exist from the middle of the third millennium B.C.E. It was not until the second millennium that horses became common south of Anatolia. This brought a revolution in warfare. Within just a few centuries the horse-drawn chariot was at the centre of combat and ceremonial events from Egypt to central Asia. At the very end of the Bronze Age, in 1274 B.C.E., the Egyptian and Hittite empires clashed at Kadesh in Syria in a chariot battle in which thousands of chariots were reported to be involved on each side. During the last millennium B.C.E. larger horses as well as cavalry units became common, and camels began to be used.

Sheep and goats, often difficult to distinguish from remains of the bones, also had a key part to play in the economies of ancient cities. Sheep were bred for longer and finer wool and could eventually be shorn of their fleeces. This made possible the textile production that was one of the first bases for long-distance trade.

Domesticated herd animals also provided the first urban societies with an important new food resource. The diets of the first farmers were not rich in fats or proteins, and urban-dwellers had even less varied diets. Dairy products were a vital supplement for populations who now rarely ate meat. Persuading sheep, goats, and cattle to produce milk when they did not have young of their own also required work. Humans had to change too. Those best able to benefit from cattle raising were the few who were able even in adulthood to digest dairy products.

Raising livestock could be made to feed back into agriculture. Many forms of early agriculture had the effect of depleting the soil of nutrients. Mixing vegetable matter and animal dung back into the soil helps restore nitrogen and phosphates (among other materials) and fertilizes the soil. A number of current research projects are trying to establish—by looking for enriched levels of the isotope nitrogen-15 in ancient seeds—just how soon manuring became widespread. By late prehistory at least, and perhaps as early as the Neolithic, some farmers had learned this way to make stock-raising and cereal agriculture mutually supportive.

Our animal partners, now more valuable than ever, thrived at the expense of others. Goats and sheep squeezed out antelope because the former were more useful than the latter. Any species that competed with domesticates for food or water was at risk. Predators too came under pressure, and this is commemorated in the art of all Near Eastern Bronze and Iron Age cultures. Near Eastern kings were portrayed as lion-killers, pharaohs hunted hippopotamuses, and the earliest Greek heroes fought monstrous boars, lions, and bulls. Cities domesticated even distant landscapes, taming the wild and limiting biodiversity.

Other societies learned to make use of secondary products. Not all were urban. Horses, for example, were milked on the steppe. But the long-distance connections that characterized the Bronze Age world-system were highly dependent on animal products and animal transport. Webs of connections linked the horse-tamers north of the Black Sea, who were constantly improving their control of their herds of cattle and sheep, with the cities of the Fertile Crescent and indirectly with other sheep-herding nomads who lived on its southern fringes. Breeding sheep to produce better wool helped satisfy local needs, but richer textiles produced from that wool fed back into the international trading systems.

The Bronze Age World-System Expands

Speakers of Semitic languages begin to appear in texts from Syrian Ebla and Sargon's land of Akkad during the third millennium B.C.E. This was a side effect of the closer links that had grown up between the settled cities of the Fertile Crescent and populations on their margins. Nomads were often treated as barbarous and primitive in ancient texts. Their societies *were* less complex than those of the city-dwellers. There were fewer ranks and classes and titles, a more even distribution of wealth, and so on. But they were definitely not the relics of a previous social order.

Nomadism was a new way of life.[15] Nomads in the Ancient Near East depended on the same domesticated animal species used by sedentary farmers—sheep and goats in particular—but they put them to different uses. Nomad pastoralists moved around large territories making use of much more inhospitable terrain than either the muddy fields of Mesopotamia or the rain-watered steppe of Assyria. Unlike sedentary farmers, they could exploit seasonal variations in the productivity of different landscapes—taking their flocks to different pastures in summer than in winter—and by moving frequently they could use land that would never have sustained a permanent presence. Their mobility also helped them deal with those bad years when drought made some landscapes suddenly incapable of supporting humans and their animals. Nomads' flocks mattered much more to them than livestock did to the sedentary farmers. But farmers too wanted meat and textiles, and some had grain and manufactures to spare, which nomads needed. So nomads traded with settled agriculturalists as well as raiding them, creating symbiotic if not always very stable relationships. Together, farmers and the nomadic partners made a better use of the varied landscapes of the Ancient Near East than either group could have done alone. This did not mean there were never tensions. Since neither nomad tribes nor city-states were particularly peaceful, it is not surprising they occasionally came to blows. Nomadism and the rise of the state were, in parts of Mesopotamia at least, two sides of the same coin.

The power of this complex of relationships expanded steadily. During the second millennium B.C.E. we begin to hear more in historical texts about the populations who lived on the mountainous fringes of the Fertile Crescent. Developments in southwest Iran, in the land of Elam, had shadowed those of Babylonia since the fourth millennium. During the second millennium cuneiform replaced local scripts there and Akkadian began to be used alongside Elamite, suggesting a closer connection with Mesopotamian states. New peoples emerge too such as the Kassites, probably originally from the Zagros Mountains to the northeast. North of Syria and Mesopotamia was the massif of the Anatolian plateau. By the early second millennium B.C.E. the Assyrians' trading posts on the plateau—the Assyrian name was *karum* and the most famous is Kanesh—had become permanent. Many Anatolian peoples had already begun to build cities of their own, but they were not great planned conurbations full of craftsmen, bureaucrats, and priests like the cities of Egypt, Syria, and Babylonia. Massive fortified wall circuits hugged hilltops, approachable only through great gates and ramps.[16] Within the defences the main monumental building was usually a great hall, equipped for a leader and his warriors. There were sanctuaries too but (unlike in Mesopotamia), they were often at a little distance from the chieftain's palaces. The first levels of Troy conform to this pattern. Citadels morphed into cities only at the end of the third millennium, becoming slightly larger and enclosing a slightly wider range of buildings, often laid out around and below the fortified hilltop. Hattusa, the capital of the Hittite Empire, grew this way.[17]

The first Anatolian cities were much smaller than those of the plains, and had none of the elaborate palaces and courtyards and gardens of the south. Their architecture was just as impressive, but different. Less is known of the origins of these cities than of some others, but it coincided with economic growth. Later than Mesopotamia, they too had now learned to use domesticated animals for things other than meat and hides; they too exploited metal resources in which they were richer than many regions; and they too engaged in long-distant trade. Beyond Anatolia and the Levant lay the Mediterranean sea and the vast continental hinterland of western Eurasia, a land of plains and forests truncated by low mountain ranges. Cuneiform writing and Mesopotamian manufactures were brought up onto the Anatolian plateau. But almost none of the products of Bronze Age core areas have been found west of Crete before the middle of the second millennium B.C.E. Up until that point Sargon's "Upper Sea" was the western edge of the Bronze Age world.

Europe and the Mediterranean in Late Prehistory

Europe was not another world, of course, but its populations had followed a different historical trajectory since the retreat of the ice, one that did not result in state-formation or urbanization. Populations of late Pleistocene and early Holocene foragers, fishers, and hunters had expanded northwards. The Mesolithic populations of Europe had developed some of the most sophisticated stone technologies ever produced: adzes for carpentry, scrapers for preparing food and hides, pointed burins to work bone, minute blades called microliths that were fixed in wooden and bone handles to make weapons and cutting implements. They made bows and arrows, wove fish-traps, and constructed rafts. They hunted and trapped smaller animals and used a wide range of plants for food and for much else.

Farming, the secondary products revolution, and metallurgy were all adopted with a slight time lag compared to the areas in which they were developed. None of the major domestications of food crops or animals had taken place in the lands around the Mediterranean Sea. But the region was similar enough to the Near East for most of the domesticated species to thrive. Wheat, barley, cattle, sheep, and goats arrived in Europe by several routes, hopping from one location to another around the Mediterranean coasts and advancing rapidly and steadily by land from southeast Europe. They reached the Atlantic just before the origin of cities in Mesopotamia.

It took longer for farming to spread into temperate Europe than around the Mediterranean. Some groups of farmers came by land, crossing the continent at a rate of maybe 25 miles a generation, mostly replacing the foragers they met on the way. But some innovations came from the south, brought by or from Mediterranean farmers. It is in general easier to move domesticated species west or east (rather than north or south) because the climates are broadly similar. If early farmers tried to move vines and olives northwards they would soon have reached their ecological limits. Many other fruit trees faced the same limits. Even among the plants and animals that did adapt to new environments, some parts of the package thrived more in some places than others. Barley and two kinds of wheat—emmer and einkorn—were all domesticated at roughly the same time in the Fertile Crescent, but barley is more resilient where water is scarce or temperatures are cold. Sheep and goats are also more tolerant of hot dry summers than are cattle or pigs; the former thrived in the Mediterranean, cattle (and especially horses) did well in the cooler, better-watered north. Across Europe and the Mediterranean farmers made use of the different characters of each species, and attempted to breed more useful strains.

By the start of the fourth millennium most Europeans were farming. In Atlantic Europe some of the first farmers built huge megalithic monuments, chamber tombs, long lines of standing stones, eventually stone circles, mounds, processional ways, henges, cursus monuments, and long barrows. These great ceremonial sites required formidable skills in technology and measurement, and the labour of tens of thousands of humans. These were central places, probably visited periodically by thousands, but they were not cities. Those societies were fatally disrupted in the middle of the third millennium by populations moving from Eastern Europe. Their DNA swamps that of earlier farmers in modern populations, suggesting that they were either very numerous or very successful in replacing their predecessors. But these groups too did not create cities or states.

Even the arrival of bronze-working, from several directions, did not bring temperate European societies closer to those of the Near East. Bronze metallurgy appears first in Mesopotamia, Egypt, and India in the fourth millennium B.C.E., around the same time as cities and the state. How fast the technology moved eastwards across the Iranian plateau and through central Asia is not yet clear. The advent of large-scale bronze-casting in China around the start of the second millennium coincides with the first cities and states along the Yellow River. Copper-working began in the Aegean in the late fourth millennium, was established in the central Mediterranean by the early second millennium B.C.E., and was evident along the Atlantic seaboard from Spain and Portugal to Britain and Scandinavia by 2000 B.C.E. The metallurgy of Bronze Age Europe is spectacular, especially the weaponry and armour made for the chiefs who controlled access to rare supplies of tin and probably most metalworkers as well.[18] Yet still none of these societies created cities or states.

This was not because populations were low nor because the chieftains that led them were isolated. During the Neolithic and Bronze Ages ancestral forests were felled with stone axes to make space for fields of cereals; the scratch marks of wooden ploughs are found everywhere, and tombs—rare from the Mesolithic—suddenly increase in number. Great quantities of labour were consumed in monument-building. As for distant connections, there was a trade in amber from the Baltic and coral and spondylus shells from the Mediterranean, and in rare greenstone from Cumbria and in the huge yellow flints of Grand Pressigny in central France known as *livres de beurre* (pounds of butter). Bronze production itself required access to rare deposits of tin and copper. Motifs on rock-cut art and the design of weaponry and helmets show how far ideas spread across prehistoric Europe.[19] Yet there was little craft specialization. Everyone farmed. There was no writing, no numeracy, no laws, and no currencies. If some of the villages were large—Neolithic Sesklo in central Greece had a population of a few thousand packed into a 20-hectare space, and there were even bigger villages in Bulgaria—none of them could be mistaken for cities.

The different paths followed by temperate Europe and the Near East offer a useful reminder of how complicated and precarious the early stages of city-building were. Some early accounts of urbanization—focused on the experience of the Near East—seem to assume that once a society had committed to farming then population growth, metallurgy, and trade would all follow automatically, with cities and states the inevitable end point of the historical trajectory. Childe's Urban Revolution was seen as a natural sequel to his Agricultural Revolution. The European sequence is one of those that shows things were not so simple. Humans might have an urban aptitude, but did not have an urban destiny. Other kinds of social worlds could be built out of farming, multispecies societies, and metal-working.

The Mediterranean, as one might expect, was somewhere between the two. Communications was the key factor here. The Mediterranean islands had been settled very early, by prehistoric mariners paddling amazingly tiny canoes.[20] As early as the sixth millennium B.C.E. their voyages connected scattered farming communities. A few made dangerous crossings to the few islands where the hard volcanic glass obsidian might be found: most important were the deposits on Melos in the Aegean, and Sardinia and the Lipari Islands in the western Mediterranean. The range of these canoes was very short, maybe 20 or 25 kilometres a day.

By the middle of the fourth millennium B.C.E.—just when the first cities were being built in Mesopotamia—there are signs that longer journeys had become more normal, between Sicily and Sardinia, Spain and the Balearic Islands, Crete and the Cyclades of the central Aegean.[21] Probably these voyages were already made in longboats, even though there is no firm archaeological evidence for them until slightly later. Around 15 to 20 metres long, and powered by twenty or so paddlers working together, these cut travel times by maybe half and allowed proper cargoes to be carried. Longboats made regular trade feasible (and irregular raiding as well). Tiny settlements of mariners appeared on the central islands of the Cyclades. As late as the middle of the third millennium B.C.E.—around the time that Sargon of Akkad was creating the first imperial state—the Mediterranean remained very marginal to the Ancient Near East. A few Egyptian artefacts have been found on Crete, but tiny villages of farmers connected only by longboats had little to offer the urban civilizations to their east, and little to fear from them too. They suffered—or were protected by—the tyranny of distance.

And then came the sail.[22] Sailing boats were invented on the Nile, and by the middle of the third millennium B.C.E. there were regular voyages made from the Nile Delta, up the Levantine Coast to the cities of Syria and Byblos in what is now Lebanon. Like many of the cities in the region these were ancient foundations, and their Copper and Bronze Age ruins stand on the ruins of Neolithic villages. But it was their location at the crucial connecting point between the Mediterranean, the forests of Lebanon and the shortest route east to the Upper Euphrates and west to Cyprus with its rich copper ore deposits, that accounts for their rise to fame. Egypt, like Babylonia, was starved of timber at least of the dimensions demanded by monumental building. Byblos was in touch with Egypt from the early dynastic period (the late third and early second millennia B.C.) and remained a key diplomatic player right up until the start of the Iron Age. Ugarit flourished a little later. For most of the second millennium B.C.E. it was the centre of a web of routes that joined up the city-states and petty kingdoms of Syria and Cyprus with the Hittite empire and Egypt. This nexus of sailing voyages extended west along the southern coast of Turkey and then to Crete and eventually the Greek mainland. Currents and winds favoured clockwise navigation, bringing Cretans to the coast of Egypt and Levantine goods to the Aegean.

Sailing changed everything. The earliest sailing vessels could carry twenty times the cargo of a longboat they were three times as fast, and easier to manoeuvre. Distances collapsed, and horizon expanded. The scattered rocks of the Cyclades became stepping stones to Greece and beyond. Sailing vessels were expensive to build, and to begin with probably carried only the most valuable of cargoes, en route to the most powerful chieftains. Bronze Age princes treated for profit as well as prestige, and all around the Aegean they were becoming rich.

In 1982 a local sponge diver came across the wreck of one of the earliest of those ships, wrecked around 1300 B.C.E. at Uluburun, off the coast of southwest Turkey.[23] Its cargo included more than 350 ingots of copper or tin, probably enough to make 11 tons of bronze. Measurement of lead isotope ratios in the copper suggest most or all of it came from Cyprus. There were storage jars too, one full of glass beads and several full of olives, but the majority containing a residue of pistachio resin (see Figure 10). Was this a cargo of resin going west? Or was this the trace of a Bronze Age retsina? Some of the pottery was Canaanite—from the Levant—and some from Cyprus. There were 175 ingots of bright blue glass—mentioned in Egyptian texts as a speciality of the coast of Palestine—and logs of hard wood from tropical Africa, elephant tusks and hippopotamus teeth, tortoise shells and ostrich eggs. These are materials often mentioned in royal correspondence of the day. There were also some bronze cauldrons, various pieces of metal jewelry, cosmetic boxes, an intricate writing board, and a gold scarab bearing the name of Nefertiti. Some of these are treasures; some the raw material needed to make treasures. The crew also had a collection of weapons, tools, weights, and some food. The excavators suggested the vessel was travelling from somewhere in Syria to northern Greece when it sank. For us, of course, it is a time capsule freezing in one moment the fruits of so much diplomatic exchange and enterprise. The Uluburun wreck is spectacular,

Figure 10 A reconstruction of the Bronze Age wreck from Uluburun
Images & Stories / Alamy Stock Photo

but it was neither unique nor the earliest find of its kind. A few Egyptian exotica reached Crete in the third millennium B.C.E.; Cypriot copper ingots of this type have been found as far afield as Sicily, Sardinia, and Bulgaria, and some date back to the fifteenth century B.C.E. The cycles of urban growth and long-distance trade that had begun in fourth-millennium Babylonia and Egypt had grown into a great complex of exchange, and Mediterranean societies would now be part of it.

PART
II

An Urban Mediterranean

7

The First Mediterranean Cities

A Sea in Fragments

For the last three decades, the ancient Mediterranean has been an object of intense scientific scrutiny. Prehistorians and anthropologists, classicists and historians, and many others have tried to understand how the inland sea and the lands that surround it worked as a human habitat. Their findings make it easier to understand why it was so long before humans tried to create cities there, and why so many of those first attempts ended in failure.[1]

Geologically the Mediterranean Sea is easy to describe. It is a remnant of an ancient ocean—now called Tethys—which once girdled the earth. As the continents moved, Tethys shrank and the lands around were buckled and twisted by immense tectonic forces. About 100 million years ago, one section of Tethys began to be squeezed between the Eurasian and the African tectonic plates. The great mountain ranges of the region, the Alps and Pyrenees, the Anatolian plateau and the Balkan ridges, were thrown up in episodes of violent convulsion. Many of the landscapes surrounding the Mediterranean are made of limestones and dolomites, the pulverized remains of marine creatures that lived and died in that ancient ocean. Tectonic forces lifted ocean floors up into mountains, folded and corrugated them into harsh, jagged karst landscapes, and baked and crushed soft sedimentary rocks into marbles.

Along the slow-moving edge between the Eurasian and African plates volcanoes have at times formed. Best known today are Etna on Sicily, Vesuvius above the Bay of Naples, and Santorini in the Aegean north of Crete. The volcanoes of the archipelago of the Lipari Islands, north of Sicily, still smoulder. At Solfatera in Pozzuoli poisonous gases bubble off pools of hot mud, staining the surrounding rocks in yellows and greens. Up and down central Italy crater lakes—the lakes of Bolsena and Bracciano north of Rome, and those of the castelli Romani to the south—are now tranquil relics of ancient eruptions. Rome itself, like many towns in Tuscany to the north, is built partly on tufa, a soft rock formed by compacted falls of ash. A few of the Mediterranean islands have rare deposits of obsidian, a shiny black volcanic glass that can be made into blades and arrowheads. Earthquakes still echo along the length of the Mediterranean, the consequence not of Poseidon striking the earth with his trident, but of the slow grinding of tectonic plates.

Glaciers shaped Mediterranean landscapes less than in other parts of the world, only a few forming on the highest mountains. But the warming of the earth during the early Holocene and the slow recolonization of postglacial landscapes by plants and animals from warmer parts has softened many Mediterranean landscapes. West-facing coasts benefit from Atlantic winds bringing rain, while east-facing coasts, especially those of southern Spain and Italy and of southern Greece, are more arid. The weather is often thought of as mild: snowfalls are rare, and so are prolonged severe droughts. But it is a fragile environment, and since the origins of farming, human action has degraded it. Forests have largely disappeared except for on mountain ranges. Elsewhere woodland has been replaced by *garrigues*, scrublands covered in plants resistant to the summer heat. Reduced tree cover and winter storms have together stripped the soil off many mountain slopes, depositing it in valley bottoms. Deforestation, the expansion of farmland, and hunting means that large mammals, predators, and prey alike have all but disappeared except in remote areas like the Abruzzi or the Pyrenees. Greek heroes hunted lions in Europe: both populations are long gone. Bears, wolves, and lynxes are on the edge of extinction.

The soils of much of the Mediterranean are poor, but its real curse is aridity. The warm Mediterranean summers are not the main problem. Egypt and Mesopotamia are far hotter at that time of year, but early farmers there were helped by the alluvium brought down in the Nile floods, and by the waters that the Tigris and Euphrates brought down from rainfall in Anatolia, on the Zagros Mountains and on the steppe. The Mediterranean world is less fortunate, since the mountains raised by ancient tectonic movements have constrained its watershed.

The sea itself is thirsty. The only major rivers that flow into it are the Rhône, the Po and the Nile. Much of its European hinterland drains into the Atlantic, the Baltic, and the Black Sea, through great rivers including the Danube and the Rhine, the Elbe, the Seine, the Loire, the Garonne, the Douro, and the Guadalquivir. On its southern borders the Mediterranean runs up against the deserts of the Sahara, which expanded since the early Holocene into what was once a landscape of savannahs, lakes, and forests. From the straits of Gibraltar to the delta of the Nile on the southern shore few rivers flow all the year round. The north coast is better, and there are a number of smaller rivers including the Ebro, the Arno, the Tiber, the Strymon, the Cayster, and the Maeander. The Mediterranean loses so much water from evaporation annually that its levels are only replenished by flows of water in from the Atlantic and the Black Sea. Those currents bring great migrations of fish. Ancient cities located by the Straits of Gibraltar and the Bosporos grew rich as a result. This was good news for fishermen, but farmers had fewer resources to work with than their counterparts in the Nile Valley and Babylonia.

The Mediterranean world we see today has not changed very much over the last four thousand years, if we can imagine it without the huge increase in population and the consequent urban sprawls and pollution. Sea levels have fluctuated a little in historic times, and some rivers have silted up. Much of the Roman port of Ostia has been lost to the shifting line of the Tiber, and the port of Ephesus now lies far from the sea. These effects varied from place to place. There are Roman villas lying in shallow water offshore in the Bay of Naples, and the Egyptian cities of Canopus and Thonis-Herakleion on the delta sank into the mud sometime in the Middle Ages.

The Mediterranean is not one world but many. Most historical geographers emphasize its fragmentation. Naturally, there are unifying features. Its warm, wet winters and dry hot summers has given the name "Mediterranean" to a climatic regime found elsewhere in the world, for instance on the Cape of South Africa and in parts of California. A range of flowering plants and trees are typical of the Mediterranean Basin and widespread within it. Yet there are differences too. The southern half is far hotter and drier than the north. Travel down the Italian peninsula and the green rolling hills of Tuscany and Umbria give way to the parched landscapes of the Mezzogiorno. Northern Greece is a land of wooded mountains framing great lakes; central Greece has some marshland, but the Peloponnese is mostly very dry in summer. The low-lying hills of Catalonia, southern France, Italy, and Greece are today plagued by wildfires every summer. In antiquity horses and cattle thrived north of the Alps, sheep and goats in the eastern and southern quadrants of the Mediterranean Basin. The pattern is neatly illustrated by the bones recovered from Roman period sites.[2]

The sea itself consists of a series of linked marine basins each with its own character. They are of different depths, different salinities, and different mean temperatures at any time of the year, and each has its own circulating currents. It is framed by mountainous peninsulas—Iberia, Italy, the Balkans, and Anatolia being the most important. They break up the littoral into a series of coastal plains with their backs to the mountains, cut off from their neighbours by rocky promontories. Some of these micro-regions are more favoured than others. Lagoons and marshes can be rich resources when they could be tapped, and there are some low-lying hilly landscapes like that of Tuscany or even Alpine pastures that provided grazing for flocks in the heat of the summer.[3] But many areas were very unproductive. Land transport between the most fertile and populous micro-regions was never easy. Some of these fertile plains might just as well have been islands, cut off as they were from each other by mountain ranges.[4]

This fragmented Mediterranean was a precarious place to live.[5] There were occasional Mediterranean-wide droughts, and years of heavy rain or cold winters throughout the region. More often good and bad years were very local. In any one year, some micro-regions would experience shortages (dearths) while their neighbours enjoyed above-average harvests (gluts). There were some regions—Attica was one of them—where wheat would fail one year in four. The most dependable harvests came from river valleys fed by spring melt waters rather than rain. The Nile floods varied from year to year but it was very rare that the Abyssinian Mountains did not provide enough for the harvest. Aegean Turkey was watered by the Maeander, the Cayster, and other rivers draining off the Anatolian plateau.[6] Many islands are still terribly short of water in summer—Malta and Sicily among them—and a few are actually waterless. Most places were neither consistently prosperous nor always on the edge; they lived with risk.

It was this unpredictability that made the ancient Mediterranean such a dangerous place to build cities.[7] Poor soils and arid summers were bad enough. Most ancient cities had to be fed from their own territory, and that imposed harsh limits on growth. The larger the city, the more vulnerable it was to crop failures and water shortages. Today we take it for granted that our greatest cities will be fed from all over the world: we bank water in reservoirs, pump it huge distances, even recycle it so we have enough to drink. None of this was easily achieved in ancient times. No ancient city of any size could do without granaries, grain funds, and tight controls on market prices. Almost all the largest cities were on the coast, where they might be provisioned more easily from a distance, and the greatest cities depended on political muscle to ensure they got more than their fair share when food was scarce.

Peasant communities around the world store food against disaster, feed livestock when there is plenty in order to slaughter it later, and borrow from their neighbours when they are in trouble with the promise of lending to them in future years. They eat food they would normally despise when needed, and will move if necessary in search of food. None of these are perfect solutions. Those who today still live in the shadow of hunger do not come out of bad years unscathed.[8] Research on more recent populations shows that in bad years fewer infants are born, and of those that are born fewer survive, and they are less healthy throughout their lives. Mortality increases disproportionately among the sick and the old, and health declines among the young. Small-scale societies survive, but only at a cost. The situation is even worse in cities, of course. Cities assemble so many more hungry mouths, many of them already malnourished and underfed and packed closer together in unsanitary conditions, and therefore more vulnerable not only to epidemics but to the endemic diseases that lurk waiting to strike down the weak and the hungry. The rulers of ancient cities often tried to shift the burden of suffering onto the surrounding countryside, so that townsfolk were the last to suffer when food was short. Even this had limited effect. Once urbanism took hold the ancient Mediterranean suffered from a lethal combination of static populations and unpredictable harvests. This, in a nutshell, is the answer to why Mediterranean farmers preferred for so long to live in villages and hamlets rather than cities. They had just the same urban aptitudes as all other human populations, but most of the ancient Mediterranean world was a terrible place to build a city.

Farmers Moving West

The Mediterranean connects three continents, and all the islands between them. Or does it separate them? Both, of course, and the balance has changed over the course of human history.

Fifteen thousand years ago the Mediterranean Basin was not a very well connected world.[9] Before and during the last glacial maximum early humans—various species of them—had roamed around the shores of the Mediterranean Sea. Few ever crossed open water, so the Mediterranean Islands remained Pleistocene idylls. A few foragers reached Sicily, Malta, Sardinia, and Corsica right at the end of the last Ice Age, when the amount of water tied up in the glaciers had lowered sea levels. The islands were bigger than today—Sardinia and Corsica were for a long time a single land mass—and some were closer to the shore. But the traces of these early foragers, hunters, and fishers are very slight. Perhaps there were visits and brief occupations, and also periods when there were few or no humans around.

Farming spread westward from the Near East beginning around 10,000 years ago.[10] It did so not as a steady wave of advance but in a series of jumps, from one favourable plain or island to another. The technical term for this kind of migration is "saltation." Colonization by saltation makes perfect sense. Why settle on a rocky headland when another day or so of travel would take you to the next little coastal plain? Farmers brought with them a subset of the crops and animals domesticated in the Near East, and they needed to find the most compatible environments for them. Good soils and reliable fresh water were major attractions. Sheep and goats were well suited to the arid environments of the Mediterranean world. Some cereals did better than others. The lands the first farmers settled were not uninhabited. Foragers were either displaced or else absorbed, presumably violently. They have left few traces in the genomes of modern populations of the region.

During the ninth and eighth millennia B.C.E. farmers settled the major Mediterranean islands: Cyprus and Crete to Malta, Sicily, Sardinia, and Corsica. The lower sea levels of the early Holocene made some of these journeys less dramatic than they would be today, but in many case groups of farmers reached new territory by longboat or canoe, bringing with them seed corn and a range of domesticated animals. Their arrival was evidently often traumatic for existing fauna. There were extinctions of insular species, including the great deer *megaloceros* on Sardinia, the pigmy hippo on Cyprus, and giant swans and dwarf elephants on Malta and Sicily. Presumably these extinctions were caused both by hunting and by habitat loss as farmers cleared woodland. Islands are precarious environments too, and it is not difficult to upset ecological balances. The first human settlers of the North Island of New Zealand wreaked havoc, especially with flightless birds. A few centuries later, European explorers of the modern period spread rats, dogs, pigs, and other mammals on the islands of the Caribbean and the Pacific. We must imagine something similar happened as prehistoric farmers spread their way of life around the Inland Sea. Mediterranean landscapes and eco-systems must have become less varied.

During the Neolithic and early Bronze Age most Mediterranean farmers lived in farmsteads of small villages. Few villages occupied areas of more than a hectare, and perhaps few had populations of more than fifty or so people. Probably these societies were organized as much by kinship as by other means, although it is difficult to establish this. Probably too individuals moved between communities, for marriage and trade and in response to conflicts, and probably too there were occasional gatherings into larger groups for ceremonials and in some places to build great monuments. During the first five millennia of farming in the Mediterranean region most people lived in small worlds.

At least some of the farming villages of the northern Balkans, of Bulgaria and Hungary, were much bigger than those of the Mediterranean, as were the larger villages of Anatolia. Some sustained populations in the low thousands. The reason is clear enough. Small communities cope much better with bad years.[11] Their environmental footprint is lighter, and they can withstand the ups and downs better than can larger groups.

Neolithic settlement on the coastal plains and islands of the Inland Sea did not necessarily make the Mediterranean a more connected place. One of the striking features of Neolithic Malta, Sardinia, and so on is how distinctive their cultural paths became after the start of farming. When communication is difficult, islands can become tiny worlds unto themselves, which give rise to strange forms. The Neolithic Mediterranean was as culturally diverse as it has ever been. Everywhere farmers lived in villages, growing more or less the same crops. But they harnessed human ingenuity to entirely local ends. Malta built extraordinary temples long before the pyramids. Sardinia developed a unique megalithic tradition of great circular tombs. On Cyprus an entirely local rounded architectural tradition persisted while all the surrounding areas developed orthogonal forms. Canoes still crossed the deep water, and eventually longboats too. Most sites of any size have produced some ceramic made in neighbouring areas. But in the first age of farming the Mediterranean remained socially fragmented. The Middle Sea divided much more than it connected, perhaps all the more so when sea levels rose slightly in the middle Holocene. During the fourth millennium the urban experiments of Egypt and Mesopotamia might as well have been taking place on the moon as far as Mediterranean farmers were concerned.

During the third millennium B.C.E. this isolation and fragmentation began to change. There were two big reasons, and perhaps a cluster of local factors too. The first big factor was a growing demand for metals, especially copper and tin, the two vital ingredients of bronze, neither of them evenly spread around the ancient world. The second was the invention of the sail. Sailing connected Egypt first of all to the northeast corner of the Mediterranean, where today Turkey, Syria, and Lebanon converge. That area was a source of timber, the famous cedars of Lebanon, and it also gave access via the Bekaa Valley to Upper Mesopotamia. Winds and currents make it easy to sail counterclockwise around the eastern Mediterranean. The earliest sailing vessels could go on easily to Cyprus and westwards along what is now the Turkish coast until they reached the Aegean. Later vessels were capable of more adventurous journeys yet.[12] But during the Bronze Age, winds and currents connected Crete and the south Aegean most easily with Egypt and the Levant. It was within this broad circuit that the first Mediterranean cities emerged.

Like other early urbanisms the beginnings of urban growth around the Mediterranean were fragile, and as a result they left few traces. Not a great deal can be said for sure before the early second millennium B.C.E., at which point each tradition had its own local linguistic, architectural, and sociological peculiarities. They were neither clones nor colonies of the cities of the Fertile Crescent. But it is impossible to imagine them except as the outer fringe of that wider Bronze Age world. A rough east-to-west chronological sequence suggests the growth of that system was gradual rather than a sudden explosion.

Byblos, in modern Lebanon, has been claimed as the oldest city in the world, admittedly in a local history written by one of its Roman period citizens. The area, on the maritime fringe of the Fertile Crescent, had been settled since the Neolithic, certainly from the end of the sixth millennium. The Upper Sea features in Sargon's proclamation, and many scholars think Mount Lebanon was the inspiration for the Cedar Forest where Gilgamesh and Enkidu slew the giant Humbaba. But it was not until the end of the fourth millennium B.C.E. that Byblos became important to Egyptians of the Old Kingdom seeking timber. A coastal location gave access to rich local resources, but little else before the arrival of maritime shipping. From the third millennium Byblos became one of the world's first port cities.

That was in the early Bronze Age. By the thirteenth century B.C.E. the ruler of Byblos was a royal correspondent of the pharaoh. It was not the only trading port in the region. Two hundred kilometres farther north was the city of Ugarit, less well connected to Mount Lebanon but an excellent gateway to Anatolia as well as northern Mesopotamia. From 1800 B.C.E. it had strong connections with the kingdom of Ebla in Syria and with the Hittite Empire, which by then was the dominant power in Anatolia. One of the most westerly of the Hittite dependencies was the city of Troy, founded around 2700 B.C.E. right at the start of the Bronze Age. Mycenaean citadels, when they began to be built around a millennium later, on the opposite (western) side of the Aegean, resembled sites like Troy with their vast walls, and spectacular entrance ramps and gates more than they did the palatial societies of Crete (see Figure 11).

These societies come into sharper focus over the course of second millennium. What makes the difference is a shift in the quality of the documentation. From the middle of the fourteenth century B.C.E. the cache of diplomatic letters from Amarna in Egypt, written in cuneiform Akkadian, includes copies of correspondence between the pharaoh and his agents and allies in the Levant. Thousands of roughly contemporary cuneiform letters from Hattusa, the Hittite capital, allow the names of places and peoples to be put on a map of Asia Minor. Troy, Miletus, and Cyprus all seem to be

Figure 11 The Citadel at Mycenae
Aerial-motion / Shutterstock.com

mentioned. The Egyptian priest Wenamun left an account of his travels, which took him to Byblos and probably to Cyprus as well. From Ebla and Ugarit there are thousands of cuneiform tablets, and on the island of Crete a completely new set of scripts was used, first to write an unknown language and then in an adapted form (now called Linear B) to write Greek.

Later generations of Greeks barely remembered this past.[13] They were impressed by the ruins of great citadels and by the complicated sprawl of ancient palaces, and the splendour of royal and princely tombs. The ancient walls of the citadels were "cyclopean"—built by giants. The palace of Minos on Crete concealed a "labyrinth," to hide the monstrous offspring of his queen and a divine bull. Around the circular tholos tombs of mainland Greece, early Iron Age populations would sacrifice horses and imagine they were feasting with the mighty dead. Their Bronze Age was an Age of Heroes, and it gave rise to epic poetry and many other myths. So splendid were these myths that it came as a genuine surprise to the first modern archaeologists who began to excavate ancient ruins in the late nineteenth century that they contained a kernel of fact. Schliemann and others overreacted, and for a while the Homeric Epics were treated as more or less historical documents. More careful excavations, and the decipherment of one of several ancient writing systems devised and forgotten during the Bronze Age, revealed a less familiar urban world but also one that can, for the first time, actually speak to us.

The Copper Island

Cyprus, the largest island in the eastern Mediterranean Basin, lies between Egypt, Syria, and Anatolia.[14] It is no surprise it was early drawn into the dynamic developments of the Near Eastern Bronze Age during the third millennium B.C.E.[15] Three sources of change are apparent.

The first was the expansion of new forms of domestication. The island had been settled by farmers from the Levant in the tenth or ninth millennium B.C.E. In the canoes with which they reached the island they had brought with them sheep and goats, the most heat tolerant and portable of the domesticated species available, and also dogs. (They also brought deer and perhaps thought they could domesticate them, but like others before and after they failed to achieve this.) The small livestock formed an integral part of the low-energy agriculture of Neolithic and early Bronze

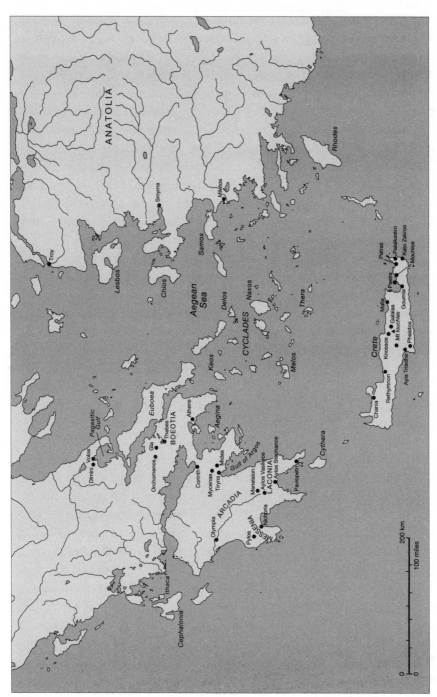

Map 3 The Aegean World in the Bronze Age

Age villages. But in the third millennium cattle were brought to the island and were used from the first to pull ploughs, transforming its agricultural productivity especially on the central plain of the Mesaoria. That increased surplus made a division of labour possible, and began to rupture the existing egalitarian social order. As in almost every aspect of Cypriot prehistory there is a fierce debate about the relative importance of local initiatives and external influence. The cattle were certainly from Near Eastern stock: societies on the mainland and in Anatolia were using them for traction before this happened on Cyprus. There is no reason to believe in an invasion of new peoples, but the new ruling groups in Cyprus must have had some connections on the mainland. However these factors were combined the net result was the same: an island of farmers had become something more complex, more stratified, and more outward-looking.

The second source of change was the increased exploitation of the copper deposits from which the island gets its name. The main deposits exploited in antiquity were in the foothills of the Troodos Mountains, a great igneous massif that occupies most of the southwest part of the island and towers over the sun-baked limestone plains. Cyprus was not the only source of copper in the eastern Mediterranean, but it was soon the most important one. Bronze Age civilizations were greedy for the metal. The Uluburun wreck shows that by the end of the second millennium Cyprus produced great quantities in standardized ingots, and sent them long distances. They are found widely around the eastern Mediterranean, and even beyond it.

The third change, and the one that made the others possible, was (once again) the arrival of sailing. Cyprus was in effect brought closer to Anatolia and the Levant and to the emerging civilizations of the Aegean at just the moment when its economic potential had become much greater. Cattle, copper, and sailing ships would eventually bring Cyprus onto the roll of great powers. It was no longer a distant territory inhabited by smallholders. By the end of the fourteenth century Cyprus was a key part of the trading world of the Near East. A kingdom named Alashiya features in records from the Hittite capital in Hattusa. Its king was the recipient of letters from the king of Ugarit, and appears in the Amarna archive too. Wenamum was shipwrecked at Alashiya on his way back from seeking wood from Byblos. Putting together all the details from these stories it looks very like this kingdom, a military power with resources of copper and a capital on the coast, was based in Cyprus.

Late Bronze Age Cyprus was a prosperous place for some. Rich tombs suggest the emergence of elites. The social hierarchy was mirrored in the landscape. A world of villages was replaced—in stages—by a landscape organized by cities.[16] During the first centuries of the second millennium B.C.E. fortresses were built at Enkomi, Maroni, Paleopaphos, and Citium. All were ports from which ships might sail to Ugarit, to the Anatolian coast, west to Crete and the Aegean. Elsewhere on the island there are signs of intensification of agriculture and mining. By the fourteenth century B.C.E. some of the fortified ports had become cities, and the capitals of city-states. All faced east, and the shortest crossing to Ugarit and the Levant.

Best known of the Bronze Age cities is Enkomi. Around 1600 B.C.E. it was a cluster of buildings, constructed of mud brick on foundations of stone. The houses were bigger than those of earlier periods, and their internal organization was more complex. Some were two-storey structures, enclosing open courtyards, and near them were chamber tombs. One, in which copper was produced, was fortified. Fragments of container amphorae from the mainland—the Caananite jars used to transport oil, aromatic resin, and wine—show some of their trading partners. Cylinder seals were first imported and then imitated at Enkomi. Someone there must have had some idea of how the palace economies of the Near East were run. Other material suggests links between Enkomi and the rest of the island. It has been suggested that a series of forts built across the island show an attempt by Enkomi—perhaps even a successful attempt—to control the entire island. During the late fourteenth and the thirteenth centuries B.C.E. Enkomi grew in size, came to be was surrounded with a defensive wall, and was replanned on a grid system. Kition and Maa did the same. Later buildings on the same site included ceramic from the Aegean.[17]

Crete and the Cyclades

Levantine travellers probably reached Crete first in the Aegean, but their sailing vessels also played a part in connecting the islands to the north as well, the Cycladic archipelago.[18] Before the maritime revolution of the third millennium B.C.E. this too was a world of tiny and fairly isolated communities, connected by canoes but largely untouched by the outside world. The first sailing vessels to reach them arrived at the end of the third millennium, shortening travel times enormously. By the start of the second millennium some of Cycladic communities had become key nodes in new networks that criss-crossed the Mediterranean, helping more prosperous societies connect, and some island societies became closely linked to developments on Crete.

On the better soils around the Aegean, as elsewhere in the Mediterranean, there had been steady demographic growth since before the Bronze Age.[19] Some village sites grew in size, and a few contained some grander buildings. At Lerna in the Argolid a two-storey building roofed in baked tiles was created in the middle of the third millennium and then burned down a couple of centuries later. What social forces lay behind either its rise or fall are obscure. Advances in metalworking and some components of the Secondary Products Revolution transformed local economies as they had done in Cyprus. Animal-drawn ploughs and new domesticated animals (the donkey) and plants (the vine and the olive) all made their appearance. Growth was guaranteed, gradual, or even secure. A number seemed to begin cycles of growth and then collapse near the end of the third millennium whether from some general cause (climatic change?), or perhaps because they were none of them very resilient. Yet movement across the Aegean steadily increased, settlements grew in size, and connections with the eastern Mediterranean steadily intensified.

The first cities and states to be created in the region were on Crete.[20] There are signs of slow settlement and population growth from the origins of farming, perhaps not continuous, but cumulative all the same. Then, at the very end of the third millennum, there was a sudden transformation. It seems to have started at Knossos, but was followed rapidly at Phaistos and Mallia. The size of the settlements grew enormously (from around 5 hectares to more than 30 hectares at Knossos around the turn of the millennia, rising to 100 hectares or more in the late Bronze Age). The villages in the surrounding plains began to be organized into hierarchies. And in the city centres themselves were built huge monumental structures: the famous Minoan palaces, with their storerooms and painted walls, and public reception spaces like the throne room at Knossos (Figure 12). .

It is an accident of the way the first excavations unrolled that we speak more often about Cretan palaces than about Cretan towns and cities. Early excavators were spellbound by the myths of Theseus and Minos, and perhaps too the lack of huge town walls also made Minoan cities seem less spectacular. Yet there is no doubt that second-millennium Crete was an urban culture.[21] The palaces stood at the centre of the cities, but they were surrounded by less elaborate dwellings and not ramshackle collections of

Figure 12 The Throne Room in the Palace of Knossos
Dan Porges / Getty Images

houses either, but properly planned districts with roads and drainage and basic amenities. There were also some smaller towns like Gournia where fifty-odd houses surrounded a small palace, and where a cobbled street runs down to the harbour. Recent studies of the size of both cities and the palaces at their heart show they are quite comparable with Levantine towns.[22] Knossos—the largest centre by far—was on a similar scale to Ebla. Its peak population in the late Bronze Age, when it covered between 100 and 125 hectares, has been estimated at between 20,000 and 25,000.[23] The other two main urban centres on Crete were each over 60 hectares in extent, not quite the size of major Mesopotamian centres of the same period nor of the contemporary Egyptian capital of Avaris in the Delta, which covered around 200 hectares, but comparable to many Near Eastern city-states. Much of the economic life of these cities probably revolved around the palaces, but not all of it. And as in every other urban system the great centres were connected both to the smaller conurbations in their hinterland, and also to more distant centres.

The exact process by which cities appeared in the proto-palatial period at Knossos, Malia, and Phaistos, in places where early Bronze Age villages had had populations of just of a few hundred, is mysterious. At this distance of course we cannot expect to recover historical details, but we can identify some factors that made the project of city-building possible. Modest demographic growth might be the least important, since that was happening in many regions where towns did not appear. There is no reason to think Crete was especially fecund. A really vital factor must have been the newly increased potential for connecting with distant places by sea. The greater speed and the greater capacity of sailing vessels allowed travellers from the Levant and Egypt to connect to southern Turkey and Crete. A final set of factors are the changes in the economy brought by metallurgy and the secondary products revolution. Crete did not have great resources of copper that Cyprus did, but it was able to produce textiles in great quantities and perhaps other agricultural products too. All this creates the potential for state-formation and city-building. How and why this opportunity was seized is more obscure.[24]

It is difficult to believe Cretan urbanism was born out of force, since there are no great citadels and few fortification walls on the island dating to the Bronze Age. Nor was it a colonial venture from the east, nor a slavish imitation of eastern models. Quite likely the idea of a city and perhaps kingship was inspired by the experiences of Anatolia and the Levant. Were Cretans already sailing the seas as merchants in the years before the palaces were built? Or were they like their descendants, visiting nearby coasts as pirates and mercenaries?

But the Cretan realization of the city, of kingship, and of writing was quite original. For starters, there were no spectacular temples in Minoan Crete. There were peak sanctuaries and other holy places, but the cities were physically dominated by the palaces.

The Greeks of the Archaic period would dispense with palaces and put temples at the centre of their cities. In Mesopotamia and Syria palaces and temples coexisted at the heart of many cities. Cretan cities are unlike both. We should conclude that below the superficial similarities Cretan societies were organized in different ways to those of their Anatolian and Levantine neighbours. Kin groups seem to have remained important in Cretan society, to judge from the tombs that surround early palace sites. Most likely the creation of cities was the initiative of one or more kin group, able to persuade others of the potential benefits of urbanism and then able to seize it for themselves.

The institution of a palace was adapted to serve local purposes. Like Near Eastern states, they made use of pottery storage amphorae and seal stones. The Minoan rulers of Crete used their palaces as the controlling centres of centralized economies, and they also made them into stages for all sorts of ceremonial. They developed a set of unique and local royal and religious symbols, not closely modelled on any others we know of, and not much imitated either. Spectacular frescoes depicted dancers and bull leaping while all sorts of marine animals appear on pottery and wall paintings. Minoan Crete made use of writing too, but they did not import either the technology of cuneiform, in which marks were impressed with a small wedge into clay tablets, nor one of the international languages of the day such as Akkadian. This is a major contrast with what happened at Ebla, or in Hittite Anatolia. Instead at least two writing systems were developed, a hieroglyphic one used in northern and eastern Crete and another created around Phaistos and used in the south of the island that used signs that stood for syllables rather than whole words. This syllabary is known as Linear A, since the documents we have use signs incised freehand (rather than impressed with tools like the cuneiform wedge) on long thin clay tablets, which do not resemble the shape of those used in the Fertile Crescent and Anatolia. Linear A is first attested around 1800 B.C.E. It gave rise to two other scripts, the Cypro-Minoan script (these are all modern names) used on Cyprus from about 1500 B.C.E., and a little later Linear B, which would be used all over Crete and in much of southern Greece to write the Greek language. A tablet written in Linear B, but found at the palace of Pylos in western Greece rather than Crete, is depicted in Figure 13.

It seems bizarre that such trouble was taken to create these scripts from scratch. It is quite likely that some Minoans, like the rulers of Enkomi, knew some Akkadian, as it was the international language of diplomacy. It is virtually certain that some of their Mycenaean successors knew the Hittite language too, since Hittite kings wrote several letters to a king of Ahhiyawa whom most experts think was a king of the Achaeans, one of Homer's names for the Greeks. But for whatever reason, Aegean rulers preferred to invent and use their own scripts rather than borrow those of their neighbours.

A major component of most early writing systems were numbers, weights, and measures, the kind of recording systems needed if one intends to accumulate surpluses through tribute or rent or tax, if you are going to organize manufacture and trade, if you need to store information for any length of time, and if you are going to deal with strangers. Neither Cretan hieroglyphic nor Linear A can be read but Linear B has been deciphered, and it

Figure 13 A Linear B tablet from Pylos
DEA / G. DAGLI ORTI / Getty Images

gives some idea of Cretan economy and society during the last generation of palaces in Crete, in the fifteenth century B.C.E.[25] Almost all the records log the movements of goods in and out of the palaces. The kings gathered in grain, and distributed much of it again as rations for palace workers. There were also royal flocks of sheep—the palace of Knossos alone controlled 100,000 animals in its last, Greek-ruled period—and there were palace workers employed in producing textiles from their wool. Where Cypriot chiefs had bought their way into the Near Eastern gift exchange system with copper, Cretan kings were apparently doing the same with cloth. It is unlikely this system was invented only in the period when Knossos was run by Greek speakers. Linear A, when it is deciphered, will probably tell us more about the earlier stages of this system.

The greatest cities were those built at Knossos, Phaistos, and Mallia. Crete was probably never politically unified, but at their height the bigger centres may have controlled around 1,000 square kilometres of territory each. Knossos was easily the major centre on the island during the Neopalatial period (roughly 1700–1450 B.C.). The foundations and ground floor walls were built of stone and mortar and strengthened with timbers; upper stories were made of mud-brick which was lighter, and the roofs were tiled. Wooden columns and occasional slabs of stone supported lintels and upper storeys. All these techniques can be found elsewhere, but they were put together in new ways that do not exactly duplicate Near Eastern, Egyptian, or Anatolian architectural styles. The public areas must have impressed with slabs of facing stone, sculptured friezes of gypsum, plaster painted with frescoes, and entrances coordinating ramps and monumental stairways that led through corridors and into a central court and great halls. Out of sight were the store rooms and workshops. Who was the audience? The elders of less-powerful kin groups bringing tribute? The rulers of rival Minoan cities? Ambassadors from overseas? The writing tablets reveal nothing about the ideology of this world. A brilliant fresco frieze from the town of Akrotiri on Santorini shows sailing vessels and galleys making their way between the islands while dolphins leap around them. On the rooftops of island towns, people stand in crowds to watch the vessels sail past. Exotic birds and animals appear on other walls. This is the closest we come to observing Minoan pageantry.

The rulers of the palaces did not try to manage the whole of the economy. Ancient seeds and grains found in excavations—sometimes called "biofacts," by analogy with "artefact," the term used for man-made objects—show that many crops were grown in Cretan farms and consumed in the palaces and their surrounding towns that do not appear on the tablets. Once we look beyond the cities and palaces we can faintly see a wider world of towns, villages, and farms, some grand enough to have been called villas. The palaces rode on the back of a more stable economic system, one that was making the most of a wider range of crops, domesticated animals, and their secondary products.

Other Cretan towns like Palaikastro and Gournia existed which either had no palaces attached, or smaller ones. These towns look very like the residential quarters that surrounded the palaces with the exception that they had little in the way of monumental architecture. They had more or less regular street plans with blocks of small residences arranged along larger roads and divided up by alleys. Palaikastro at least had a drainage system too. Some houses were two storeys in height, there is usually a definable centre around a square, and at the edges they fade out into suburban scatters of workshops of farms. Depending on how much of this periphery is counted, their areas were between 20 and 40 hectares and their populations probably in the low thousands. Settlements very like them appear on neighbouring islands. Minoan objects and Minoan style became more and more widespread across the southern Aegean during the Neopalatial period, in significant quantities from Cythera off the southernmost cape of Greece, from Akrotiri on Santorini, from Phylakopi on Melos and Kolonna on Aegina, from Rhodes, and at Miletos on the west coast of Turkey. A few stray finds have been made in the northern Aegean, on Samothrace and at Troy. Frescoes in a Minoan style have even been found at Tell el-Dab, a short-lived Egyptian capital built in the Nile Delta.

During the fifteenth century B.C.E., most of the major sites on Crete were destroyed. The reasons for the collapse are fiercely debated. Volcanoes, climate change, peasant revolts, and invasions have all been suggested. It is also possible that these first urban societies were inherently precarious, perched on a set of economic transactions that could easily be upset. Knossos itself did survive for around a century, and it probably ruled most of the island. Smaller towns seem to have survived this crisis better than the palaces. At some point control of Knossos and Phaistos passed to Greek speakers, those who used Linear B. The first investigators of Bronze Age Crete interpreted this as a wholesale conquest by mainlanders. It no longer looks so simple, and there is no real sign that mainlanders were responsible for the destruction of other centres rather than arriving to take charge of an island that had already suffered some crisis. A takeover of some sort seems likely, although a great deal was preserved. Knossos remained the main centre, but someone either taught palace scribes Greek and helped them produce a new version of script suitable for writing it, or else taught Greek speakers how to write and how to manage the complex palace economies. It is easy to think of historical parallels for invaders adopting the ways of the conquered, or for subject peoples taking control, but it is more difficult to decide exactly which parallels apply.

Mycenaean Greece

The southern portion of the Greek mainland lay on the fringes of the Minoan World, connected to it through the Cycladic island chains. There was a lag of a few centuries in the arrival of bronze-working and a few other technologies. Around the turn of the third and second millennia when a few Cretan centres were expanding rapidly and reorganizing their surrounding landscapes, nothing similar is visible on the mainland. Small settlements of a hectare or so in size were the norm, often located on hilltops, and over the next few centuries the largest were only around

seven hectares in size. There had been and would be again a few exceptions to this rule. Grave goods suggest that although some individuals
ended their lives richer than others, there was nothing yet really resembling an elite.

This changed around the seventeenth century B.C.E., the great age of the
Cretan palaces and of Minoan urbanism. Very rich burials appear in several
areas of the mainland. The shaft graves of Mycenae are the most famous,
but elsewhere in the Peloponnese and in parts of central Greece similar
dynamics were underway. At least some families were gaining access to
supplies of precious metals that they could afford to put out of use in the
graves of the dead. Some of those receiving rich burial were women and
children. This is a sure sign that particular families had gained hereditary
power, and that there were chiefdoms. Among the grave goods are swords
and daggers and spears and arrowheads. There is ornate drinking equipment too. Baltic amber and the design of weapons illustrate regular contact with central Europe. The difference is that the emergent chiefdoms
of southern Greece found themselves on the fringe of an international
trading system in a way those of central Europe did not. These Mycenaean
chiefdoms were open to the world, but in more than one direction. The
emerging chiefs of Sparta and Messenia probably encountered Cretan
culture via Cythera. Others looked across the Aegean. The fortifications
and monumental gate at Mycenae resemble those of Anatolian towns,
Troy and Hattusa included, much more than anything on the island of
Crete. Tomb-building—including the creation of beehive tholos tombs—
carried on without any sign of influence from Crete. Cretans had picked
what they wanted from the Near East and suited it to their own needs.
Now mainland populations did the same with Minoan and Anatolian
culture.

At least one thing the mainland chiefs clearly wanted to do was to signal their power. Rich funerals make a major splash locally, but it is always
temporary. The treasures buried in the shaft graves at Mycenae were
invisible for millennia until Heinrich Schliemann "gazed upon the face
of Agamemnon." Much more impressive were the great citadels built at
Mycenae and Tiryns. Despite the fact that they were much smaller than the
largest Cretan palaces, they seem designed to make more of an impression
on those who approached them. Within the Cyclopean walls there were
some reception spaces, but nothing like the great ceremonial courts of
Crete. Both citadels towered above sprawling lower cities of more humble

residences, less obviously planned than the towns and cities of Crete and made up of simple one or two room houses. The gap between rich and poor was advertised more bluntly in mainland Greece than on Crete. At least some of the Mycenaean citadels were designed not just to be easily defended but to be visible from a distance. There was a citadel at Athens too, but the Mycenaean remains are buried beneath the Parthenon and its associated structures, and another on the hill of the Kadmeia at Thebes. There is a lost landscape of Bronze Age fortress capitals, lying beneath classical sites, the palaces themselves often lying under grand temples of the kind the Mycenaeans did not build. The dim outline of a political geography of Mycenaean Greece can be picked out, often based on the same centres as would dominate Iron Age and Classical Greece, or else close by their future locations. These polities were much larger than those predicted for Crete. Linear B at Pylos at least was used to organize military detachments, as well as textile weavers and sheep.

Towards the end of the Bronze Age Linear B was brought back from Crete and eventually used at dozens of centres in southern and central Greece, including Mycenae and Tiryns, Athens and Sparta, Thebes and Gla, Pylos and Iolkos. The mainland palaces were much smaller and less elaborate than Knossos or Phaistos, but they have produced plenty of evidence of wealth and they too were at the centre of small cities. Seal stones, elaborate ceramic drinking vessels, exotic imports, and splendid display weapons show the power of local chiefs to mobilize resources and establish long-distance relations with their peers. The tablets show attempts to import some of the administrative tools developed on Crete, and they were also modified to organize military deployments. During the fourteenth and thirteenth centuries mainlanders travelled much greater distances than their Cretan predecessors. A faint scatter of Mycenaean material stretches from the Levant to Sardinia and right up to the northern Aegean.[26] It is found in large quantities at Troy and on Cyprus and in the Levant, and a very small amount was thinly scattered in southern Italy, Sicily, and even Sardinia.[27] The basis of these exchanges is unknown. Mainland Greece, especially the area in which the new palaces were founded, is poor land and produced little in the way of agricultural surpluses. It had little to rival the cedars of Ugarit and Byblos, the oils and resins of the Levant, the copper of Cyprus, or even the textiles and grain of Crete. Were the mainlanders simply middlemen, making their profit from trade? Or were they like their Iron Age descendants, swords for hire?

Collapse

The collapse of Minoan states on Crete and their takeover by the Greek-speaking rulers of Knossos was not the last disaster to strike Bronze Age urbanism in the Mediterranean. There were always local disasters, the most famous being the explosive eruption of Santorini at a date that is fiercely debated. But at the end of the Bronze Age something much more dramatic happened all over the Aegean world, Anatolia, and the Near East. It has become known as the Late Bronze Age Collapse. The collapse affected the Mycenaean chiefdoms with their citadels and towns around 1200 B.C.E. and Ugarit, sacked around the same time; it engulfed the Hittite Empire (which collapsed around 1178 B.C.E.); and has been linked to the chaos of the nineteenth and twentieth dynasties in Egypt (1292–1077 B.C.E.), a period marked by civil wars, foreign invasions, and the collapse of pharaonic power. There were population movements on a large scale, some of them more like refugees in flight, others more like invasions. Egyptian records speak of the Peoples of the Sea, and there have been many attempts to identify who was moving where.[28] Many possible causes have been proposed including environmental disasters, social revolution, and invasions from outside the region. It is not completely clear whether we are dealing with one disaster or a number coinciding, a perfect storm at the end of the Bronze Age.

Local sequences differ. Most agree that on Crete the Minoan palace civilization ended around 1450, but that Knossos survived for nearly a century after the other palace centres. The rule of the Greek speakers who used Linear B lasted until the middle of the fourteenth century, but several sites had a postpalatial afterlife. At Troy in the northeast Aegean, a series of cities were built on top of each other's ruins between 2700 and 950 B.C.E. Conventionally it is divided into seven periods—Troy I to Troy VII. Troy VI was a large and impressive city, built around a citadel protected with massive walls, towers, and monumental gates. Weaving, the manufacture of purple dye, and other craft manufacture were concentrated here around a great structure that was probably a palace. Only the foundations survive. Other great halls, two storeys high, did survive. Below the citadel stretched out a lower town, like those that surrounded Mycenaean centres, and that too was protected by a wall. Troy VI was destroyed, probably by an earthquake, around 1300 B.C.E. The succeeding occupation—Troy VII—was much more modest. Enkomi on Cyprus was also destroyed, but a century or so later, sometime around 1200 B.C.E. By this stage much of the pottery looks Mycenaean, and perhaps Greek was already being spoken widely alongside the other languages of the island. It was not such a sudden end. Enkomi was rebuilt in style with a great hall at its centre made of ashlar construction—a Mycenaean technique. A new centre at Salamis did eventually replace Enkomi but not until the eleventh century, and much continued into the Iron Age. Cyprus was the only place where a script descended from Linear A—the Cypro-Minoan syllabary—survived. It was already being used to write Greek before the evidence for it disappears between the tenth and eighth centuries B.C.E.

What followed political collapse in Asia Minor and the Aegean world was a dramatic downscaling. Large centres disappeared for a few centuries, while villages with less specialization of labour continued to farm. Without palace economies, writing disappeared from the Aegean world. If it had mostly been used to organize the Bronze Age states, it is easy to see why the skills of reading and writing nearly two hundred signs were lost. Ceramic styles became more localized. Monumental building disappeared. For centuries most of the Mediterranean Basin was once again a world of villages. Bronze Age urbanism was never completely forgotten, but most memories were unreliable. Homer, probably writing in the eighth century, knew there had been cities and palaces and some of their locations, but he imagined them just as larger versions of the citadels and megaron-halls of his own day.

Bronze Age Urbanisms in the Mediterranean World

Historians are often drawn to catastrophes, as their narratives are drawn to closure. But the most remarkable thing about the Bronze Age urbanisms of the eastern Mediterranean is that they got started at all. No system lasts forever, after all, and the cities of Crete lasted for nearly a millennium. It is more important to ask why urbanization was attempted at all, given that Mediterranean farming communities had been living happily without cities for millennia.

One approach is to see urbanism as unleashed by a range of new technologies—bronze metallurgy, sailing vessels, perhaps writing—that enabled Mediterranean populations to overcome the obstacles placed in their way by a relatively hostile environment. But this only works if we imagine some sort of inner drive towards cities, states, and social complexity. There is no evidence at all for this sort of urbanizing imperative. Nor— to dispose quickly of some other bad answers—is there any evidence that urbanism is contagious, that nonurbanized societies are inevitably trans- formed by contact with urbanized ones, nor that economic or demographic growth always leads, eventually, to the city. It is not plausible either, however, that it was just an accident that the first Mediterranean cities appeared first in that part of the region that was closest to Egypt and the ancient Near East. Autonomous, endogenous growth is not a good answer either.

Cyprus, Crete, and the rest of the Aegean world came to form part of a broad nexus in which the extension of long-distance networks of exchanges and experiments in urbanism supported each other. The growing potential for these developments arose in part from the elaboration of the multi- species societies humans had been engaged in since the late Pleistocene. The Secondary Products Revolution—the more resourceful use of domes- ticated animals to provide wool, milk, and labour—is a manifestation of this, but not the only one. Not all textiles came from animals. Linen had been produced in Egypt since the fifth millennium B.C.E. and was essential for the construction of sails. I have made a good deal of the importance of sailing in shortening travel times and reducing transport costs within the eastern Mediterranean. Not all long-distance connections were made by sea. The early second millennium B.C.E. also saw the establishment of Old Assyrian trading posts in Anatolia. More than forty are known. The long-distance exchanges that they organized in metals and textiles, richly documented by an archive found at Kültepe, were managed by caravans of hundreds of donkeys that carried piles of textiles up from the city of Assur to the trading colony at Kanis, and returned laden with metals.[29] Donkeys were probably first domesticated in or near Egypt in the fifth or fourth millennium B.C.E., and by the fourth millennium were used all over the Fertile Crescent.[30] All these exchanges—and we could add the trade in precious wood from Lebanon or lapus lazuli from Afghanistan[31]—depended on complemen- tarities of resources. At a smaller scale this had been conducted between pastoralists and farmers in Mesopotamia and elsewhere as well. These com- plementarities presented opportunities for any community to seize on the potential of the transport mechanisms and resources at their disposal to begin the process of interregional exchange and accumulation.

No doubt some opportunities were missed, and there must also have been many ventures that failed. At the fringes of these Bronze Age world-systems there must have been some contingency, and places and peoples that chose not to get involved when they could have, and societies simply organized in a way that made this kind of change difficult.[32] All we see are the cases where changes did take place, creating in the process artefacts and structures that are more visible than what went before. Urbanism marked the limits of success, not the limits of endeavour. In some cases—Crete is an example— the energy unleashed by these exchanges was so great that it obliterated most of the traces of what went before: prepalatial society is so difficult to see because palatial society has blotted it out. This is an evolutionary truism as well: that we see the variations that were successful, not those removed by selective pressures. In other cases the energy released by Bronze Age intensification and exchange may have had more disruptive effects. All these systems were unplanned, of course, and therefore were by definition chaotic. If what some groups were trading into the system was neither exotic materials (cedar wood, lapis lazuli, gold) nor manufactures (stone vessels, textiles, metalwork) but instead military energy, then that might explain some local collapses. But the failure of one trading partner does not usually bring down the whole system. However the Bronze Age Collapse is to be explained, it should not distract us from the energy and success of centuries of urban experiments that preceded it.

8

Mariners and Chieftains

Interlude

For four hundred years after the collapse of the Cretan palaces, there were no cities west of Cyprus and the Aegean coast of what is now Turkey. This chapter tells the story of the interlude between late Bronze Age urbanism and the appearance of new urban traditions around the Mediterranean, some in landscapes that had never been part of the Bronze Age world-system. The sense of rupture is unavoidable, especially in the east. Population levels there had plummeted, there were few settlements of more than a few hundred people, and the quality and variety of material culture was impoverished. Ships still sailed the sea but regular contacts between neighbouring cultures were attenuated. The volume of goods moving had dropped dramatically.[1] Some technologies had been lost or gone out of use, including writing. Cyprus and the Levant recovered more quickly from the Bronze Age Collapse, and in northern Mesopotamia the Assyrians were laying the foundations of the first of a long series of Iron Age Empires. But for around a dozen generations little of this growth touched the Aegean world let alone points further west.[2]

Over the last few decades archaeologists working in the Aegean have worked to nuance the picture of a dark age intervening between the Bronze Age palaces and the rise of the polis. Not all places had the same experience, and things were not static for four centuries, but the cumulative picture is still pretty grim. Immediately after the collapse of the palaces there was a short afterlife with settlements still living around some of the old centres, including Mycenae and Tiryns. Even when palatial sites were abandoned rapidly—as happened at Iolkos in Thessaly—the inhabitants seem to have moved to settlements nearby. On Crete too there was some continuity of settlement and also some local shifts, often to inland sites with some, like Karphi, quite large. During the twelfth century B.C.E. it looks as if there was a realignment of connections as well as more permanent population movements. Imports into southern Italy suggest that contacts intensified with the former kingdom of Pylos in the western Peloponnese. Mycenaean ceramic appears at new sites on the islands of Euboea, Chios, and Rhodes, and at Cyprus. Much of this reflects the movement of refugees, but perhaps some were just adventurers freed from the control of the palaces. The postpalatial cultures did not last for long. Within a generation or two writing was gone and with it presumably the last traces of the administration it had sustained. Surveys of Greek landscapes find few traces of settlements from the Early Iron Age. Those we do know of were very small. The largest centres probably had fewer than 1,500 people, whereas the largest Mycenaean centres had had up to 10,000. Population levels as a whole also fell, whether through migration or hardship: on some estimates they dropped by 50 per cent.[3] Mostly, the absence of artefacts and structures indicates impoverishment and stagnation. Over most of the area this stagnation lasted until the late eighth century B.C.E.

Much of this was a consequence of political collapse. The webs of exchange created by the city-builders of the Bronze Age had sustained the employment of textile-workers, herdsmen, palace attendants, store managers, scribes, and soldiers, not to mention the craftsmen who specialized in painting frescoes or building in ashlar, or in painting the gorgeous octopus-style ceramics of Crete. All now became farmers as their ancestors had been. Specifically they became subsistence farmers, working small areas intensively, growing a little of everything, storing what they could, and trying to reduce their dependence on the wider world. A great mass of knowledge vanished because the contexts in which it was deployed disappeared, and because oral societies rarely pass on much more about the past than their children need. There is some suggestion too that these communities lost interest in the past, investing instead in relationships in the present. It is easy for us to forget that not all societies are very concerned with conserving traditions. The rulers of Bronze Age cities had taken the lion's share of the profits of long-distance exchange, but others had had a small share. Not anymore. Imports more or less disappeared. Almost everywhere in the Aegean world we see small worlds, flat societies, and the most basic locally made forms of material culture.

Cyprus had emerged from the chaos in a different way.[4] The quantity of Mycenaean-style ceramic that appeared there, along with the arrival Mycenaean techniques of building in stone and especially the use of the Greek language, makes it seem certain there was some movement of population to the island. Enkomi was reoccupied after the destruction of 1200, sanctuaries were rebuilt, and its final phase lasted a century and a half, until it gradually lost out to the new royal capital at nearby Salamis. Writing continued to be in use—even if we have no examples after 1000 B.C.E. for a couple of centuries—and Cypriot cities continued to trade with older and newer Canaanite cities along the Levantine coast, Byblos first and then the rising centres of Tyre and Sidon in the area Greeks called Phoenicia.[5] Some connections remained between Cyprus and Crete, but only a few other sites in the Aegean world kept up links with the Near East before the ninth century.

It is difficult to write about this period without using the language of collapse, failure, impoverishment, and isolation. We have an inherited prejudice against societies that leave feebler physical remains, and produce neither lasting art nor texts. When we encounter them in the present-day world we try hard not to call them barbaric or primitive or underdeveloped. When we encounter them in the past—especially when they occur chronologically after societies that are more visible and legible to us—we speak of dark ages. Small-scale and simpler societies like these offend our expectation of a gradual progress towards civilization. Even worse, they often shamelessly coexisted with more complex civilizations, in this case the city-states of Cyprus and Phoenicia, and the empires of Assyria and Egypt. It is as if they had deliberately and recklessly turned their backs on a system of urban values we still hold dear today. The Aegean in the early first millennium B.C.E. is not the only Dark Age–society to be treated in this way.

No doubt there were many in the early twelfth century B.C.E. who bitterly lamented the end of palatial civilization, but perhaps not everyone agreed. The Bronze Age kingdoms had enriched very few—especially on the mainland—and the splendour of the palaces depended on organizing and coercing many others. Linear B tablets from the palace of Pylos record slave women. It is a reminder that the creation of Bronze Age cities came at a cost. Perhaps too they were risky as well as expensive endeavours. Small-scale communities like those of the Early Iron Age were both cheaper and more sustainable. Tombs from the tenth century and after suggest that the postpalatial world was much more egalitarian, organized by families and villages rather than elites. Less work had to be devoted to supporting the great long-distance exchanges of exotica that the palaces had organized. As a result, their homes and graves seem less rich. Perhaps most people were not worse off. In the contrast between the late Bronze Age and the Early Iron Age we observe one of the recurrent dilemmas of Mediterranean urbanism: in order to create a higher standard of living for a few, more labour had to be extracted from the many, and what was built with that labour was almost always less resilient than simpler systems. From the eighth century onwards Mediterranean communities got better at mitigating the risks of urbanism but were unable to reduce its costs which fell, in all periods, mainly on peasant families and slaves.

One thing that made it a little easier to do without long-distance exchange was the gradual replacement of bronze by iron.[6] Because there were only a few good sources of copper and even fewer of tin, kings and paramount chieftains across the Near East and Europe had often managed to control access to distant sources of copper and bronze. Metals were not the only materials the exchange of which resembled diplomacy more than commerce, but they probably mattered more to most people than the supply of lapis lazuli or cedar wood. Iron ore is much more widely distributed, and the key barrier to its use was learning the more complicated skills required to create iron objects that were hard but not brittle. Once these were mastered, the shift to iron did not just free regions from their dependence on long-distance trade. It also freed some communities from their dependence on their overlords. The "democratizing" effects of iron can be traced all over the Old World, as the shift from bronze to iron took place again and again. By 500 B.C.E. there were Iron Age societies from the Atlantic to the China Sea.[7]

Iron first appears on Mediterranean sites in the second millennium B.C.E., but it was only in the eleventh century that it began to be used to make everyday weapons and tools. The process started in Cyprus and by 1000 B.C.E. was underway across the Aegean. At first it was an exotic metal, and it took some centuries before smiths learned how to produce tools that were significantly harder and more reliable than bronze. Once the processes of carburization were mastered, iron blades could be made that were sharper and more flexible than bronze. The technology was applied to weapons, tools, and utensils of all kinds.

One common thread brings together the collapse of palace economies, the movement of populations, and the spread of iron-working: this is the disruption of social power. These disruptions were not planned and they were certainly not coordinated, but their combined effects were to return Mediterranean societies to a condition rather like that of the middle Bronze Age, before the first urban experiments in the Aegean world. This was a relatively stable state, as four centuries without states or cities demonstrates. This interlude seems to show that the ancient Mediterranean was a world that lay on the cusp, urbanizable but equally easy to inhabit by other means. The Early Iron Age was a time when most Mediterranean populations did the latter. This was not the result of a deliberate choice. They had not collectively turned their backs on city life or consciously rejected their urban destiny, but there is no sign they hankered for it or struggled for centuries to regain past glories, either. Their lives had simply become routinely non-urban, and there were no very pressing forces urging them to change.

Experiments

Fewer settlements are known in the Aegean World around 1000 B.C.E. than at any time in the Bronze Age or at any time afterwards. What makes settlements visible to archaeologists are buildings and possessions. When the occupied area is small, when the buildings are simpler and no longer built of massive ashlar blocks, and when local ceramics are difficult to identify, ancient settlements are more difficult to find. When those who lived there had few exotic or rich possessions, settlement sites do not attract much attention. The early Iron Age in the Aegean world was mostly unspectacular.[8] That does not mean nothing was happening. It was also a decentralized world, one in which different communities were free to experiment and some pretty unusual local forms emerged.

A sense of what surprises might lie in store is given by the discovery, in 1981, of a 50-metre-long building dating to around 950 B.C.E. at Lefkandi on Euboea.[9] In the centre of it was a rich double burial—a man and a woman—and beside them a pit holding the remains of slaughtered horses. The man's cremated remains were placed in an elaborate bronze vessel imported from the Levant, with weapons wrapped in cloth. Beside him was buried a woman laid out and dressed in gold jewelry. The scale of the structure alone is extraordinary, and its design owes nothing to Mycenaean precedents. It was constructed of mud brick on stone foundations and was surrounded with a stockade or colonnade of wooden posts. Soon after the burial was finished the building was covered with a great mound. For a century or so other rich graves—although none as rich as this one—were laid out around the mound, some containing objects suggesting connections with Cyprus. Contemporary graves on the mainland in Locris also have some eastern imports. Pottery similar to the local productions of Lekfandi are found on a number of sites in the Aegean. Then, before the end of the ninth century, the cemetery went out of use and Lefkandi vanishes back into obscurity.

The great mound at Lefkandi poses more questions than we can answer at the moment. Who was the person buried there: a king, a founder, a hero? All have been suggested. Was the building raised simply to cover the tomb, or was it first used for other purposes, such as a hall or a local palace? Connections have been made to the Homeric epics, written down centuries later on the basis of orally transmitted tales, but we cannot tell whether the burial of Lefkandi imitates those attributed to heroes or was a model for epic composition. What is certain is that some person or family was able to persuade a community to devote resources and time to organizing a spectacular funeral, and then a spectacular burial mound, and that that community persisted in some sense for a few generations after the event. This sort of effort usually means someone is making a claim to succeed the dead chieftain. His life remains obscure, but it does seem as if we are observing an attempt to build a more lasting power base. For a while, it worked.

It is possible that there are other grand burial monuments of this kind waiting to be discovered, although archaeologists have been looking for them for a generation without success.[10] There were certainly alternative ways of building communities and asserting control over them. At Kalapodi in Phocis great gatherings took place on the site of a former Bronze Age shrine.[11] No temple existed in the tenth century, but the ground was terraced and landscaped to make a large space for participants to gather, perform sacrifices, make offerings, and feast together. Warfare offered another route to social power. Among the earliest iron objects found at sanctuaries and in graves are weapons. Weapons may have been a priority for the first iron workers because bronze—especially when it was made with more than 90 per cent copper—is soft and easily blunted, fine for cauldrons or other vessels but not so good for swords, daggers, and spearheads. Iron was to begin with a rare and mysterious substance, a new exotic that only the powerful could afford. It is difficult to miss the prominence of warrior culture in Iron Age Greece. By the eighth century the cult of the warrior was well established.[12] Arms and armour (and miniature versions of them) appear among votive offerings. Geometric vases begin to include depictions of soldiers and chariots, the richer graves armour as well as weapons. The *Iliad* evokes an idealized—if implausible—past in which great chariot armies massed, alongside thousands of infantry, clash alarmingly while individual heroes match themselves against each other in combat. Gathering and arming a war band is a common enough feature of late prehistoric societies. A war band maybe be used to secure power at home, to intimidate neighbours, or to go on long-distance raiding expeditions. Perhaps all three were attempted in the tenth and ninth centuries. By the end of the eighth century Greek pirates were turning up in the records of the Assyrian Empire, and Odysseus presents himself as a raider on more than one occasion. Without the sort of records preserved in the time of the Hittite Empire or at Amarna in Egypt it is more difficult to write a political history of the tenth century, but there were certainly episodes of violence. The great city of Troy VII was destroyed in 1300 B.C.E., probably by an earthquake. The site was reoccupied, although the great buildings within the citadel were never repaired, but it was abandoned definitively in the middle of the tenth century, around the time of the great burial at Lefkandi.

Burial and tomb cults, feasting and sacrifice, war bands and raiding. Probably all of these strategies—and maybe others—were used in attempts to establish the power of individual leaders and their families. A few imagined themselves the equals of the dimly remembered Bronze Age kings or of the distant rulers of foreign states. Some tried to re-establish contact with distant trading partners. The Lefkandi grave goods show this was not impossible, but the total quantity of goods of eastern origin that has been found is tiny compared to what was being brought back in the age of the palaces or even the twelfth century.

One thing no one seems to have tried—or at least not successfully—was to create a city. Within a hundred years of the fall of the palace economies, the populations of sub-Mycenaean towns dispersed. No doubt the greatest of the new chieftains gathered retinues around them, but there is no sign that their activities generated permanent settlements of any size. A few chieftains built halls like the structure under the mound at Lefkandi, but there are none of the monuments or public structures that indicate urban rather than village life. Most people in the Aegean world lived in small groups, depending on neighbours and kinsmen, and continued to do so for most of the eleventh, tenth, and ninth centuries B.C.E.

The Kindness of Strangers

A thin but broad scattering of Mycenaean-style pottery is virtually the only trace left of mariners from the eastern Mediterranean sailing west of Greece in the Bronze Age. Between five and six thousand sherds of pottery have been found, some from the sixteenth and early fifteenth centuries B.C.E., most from the period when Greek speakers ruled palaces on the mainland and on Crete. Some at least was manufactured locally in the west. So far fragments of this kind of ceramic have been found on nearly a hundred sites, most in southern Italy and Sicily, but a few on Sardinia and even central Spain. It might sound impressive but it amounts to only a handful of pieces of pottery each year.[13] We have no shipwrecks from this period, and there is no certain sign of settlers—no graves, no buildings, no texts. If Mycenaean visitors brought exotic treasures from the east, they have not survived. If they were looking for metal sources they were mostly looking in the wrong places. A similar pattern emerges from the finds of Mycenaean pottery in Asia Minor: even sites like Miletus and Troy, Sardis and Ephesus have yielded only a few hundred sherds. Almost no Aegean manufactures have been found in inland Turkey.[14] All this amounts to the faintest of faint fringes of activity. From the preceding Minoan period there is even less.

The situation in Cyprus and the Levant is quite different.[15] There are more than a thousand Mycenaean vessels known from Ugarit alone, and contact with Cyprus grew ever more intense until 1200 or even later. For the whole of the late Bronze Age the main axes of trade were from southern Greece and Crete to Egypt, Cyprus, and the Levant. Beyond this were not exactly unexplored seas, but there is not much sign of traffic across them. To the west that faint background noise seems to disappear more or less completely during the twelfth century with the end of sub-Mycenaean contacts with Otranto.

The beginning of the last millennium B.C.E. sees all this change. At Huelva, on the Atlantic coast of Spain just beyond the Straits of Gibraltar, there are unmistakable signs of visitors not just from the eastern Mediterranean but from its easternmost end, from the coastal cities of the Levant.[16] First contact probably dates to the tenth century—more or less contemporary with the great burial mound at Lefkandi—but between 850 and 825 B.C.E. there were some easterners living in local Iberian communities, working iron there, making their own kinds of pottery. The exact route they followed is still being pieced together; the early dates have only just been confirmed from a mixture of the study of their material remains and radio-carbon 14 dating. Already we can be sure that they did not gradually advance east to west across the Mediterranean. Like the first farmers to paddle across the middle sea, they came by saltation, leaping from one convenient stop to another. One stop was almost certainly the port of Kommos on southern Crete. Another was in Sardinia. They followed as direct a route as they could, because they had a definite objective. Around Huelva are rich metal resources, especially of silver. The greatest demand from metals was from the urban economies of the Near East, now growing again after the disruptions at the end of the Bronze Age. The earliest levels of occupation at Huelva included pottery from Greece and Cyprus, Italy and Sardinia. The Mediterranean world was being reconnected.

The cities from which these mariners came were the Iron Age successors of the Levantine cities that had played a key role in coastal trade from the third millennium B.C.E. and had connected it to the Fertile Crescent. Ugarit

Figure 14 A Phoenician sailing vessel
Elie plus / CC BY-SA 3.0

was destroyed just after 1200, but Byblos had continued to thrive. Since then
a series of other Canaanite cities had come to face seawards. The Greeks
called these people Phoenicians, but there is no sign that this was an identity
they shared, or even that they felt they were a single people as opposed to a
group of cities equipped with the same navigational expertise.[17] Depictions
of their small sailing vessels appear on all sort of media from western Syria
to Atlantic Spain (see Figure 14). The most important 'Phoenician' city in
the last millennium B.C.E. was Tyre, whose king Hiram I appears in the
Hebrew Bible. The Tyrians had been in contact with Cyprus since the start
of the Iron Age. Objects made in Tyre in the eleventh century B.C.E. have
been found at Paleopaphos on Cyprus. Figure 15 shows a spectacular silver
cup found at Idalion, also on Cyprus. Around 820 B.C.E. the Phoenicians
founded a city of their own on the island at Kition. Assyrian records make
it clear that the kings of Tyre claimed to be overlords of all the island in the
late eighth century.[18] Perhaps they already did in the ninth.

Figure 15 A Phoenician silver cup from Idalion in Cyprus
Photo © Musée du Louvre, Dist. RMN–Grand Palais / Raphaël Chipault

Another staging post to the west was Carthage, near modern Tunis. The first occupation levels there have been dated between 835 and 800 B.C.; as at Huelva the earliest archaeological contexts contain Sardinian and Greek pottery. Two more settlements were established in Spain around 800 B.C.E., one at Moro de Mezquitilla and another at Toscanos. Objects of Phoenician manufacture turn up in contemporary indigenous settlements in both Spain and Sardinia. Over the next two centuries more bases would be established in North Africa, in western Sicily, in Sardinia and in Spain. None were cities. Probably the number of Tyrians resident at any one site was quite small. Each base was probably rather like what the Greeks would later call an *emporion*, a trading base without much internal political structure and certainly not a new city. They probably functioned like the Assyrian institution of the *karum*, the trading ports in Anatolia that had been the northern destination of all those donkey caravans. The idea was that a self-governing enclave of merchants would be based in or near an indigenous centre, with the permission of the local chieftains.[19] It is quite likely that the Phoenician city-state of Kitium on Cyprus was originally a base of this kind, nestled inside the old Bronze Age city with its great cyclopaean walls and its acropolis. Bases like this coexisted on the island with Greek foundations like Kourion (see Figure 16) and with indigenous communities as well.

Figure 16 The site of Kourion on Cyprus.
leoks / Shutterstock.com

Another place where bases of this sort existed was Crete, the only part of the Aegean world to maintain much of a connection with the Levant after 1100.[20] One area where eastern material has been found is on the north coast of the island around the former palace site of Knossos. The other is Kommos. Kommos is on the south coast of the island, a former Minoan harbour that gave access to the Mesara plain, one of the richest agricultural regions on the island. Perhaps travellers from the east were drawn here by the search for trade goods, but it is also a rare safe stopping place for vessels heading west that did not wish to navigate through the Cyclades. Around 800 B.C.E. a temple was built on the site which seems to echo in its design some of the temples of the Levantine coasts. There are also Phoenician storage vessels. Graffiti from a little later suggest several languages being spoken there, and a mix of ethnic names. Polyglot populations turn up again and again in the ports of trade of the Iron Age Mediterranean.

Trading bases of this kind have been common in world history, wherever indigenous populations and foreign traders find an interest in more than casual connections.[21] The most developed form is the modern treaty-port, sites where some license was given to foreigners to manage their own affairs within limits set by local authorities. The term "port-of-trade" was first coined to describe ancient near eastern institutions of this kind, in which a king or imperial power set boundaries on where and how foreigners might live and trade.[22] Quite likely the city of Naukratis in Egypt belongs in this category: from the sixth century (and probably earlier) it was home to thousands of Greeks and Carians, resident by permission of the Egyptian authorities. Foreign influence was confined and controlled while the pharaoh could profit from and control foreign action in his realm.[23]

The trading arrangements made in the early Iron Age Mediterranean were probably less formal than this, but more vital. Less formal because visitors from Tyre and other eastern centres found no states, no laws, no written treaties in most of the lands they visited. Often they must have made personal arrangements with the local chiefs, arrangements which began through exchanges of gifts and developed into something more commercial and perhaps included their services as craftsmen too. Yet arrangements of some sort were more vital because of the conditions of navigation. Vessels were between 12 and 15 metres long, and crews were small. Carrying enough food on long journeys or stays overseas was a major problem. Long-distance voyages could only safely take place between May and September. Estimates of journey times vary, but a recent simulation project estimates that it would take between thirty and forty days of sailing to travel the four and a half thousand kilometres from Tyre to Huelva beyond the Straits of Gibraltar. Getting there and back within the sailing season (roughly May to September) was just possible, so long as adequate arrangements could be made for provisioning at each end and along the way. This is why staging posts were so important. Mariners on these routes must have relied upon a knowledge of safe beaches to weather a storm, places where fresh water could be reliably fetched, perhaps even good hunting and fishing grounds along the way. Many mariners heading to the western Mediterranean must have overwintered there. They brought with them many skills the locals did not possess, such as the production of fine painted pottery and some metalworking techniques, wine production and tree cultivation and much else, but they had no superior weaponry or armour. Add to this their tiny numbers, and the great distance between their entrepôts in the west and their home cities, and it is clear there can have been no land grabs or conquests, no massacres of locals by colonizers, no catastrophic depopulations. The newcomers were dependent on local allies for protection and support both along the way and at the final destination. In return they offered access to a distant and enticing world.

Very few peoples took to long-distance voyaging in the archaic period. Most of the cities where Greek or Phoenician were spoken did not. Until at least 700 B.C.E the mariners belonged to a handful of communities in Greece and the Levant, and perhaps a few from Cyprus. There is no sign of Sardinian, Sicilian, or Etruscan sailing vessels before the coming of the Phoenicians. This does not mean that communities all around the Mediterranean did not use sailing vessels locally, but long-distance navigation requires special skills and knowledge and significant investment too, given the time gap between a vessel setting out and it returning with goods that might be sold for a profit. Just as in the early modern period, few communities specialized in long-distance navigation. Most sea travel was local and coastal.

The biggest mystery is why this symbiosis between local chieftains and long-distance mariners came about exactly when it did. Mycenaean sailors and perhaps others had been occasionally sailing western seas since the late Bronze Age. One popular idea—that Phoenician expansion westward was in some way a consequence of the expansion of the Assyrian Empire to their east—has for the moment been made less likely by the new dates.[24] Huelva and other western sites were being visited long before Assyrian pressure was applied to the Caananite cities of the coast.

One possibility is that the answer lies in technical advances in navigation.[25] Few hulls survive from the second millennium B.C.E., and few illustrations of ships either. As well as the Uluburun wreck (about 15 metres long and dating to around 1300 B.C.) there is the Cape Gelidonya A wreck, about a century later and a little shorter, and the cargo of what was probably a smaller vessel off Point Iria in Greece, on the approaches to the Argolid. Most often wrecks are detected today by their cargo alone, since little survives of wooden hulls underwater. The earliest vessels we have from the Iron Age are within the same size range as their late Bronze Age predecessors. Two eighth-century vessels were recently found by remotely operated vehicles in deep water off Askelon in Israel. Each was about 15 metres long and half as wide, and each carried several hundred container amphorae, suggesting cargoes of about 10 tons. All these ships were constructed in the same way, with a hull built up first, like a shell, from timbers fitted together with mortice and tenon joints. One probable innovation concerns the sail. Paintings of Minoan vessels from Thera show great sails attached at the bottom to a wooden beam, and this is similar to ships depicted on Egyptian monuments like the ships of Punt depicted on the female Pharaoh Hapshetsup's temple at Deir al Bahr. At some point before 1200 a new design spread, in which there was no boom. Instead the sail was controlled by brails, a set of rigging that made the ship much easier to manoeuvre, especially when winds were against it. Was this enough to make the difference when it came to long-distance journeys far from shore?

From the eighth century B.C.E. both the archaeological and the iconographic record improve. More changes in maritime technology appear, including the development of specialized warships, some powered by two, three, or even four banks of oars. Mediterranean shipbuilders continued to experiment with new design features into late antiquity, eventually creating much larger merchantmen that could carry from Egypt to Rome the enormous granite columns required for imperial Roman monuments, as well as deep-hulled grain transporters that required special harbours.[26] But in the early Iron Age and archaic periods sea travel was always conducted in tiny vessels, ones that could be dragged up onto a beach if necessary. Boomless brail sails must have made navigation a little quicker, but hardly revolutionized sea travel the way that the appearance of sailing vessels had in the third millennium. Bronze Age mariners had reached southern Italy and Sicily well before the new sail is thought to have been invented. Technology does not seem to explain the renewed interest in the west in the early Iron Age.

One other possibility exists, and at the moment it looks the most likely one. Mariners from the eastern Mediterranean sailed west because news had reached them of changes there. After centuries of relative poverty and isolation, the west had suddenly become of new interest to the urban societies of the Near East. Metals were almost certainly the main lure. Silver in particular drew explorers to Spain, but as the west opened up routes were found to sources of tin and gold and high-quality iron ore as well.[27] But it also seems that over the last millennium population levels had been rising steadily. Even a tiny growth rate of 0.1 per cent could have quadrupled the population of the region between the late Bronze Age Collapse and the second century C.E., usually taken as the ancient demographic high point before a series of plagues.[28] Others have argued for even high rates of growth, at least in the Aegean world. Demographic growth translates often into greater production and surpluses of many kinds attracted traders.

Meanwhile, mariner societies in the eastern Mediterranean must have been organized in such a way that promoted risk-tasking and rewarded adventurers. Local economies in the east must have been geared to provide the capital needed for these ventures, for the acquisition or building of a vessel, for equipping it, for hiring a crew, and for providing them with supplies and trade goods. The history of early modern exploration shows the importance of all these factors. Luck was probably needed too, and there were presumably many voyages that failed and local partnerships that collapsed. We will likely never know. But enough of these precarious partnerships succeeded to encourage imitators. Once successful connections were made we can expect migration flows to be set up, and this is where communities that had been pioneers in exploring the west really began to benefit.

The West Awakens

The appearance of easterners beyond the Straits of Gibraltar in the tenth century B.C.E. tells us that all parts of the Mediterranean Sea could now—in theory—be connected.[29] In practice, just as only a few eastern societies invested in long-distance seafaring, so there were at first only a few preferred destinations in the west. Southwest Spain was one; Sicily and Sardinia were also important, and central Italy was another. Perhaps explorers did visit the southern shores of France, northwest Italy, or eastern Spain very early. If so, they made no lasting connections. Visitors came where there were hosts ready to receive them, and goods they wished to trade for. This was the same pattern as in the Aegean world. Kommos and Knossos on Crete and Lefkandi on Euboea reconnected to the east long before other areas. Entrepôts only worked when local chiefs were able and willing to help, and could muster a surplus of something mariners desired. Phoenicians seem to have been willing to go almost anywhere in search of trade goods. Local initiatives made the difference.

At one time archaeologists wrote this story in a different way, looking back from what they felt was the densely urbanized classical Mediterranean in the fifth century. That urbanized world had its roots, they believed, in the sowing of colonies by Phoenicians and especially Greeks, and the eighth and seventh centuries were presented as something like the nineteenth-century scramble for Africa when Great Powers in Europe competed to claim different parts of the continent. The creation of new cities in the west was described in terms of colonization, while the century or so before was described as an epoch of proto-colonization or precolonization, or with the phrase "trade before the flag," another allusion to modern European imperial expansion.

Antiquity was not like that. Not only was the ancient Mediterranean never densely urbanized, but there was no great plan to claim different portions for Greeks or Phoenicians.[30] Only a few Greek communities ever explored the west. Euboeans and Corinthians and others did not consistently work together nor make common course against the interests of Tyrian and Sidonian explorers. The idea that Phoenicians sought trade and Greeks land has long been discredited.[31] In fact most early sites that have been carefully investigated—like Huelva—have produced a very mixed assortment of ceramic and metal objects. In some places Greeks, Phoenicians, Cypriots, and others lived side by side with indigenous peoples. It goes without saying too that mariners from the eastern Mediterranean and local chiefs never set out to urbanize new regions. All participants wished for was to enrich themselves in the here and now. Local chieftains perhaps also wished to entrench their power, and pass it on to their descendants.

At Huelva it was all about metals. Southwest Iberia was at the southern end of a great arc of rich Bronze Age societies stretching north to Ireland and Scandinavia, participants in the so-called Atlantic Bronze Age.[32] All these societies made, displayed, and exchanged rich treasures of gold and bronze. Huelva itself was near the mouth of the Rio Tinto, a major silver source in antiquity. Later legends of the kingdom of Tartessus are difficult to

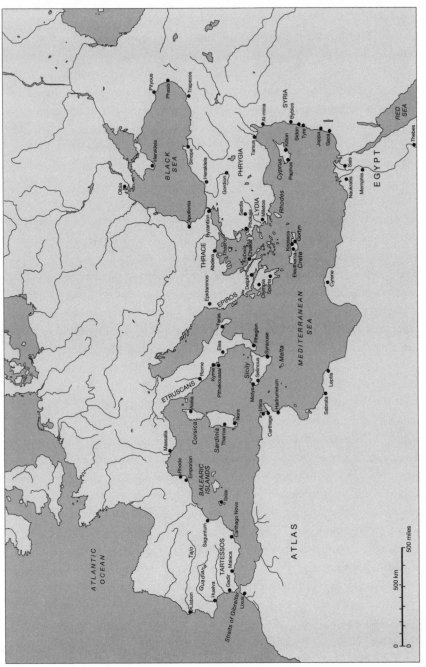

Map 4 The Phoenician Mediterranean

pin down exactly in space, but between the middle Guadalquivir Valley and the Atlantic coast several late prehistoric societies exploited metal resources. Tin was to be found here as well. Crucially for eastern visitors, some of the local chieftains had been skilled at amassing power over this resource. Easterners brought exotic oriental manufactures which for centuries turn up in rich graves, showing that local chiefs had made them into symbols of their power and prestige. Among them were wine and oil, and the taste they inspired for these products led to other exchanges, exchanges of knowledge. Phoenicians were working iron at Huelva from the beginning. It took some centuries before local societies underwent the same changes Cyprus had undergone in the eleventh century—systematically replacing bronze tools with iron ones—but eastern smiths must certainly have helped.

Even more significant in the long term was the ecological impact of visitors from the east. From the early Iron Age the societies of southern Spain were instructed in how to plant vines and cultivate olives for themselves.[33] Other new crops that appeared in the ninth, eighth, and seventh centuries include hulled barley, hulled wheat, bread wheat, peas and lentils, and peaches. Little by little what had begun as exchanges of valuables led to a transformation of southern Iberian landscapes. Olive oil would in time make the fortune of Andalucia. Phoenician potters were also at hand to teach the production of clay amphorae in which to store and transport these new commodities.

Not all western societies were as receptive. On the island of Sardinia, Neolithic and Bronze Age societies had also been growing in scale and complexity. A distinctive architectural form appears: the dry stone tower house called the *nuraghi*. The first *nuraghi* appear around 1800 in the middle Bronze Age, but from 1300 construction speeds up and more and more complex versions appear with multiple towers and occasionally a walled outer circuit. Around 7000 of these structures are known from all over the island, although there are regional differences between them. The proliferation of towers suggests both the social power available to Sardinian chiefs and leading families, and also how geographically fragmented it was. During the late Bronze Age different parts of the island had sporadic contact with Mycenaean visitors, with the Italian mainland, and perhaps also with Cypriot visitors, to judge from the ingots of copper found on the island. Phoenicians must have visited in the tenth century, since they brought some Sardinian ceramic to Spain. Most likely they used Tharros on Sardinia as a staging post, as they had used Kommos on Crete. Phoenicians are more in evidence from the late eighth century, when Sardinia enters the Iron Age and the *nuraghi* are mostly abandoned. There is no sign, however, of anything corresponding to the centralizing chieftains of southern Spain. It looks as if, offered some of the same opportunities as Iberians, local chiefs were uninterested or incapable of taking them.[34]

Sicily had had stronger connections with the Aegean world during its middle Bronze Age (1450–1250 B.C.E.). In the preceding early Bronze Age, the population of the island lived in tiny villages and used handmade ceramic. They had little regular contact with the wider world. Visitors from the east began to visit Sicily in the middle of the second millennium B.C.E. At some point in the fifteenth century—the period when Greek speakers ruled the palaces of Crete and had set up their own palaces in southern and central Greece—mariners from the eastern Mediterranean established some sort of base in Sicily at Thapsos, not very far from the later city of Syracuse. Across Sicily and the Aeolian islands this was a period of population growth, and the appearance of rock-cut monumental tombs may suggest that a few families were succeeding in elevating themselves above the rest. On the eastern and southern coasts of the island there was even some local imitation of Greek and Cypriot pottery, and perhaps of Cypriot metalwork too. How much difference these connections made is still uncertain. From the thirteenth century contacts became attenuated, although the influence of Aegean styles persists. There was apparently no dramatic collapse, and Sicily slipped from the Bronze to the Iron Age with no major transformation in society.[35]

Things were moving faster on the Italian peninsula. The middle Bronze Age there was a period of growth. Western central Italy—the territory of modern Tuscany, Lazio, and Campania in particular—was one of the most productive areas in the Mediterranean Basin for farming. It is well-watered by winds from the Atlantic, has rich volcanic soils in many parts, and its gentle hills slope back onto the low wooded mountains of the Apennines and Abruzzi. Bronze Age farmers made use of the full range of domesticated crops and animals here, and of their secondary products as well. Some had begun to make use of complementary environmental niches in this landscape. Upland meadows were being cleared to create summer pastures. As far as we can tell from burials and a few settlement sites, most people lived in small villages and there were no great differences in social status. Those simple, egalitarian societies began to change during the late Bronze Age, which in central Italy began around 1300 B.C.E. and lasted until the ninth century.

The best known settlements were still villages with populations in the low hundreds, often gathered on low outcrops of tufa, a soft stone formed in central Italy's volcanic past. The inhabitants buried their dead in flat cremation ceremonies, very like those used by other Bronze Age societies all over northern Europe at this time. This is the first stage of a process of settlement nucleation and centralization that would lead to the Etruscan cities. Between the hilltop villages a more scattered population farmed the land. Some sectors of society at least were becoming rich, as we find more and more wealthy graves. Wooden longhouses began to be replaced by more substantial houses built on stone foundations. The amount of metal found increases in quantity and stone tools were replaced entirely by bronze ones.

None of these changes seems to be prompted by contact with foreign civilizations. Central Italy had fewer contacts with Mycenaean visitors than many other parts of the central Mediterranean. The processes of growth here seem similar to those in the European interior, based on more and more skillful farming techniques, and gradual improvements in technology. Prehistorians used to write of a Neolithic Revolution as if the world changed overnight with the discovery of farming. Agriculture was, in reality, more of a slow burn. Landscapes were changed incrementally, and the range of cereals and legumes and later fruit trees diversified slowly. Population after population found new ways to get more out of their closer relationship with domesticated animals. Sedentary populations became better at accumulating possessions and transforming them. Wood, stone, amber, bone, gold, bronze, iron. The material world became more and more diversified, and by manipulating it and by organizing exchanges with neighbouring peoples, a few became rich. No area of the ancient Mediterranean illustrates this better than central Italy.

Mariners from the east had been sailing the western Mediterranean for more than a century before central Italy attracted their attention.[36] The first Iron Age civilization of the area just north of Rome is today termed "Villanovan": as they enter history the same people tend to be called Etruscans. A similar group to the south is now known as the Latial culture, while to the north the Golsecca culture appears in Lombardy and the Este culture in the eastern Po Valley, both with strong connections to societies north of the Alps. This mosaic of late Bronze Age and early Iron Age cultures can be followed down the Apennines and into southern Italy. It is, up to a point, a product of the way the archaeology of the peninsula has been studied and we can now see more and more clearly the networks of exchange that connected all these peoples and ensured that new technologies, when they appeared, spread rapidly up and down Italy. These Iron Age civilizations, all of which appear in the tenth and ninth centuries, are easy to distinguish stylistically since all were now characterized by elites with the wealth and power to acquire beautiful things, many associated with the cultures of hunting and athletics and above all, formal dining.

Eastern manufactures eventually found their way into most of the societies of the west. Towards the end of the sixth century B.C.E. the grave of a princess at Vix in Burgundy contained a magnificent Bronze mixing vessel, more than a metre and a half in height that could have contained 1000 litres of wine, a piece of art probably made in distant Sparta. The web of connections that brought it there was thinner and more narrowly spread in the tenth and ninth centuries B.C.E., but we can already detect the beginnings of a kind of economic growth that traded in luxuries and skills. That networks of exchange extended right across the Mediterranean world in the early Iron Age, already reaching places well beyond the limits of Bronze Age world-systems. Some of its anchors were urban centres, such as the cities of Byblos and Tyre and Sidon in the Levant and the new cities of Cyprus. Others were enclaves of traders, living close to indigenous chieftains; yet others were simply places of habitual change. These exchanges did not articulate an urban world, and indeed they showed how much could be achieved in the Mediterranean world without a network of cities. In the background the spread of skills in working metals, in ever more sophisticated domestications, and also the hum of a slowly growing population, provides the background noise for a set of urban systems that would be much more resilient than the palace economies of the Bronze Age. But for the early Iron Age pioneers, in their citadels and on the water, the cities of the past were forgotten and those of the future not even a dream.

9

Western Pioneers

A Different Road to Urbanism

One of the key findings of the comparative study of early cities is that there was no single route to urbanism. City-building offered solutions to many different problems, served many different interests, and emerged from all sorts of different un-/pre-/proto-urban situations. Some urban communities came together spontaneously; others were assembled by force. Large villages were in some places transformed into small cities through a subtle transformation of their parts and a recalibration of relations within them. Others appeared suddenly, collective responses to crises or simply ordained from above. Urbanization is a convergent process: there are many evolutionary roads that lead to the city.[1]

The new cities that appeared during the Mediterranean Iron Age were unlike their Bronze Age precursors in many ways.[2] They had at first no great monumental quarters and temple precincts, no royal palaces and no government offices. Nor were they like the contemporary cities of the Fertile Crescent. The first cities of Egypt and Babylonia had to manage abundance: an abundance of people, an abundance of alluvial mud and flood water, an abundance of crops. The Mediterranean was a harsher mistress. The cities built around its shores had to deal with scarcity, and with shortages of manpower, food, even of water.

There is another difference worth considering. The Bronze Age urbanism of the Aegean was arguably an experiment in transplanting an established economic system into a new environment. This sort of thing has been tried many times in history, and successful transplantations are rare. That particular experiment was never repeated. The graft did not take. The urbanisms that emerged in the Mediterranean Iron Age had a different evolution, one more rooted in indigenous institutions. Perhaps this explains why they were, in the long run, more successful.

The maritime voyages of the first two centuries of the last millennium B.C.E. connected the urban economies of Cyprus and the Levant to a scatter of entrepreneurial chiefdoms in Crete and Aegean Greece, in distant southern Spain, on the major Mediterranean islands, and in central Italy. The first of these places where those chieftains began to build cities was central western Italy.[3]

The Etruscans inhabited the gentle landscapes between the Apennine mountains and the sea, bounded to the north by the Arno and the south by the Tiber rivers. Their landscapes were gentle because Tuscany was west-facing and therefore well-watered, and because much of the soil was deep and fertile—the gift of a vulcanism that no longer troubled them. The inhabitants probably called themselves Rasenna, but they were known to Greeks as Tyrrhenians and to Romans as Etruscans. Archaeologists today distinguish Etruscan culture from an earlier Villanovan culture (roughly the ninth and early eighth centuries, named for the site of Villanova where the phase was first identified). Earlier levels yet are labelled proto-Villanovan. There is little doubt now that all these names refer to the same people, and that most were descendants of the Bronze Age inhabitants of the region.[4]

Etruria was far from the cities of Cyprus and the Levant. It had not been visited much either by Mycenaeans in the late Bronze Age nor by Phoenicians in the tenth and ninth centuries. Cities here were a local development. They were not planted by strangers nor did they emerge through the expansion of an existing urban network, nor the contagion of ideas. Across Europe, most Bronze Age societies had been growing slowly. Iron made much more of a difference to agriculture than had bronze, since iron tools were often superior to stone ones in a way softer and more expensive bronze was not. Iron technology added to the power of societies already discovering how to make more use of living animals for pulling ploughs, as beasts of burden, and to produce wool and milk. Iron also made better weapons. More land was cultivated, populations grew, and chieftains became more powerful. When local growth intersected with the loose network of maritime connections being stretched across the Mediterranean by eastern mariners, new opportunities presented themselves. The Etruscans, some of them at least, were among the first to grasp the potential of connecting economic growth to trade routes.[5]

Map 5 Etruscan Italy

We can now trace this process in some detail. During the tenth century B.C.E. most villages were smaller than 5 hectares, with just a few reaching 10 or 15 hectares. During the ninth century a small number of much bigger settlements appeared. This is the period termed Villanovan. Most were new sites, created on tufa plateaux or on promontories protected on most sides by steep ravines. The shift was most pronounced in southern Etruria where Tarquinia, Veii, Caere, Vulci, and Volsinii each covered between 100 and 200 hectares. But sites were growing in size everywhere. There were settlements of more than 30 hectares at Populonia, Vetulonia, and Volaterra in northern Etruria. Another cluster of sites appeared on the hills of Rome.

On the larger plateaux occupation was rarely continuous. There were clusters of houses, interspersed by open fields and connected by tracks. It looks as if clans lived in separate zones, each with its own cemetery, and coming together now and again to worship together or for their common defence. The larger centres tended to be located close to where there were rich resources to exploit. That might mean rich farmland below the plateaux or it might mean metals as around the Colline Metalliferre in northern Etruria. It is probably not a coincidence that these changes took place around the very start of the Iron Age in an area where iron resources are especially rich. A few seem to have grown simply because they commanded key points of communication: Rome sat on a crossing point of the Tiber and on the salt route that ran beside it. Exchanges grew more important, and so did ports of all kinds.

We do not know exactly how cities coalesced in the Villanovan case. It is common enough in Mediterranean history to find an alternation between periods when settlement in any given landscape is scattered, and periods when populations are suddenly concentrated together. This happened at least twice during the Iron Age of temperate Europe too. Italy itself has experienced several episodes of *incastallamento*—periods where populations left the fields for a few generations and gathered together behind the ramparts of hill towns—since the Middle Ages. Many Mediterranean islands have a town in the interior and a coastal port as well, each important in different periods, reflecting changes in conditions of security. Something similar might lie behind the settlement centralization of Early Iron Age Italy, but we do not know for sure. However it was engineered, it must have helped that populations were gradually growing and the seas opening up to trade.

Perhaps charismatic leaders persuaded groups of Villanovan villages to merge or cluster. If so, they did not noticeably profit from the move. Burials suggest these societies were still relatively egalitarian. These local grandees were not yet buried with luxurious imports from the east. They built no palaces or citadels. In fact there is almost no sign of a public organization of space before the seventh century. Whatever institutions the Villanovan communities had—assemblies, meetings of elders, collective worship—have left no physical traces. But these populations had urban potential, the critical mass out of which cities might be formed.

Cities of the Dead

That potential was barely realized until the middle of the eighth century B.C.E. From this point on we usually write of Etruscans. The first signs of social transformation are revealed in burials. At the best studied cemeteries, like that of Quattro Fontanilli at Veii, it is possible to see a shift in rituals and the appearance of small number of much richer burials. It looks as if there were some rather grand public funerals now, presumably including a display of the rich goods that would be consigned to the grave along with the cremated bones of the dead. Etruria was the site of the grandest examples but the phenomenon was general to central Italy. There are four chariot burials at Castel di Decimana in Latium: chariots were a new arrival in Italy in the eighth century, associated with warrior ideals, and maybe already with myths of an heroic age. At Quattro Fontanili one individual was buried with a complete set of arms and armour, his bones sealed in a bronze casket. Among the precious objects were a faience scarab from Egypt, and Greek ceramics. The richest burials at Osteria dell'Osa near Gabii in Latium were accompanied by intricately miniaturized bronze tools and weapons. Earrings, jewelry, and razors appear. Some of the rich graves are for women, a sure sign that an elite family was being celebrated and not simply a charismatic individual. The wealth of this minority of tombs is the clearest sign that these societies were becoming more complex.

Over the course of the seventh century B.C.E. the wealthy burials became richer and more numerous. Increasingly they contained exotic imports from the eastern Mediterranean, or locally made objects that imitated them. Etruscologists often term this the Orientalizing period.[6] The models for new styles of pottery are to be found in Greek pottery, in Phoenician silverwork and even in metalwork from Urartu in eastern Anatolia. Sphinxes, female demons with wings, and human-headed birds all recall the animal–human hybrids of Near Eastern and Egyptian art.

The term "orientalizing period" does not mean the elites of the emerging Etruscan cities were really trying to imitate Near Eastern rulers, and they were certainly not becoming more like them. Most westerners can have had no real idea about the actual societies from which their treasured scarabs, painted pottery, and worked silver and gold bowls came, any more than they knew about the Baltic origins of their amber or the African animals that were the ultimate source of the ivory they imported through middlemen. Exotica offered them something different but equally important. Possessing and displaying these unusual treasures made their owners feel part of an international culture of prestige that extended beyond their social horizons: some also had resonances of a vanished world of heroes. These bright and rare objects made clear their owner's status to others. By obtaining and displaying exotica advertised their power and literally how well connected they were. Eastern goods made local chieftains into aristocrats. Most graves contained no such treasures, indeed some of the population did not even have graves that we can find. The combination of high status at home and a sense of belonging to a global elite formed a new identity for the rulers of Etruscan cities. Their ancestors may have lived much as their subjects still did, but oriental exotica set them apart, made them feel different, and perhaps better too.

More than most ancient Mediterranean peoples, the Etruscans are known through their tombs. This does not mean they had a morbid fascination with the afterlife. Some tombs cut into the soft rock, with passages, doors, and furniture carved from tufa and then painted with bright scenes of the lives of the living and images from myths now lost. Others were covered with grand mounds. The cemetery of Banditaccia outside Cerveteri, Etruscan Caere, grew over the centuries until it contained thousands of tombs including the grand tumuli of princes and then entire quarters of much smaller graves laid out like a city (see Figure 17). The most splendid wall paintings deal with ways of life that for other societies we know through other kinds of evidence: athletics, hunting, and procession.

Banquets and drinking parties (*symposia* in Greek) are a case in point.[7] The great feasts of Babylonian and Persian kings are described in the books of *Daniel* and *Esther* and the *Histories* of Herodotus (among many other witnesses). Homer's heroes devoted great care to mixing wine, preparing meat,

Figure 17 Necropolis of Banditaccia at Cerveteri
DEA / G. CARFAGNA / Getty Images

and extending hospitality to friends and strangers. There is an entire tradition of first Greek and then Latin "sympotic" literature in which discussions of philosophy, literary criticism, or erotic or obscene verse are put into the mouths of celebrities dining or drinking together. No Etruscan literature of that sort has survived, but the walls of the tombs have preserved many images of meals and drinking parties, and the tombs themselves contain elaborate collections of cups, bowls, and other drinking goods. Silver bowls were among the richly decorated objects that must have been displayed and admired among the wealthy, passed around at drinking parties, perhaps given as gifts. Wine-drinking brought with it specialized equipment too: strainers and cauldrons and tripods, and jugs and mixing bowls and cups.

The same is true, as it happens, of societies farther north. During the sixth century B.C.E. a tradition developed in an arc around the head of the Adriatic Sea of making elaborately decorated bronze "buckets," now named *situlae*.[8] The buckets were used like cauldrons or mixing bowls to hold wine at drinking parties, although what we have are those that were reused as grave goods. On them are portrayed chariot races, and boxing matches, battles and hunts, religious processions and banqueting scenes (see Figure 18). The dress of the figures recalls Greek and Etruscan art.

Figure 18 Situla from Vace
© National Museum of Slovenia Photo Tomaž Lauko

These images are arranged in friezes resembling the processions painted on Geometric Greek pottery from ninth century Athens. The posture of figures at drinking parties echoes seventh-century Etruria. Some of the weaponry looks like that used by other peoples north of the Alps. And here too there are sphinxes and other mythical beasts whose ultimate origin was the eastern Mediterranean but that probably came by way of Etruria. West of the Alps the Iron Age populations of what is now France would also develop a culture of great feasts, and distributions of wine and meat, and they too would collect Greek and Etruscan metalwork and pottery for serving it.

The idea of belonging to an international elite was not entirely a fantasy. From Babylonia to the Atlantic there were huge differences among Iron Age societies, but we can pick out some motifs and customs like these that were widely shared. During the eighth and seventh centuries, when the Etruscan engagement with the wider Mediterranean was at its height, a range of aristocratic "markers" widely disseminated. One was the chariot, used in the Near East in the Bronze Age, but rare in Europe until the early first millennium. Chariots feature in epic poetry and in art, and there were chariot burials from Salamis on Cyprus, from northern and central Italy, Germany and northern France, and even (eventually) Britain. And there was warfare, fought in a range of ways, but using the same basic equipment of helmet and shield, sword and spear. Finally, there was the hunt. Near Eastern origins can be found for many of these markers, although most were transformed in their translation to new peoples and new lands. And there was wine. Probably there was no one group of people who knew how widely these themes were disseminated, yet they all participated in this culture that separated them from the rest of the population at home and claimed kinship with distant elites unknown to them.

Each people customized these global fashions to suit local circumstances. At Athens drinking parties become more important than eating together, *symposia* were all-male events for the wealthy, safe spaces perhaps for undemocratic thought and speech. Sparta organized its male citizenry by messes (*sussitia*), groups of warriors who ate together, each member contributing to the common cost. Commensality in Greek cities was about asserting common status, or celebrating the solidarity of family or clan. The chiefs of the European Iron Age made great gifts of food and wine to their followers, demonstrating their superiority and power in lands where vines were not yet cultivated and so all wine was an exotic import.

The Etruscans made their own appropriations, domesticating a warrior lifestyle within a society now more orientated on production and trade. Women shared in the new cultures of the elite, even joining their relatives at meals in Etruscan society. Across Latium and Etruria grand houses began to be built from the seventh century on, places where the powerful could welcome and entertain guests, and display their taste as well as their wealth. Along with exotic goods came a new repertoire of images. Probably some Syrian sculptors, Greek potters, and Phoenician silversmiths actually lived and worked in the larger Etruscan centres, sometimes passing on their skills to local craftsmen. Some local craftsmen were soon making extraordinary metalwork on which sphinxes and lions featured. On some Etruscan mirrors there are images of heroes who seem familiar from Greek myth, but are labelled with Etruscan names.[9] The alphabet was another import, arriving probably around 700 B.C.E. and modified to write Etruscan and other Italian languages. The first uses of writing in the west were for religious dedications and owners' marks—private uses, rather than the administrative tasks of the kind for which they had been used in the Bronze Age palaces. Even when it came to the alphabet Etruscans found new uses for an imported technology.[10]

Etruscan Cities

Etruscan potters imitated Greek vessels. Their appetite for particular designs would in the classical periods have a discernible effect on what Athenian workshops were producing for export. Meanwhile the rise of Etruscan pottery production is one sign of how far the major centres had come from their origins as agricultural villages. Craft specialization, literacy, and commerce show that these archaic centres were functioning as cities. They had become complex social worlds at the heart of differentiated social landscapes, and they were also now part of an open ended international network. Like many early cities they were probably rather ramshackle social organizations, thrown together over a few generations to manage the growing energies unleashed by economic and demographic growth, an accumulation of political fixes made to hold together communities undergoing rapid change.

The first Etruscan cities did not look very grand. There were no ziggurats, no monumental precincts or palaces. Most houses were small round huts made of wattle and daub, replaced over time by longer wooden structures. On the plateaux tops there were clusters of houses with their fenced yards, arranged along winding lanes. Between these urban hamlets were patches of open ground before the buildings began again. The only public structures were temples, and they were (by later standards) small and not very imposing. Some of this probably reflects the social basis of Etruscan communities. These were not directed by kings and priests in the way some Bronze Age societies had been. Etruscan cities were assembled by societies organized first of all by kinship. The clans had not disappeared from view. This why the most visually striking buildings in eighth- and seventh-century Etruria were the great family tumuli that dominated the cemeteries that surrounded the cities, not palaces or public buildings within them.

This would soon change. During the sixth century many of the cities of Etruria were replanned. So too were their necropoleis, the cities of the dead. Streets were laid out in the cemeteries, lined by rows of smaller tombs, often shaped to resemble simple houses. This was not egalitarianism. It was a sign that others in Etruscan society apart from the very rich wanted to belong to a wider Mediterranean world. Urban street grids appeared in the cities of the living too during the late sixth century. Masonry houses were built in blocks. This is clearest in new cities like Marzabotto, but even older foundations like Veii were affected. The main streets were paved, and some had pavements too. Drains and water supplies began to be built into urban design. Large public buildings appeared, and perhaps open piazzas. Around the cities the wooden palisades and mud brick walls were replaced by with polygonal stone walls. At Vetulonia a citadel was fortified; at Veii monumental stone gates were built. The traces of sixth- and fifth-century urbanism is, on many sites, obscured by the Roman and mediaeval cities built over them. But enough remains to show that across Etruria the disordered conurbations of the eighth century were, by 500 B.C.E., in the process of being replaced by monumental, planned cities.

An Urban Network

The cities of central Italy developed as a cluster of more or less independent states. How far and how often their inhabitants felt part of a wider nation is impossible to say in the absences of texts, so our view is always that of the outsider, whether than means Greek or Roman authors or modern analysts. At the peak of the system there were around fifteen city-states, some much larger than others. In the south there were big centres, notably Tarquinia, Caere, and Veii. To the north cities were not quite so grand. In some polities there were two or three smaller subordinate towns as well, which means that depending on how we count, them there were perhaps twenty to thirty Etruscan cities in total.[11] There were alliances, some rather shadowing leagues, but the area was never politically united before the Roman conquest. Political territories shifted a little over time and there were probably a few areas not firmly under the control of any single state. All the same it is helpful to think of Etruria as a mosaic of city-states, a landscape divided into smallish cells, and also to think of the cities of Etruria as forming a network, connected to each other by roads and rivers, by the movements of soldiers and traders, or the very wealthy and of their slaves.

City-state systems are quite common in world history. A recent comparative study found around thirty examples, and even that it was possible to generalize a little about them.[12] A few clusters did eventually end up rolled up into one larger state, but usually the competitive tensions between them meant that if any one city became too powerful its neighbours would gang up against it.[13] Neighbouring cities tend to be rivals, argue over borders, shelter each other's exiles, and so on. Unification more often comes with conquest from outside, as when Alexander of Macedon and his father extended their power over most of the city-states, the poleis, of southern Greece, or when the Qin on the western margins of the Chinese world ended the warring states period and created the first Chinese Empire. For Etruria, the conqueror from the margins would be Rome in the fourth and early third centuries B.C.E.[14] But until then Etruscan cities fought, allied, squabbled, and competed like any other group of city-states in history.

Competition within a cluster of city-states can have some positive effects too. Each city tends to be well informed about what is going on in its "peer polities" so it can imitate successful innovations and avoid replicating failed experiments.[15] The members of a cluster of city-states tend to change and grow in parallel, developing common cultural traits as they go. So during the sixth century B.C.E. communities all over Etruria and its southern neighbour Latium threw their energies into temple-building until every community had at least one huge building towering over the small low houses out of which settlements had been mostly composed until then. Later on we can see new ways of burying the dead, new pottery styles, new kinds of warfare spreading rapidly within the system. This is one of the things that makes it possible to write a single cultural history of the Etruscans, and perhaps they did become more alike in the process. Roman writers at least wrote of them as if they had a single language and a single set of religious institutions (the *disciplina Etrusca*).

What the ancients knew as Etruria more or less coincides with modern Tuscany and a little portion of northern Lazio. Its limits were probably less clearly marked out in the tenth and ninth centuries. The material culture of Villanovans is in most respects part of a continuum with that of other peoples all the way to the Alps, and in some respects with those beyond them too. To the south other peoples, like the Latins, were also building bigger and bigger settlements, led by elites who were also using exotic trade goods from the east to signal their social distinction.[16] Rome, Palestrina, Gabii, and some of the cities of Campania had at one time or another close relations with Etruria. Etruscan was never spoken by the majority population in these areas, but perhaps some of their rulers knew the language. Romans believed that some of their kings had been Etruscan. The picture is scrambled however because by the time our first historical records about the region were composed—in the fourth and third centuries in Greek and the second in Latin—Italy was imagined to be partitioned by a series of firm ethnic boundaries. Latins, for example, lived south of the river Tiber. North of the river was where the people they called Etrusci resided. Umbrians, Sabines, Samnites, Gauls, and others each had their territories. Roman writers spent some energy explaining the ways in which they were not exactly Etruscan or Greek, let alone Samnite or Gallic. Almost certainly the boundaries were more blurred in reality.

The wider influence of developments in Etruria is undeniable.[17] North of the Apennines a few cities like Marzabotto and Bologna were heavily influenced by Etruscan culture. Later writers explained these relationships in terms of Etruscan colonization in the Po Valley, and likewise to the south in Campania. That idea is anachronistic, and some ancient writers knew it. Alongside the insistence on sharp ethnic differences, historical records speak repeatedly of individual aristocrats who moved back and forth from one community to another, as if their high birth somehow trumped ethnicity or allegiance to one particular city-state. The fifth king of Rome, for instance, was said to have been an Etruscan named Tarquinus Priscus whose father, Demaratus, was a noble exile from Greek Corinth. The Roman general Coriolanus, when himself driven out of Rome, supposedly became a general for the Etruscan Volsci. There are many stories like this, which of course fascinated later ages concerned about the patriotic duty expected of citizens. It follows that this network of city-states was in some respects open, that cities like Rome might well be considered part of it, and that the network connected outwards to the cities of Latium and Campania. It reached out to the port of Spina at the head of the Adriatic, and through Etruscan port cities like Populonia and Pisa in the north that lay opposite Elba and Sardinia, and through Graviscae and Pyrgi in the south to Phoenician and Greek mariners of the western Mediterranean. The emergent cities of Etruria were sustained by both long-distance connections and by the increasingly tight control they exercised over their own hinterlands. Their ports had mixed populations, with resident craftsmen and traders bringing their own languages, burial customs, and material culture.

By the early sixth century at the latest some of these traders were themselves Etruscans. Tyrrhenoi do not appear in Homer but they are mentioned by Hesiod and by the Homeric Hymns written not too long after, by which stage they sometimes feature as pirates, rather as Phoenicians sometimes did in Greek writing, and Ionian Greeks (Yavana) in Assyrian texts. As among the Phoenicians and Greeks it was at first probably only a few Etruscan cities that took part in long-distance trade.[18] The boats they used were identical to those used by Greeks and Phoenicians, so it is not usually easy to know who we are looking at when it comes to shipwrecks. But a number of wrecks have been found off the coasts of Italy and France with cargoes almost entirely consisting of Etruscan products. Ships appear on tomb paintings, and there are accounts of naval battles off Corsica and in the Bay of Naples in the fifth century.

Why did Etruria stand out among other Iron Age societies in the Mediterranean world? Older accounts claimed they were influenced by the Greeks, but the chronology is all wrong. Etruscan urbanism either came first or emerged about the same time as the cities of Greece.[19] The concentration of settlement on a few larger sites, and the separation of the world of the living from the surrounding world of the dead happened earlier in central Italy than around the Aegean, although other parts of the "package" began earlier in the east. In reality, none of these events happened in isolation.

It does seem clear that it was economic growth in Etruria that attracted foreign visitors, and not chance visitors who initiated growth. We might also ask why the first western Mediterranean urban experiments took place here rather than, say, in southern Italy, or in Spain or Sicily. Part of the answer must lie in the natural resources of Tuscany, in agriculture as well as in metals. But Tartessos in Spain had wealth too, and it just lagged a little behind the Etruscans. The Etruscans' central location may have helped, especially in the second stage of growth when contact with outside peoples—in northern Europe and in Sardinia, as well as the Phoenicians and the Greeks—mattered more. Perhaps too there were particular features of Villanovan society that gave their descendants some slight advantage over other Iron Age societies, perhaps something about local kinship structures that made it easier for powerful families to mobilize larger populations to projects of town-building, mining, trade, and warfare. One recent study of Sardinia, which enjoyed many of the advantages of nearby Etruria, concluded that the reason it did not make more of its rich metal resources in the early Iron Age was that the island tradition of extreme local fragmentation hampered any efforts to organize at a larger scale.[20] Whether or not this was the case—and it seems plausible—it looks as if urbanization in central Italy was driven by local power dynamics.

Myths of Origin

There are very few sites in the western Mediterranean which we know for sure were visited by easterners in the ninth century B.C.E. Over the course of the eighth century this changed. Material from the Aegean and from the Near East begins to appear in abundance on sites in southern Spain and North Africa, Sicily and Sardinia, and coastal sites around central and southern Italy.[21] This must have been a world of constant cross-cultural encounters, testified to not only by the spread of objects but of techniques and technologies as well. Over the centuries that followed more and more communities would become engaged in viticulture, start using writing, create monumental statues, and mint coins. It would be wonderful to know how all this began.

Unfortunately, the first stages of this story is still very unclear. One huge obstacle is that ancient writers thought they knew already what had happened. Although they were wrong about that, their guesses misled generations of scholars. Only recently has it been clear how untrustworthy ancient historical accounts of this period were, and how much more can be learned if we begin from the archaeology.[22]

The Greeks did not begin to write history until the fifth century B.C.E., and for a long time the focus was very much on the cities of the Aegean world and their neighbours. The peoples of the west had been using writing since the end of the eighth century, but it is unlikely they wrote any reliable records that later authors might use. Most early examples of writing that have survived are names scratched on pottery or dedications on objects deposited at sanctuaries. A few fascinating early inscriptions record lines of verse, traces of the oral poetry that provided those generations of mariners and kings alike with the nearest thing they had to a literature.[23] The first surviving letter written in Greek dates to the late sixth century B.C.E. It is inscribed on a lead tablet found on the island of Berezan in the northern Black Sea. Around the middle of the fifth century there was an explosion of prose. Works of medicine, philosophy, science, and historical writing appear. Along with an interest in recovering the past, we see a new interest in preserving documents for the future. Monumental public inscriptions began to be used in Greek communities (and some others) to record decrees and treaties. From the early fifth century B.C.E. we have the fragments of a stone inscription of the great law code of Gortyn in Crete. Some law codes attributed to the sixth century were probably written down as well. This is a fascinating story. The near simultaneous appearance of an interest in both the past and the future, the explosion of kinds of enquiry, and the appearance of public documents alongside private ones all show a profound shift in priorities. But it also means that virtually all ancient accounts about events much before 600 B.C.E. were guesswork.

Prior to the sixth century, the Greeks treated the past in a different way.[24] Stories of the heroic age circulated, but it was treated as an age apart, separated from the present by a vaguely imagined gulf of time and also by a great moral distance. The earliest Greek literary works are Homer's epics. They were probably written down around 700 B.C.E., based on oral poetry composed in the preceding generations. The *Iliad* in particular occasionally draws comparisons between the present day (of Homer and his audience) and the past in which the events narrated in the epics took place. Men in the past were stronger, heroes encountered gods face to face, and so on. Everything—cities, palaces, warriors—was bigger and better, and at the same time the author of the *Iliad* was dimly aware that some things, such as iron and writing and massed infantry warfare, should maybe not feature in his narrative. A near contemporary, the poet Hesiod, described five ages of mankind in his *Works and Days*. The Golden, Silver, and Bronze Ages marked a progressive decline from an original period of abundance to shorter and shorter lived generations of less and less perfect humans. The men of Hesiod's Bronze Age were more warlike than their predecessors, more sinful, and after their deaths all went straight to the underworld. Then came the Age of Heroes, a brief return to form and the period of the Trojan War, but it was followed by an Age of Iron, the grim present day of Hesiod and his audience. Present-day men lived only a short time, were beset by vices and conflict, and had consequently been forsaken by the gods.

Myths of an heroic age are common enough around the world, as are myths of an even more distant time of creation. In many oral cultures the events of the previous three generations are seen as important because they explain or justify the present order of things. How long elapsed between the limit of living memory and the time of origins is usually very unclear.[25] Homer's heroes are transparently larger-than-life versions of the Iron Age chieftains who patronized the poet, rather than approximate depictions of actual Bronze Age kings sitting in their palaces surrounded by scribes and textile workers.[26] Some social memory had been preserved. Mycenae and Troy were indeed prominent centres in the late Bronze Age, just as Homer said. Now and again the description of a piece of weaponry or armour really does seem to be an echo of the real Bronze Age. Did heirlooms or chance finds give Iron Age Greeks a glimpse of their real past? Or were these details passed on for generations in songs? Most things, however, were forgotten, simply because they were no longer relevant to early Iron Age societies.

During the sixth and especially the fifth centuries B.C.E., the societies of the Greek world were utterly transformed. Changes included increasing urbanization, state-formation, and new uses of writing. Interest in the past increased. But no records survived of the first generations of explorers of the west. For Etruscans and Phoenicians and all the other peoples involved in the process the situation is even worse. For whatever reasons, their languages seem to have been used to write historical works very late indeed (if at all). No prose works in either language survive. Around the Mediterranean most people who developed literatures did so in Greek, and mostly not until after Alexander's conquest of the Persian Empire.[27]

A few traces of local myths were picked up by Greek writers, and found their way into later historical writing. There have been heroic modern attempts to sort out which stories derived from local traditions and which from Greek myth.[28] Rome, with its two foundation myths, provides a good example. The story that makes Aeneas, the Trojan refugee, the founder of the Roman race is most likely Greek in origin, because it resembles many other myths told about travelling heroes in the aftermath of the events related in the *Iliad*. The version we most often read, that written by the Roman poet Virgil at the turn of the millennium, is strongly influenced by Homer's *Odyssey* and also by many other epic poems composed and circulating in the seven centuries that separate Homer and Virgil. The story of Romulus and Remus, on the other hand, which places the foundation of Rome in 753 B.C.E., is probably Italian in origin. Here again it is not so simple. By the time Diodorus of Sicily wrote his *Library of World History* (in the generation before Virgil) there were dozens of versions of this myth, some with one, others with two, others with even more brothers. The version of twins raised by a wolf, one of whom killed the other, only became canonical at a late date. By the last century B.C.E. ancient writers were already finding ingenious ways to reconcile the Aeneas cycle and the Romulus and Remus legends. The monuments of the first emperor Augustus were carefully engineered so that both he and the Romans could claim descent from Venus (via her son Aeneas) as well as from Mars (the father of the twins).

The last century B.C.E. was the great age for the invention of western foundation stories. A century beforehand the Roman senator Cato the Elder had gathered up from the cities of Italy a series of foundation stories, a few of them very ancient, others we suspect more or less made up on the spot. Celts, Umbrians, Greeks, and Etruscans all contributed to what was one of the first Latin prose texts, entitled *The Origins*. It does not survive, but we can get a good idea of its contents from later authors who used it. Local populations were connected to peoples or places from the history of mythology of the eastern Mediterranean either because their names sounded similar, or because some local cult could be connected to a Trojan or Greek hero, or simply because one genealogy suited them better than another for political purposes—that is, to claim kinship or ancient enmity with one or another group of neighbours. The Romans were no means the only ones to claim descent from the non-Greek Trojans.[29] The Etruscans claimed to be descendants of the Lydians, from Asia Minor, who had featured prominently in Herodotus' *Histories*. The Celtic-speaking peoples of northern Italy were sometimes said to be the descendants of invaders, sometimes from ancestors who had been invited to cross the Alps. Many of these traditions were new, and around the Mediterranean there was a fashion for recording them. Polybius, writing around the same time as Cato, but in Greek, complained of the number of foundation stories and local histories being composed. Few have survived, so we mostly see their results in the synoptic, common, or "universal" histories compiled by Polybius and later by Poseidonius, Diodorus, and Strabo. Some of these origin myths found their way into the work of Latin historians such as Livy as well, or are known to us only through poetry that from the third century B.C.E. was often highly learned. By the end of the last millennium, almost every city seems to have had a detailed account of the names of particular founders and the reasons that led them to pick on this or that spot for a future city.

The foundation stories that survived are rather generic and repetitive. A noble leader is forced to leave home, often because of a crime or a quarrel or an accidental killing; receives guidance from an oracle or portents; travels with his followers to strange lands, often making a few false stops before reaching his ultimate destination where he regularly becomes involved in resolving local conflicts; and ends up marrying a local princess. Even more suspiciously, if we look at the various versions surviving for better-known cities—Marseilles in the south of France and Taranto in southern Italy are good cases in point—we find that the later the version, the more details

there are. It is very difficult to avoid the conclusion that these civic foundation stories grew with each retelling, and not because of new research
or discoveries. Tiny kernels of tradition—or just plain guesses—were elaborated until they filled entire books, as in the case of Rome. By this stage
more than seven hundred years separated the authors from the eighth century B.C.E., and even longer from the fall of Troy, which is featured in many
stories.

We should not despise those first Greek attempts to reconstruct human
history. Many were honest attempts to understand the past on the basis
of very little information. Long before the political manipulations of the
Augustan age, serious attempts were made to work out why Greek-speaking
and Phoenician-speaking communities were located where they were, why
some old place names appeared in the New World, how the distribution of
dialects and cults might be explained, and whether any myths did contain
kernels of fact. *Historie* to begin with simply meant research or enquiry. It
was several centuries before labels like "natural history" (as in Pliny's *Historia
Naturalis*) were created to differentiate biological research from research
into human antiquity. Herodotus and other early historical writers often
seem to us to include all sorts of geographical and anthropological material
that would not find a place in most nineteenth- and twentieth-century
histories. Our loss, perhaps. A major trend in twenty-first-century studies
of the human past is to reintegrate the human story into the history of
the natural world, whether that means environmental history, evolutionary
theory, or the history of human–animal relations. But even if we admire
the ambition of those early researchers we can no more trust their guesses
than we would apply ancient medical remedies today. Before 600 B.C.E.—
the limit of human memory for the first generation that wrote it down—
Mediterranean history is prehistory.

The western Mediterranean illustrates this perfectly. The Homeric epics
mention absolutely no real places west of the Adriatic Sea. From the fifth
century on Greek geographers tried hard to find Calypso's island, Trinacia,
Scherie, Circe's home, or the Cimmerians in various locations. Many
modern writers have followed them. Yet the astonishing truth is that these
poems, composed in the eighth century, do not mention Sicily, Sardinia,
Corsica, Spain, North Africa, the Etruscans, or the Straits of Gibraltar.
Nor for that matter do they show any sign of knowing about the Black
Sea. Ithaca is the westernmost real place; otherwise, all the action takes
place around the Aegean with just a few references to Egypt and Cyprus.

Phoenicians are mentioned but there is no trace of either the Bronze Age empires of the Hittites and the Mitanni, nor of their main Iron Age successors, the Assyrians, whose power extended by Homer's day as far as Cyprus. Centuries after the great finds at Lefkandi, and even longer after Phoenician voyages to southern Spain, the world beyond the Aegean remained almost entirely a blank for Homer's audiences.

The Early History of the Western Greeks

Early Greek poetry also has little to say about the far west before the fifth century, when Pindar and his contemporaries began to compose victory odes in honour of successful athletes at Panhellenic games.[30] The games all took place in Greece—on a complex cycle rotating between Olympia, Delphi, Nemea, and the Isthmus of Corinth—but from an early date they attracted Greeks from much further afield. Some of Pindar's odes celebrated victors from Sicily and cities in southern Italy. His first Pythian Ode, composed in 470 B.C.E. just after the Persian Wars, celebrated King Hieron of Syracuse. This is close to the date when Aeschylus was composing the *Persians,* a tragedy based on the war against Xerxes and a foundational text of ancient orientalism.[31] From these poems we know that by the fifth century at least myths were circulating about heroes and founding fathers, and some recent traditions too. The first Pythian Ode associated the western Greeks with contemporary wars against the (Persian) barbarian by recalling victories against Phoenicians and Etruscans. Material like this must have been difficult to convert into a proper history of the west, although several ancient historians tried to do just that. Timaeus of Tauromenium, another Sicilian but one who wrote in Athens during the third century B.C.E., struggled to produce a comprehensive history of the western Mediterranean that might compare to what was available for the east. He evidently had almost nothing usable from before the fifth century B.C.E.

The first historical account of the western Greeks we do have is a few chapters at the start of book 6 of the *History of the Peloponnesian War* written by the Athenian historian Thucydides. They formed part of his introduction to an account of the great military expedition launched against the city of Syracuse by the Athenians in 415 B.C.E. Thucydides was extremely sceptical of the myths circulating in his day, but he did provide a list of foundation dates for the Greek cities in Sicily. This was probably based on the very recent work of Antiochus of Syracuse, a slightly shadowy figure who seems to have written accounts of early Sicily and southern Italy in the 420s soon after the appearance of Herodotos' *History*, which had said little about them. Thucydides' version summarizes the names of various inhabitants of the deep past, beginning with two peoples named by Homer, and then goes on to tell the stories of ancient migrations from Spain and Africa and Italy and the arrival of Trojan refugees before moving on to the supposed ancestors of the Phoenicians and Greeks of his day. He then produces foundation dates for the cities of Naxos (734 B.C.E) Syracuse (733 B.C.E.), Leontini (728 B.C.E.), Megara Hyblaea (727 B.C.E.), Gela (688 B.C.E.) and Akragas (580 B.C.E.), Acrae (663 B.C.E.), Casmenae (643 B.C.E.), and Camarina (598 B.C.E.). Foundations are also mentioned for Catana, Zancle, and Himera, but no exact dates are given. In most cases Thucydides tells us the name of the founder, the people or peoples from which the population came, and sometimes the dialect they spoke. In a few cases there are other details, such as that the Camarineans were expelled from their original site by the Syracusans, that the tyrant of Gela acquired their territory from Syracuse in a prisoner exchange, or that he resettled the city but it was depopulated again by the tyrant Gelon and resettled a third time from Gela. Significantly these snippets of narrative mostly relate to the more recent past of the Sicilian cities.

What Thucydides' account really tells us is what seemed most important to Sicilian Greeks in the late fifth century B.C.E. They cared about their relative antiquity, which conveyed some prestige. Naxos, supposedly the oldest, had an altar to Apollo the Leader, at which Sicilian delegates to the Panhellenic games of Greece would sacrifice before they set sail. They cared about the identity of their founders—many of whom were paid cult as if they were heroes by the fifth century—and about which cities they claimed as mother-cities (metropoleis). We know this mattered because it had some influence on whom they sided with in subsequent wars. Syracuse was an enemy of Athens because it had sent help to its Doric "kin" the Spartans. Kinship in this case trumped ideology and culture, for Syracuse was, like Athens—and unlike Sparta—a naval democracy, and one of the few places apart from Athens where Athenian dramas were performed. Most of all they cared about the recent history of intercity strife on the island. Perhaps Antiochus, like Timaeus after him, was keen that the antiquity of his island be recognized within wider Greek history. Only four short fragments of his works survive, quoted in much later writers, so it is difficult to be sure.

Last of all, they cared exclusively about Greeks. During the fifth century there were Phoenician communities on the island, and several indigenous peoples, at least one group of whom, the Elymians in the west of the island, had already begun to create cities of their own. Yet the non-Greek inhabitants of Sicily rarely enter historical writing except as enemies of the Greeks. There is good reason to think ethnic identity was becoming more and more important in this period, at least to Greeks.[32] A slow and complicated debate about pure descent, moral and intellectual superiority, and the justification for slavery and conquest was taking place in the darker corners of the Greek Mediterranean.

How much of Thucydides' pocket history of Sicily can we trust? Some elements are certainly anachronistic. We should be sceptical of the way the history is told entirely in terms of city-states.[33] These barely existed in Greece in the eighth century B.C.E., but they dominated the world Antiochus and Thucydides had grown up in. That part at least needs to be imagined away, and so does the model of state-led foundations that is tied to it. Eighth- and seventh-century communities did not have the demographic power or organizational capacity to organize colonial projects of the kind that a few fifth-century city-states did occasionally undertake.[34] In a world without law and politics most big ventures were a blend of the private and the public, and charisma mattered more than due process.

The *precise* dates also seem dubious. It is difficult to imagine records being kept in new foundations in the west given how little of this was done in Greek cities around the Aegean. Perhaps, it has been suggested, the precision served another purpose: to reinforce Thucydides' complaint that the Athenians resolved on invading Sicily without any idea of how big it was, or how many people lived there. See how much good data *is* available, he seems to be saying, if they had only bothered to look before they leapt to a tragic debacle. On the other hand, if the earliest ceramic known from the major sites is examined, not only is the relative order of foundations more or less correct, but so is the rough chronology. Potsherds do not prove a colony or a city, but the earliest material is from the later eighth century and the earliest cemeteries with Greek material in them are from the early seventh. Soon after this, almost all the material culture found there was Greek in style. Something was happening, then, even if it was not the official creation of new city-states, and Thucydides (or Antiochus) has got the dates about right. The big question is, what was happening on the ground? To answer that we have to unthink the mythology of heroic leaders founding new poleis in alien territory—both the original myths and those created in the nineteenth and twentieth centuries—and ask what the material evidence suggests about encounters between eastern mariners and local chieftains around the western Mediterranean.

The Contact Zone

The island of Ischia in the Bay of Naples has a central place in this story, because evidence of eastern visitors appears there so early, and because it has been investigated in such detail.[35] A site named Pithecusae was created in the middle of the eighth century—some think even earlier—and within a generation became one of the largest urban centres in the western Mediterranean. Estimates of its population range from 5,000 to 10,000. Well over a thousand graves have been excavated, as well as portions of the town and its acropolis. Buried within the graves are Greek, Syrian, and Italian objects, and sometimes a mixture of these. It is almost unmentioned in classical literature, featuring briefly as a staging post in two early first-century C.E. accounts of the foundation of other cities. But it may have been the beachhead for a whole series of encounters between easterners and Italian peoples.

Ischia lies just a few kilometres off the coast. It is a rich source of metals, and also has access to other rich sources on the mainland. At the very least it was an entrepôt, like the Phoenician base at Huelva, but it was much larger. It was also short-lived, perhaps already in decline by the end of the eighth century, and unlike many other early sites it never developed into a city-state with its own political system, laws, and foundation myths. The site is incredibly valuable in giving a glimpse of how Greeks and others began building relations in the contact zone during the eighth century B.C.E.

Many early bases were created on islands close to the shore, or on promontories mostly surrounded by water.[36] That is true of the Phoenician bases at Cadiz in Spain and Motya in Sicily, of Greek bases at Berezan and Borysthenes in the Black Sea, Ortygia at Syracuse, and Eusperides off the coast of Benghazi in what is now Libya, and it was also true of Pithecusae. Islands are easy landmarks, and provide a little security, but visitors always came to make contact with the locals, not to avoid them. Almost none of these islands has enough territory to feed a population of any size. We may be sure that they were not intended to be the urban kernels of city-states, nor self-sufficient in food or other resources. At one point these sites were described in the language of precolonization, as if mariners were guided by a long, multigenerational plan of settlement, occupying island strongpoints as a first stage towards acquiring territory in the next generation and founding a city in the one that followed. This is wildly anachronistic.

Any grand scheme of settlement would in any case have faced huge practical difficulties. How would the small populations of easterners that ancient vessel could have transported feed and protect themselves until the first crops they sowed could be harvested? The seas were closed during the long winter months between October and the end of April and it would have been impossible to summon help, and nearly as difficult to flee. Besides, these were not empty lands. Most were inhabited by peoples whose technologies were on par with those of the newcomers. Even the first European settlers in the New World—for all their guns, germs, and steel—had huge difficulty in establishing themselves. Many early modern colonies perished, and others survived only with the help of indigenous peoples. The same must have been true in antiquity. Entrepôts survived not in the face of local opposition, but thanks to the support of indigenous chiefs. These were not Greek or Phoenician colonies. They were joint ventures from the start.

The archaeology of Pithecusae gives some sense of the range of possible collaborations. There were both Greek and Phoenician speakers resident on the island, since we have graffiti in both their languages from the site. Probably there were Italians present too. Many graves contain Italic *fibulae*—metal pins for fastening clothes—and strongly suggest an origin on the mainland. One suggestion is that easterners "acquired local wives"—a conventional euphemism—but it just as likely there were indigenous craftsmen and traders based there. The ceramic on the site is quite varied. It looks as if some local potters were trying to produce imitations of foreign ware, and maybe some incoming potters were trying to reproduce traditional forms too. The styles suggest links not just with the Euboean cities of Eretria and Chalkis mentioned in later testimony, but also with communities from the east Aegean, including Rhodes. Pottery made on Pithecusae has been found in Phoenician bases in Spain and Carthage. Metals were clearly important to everyone.

Most likely Pithecusae was just one gateway through which the elites of southern Etruria and Campania obtained exotic goods to the rest. As it happens, the Greek ceramic in contemporary Etruscan and Latium is not an identical selection to what we know of from Pithecusae. There were alternatives. The Etruscan port of Pyrgi has a Greek name that means "towers." At the start of the fifth century a set of famous gold bilingual tablets reveal a local Etruscan prince performing ceremonies there jointly with Phoenicians. This is about the same time as Polybius tells us the first Roman treaty with Carthage was made, a treaty that deals with where different peoples are allowed to trade. Another route into Etruria was via Sardinia and Elba, from which it is easy to connect to the iron-producing hinterlands of Populonia. The Tiber and a series of sites around the Bay of Naples also offer easy access to central Italian peoples. Quite likely other bases like this will be identified in the future. There must also have been many failed joint ventures: sites which could not be made profitable, places where relations between locals and visitors broke down, or simply locations that were poorly chosen in relation to where people lived, what local exportable resources were available, and where ships could safely be harboured. Failed collaborations would be archaeologically almost invisible, and they would also be unlikely to feature in later foundation myths.[37]

Bases like Pithecusae and the first-generation Greek settlements at Sicilian Naxos and Syracuse would not have looked very like the much grander city-states of Phoenicia and Cyprus, ancient cities rebuilt repeatedly since the Bronze Age by kings. Nor were they very like the more loosely organized early cities of Etruria, still largely agricultural in nature and with a much lower density of population. How people of different origins got along—and what happened when they did not—are mysteries. It was likely in places like these that alphabets were learned, adopted, and adapted. It must also have been in places like these that skills in making pottery on the wheel and achieving a high gloss were perfected. Perhaps it was in places like these too that a few Italian peoples learned to make their own long-distance sailing craft.

During the early seventh century a new style of pottery was created at Caere, a south Etruscan port city. *Bucchero* developed from the Villanovan *impasto* pottery, but in its range of shapes and its hard shiny black surface mimicked metal tableware and the fine ceramics and the metalwork of the eastern Mediterranean (see Figure 19). Soon it was manufactured across southern Etruria and was exported in large quantities to Phoenician Carthage. Working out the precise ways in which this product was created, perfected, and marketed is almost impossible at this distance, but it is difficult to imagine this arising except in a contact zone like that created around the western Mediterranean Basin in the late eighth and early seventh centuries

Figure 19 Etruscan Bucchero
DEA / E. LESSING / Getty Images

B.C.E. What had begun as a trade in metals was now a much more complex relationship. As more and more bases of this kind were created in Sicily and Sardinia and then in southern Italy and Africa, by locals in collaboration with eastern visitors, so the basis of an urban network began to appear.

10

A Greek Lake

The Thirsty Greeks

It was the Phoenicians who lead the reconnection of the Mediterranean world after the late Bronze Age collapse. By the eighth century the Etruscans were already creating cities of a new kind in central Italy. Yet by 500 B.C.E. the coasts and islands of the inland sea were dominated by the Greeks. The Greek language and alphabet, Greek myths and Greek sculpture, Greek painted pottery and Greek architectural ornament were everywhere, from the frozen Crimea to sun-baked Egypt and from Syria to the southern coasts of France. The Mediterranean had become a Greek lake.[1] And around the Greek lake, everyone was building Greek cities.

On the shores and islands of the Aegean Sea the first centuries of the last millennium B.C.E. were unspectacular.[2] The last flicker of Bronze Age civilization guttered out in the twelfth century, leaving just a few unreliable memories. Writing, long-distance voyages, and monumental building were all gone. There were no rich graves, perhaps no rich people either. Most settlements were villages with populations in the hundreds. There is not much sign of connection with a wider world. Iron technology spread through this world, but its economic impact was slow. After a couple of centuries there are signs of tentative reconnections. The princes of tenth-century Lefkandi and their contemporaries welcomed infrequent visitors from the Levant. The weaponry of the period suggests some connections with the European interior, perhaps through intermediaries. But Aegean societies did not produce large agricultural surpluses. Most families lived simple lives, mostly self-sufficient, and by later standards poor. Demographic growth was small. Century by century we know of more and more inhabited sites, but most remained tiny.

One of the largest sites was Athens, which probably had a population of around a thousand people at the start of the millennium.[3] Who can tell what its inhabitants remembered of the Bronze Age? Their scattered hamlets clustered around the Acropolis, the hilltop on which a Mycenaean palace had once stood, surrounded by a Cyclopean Wall. The first version of the Parthenon was not built until the middle of the sixth century, but perhaps its site was already a sacred place as well as an occasional refuge. By 700 B.C.E. the population had grown to around 7,000—about the same as Pithecusae far to the west. Probably nowhere west of Cyprus had a population as high as 10,000 people. Corinth in the eighth century was no more impressive, again a dispersed settlement around sacred sites, a focus for a larger community to be sure, but not a functioning urban centre. Even the largest settlements were no larger than the biggest villages of Neolithic Anatolia built six millennia before.

As in Etruria, the early Iron Age settlements of the Greek world were low-density and discontinuous. At Athens, Corinth, Eretria, and Lefkandi each cluster of houses with its graves and farmland stood alone, connected by paths and a few roads to each other and sometimes to a central sanctuary as well. There is no sign of urban planning, no zoning, almost no public areas, and certainly no street blocks with drainage and pavements of the kind that Minoan towns had. Physically they did not resemble Villanovan settlements either. The east-facing coasts of mainland Greece were arid and the soils poor. Houses clustered near springs and summer watercourses and sheltered where they could beneath an acropolis. Most communities had one or more central temples. Building these and defending the settlement required some common effort and conflicts needed to be adjudicated too, so we presume there were councils of elders or chiefs and occasional assemblies as well as religious ceremonials. As yet there were no monumental structures to house these.

Low-density urbanism has many parallels around the world, from the forests of Central America to the larger hill forts of late prehistoric Europe.[4] Geography often plays a part. The larger hilltop sites of Iron Age Europe and the low tufa plateaux of Tuscany lend themselves in different ways to loose clustering. Low fertility also militates against dense settlement. If townspeople are still mostly farmers, they need access to fields. Low-density urbanism has sometimes been the result of gradual growth, the slow and piecemeal accretion of residential areas around a single focus. This was probably the case at Athens. Coming together offered some advantages—efficiencies of production, safety in numbers—but there was less concern with ordering space. Perhaps too this messy, loose urbanism reflected very diffuse social power. Heads of households might get together occasionally, but mostly each family was left to its own devices. There were exceptions. Athens and Corinth spread out around their acropoleis, but some coastal sites were more densely packed. Old Smyrna on the other side of the Aegean was built on a promontory surrounded by the sea. It acquired a fortification wall around 700 B.C.E. and its first monumental temples were begun soon after. The settlement of Zagora on the island of Andros, built on a steep headland, had a wall even earlier.

The first cities of the Iron Age Aegean would probably not have impressed visitors from the east. Few had anything that we would consider monumental before 700 B.C.E. Compared to the imperial cities of contemporary Assyria or Egypt of the New Kingdom and Third Intermediate period, the cities that Homer and Hesiod knew were unimpressive. Houses were mostly small, just a few rooms, single storey, built of wood and mud and roofed in thatch. Where soil was thin and wood was scarce, dry stone walls were used. Where timber posts could be found they supported roofs. The postholes they left behind are among the most prominent archaeological traces on many sites. From central Italy there are models of small houses like this in pottery, called "hut urns," used in the ninth and eighth centuries B.C.E. as containers for the ashes of the dead. Connections between the houses of the dead and the houses of the living crop up all over prehistoric Europe. In Italy we can trace the creation of more and more elaborate houses for the living through the provision of more and more elaborate tombs for the dead. The Aegean world was at the poorer end of the spectrum.

It is easy to understand why the Aegean world lagged behind other regions. In the end it all came down to water.[5] Central and northern Italy have not only significantly greater rainfall than the Aegean world but are also irrigated by rivers draining from the Apennines and in the Po Valley from the Alps as well. The same is true of Aegean Turkey, where rainfall is a little higher and where the Cayster, the Maeander, and other rivers brought water down from the Anatolian plateau. Where rainfall is not only low on average but also unreliable from one year to another—as in Attica—both tree crops and less resistant cereals like wheat also suffer.[6] Water poverty made it more or less impossible to raise livestock of any size or in any number. The range of domesticated crops and animal species available to these populations was much reduced as a result. Southern Greece and the islands have never produced great agricultural surpluses. Nor did they have the kind of metal resources that drew eastern visitors to the bay of Naples, to Elba, and to southern Spain. The Aegean is rich in metamorphic rocks—in obsidian, marble, and other hard building stones—but these were barely exploited in the early Iron Age. The poverty of Greece was certainly one thing that motivated Greeks to sail to areas rich in timber, like the coasts of Macedonia and Thrace, to sources of copper in Sardinia and Cyprus, and iron in Anatolia and northern Tuscany. During the sixth century they began to visit southern Russia and Egypt in search of grain.[7] But before they became long-distance mariners, the villages of Greece lived on the margin.

The Greeks believed they were poor. At one point in his narrative of the Persian Wars, written in the middle of the fifth century B.C.E., Herodotus has the Spartan exile Demaratus tell Xerxes, the Great King, that Greece and poverty had grown up together, were stepsisters, and that this had made Greeks hard and strong. Spartans, added Demaratus, were poorer and stronger than any other Greeks. They would resist the wealth of Persia because of their poverty, not despite it.[8] Perhaps this was a reassuring myth during the Persian Wars. It was a more disturbing one in Herodotus' own day when wealthy imperial Athens was itself periodically at war with those same poverty-hardened Spartans.

The story also seems to reflect a common wisdom. The Hippocratic text *Airs, Waters, Places*, written around the same time, describes the effects of local climatic conditions on the physiques and health of different peoples and on crops and animals as well. Everything in Asia grows to greater size and is more beautiful than in Europe. European populations suffer violent seasonal variation, heat waves and icy winters, droughts and winds, and this makes them more courageous than Asiatics. Perhaps too it made them more willing than others to risk the dangers of seafaring. By the time these books were being written, the Greek world was in fact in full recovery. From the eighth through the fourth centuries there was remarkable growth in the standard of living and in the size of the population, sure signs of growing wealth. But for a moment, at least facing Persia, this was not how Greeks thought about themselves.[9]

Dreams of the City

The first long texts written in Greek were the poems of Homer and Hesiod. Their works are literary compositions deeply marked by traditional ways of composing and performing without the use of writing. Songs first sung to the mighty and their followers gave birth to long and elegant scripts written in ink on papyrus rolls. These books were a new kind of treasure, expensive to make, jealously guarded, and enjoyed silently, as well as read out or recited from memory in great public gatherings. Most experts think that the first written versions of epic appeared between 750 and 700, with the *Iliad* a little earlier than the *Odyssey,* and Homer a little earlier than Hesiod; the age of mariners, in fact. The exact connections between the expeditions of traders around the Mediterranean and the creation of Greek literature are difficult to tease out. One of the most famous of early Greek graffiti was scratched on a clay cup found on Pithecusae in 1954, and begins: "Nestor had a cup good to drink with." The cup was made between 750 and 700 B.C.E.; the script is that used by Euboeans and the dialect is not the same as that in which the Homeric songs were written down, but the story of Nestor's cup is told in book eleven of the *Iliad.* Were several versions of the poem, perhaps still oral rather than written, already well known?

The text of Homer that we use today shows only a few later additions and changes, despite stories of politically motivated tampering in the sixth century B.C.E. Mostly the poems speak from an age that was only just literate, a world with close horizons but a growing consciousness that much lay beyond them, an age more interested in myth than history, and societies that were barely urban. The oral precursors of the poems were sung at open-air festivals or in the *megara*, the great halls, of Aegean chieftains. Hesiod claims that he won a tripod for a song sung at funeral games held in Euboean Chalkis. Elaborate bronze tripods are a familiar item of treasure in the poems, were frequent prizes at athletic competitions, and were often dedicated to the gods. Funeral games are described in the *Iliad* and the *Odyssey.* There is a scene in the *Odyssey* when Odysseus, washed up on the distant (and mythical) isle of Scherie, is taken to the palace of king of the Phaeacians, where he hears the bard Demodocus singing songs about the Trojan War and the Greek gods. Writing, by contrast, is almost completely absent from the poems, as if to mark the distance between the age of their composition and the heroic period they describe. Odysseus on his travels

encounters gods and monsters, cannibals and a witch, people who live on
terms of familiarity with the gods, and he even visits the land of the dead.
But he never visits a city, except of course for the one that he sacked, Troy.

The city of Troy stands at the very centre of Homer's *Iliad*. Not only is
its imminent destruction the backdrop to most of the action of the poem,
but images of urban life are constantly evoked. Achilles, raging against King
Agamemnon, provides one gripping example.

> I hate his gifts. I hold him light as the strip of a splinter
> Not if he gave me ten times as much, and twenty times over
> as he possesses now, not if more should come to him from elsewhere,
> or he gave all that is brought in to Orchomenos, all that is brought in
> to Thebes of Egypt, where the greatest possessions lie up in the houses
> Thebes of the hundred gates, where through each of the gates two hundred
> fighting men come forth to war with horses and chariots;
> not if he gave me gifts as many as the sand or dust is,
> not even so would Agamemnon have his way with my spirit
> until he had made good to me all this heartrending insolence.

The Iliad 9. 374–387 (trans. Lattimore)

Achilles—who at the time of his outburst has lived for ten years in a military
encampment below the walls of Troy—reaches out for images of unsurpass-
able wealth. Among them he mentions the city of Orchomenos in central Greece and then hundred-gated Thebes, the Greek name for Egyptian
Luxor. The Greek city of Thebes—near Orchomenos, as it happens—was
famous as *seven*-gated Thebes, and the subject of another epic cycle of
poems. Egyptian Thebes was of a different order of magnitude: one hundred gates from each of which come two hundred warriors, a city that
contained an unimaginable army of 20,000 men all mounted on chariots,
the ultimate prestige vehicle of the later Bronze Age.

Then there is Troy itself, fated to fall to the Greeks soon after the end
of the poem and Achilles' death.[10] Its walls are presented as impregnable.
There is no siege warfare here of the kind that features on the reliefs placed
by contemporary Assyrian kings on their palace walls (see Figure 20). They
brought battering rams and towers against city walls, and portrayed captured
cities surrounded by moats full of the corpses of their defenders. In the *Iliad*
the war is fought entirely on the plains in front of the city. We are treated
to scenes of the women of Troy watching the combat below, anticipating
their fate at the hands of the Greeks when Troy falls. There is an awful lack
of symmetry between the two sides.

Figure 20 The siege of Lakish on a relief from Nineveh
akg-images / Erich Lessing

The Trojan citadel shelters not only the Trojan heroes but also their families. Hector's exploits, and his death at Achilles' hands, are watched from the
battlements by his aged parents, his wife Andromache, and by his infant son
Astyanax (the name literally means "lord of the city"). The Greek camp, by
contrast, is a masculine world, and an entirely adult one. The only females
present are slaves, like the captive Briseis, who is the cause of the rift between
Achilles with Agamemnon. There are no children in the camp; the Greeks
have left them behind. A central theme of the *Odyssey* is the estrangement
of the returning warriors from their wives and children. The war has broken Greek families as surely as it shattered the city of Troy itself. The Greek
beachhead in the *Iliad* is an anti-city, a place where civil society is replaced
by the pecking order of the chiefs, where there is an undercurrent of antag-
onism against the heroes on the part of some of their followers. As Greeks
and Trojans slug it out between the city and the camp, the poet occasionally

recalls the time when the battlefields were just fields, when it was safe for men to sow and plough.

The distant cities of the Greeks also figure in the poems. Mycenae, the capital of Agamemnon's realm, is several times described as "rich in gold," and it is a "strong-founded citadel." Like Troy, it is described as "wide-streeted." Corinth is "wealthy," Tiryns "well-fortified," and so on. These epithets are not unique to particular cities. Troy is called "holy" but so are Athens, Pylos, Sounion, and a few other places. Several cities are described as "lovely." Troy naturally has the lion's share of the epithets, both because it dominates the scene of the drama and because its magnificence is all the more poignant given its coming destruction. Its location on a hilltop is mentioned again and again. Troy is "high-gated" and "high-throned," and it is often described in words that mean "steep" or "precipitous," and as "windy." Most of all, Troy is praised. As well as "holy" and "wide-streeted" it is "well-towered," "well-built," "well-walled," "well-peopled," and "rich in horses." And doomed, of course.

The doom of Troy hangs over the entire poem, but it is delayed while Achilles, the greatest warrior of the Greeks, refuses to take part in battle because of his quarrel with Agamemnon. It is not until his friend Patroclus is killed by the Trojan hero Hector that the grief-stricken Achilles returns to battle. At this point his divine mother Thetis gives him a wonderful shield made by Hephaistos, the smith of the gods. On the shield is depicted a microcosm of the entire world. It is framed by the sky and the stars and by the great stream of ocean that surrounds the earth. At the centre Hephaistos has depicted two cities, one at peace and the other at war. In the first there are wedding celebrations, dancing, and music, and also a scene in which a group of elders calmly adjudicate a dispute over the blood price owed for a killing. The other city is under siege, and the defenders have set out, led by Ares and Athena, to save it, leaving their women and children and the elderly behind the walls. There is an ambush scene too, and a vicious battle. The cities on the shield crystallize an opposition that appears throughout the poem, between Troy's peaceful and productive past and its savage present when the rich farmlands have become killing fields, and marriages have been replaced by funerals. Around the cities are depicted other scenes of agriculture: the ploughing of a field, the harvesting of a king's estate, grape-picking, the herding of cattle and sheep, and finally the harvest festival, with dancing on the threshing floor.

This world recalls that of Hesiod's *Works and Days*, which also celebrates the farmer who knows the agricultural year and what tasks are appropriate to each season. Hesiod too is preoccupied with justice in the city:

> But when the judges of a town are fair
> To foreigner and citizen alike,
> Their city prospers and her people bloom;
> Since Peace is in the land, her children thrive;
> Zeus never marks them out for cruel war.
> Famine and blight do not beset the just,
> Who till their well-worked fields and feast. The earth
> Supports them lavishly; and on the hills
> The oak bears acorns for them at the top
> And honey bees below; their woolly sheep
> Bear heavy fleeces, and their wives bear sons
> Just like their fathers. Since they always thrive,
> They have no need to go on ships, because
> The plenty-bringing land gives them her fruit.

Hesiod *Works and Days* 225–238 (trans. Wender)

The poem goes on to describe the opposite fate that lies in wait for a city beset by the proud and evil-doers. Plagues, famines, sterility, and depopulation follow. Zeus may destroy their armies, shatter their walls, and destroy their ships at sea. Crooked judges are especially singled out for divine punishment.

Homer and Hesiod do not describe a real world, or at least not the one that they themselves knew. Nowhere in the eighth century was as grand as Homer imagined Troy, and nowhere in the Greek world was really the self-sufficient idyll Hesiod admires. Those worlds were carefully constructed from traditions about the Bronze Age mixed with a grandiose exaggeration of the present day.[11] They have been carefully edited as well. Almost everything beyond the Aegean has been removed. These texts were first written in an alphabet adapted from that of the Phoenicians, on rolls of papyrus imported from Egypt. The shield of Achilles recalls Levantine metalwork. The more fantastic tales of the *Odyssey* and Hesiod's weather lore both have analogues in Near Eastern literature. There are even themes shared with Gilgamesh, such as the poignancy of mortality or the terrifying enmity and favoritism of individual gods for particular heroes. And of course there is the traditional motif of walled cities at war. Yet all these foreign elements have been absorbed, domesticated, and familiarized.

The *Iliad's* world is tiny: it hardly extends beyond the coasts and islands of the Aegean Sea, except in occasional remarks like Achilles' evocation of Hundred Gated Thebes. There is no consciousness either of the great Assyrian empire of the poets' own day, nor of the historical Hittite Empire of which the actual city of Troy was for a while probably a dependency. There are a few allusions to the story of the Argonauts, who sailed to mysterious Colchis in search of the Golden Fleece, but no real knowledge of the Black Sea. The *Odyssey* used a larger canvass, but the western Mediterranean remained a fantastical realm of monsters and witches, even though there were Greek merchants and craftsmen working in Etruria before the poems were written down. The Phoenicians appear in some of Odysseus' fictitious stories, but only as occasional visitors to the Aegean. At best the poems reveals the dreams some of their audience shared about the past, and also their projects for the future.

The Widening Horizon

The eighth-century world of Homer and Hesiod was in reality no longer isolated. Its communities remained relatively small and were not yet splendid, but its centres were much more connected than they had been in the tenth century. Archaic Greece was open to innovation and to new technologies.[12] Its population was also growing fast, at least recovering from the devastating crash at the end of the Bronze Age.

Many of the new technologies picked up in the eighth century had an eastern origin. The alphabet, invented in North Syria by Phoenicians or their close neighbours, was adapted to write Greek somewhere in the broad contact zone where Greeks and Near Easterners met and worked alongside each other. Researchers have proposed Syria or Cyprus, Crete or central Italy, and half-dozen other places. Once invented it spread very rapidly, a clear sign of how connected the Greek Mediterranean was becoming. Dozens of local versions were created, as sign of how fragmented that world remained.

There were other borrowings too. Greeks became fascinated with the monstrous human–animal hybrids featured on Near Eastern art. Centaurs, chimaeras, sphinxes, gorgons, and harpies entered their myths and their art.[13] The tyrants of the sixth century—in Corinth, in Samos, in Athens, and other major centres—modelled some of their behaviour on that of the Iron

Age monarchs of Lydia and Egypt. *Tyrannos* was itself a loanword, meaning an autocrat who in one way or another it did not seem right to call *basileus* or *anax*, the traditional terms for king or overlord. The Iron Age autocrats of Lydia and Corinth, Egypt and other Near Eastern states surrounded themselves with heavily armed mercenaries, some of them Greek, some of them Carians. Around the same time Greeks adopted coinage, also from Lydia. Weapon technology increasingly drew on eastern models. Tyrants undertook grandiose building projects, temples, harbours, and fortifications. The Aegean was becoming part of a wider eastern Mediterranean cultural sphere.

The eighth century was also the age in which Greeks really began to travel widely beyond the Aegean Sea. Mycenaean journeys to the west were long forgotten; so too were the confused refugee movements that followed the Bronze Age collapse. At the start of the Iron Age the Aegean had had only occasional visitors from outside the region and movement within it was limited. Now there was more of a hum of mobility between the islands. Hesiod, who lived at Ascra in Boeotia in central Greece, wrote that his father had emigrated from the city of Cyme on the other side of the Aegean. The archipelago of the Cyclades was full of staging posts for travellers, and not all of them were locals.

Long-distance voyages had for centuries been the preserve of the Phoenicians. Only a few cities in the Levant were involved, and for this reason the volume of traffic was low. It carried treasures and metals; in other words, items with a high value per unit of weight or size. Now Greeks— some at least—followed their example, sailing to the metal-rich regions of Italy and Spain. Aegean Greeks also visited Cyprus, where there had been other Greek speakers since at least the end of the Bronze Age, and also the ports of the Syrian mainland near the mouth of the Orontes. Egypt and the Black Sea were next. Some Greeks had seen "hundred-gated Thebes" for themselves. Around the Mediterranean and Black Seas there were more and more places where Greeks settled for long periods. Some would become permanent residents, and some of their centres would become cities. But not at first.

The expansion of the Greeks was once imagined as the planting of hundreds of poleis around the shore sand islands of the Mediterranean and Black Seas. That was one ultimate result of the explorations of the archaic era, but it did not begin in this way. For a start, during the period of most intense explorations in the eighth and seventh centuries B.C.E., there was not much that could be called a polis in the Aegean world. There were places where villages clustered, often around ancient Bronze Age centres, but the only public buildings were small temples, which were first of all homes of the gods. A few sites had early walls—Zagora in the Cyclades, Old Smyrna on the coast of Asia—which were usually improving on natural defences. Some of the earliest planned cities—featuring blocks of housing organized by a road grid, with a central area for meeting and public business, and a wall circuit—were created far from the Aegean, at sites like Megara Hyblaea in Sicily. It is has been speculated that it was often in new territory that the opportunity and need to divide up the land and organize a citizen body first presented itself. There are plenty of modern parallels for new foundations capturing the idea of a city long before it was realized at home, among the messy accumulation of organic growth and vested interests. The first explorers carried with them dreams of the great cities of the heroic age and of barbarian empires, but their priorities were profit, then later safe bases for trade, and only later places to live and farm. The urbanization of the Mediterranean was an unforeseen consequence of those expeditions, another example of the way cities have so often appeared as solutions to problems caused by other kinds of growth and the threats they evoked.

The first great overseas expeditions required much more preparation and planning than island-hopping across the Cyclades or short journeys along a coastline. Long-distance navigation required superior geographical knowledge. More importantly, each voyage was a major investment for the community where it originated. Not only did the vessel have to be prepared but equipment too, if its crew were to be self-reliant for months away from home. Long-distance vessels carried carpenters with their tools, equipment to repair sails and rigging, perhaps a portable forge. If they were traders, they needed cargo. If they hoped to settle they would need agricultural equipment, weapons, seed corn, and animals. Some expeditions certainly carried potters, metal-workers, and other craftsmen, because we find them at work far from home. Then there was food for a journey of several weeks, containers for water, and so on. Vessels were typically small and so were their crews, perhaps just a few dozen people in boats only a few tens of metres long which had to have space for cargo, supplies, and equipment as well. One fourth-century shipwreck of a boat about 50 metres long had equipment in it that suggested a crew of only four people. Its hull is now preserved in the Hecht Museum in Haifa. This was a merchant vessel; the larger the crew, the smaller the cargo.

Launching expeditions of this kind meant that home societies had to be re-engineered even if they were long familiar with the sea through fishing and local trade. Long-distance maritime expeditions demand much more preparation. Many more people must have been involved in shipbuilding and provisioning than ever sailed, and these were either recompensed in advance or expected a share of the profits when the vessels returned. It is quite unlikely that this was organized by civic institutions.[14] For a start, few Aegean communities had much in the way of political institutions in the eighth and seventh centuries. Most likely expansion was led by families and clans, by charismatic individuals and relations based on trading partnerships. This was remembered differently, of course, in the fifth century and after when cities like Athens and Corinth competed to claim a sort of ancestral authority over settlement ventures that had succeeded.

To begin with it was just a few communities that made the transition from local living on the sea to long-distance travel. That had been the case in the Levant, and would be again in the great age of exploration of the fifteenth century. The Euboeans of Eretria and Chalkis were among the first to regularly make long voyages. For this period we can often identify different origins by the pottery forms they carried with them, as well as by their dialects and the scripts they used when we find traces of their writing. It is not always possible to say for sure whether Attic pottery was carried by Athenians or Euboeans, or even whether Greek painted pottery was occasionally traded in Phoenician vessels. Later traditions, place names, and cults sometimes make one reconstruction more likely than another. But it is fairly certain that Euboeans were already exploring the north Aegean in the ninth century.[15] Euboean pottery appears in large quantities at the enigmatic site of Al Mina at the mouth of the river Orontes in Syria at the end of the ninth century B.C.E. and also on Cyprus. Euboeans were among the first Greeks at Pithecusae in the middle of the eighth century. Some place names in the far west seem to refer back to Euboea.

When distributions of the different exotica traded in this period—seal stones, painted pottery, metalwork, faience beads, and scarabs—are compared, they do not completely coincide.[16] The most likely explanation is that we are observing the faint traces of alternative trade routes or carriers, of different webs of connections laid over each other but not perfectly aligned. One strand seems to link Euboea (and Attica) with north Syria to the east and central Italy to the west. A slightly different strand links Phoenicia with southern Italy, Sicily, and the far west. There were overlaps, places touched by several networks such as in Crete and in southern Etruria. Pithecusae was a major nexus in the second half of the eighth century. Euboeans were soon joined as mariners by Corinthians and by some of the Greek cities of the west coast of what is now Turkey, sailors from Miletus and Rhodes among them. Those peoples were termed Ionians or Yavana in some Near Eastern texts, which refer to them mostly as pirates and mercenaries. Their ceramic signature is called Eastern Greek, and it occurs in Egypt and also around the Black Sea.

At first the major focus of Greek exploration was the west.[17] Thucydides' foundation dates for Sicilian cities (listed in the previous chapter) begin in the 730s and ended in 580 B.C.E. Similar dates were claimed for the foundations of cities in southern Italy. Cumae, Sybaris, Croton, and Tarentum were said to be founded in the late eighth century, with others following. Among the communities joining in exploration were Naxos and Megara, and we find cities with those names in Sicily too. Farther north and west, around Sardinia and Corsica and the coast of France, Phoenicians, Etruscans, and Greeks sailed the same seas, occasionally fought, and probably traded with each other, and cohabited in each other's bases and in indigenous settlements. At this point the difference between Greeks and barbarians cannot have mattered that much, and from the point of indigenous peoples a more significant difference was between peoples they had known forever and new arrivals who came over the horizon in ships.

During the late seventh century Greek material began to appear in some areas that the Phoenicians did not visit. Greek pottery appeared in Egypt for the first time since the Bronze Age. Some sort of entrepôt was licensed by the Pharaohs in the city of Naucratis in the Nile Delta.[18] Eastern Greeks took the lead, although others joined in. At Naucratis most of the pottery was Eastern Greek, but there are also vessels from Attica and Corinth and Laconia, and some seems to have been made locally. Around the same time Greek material appears on the northern coasts of the Black Sea. There are also mentions in Assyrian texts and graffiti from Egypt of Greek raiders and soldiers around the Near East, some serving as mercenaries. Carians from western Asia Minor served alongside Greeks in Egypt. There were Cypriots fighting for local princes in the Kingdom of Judah.[19]

Moving north and south took the explorers into new ecological zones. Phoenicians had travelled thousands of miles west but hardly ventured out of their latitudinal comfort zone. Some Greeks at least were more adaptable, prepared to shelter in semisubterranean huts at Berezan during the freezing

Black Sea winters, to march far from the sea in Syria, and to go inland into in Egypt, where Greek graffiti have been found on the temples of Abu Simbel south of the first cataract. Were they bolder and more entrepreneurial than the Phoenicians? Or just more desperate? Egypt and southern Russia both produced great grain surpluses. The Phoenician cities were in a more favourable ecological zone: they craved metals, not food. By the fifth century grain was being regularly traded from both Egypt and the northern Black Sea to the larger centres of the Aegean world. This was a different kind of trade than that in silver bowls and rich textiles: it was a trade in bulk, and one destined for consumption by more than just the elite. Greece had, in any case, by the fifth century more egalitarian societies, which were becoming prosperous. They put different demands on their traders than had the princes of the early Iron Age.

By the beginning of the sixth century Greeks were found almost everywhere in the Mediterranean world. There were other mariners. Phoenicians, Etruscans, and probably Cypriots, Syrians, and Sardinians sailed in small numbers, all making use of more or less the same maritime technology. But the overwhelming majority spoke Greek, called the gods by Greek names, and shared a common set of myths that surface in painted pottery, on architectural reliefs, and in the lines of verse that were for a long time among the most common archaic inscriptions. The numerical dominance of Greeks in part reflected demographic growth in the Aegean world.[20] It also reflected the participation of growing numbers of cities in maritime expeditions. There remained Phoenician and Etruscan cities orientated on the sea right up until the third century B.C.E. Many languages were still spoken around the Mediterranean, and bilingual texts are known from all periods of antiquity.[21] Yet it was Greek that had become the lingua franca, everybody's second or first language, while Greek imagery, enriched by its own engagement with Near Eastern art, was now the dominant cultural style.

Greeks and Others

At the same time as this the Greeks were becoming more preoccupied with what set them apart from other peoples.[22] Travellers from different Aegean communities met in various foreign places. Corinthians and Eretrians visited the same mining regions or trade entrepôts. Eastern Greeks from various cities served alongside each other as mercenaries in Palestine, Syria, and

Egypt. Ceramics from the new communities outside the Aegean world suggests that even if many cities later claimed one mother-city, in reality new foundations attracted settlers from many different parts.[23] A sense of wider kinship must have developed when Greeks encountered each other in the cold ports of the Black Sea, up country in Andalucia, or around the shores of Sicily and southern Italy. They spoke more or less the same language, if in several dialects; they worshipped the same gods and shared some myths and festivals that marked them out as different from Carians, Lydians, and others. Perhaps these encounters made them feel just a little bit more Greek, and a little less Milesian or Corinthian or Euboean. The burial customs and temple architecture of Sicilian cities shows how different Greek traditions cross-fertilized in the west. Attachment to a single founding city became part of the city-state diplomacy in the sixth and fifth centuries, but in the first two centuries of settlement allegiances and genealogies were much more fluid. Probably most of the settlements that succeeded and grew drew in new members from non-Greek populations as well, although their material culture was masked by the dominant international styles. The descendants of mariners continued to explore new land and began to weave new senses of kinship. Being Greek found a new meaning and importance beyond the Aegean.[24]

It followed that barbarians were an invention of this age. The term "barbarian" came for many to mean "the opposite of Greek." The *Iliad* describes Carians as "barbarophonos," meaning "speaking in an alien tongue." But in general the Trojans, Lycians, and their other Anatolian allies seem morally and culturally indistinguishable from the Greeks. They worshipped the same gods, had no need of interpreters, fought in the same way, even wore the same sort of armour. Bizarrely, many of the Trojans have names that make sense in Greek, like Astyanax (city lord) and his mother Andromache, whose name combines the Greek words for "man" and "battle." That fundamental equivalence between the enemies serves a poetic purpose too, as in the moving scenes when the aged king Priam visits Achilles by night to beg him for the body of his slaughtered son Hector.

It is interesting that it is the Carians who are singled out as barbarians. Carians and Greeks often found themselves together in Homer's lifetime, serving in the same armies around the Ancient Near East or cantoned together in Egyptian cities. In historical times they lived in southwest Anatolia, but later Greek writers believed they had once lived on the coast and on the Cyclades and other islands in the Aegean. Perhaps Homer preserves an early stage of the process by which Greeks came to think of themselves as unlike their closest neighbours.

A heightened sense of the difference between Greeks and others must have been connected to a shift in the collaborative relations through which most new settlements had come about. The first permanent bases—perhaps accidently permanent in many cases—were very small. A few crews over-wintering in an indigenous centre must have given rise on several occasions to the creation of new settlements of a few hundred people each. Seeing this process in detail is really difficult because little was written at the time, and later accounts think only in terms of civic foundations. But tension is suggested by the appearance of wall circuits, by the apparent takeover of large tracks of arable land, and by the enthusiasm to welcome new arrivals from the Aegean world. Perhaps in these circumstances it was safer to live more closely together, and more important to have the means of organizing common action. The first Greek cities in the west did not exactly rival Troy or Hundred-Gated Thebes, but they were practical expedients in a world increasingly based on Greek dominance of surrounding populations.[25]

During the late sixth and early fifth centuries that notion of a moral difference between Greeks and Barbarians was weaponized. Greeks and Phoenicians came to blows over control of Sicily, and also in the seaways of the western Mediterranean. After the Persian Empire conquered Lydia in 546 B.C.E. and Cyprus in 526 B.C.E., Persians came to be the quintessential barbarians.[26] Many researchers think it was the shock of war with Persia, and the unique emphasis it created on Greek cities cooperating with each other, that really entrenched the difference once and for all. Herodotus and his contemporaries wrote in a world where barbarians were often expected to be the opposite of Greeks in every respect. Their men were soft, their women ferocious, and so on. Greeks who had sided with the Persians were accused of "Medizing"—that is, siding with the barbarian Medes against fellow Greeks in the Persian Wars. By the fourth century Aristotle was pro-ducing rationalizations of the common view that barbarians were "natural" slaves and Greeks their "natural" masters. That prejudice was never com-pletely accepted. The third-century B.C.E. polymath Eratosthenes pointed out that many other people, including the Phoenician Carthaginians, had political institutions, laws, and other things generally associated with civi-lized peoples rather than barbarians. Yet a strong sense that Greeks were a people apart persisted. The fact that so many barbarian peoples now made art that depicted Greek myths (as the Etruscans did), claimed Greek origins (as many Asian peoples would), and even adopted Greek as a language for public affairs (as the Lycians did) must have helped bolster that view. What had begun as a lingua franca, a common language of convenience in a world were most mariners spoke Greek, gradually became a hegemonic culture.

An Urban Mediterranean, a Greek Mediterranean

What was it that meant that the Mediterranean became a Greek lake? No one would have predicted it in the tenth century, but by the end of the fourth it was almost a fait accompli. It will not do, any more, to claim that Greek culture was in some way superior. Many of its components were in any case recent appropriations. What made the difference was the way a cluster of key symbols and technologies were disseminated, and central to that process was the transformation of hundreds of settlements (whose origins were quite diverse) into Greek-style city-states.

Many of the ways in which the Mediterranean went Greek reflected transfers of technology. The alphabet is a good example, devised near the beginning of the millennium in northern Syria, adapted and spread first by Phoenicians and then in the eighth century adopted by dozens of Greek communities, from whom first Etruscans and then other Italian and peoples adopted it. Alphabetic scripts were adopted, adapted, and used for new purposes in southern Spain and then in continental Europe, until they were widespread in the second century B.C.E.[27] A similar story could be told of coinage, almost certainly invented in Lydia, adopted by Greek cities, and from them adopted by Italians, Gauls, Spaniards, Africans, and many others. Carthaginians did not begin to mint their own coins until the fourth century B.C.E. and Rome not until the third, but they had known Greek coinages in Sicily for centuries. Presumably they felt no need for coinage of their own before then. Olive cultivation and much else followed similar patterns.[28]

None of these technologies were invented in the Aegean world, but Greeks were the vectors through which they became widely known. This illustrates one important feature of the Greekness of Mediterranean culture: it depended as much on the fact that from the eighth century Greeks dominated the seaways as on anything intrinsically Greek about what they brought. The same case could be made for life-size statuary or temple architecture. Phoenicians had been the first long-range mariners and their influence is clear in Etruscan and Greek engagement with Near Eastern styles. But by the seventh century there were so many more Greeks overseas than Phoenicians that their influence was drowned out. When Etruscans too took to the sea, a little later they were already sailing in Greek waters. A Phoenician Mediterranean or an Etruscan one is imaginable, but only if no Greek communities had taken to the waves. In the end it came down to numbers.

Getting those numbers right, however, is difficult. What seems certain is that traders and other temporary visitors were much more important than settlers in acting as conduits for new styles and technologies.

The scale of settlement and migration as a whole has been hugely over-estimated. One constraint is the small scale of urban centres in the eighth-century Aegean and the limits on what these early polities could organize. Herodotus' world contained a few major cities in it, the great maritime powers like Athens and Syracuse, Corinth and Samos, and ancient land powers like Sparta and Thebes. But in the period of expansion maybe none of these centres had more than 10,000 inhabitants and were therefore inca-pable of "budding off" many new cities. One recent estimate based on a modern understanding of demography suggests that the number of Greeks who left the Aegean world for new homes elsewhere in the Mediterranean or Black Sea basins between 750 and 600 B.C.E.—the period when most overseas settlements were created—was between 500 and 1,000 persons a year.[29] Even that low level of migration poses some challenges for would-be settlers. For a start, their vessels were very small. One of the most common types of warship was the penteconter, which carried a crew of fifty and was about 30 metres in length, but these were not built for long expeditions and fifty men needed a lot of food and water if they were to row for hours every day. Merchant vessels were only a little larger, with less than 100 tons. They carried many fewer people, partly because they relied on sail rather than oars, and partly because they needed space for cargo. How many ves-sels would it take to carry the few hundred people needed to found a new settlement? Quite apart from all the equipment needed to start a settlement from scratch, there are other questions about the settlers. One issue concerns the ratio of men to women. Taking entire families would have been even more expensive in terms of transport, especially if oared vessels were used, and increased the demand for food and water in transit and afterwards, but could a mostly male expedition really rely on finding sufficient indigenous princesses (or female slaves) to ensure the future of a new foundation? Even without families, the first wave of settlers had to survive the period between their arrival and when they could harvest their first crops. The horrific experience of the first European colonies in the New World gives pause for thought. And those European settlers had far superior technology, both in absolute terms and in relation to the locals. Greeks had not much of a military advantage over the local populations of the western Mediterranean. Superior skills as navigators might enable a quick escape if things became tense, but in terms of conquest and occupation of land, the incomers were few in number and had the same sort of Iron Age weapons as the locals.

Yet by 500 B.C.E., there were communities all around the Mediterranean and Black Sea coasts who thought of themselves as Greeks. Quite how many is unclear. One estimate suggests there were between 800 and 900 poleis (city-states) a century later, in 400 B.C.E.[30] That total included some communities that had probably never included Greek settlers: the cities of fourth-century Caria, for example, were no longer "barbarian-sounding" and used Greek language, Greek institutions, and local appropriations of Greek architecture.

Two more recent surveys—this time only of new settlements beyond the Aegean—came up with between 100 and 150 settlements that lasted long enough to leave traces.[31] It still seems impressive, given the enormous difficulties facing overseas expeditions, that this many foundations were successful. One response has been to see this activity as just a small part of something bigger, the fringe of processes of settlement mobility and refoundation that was most intense in the Aegean itself. There is no denying that the success of eighth-century expeditions to the western Mediterranean built on that of ninth-century expeditions to the north Aegean, carried out in both cases by Euboeans. Yet distance does change things. Small groups of settlers beyond the Aegean were far more vulnerable than the population of a new settlement on the Greek mainland and their relations with the locals were more precarious, especially if we imagine expansion as a kind of land grab. The Mediterranean was effectively closed from September to May, cutting them off from support and from supplies and making retreat very difficult. Conditions in the Black Sea were even more brutal.

The only plausible solution is that just as in the western Mediterranean, most of these foundations did not begin as colonial implantations in a modern sense but as joint ventures with the locals. Whatever tales their descendants would tell the historians and geographers of the fifth century and later, most of these communities must have depended on indigenous founders at least as much as incomers. It was because the Mediterranean had become a Greek lake that they claimed to have been founded by Greeks, not the other way around. These early conditions soon changed. Powered by economic and demographic growth in Greece, these joint ventures soon became thoroughly Greek communities. Their citizens probably included descendants of some locals as well as of successive groups of incomers. Beyond their territory, other descendants of former partners were now regarded as barbarians. By the time the first historians began to collect foundation stories they were already permeated with stories of original violence, epic city foundations, divine legitimation, and of theft and murder.[32] The Greek polis had appeared with its antithesis: the lawless tribes of barbarians fit only to be ruled by tyrants or purchased as slaves.

11

Networking the Mediterranean

A Networked World

By 600 B.C.E. there were hundreds of cities scattered around the islands and shores of the Mediterranean and Black Seas. Some were ancient. The cities of Phoenicia and Cyprus had roots in the Bronze Age. Others had grown slowly, as happened in parts of Etruria, or else appeared in sudden bursts of energy during the Iron Age. All were very small, with under five thousand inhabitants in each.

Urban life had not spread out from a single point of origin, developing local peculiarities as it spread. Around the Mediterranean cities had become in fact become more alike, not less, over the centuries. Urbanization progressed faster in some parts than others: earlier in the central Mediterranean than in the Black Sea or southern France, for example. Mostly they had their origins in collaborations between locals and visitors, but every story was different. Some were more violent than others, and some ended in failure and for that reason are mostly lost.

Whatever their origins, these cities were networked. This was true of virtually all early urbanism. In the ancient Mediterranean we can imagine that network as a mass of sailing routes superimposed over each other. Together they formed a loose web across which people, goods, and ideas moved back and forth. Some sea routes—those crossing deep water or covering long distances—really were seasonal. Homer's *Odyssey* is haunted by the perils of storms and shipwrecks, and Hesiod portrayed seafaring as a ridiculously risky way to make a living. Other routes were very local, connecting islands that were never out of sight of each other, or coastal communities with their nearest neighbours. Many journeys consisted of a series of short hops along the coast that allowed crews to pull up their boats each evening. This kind of shipping is often called *cabotage*. Many coastal communities lived off this sort of connection, and some were located where the sea routes intersected with rivers or trackways connected the uplands with the coast, the woodland with the beach, or pasture with salt pans. The maritime network itself connected many older local webs of communications. Long-distance maritime voyages had been something only a few communities attempted in the eighth century. That had changed. By the sixth century there were many maritime nations, and many landscapes had reorientated themselves to face the sea.

This web was thicker in some places than in others. Routes back and forth across the central Aegean were busy. Dedications by western Greek cities at the sanctuaries of Delphi and Olympia show lively traffic between mainland Greece, southern Italy, and Sicily. Corinthian and later Attic Black figure pottery was produced for overseas consumers as well as domestic markets: their distribution illuminates some connections. Soon local potters in the west imitated the most popular imported wares. A boom in temple-building in the sixth century provided a stimulus for the development of marble quarries. As urban populations rose some cities began to import food, at least during bad years.

Some sea-crossings were more popular than others, and coastlines and currents created bottlenecks. Traffic came together south of Cape Malea in southern Greece, at the isthmus of Corinth and when it passed through the Straits of Messina between Sicily and Italy, or the Dardanelles and the Bosporus to the Black Sea. Where there were many cities there would have been a constant back-and-forth of small vessels. There remained some less travelled seaways. It was not so easy to hop around the western shores of the Mediterranean, nor along much of its southern coastline. Even the northern Adriatic was probably rarely visited until the Etruscan ports of Adria and Spina near the Po Delta were created during the sixth century .

Little by little the network ramified, redundant elements dropped out, and settlement consolidated on sites that were well connected. The cities along the east coast of the Adriatic and those dotted around the Black Sea were eventually located at distances of roughly one day's sailing. That created ladders that small vessels could use as they hugged safe shorelines. Some cities became important nodes. From Etruscan Spina near the Po Delta or Greek Marseilles near the mouth of the Rhône, it was possible for Mediterranean merchants to connect to the continental hinterlands of Europe. Grain came from southern Russia, timber from the northern Balkans, metals and metal work from the Alpine regions, and slaves from everywhere. In the other direction went silver and gold, Etruscan jugs, Greek mixing bowls and wine. During the sixth century Mediterranean manufactures begin to turn up in the burials of chieftains and their relatives, in a broad belt from central France to the northern coasts of the Black Sea.

Phoenician and Greek explorers had sowed the seeds from which many cities developed. Etruscan cities appeared north of the Apennines in the early fifth century, forming a network within a network. There were others groups too. The Elymians of northwest Sicily built cities at Segesta, Eryx, and Entella. Already by the middle of the sixth century they were building monumental temples like those of their Greek neighbours. By the early fifth century their elites were amassing imported Greek ceramic, but examination of small sites makes it clear the routes of urbanism were local. Like the Etruscans they traded with Phoenicians, and they also adapted the Greek alphabet to write inscriptions in their own language, so far deciphered. The Tartessians of southern Spain exchanged metal ores with the Phoenicians even earlier. By the eighth century they had developed indigenous styles of art that made use of eastern and Greek motifs, but in slightly different ways from other western peoples. The location of their major settlements is uncertain. Probably one lies under modern Huelva, buried by sands brought down by the Guadalquivir, but it is too soon to say much about the first indigenous urbanism of that region.

New cities attracted visitors, and visits from foreigners helped stimulate urban growth. Communities did many things: they farmed, they defended themselves, they collaborated on building projects, and they kept the peace. But the thing small cities could do much better than large villages was to connect. Because they typically had specialist craftsmen and traders, because they had larger disposable surpluses, and because they were organized more centrally, it was easier for them to form effective alliances with others. In many cases it was the arrival of foreigners that nudged a few villages into becoming urban, or made clear their urban potential. Sometimes it was the emergence of cities that attracted visitors. There was a positive feedback, in other words, between the local development of cities and the ramification of networks of exchange.

What about the failures? We know little about them, because it was only the successful ventures that left traces prominent enough to be recoverable today. Since most myths of origin were created much later, they tell us little or nothing about foundations that failed or—like Pithecusae—were

short-lived. Some must have failed because they were built in poor locations. The foundation stories told about the origins of Byzantium say that
its founders were told by an oracle to build a city opposite the land of the
blind, the point being that the existing city of Chalcedon on the Asian coast
opposite was much less well suited for exploiting commercial connections.
Some locations were not bad in themselves but difficult to connect to urban
networks. Finally, there was the work invested in sustaining local collaborations between chieftains and travelling warriors, miners, potters, and traders.
Sometimes the location of the node is clear, but it seems a matter of chance
which community seized it. It is easy to imagine a counterfactual world in
which it was Veii and not Rome that came to control the Tiber salt road up
from the sea and the connections between Latium and southern Etruria.

An actual historical example is provided by the cluster of Greek cities founded on or around the Bay of Naples.[1] Cumae, Neapolis/Naples,
Dikaiarcheia/Pozzuoli, and south of the Sorrento peninsula, Poseidonia/
Paestum are all prominent in historical records, which effectively begin
in the fifth century B.C.E. around three centuries after their foundation.
Throughout their histories each had close connections to cities in the interior including Capua, Nola, and Nuceria, which were apparently indigenous creations influenced at times by connections with Etruscan cities, to
judge from burial evidence. Around them were a cloud of smaller centres
including Herculaneum, Pompeii, and Sorrento, which had both Greek and
indigenous features, and less well known centres like Suessula. Separating
this local urban network into Greek and native would be impossible by
archaeological criteria alone, and it is not easy on the basis of inscriptions,
written in Oscan, Greek, and some other languages. Over the centuries the
fate of individual cities rose and fell. Cumae dominates the history of the
first centuries. It was credited with destroying an earlier Greek foundation,
Parthenope, and with founding Naples in its place. Its sixth-century tyrant
Aristodemus allegedly fought off an Etruscan-led invasion of Campania. In
474 Cumae and Syracuse together won a naval victory over an Etruscan
fleet. The dates and details of all of this are very uncertain. By the end of the
fifth century Samnites and Lucanians from the Italian interior seem to have
captured Cumae, Naples, and Paestum. Yet these shifts in political balance,
except when they led to the obliteration of cities, did not change the fundamental organization of the territory in which larger centres on the coast
connected the inland populations to a wider world. Pozzuoli remained a
major centre even into the first centuries C.E. when its good harbour made

it a point where many visitors from the east alighted en route to Rome. Who profited changed, of course, but in the end it was the geographical logic of the sites that determined which centres remained crucial to the urban network and which were backwaters. Roman conquests humbled Capua and led to a mild resurgence in Naples, but it was only the construction in the first century C.E. of major harbour facilities at the mouth of the Tiber that made a real difference to the way the cities of Campania worked together.

Myths of the Net

Networking created its own community of knowledge. That included the navigational lore that was of interest to mariners, and also shared myths about an age of travelling heroes.[2] By the sixth century, the point at which Greeks began to take more of an interest in their past, many communities beyond the Aegean were already claiming to have been founded by Greeks. The reality, as I have shown, was probably more complicated. But since the language of the emerging network was Greek, so were many of the myths and images that were exchanged across it, and Greek styles and Greek ways of doing things had come to have enormous prestige. Add to this the fact that the Greeks alone had become historians, and it is no surprise that Greek elements of heritage were remembered and celebrated. There were other ethnic identities in play. Several peoples eventually claimed descent from Trojans rather than Greeks, a tribute to the primacy of Homeric poetry.[3]

Those connections were often imagined in terms of one of the oldest bonds of Greek society, the ties formed by kinship. Many cities in the west claimed Corinth or Sparta as mother-cities (the Greek word is metropolis). Corinth seems more plausible, as it was a sea power in the archaic period and Corinthian painted pottery was to be found all around the Mediterranean. But Sparta was by far the most prestigious of ancient Greek states, which is what made it an attractive parent.[4] Around the Black Sea many cities claimed to have been founded by Miletus. One much later Roman author claimed there were ninety Milesian colonies. Given how small most Greek cities were, claims like this are quite incredible. At best some cities played a larger role than others in exploration. More likely most of these stories were simply made up. What they tell us is that new cities overseas that felt themselves Greek wanted to have stories that connected them to the ancient cities of the Aegean, and at least some of those cities were prepared to acknowledge those claims, perhaps because being a metropolis conveyed some prestige in their rivalry with other ancient cities. Genealogical myth-making gave cities ways to form families and express enmities.

Links of kinship were celebrated in ceremonial. Sacred ambassadors would travel to be honoured guests at the major festivals of cities connected to their own by alliance or descent. Connections of this kind had real consequences for interstate relations. When the Athenians sent a great expedition to Sicily in 415 it was partly because the Syracusans were regarded as kin of the Athenians' enemies the Spartans, fellow Dorians in this case. Those ties of kinship mattered more than political ideology or cultural allegiance.

Wars and alliances, foundations and migrations fascinated the first historians. We know far more about spectacular disasters and threats, about coups and counterrevolutions, than we do about normal life, even normal political life. Those campaigns and coups were real enough. The historians' interest reflects the fears and hope of a much larger group involved in them, since everywhere warfare was a matter for male citizens and the risks were born by their families too. This was a violent world, and most political change was violent as well as noisy. But in the background we sometimes can hear the faint noise of routine traffic across the urban web. People moved, things moved, ideas moved.[5] Those circulations knitted the Mediterranean up into a single social world far more effectively than any wars of conquest or diplomatic triumphs could have done.

Most vessels carried trade goods, but some had passengers, many travelling for religious reasons. Local festivals were probably more ancient than the city-state itself. Both Homer and Hesiod mention funeral games. Several myths feature heroes gathering for competitions, like the race in which Melanion won the hand of the princess Atalanta, or the games in which Pelops won the kingdom of Olympia. During the seventh and sixth centuries a few festivals began to stand out from the rest, drawing competitors from all over mainland Greece and eventually the new cities of the west as well. By the early fifth century B.C.E. there was a set rotation of games held at Olympia, Delphi, the Isthmus of Corinth, and Nemea.[6] Meanwhile, some ancient local oracles also acquired an international reputation: the oracle of Zeus at Dodona, that of Apollo at Delphi, and that of Amphiaraus at Oropus were the most famous, and they attracted visitors from surprisingly far afield. New oracles, often connected to Apollo, continued to appear throughout antiquity. Sanctuaries dedicated to Apollo's son Asclepius the healer drew visitors in search of cures. Epidauros was the oldest, but cults of Asclepius and his father spread west to Italy and east through Asia Minor. Mystery cults, in which individuals prepared for days to be initiated and learn secrets about the world they could not then reveal, appeared in the fifth century. Those of Demeter and the Maiden at Eleusis and of the Great Gods on Samothrace eventually drew visitors from all over the Greek world and beyond.

Once vessels were making regular voyages, others could hitch a ride. Hitchhikers on trading vessels included craftsmen, poets, philosophers, teachers, sculptors, adventurers, tourists, and also ambassadors and envoys. Few Greek intellectuals lived all their lives in one city: Herodotus and Thucydides, Plato and Aristotle, Xenophon and Protagoras all moved about, seeking patrons or avoiding enemies. Greeks and Carians had travelled as mercenaries since the archaic period, and this continued into the fourth century B.C.E. and beyond.[7] We should not exaggerate the scale of mobility. Ships remained small, and there were no dedicated passenger services. Mass movements were almost always military and many were made on foot, like the long march of a mercenary army of over 10,000 Greek soldiers in 401 B.C.E. from what is now western Turkey to Babylon and then back over the Anatolian plateau to the Black Sea. Perhaps only a few thousand travellers made really long-distance journeys each year, but their impact was disproportionate to their numbers. A network of cities can function even if the numbers of individuals crossing it are relatively few.[8] It is what they carried with them that mattered most.

Information Exchange

From the middle of the eighth century B.C.E. we can see information flowing across the network. Maritime networks had their own technical knowledge: information about currents and winds, about which shores were safe to approach, about where there were deeper or more sheltered anchorages, and which populations were friendly. Knowing how to repair and build boats was also at a premium. Explorers might benefit from experience in contact diplomacy, and traders from a fuller sense of what each microregion had to sell and wanted to buy. Language skills must have been at a premium. Other kinds of expertise travelled with settlers and travelling craftsmen. It is not possible to document early transfers of knowledge about how to cultivate olives and vines, about how to use the potter's wheel, and how to make kilns that could safely fire pots at high enough temperatures to produce hard shiny tableware that was almost as good as the metal plates used by kings and heroes. There was information about calendars, about weights, and about calendars.

Alongside this practical knowledge came the information that wine-drinking was something elites did, that a knowledge of myth was a necessary cultural accomplishment, and that athletics were the noble companion of warrior culture. Around the Mediterranean Sea in particular a shared aristocratic culture was emerging, the basis for forms of hospitality that crossed ethnic or linguistic divides.[9] What began with a shared sympotic culture would end up with Roman nobles learning Greek philosophy. Some Greek manufactures still travelled farther than the information they set out with. We find strange and un-Greek uses of things on the fringe of the Greek lake. It is thanks to the barbarous Thracian practice of hoarding and burying Greek silver plate that so much of it has survived. For similar reasons much of the finest Attic pottery comes from rich graves in central and southern Italy. But in most cases, those who had acquired a taste for Greek things and had learned how to make them for themselves soon internalized Greek ideals and adopted many Greek habits, such as the symposium, the aristocratic drinking party.[10]

Greek temple architecture provides another example of this process. Greek temples appear in the eighth century B.C.E. and to begin with were small structures built of timber and mud-brick that closely resembled the *megara*, the halls of Iron Age chieftains. Within a few generations temple-building had become *the* communal activity around the Mediterranean, rivalled only by warfare. By the early seventh century temples were by far the biggest buildings being built by Greek communities, and some non-Greek ones as well.

The centre of the Greek temple was a *naos*, a room for the gods and for his or her possessions. Many contained statues made of terracotta, bronze, or stone, some of which the gods were believed to inhabit. Prayer and sacrifice typically took place in front of this building, but within the sacred precinct, the *temenos*. By the start of the sixth century the largest were being built in stone—local limestones in some areas, marble in areas that had access to it. Their roofs were made of stone slabs or terracotta tiles.

Greek builders drew on construction techniques developed in Egypt and elsewhere in the Near East, but they did something different with them.

Around the *naos* was a portico supported by columns. The temple might be approached by steps on each side. The buildings were visually entrancing. Temples became elaborate scaffolds on which to display sculpture of various kinds. The tops of the columns could be elaborated as in Egypt, with flowers, geometric shapes, or later scrolls. Space was soon found for *metopes* (blocks of relief sculpture) and friezes, which often depicted battles—Greeks versus Lapiths, Lapiths versus centaurs—or processions in a way that invited viewers to walk around the temple following the action. Sculptural groups might be placed in the triangular spaces under the pitch of the roof at either end, or on the roof itself. Scenes from myth or gatherings of gods looked down on their mortal worshippers. The ornaments, tiles, and statues were painted in bright colours and gods and heroes given bright metal spears and weapons. They must have been an impressive sight in the middle of small towns of mostly rather simple houses.

Temple-building projects of this kind consumed vast quantities of labour. They could only be undertaken by entire communities, and their construction brought communities together. The largest took decades to construct, and each was literally the work of an entire generation. How did you know you were an Aeginetan at the end of the sixth century? Because in one way or another, you had contributed to building a splendid new temple for your goddess Aphaea to replace one that had burned down a generation before. On one pediment was a battle scene showing the local hero Telamon fighting Laomedon at Troy; on the other his son Ajax during the Trojan War. The temple was built on a hilltop visible from all over the island and beyond it. For a generation that had seen the Persians retreat from their invasion of Greece, it was a spectacular display of civic pride.

This idea of a temple—a home for a god, equipped with columns and roof of marble or tile, and lavishly decorated—spread rapidly around the Mediterranean. The Elymians of Segesta built a huge temple in the sixth century, their eyes drawn by the great temple-building projects of Greek cities in Sicily. Etruscans borrowed the Greek design around the same time, but adapted it. The typical Etruscan temple was approached only from the front and often stood on an artificial podium of stone. As in Greece, there were close relations with domestic architecture. Unlike in Greece, the classic Etruscan temple continued to be built of wood and brick with ornament in stucco. Etruscan statuary was more likely to be of terracotta than stone, but there were the same columns at the front and the statues on the pediment and roof were often spectacular. Some of these differences were simply adaptions to the different resources of Tuscany, which had no marble but was rich in clays and in soft volcanic tufas that were good for providing foundations and podia. There were differences in taste and aesthetic at play too. The marked frontality of Etruscan temples and the style of their decoration recalls that of the grand tombs and houses of Etruria.

Imitation, borrowing, appropriation. How should we imagine the traffic in ideas and styles across this network of tiny but closely connected cities? Some travellers must have been inspired by what they had seen abroad, and tried to recreate it at home. This is still the best explanation for how Egyptian temples and Egyptian statues became the models for their distinctively Greek counterparts. Probably there were effects that Greeks were at first unable to duplicate exactly, but soon they were not trying to make exact copies. The Greek temple, in which Egyptian monumentality was grafted onto the *megaron*, is a good example of this planned hybridization. The development of monumental nude statues in the sixth century—the *kouroi* and *korai* that were set up in sanctuaries and also as grave markers— had a similar descent from Egyptian sculpture. Techniques were learned and some stylistic components retained, but something new was also added, most likely reflecting features of earlier images made in perishable materials like wood. Admiration inspired imitation, working with new materials produced innovation, and an established sense of what was beautiful found compromises with a new alien standard. Presumably there was no deliberate or conscious attempt to create a new set of standards. But the existence of a network of cities meant some early experiments were bound to be canonized and imitated in turn.

Sometimes rivalry *was* the object. Temple-building around the Saronic Gulf in Greece in the sixth and fifth centuries B.C.E. looks a little like an arms race, each city trying to create bigger and better temples on points of high visibility. The temple of Poseidon at Sounion remained a landmark for centuries: it was the first sight of Greece for Pausanias, travelling from Turkey in the second century C.E. The temples on the Acropolis and Acrocorinth in Athens and Corinth, the Temple of Aphaea on Aegina (see Figure 21), and several others proclaimed the achievements, wealth, and piety of the communities that had built them. Those communities watched their neighbours and tried to outdo them, particularly in the public sphere. Less obviously, they also watched their neighbours' mistakes and tried to learn from them. Some anthropologists think that social change is actually

Figure 21 Temple of Aphaea on Aegina
orangecrush / Shutterstock.com

accelerated when a group of autonomous communities works in parallel in this way.[11]

The story of the spread of the temple finds many parallels. The development of arms and armour followed a similar pattern. Sometime around the end of the eighth century B.C.E. Greek warfare came to rely more and more on massed groups of infantrymen, fighting with spears in a tight formation called a *phalanx*. When this was fully developed each soldier carried a very heavy shield, wore a bronze helmet, and carried a sword as well as his heavy spear. Infantrymen of this kind are called *hoplites*. Some were also equipped with body armour and greaves. Elements of this package were inspired by weapons in use in the Assyrian Near East, in Anatolia, even in central Europe. But it was the Greeks who put them all together into the hoplite panoply. Many aspects of the rise of the hoplite remain controversial. Some researchers think this style of fighting can already be detected in Homer's poems in the great surges of foot soldiers that form the background to the duels fought between heroes mounted on chariots.[12] Was hoplite equipment invented to make this sort of scrum warfare more effective? Others think equipment and tactics were developed together, perhaps very rapidly as part of a revolution that also affected politics, by making it essential to involve the hoplite class in the political order.

However the hoplite panoply arose, it was immediately imitated and modified around the Mediterranean world including in some societies that were not organized at all like Greek poleis. By the fifth century there were Carthaginian and Etruscan hoplites, and Carians, Lycians, and Lydians were apparently equipped this way as early as the Persian Wars. Not all these peoples fought in phalanxes. Few had political institutions like those of classical Greek cities. Etruscans fought in loose war bands, even when clad as hoplites.[13] Some Italian warriors gradually lightened the weight of the full hoplite panoply to make it easier to fight on rough ground or in more open formation. Early Roman armies replaced the thrusting spear with a heavy javelin and relied more on their swords when they came to close combat. By contrast to the north, in Macedonia, a version of the phalanx appeared in which a much more dense body of infantrymen used even longer spears, which had to be held with two hands. This was the core of the armies with which Philip and Alexander would humble the Greeks and then seize control of the Persian Empire. The advantage was a dense mass of spears at the front; the cost was that the shield had to be lightened. Information flowed back and forth and technologies were rapidly shared, but the result was not a broad homogenization because in the end, local priorities prevailed.

The traffic in people, goods, and information resulted in an acceleration of technological change. These changes were once termed "Hellenization," rather as the appropriation of Near Eastern motifs and craft technologies in the archaic period was once called "Orientalizing." But the emergence of distinctive local traditions in regions like Etruria and Macedonia shows the aim was rarely simple imitation. Instead we can see how new ideas were exchanged across a broad but loose network, and then time and again adapted to suit local needs and local tastes. Socially and politically the Mediterranean in the age of the city-state remained fragmented. There was no pressure to standardize. Regulation, such as it was, never reached beyond the limits of the city-state. Production of most things was local, so there were no industrial pressures to conform. Some convergence came about simply because one kind of shield or sword was superior to its competitors. Otherwise it was all about local choice, and even when they chose to do things the same way as their neighbours, that was a local choice too. The connecting of the Mediterranean world has been compared to modern globalization. There are some similarities, but in antiquity goods escaped the control of their makers much more quickly. Communication did not create multinational companies nor huge inequalities of wealth. The network connected many small worlds, in which power and authority was fundamentally based in small polities.

Cities provided the centres for those polities and the nodes of this network. When we look at its power to connect and see common forms like the alphabet, coinage, temple architecture, or the hoplite panoply spread across the Mediterranean it is easy to imagine the cities were great economic powerhouses. This was not the case. Most cities remained tiny, with populations in the low thousands. Most buildings within them were extremely small-scale compared to the temples at their hearts.

By the sixth century a few cities were emerging from the pack. Some were central nodes, better connected by geography or human effort than others. Some of the new leading cities possessed precious resources in land, crops, metals, or stone. Competition, communication, and interaction all allowed some to pull ahead. The network restructured itself, acquiring centres and creating peripheries. This process is too familiar from the modern world to require more explanation.

But there are some extraordinary examples. Corinth, just south of the isthmus that connects the Peloponnese with the rest of Greece, had two harbours: Cenchrae, which opened onto the Saronic Gulf and therefore to the seaways to Attica and the Aegean, and Lechaeion on the Gulf of Corinth, which opened west to the Adriatic, Sicily, and Italy.[14] It also controlled the isthmus that linked joining the Peloponnese to central and northern Greece. From around 600 B.C.E. a paved drag way called the *diolkos* allowed ships to be pulled across the isthmus from one sea to the other, so that sailors could avoid the hazardous circumnavigation of Cape Malea to the south. Corinth became a byword for wealth. There was also the great sanctuary at Isthmia where games honoring Poseidon were held every other year beginning in the early sixth century. Corinth flourished early and was hailed as mother city by many new foundations in the west. The centrality of Corinth in the emerging network was a product both of good fortune and design. Its great period of growth in the late seventh and early sixth centuries coincided with the rule of the Cypselid tyrants, who made the most of its geopolitical advantages. Athens, Samos, and Syracuse all had archaic tyrannies. Economically most did well from them.

Island cities were generally less populous just because they had less territory to farm, but in some cases their natural resources made them prominent. By the middle of the last millennium B.C.E. marble quarries were opened up on Naxos and Paros, and these cities too became briefly rich. Some larger islands were divided between a number of city-states: that was the case with Rhodes and Lesbos. But Samos, populous and rich, and lying just off the coast of Asia Minor, was unified early. The city was wealthy from archaic times through to the Roman period.[15] Farther west Etruscan cities with ports flourished—Caere, Tarquinia, and Vulci—as did the best connected cities of Sicily, Greek Syracuse, and Phoenician Motya. The greatest of the Phoenician settlements in the west was not the earliest, but Carthage was well placed to exploit the agricultural riches of North Africa and to dominate the western seaways to Sicily and Etruria. All around the Mediterranean Sea a shallow hierarchy of cities began to emerge, one based not on imperial power but on good connections.

Cities of Stone

A node is an abstract concept. What about the hardware on which the network was run? What did the first Mediterranean cities look like as they came to be connected across the waves? The temples that dominated their low-rise cityscapes were perhaps the only sign that something more was going on than village life. But there were other changes too, first gradual and then more and more striking, until the urban world was visually completely different to its rural counterpart.

One of the first signs of this transformation was the appearance of a sharper boundary between the area occupied by the living and the area occupied by the dead. At first, in central Italy as well as in Greece, the dispersed areas of housing that were growing together into cities were separated not only by fields and gardens but also by small graveyards. From the seventh century on this began to change. Cemeteries began to be placed at a distance from where people lived and worked, until they surrounded an area that was still not densely inhabited or built-up but was recognisably a bounded space. Some necropoleis—literally cities of the dead—began to be organized in the same way as cities were, with street grids and rows of near identical plots. Spend a little time walking among the tombs at Cerveteri or Orvieto and you can see why the term "necropolis" seems appropriate. Beyond the cemeteries the landscape was farmed, with a mixture of arable crops and fruit trees, dotted with little houses and hamlets. It was now recognizably rural. Homer's vision of mighty walled cities surrounded by grain-giving fields dotted with the funeral mounds of heroes was—on a small scale—coming to life. There would be no palaces in the interiors of the cities of this period, but slowly the size of houses was increasing.

Three developments made this possible.

First, populations were growing. We have no exact figures for ancient populations but archaeologists and historians are agreed that populations were rising very slowly throughout the late millennium B.C.E. We can see this in the number of settlements known from each period, in the size of the larger cities, and in the scale of cemeteries. We know for certain that the classical world of the fifth and fourth centuries was much more populous than that of the early Iron Age.[16] The landscape had filled up; the urban network had grown, as had its largest nodes; and the scale of what could be achieved in building or warfare or agriculture had grown enormously. The best current estimate is that the population of the Mediterranean Basin grew on average at roughly one-tenth of a per cent per annum. That does not sound like much, but over the centuries the cumulative effects were significant. A population of around 15 million at the start of the Iron Age might have grown to one of around 60 million by the middle of the second century C.E. (this estimate includes the areas of temperate Europe that eventually became part of the Roman Empire).[17] All this is very approximate, of course. But if we combine that slow underlying upward trend with the way larger centres emerged by concentrating populations that had formerly lived scattered in smaller villages, we get some sense of how urbanization was possible. It has been estimated that Athens had maybe 1,000 inhabitants in 1000 B.C.E. and perhaps 7,000 in 700 B.C.E. At its peak, in 400 B.C.E. after nearly a century of leading a regional hegemony that became a maritime empire, the population maybe rose as high as 35,000 and it was the biggest city in the Aegean world, as Syracuse was in the western Mediterranean.

Demography drove everything, because people power was fundamental. This was a world without many sources of energy beyond the muscle of humans and their companion species. More people meant more energy to farm, to mine, to build, and to fight. As late as the fifth and fourth centuries B.C.E.—the classical era—we can see from inscribed records of expenditure on building at Athens that much of the hard labour had to be done in the quieter periods of the agricultural year.[18] That was true of warfare too. Archaic warfare involved only a small proportion of the population.[19] Over time more and more adult males were involved. Even so, classical warfare was almost always a matter of annual campaigns of a few weeks at most. Ancient states did not have the infrastructure or resources to supply armies in the field for long. There were no professional soldiers, and so even in long drawn-out conflicts like that between Athens and Sparta in the fifth century, there was generally an annual pause to farm, repair, recoup, and prepare for the next campaigning season. When there was no war to be waged, those same adult citizens (with their slaves in Athens at least) might take part in public works. Domesticated animals could help a little. Oxen helped plough larger farms, donkeys and horses helped with larger loads, and some elite soldiers even rode to battle where they dismounted to fight on foot in the phalanx. When conflict moved to the sea, as it did in the Peloponnesian War between Athens and Sparta in the late fifth century or in the first Punic War between Rome and Carthage in the third century B.C.E., the warships were mostly powered by oarsmen. In the end, it all came down to people power. That is the reason population growth—and slavery—underpinned all other changes in the archaic and classical periods.

The second key factor that allowed for the physical transformation of cities was a series of architectural and technical developments. The Greeks had learned many of these from neighbouring societies, and the skills moved rapidly across the urban network that connected the Mediterranean world. They had learned to manage the fantastically hard marbles that occur around the Aegean coasts and islands, to quarry and saw and transport and carve and polish huge masses of stone. Quarrying alone required new metal tools, and a better understanding of pulleys and other transport devices. Making use of very heavy stone was no mean feat. Meanwhile in Italy, Etruscan architects were applying some of the same skills to master a different set of rocks, soft tufas, hard basalts, and so on. By the sixth century terracotta roofing tiles were in use for the first generation of monumental temples and for some houses as well, from Anatolia to central Italy. Some of the larger buildings required timbers that had to be obtained from some distance, since the dry lands of much of the Mediterranean had no great forests.

All these developments recapitulated technical advances made during the Bronze Age in Egypt and the Levant. It is certain that the knowledge of how to create monumental buildings was acquired from those sources, along with the inspiration for life-size and larger statues of humans and mythical beasts. Greeks and Etruscans used these skills, along with the new power their growing populations gave them, to make something new. All the same, we can often sense the source of this or that idea. Origins do not explain that much, of course. Greeks had been going back and forth to parts of the Levant for centuries before they began to build cities in stone. Only when they had the manpower to use these techniques was it useful to know how to apply them.

The third key development was in organization, in the management of people. A large population makes little difference if it cannot be marshalled to work together. Near Eastern cities were often built at royal command, with entire populations moved to construct, inhabit, and feed a new city. Greeks could see this for themselves if they travelled up the Nile to Luxor and Karnak, where a great processional way lined by sphinxes led visitors into a series of vast spaces, internal halls supported by columns, outside courts, even vast artificial pools. Any Greek or Carian mercenary who found his way into the Assyrian heartland would soon encounter the massive wall-circuits and gates of Assyrian royal cities, each enclosing vast areas of housing for the transplanted populations that serviced imperial palaces. Yet this inspiration would have meant nothing if it had not been possible to organize quarrying and transportation and building projects, to decide on priorities, to gather workforces at times it was practical to do so, and subordinate all that energy to a particular goal. Many traditions about the archaic Mediterranean link great building projects with periods of tyranny. Polycrates, tyrant of Samos in the 530s and 520s, was reputed to have organized the building of a massive harbour wall, a great temple to Hera, and a water supply for his city. The Tarquins who ruled Rome off and on for much of the sixth century were credited (or blamed) for carrying out great drainage projects in the Forum and for commissioning the Temple of Jupiter on the Capitoline Hill. Peisistratos, tyrant of Athens in the middle of the sixth century, was credited with temple-building at Eleusis and in Athens and providing a water supply as well. There are many other anecdotes of this kind.

Almost none of the stories about builder-tyrants can be verified for certain. They ruled in a period when there were virtually no public inscriptions, and several generations before historical writing began; they were hugely controversial figures after their deaths; and debates about their contribution were already raging when history writing began. The archaeological traces of their monuments are difficult to date precisely in the absence of coinage or inscriptions. Most of these cities were rebuilt later in any case, in much more spectacular styles in the centuries that followed. All the same, we can be pretty certain that none of these projects could have been brought about by the sort of small-scale decentralized communities that populated Greece and Etruria in the tenth, ninth, and even the eighth centuries. Political communities that could not prevent sections of their population moving away every so often to create new homes could hardly have planned and carried out some of the most spectacular building projects of the sixth century. One reason that the creation of new settlements overseas petered out in the late sixth century is that it was precisely then that states became strong enough to contain and manage internal conflict. Tyranny, law codes, and constitutions held together communities that in earlier times would simply have fallen apart.

There are several indirect signs that the newly urban communities were coming to prefer a more organized and egalitarian existence. The segregation of cemeteries from living areas was just the first sign of this: it must have required either consensus or authority to bring about. Spatial divisions also became more fixed inside cities. By the sixth century both newly founded cities and their necropoleis were being organized on street grids. Attention was being given to drainage and water supply. Hydraulics is an important test of a community's commitment to organized living together, since typically canals, wells, aqueducts, and drains take time to create and rely on a long-term commitment to their maintenance. Some water channels cross the lands of several owners and villages, and often each group has to look after them or all will suffer. Growing communities also need places to meet for markets, for assemblies, for conflict resolution, and for collective rituals. Public squares began to be laid out, and their usage regulated. Mediterranean cities would by the fifth century have market officials, *agoranomoi, aediles,* and the like, with the responsibility of making sure markets could operate without dispute. They would regulate weights and measures, adjudicate disputes between buyers and sellers, and generally keep order. Eventually each square—an *agora* in Greek, a *forum* in Latin—would come to be surrounded by public buildings, indoor assembly areas, law courts, and offices. More permanent houses began to be built in stone and roofed in tiles, larger than had been made before but now respecting common roads. Potters' quarters and other messy industries like leather-working would be located a little way away from where people lived. Elegant gymnasia with gardens would also appear a little way away from the centre. The larger cities of the sixth century had little of this yet. But what we can see of their evolving topography shows that the first steps towards communal organization had been taken. Political communities with an urban consciousness were emerging.

12

Cities, States, and Kings

Getting Political

Herodotus tells a story about how the Phocaeans abandoned their city in 546 B.C.E., when it was attacked by the Persians. Putting all their families into fifty-oared vessels, they fled, leaving the Persians to take an empty town. Phocaea was one of those Greek cities that had been an early base for voyages of exploration to the western Mediterranean in the seventh and sixth centuries. The Phocaeans were remembered as among the first to contact the Tartessians of what is now southern Spain, and as the founders of cities on Corsica, in southern Italy, in Spain, and at Marseilles in France. All the same the refugees had difficulty in finding a new home, rejected first by the Greeks of Chios, and then defeated in a sea battle off Corsica by an alliance of Etruscans and Carthaginians. A few did end up with their kin in Corsica all the same, some others went to Elea in Italy, and few returned home and participated in the great Ionian Revolt again Persia in 500 B.C.E.[1] In Herodotus' *History* the relations of the Greeks of western Asia Minor with the Persian Empire form a prelude to the main subject of his investigation, Persia's unsuccessful invasions of the Greek mainland in the early fifth century B.C.E. The decision of the Phocaeans to abandon their ancestral home foreshadows the decision the Athenians would make at a key stage in the war, to abandon Athens and Attica and to depend on their naval power to resist the Persians.

These incidents introduce us to a new dimension of ancient Mediterranean urbanism. For the first half of the last millennium B.C.E. we have to reconstruct the history of urbanism entirely from material remains. Even when writing spread through the network of emerging cities, it was not used to record events, laws, constitutions, or histories. We can see very clearly the growing size of the larger centres, the concentration of settlement, the construction of temples and walls, and then the division of the city of the living from the city of the dead. Artefacts reveal trade and other exchanges across the networked seas. But alongside these material transformations there were other invisible changes underway. The inhabitants of these emergent cities were beginning to think of them in new ways. The Greeks of the fifth century had begun to imagine the city not just as a collection of buildings, but also as a group of families bound together by intermarriage and kinship, and a sense of common past in short as a political community. Those communities were imagined as extending back in time to the mythical age when gods walked the earth. They had relations with particular gods that lasted far longer than human lifetimes. So for example Athens was not just a place; it was the city of the Athenians who had always lived there, and the city of Athena too, who took special care of the Athenians even though she was worshipped everywhere.

At Athens the idea grew stronger over time. Athenians were a collection of families whose members owned all the land in the territory, and they did not marry strangers. It was this community of citizens which might, in principle, uproot itself and move to a new location, and yet still remain the Athenians. Uprooting was rare and never undertaken lightly. For the Athenians their common myths were linked to particular places. Athena and Poseidon had competed for the Athenians' favour on the Acropolis itself. Ancestral cult was paid by Athenian tribes at the tombs of the heroes all over Attica. Yet in the end the polis was portable because it was made of humans, not simply of buildings.

This strong sense of community comes into focus for us in the sixth century B.C.E., but that just is an accident of the evidence. The first histories were written in the fifth century B.C.E., reflecting a wide interest in the historical past that surfaces in other media.[2] Most of the Greek plays that have survived are set in mythical times: the lifetimes of Hercules and Theseus, events around the voyage of the Argonauts and the Trojan War, the story of Oedipus. But in 494 B.C.E. the poet Phrynichus presented his *Sack of Miletus*, inspired by the recent Persian conquest, and Aeschylus' *Persians* performed in 472 B.C.E. included an account of the Battle of Salamis. Recent events also appear—juxtaposed with myth—in some of the victory odes written by Pindar for aristocratic victors at Panhellenic festivals. Speeches made in the fifth and fourth centuries included allusions to past events, and quotations from the poems of Solon. There were memorials set up too, like the statue of Harmodius and Aristogeiton, heroes of the Athenian struggle against tyranny (as it was later remembered). By the middle of the fifth century when Herodotus of Halicarnassus, Hellanicus of Mytilene, Antiochus of Syracuse, and others started to gather a mixture of oral testimony and written records, there was a growing interest in knowing about the past of cities. Their work reached back into the sixth century because it could draw on individuals' memory and collective tradition.[3] But for the period before 600 B.C.E. they had very little information. What we have about that period has often obviously been made up later.

From this point on we can tell completely different kinds of stories. The names of real historical individuals appear for the first time. Sometimes we can even read their own words. This is where the political history of the ancient Mediterranean begins, and this is where the institutions of the state first come into sight.

Solon of Athens produced his famous law code while he held the office of archon. The date, according to the traditional (and very unreliable) chronology, was 594/593 B.C.E. This is around the same time the earliest of the Cretan law codes were drafted. Athens and Crete supply most of our evidence for early law codes, but there were many more examples. When Aristotle and his pupils began, at the end of the fourth century B.C.E., to gather constitutions from around the Greek and non-Greek world, they found hundreds of examples. Modern scholars have made their own collections of decrees, treaties, laws, and other public documents. Most date from the middle of the fifth century onwards.

For sixth-century Greeks the big issue was justice. Solon composed poems which presented himself as an honest broker, establishing a fair settlement between social classes, between owners and tenants, and other opposed groups. The surviving fragments of the Gortyn Code are also about justice, in this case largely the rights of husbands and fathers over their wives and children and slaves. Slavery is the pervasive background to many early laws, but not for humanitarian reasons. One major stimulus for law-making were disputes arising from property, and slaves were property. Law also emerged as a solution to faction fighting of all kinds: tribes, clans, different regions, rich and poor, followers of one charismatic leader or another. Solon was most concerned with tensions between the rich and the poor, a sign incidentally of economic growth. Only a part of Solon's laws dealt with what we would call constitutional matters. He defined the powers of the assembly relative to the magistrates, probably set rules for the councils, and most importantly, he proposed laws about citizenship. Solon's own poetry shows he was proud of marking citizens out clearly from slaves, of dividing the male citizen body into categories based on the property each owned, and of establishing an order that was fair for everyone. It was far from democratic and nothing to do with human rights, but it explicitly offered social justice. Probably that was common in the rhetoric of archaic state-builders across the Mediterranean.

Archaic Greek communities were not only divided along economic lines. Some cities—Sicyon for example—contained within them people who belonged to different tribes, different kinship groups perhaps. Now and again we hear of groups of families who claimed noble birth, like the Bacchiads who ruled Corinth or the Penthilids who ruled Mitylene. Those families in Rome who called themselves Patricians are another example: they claimed a monopoly of some priesthoods and for a while the greatest magistracies. "Good birth" is not the same as wealth. Some tensions probably arose from the impoverishment of some old families and the rise of new ones. There were also regional tensions in the larger communities. Attica in the sixth century was riven by conflicts between groups associated with the mountain, the plain, and the coast. Each was led by a major aristocratic family, and it is not easy to know how far they mobilized regional identities and how far they created them. What we do know is that at the end of the sixth century another Athenian archon, Cleisthenes, developed a fiendishly complicated set of constitutional measures designed to ensure equal representation for all the regions of the Attic state. His system relied on the creation of ten new tribes which were not territorially contiguous; that is, each included villages from all three divisions of Attica. This is a remarkable scheme. Greeks had gotten into the habit of trying to solve civic conflicts through political change. Many of these experiments were short-lived, and some failed, but the project—this faith in a political solution—really was revolutionary.

The invention of politics is just another term for state-formation. What these fragmentary law codes and accounts of civic strife reveal is an advanced stage of state-building around the Mediterranean. The early stages are not always well documented. Not much is known about how Etruscan city-states emerged in central Italy, because they did not use writing (or at least not monumental writing) to manage the process. But by the time the historical records of other peoples shed light on ancient Etruria the cities had magistrates, institutions, and laws just like their Greek contemporaries. The same applies to the Phoenician city-states of North Africa, Sicily, and southern Spain. Perhaps they brought with them some institutions from the Levant—kingship and the *karum* have both been suggested—or perhaps they worked it out for themselves on colonial grounds. But by the historical period they certainly had assemblies, councils, magistrates, and so on. There are not many signs, in fact, that in their essentials the political systems of Etruscan, Greek, and Phoenician city-states differed more among each other than, say, Greek ones did among themselves. City-states have been invented dozens of times in world history.[4] It is no surprise, given the ubiquity of urbanism and the needs that urban communities have always had for regulation, from within or without.

States generate documents. As a result, the origins of early Mediterranean states are much less well documented than their later stages. But there is indirect evidence we can use. For a start, civil strife was impossible before a community existed that could be disunited or reconciled. And before the archon Solon could propose new laws to regulate social injustice in Attica, the Athenian people must have existed, and his archonship shows there were already elected offices and so there was also some kind of assembly. Both in Attica and Etruria burial evidence suggests the emergence of broader-based groups within the seventh century, establishing their power against that of princes or chiefs.[5] These were not yet citizens and not yet everyone, but it shows a broadening based of power and wealth. Then there are the patterns revealed by the monumental temple-building, which began in the seventh and took off in the sixth century. Sanctuaries began to appear on the disputed borders of emerging states, and also at their centres. Often processions or "mirror cults" linked extra-urban sanctuaries with the centre, providing a spatial means of weaving the population together. This shows not just an increased capacity to organize the biopower of the community, but also that territory was being reorganized at the same time as society.[6]

These new practices can all be thought of as responses to the new difficulties posed by living close together as a result of demographic and economic growth. In all these ways and others, states came into existence around the Mediterranean. The numbers living even in cities of just a few thousand had crossed the threshold where humans' super-evolved sociality could resolve all problems. Bees or ants can form colonies of tens of thousands of individuals because there are in effect no interpersonal relationships to deal with. Our sociality depends on a web of one-to-one relations, and beyond a certain limit this becomes difficult to handle.

Alternatives existed, such as the old primate strategy of fission, the splitting of large groups to reduce tensions often followed by dispersal. The tactic worked—and still works—for mobile hunter-gather populations. But it is less and less feasible as the landscape fills up and as groups of humans acquire possessions. Perhaps some of the impulse for overseas migration came from this, but if so then those who departed left a good deal behind. Once a group invests in sedentarism, sows fields, plants trees, and builds houses, then fission and migration is a much more expensive way to reduce tension. Conflict resolution, which does not also entail a loss in biopower, is to be preferred. Greeks sometimes thought of this in terms of law replacing feud, of civic obligations superseding familial obligations. Yet in larger communities solutions also needed to be found to the problems of negotiating conflicts between groups of people, such as the Hylleis, the Pamphyli, and the Dymanatae at Sicyon, or the people of the plain, the coast, and the hill in Attica. State-building required different lineages, classes, tribes, and families to work together in peace and fight alongside each other in war. It depended on politics.

There is some reason to think that state-formation around the world has often been a response to issues of this kind, an attempt to manage change and minimize conflict in times of rapid change.[7] Many anthropologists and prehistorians used to think that states arose when one group of fairly peaceful and egalitarian villages persuaded the rest that state-building would allow a community to do something new such as irrigation farming, self-defence, or monumental building. Now it looks more like it was the violent conflicts arising from, among other things, population growth and sedentarism that forced societies to invent the state and develop laws. Tyrants could keep the lid on things for a while, but in the end laws and constitutions were needed to keep the peace. The state, like the city, was an equifinal solution to all sorts of problems. In the early Iron Age Mediterranean it looks as if it was most often a solution to the toxic consequences of demographic growth in a harsh environment.

Thinking It Through

Greek political thought began as a reflection on these processes, but its main concern was different and practical. Assuming one lived in a state—as all Greeks soon did—what was the best way for it to be organized?

Solon and his generation had argued for social justice, understood as an equitable distribution of privileges and property among the citizens. But defining justice was not always easy. Should it be the same for everyone? Or should it be proportional, perhaps to wealth as in those states where hoplites or the *prima classis* (the first division of citizens in Rome) had more say than the poor? Should some families have special privileges because they were hereditary priests, or had good birth, or were descended from the founders of a city? How could the property rights of the rich be reconciled with the rights of the poor to a living and a livelihood? Should the wise have more of a say than the uneducated, as Plato suggested? These were not esoteric intellectual games.[8] Politics provided a framework for making changes, however much one respected ancestral custom (*patrios nomos*). It followed that people wanted to know what happened to states where the masses ruled, or where the rowers were more powerful than the soldiers. What were the risks in entrusting power to the few or to a single person? What was the best size for a state? The debates could be endless, and in Greek cities where competition of all kinds—the *agon*—was central to individuals' pursuit of glory and honour, those debates were fierce. The texts we read are probably just a by-product of verbal discussions conducted at many levels of society.

Even before Aristotle began to compare civic constitutions systematically, there was debate over the rival merits of different political systems. Herodotus tells a very implausible story of a group of Persian noblemen debating whether their empire should be ruled by the many (a democracy), by a small group (an oligarchy), or by a king.[9] The idea of a democratic empire seems fantastical to us. Perhaps the foundation of the Persian Empire was just too good an opportunity for Herodotus to miss. Xenophon, writing a little later, offered up an equally fantastic story of the education of the first Persian king, Cyrus, as a contribution to the growing literature on what made a Good King. He also wrote an idealized account of the Spartan way of organizing the state, while Plato's *Republic* and his *Laws* are among the most early of utopian literatures. The debate over the "three constitutions" appears in Attic drama from the fifth century, in a passing reference in Pindar's second Pythian Ode, and in the political pamphlet known as the Old Oligarch, which may be our oldest piece of prose literature in Greek. All these texts assume that the differences between those three kinds of constitutions were *already* widely understood, and not just by those who read literature. This vocabulary obviously also belonged to the practice of politics. Political struggles in Mediterranean city-states often took the form of attempts to broaden or narrow the direct power of the citizens. Internal conflicts were sometimes connected to external ones, so that many cities sheltered groups of exiles from their neighbours and looked for a chance to support a coup. When Alexander the Great defeated the Greeks and imposed peace on them, one of his first demands was that exiles be allowed to return home.

Athens in the middle of the fifth century experimented with one of the most radical forms of direct democracy ever attempted. All male citizens might vote, all might serve on juries, and political office was (mostly) determined by lot. So powerful was the ideology of male citizen equality that it was dangerous to parade one's noble ancestry or one's wealth. Exile was a risk run by those who expressed antidemocratic sentiments. Some occasions were more suited to radical politics than others. The critique of democracy that surfaces in almost every prose text we have was probably elaborated in exclusive drinking parties, the *symposia,* where the wealthy could voice their dissent in private. By contrast, arguments for the merits of democracy were put forward by speaker after speaker at the assemblies and the law courts, where a broader public was assembled. Civic drama offered a rare place where political issues were considered in a more discursive mode. The questions were a little different. Aeschylus' *Oresteia* and Sophocles' *Antigone,* for example, both dealt in part with the issue of how to reconcile the overwhelming demands of family obligations with the duty of citizens to submit to the authority of the state. Athenian literature shines a particularly bright light on debates that must have been taking place much more widely, to judge by the alternation of democracies and oligarchies around the Mediterranean world. Perhaps this is one reason that these dramas, although written to be performed at civic festivals in Athens, circulated widely around the Greek world.

There was no general progression to or away from democracy. Local sequences varied, and some cities oscillated wildly. The cemeteries of Etruscan cities like Tarquinia suggest there was a period in which princes, or princely families, were dominant and that later period power became more widely shared. But the Etruria that emerges in the first historical accounts—some Greek, some Roman—is a landscape in which semifree peasants worked for a broad ruling class. Etruria had its own share of tyrants, among them some of the kings of Rome. Syracuse in the fifth century alternated between tyranny and democracy and was an oligarchy for part of the fourth. Other city-states never had constitutions that Greeks would have considered democratic. The earliest legends about Corinth record the names of kings. Their power was allegedly seized by the aristocratic clan of the Bacchiads in the middle of the eighth century. The Bacchiads were in turn overthrown by Cypselus, who with his sons created a tyranny that lasted from the late seventh until the early sixth century. From the 580s on Corinth was ruled by an oligarchy based on wealth rather than birth, one that endured with few changes until the Roman sack of 146 B.C.E.

Athens too had a convoluted political evolution. There was an attempted coup by Cylon, supposedly in 632 B.C.E., and between Solon's archonship and that of Cleisthenes there was nearly a century of chaotic conflict. Peisistratus ruled as tyrant on several occasions. He was twice expelled by one aristocratic family, the Alkaemonids, of which Cleisthenes was a member, and at least some Athenians thought Cleisthenes' political changes were primarily a populist measure or a strategy of desperation because he could not win within the existing system. Herodotus' remark "He took the people into his party" shows the controversy that still surrounded the origins of Athenian democracy nearly a century after its creation. Radical democracy looks almost an accidental product of a solution to a different problem: conflicts between regionally based factions in Attica, each of which was associated with particular aristocratic clans. Cleisthenes devised a complicated constitution involving the creation of ten tribes, each of which include a noncontiguous selection of villages (demes), to break up those power blocks. The effect was to give more power to the assembly of citizens, and especially to those in or near Athens. Cleisthenes' political system was not left unchanged: nothing legitimates revolution like a tradition of revolution. There were several modifications, led especially by those who used the assembly to expand citizen rights beyond the propertied classes, who had had a special place in the state since Solon. The creation of the radical democracy is usually dated to the 460s. There was then a brief attempt to reverse this after Athens' humiliation in the Spartan War, but this was followed by an even more radical version.

During the fourth century (when Athens no longer had a naval empire) the restored democracy was bankrolled by the richest few hundred families, who paid for everything from ships to drama. It was one of the few ancient states where the rich got poorer over time. That system lasted less than a century. After Alexander's conquest of the Greeks, Athenian democratic institutions began to be limited. Under the influence of first Macedonian kings and then of Rome, Athens became much more of a conventional city-state, to the advantage of the wealthy. Many of its peculiar institutions, such as two councils and annually elected magistrates, endured for centuries, but the assembly no longer called the shots. The political evolution of Athens was more complicated than that of many other cities, as well as being better known. It was among the biggest cities in the Greek world, and at the centre of political conflicts from Sicily to Egypt. But on a smaller scale, political dramas were played out around the Mediterranean on hundreds of local stages. *Stasis*—civil conflict—was completely characteristic of the polis and only diminished when external power imposed order.

Kings

City-states were not the only kind of polity known to ancient Mediterranean peoples. There were also federal and tribal states, some of them quite urbanized, some not at all. There were leagues of cities dominated by a single city such as the Boeotian League, led by Thebes. In northern Greece and on the slopes of the Apennines were tribes with a few urban centres that came together at common sanctuaries.[10] Interspersed between all these systems—and sometimes taking them over—there were also autocracies of various kinds.

Plato, Isocrates, and Xenophon all reflected on what made a successful king. This too was a very practical consideration for many Greeks. From the archaic period on there were always some cities ruled by kings or tyrants.[11] The tyrants of Corinth and Samos had diplomatic connections with their Iron Age counterparts in Lydia and Egypt. The last tyrant of Corinth was named Psammetichos, a compliment to the pharaoh of the same name that was his father's guest-friend. The title *tyrannos*, as I have mentioned, was probably a Lydian term. Other titles were used too, including *asymnetes*, which seems to have meant something like an arbitrator. Many tyrants had hoplite bodyguards. At least some tyrants seem to have come to power because they could broker peace between social or tribal factions, and some used bodyguards of hoplites to enforce their settlements. The same was true of those Iron Age kings of Lydia, Palestine, and Egypt, who hired Greek mercenaries. There are example of this from western Asia Minor in Mitylene; Samos and Miletus; from mainland Greece where Athens, Sicyon, and Argos had famous tyrannies; and from the cities of Sicily, southern Italy, and Etruria. The city of Cumae on the bay of Naples had a famous tyrant, Aristodemos, who is said to have had some sort of alliance with the exiled tyrant of Rome, Tarquin the Proud. Roman legends describe various tyrants or kings. There were also hereditary kings (usually called *basileis*) in Sparta, in the Crimea, and on Cyprus. Autocracy was not simply a feature of the archaic period. Plato travelled to the court of Dionysius, tyrant of Syracuse; Xenophon spent a long period campaigning with Agesilaos, one of the kings of Sparta; Isocrates wrote speeches offering advice to the king of Salamis on Cyprus, to Archidamus, king of Sparta, to Philip of Macedon, and to Alexander of Pherae in Thessaly. Critics of democracy sometimes wondered whether well-directed kings might offer better solutions to some of the problems of their own day than could the masses.

Most of these tyrants and kings ruled in cities, taking on some of the functions of magistrates and sometimes priests, and making decisions that elsewhere were made by councils or assemblies. But in the Balkans there were kingdoms that had developed from a kind of chiefdom that was common in temperate Europe. Some came to include and dominate Greek cities, but they remained fundamentally tribal states. The central and northern Balkans were home to the kingdoms of the Illyrians, the Molossians, and the Macedonians. Macedon was briefly the westernmost province of the Persian Empire; later it expanded to unite under its rule Balkan and Thracian tribes and coastal Greek cities. During the middle of the fourth century Philip II became the dominant political force in mainland Greece and his son Alexander, who succeeded him in 336 B.C.E., led the great expedition that led to the capture of the Persian Empire.

Less famous is the Bosporan kingdom that under two dynasties ruled the Crimea for most of the fifth, fourth, third, and second centuries B.C.E. The Spartocids who ruled for most of this period were probably Thracian in origin, but their kingdom included Greek cities as well as a substantial hinterland. Their control of access to the grain lands of what is now the Ukraine and southern Russia made them rich and won them honours from Athens, which depended on the region for wheat. Hybrid states of different kinds existed elsewhere too, including in southern Italy and in the western Mediterranean. Sometimes the ruling class identified as Greek, sometimes not, but their economic rationale was based on harnessing the potential of local resources—grain, timber, and slaves in particular—and using the cities under their control to make connections to distant markets.

Empire

One monarch eclipsed all the others, so much so that he is often referred to in Greek texts simply as The King.

The Persian Empire, founded by Cyrus of the Achaemenid dynasty, was the largest political entity on the planet from the middle of the sixth to the end of the fourth century B.C.E. At its maximum extent the Achaemenid Persian Empire extended from Macedonia to the Hindu Kush, and included Egypt, Syria, Mesopotamia, and most of Anatolia, as well as the Iranian plateau and central Asia including Afghanistan. Like many early empires it was created relatively quickly through the conquest of a series of pre-existing kingdoms, in this case including those of Egypt, Babylon, the Medes, and Lydia. The Greek cities it encountered in the middle of the sixth century were first of all those that had been ruled by the kings of Lydia, and then those of the Aegean islanders and mainland Greece, which had never been ruled by others. The great theme of Herodotus' *History* is how Persian expansion faltered under the kings Darius and his son Xerxes. The defeat of their invasions of mainland Greece in 490 and 479 became for a while central to Greek political culture. It bolstered a sense of the superiority of Greeks over so-called barbarians. It provided foundation myths and justification for the local hegemonies led by Athens and Sparta in the fifth century. Eventually it inspired a series of kings, including Agesilaos of Sparta, Philip of Macedon, and Philip's son Alexander, to challenge Persia. Alexander's invasion in 334 B.C.E. led to the collapse of the Achaemenid dynasty, and his death marked the fragmentation of the empire he had conquered. Yet the Persian Empire has a good claim to be the inspiration for a whole series of later imperialisms in western Eurasia: those of the Kushans of Afghanistan and the Mauryas of North India, as well as the Macedonian dynasties of the Seleucids and Ptolemies, various Anatolian kingdoms like those of Pontus and Bithynia, and later Iranian powers including the Parthians, the Sassanians, and the empire of Rome itself.

Empire did not really offer an alternative to the city as a political form. They were built on different scales. It was never quite true that everyone in a polis knew everyone else, and so it was not really a face-to-face society. But even a polis as large as Athens could, through a complex coordination of local village politics, kinship, aristocratic friendship networks, and the institutions of the Cleisthenic state—deme assemblies, tribes, the gathering of all citizens, the two councils and the law courts—create a political community of several tens of thousands that had an intimacy difficult to imagine today.[12] Small cities, those typical cities of a few thousand inhabitants, must have found it even easier.

Empires, by contrast, were vast. All early empires included within them enormous social diversity, and most were so institutionally weak that they tended to use as much as possible of the governing machinery of previous states.[13] This was true of Rome and of the Macedonian kingdoms, and it was true of Persia as well. From the reign of Darius (521 and 486 B.C.E.) the empire was overlaid at the highest level by a series of provinces called *satrapies*, each with a governor and a corps of Persian soldiers and officials who communicated back to the king and his central bureaucracy at Persepolis, organizing tax, levies, and the provisioning of officials and soldiers. This structure applied from Egypt to Afghanistan, and a few precious archives of satrapal correspondence, together with records from Persepolis, show broad similarities in the way each part related to the centre.[14] Below this surface uniformity the empire was enormously diverse, and its success depended on its ability to adapt to local circumstances and make the most of local resources.[15]

Many satrapies contained within them urban systems of great antiquity. This was true of Babylonia, where city-states with their temples continued a tradition that went back to Sumerian roots. It was also true of Egypt, where the centralized Pharaonic state contained some of the largest urban settlements in the region but where nothing like citizenship existed. Egypt was divided into nomes, each of which had an administrative capital controlled by royal appointees. The pharaohs occasionally built vast cities for themselves, and by the Persian period the capital had come to settle at Memphis, near modern Cairo. The Levant and Syria had been divided into city-states since the end of the Iron Age. Most were subject to local kings or powerful temples. For much of the early first millennium B.C.E. this area, along with Mesopotamia, had been ruled by the New Assyrian Kingdom. This was in many respects the predecessor of Persia as a regional hegemon, and the Persians had adopted many of its technologies of control while presenting a very distinctive imperial style. Cities appear frequently on the royal reliefs of Assyrian palaces, often under siege by Assyrian armies deploying huge siege engines as well as great numbers of archers. Assyrians also moved subject populations around, especially when creating great dynastic cities like Nineveh, on the outskirts of contemporary Mosul. The royal cities of Assyria were enormous, provided with palaces and libraries and great irrigated gardens enclosed within huge wall circuits. Nineveh was built by Sennacherib in around 700 B.C.E. It covered an area of between 1,500 and 2,000 hectares, and according to the *Book of Jonah*, its population was more than 120,000. The Persians, whose territory in Iran was barely urbanized, also created a city for themselves, Persepolis ("City of the Persians") (see Figure 22). At the centre of Persepolis was an extraordinary palace decorated by sculptures drawing on a great range of traditions. But there were many other parts of their empire where cities were few and far between.

Greeks travelled extensively within the Persian Empire, especially in its western provinces, and some of what they saw found its way into historical writing. Greek cities were among the communities governed by the Persian king's western satraps, especially in what is now Aegean Turkey, and also in Cyprus. There were Greek craftsmen at Persepolis; Greeks served in Persian armies as levies and as mercenaries; the Greek doctor Ctesias attended the Great King; there were certainly some Greek slaves at court and some Greek exiles too, while travellers like Herodotus wandered around the provinces. After the shock of conquest, both the successful takeover of Ionia and the

Figure 22 The Achaemenid Capital at Persepolis
M Selcuk Oner / Shutterstock.com

less successful expeditions across the Aegean, relations between powerful cities and the King became a matter of diplomacy. During the fourth century Persian Kings and their satraps were often able to shape Greek politics using royal money to play one city-state off against another, or alternatively by imposing peaces.

Greek city-states were useful organs of government, and the hoplites they could supply were valued. Persians dealt similarly with Phoenician cities that supplied them with naval forces. Those too close to Persia to hope for freedom settled for a degree of local autonomy. Some received privileges, like Magnesia on the Maeander, which preserved for centuries a letter from the Great King assuring the rights of its great sanctuary. The temple city of the Jews at Jerusalem was rebuilt with royal support. There is no sign that the Kings tried to create cities where there were none, nor that they tried to promote urbanism except in their royal foundations. Their approach everywhere seems to have been more pragmatic. They worked with what they had.

City-States and Kings

By 400 B.C.E. there were around 800 Greek poleis in existence, most around the Aegean but also on the coasts of the Black and Adriatic Sea, in Sicily and southern Italy, in France around the mouth of the Rhône, on Cyprus, and in Cyrenaica.[16] Most of these thought of themselves as Greek by descent, although many had absorbed other elements and some were in fact joint foundations sponsored and protected by local chiefs. Real origins mattered less than the fictive ones that were already the stuff of religion and diplomacy.[17] Then there were the city-states created by other peoples. The oldest were the city-states of the eastern Mediterranean, Phoenician, Canaanite, Syrian, and a few others. In the southern and southwestern parts of what is now Turkey there were fifty-odd Carian and Lycian city-states. Like those in the Levant they were a part of the Persian Empire, but their architecture, their temples, their myths, and public inscriptions look increasingly Greek. At the other end of the Mediterranean the Etruscans, the Elymians, and perhaps others had city-states. Scattered among them were those cities of the Phoenician diaspora, as different among themselves as were the Greek poleis.[18]

Aristotle in his *Politics* concluded that human beings were social animals who reached their full potential for well-being when they lived in poleis. It is easy to see why he thought the city-state was the most natural form of political community. It seemed to have sprung up everywhere, and even kingdoms and empires—from his perspective—rested on urban foundations. Greek drama, even when set in the ancient past, imagined that past as a world of city-states. Thucydides, tracking the intricacies of the Peloponnesian War, thought he his work would be of permanent value. A future without city-states was as unimaginable as a past without them.

City-states did well in the ancient Mediterranean for several reasons. The political institutions that made up a democracy or an oligarchy were perhaps quite recent—like the great temples that expressed the centrality of the gods in the community—but they had their roots firmly in the period of regrowth after the Bronze Age collapse. As populations grew they often coagulated around Bronze Age centres, drawn to the tombs and citadels of their heroes. Tradition had a heavy inertial effect. Yet it was also the case that the corrugated landscapes of much of the Mediterranean created niches suitable to smaller political units. Good farmland was rare in many parts of the region, and snapped up in every period. Not every shore or island was composed of small coastal plains flanked by arid karst hillsides. Yet there were few rich river valleys to support the early development of larger states like those that had appeared in Bronze Age Mesopotamia and Egypt, or in the valleys of the Indus, the Yangtze, and the Yellow River. The low carrying capacity of the Mediterranean Basin and its geological fragmentation made city-states a common solution once population sizes began to grow. By the time larger states appeared—generally expanding into the Mediterranean from larger land masses, as had been the case with Lydia and would be with Macedon—it was easier to rule through city-states than to attempt to sweep them aside. These tiny communities had formidable institutions. Their economic success was extraordinary given their size. This made them tempting targets as well as useful tools. That meant that in a world of empires, the long-term success of the Mediterranean city-state was assured.

PART
III

Imperial Urbanisms

13

City and Empire

Imagine the Persian Emperor Darius surveying the Mediterranean world on the eve of his failed invasion of Greece, the Marathon campaign of 490 B.C.E. Behind him the Achaemenid Persian Empire stretched back eastward over Anatolia and Mesopotamia onto the Iranian plateau and beyond to Afghanistan, and south as far as the Hindu Kush and the borders of India. Looking westward, the shores and islands of the middle sea were divided among hundreds of cities and tiny tribes. It was not just the Aegean world that lived, fought, and died at the small scale. If he could have seen beyond to the valleys of the Balkans or to Italy on the other side of the Adriatic, it would have been the same. All around the Alps and the Atlas, along the Mediterranean coasts of France and Spain, on Sicily and the other islands, the Iron Age Mediterranean was a mosaic of tiny territories. Tiny cities—Greek, Phoenician, and Etruscan among them—lay along the shores. Behind them in the valleys and high plateaux were territories of villages, hill forts, and loose tribal federations. Darius' empire measured nearly 4,000 kilometres west to east. Attica on its longest axis was less than a 100 kilometres long, and it was a giant among city-states. The western frontier of Persian power marked the boundary between two worlds.

During the next half-millennium, that boundary collapsed. The political map of the Mediterranean was transformed as bigger and bigger political units appeared. These larger units were at first quite various. There were alliances, some relatively stable like the Peloponnesian League created by Sparta, some quite short-lived like the Greek alliance against the Persians. There were federal states like that of the Aetolians within which cities grew up, and leagues of cities like that in Boeotia or later Achaea, with formal constitutions. Powerful cities like Athens, Rome, Sparta, and Syracuse dominated their neighbours in informal ways we sometimes call hegemonies.

Sometimes these evolved over time into micro-empires, sometimes they fell apart. There were monarchies too, and groups of chiefdoms connected by dynastic marriages, as happened in the north Balkans. There were a few hybrid states like those of the northern Black Sea or the south of France, where cities and chiefdoms were closely connected. The city-state and the kingdom were the two fundamental building blocks in Mediterranean politics. Imperial projects arose from both. Most were short-lived, because the geographical pressures towards fragmentation were very powerful and because local identities and loyalties were so strong. Yet by the turn of the millennia the Mediterranean Basin had become a single political entity, one vast system of domination in which one monarch, the Roman emperor, ruled over and through two thousand cities and a cluster of lesser kings. This chapter takes the long view, from the empire of Darius to the empire of Augustus, and seeks to understand how the extreme fragmentation of the Mediterranean world was overcome.

A World in Pieces

Historians of the premodern Mediterranean world have returned again and again to fragmentation.[1] One reason the city-state has been such a successful form in the Mediterranean world was that it recognized and built on local particularities. It is the ultimate political manifestation of the idea that small is beautiful. More than in almost any other political system there is the possibility of local self-determination, or at least politics based on fairly broad participation. From a social evolutionary point of view we might see it as the most successful of the different local political experiments of the last millennium B.C.E. There were attempts to create tyrannies and kingdoms, short-lived mergers of cities in Sicily, and tribal states, but city-states were throughout antiquity and much of the Middle Ages the most durable feature of the human landscape around the Aegean and Adriatic Seas, in the western Mediterranean, and on many of the islands. Kingdoms and alliances have come and gone. But there are Mediterranean cities today that are more than three thousand years old.

The geography of the Mediterranean Basin makes all the difference. Prehistorians and historians rightly stress the small scale of most islands and the tiny coastal plains divided by bare mountains. Communities are caged, confined, and shaped by the terrain. Sea travel between nearby cities has often been easier than land travel. It has been remarked that even parts of the coast might as well have been islands in terms of how they were connected to the outside world.[2] Geographical fragmentation and its consequences have been especially important in recent work on Mediterranean history and archaeology.[3] Much of the ancient Mediterranean was impoverished and precarious, at least when we compare it to adjacent regions like the European interior or the Fertile Crescent. Mediterranean soils were often hard to farm, and regularly at risk from drought. But its fragmentation was also a blessing. Because the micro-regions into which it was divided rarely all suffered environmental stress at exactly the same time, help—or at least food—might be found just around the next headland.[4] The history of the Mediterranean has become the history of necessary connections—by canoe and sailing vessel, by trade and migration, by piracy and war, and last of all by empire.

The Mediterranean Basin is not uniformly fragmented, and not all populations face the same levels of risk. The Aegean coast of mainland Greece faces droughts far more often than the Tyrrhenian coast of Italy. Its soils, eroded off karst mountain ranges, have none of the fertility of the volcanic earth of Tuscany or Campania. Mediterranean summers are much fiercer in the south than on the northern coasts and many northern coasts are closely connected to low mountain ranges that provide water and timber. There are some relatively well-watered Mediterranean landscapes: the lower Rhône valley in southern France, the plain of the Po in northern Italy, parts of the north Aegean and the delta of the Nile, the valleys of the larger rivers that drained the Anatolian plateau into the Aegean. Not all the islands were small. The hundreds of small islands of the Aegean archipelagos are dwarfed by Corsica, Sardinia, Sicily, Crete, and Cyprus. Equally, there are regions that significantly less fragmented: the plain of Thessaly for example, or the Maghreb.[5] Some islands were not well connected, for example the Maltese and Balearic archipelagos. City-states thrived on the Aegean islands but they also did well on the shores of rich agricultural regions like the north coast of the Black Sea, and in Cyrenaica in what is now eastern Libya. "Mediterranean" is a formal description of a climate type, and is regularly applied to plant and animal species characteristic of the region, but historically it is a convenient but elastic category. The inland sea has certain unities, but it is also an empty space between three continents with characters of their own. Europe is also a promontory of the larger entity of Eurasia, open to the steppe as well as to the sea. Equally, the Levant is a margin of the Fertile Crescent, while its southern shores are as connected with other African societies by the sand sea of the Sahara, expanding and shrinking over time, as they are with other maritime peoples.

Tributary Empires in Western Eurasia

The combination of these alternative and intersecting geopolitics still made the Mediterranean a difficult world to connect up politically, at least in a stable way. The Persian Empire and its predecessors in southwest Asia did not offer much of a model for Mediterranean empire builders. Darius' defeat of the Asian Greeks and his and Xerxes' failed invasions meant that no Greeks would explicitly try to imitate Achaemenid Persia in the way some archaic tyrants seem to have looked to Lydia and late-period Egypt as models. During the years that followed the failure of the Persian invasions of the early fifth century B.C.E. "medizing" became a term of political abuse directed at Greeks, who it was claimed had taken the barbarians' side. Herodotus' *Histories* were written in the shadow of worsening relations between Sparta and Athens, the two cities that had led the resistance to Persia. His account is full of accusations and insinuations that this or that state had not done as much as it could have in the Great War. Not all Greeks agreed, and some were frustrated by the politics of their city-states. But those like Xenophon, who expressed their admiration for some Persians, were unlikely to be persuasive.

The great inland empires of Asia would in any case have been difficult to transplant into a Mediterranean setting. Herodotus' explanation for the defeat of Persia is subtle and complex, and at least part of it comes down to moral contrasts between Asians and Europeans, which were widely held in his day but read very uncomfortably today.[6] Yet his theme that Persia was defeated *because* of its wealth, not despite it, rings true in some respects. The logistical demands of supporting a huge army of levies were considerable. Darius had tried attacking across the Aegean, but there were limits on how many troops could easily be transported, and at Marathon his army was unable to establish a beachhead. Xerxes came by land as well as sea, but crossing the Hellespont and marching across the north side of the Aegean and down the eastern coast of Greece took far longer than expected. When the main part of the fleet returned—after defeat at Salamis, fought in late September 480 B.C.E.—the sailing season was almost over. A large part of the fleet was lost in storms on the way home. Overwintering in Greece was not much easier. The remnant Persian land army was defeated at Plataea quite easily the following spring. Darius' invasion of southern Russia in pursuit of the nomadic Scythians had also run into logistical problems. Both campaigns exposed the limits of this kind of empire.

The Persian Empire of Darius is an example of what historians call a tributary empire. Its economy was not that of a classic "conquest state," one based on constant raids that cowered their neighbours, supplied the army with booty, and the rulers with glory. Instead the Persians sought a more sustainable kind of rule. Subject peoples were required to provide regular payments of tax, along with levies of troops and labour, and in return were allowed a level of local autonomy under the oversight of Persian satraps.[7] Tributary empires provided virtually nothing else for their subjects, and mostly left them to run their own affairs so long as they remained loyal.

The Assyrian New Kingdom had pioneered this form of empire from early in the last millennium B.C.E. Assur was in origin a city-state ruling a territory, but Assyrians, including their king, seem to have thought of themselves as servants of the god Assur in the central temple of the city. Their wars were religious expeditions to add provinces to his territory or to compel clients to send him tribute. Clients were rewarded and some local princes and city-states were effectively treated as if they were Assyrian governors. Those who refused to send tribute or rebelled were punished with extravagant force. Whole populations were moved about, many deported into Assyria proper to work royal or temple land or build cities and palaces. On the walls of their great palaces, constructed in cities built by conscript labour, the dominance of Assyria is expressed in visual narratives of sieges, battles, and slaughtered enemies.[8]

Persian emperors were more likely to seek alliances with local rulers and peoples and to patronize local gods: Marduk in Babylon, Apollo on the Maeander, and Yahweh in Jerusalem all received favour despite the strong Zoroastrian monotheism of the Persian kings.[9] Tribute was raised and troops were levied, but neither monumental art nor literary accounts convey a sense of an empire built on terror. The contrast can be overdrawn, and violence always remained an option. All Persian governors had military forces at their disposal, and their kings had their share of revolts to deal with. But the palace at Persepolis was decorated with friezes of tribute bearers, and records there show that members of subject populations could sometimes find a place in the imperial administration. Doubtless the ultimate failure of

Assyria and the horrendous sack of Nineveh influenced the imperial strategies and styles of the Achaemenids, just as Macedonians and Romans would
later learn from their mistakes and build on their successes.[10] Empire was a
millennium-long work in progress.

Tributary empires have been invented several times in world history, in
the Far East and India as well as in the Near East, and in the Americas as well
as Eurasia.[11] One key to its success was communications. The Grand Canal
in China, the running paths built by the Inca up and down the Andes, and
the famous Roman roads are good examples. Darius built the Royal Road
from Sardis in the west to Susa in southwest Iran along which messengers
and more rarely armies could move at great speed. It was said that mounted
couriers could travel the whole distance of 2,700 kilometres in just seven
days. In reality the empire depended on an entire network of roads, but the
idea of a single royal road fascinated Greek writers.[12] There is a story that
the first Macedonian ruler of Egypt, Ptolemy the First, asked Euclid if there
was a quicker way to learn the subject, only to be told the was "no royal
road to geometry."

Building a royal road across the Mediterranean was not an option. Even
if a power did have the naval capacity, the open sea could be terrifying
in winter. Near Eastern emperors could levy vast armies and march them
into rebel territory, could move entire populations to distant places, could
demolish and rebuild cities and redraw borders at will. Their power was
phenomenal in those places where they could effectively apply it. None of
this was so easy across the fragmented lands around the Mediterranean Sea.
Perhaps it would not have been impossible. But Persian kings had other
concerns than conquering troublesome western barbarians, whom in practice they could manipulate quite easily by sheltering exiles and funding one
or other side in interpolis warfare. The Cypriot and Phoenician cities found
a place in the Persian Empire that was not too onerous. But presumably
the potential rewards of control of southern Greece were too few to com-
pensate for the costs and risks. After Xerxes there were no serious attempts
to extend Persian rule (as opposed to Persian influence) across the Aegean.

The key to all tributary empires was establishing strong ties between
local elites and the imperial court, relations that devolved most of the cost
of government in return for supporting the institutions and individuals on
which empire depended. There were many variations: some extracted profit
mostly through military levies, some imposed taxes on communities, some
extracted land to distribute to settlers from elsewhere in the empire, and

some used tax farmers. Most tributary empires had to rely on different local arrangements from one area to another. Assyrian, Persian, Macedonian, and Roman empires all began with a mixture of direct and indirect rule, of client princes, settlers, and local chiefs. But in the Mediterranean world one institution out-competed all others to become the building block of empire: the city-state.

Tyrant Cities

A good deal of confusion about the nature of early empires has come about by the habit of later empires stealing the clothes of their predecessors to try and seem more legitimate. The differences between modern and ancient imperialisms are usually profound. Modern European empires had dual origins. Economically they rested on the private ventures of sixteenth and seventeenth entrepreneurs. Trading posts, factories, settlements, and overseas colonies often operated under royal licenses. Explorers, settlers, and companies took the initial risks and decisions. Only when the consequences of those decisions began to impact on national politics did this intersect with the second pillar of modern empire, the rivalry between the monarchies of emerging European nation-states. Mercantile ventures became militarized and entirely new formations were created that straddled the globe. Yet few wanted to seem new, because ancient analogies conveyed some legitimacy. As a result, when they wanted a way to describe what they were doing, they often turned to the classics. Many chose some version of the Latin term *imperium* (empire), which in Europe had survived as a label for various mediaeval kingdoms.[13] Their new empires were as different from those of Charlemagne and Rome as they could have been. The empires created in the Industrial Age, strongly shaped by the hunt for raw materials and markets, were another thing entirely. It is confusing that we use this same basic Latin terminology to describe the global economic networks of the Victorian Age, the results of mediaeval and early modern competition for European primacy, and the Roman and pre-Roman domination of the Mediterranean. Classicism served different political ends in revolutionary France, Victorian Britain, and Fascist Europe: an accidental by-product is that it has made modern imperialisms seem much closer to ancient empires than they were in reality.

The language of empire in the fifth century B.C.E. was fundamentally different. For a start, it was extremely rare for anyone to attempt to destroy an existing city-state and annex its territory. Most Aegean poleis and Levantine city-states had ancient and deep roots. Even when their political institutions had changed over the centuries, the peoples in question—the Corinthians, the Lacedaemonians, the Romans, the Sidonians, the Athenians, and all the rest—believed their origins lay in a period accessible only through myth. Some felt they had been there forever, and most believed they were there to stay.

There were exceptions. The island of Lesbos in classical times had five city-states on it. Once upon a time there was a sixth, Arisbe, but Herodotus says its inhabitants had been made into slaves by their relatives in the city of Methymna. But this was a horror story about a rare kind of atrocity. From another story in Herodotus we can infer that Eleusis was an independent city before it was conquered by Athens, sometime before Solon's day. Then there was the series of wars that the Spartans waged against their westerly neighbours the Messenians. The land of Messenia was first conquered in the archaic period, before there were city-states as later Greeks understood them, but the Messenians did not forget who they were. The Third Messenian War was a long and bloody attempt to win independence in the 460s. It failed, but a polis of Messene was at last established with the help of Sparta's enemies in 369 B.C.E. In most cases, however, once a city-state was entrenched in the landscape it endured, often until the end of the Roman Empire.

Another category of city-states were aware of their origins in historical rather than mythological time. The poleis of Sicily and the west and those around the Black Sea did not feature in Homer and were not remembered as the birthplaces of the heroes. Some responded by developing mythic prehistories of their own. Hercules turned out to have visited many famous sites, Rome included, long before the date the city celebrated as its foundation. Trojan refugees and Greek heroes swept a long way off course on their journeys home, peopled the western Mediterranean and the Adriatic. Tarentum, Marseilles, Carthage, Syracuse, and Rome had dug their roots deep well before the fifth century B.C.E.[14] All the same it does seem that some Sicilian and south Italian cities were a little more prone to redrawing the political map. There were destructions, as happened at Sybaris, but there were also mergers. At the start of the fifth century the tyrant of Gela conquered a number of other Sicilian cities and his successor used their combined army to conquer Syracuse, which he then made his capital by transferring populations from other cities to make it the most powerful city-state on the island, especially after a marriage alliance with the tyrant of another major city, Akragas. Yet even in the west the durability of cities—and civic identity—is really striking. Almost all those we know to have been created in the eighth and seventh centuries were not just still surviving, but also still organizing the human landscape half a millennium later when they began to be incorporated into various Roman territories.

Mediterranean empires rarely abolished city-states and unlike their Near Eastern analogues, they rarely transplanted populations.[15] Instead they exercised their power through them, in the time-honoured manner of tributary empires. Generally they left them in the hands of local allies and allowed them to manage local affairs in their own way, so long as they complied with commands and provided whatever tribute of crops, money, or troops was demanded. The original terms used for that power—*arche* (rule) and *hegemonia* (leadership)—were words that could be used of the power of individuals too. The same was true of Rome: *imperium* literally means the power to give orders. City-states and their populations were imagined in the same terms as individuals: as leaders, subjects, or slaves.[16] Time and again around the Mediterranean city-states and kingdoms exported their domestic power relations onto the international stage until there were cities that were enslaved to other cities, client cities, and even tyrant cities.

Hindsight allows us to see how these proto-empires emerged from their different origins, becoming more alike over time as they each learned—sometimes the hard way—what strategies worked for a tributary empire. To begin with, *arche* meant power exercised over a group of existing city-states. The beginning was often alliances between unequal partners. This was true of Rome and it was true of the great alliance between southern Greek states that faced the Persian invasion of 479. Sparta provided the commanders, although matters of tactics were debated in battlefield councils and matters of strategy—such as where to face the Persians—were decided by interstate diplomacy. All of this we see through the eyes of Herodotus, who had to deal with rival accounts of which generals and states had done the most (or least) on the day. He was convinced the Athenians were chiefly responsible for Greek resistance, but even so he made it clear that Sparta had the place of honour in the alliance. Spartan leadership was based on their military reputation and on the fact that a number of smaller poleis south of the Isthmus of Corinth were already in effect unequal allies.

Why Sparta? Because by the time of the Persian Wars the Spartans—
properly the Lacedaemonians—already controlled two-fifths of the
Peloponnese, making them the largest polis by far. This was the result of
a kind of internal imperialism in which the city of Sparta had created an
elaborate state within the valley of the river Eurotas, the heart of the land of
Laconia.[17] Their state included not just their full citizens—the Spartiates—
but also inhabitants of some surrounding town, the *perioecoi*, and a great
mass of subject people, the helots. Helots were in many respects like slaves,
although they were not owned by individual Spartiates. They worked the
land and their labour allowed Spartiates to specialize in war, undergoing a
ferociously fierce training regime and living in military messes apart from
their family for much of their adult life. How that system emerged is lost
in prehistory. Some features of Spartan society—the common messes, for
instance—are known from other states. But what the system the Spartans
made of them was unique. The key elements seem to have been in place
by the middle of the seventh century, when they are listed in a document
known as the Great Rhetra. But there is a strong sense that Sparta became
more and more different over time, and perhaps the totalitarian militaris-
tic society that fascinated and appalled other Greeks only really appeared
in the sixth century. That particular local combination turned out to be
fantastically powerful. Sparta exported the helot system to Messenia early
on, and fought a series of wars around the Peloponnese in the seventh and
sixth centuries. Almost all the states south of the isthmus eventually came
to accept Spartan leadership. Only the Corinthians maintained much independence within the group that came to be known as the Peloponnesian
League.

Spartan leadership was already acknowledged far and wide in the sixth
century.[18] Croesus, the last king of Lydia, and the Ionian rebels both sought
alliances with the Spartans and also with the Athenians. Sparta was also
prepared to take on Polycrates, the tyrant of Samos. During the reign of
Cleomenes (519–490 B.C.) the Spartans were the major power in mainland
Greece and beyond. Sparta was behind the end of the tyranny of Peisistratus'
son Hippias in Athens. It was Spartan pressure that led to the exile of
Cleisthenes' family, the Alkmaeonids. Sparta defeated the city of Argos and
intervened in the politics of the city of Aegina. When Xerxes' invasion
began in 480, Sparta was persuaded not to fortify the isthmus so as to leave
central Greece to its fate. The heroism of Leonidas and the three hundred

Spartiates at Thermopylae, and the victories at Salamis in 480 and Plataea in 479, both under Spartan leadership, consolidated Sparta's reputation.

Sparta's main rival in the fifth century was Athens. Attica, like Laconia, was a territory far larger than most city-states. Athenians fought and won a number of land battles over their neighbours. But their imperial ambitions rested on sea power. Athens had staked a claim to Sigeum in the Troad (in northwestern Turkey) before 600 B.C.E. The general Militiades seized the Thracian Chersonesus, on the European side of the Dardanelles, on the instructions of the tyrant Hippias in 524 B.C.E. Both sites were important as they gave access to the Black Sea, from which Athens was already importing wheat before the Persian invasion. During the sixth century Athens captured the island of Salamis in the Saronic Gulf. From the early fifth century the profits of the silver mines at Laurion in Attica were hypothecated to building up the Athenian fleet. The growth of the fleet proceeded at the same time as the growing influence in politics of the poorer citizens, who provided the crews. Reactionary figures deplored the "rowers' democracy" and at the end of the fifth century there was an attempt to limit political participation to the hoplite classes.

One thing the primacy of Sparta and Athens shows is that hegemony did not arise from one particular kind of political system. The two poleis were not as completely different as was sometimes claimed: both were based on broad participation, both depended on subjected noncitizens, and their religious differences were slight. But they did represent different political formulae and also ones that diverged in the course of the sixth and fifth centuries, as Athens extended full participation well beyond the hoplite classes and subjected its elites to more and more scrutiny while the number of full Spartiates shrank and the power of its kings rose.

Around the Greek Mediterranean city-states were experimenting with a wide range of constitutional and political forms. Yet when it came to building power beyond the city-state, they all behaved in more or less the same way. These micro-empires all consisted of clusters of bilateral alliances and treaties, necessarily calibrated to the different scales and locations of lesser allies, and they extracted military support above all else. Athens was unusual in extracting financial tribute as well, and Athens is the only case where the city-state came close to being transformed into some other kind of imperial nation, one with a common coinage, a common myth of origin, and perhaps even a common identity.[19]

Athens was not the only naval power in fifth-century Mediterranean. Corinth, with its twin harbours giving access to the Aegean and the Adriatic via the Saronic and Corinthian Gulfs, provided a major part of the Greek naval effort against Persia. Three of the larger east Aegean islands—Chios, Lesbos, and Samos—also had navies. Farther west the Corinthian colony of Corcyra and the city of Syracuse were major powers. But none could rival Athens in the number of ships it could field. At its height the Delian League numbered several hundred members. Most were tiny, and it was possible from the beginning for them to make an annual contribution in cash rather than provide ships of their own. Of the two hundred-odd members in 441 B.C.E. around 70 per cent contributed a talent or less each year.[20] The money went to a common treasury, first held on Delos. Athenian citizens were paid to man warships. By stages this league became more like a tributary empire, if a very small one indeed. An early sign of its coercive nature was when first Naxos in 471 and then Thasos in 465 were prevented by force from leaving. Then in 454 the common treasury was moved from the island of Delos to Athens. Around 449 peace was made with Persia, removing the original pretext for the alliance. Yet payments continued, and at the same time the Athenians began to build impressive new monument on and around the Acropolis (see Figure 23). Meanwhile, relations between Athens and Sparta deteriorated. Short episodes of warfare alternated with peace treaties, but

Figure 23 The Athenian Acropolis
Aerial-motion / Shutterstock.com

the multiplicity of arenas in which the interests of one state clashed with those of the another or its allies multiplied, and fulloblown war started in 431 and lasted until Athens' comprehensive defeat in 404 and involved powers from Sicily to Persia. It was the first Mediterranean-wide conflict in history.

Hegemonies

Why was it that during the second half of the last millennium B.C.E. the Mediterranean become a battleground for great powers, after its millennia of splendid fragmentation?

Ancient testimony is not much help here. Most ancient writers were more concerned with explaining the outbreak of individual wars than shifts in their scale. Thucydides, the historian of the Peloponnesian War, is a partial exception. He argued that despite myths about King Minos of Crete's naval power and the Trojan Wars, the Greek world had until recently been far poorer and weaker than in his own day. He was correct. The most recent estimates suggest the Mediterranean Basin had a population of around 15 million after the Bronze Age collapse, which grew to more than 60 million by the second century C.E. That assumes a growth rate of 0.1 per cent per year, and it might have been a little higher.[21] The fifth century lies roughly at the halfway mark, which would mean a figure of around 30 million. One thing that made larger scale conflict possible was that there were simply more people around.

Another dimension of change is offered by settlement size. There were almost no cities in the Mediterranean world at the start of the last millennium B.C.E. The only real exceptions were on the Levantine coast and Cyprus. Five centuries later there were nearly one thousand cities, about half in the Aegean. Most were still settlements of only a few thousand people; some reached 10,000 or so, and a few—Athens and Syracuse are the best candidates—were pushing close to 50,000 inhabitants during the fifth century. It was the cities with the larger populations which were the first to exercise influence over others. What does this correlation mean? In later periods of history large cities tend to be sustained by their capacity to extract food, fuel, metals, and other goods from their empires. National and imperial capitals or major industrial centres all do this. Yet in 500 B.C.E. it is pretty clear that even Athens was not usually dependent on imported

food.[22] In other words, it was already one of the largest cities in Greece
before it became a regional power. Syracuse, Corinth, Sparta, Argos, Thebes,
Miletos, Samos, and the other major centres had also grown without the
support of empires. Large cities won empires; empires did not (yet) create
large cities.

So how did they grow? Most did not, of course. Most Mediterranean
cities were the same size as the larger villages that had occupied the same
landscapes for millennia. But a few of them had, through luck or design,
crystallized into larger poleis than their neighbours. There was no single
route to growth, but marginal ecological advantages made a real difference.
Sometimes this was a product of how the physical geography provided different sized frames for emerging political communities to fill. The Attic
plain, with the Acropolis at its centre, formed a landscape easily united.
Once it was unified it is not surprising it extended its power south and
west towards the isthmus, along the coast facing Euboea and to the borders
of Boeotia. Laconia was perhaps another natural unit, or perhaps better
a geographical space with special potential for state-builders. Sparta, near
the centre of the Eurotas valley, was in a good position to control it. Once
it did so, the scale of the state gave it a competitive edge over its smaller
neighbours. Both Athens and Sparta had also been the sites of Bronze Age
states. Maybe this shows that the same locations had a geopolitical advantage in both eras. Maybe the dimly remembered prestige of the palaces also
helped Iron Age state-builders to promote their centre over others, but this
was not always the case. After the fall of Mycenae and Tiryns the plain of
the Argolid did re-emerge as a political territory, but focused on the new
centre of Argos.

Geography constrained as well as promoted state-building. Many city-
states were limited by the small size of the island they were on, or by the
poor resources of a particularly small coastal plain. These cities were never
going to rule the waves. Yet geography does not explain all the variation.
Chios and Samos, two of the larger islands off the western coast of Turkey,
were each unified by a single polis. Lesbos, by contrast, had first six and
then five poleis. Rhodes had three in the archaic age. Only after they came
together to create a single federal state in 408/7 B.C.E. did they begin to
grow into one of the major naval powers of the east Mediterranean.

Perhaps sometimes it was just chance that gave one city-state an initial advantage over its neighbours. Once any difference existed it is easy
to see how it might be perpetuated, especially as the population of the

Mediterranean world grew. Hoplite warfare depended most of all on man-power. Small poleis had little chance against larger ones. The first wars between city-states probably did help states to define their boundaries and solidify that sense of relatedness among citizens that underpinned citizenship. Greeks remembered as the first war between poleis the struggle between the Euboean cities of Eretria and Chalkis for control of the Lelantine plain that lay between them. Land was always the key resource, along with people to work it. Agricultural production was very dependent on manpower, given the small part played by beasts of burden in traditional peasant agriculture. A sense that Greeks should not enslave Greeks never quite became the norm, even if the idea that barbarians were natural slaves did catch on. There is not much sign of wars fought for other key economic resources, for grain or metals or timber or water. What Sparta got out of leadership of the Peloponnese was security. Even then some allies—the Corinthians in particular—still had a say in matters of war and peace.

There were also less tangible motives for expansion. One was pure competition. The plot of the *Iliad* revolves around a conflict for honour between Agamemnon, the leader of the Greeks, and his greatest warrior, Achilles. Agamemnon had been compelled to give up a slave girl who was his share of the booty of a raid on one of Troy's allies. Feeling his honour was hurt by this, he deprived Achilles of his share. Achilles then refused to fight, bringing disaster on the Greeks and the death of his best friend Patroclus. The quarrel seems so petty that it is tempting to over interpret it to find a better explanation. Does the dispute reflect the fragility of Bronze Age political alliances? Perhaps Achilles was in love with the girl he had to give up? Maybe Agamemnon was never worthy to rule and the quarrel derived from the disparity between the public status of the two men and their actual worth. The alternative is that Homer meant what he said, that face really did matter.

Classical Greece is often described as an agonistic society, one driven by competition. Athletics, rhetoric, and politics all seem to exhibit an extremely competitive ethic. Most Greek states had poor relations with their neighbours. Reading Herodotus' accounts of Greek assemblies during the Persian War, there is a strong sense that the relative status of city-states and their leaders were constantly at stake. Perhaps in a world as competitive as the world of the polis, imperial ventures might draw power from envy as well as from fear of one's neighbours, and from a fierce loyalty to the few thousand people who were one's kin as well as one's fellow citizens. Kinship mattered far more than political ideology. Athens sometimes promoted democracies in the smaller poleis it dominated, but it also made a good deal of the myth that Athens had originally sent out the Ionian migrations that settled much of the eastern Aegean in the years after the Persian Wars. Syracuse was, for much of its history, a naval democracy just like Athens, but in the Peloponnesian War it sided with its Dorian kinsfolk the Spartans.

Maybe competition was even more important than the hegemonies that resulted from it. None of these imperial ventures seem to have been designed to set up stable institutionalized empires like that of the Persians. The Athenians did, in the end, gather regular tribute and spent some of it on glorifying the city of Athens. But it was far from an organized fiscal system. Mostly they wanted to command, and to be recognized for that. Sometimes their commands seem to reach for something more. Around 450 B.C.E. a decree of the Athenian assembly required all their allies to use Athenian weights and measures and declared Athenian silver coinage to be the currency of the empire. Symbol of imperial domination, or just compelling subjects to suit the convenience of their masters? Athenian citizens and key allies benefited individually from the empire as military settlers, through access to the courts in Athens with their juries of citizens, and in a few other ways. Yet this was as far as imperial unification ever went.

The western Mediterranean followed a similar pattern. A small number of city-states drew ahead of the pack and used their muscle to create regional hegemonies like those of Sparta and Athens.[23] Some of the earliest documents of Roman imperialism are a series of treaties made with the city of Carthage. They do not survive, but they were seen and recorded by the Greek historian Polybius in the early second century B.C.E.[24] Polybius presents a Greek translation of the first one but adds that the archaic Latin was very difficult even for Romans to understand. There is a risk, then, that he has interpreted it in terms of more familiar treaties. It was dated to the first year of the free Republic after Rome's kings had been expelled and to twenty-eight years before Xerxes' invasion, around 509-507 B.C.E. It asserts friendship between the Carthaginians and their allies on the one side, and the Romans and their allies on the other. Each city or people presents itself as leader (*hegemon*) of a regional alliance. What follows defines spheres of influence, apparently in an attempt to limit future disputes: Romans must not sail beyond the Fair Promontory (next to Carthage), nor land in Africa unless forced ashore. If they are forced to land they must not stay for long and must not trade in Africa or Sardinia, except in the presence of the town clerk or herald. Romans shall have the same rights as anyone else if they visit the area of Sicily controlled by Carthage. Carthage for its part will not harm Rome's subjects or allies in Ardea, Antium, Laurentium, Circeii, Terracina, or anywhere else in Latium, and they shall not pass a night in Latium if they arrive with weapons. Many areas are not covered by the treaty, notably the remainder of Sicily, Etruria, and much of southern Italy. Were these other areas fair game? Or just areas in which neither side had any interests at the moment of signing?

There has been much speculation about the exact context of this treaty and the two that follow it, one probably dating to the fourth century, the third to the period just before the Epirote king Pyrrhus crossed the Adriatic and campaigned in southern Italy between 279 and 275 B.C.E. Historians have tried to link the first treaty to the end of the Roman monarchy, and to various ill-documented and poorly dated wars and peaces between Rome and the various Etruscan cities. Carthage also allied and fought with Etruscan cities in this period, and there are the Greek cities of Sicily and of Italy and tribal peoples like the Samnites, Oscans, and Siculi to be factored in. It will never be possible to write a history of the fifth century in this region that can be compared in detail with that of the Aegean world. Ancient attempts to do exactly this arouse suspicions. Some historians decided that the origin of the Roman Republic coincided pretty much with Cleisthenes' reform of the Athenian constitutions, that the Greek defeat of Carthaginians at Himera in Sicily happened at the same time as the Greek defeat of Persia at Salamis, and that Rome's long war with Veii corresponded in time to the struggle between Athens and Sparta. The desire to establish synchronisms of this kind may well have distorted historical narratives beyond repair.

All the same, the treaties between Rome and Carthage give us a sense of the kind of imperial or hegemonic ventures taking place in the western Mediterranean in the fifth and fourth centuries. Each city presents itself as heading an alliance of cities that was reasonably stable, and also enjoying a sphere of influence that extended beyond those allies. The treaty envisages a world in which trading and raiding were common, and it tries to regulate them. In the second treaty it is agreed that if the Carthaginians seize a Latin town that is not subject to Rome, they should be content with the movable booty (including the population) and hand the town over to Rome. And these treaties envisage a wider world in which they interact with third parties. The last treaty includes a clause on what to do if either city makes an alliance with Pyrrhus. Even allowing for Polybius' translation and interpretation, all this seems familiar from the treaties and conflicts of the Aegean world. At one point the Athenians banned their neighbours the Megarians from access to the markets and harbour of the Athenian Empire. Spheres of influence formed part of the various settlements between Athens and Sparta.

Regional hegemonies led by powerful cities continued to exist through-out the fifth and fourth centuries. The balance of power shifted from time to time. The defeat of Athens in 404 limited the scope of its maritime ambitions. A second Athenian confederacy was created in the fourth century, but it was much more like the original Delian League and much less like an Athenian empire. Sparta's influence expanded briefly but in 395 a brief alliance against it was formed between Corinth, Argos, Thebes, and Athens. An end to the Corinthian war was brokered by the Persians the next year. Thebes had its moment as *hegemon* in the 370s and 360s. The creation of a polis in Messenia and a great city for the Arcadians, Megalopolis, perma-nently limited Spartan power in the Peloponnese. Meanwhile in the west, the fourth century saw the rise of Syracuse. Athens had attempted to take the city in the last years of the Peloponnesian War, but the expedition ended in disaster in 413. The years that followed saw Carthage and Syracuse fight-ing to win control of various Sicilian cities. Under Dionysius I, Syracuse became briefly the dominant Greek city not just in Sicily, but also in south-ern Italy. During the rest of the fourth century Carthage and Syracuse, Tarentum and Acragas fought, made peace, and fought again. Farther north, Rome fought wars with Etruscan cities and with the Volci, then with the Gauls and the Samnites and other peoples south of the Apennines. At the mouth of the Rhône the city of Massalia (Marseilles) exercised a loose lead-ership of a dozen of so Greek cities and entrepôts along the Mediterranean coast of France, and grew rich from trade with the interior and with Spain. Far to the east Panticapeum in the Crimea had a similar history.

Seen up close, these regional hegemonies seem fantastically precarious. Few lasted more than a couple of generations, some much less. They had few institutions and were constantly at war. Ancient writers typically attributed the ups and downs of various states to the failings and virtues of their gener-als. Dynamic generals like the Thebans Epaminondas and Pelopidas get the credit for episodes of success; the supposed failing of the Spartans' Pausanias and Agesilaos the blame for Sparta's fourth-century decline. Occasionally the intervention of a military adventurer from outside like Dionysius,

Agathocles, or Pyrrhus disturbed the balance but none established lasting control of the cities they allied with.

In a slightly longer perspective, however, the situation looks more stable. The same set of larger cities remained prominent throughout the period. If one became briefly more powerful, its neighbours ganged up to pull it down. Persian satraps and kings were usually ready to help break up any hegemony in the Aegean world. But the rules of the game—and its objectives—remained pretty much the same throughout the fifth and fourth centuries. A kind of dynamic equilibrium existed. Most Greeks seemed to have shared the view of Aristotle and Thucydides that their world would last forever.

14

Europe Awakes

Beyond the Mediterranean

Demographic growth within the Mediterranean world was just one part of a larger phenomenon. In the continental interior of Europe populations were also growing during the second half of the last millennium B.C.E. Some of the clearest signs are an intensification of agriculture and metal production. Iron moved from being a rare find to becoming ubiquitous in late prehistoric sites, providing tools, weapons, and building materials. Iron tools made it easier to clear forest and plough deeper soils. Livestock breeding was intensifying. A few new domesticates were introduced. Fruit trees were being acclimatized to new environments, first in the western Mediterranean and then north of the Alps. It seems likely that this growth was partly made possible by a slight climatic amelioration. Human populations—still the main source of energy—were also growing. Most of this is difficult to see in detail because these societies did not yet make their own historical records, although some adopted writing along with coinage in the last centuries B.C.E. But the scale of building, the size and complexity of the largest settlements, and the numbers attested in battle narratives all suggest the late Iron Age witnessed major transformations.[1] That growth spilled out in all directions. Commerce with the Mediterranean increased in scale. Exchanges with nomad populations to the east increased. A technological gap between Europe and the Mediterranean that can be traced back to the Neolithic was being closed. Looking ahead, by the Middle Ages northern Europe would have an economic lead over the Mediterranean it has not yet lost.

From the seventh and sixth centuries B.C.E. we begin to hear of population movements in forest Europe and on the adjacent steppe. Cimmerians swept across the Near East in the last days of the Assyrian Empire. Achaemenid emperors fought wars with Scythians, Massagetae, Sakae, and other nomad groups from southern Russia to central Asia. Migrations within central Europe led to the establishment of the Celtiberians in the upper Ebro Valley and the Volcae in southern France. There were certainly other movements we do not hear about. The balance of power seems to shift in several areas between highland populations and their neighbours on the coasts in favour of the former. Why exactly this happened—in Apennine Italy, in the Balkans, and elsewhere—is not clear. Climate change might be a factor, but it is also possible that highland peoples were benefiting from an intensification of ecologically complementary exchanges. Lowlanders often depended on highlanders for timber, for summer pastures, for water, and even manpower. Samnites and some other Oscan speakers began in their turn to construct sanctuaries, and to adopt military equipment from the urbanizing societies flourishing on their fringes. Macedonian kings and Gallic tribes put pressure on Greek cities in order to control and profit from these exchanges. Up and down central Italy we see new power dynamics. Greek Posidonia, south of the Bay of Naples, was probably captured by Lucanians during in the fifth century.[2] Pompeii was a Hellenized Oscan city before a Roman colony was implanted on it. This was part of a wider pattern.[3] Historical narratives emphasize military aspects of these changing relationships. Rome fought long wars with the Samnites during the late fourth and early third centuries B.C.E., but there were other dimensions to those relationships, many of them contributing to the creation of a more integrated social system in Italy.[4] Ancient writers liked to think in terms of migrations and there was even the idea of a "sacred spring," the moment when a new people arrived in a land for the first time. Mass migrations were a reality, but they were only a part of a more complex story.

No case illustrates this better than Rome's relations with peoples they usually called Gauls and the Greeks called Celts, especially with those who inhabited the Po Valley and other parts of Adriatic Italy north of the Apennine ridge.[5] There are implausible myths (written down much later) about great organized migrations from central France. In fact there is no way to decide whether the Gauls of northern Italy were the descendants of one or more great migrations or simply the product of constant movements and exchanges back and forth around the Alps that created an island of central European society in one of the best-watered parts of the Mediterranean.

Villanovan culture also shared a good deal with the Urnfield cultures of northern Europe, so this kind of connection is not implausible.

Things began to change in the later Iron Age. Our historical narrative begins early in the fourth century B.C.E. when Rome was sacked by a Gallic army from across the Apennines, and there were other incursions into parts of Etruria and Campania.[6] Early in the third century there was a great raid on Delphi in central Greece. Three Gaulish tribes established themselves on the Anatolian plateau soon after, and a tribe called the Scordisci took control of the middle Danube. Probably there were other movements we cannot reconstruct happening beyond the sight of classical observers. The Cimbri and Teutones who invaded Italy and France in the late second century may have come in part from northern Europe. Caesar's invasion of Gaul was opportunistic, of course, but it was also a response to the next generation of these migrations, an attempt to fix a world more fluid than the one familiar to the inhabitants of Mediterranean city-states.[7]

What these conflicts remind us of is that the Mediterranean Basin has never really been a closed system. There is a long history of movements of technologies and crops back and forth across its margins. Weaponry shows this amazingly well, as does the history of ritualized dining and drinking, the spread of writing and coinage, and a whole series of stylistic motifs and forms. There must have been many vectors for these connections. Some trade probably did pass through intermediaries, circum-Alpine populations with connections both south and north. Perhaps there were some bold Mediterranean traders making their way up the rivers into central Europe. Warriors from temperate Europe served in many Mediterranean armies as mercenaries from the fourth century and perhaps earlier. Some will have returned home with wealth and with tales of wealth. Wine, metalwork, painted Greek pottery, and occasional caches of Mediterranean coins appear in princely graves and on hill forts from central France to Romania. These connections had ancient roots, but contacts intensified during the Iron Age.[8]

Hungry Cities

During the archaic period many of the first cities created around the Mediterranean had been built on a fine network of connections through which luxuries were exchanged for material of great value, metals in particular. Phoenician, Greek, and Etruscan traders played a key role in stitching the Mediterranean world back together. The origins of many Mediterranean cities lay in entrepôts established on favourable location on the networks established in this period. During the sixth and fifth centuries this changed, as a mass trade in commodities appeared on some of the same routes.[9] The demand for some commodities also led some traders outside the Mediterranean, seeking grain from Egypt and south Russia and exploring areas like the Adriatic and southern France that gave access to the resources of temperate Europe. There is no doubt that the growth of states and the spread of cities within the Mediterranean was a powerful factor in making the trans-regional trade in mass commodities profitable. Bigger cities were the hungriest. Athens sought suppliers of bread wheat from the Black Sea and the Nile Valley. But nonurban societies could generate demand too. Wine began to be produced in bulk and exported especially to the west. The increasing use of coinage from the sixth century meant there was increased demand for silver, gold, copper, and tin even after iron replaced bronze in many used. New technologies in water management made lead more valuable. The use of olive oil for food, for light, and for bathing increased. Timber, stone, and eventually livestock would join the list of commodities traded long distances. So would humans.

Shipbuilding and the construction of larger and larger temples created a demand for timber. There are few forests of tall trees in the central and southern Mediterranean, but fir and pine could be found in Macedonia and from the southern coasts of the Black Sea. Western Mediterranean cities turned to Corsica and to the wooded slopes behind Genoa. Classical urbanism did not result in widespread deforestation in all regions, but long timber became increasingly rare. Urban appetites extended beyond food and raw materials. Slaves were imported from southern Russia, from central Europe via the Adriatic, and from Western Europe via the Rhône Valley. Mercenaries too found their way from these regions into the central Mediterranean.[10]

A new generation of trading cities grew on the back of this trade. Marseilles and its daughter cities in southern France did not just connect Mediterranean Gauls with the urban network; they also provided a connection to routes up the Rhône valley. Greek ceramic has been found as far north as Burgundy and also in the Berry region. Classical writers credit the Massiliots with introducing viticulture and in general civilizing the Gauls. From around 500 B.C.E. the cities of Adria and Spina at the head of the

Adriatic provided Etruscans and Greeks with access to the Po Valley and also to central Europe east of the Alps.[11] A series of small cities up the east coast of the Adriatic connected the Illyrians of the northwest Balkans with the wider Mediterranean world. Apollonia, also founded in the sixth century, was the most famous of these. In the north Aegean Torone, on the peninsula of Chalcidice, was a major shipper of timber. The area became a strategic priority in the fifth century when Sparta tried to limit Athenian access to the resources it needed to renew its navy. A string of Greek cities from Amphipolis in the west to Byzantium in the east provided access to the many Thracian tribes. Slaves, timber, soldiers, and metals passed back and forth through them. Beyond Byzantium the Sea of Marmara opened up into the Black Sea. The most important trading cities here were on the Crimean peninsula and along the south coast. The most successful trading cities of this period had deep harbours, suitable for the larger vessels needed for this kind of trade in bulk. Politically they mediated between powerful chieftains and various Greek alliances, mostly trying but often failing to avoid being controlled by either.

Economic and demographic growth in Europe, coupled with urban and political growth in the Mediterranean world, provided the perfect conditions for closer connections between the two regions. Northerners desired some southern manufactures, while Mediterranean peoples wanted the raw materials and slaves available from the north. The relationship was not always a stable one. Perhaps, as happened in other places and times, increased contact only made mobile populations more aware of what else was available in the Mediterranean world. The consequences were unpredictable. Barbarian invasions were certainly disruptive, but powers that resisted them—like Rome in the west or Pergamum in the east— might use the prestige they won to assert their hegemony. Dying Gauls in statuary proclaimed the success of Pergamon in keeping the Anatolian Galatians under control. The triumph of 187 B.C.E. that followed their defeat by the Roman general Manlius Vulso was remembered as especially spectacular. As late as the last century B.C.E. the Roman Senate reserved the right to declare a *tumultus Gallicus* as a kind of state of emergency. Well before that point, however, economic growth on the edge of the Aegean world had shifted the balance of power fundamentally. A tribal kingdom in the northeast Balkans had realized its economic potential and as a result moved from the margins to the centre of Greek politics. Its name was Macedon.

Macedon

The heart of the kingdom of Macedon was a large inland plain northwest of the Aegean Sea. To its south was Mount Olympus, and beyond that the smaller plain of Thessaly and the city-states of central Greece. To the east were the Thracian tribes—famously ferocious and equally famously impossible to unite—and to the west a series of Balkan valleys, each occupied by smaller or larger tribal territories. The nearer of these eventually became known as Upper Macedonia. At the end of the sixth century Macedon had briefly been an outlying part of the Persian Empire. Greek texts from Hesiod on placed the Macedonians on the fringe of the Greek world, cousins of the Greeks rather than brothers. Their royal family cultivated Greek culture, used Greek names, and patronized Greek poets and writers in the fourth century. The population of the hinterland had a different lifestyle. The historian Arrian tells the story of how Alexander, in a moment of anger, told his army that they had been virtually barbarians until the reign of his father, Philip II.

> He found you wandering about in poverty, many of you dressed in sheepskins and pasturing small flocks in the mountains, defending them with difficulty against the Illyrians, the Triballians and the neighboring Thracians. He gave you cloaks to wear instead of sheepskins, brought you down from the mountains to the plains, and made you a match in war for the neighbouring barbarians, owing your safety to your own bravery and no longer having to rely on your mountain strongholds. He made you city-dwellers and civilized you with proper laws and customs.[12]

This was an exaggeration, but not completely untrue. Macedon was another of these regions that straddled the divide between temperate Europe and the Mediterranean and therefore had the potential to link the two. Their territory was not subject to the arid summers of the central and southern Mediterranean and it had timber, metals, horses, and grain in abundance. But it also touched the sea and connected easily with the Greek city-states. Macedonian kings were able to employ Greek craftsmen and intellectuals as well—both Euripides and Aristotle spent time at court—and built palaces and tombs in a style that recalls that of Sicilian tyrants and Etruscan princes. During the fifth and fourth centuries these kings fought off Thracian raids and consolidated their control of the regions to their west and north with warfare and dynastic marriage alliances. Progressively they played a larger and larger part in the politics of the Aegean world. Perdiccas II (450–431), Amyntas III (393–370), and Philip II (359–336) in particular created a state that harnessed European power to Mediterranean ambitions. Their army became experienced and disciplined, its strength resting on a new type of phalanx in which many more ranks of infantrymen could engage with long two-handed spears. They were supported by cavalry and by Thracian and other levies and allies. This was a national or ethnic levy, not a citizen army, and it was focused on the person of the king. Only a few Greek observers realized how fast the balance of power was changing.

Once Philip's position as king was established he quickly took control of the Greek poleis that fringed the coast of Macedonia. He then went on to annex Thessaly. By 346 he was the dominant power in mainland Greece. Sparta was contained within Laconia. Other alliances were broken up. Following diplomatic failure after failure, the Athenians allied with Thebes against him only to be comprehensively defeated at Chaeronea in 338. Garrisons were installed in the major Greek cities. Peace was imposed and Philip accepted as hegemon of a new league declared at Corinth. A war against Persia was declared, and the first detachment crossed the Hellespont. Philip's assassination in 336 meant leadership of all that passed to his son Alexander. Like most Macedonian kings on their accession, Alexander had first to prove his credentials as a warrior by fighting in the north. Thebes took advantage of his absence to revolt. Alexander returned and destroyed the city and enslaved its citizens.

The career of Alexander the Great has mesmerized later generations. He was only twenty-two years old when he led his army across the Hellespont from Europe to Asia in 334 B.C.E. Spectacular victories later that year on the river Granicus and the next year at Issus shattered the power of the Persian Emperor Darius III. Alexander took Egypt in 332, invaded Mesopotamia in 331, and won the third of his great victories at Gaugamela. Babylon, Susa, and Persepolis fell without a fight. Darius was murdered in 330 and Alexander led his army on a long circuit of the empire's eastern provinces, reaching what is now Afghanistan and the valley of the Indus before returning to its Iranian heartland in 324. Stories of his ambitious projects, for a multicultural empire and for further conquests, circulated soon after he died at Babylon in 323. He was thirty-three years old.

In one sense Alexander's conquests changed little; in another they changed everything: little, because throughout the ten years of conquest and exploration the Achaemenid Empire carried on as normal to the extent that

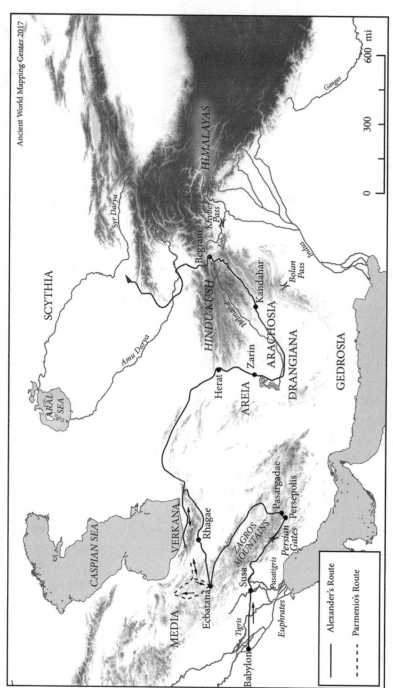

Map 6 Alexander's invasion of Persia's eastern satrapies

some researchers reasonably consider him to be the last Persian emperor.[13] And everything, because the kingdoms that emerged from the wreckage were transformed into fusions of Macedonian kingship and Persian rule. The history of the first decade or so after Alexander's death is a confusing narrative of rapidly shifting alliances and territories. His relatives and generals struggled first to preserve the empire as a whole, and then to carve out kingdoms within it. Some kingdoms barely lasted a generation. By the beginning of the third century B.C.E. it was more or less clear who the winners would be. The old kingdom of Macedon, considerably enlarged, was in the hands of a dynasty known as the Antigonids after its colourful founder Antigonus, the One-Eyed. Egypt, always one of the most easily detached parts of the Persian Empire, was the power base of the Ptolemies, descendants of another of Alexander's generals. Asia was more chaotic. The largest kingdom was that created by Seleucus, based in Syria and Babylonia. In periods of strength it also controlled the Iranian and central Asian parts of the Persian Empire to the borders of India. But there were many periods of weakness. Frequent rebellions occurred in the eastern provinces, and an independent kingdom of Bactria was set up in what is now Afghanistan.

Elsewhere, no stable political geography ever emerged. Asia Minor was gradually broken up into smaller kingdoms, among them that of the Attalids based on the city of Pergamum, near Troy. Then there were the tribal territories of the Galatians on the Anatolian plateau. Smaller kingdoms on the northern shores included Bithynia and Pontus. Some were more Persian than Macedonian in flavor; most were a mix of some kind. The Ptolemies attempted to maintain control over Cyprus and Cyrenaica, and during the second century maintained a string of naval bases across the southern Aegean and southern Asia Minor, but their naval hegemony was short-lived. Energy was spent (or wasted) on endless border wars with the Seleucids over the part of Syria that lay between the two kingdoms. All the kings competed fiercely to influence the Greek cities of the Aegean, and major Greek cities tried to win the support of the kings. When Macedon was strong it installed garrisons in mainland Greece, and its armies occasionally marched south to impose their will.

Not much more than a century elapsed between the death of Alexander and the first Roman interventions east of the Adriatic at the end of the third century. The last of the Macedonian monarchies to remain independent was the Ptolemaic kingdom of Egypt. It was finally absorbed by Rome after Octavian—the future Augustus—defeated its ruler Cleopatra and her

Roman ally Mark Antony in 31 B.C.E. Even before the Macedonian kingdoms were dismembered, they were progressively forced to follow Roman
commands. Yet in their different ways these short-lived empires pioneered
new relations between empire and city that would last for centuries. Old
Greek cities mostly flourished under their rule; some new ones were
founded, most of them military colonies; and many ancient indigenous
cities remodelled themselves as poleis. By the time Rome took definitive
control of the east, cities like Baalbek and Jerusalem were halfway towards
becoming Greek cities. Their politics changed in the process, and many cities flourished under first Macedonian and then Roman rule. It is crude to
say they won prosperity at the price of their freedom, but not completely
false, either.

Each Macedonian kingdom had its own character, but their central institutions had a family resemblance. That reflected not only their common
descent from the kingdom of Philip and his predecessors, but also a process
of convergence as new norms of diplomacy and politics became established.[14] At the heart of each was the king and his court, which consisted of
his relatives and a group of friends, mostly Macedonians and Greeks chosen
to support and advise the monarch. Over time court hierarchies became
more elaborate and ministers appeared, with different titles in each kingdom. Each kingdom had at least one capital with a spectacular palace, and
this was the normal base of the court. A second pillar of the king's power
was the army, meaning the Macedonian hoplites and cavalry who formed
the core of all their armies. The army was mostly hereditary, and soldiers and
their families settled in colonies or land allocations scattered throughout
the kingdom. The army could make or break a king, so a strong personal
bond between the king and his Macedonians was essential. Like Alexander
and Philip before them, most kings began their reigns by making war.[15]
Macedonians were a privileged population in each kingdom, and each also
had many Greeks in their employ. Lastly, there were the local elites and subject populations. This is where the kingdoms differed most.

Macedon itself was least changed. Its ancient capital, Pella, was more
splendid than ever and the Antigonid kings were far richer than their predecessors, but the institutions of the kingdom remained much as Philip II
had left them. The success of Alexander inspired other Balkan monarchs to
flex their muscles. Pyrrhus of Epirus was born in 319, just four years after
the death of Alexander, and became king in his teens. Supported at different times by Ptolemy of Egypt, the tyrant Agathocles of Syracuse, and the

Antigonid Demetrius Poliorcetes, he managed to enlarge his kingdom in the western Balkans with parts of Illyria, Macedonia, and Thessaly. He is most famous for crossing the Adriatic in 280 at the request of the Greek city of Tarentum, then at war with Rome. After costly victories over the Romans at Heraclea and Ausculum he crossed to Sicily to assist Syracuse against the Carthaginians and the Mamertines, before returning to fight Rome again. Between 275 and his death in 272 he waged campaigns against Macedon, Sparta, and Argos. There were others too, some of them Alexander's generals, some local dynasts whose attempts at empire-building flared up only to fail.

The Seleucids relied, as Alexander had, on the Persian administration.[16] Like the Persian Empire their kingdom had multiple capitals, among them Antioch on the Orontes in Syria and Seleuceia on the Tigris in Babylonia. Their empire continued to be divided into great territorial units called satrapies, each with its own governor referred to by the Greek word for general, *strategos*. The complex tax-system of the empire, the system of raising local levies, and even the use of Aramaic in government were all remnants of the Persian system. Successive kings tinkered, dividing some of the larger satrapies and adding more ministers in the centre. In essence, though, the Seleucid Empire remained a Macedonian court and army grafted onto the Achaemenid Persia administration.

When the Ptolemies took over Egypt they found a Persian administration that had itself been grafted onto a more ancient system. Macedonian kings—like Persian kings before them and Roman emperors after them—were regarded as pharaohs by the locals, worshipped in major temples scattered throughout the nomes, the ancient districts into which Egypt was divided. The kings and the temples were rich. Although there were administrative centres in the nomes and the Nile valley compressed its population into dense villages, there were few urban communities that managed their own affairs in the way a Greek polis did. The Ptolemies ruled from a court staffed by Macedonians and Greeks, based first in the Pharaonic capital of Memphis (close to modern Cairo) and then in their new foundation of Alexandria. They too depended on a Macedonian army, supplemented by local levies and mercenaries. Just as the Seleucids had difficulty maintaining control of the Upper Satrapies of Iran and all points east, so southern (Upper) Egypt was the site of occasional revolts. The Ptolemies made more changes to the governance of Egypt than the Seleucids did in their territories. Egypt had, after all, been a single satrapy under Persia, and its government had been highly centralized for millennia. Centralization made it easier for the Ptolemies to dictate change. A new census was carried out and a new tax system imposed, managed from the palace. Greek replaced demotic Egyptian as the language of administration. A bureaucracy using papyrus records began to grow. Macedonian and Greek officials controlled everything but the temples. Even the indigenous priesthood was weakened in influence. Ethnic status—Macedonian, Greek, Egyptian, Persian—became the basis of legal distinctions.

When they could, the smaller kingdoms imitated the larger ones. Attalus I of Pergamum declared his independence simply by taking the title of king. The founder of the dynasty was Philitaeros, a military commander in the service first of Antigonus I and then Lysimachus king of Thrace, who defected to Seleucus in 282. He and his successors extended their power and influence, partly by taking the lead against the Galatian invaders, partly by exploiting the collapse of Seleucid power and allying first with the Ptolemies and then with Rome. The kingdom of Pergamum became the core of the Roman province of Asia in 133 B.C.E., more or less peacefully. Its rich epigraphic record shows how the kings managed their relations with the city of Pergamum itself, with the various tribes in the kingdom, and with a series of rich poleis that enjoyed a semiautonomous status. The city of Pergamum itself was covered in spectacular monuments including a vast theatre and a great outside altar, now the centrepiece of the Pergamum Museum in Berlin. A royal library was created, and the kings made great gifts to Athens, in competition with the kings of Egypt and in defiance of Macedon. Trade in and out of the kingdom of Pergamum was taxed at specified border posts. Greeks and cities like Pergamum had become Greek, enjoying a special status relative to locals.

Pergamum in some ways resembles the kingdom created in eastern Sicily by successive tyrants of Syracuse. Both were ruled from one city but included Greek cities and non-Greek peoples. Where Pergamum had won the support of Greek cities by protecting them against the Galatian tribes, successive tyrants of Syracuse from Dionysius onwards had led the Greeks against Carthage. Both cities promoted Greek culture, building temples and theatres and patronizing sculptors and poets. During the third century both formed alliances with Rome, and that of Syracuse survived the conversion of Sicily into Rome's first province in 241 B.C.E. This relationship came to an end in 211 when the Roman general Marcellus sacked the city after it had become too friendly with Carthage. The city continued to thrive under Roman rule, and the system of tithes created by its tyrant Hieron II in the middle of the third century became the basis for Roman taxation. The Attalids remained favoured allies for longer. On the death of Attalus III it was found he had left his royal prerogatives to Rome, which made most of the kingdom into the basis of their first Asian province. Again, fiscal institutions were preserved and Greek cities simply turned their attention from the king to the Roman governor and behind him, the senate.

Empire Resurgent

During the fourth century B.C.E. the political landscape around the Mediterranean Basin underwent a transformation.

It took contemporaries a little longer to realize that the fragmented world of the early fifth century was passing away forever. The speeches of Athenian orators and the emergent political philosophy of Plato, Xenophon, and Aristotle all convey a picture of a world still fundamentally divided into city-states, each autonomous and independent, even if some were a little bigger than the others and exercised a little more influence in alliances that were mostly voluntary and temporary. The polis was deeply entrenched in the citizen ideology of the Greek world, more deeply than it was in the ecology and geography of the Mediterranean Basin. What the leaders of Etruscan city-states thought is now lost forever, along with the political culture of Phoenicians, Elymian, Tartessians, and all those other peoples—hill people and coastal tribes, islanders and mountaineers who formed part of the Mediterranean's human geography. Romans, by they time they records their thoughts on the matter, were deeply influenced by Greek thought. Polybius, when he wrote his history of the unification of the Mediterranean in the late third and early second centuries B.C.E., still worked within a framework drawn up by Aristotle.

The story we can now tell is quite different. Seen in the long term, the Mediterranean hegemonies created by the larger city-states were never that stable. Demographic growth, the creation of new settlements, and state-formation all continued throughout the last millennium. While geography and ecology help explain the political fragmentation of the region, they also make clear that the Mediterranean was never a bounded entity, nor a self-sufficient one. There was always traffic back and forth between the coasts and islands on the one hand, and the upland massifs and continental hinterlands on the other. During the fourth and third centuries the Mediterranean political system was profoundly disrupted. Ancient writers usually pointed the finger at the empire-building ambitions of groups like the Athenian demos, the Roman aristocracy, or the king of Macedon. But this is also the period in which the Mediterranean suddenly got swept up in the dynamics of continental Europe, and was equally overturned by the new union of Macedonian kingship and Near Eastern empire.

Meanwhile in the west, a Roman state strengthened and reinforced by absorbing the manpower of nonurban populations within Italy, succeeded in establishing a durable hegemony first in the west and then across much of the Mediterranean world. Rome and Carthage finally came to blows shortly after the last of the three treaties recorded by Polybius. This first Punic War lasted from 264 to 241 and was a struggle for influence beyond the core territories of either state. There were raids on Italy and Africa, but most attention was focused on Sicily and the seas that surrounded it. At the end of the war Rome took over the island. Shortly afterwards they took Sardinia as well. The war—exactly the kind of conflict the three treaties seemed designed to head off—was about hegemony and influence, and a little bit about trade as well, but it also resulted in overseas possessions. This model of rule—quickly evolving into a tributary empire on a very small scale—would also become a laboratory within which Rome would discover that by far the best instrument of government was a repurposed city-state.

Carthage had made herself leader of the Phoenician cities of the west as early as the fifth century B.C.E., but her hegemony was not much more than a system of alliances with other cities.[17] Conflict in Sicily probably made the alliances led by both Carthage and Syracuse more durable than they would otherwise have been. Roman expansion into Italy took a parallel route. No taxes or tribute were levied from defeated Latin, Etruscan, and Campanian cities, nor from the tribal peoples that surrounded them, but they were obliged to provide troops to assist Roman armies.[18] Roman leadership of Italy consisted of a series of unequal bilateral treaties, supported by personal relationships by Roman aristocrats and local elites. Allies supplied troops as commanded to and did what they were told. Not all of Rome's allies were city-states, but most of them were. Up until the end of the third century the hegemonies that Carthage and Rome had created were in many ways similar to Sparta's long leadership of the Peloponnesian league. From that point on, Rome at least began to coordinate a much more diverse group of peoples and polities.

By the end of the First Punic War it was apparent that city-states would be an essential part of the empires of the future. Apart from fighting off Pyrrhus, Rome's first military contact with kingdoms east of the Adriatic was in 229 (not quite a century since Alexander's death). The consuls depatched to Illyria ended up expelling royal garrisons from the Greek cities of the coast, Apollonia and Corcyra among them. Cities were easier to deal with than kings. The reason is not hard to find. Ancient empires depended most of all on manpower, and city-states organized this better than any alternative. The ruling elites of Mediterranean cities were mostly content to take on the burden of government in return for *autonomia*, the right to use their own laws, which they tended to do at the expense of their fellow citizens.[19] Kings might be allies for a while, and Rome never completely stopped making friends of useful monarchs, especially in geographically marginal zones like mountains and deserts, but they brought with them succession crises and worries about disloyalty. Cities, especially if their democratic elements were suppressed, were more stable. The kingdom of Hiero of Syracuse became the first Roman overseas territory to be subjected to a governor. From 241 the city of Sicily collected a grain tithe for the Roman state and managed justice and security throughout the island. When the kingdom of Macedon was finally abolished in 167 the Romans replaced it with four city-states. The transformation of the kingdom of Attalus of Pergamum into a province in 133 went almost as smoothly, and there too the cities were eventually given the main role in running and taxing the province. Pompey divided up Pontus into city-states after the defeat of King Mithridates.

The wars that Polybius documented in the early second century B.C.E. must have seemed to many like a contest to see whether the Mediterranean would be ruled by kings (like Antiochus of Syria and Perseus of Macedon) or by cities like Rome and Carthage. The humbling of successive Macedonian dynasties by Roman armies seemed to show that the victory of the city, but in fact the Roman state, soon morphed into a monarchy, ruling a tributary empire through city-states wherever it could. For that reason Romans typically strengthened civic institutions, and even promoted the creation of new cities where they needed them. En route they did try many alternatives—alliances, client kings, handing over tax collection to private companies—but trial and error led them repeatedly back to the city-state. No other political institution provided as stable and effective control of Mediterranean landscapes and populations at the local level. The future of the city under imperial rule was assured.

15

Cities of Marble

Wandering the Ruins

The history of Mediterranean cities as human communities is a long one, but for much of that time they were not much to look at. Buildings came long after people, and it took centuries for most ancient cities to acquire the range of architectural ornaments by which we most often remember them. During that time most ancient cities remained tiny, with populations of just a few thousand people. Monumentalization represented not the growth of urban populations so much as the power of their rulers to concentrate resources in a few locations. Most of the grandest buildings were designed for public, collective use. There were places this process began in the fourth century B.C.E. but when we visit archaeological sites in Greece or Turkey, in Egypt and Italy, Spain, North Africa, France, Germany, or Britain the most impressive urban monuments are usually those of the second century C.E., that period in which under Roman rule, the Mediterranean was at its most prosperous and most peaceful.

Many ancient cities lie under modern metropoleis, so only fragments of them can be glimpsed. Take the steps down into the basement of the Guildhall in the city of London (see Figure 24) and suddenly you are at one end of a buried amphitheatre, where gladiators once fought to entertain provincial notables and perhaps the odd bored governor who had seen much better in Rome.

Most of Roman London is not visible above ground, but if you walk along the right streets every so often you find a stretch of ancient wall. It is often possible to walk above the main streets of a Roman city. A series of shopping malls in Cologne still follow the lines of ancient highways, and a couple of Roman towers still survive with characteristic brick and stone decoration.

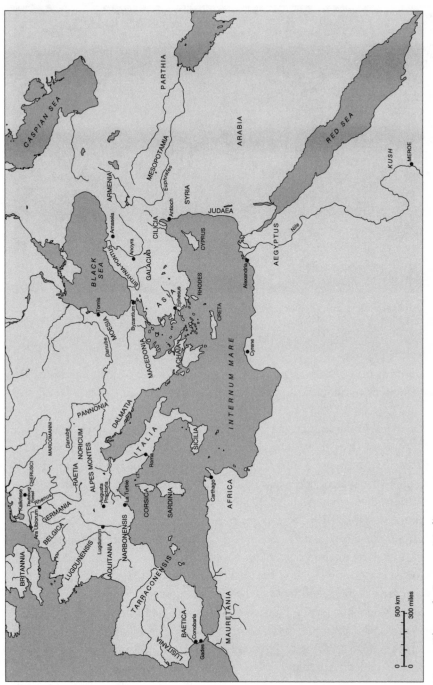

Map 7 The early Roman Mediterranean

Figure 24 The amphitheatre under London's Guildhall
Steve Vidler / Alamy Stock Photo

The most impressive remains of Colonia Claudia Ara Agrippinensium are also underground, buried under the accumulate remains of mediaeval and later urbanisms.

Sometimes the street plan of an ancient city survives as a ghost in the plan of a modern city. All over northern Italy and southern France there are cities that at their heart have the traces of a square grid. An oval *piazza* in Lucca occupies the space once enclosed by the amphitheatre. The mediaeval city first flowed up to the walls of the building, and only after it was demolished was the space filled in, forming a perfect oval of housing. Once that was cleared again a piazza in the exact shape of the amphitheatre reappeared, now surrounded by mediaeval shops and houses. At Damascus and Jerusalem long covered souks now occupy the spaces once framed by colonnaded streets What Jerusalem looked liked before this transformation is vividly depicted on the Madaba map (see Figure 25). When civic authorities lost the power or will to protect public space, commercial and private interests encroached until the great boulevards were covered over.[1] By a similar process waterfronts extended farther and farther out from river banks where great quaysides were once maintained. Bridges and gates often survived for centuries,

Figure 25 Jerusalem on the mosaic map from Madaba
Mondadori Portfolio / Getty Images

encrusted with later building. The Porta Nigra at Trier has survived because
the great monumental gate of the city was converted into a church. The
filled-in shape of Roman gates can be seen in many mediaeval wall circuits. Most ancient buildings of any size were converted during the Middle
Ages—quite a few into castles—and later demolished or else plundered for
stone or to free up prime real estate in the centre. Some sections of town
wall survived for centuries inside buildings constructed against them.

Often only the foundations are visible. The Piazza Navona in Rome preserves the shape of the stadium built by the Emperor Domitian for his
Capitoline games, but if you want to see actual Roman masonry you need
to visit the excavations of the substructure at one end. Pompey's great theatre in Rome's *centro storico* survives only as a shape in the street plan, and in
the cellars of some buildings on the site. At Istanbul the Byzantine walls still
frame the city, and Justinian's great church to Holy Wisdom, Haghia Sophia,
is now a spectacular mosque. Otherwise the most impressive Roman
remains of Constantine's new Rome are subterranean; the vast cisterns built
to store the aqueduct delivered water on which the city, built on a riverless
promontory, depended.

Sometimes an ancient city seems very present at the heart of a modern capital. This is rarely an accident. Today Rome and Athens seem like architectural palimpsests, spaces on which many city-scapes have been inscribed. But many ancient civic centres are only visible as a result of clearance projects in the nineteenth and twentieth centuries designed to reveal and highlight their classical ancestry.[2] Traces of minarets and mosques are mostly gone from the Athenian Acropolis and the districts around it, which were once Ottoman villages. Renaissance Rome still stands over and around the ancient city, but Mussolini removed much of its mediaeval predecessor to expose the imperial fora and great monumental stages for his own parades. The city has been edited, with some periods stripped out and others restored. Archaeological parks are increasingly common: in Mérida in Spain and at Lyon in France extensive areas have been excavated and conserved.

If we want to get a sense of the original physical impression of an ancient city we usually need to visit cities that were abandoned at the end of antiquity or even earlier. It is still possible to walk through block after block of Pompeii and Herculaneum, both preserved by the cataclysm of the eruption of Vesuvius in 79 C.E. and by the happier accident of their rediscovery in just

Figure 26 A street in Herculaneum
Gerard Puigmal / Getty Images

the period when Grand Tourists from northern Europe were beginning to visit Italy in search of sites and antiquities. Herculaneum is much smaller than Pompeii. Because it was covered in mud rather than ash, some of its most famous monuments were actually explored by tunnelling rather than conventional excavation from above. The Villa of the Papyri, in which a mass of classical sculpture and the charred remains of a private library were recovered by the first excavators, is one example. The famous "underground" theatre of Herculaneum is another. Unusually, some private housing survives to the second storey (almost unheard of in ancient cities), and we have some sense of the tall enclosed side streets of an ancient city (see Figure 26).

The excavated portions of Pompeii include several public spaces, some great thoroughfares, the temples of the gods, the mansions of the local gentry, and all the shops and taverns and public baths and fountains needed in any Roman city. Ostia, at the mouth of the Tiber, one of the ports of Rome, preserves huge brick warehouses and lock-ups. Spice, textiles, aromatic woods, sculptures, and perfumes would all have been stored here. Less visited today than the Vesuvian cities, Ostia is a good place to lose oneself among overgrown streets and forgotten houses. In a few ruined cities it is possible to get some sense of what it was like to wander through a suburban cemetery. The Cerameikos at Athens, just outside its Dipylon Gate, is one. Aquileia and the Isola Sacra in Italy and the Alyschamps outside Roman Arles preserve examples of Roma "grave streets." Long rows of funerary monuments were built along the approach roads to ancient cities, the richest commanding the widest frontages. The facades of house tombs and other monuments greeted travellers. Once or twice a year many of the city-dwellers would come out by the same roads to celebrate meals with their dead ancestors. A few Roman tombs have small holes built into them so that morsels of food and drink could be shared with the dead.

The grandest ruined cities are in places where postclassical populations did not reoccupy or dismantle old buildings. Many are in North Africa, Turkey, and the Near East. Dry conditions and drifting sand slowed the effects of environmental degradation. Across the areas conquered by the Arabs some cities thrived, but many others were abandoned. Alexandria, Seville, and Cordoba became great centres, and although Carthage was destroyed in 698 C.E. after the defeat of Tiberius III at the battle of Carthage, neighbouring Tunis soon grew to take its place as a regional centre. Yet many second-ranking Roman cities in North Africa, some already probably shrinking well before the Arab conquests, were abandoned or as good as abandoned.³ Most of the monuments at sites like Dougga and Timgad date to the early imperial period. There are a few late antique churches and occasionally a much later mosque. Many of these centres survived more or less intact until the nineteenth century. Economic and demographic growth was much faster in the early modern period than in areas south of the Mediterranean, so ancient cities in the Islamic world often survived longer before they were raided for stone or built over.⁴

The situation was broadly similar in the Near East. Antioch, Jerusalem, and Damascus have had their long and complex mediaeval and modern histories, but it is still possible to wander for hours among the excavated ruins of Jerash or Caesarea Maritima; the same was true until recently in Syria. Turkey had a different history in late antiquity and the early Middle Ages. Some cities thrived under centuries of Byzantine and Turkish rule, and lie beneath major Ottoman cities such as Bursa and İzmir or more modern ones like Ankara. There are also extraordinary cities in ruins: Ephesus and Pergamum, Miletus, Priene and Sardis in the west, many Lycian cities on the southwest coast and to their east Perge, Aspendos, and many others. Mostly it is their monuments and street plans that are easiest to see, but now and again we catch a glimpse of other aspects of the ancient city in a row of shops at Sardis, the grand houses at Ephesus, or the spectacular overgrown mountain city of Termessus. Ruined cities are among the most evocative traces of the ancient world. What we see is the hard matter: the skeletons of dinosaurs, not their flesh. For much of antiquity cities were soft-shelled boneless organisms, communities of souls that were born, grew old, and died without leaving fossils of stone and brick. For just a few centuries around the turn of the millennia their inhabitants devoted huge amounts of energy to building monuments they hoped would last forever.

Each ruined city is different, but some motifs appear again and again. Every city had a monumental centre, one or more areas from which ordinary housing and business was excluded. Those centres were often built around one or more public spaces: usually called a *forum* in Latin or an *agora* in Greek. These were the descendants of the multifunctional open areas of archaic cities, areas kept free for markets, assemblies, and religious ceremonies to take place on different days. Now they were clearly demarcated, provided with grand entrances, paved surfaces, and regular outlines formed by the facades of temples and other public buildings. They were often filled with statues and elaborated texts inscribed on bronze or stone. The larger cities had multiple public spaces, sometime including a permanent market for food and other goods. Structures called *macella* are common in some western cities, marble stalls for selling foodstuffs. The public buildings in the centre included a range of different meeting places including law courts; offices for civic officials and their slaves, who kept the public measures and weights; sometimes public dining rooms, in Greek cities. Many buildings still served multiple functions. A *basilica* was simply a vast roofed area which could be used for political meetings or a law court (*dikasterion* in Greek). Great circular banks of seats, mostly set into a hillside, are usually labelled theatres, and drama and other entertainments did take place there, but they were sometimes also used for political gatherings or religious ceremonies. In some cities a meeting place was built for the town council to sit in, a *curia* or *bouleuterion*. These could double as entertainment spaces. There were also specialized *odea*, covered halls where smaller crowds could listen to music or perhaps poetic performances.

The monumental centres of the first centuries C.E. were much larger than the open areas reserved for communal business in earlier cities. So were the grandest temples, themselves often standing in grand sacred areas. Care was usually taken to organize the approach routes to public spaces and the larger temples. Great paved boulevards were created, sometimes lined with colonnades, forming the backbone of planned streets. Processional ways had existed before cities were properly planned. Now they were grander and often articulated with spectacular vistas.[5] Great monumental fountains were sometimes located along the way, fed by aqueducts which also supplied ornamental pools and reservoirs as well as providing drinking water, water to flush out drains and even water for gardening. Elsewhere in the city great complexes were provided for public spectacles of different kinds: circus racing, athletics, drama, and music. There were gymnasia, bathhouses, and many utilitarian structures such as river ports, warehouses, and shops that rebuilt on a monumental scale. Every opportunity was taken to provide spaces in these structures for statues of emperors and civic benefactors.

The history of urbanism in the ancient Mediterranean is a long one, when we are considering cities as human communities or political entities. The monumental city had a much shorter history. A few communities began to transform their civic spaces in the fifth and fourth centuries but most of what we see today was created later, and the vast majority of these buildings date to the centuries around the turn of the millennium. Their creation depends on economic growth, technological advances, peace, and the transmission of skills, but most of all on a new desire for monumentality on the part of the masses and a willingness on the part of the wealthy few to fund those dreams.

Civic Patriotism

Citizens of all ranks expressed passion for their native cities. That passion extended to the cults and festivals, the stones and spaces of the city, its history and myth, its institutions and traditions. It went far beyond political loyalty. Indeed a prejudice in favour of one's home town—what in Italian is called *campanelismo*—is even more visible in periods of antiquity when city-states had little say over their foreign relations or even their constitution, because they were dominated by kingdoms or empires.[6]

Gaius Vibius Salutaris provides an example. His names shows he had Roman citizenship and he was very wealthy indeed, but he was also a citizen of Ephesus, an ancient Greek foundation that was by some measures the most important cities of Roman Asia Minor. In 104 C.E. he created a foundation to fund a regular festival that included processions in which statues of the founders of the city—mythical and more recent—were carried through all the public spaces. The details were inscribed in an inscription of more than five hundred lines set up by the theatre on blocks of marble. It included letters from Roman officials and resolutions by both the council and people of Ephesus. Salutaris had inserted himself into the festival life of his city and created a celebration of a civic identity that was Roman and Greek, ancient and modern. The monumental routes, squares, and buildings provided the stage for his procession, and the inscription was another addition to those monuments.[7]

Salutaris' generosity was spectacular, but not unique. Many of the cities of Asia inscribed the texts of diplomatic letters that confirmed their ancestral links with the ancient cities of Old Greece.[8] The pasts they chose to celebrate often look a little surprising to us. The Persian Wars loomed large in some traditions, the defence of Delphi from the Gauls in others.[9] Athenians continue to celebrate their military past, especially their victories at Marathon, Salamis, and Plataea, well into the time of the Roman Empire. We know this not just from their annual festivals that celebrated these events, but also from the terms in which the second century C.E. orator Aelius Aristides chose to praise them in his speech *To Athens*.[10] Inscriptions in Italy and the West recorded local benefactors who had paid for theatres or the repair of temples, and created foundations to feed citizen children or established annual feasts.

Citizens everywhere wished to see and hear their home cities appreciated. Visiting orators performed speeches praising the cities that hosted them, and some grew rich on the gratitude of those they praised. Even when they were trying to persuade the councillors or citizens to some course of action, orators made sure to reflect back to their audiences their love of their home town. A number of these speeches have survived from Roman period orators. They include a speech made by Favorinus to the Corinthians (asking for a statue in his honour to be restored) and speeches to Rome, Athens, Smyrna, and Cyzicus by Aelius Aristides. Some speeches even tried to calm down the fierce rivalry that *campanelismo* could create. Dio of Prusa tried to bring about harmonious relations between the rival neighbouring cities of Nicomedia and Nicaea, and spoke firmly to the Alexandrines about their rowdy behaviour at the circus, taking care also to praise their city as the second greatest in the empire, to celebrate its wealth and commerce and its god Serapis. Apuleius spoke at Carthage praising the god Aesculapius in his temple. Speeches in praise of Athens and Sparta were performed in memory of the Persian Wars. These events attracted audiences well beyond the few hundred members of the landed elite that ran even moderately sized towns.

A darker side of civic patriotism emerged when it occasionally erupted into intercommunal violence. Barcino and Tarraco in Spain, Vienne and Lyon in France, and numerous neighbouring cities in Asia Minor sometimes inclined to different sides in a Roman civil war. Citizens of Nuceria attending gladiatorial games in Pompeii in 59 C.E. came to blows with the locals in a riot recorded by Tacitus and depicted on a wall painting from the city. Aristides addressed the provincial council of Asia to argue that the virtues of Ephesus, Pergamum, and Smyrna all be appreciated.[11] A series of inscriptions and local coins celebrating harmony or consensus among the orders obliquely refer to the threat of the reverse. A treatise on civic statesmanship by the philosopher Plutarch reminds cities that the disputes they could not sort out among themselves might end up being resolved by Romans. Embassies to the emperor and to his governors were common enough in fact, and many did concern local struggles for status. Cities competed for the privilege of building the provincial temple to the latest emperor to have been deified, and they argued over which cities the governors should visit when they made their annual tour of the assizes, even over which city newly appointed governors should arrive in when they went to their provinces.[12] In all this we see the propertied classes, the educated, and the civic masses making common cause around the merits of their home city. Benefactors won great prestige at home when they paid for monuments or festivals. Those of the wealthy not believed to be paying their way faced huge unpopularity, as a few trials and imperial letters reveal. The dossier of inscriptions and one biography of one of the richest private individuals we know of, Herodes Atticus of Athens, reveal how much animosity his own extreme wealth (and arrogance) aroused. He is not the only provincial grandee who survived local intrigues mainly because of his friendship with the emperor.[13] He built great monuments in Athens, Olympia, and elsewhere. But the people expected more.

Local identities probably mattered much more to many people than whether they were Romans or Greeks or both.[14] Tombstones proudly declared the deceased were citizens of Laodicaea or Antioch, Lepcis or Sabratha, Arles or Trier. Cities were often represented on local coins by images of their most spectacular buildings or their patron deities.[15] Descriptions of cities, and especially of their monuments, fill works like Pausanias' *Journey around Greece* and Strabo's *Geography*. Cities remembered (or invented) foundation myths and traditions about local heroes, some of which became the basis for local histories.[16] Athens naturally generated a mass of local histories. Hellanicus of Lesbos wrote one with which Thucydides was familiar. There were at least six more Atthidographers— historians of the Athenians—mostly writing in the late fourth and early third century B.C.E., each compiling a collection of myths and historical events, accounts and explanations of local institutions.[17] They shared a fascination with early myth and with the political and military history of the fifth and fourth centuries.

The public spaces of even quite modest cities came to be filled with statues and inscriptions honouring local benefactors. Often the statues are so alike in their clothing and posture that only the accompanying text distinguishes them. Since most citizens could not read, they moved through a city filled with memorials to anonymous benefactors. The statues were at the same time a reproach and an incentive to those of the wealthy who had not yet provided evidence of their local patriotism. There were many ways to be generous.[18] Occasionally we know of a magistrate or orator who had gone on an embassy at his own expense, or paid for the repair of a temple or a bathhouse. Buildings were a big expense, but it was also possible to pay for regular feasts or games or athletic or musical competitions, to establish schools or libraries, or create foundations to feed children or be reserved for use in time of food crises to buy or subsidize grain. Wealthy women as well as men were honoured for their benevolence—their *euergetism*—towards their fellow citizens.[19]

Civic generosity reached a peak in the first centuries C.E. Peace and prosperity had made the rich especially prominent, and perhaps also especially vulnerable to social pressure. It had various roots. Some western cities imposed contributions (*munera*) on magistrates when they were elected, and sometimes magistrates made promises (*pollicitationes*) before the election about what they would provide if successful. Those promises were legally binding. Republican Roman generals had often made battlefield vows of a portion of their booty in the event of victory: formally the temples they built were gifts to the gods, but they also beautified the city. In fifth- and fourth-century Athens and in at least some other cities, there were regular liturgies: a wealthy citizen was required to pay for a trireme or for the performance of a play or some other festival. There was quite a difference, naturally, between being compelled to subsidize Athenian democracy—the liturgies do actually seem to have impoverished some families in the fourth century—and simply handing over a share of the plunder after a victory. After democracy, and especially after the imposition of the Roman peace, we begin to see the emergence within the propertied classes of a small number of families with spectacular wealth. The most foolish of the super-rich could even compete with emperors in their benefactions. Even in the Roman Empire there were some benefactors who needed to have their arms twisted to do the decent thing.[20] Monumental inscriptions say nothing about how spontaneous each gift had been.

The Monuments of Athens

Monumentalization was always expensive. When it depended on private benefactors its progress was uneven and sometimes idiosyncratic. Some cities built faster than others. There are some broader patterns in the order in which different kinds of monuments appeared.[21] Those patterns reflect changing priorities about what made a city great, and also the growing capacity—economic and technological—to create spectacular public works. But benefactors had a lot of freedom of choice. If the richest man of town wanted to build a library rather than fund a feast, his fellow citizens were likely stuck with it. A case study helps reveal some of the complexities. Athens, atypical as it is in many ways, is a good place to start.

The city of Athens has some claim to being one of the oldest continuously occupied cities in Europe. Its topography is better known than most other cities from archaeology and travellers' tales, as well as from ancient testimony. It follows that here have been many monumental cities of Athens. The first was the (now lost) Athens of the Bronze Age. Contemporary with the great centres known from excavations at Mycenae, Tiryns, and Pylos, there was a citadel on the Athenian Acropolis and within it, a palace. Almost no traces survive, but there are tombs from the fourteenth century and a fortification wall from the thirteenth, as well as the remains of a water supply. Bronze Age palaces were never completely isolated. We should imagine a community living around the Acropolis too, most likely around the later *agora*, and perhaps elsewhere as well. Three millennia of urbanism has almost completely erased this first monumental Athens.

The early Iron Age settlement consisted mostly of scattered farms interspersed by fields and cemeteries. The Acropolis with its Bronze Age ruins provided a visual focus and a refuge if needed. Myths about the founding kings—Cecrops, Theseus, and others—were associated with the citadel. Its inhabitants now were gods, not kings. Collective cults must have taken place on the Acropolis but—just as elsewhere in this period—no major structures seem to have been built for it. It is always possible, of course, that there were some sort of temples underlying later buildings. The archaic city will always remain a little mysterious.

The first major monuments of the classical city appeared in the sixth century B.C.E. and were two massive temples built on the Acropolis. One was a structure built in limestone in the Doric style, probably where the Parthenon now stands; a second later one was built between there and where the Erechtheion now stands. Both were dedicated to Athena Polias, Athena of the City. These structures were local manifestations of the trend for temple-building we can see across much of the Aegean world in the sixth century B.C.E. Quarries were being opened up and architects experimented with larger and more elaborate structures. By comparison, most domestic housing must have seemed quite humble. Nor was there much town planning in sixth-century Athens. There were probably no major roads, apart from the sacred way that led from the Dipylon Gate across the *agora* to the approaches to the Acropolis. There must have been some collective agreement to keep some spaces like the *agora* open for communal use and to maintain the boundary between inhabited space and land given over to the dead. By Solon's day we know boundary stones were being used for other purposes, so perhaps there was already a clear demarcation of public space. Once again the long history of later building makes this difficult to decide for sure. The same is true of Athens' earliest walls. Many Greek cities began to build walls in the ninth and eighth centuries, and Athens certainly had one. But the first version of the city's fortifications is barely known, and they were replaced by larger and more complex structures in the fifth and fourth centuries.

Athens in 500 B.C.E., on the eve of the Persian Wars, remained a loosely settled conurbation covering around 200 hectares enclosed by a wall. Tyrants and others had begun to give the city some shape. The agora was the main public space, used sometimes for political or religious purposes, sometimes for markets. The hill of the Pnyx was probably already reserved for assemblies (although what they did under the tyranny is a bit unclear). On the southeast slope of the Acropolis a natural depression had been sculpted into a cavea, or enclosure, to form the first Theatre of Dionysus. Here civic dramas were performed during the festivals of the Greater Dionysia and the Lenaea. The only monuments of any size remained the temples on the Acropolis. Work had already begun on replacing them before the Persians sacked the city in 480 B.C.E.

The Persian sack and Athens' subsequent age of imperial greatness enabled a modest expansion of the monumental city. New walls were built around the city, and extensions were later added all the way down to the harbour at Piraeus. Behind its Long Walls Athens was an inshore island, one that could be protected and provisioned from the sea. During the first summers of the Peloponnesian War, Athenians would shelter within the walls while Spartan armies marched around the Attic countryside. On the Acropolis the Parthenon and the Erechtheum were constructed at great expense, partly paid for by allies. A monumental approach to the sanctuary, the Propylaea, was constructed. Pericles had a small covered odeon raised beside the Theatre of Dionysus in 435 B.C.E., allegedly from timber taken from captured Persian warships. Around the *agora* a series of small public buildings appeared. The law courts were the largest structure. There was also a council chamber, a public dining room, and some other buildings. Sanctuaries and smaller temples were set up elsewhere around the city.

This monumental city was almost entirely public. The fiercely democratic ideology of the fifth and fourth centuries meant that the wealthy were careful not to create ostentatious mansions and for a while even stopped building magnificent tombs for themselves. This marks a real contrast with the cities being built in central Italy at the same time, where aristocratic housing and grand necropoleis were widespread. Naturally some Athenian houses were more spacious than others.[22] Behind their closed doors occasions were found for luxurious display, rich meals, and the elaborate drinking parties known as *symposia*. But the greatest buildings of the city were all about citizen solidarity. Outside the Dipylon Gate a public cemetery for the war dead—the *demosion sema*—was laid out. It was the site of annual speeches in their memory, speeches that constantly reformulated and reproduced the ideological foundations of democracy. Pericles' *epitaphios* (or at least Thucydides' version of it) is the most famous example, but honouring the citizen dead was a sacred routine in Athens.[23]

Modern visitors to Athens tend to head straight for the Acropolis to admire the temples built in the middle of the fifth century B.C.E., the age when Pericles was in the ascendant. Yet much of what they actually see is more recent. Even imperial Athens had limited resources to expend on public works, and the techniques and material to construct much larger buildings were still not available. Building classical Athens was the work of many generations. The marble aesthetic spread gradually. The Theatre of Dionysus was rebuilt in the fourth century B.C.E. with marble seats and permanent stage buildings. Marble thrones for dignatories were not added until the third or second century. This is also the period in which marble inscriptions become common. Larger projects awaited the patronage of kings. For a while, in the third and second centuries B.C.E., the historical prestige of Athens—and the fact it already attracted visitors—meant it became *the* place to build if you wanted the world to know about your support for Greek culture.[24] The Royal Stoa (*stoa basilike* from which the Latin equivalent *basilica* derives) housed the Areopagus, the old council that was mostly concerned with religious offense. The Painted Stoa, built in the early fifth century, was a rather splendid colonnaded structure decorated with scenes of Athenian victories and captured spoils. Legal cases were heard there, but at other times it was a sort of gallery open for public use.

The kings of Pergamum were particularly generous in funding monumental building in Athens.[25] A series of statues were set up on the south side of the Acropolis, probably a gift from Attalus I to commemorate—and advertise—his defeat of the Gauls. Like Sicilian tyrants who capitalized on keeping the Carthaginians at bay, the kings of Pergamum liked to present themselves as protectors of the Greek cities from the barbarian hordes on the Anatolian plateau. Quite often the most generous kings were those whose own credentials as Greeks might be called into doubt. Macedonians were not really Greeks in the eyes of some. The Attalids, and later the kings of Pontus, were even less certainly Hellenic. Greek inscriptions tend to reserve the label "philhellene" (lover of the Greeks) for those they regarded as friendly barbarians.[26] Monumental Athens owed a lot—over the centuries that followed the end of democracy—to friendly barbarians.

Successive building projects extended the public area of the city, framed public spaces, and created backdrops and stages for civic ceremonial. Eumenes II of Pergamum built a long covered walkway leading west from the Theatre of Dionysus. His brother Attalus II funded a great stoa flanking the agora on one side. It was reconstructed in the 1950s as a base for American excavations and today also houses a museum. Those excavations have revealed the stages by which the agora developed from an open space with a few public buildings on its fringes to something approaching a great enclosed monumental piazza. Other kings turned their attention to other parts of the city. A great monumental gymnasium was provided by one of the Ptolemies. Antiochus IV, the Seleucid, provided funds to resume work on the vast temple of Olympian Zeus in the southeast.

Eventually the Romans joined in. Relations between Rome and Athens were not always good in the Republican period, and Athens was actually sacked in 86 B.C.E. by Sulla after the city allied with Mithridates, king of Pontus. The city picked sides badly during the Roman civil wars too. But at the very end of the Republican period things changed for the better. A great marketplace—now called the Roman agora—was built in marble, funded first by Julius Caesar and then by Augustus. Next to it stands the Tower of the Winds, a marble tower bearing sundials, a water clock, and a wind vane. An odeon, funded by Augustus' friend Agrippa, was built in the middle of the agora. The Roman period agora was no longer a multipurpose open space; tt was a monumental park more like the Field of Mars in Rome, also being monumentalized by Agrippa. From the second century C.E. Athens became once again a spectacular site for architectural display. Hadrian founded a vast library with lecture halls and colonnades. He also completed the Olympeion, which Antiochus IV had promised to build but failed to do. It dwarfs the Parthenon in scale, although not in location. Herodes Atticus created an odeon, both larger and more elaborate than the theatre of Dionysus. It remains in use today for concerts and other performances. Herodes also rebuilt the fourth-century B.C.E. stadium in marble: it was refurbished again to be used for the first modern Olympics. By now the city had expanded well beyond its fifth-century B.C.E. limits. The arch of Hadrian, built on the edge of a newly developed district, claims the emperor as a second founder of the city, after Theseus. The new quarter was planned in a way the old city, which had grown organically, was not. Roman visitors to Athens encountered a whole series of gymnasia and schools. Pausanias began his account of the marvels of Old Greece with a description of what a second-century C.E. visitor would see if he arrived in the Piraeus and went up to the city. Grave marker by grave marker, colonnade by colonnade, painting by famous painting, the passage through the city constantly triggers memories of great episodes of Greek history.

The monumentalization of ancient Athens reached its peak in the second century C.E. Where the inscriptions of the fifth and fourth century document the decrees of the *demos*—the people—those of the Roman city describe the benefactions of the rich. Local grandees led its cultural life and its increasingly undemocratic politics, with a lot of financial help from the emperors and from rich foreign residents.[27] The last big building project was a circuit wall built after the city was sacked in 267 C.E. by the Heruli, a group from north of the Black Sea who had broken through the imperial frontiers, but it was not the result of a spectacular benefaction. Like many third-century C.E. circuit walls, it was built in a hurry out of fragments of earlier buildings and protected only a small area of the city: the Acropolis was inside the circuit, but most of the agora was outside it. Athens did recover, and was still a major educational centre in the fourth century when the orator Libanius of Antioch studied there. It continued to be a centre for the teaching of philosophy until the emperor Justinian closed the schools in 529 C.E. on the grounds they were incompatible with Christian culture. But the epoch of monumental building that had begun slowly with temple-building in the sixth century C.E. had diversified in the fifth and fourth centuries, and experienced a boom under the patronage of Macedonian monarchs and Roman emperors between the third century B.C.E. and before the second C.E. was over.

Marbling the Med

The monumentalization of Athens progressed by fits and starts. The imperial age of Pericles was one high spot, and Pergamene benefactions another. The Augustan age and the reign of Hadrian also stand out. Between them there were long periods when no great projects were conceived and completed. Political ups and downs played a part, but what made the most difference was the varying supply of funds. Even the Athenian state, with a much larger territory than most Greek poleis, depended on outside income for its most spectacular building. Economic growth and political growth were the engines that powered monument building, or better could power it when the will was there.

Athens was not typical, of course, but its monumentalization reflects some wider trends. First there was a gradual expansion of the range of monuments built, beginning with temples. During the fifth and fourth centuries B.C.E. buildings for the gods were supplemented by buildings for the city. Law courts, dining rooms and council chambers, assembly places, theatres, stadia and odea all provided grand locations for civic populations to share. Then, from the third century onwards, the patronage of monarchs began to transform a tiny number of cities. Vast theatres were constructed in Syracuse and Pergamum, gifts given to major temples, great civic buildings like stoas added. As well as patronizing ancient cities like Athens, the kings built spectacular capitals of their own at Antioch, on the Orontes; Seleuceia, on the Tigris; and Alexandria, on the Nile.

Another direction of movement we can identify in urban design was the tendency to imagine urbanistic projects in ever larger units. Reserving an area like the forum or the circus maximus as a zone in which private building was not allowed was just the first step. There was also the appearance of planned street grids, first used in new cities but soon applied to old as well. It is probably not true that these were invented by the famous fifth-century architect Hippodamus of Miletus, but he did use a grid plan when developing the Athenian port of the Piraeus, and soon most new precincts and some new cities were planned this way from the start. Hippodamian-style grids were orthogonal: they were made up of roads laid out at right angles to each other, even if the blocks formed were not necessarily square. It was new districts like Hadrian's extension of Athens, and especially new urban foundations, that were more likely to be built on a grid plan.

Corinth provides a wonderful example of these changes. At the centre of the city the archaic temples and agora on the plain below Acrocorinth are on their own alignments. Around this area the lines of the first orthogonal grids can be seen. Although the main processional routes to the city's two ports structure much of the city, farther out the characteristic square-planned blocks and centuriated fields of the Roman colony founded by Julius Caesar are visible. Each stage of its development introduced new regularities. New cities were much more ordered. Some of the most regularly planned Greek cities were those created in the seventh and sixth centuries in Sicily and southern Italy. As Rome created daughter settlements up and down Italy, and then in her western provinces, more and more orthogonal grids appeared.

It is not entirely clear what functions this kind of planning served. Conceivably, in newly settled areas dividing up the agricultural territory between settlers was easier within a grid, but that hardly applied to city blocks. Sometimes the use of an orthogonal plan seems perverse. At Priene it stretches up a steep hillside in a way that pays no attention to the relief. Planning whole districts or entire towns is a sign of authority, the power to impose order on space. Hadrian's city looked different than that of Theseus. The new cities created by the founders of military colonies in the Seleucid east or the Roman west reflect the power of a new ruler to declare *terra nullius*, the complete abolition of prior property rights. Perhaps a similar aesthetic of regularity is reflected in the way many public spaces came to be enclosed with buildings that gave them clearer boundaries. In new cities, the agora or forum often occupied one or more blocks in the centre of the street grid.

By the second century B.C.E. a few cities were also having entire monumental quarters planned and laid out. Alexandria was probably one of the first. At Rome the transition from planning grand buildings to planning grand districts took place somewhere in the last century B.C.E. with Pompey's Theatre and the Forum of Julius Caesar, although a few of the larger temples on the campus Martius had had quite large precincts in the second century. The Roman Market at Athens is another example of this kind of coordinated structure. Centralized control, especially from a monarchy, definitely made this sort of project easier to achieve. It rapidly became a feature of planned urbanism in early imperial Italy and the western provinces.

Underpinning this was not just economic growth and the appearance of very rich benefactors. There was also technical and architectural experimentation. From the sixth century B.C.E. on we can see cities imitating their neighbours and trying to outdo them. There are many anecdotes about architects who worked in more than one city, and by the last century B.C.E. Roman generals were quite explicit that their domestic building projects were inspired by theatres and other structures they had seen in subject states. Less glamorously there was the exploration of different sources of stone and of long timbers; the opening up of quarries; the development of a trade in marbles, hard stones, and timber; and eventually innovations based on architecture in brick and concrete.

Herodes' Odeon on the slopes of the Acropolis could never have been built by Pericles, even if he had been able to raise the money, because it employed design and constructional techniques simply not available in the fifth century B.C.E. Some parts were traditional—the curved seating set into the hillside, the monumental backdrop modelled on Roman theatres—but the scale was unprecedented. It could accommodate 5,000 people, whereas the odeion built by Agrippa in the agora in 15 B.C.E. had room for only a thousand. The roof of Pericles' odeon had been supported by a forest of pillars. Those of Agrippa and Herodes did without internal supports, in the latter case roofing a pace with a radius of 38 metres. Athens is a laboratory in which we can watch eight centuries of ancient building techniques being developed.

Finding ways to create large free-standing structures was a particular technical challenge. The first stone theatres were almost all built on hillsides; anything built in the round had to use temporary seating of wood. The development of arches and vaults and eventually domes made it possible to support much larger buildings without making them prohibitively heavy. They also opened up new monumental possibilities. From the late Republic great basilicas soared up above the Roman forum just as stoas had begun to enclose the Athenian agora. The circus Maximus at Rome was surrounded by multistorey arcades at the turn of the millennia.

Grandiose designs demanded some new materials. Marble is very heavy. The same hardness that makes it durable and polishable makes it difficult to quarry and work, even with iron tools. Deposits of marble are unevenly distributed around the Mediterranean world. Much of the rocky basin containing the Mediterranean originated on the bottom of a shallow prehistoric sea. As a result it is largely composed of soft and crumbly limestones, karsts, calcites, and dolomites. Marble results when these sedimentary formations are put under enormous pressure and heat by tectonic activity.

Outcrops of marble are found on many of the Aegean islands, in parts of southern Greece and northwest Turkey, and in a few places in Tuscany and North Africa.

Small pieces of marble were used to make figurines in the Aegean Bronze Age. Larger-scale work began with the creation of *kouroi* and *korai*—larger than life-size sculptures of youths, male and female, used as grave monuments and dedications in temples—and they probably first appeared in the seventh century, an adaptation of Egyptian statuary. Marble as a building material came a little later. At first just a few islands—famously Paros and Naxos—supplied the modest demands of many cities. As the desire to built large temples from hard stone spread, so did marble production. Deposits of marble were found in western Turkey. Quarries near Ephesus were exploited from the sixth century B.C.E. Athenians probably began to exploit Pentelic marble on a large scale only in the fifth century.

It is impossible not to be impressed by the speed with which the construction of massive stone temples spread around the Aegean. Monumental building of this kind was fantastically expensive in labour. The construction of the Parthenon we see today took fifteen years, from 447 to 432 B.C.E. The structure was big for the period—about 70 by 30 metres in plan—and elaborate, especially on the outer friezes. Pericles' project had the resources of imperial Athens behind it; it was the prestige project of the greatest city of its day, and even so it took half a generation to complete. Revenue from the empire was used to pay the day labourers (or more often their owners since much of the work was carried out by slaves). The scale of work that went into the Parthenon is staggering. The construction of the first archaic temples must have absorbed the energy of entire city-states for a generation.

At first only white marbles were used in building, and a limited number of quarries supplied the cities of the Aegean. Over the last centuries B.C.E. more and more quarries were opened up as appetites increased. The taste for building in marble spread to many areas without local supplies. The archaic and classical temples of central Italy were built of different materials, especially tufas, and brilliant decorative effects were achieved with terracotta. Complex statues were made first in parts, and then assembled and painted. The rooftops of Etruscan temples were brilliant displays of colour, and gods and heroes stood on the summits or peered down from friezes. Marble friezes and statuary were painted as well, but what could be achieved with the lighter material of fired clay was different to what could be worked in hard stone.

Rome began to use white marble in the late second and early first centuries B.C.E. Both materials and sculptors travelled there from the Aegean, especially from Attica. Marble was scarce in the western Mediterranean and was imported long distances until quarries were opened up at Luni in the Augustan Age. A fashion had already begun for coloured marble. In the middle of the first century C.E. Pliny the Elder listed many varieties in his *Natural History*. There were brescias, green and red marbles, marbles in which white stone was mottled in grey. A new aesthetic had brought an international marble trade into existence.[28] At Chemtou in Numidia a range of brilliant yellow marbles were produced from the end of the second century B.C.E., loaded on shallow barges, and floated down the Mehjeda River to the port of Utica, from which they could be shipped to Rome. Something similar happened a century later in Egypt when the hard granites of the eastern desert became popular. These quarries were so inhospitable that bread and water had to be transported in for the workers and the columns moved for hundreds of kilometers overland, until they reached a point on the Nile where the first of a series of specially designed vessels could carry them on their long journey to Rome and other centres. The most famous Egyptian granite was porphyry, the colour of imperial purple. There was more to the marble trade than quarrying. Islands like Thasos and Paros, famous for their marble, also produced celebrated sculptors. Methods of cutting, transporting, and finishing marble improved over time. Some marble was moved in the form of blocks or column drums, which were individually easier to handle. But a complete column of porphyry could only be moved using specialized river vessels and shipping. The major ports developed expertise with cranes and salvage, divers and porters.

Very large buildings also required long timbers, and there were not many forests in the Mediterranean Basin that could supply them.[29] The forests of Macedonia were an early source of fir and mountain pine for Aegean cities. Rome and Italy used timber from the Apennine slopes behind Genua, and also from the Alpine areas at the head of the Adriatic. There are some indications that by the reign of Hadrian the cedar forests of Lebanon were famous, and reserved for imperial use.

Not all great buildings could be built of hard stones. Architecture of brick and tile made possible the tower blocks and commercial buildings we can still see in Ostia. Great brickyards grew up in the first centuries C.E. along the valley of the Tiber, where river clays were easily extracted and fired in standardized sizes.[30] Some were stamped—originally to help control different batches in complex production systems in which several owners might collaborate at various stages—and this has allowed historians to track the growth of the brickyards and see which families profited from them. Brick was also an important material for building baths, because of its insulating qualities. The other vital material was concrete, and the hydraulic waterproof concretes developed in the last century B.C.E. also made possible swimming pools, fish tanks, harbour construction, and food processing plants, among much else.

The development and spread of new building technologies is a rapidly moving field of research.[31] The exact origins of many stones can now be found by petrology and other scientific techniques. The most spectacular examples of architecture were those funded by the emperors. The Roman *thermae* (baths) are a revelation with their soaring domes and vaults, their complex heating systems and hydraulic engineering, and their spectacular use of coloured stones and of glass. Walk around the Baths of Diocletian near Stazione Termini or wander the park in which the Baths of Caracalla stand, and you will have a master class in ancient architecture.[32]

Urban Essentials

There is a famous passage from Pausanias' *Journey around Greece,* compiled under Roman rule in the second century C.E., in which the city of Panopeus is held up as the most feeble kind of polis:

> If someone can use the word *polis* to describe a community who have neither government buildings (*archaia*) nor a gymnasium, neither theatre nor agora, who do not even have a water supply feeding a fountain and who live in bare shelters like mountain cabins right on a ravine.[33]

Panopeus was a community and an old one. Juridically, it remained a city-state. It sent envoys to the Phocian assembly and it had its own boundaries and a temple. It had foundation legends and was even mentioned by Homer, the ultimate pedigree for a Greek city.

Pausanias' dismissive remarks shows how far urban ideals had changed over the centuries, although perhaps they also reveal the prejudice of a citizen of a smart "new" Asian city about a shabby one with an ancient name.[34] No sixth-century B.C.E. polis boasted all the amenities second-century C.E. Panopeus lacked. Irregular housing with a temple at its centre was pretty much the physical definition of a city in the archaic period. Now, near the end of the long centuries of architectural elaboration, a city was also to be judged in terms of its monuments, of its physical presence in the landscape.

Pausanias' list begins with buildings devoted to communal uses that were not religious. The term he uses—*archaia*—is a little vague. Probably this denotes buildings like the public dining room (the *prytaneion*), the mint, the law courts and any council chambers, and perhaps stoas, a general term for a covered colonnade that allowed business to be conducted when the weather meant doing business out of doors was less practical.

The next amenity that Pausanias mentioned was communal but less overtly political: the gymnasium. Training of various kinds was an important part of the way young men became citizens, and becoming a citizen in many cities involved a period of apprenticeship that involved physical training and military service of various kinds. Yet as far as we can tell these cohorts of youths—*ephebes* in Athens, youths undergoing the *agoge* in Sparta, and aristocratic *iuvenes* at Rome—trained in open spaces until the fourth century B.C.E. Only at the end of the classical period are there references to spaces set aside for sport and education, the prototype of the gymnasium. The original Lyceum in which Aristotle taught was probably not very grand. Soon gardens and colonnades were created, as well as exercise spaces (*palaestrae*), running tracks, and bathing facilities. There were sometimes one or more rooms for lectures and perhaps small libraries. The wealthier cities of Asia Minor in particular (from where Pausanias himself originated) often had grand gymnasium complexes that were civic monuments in their own right, with statuary and inscriptions around the training spaces and sometimes great bathhouses attached.[35] Naturally these too were paid for by benefactors. This is true at Pergamum and Ephesus and Sardis, where a great bath-gymnasium complex has been partly reconstructed. The culture of the gymnasium seems to have particularly taken off in the Greek cities contained within the Macedonian kingdoms founded by Alexander's successors. Democratic structures, by contrast, were less prominent. In Egypt a gymnasial class emerged in the Roman period—shorthand for those families that could afford to give their sons an athletic and intellectual education in the gymnasium. Athleticism had been one criterion of aristocratic identity for centuries, celebrated in literature, incorporated into the designs of grand houses, and illustrated on their mosaics floors.[36] Now it was a sign that one had signed up for a set of international values connecting Greek-speaking elites. Gymnasia flourished from Sicily to Asia in the second century B.C.E. By the second century C.E. Greek games had spread over much of the western Mediterranean, and there were athletic contests not just in ancient Greek cities like Naples and Marseilles but also in Rome and Vienne.[37]

Theatre, in Pausanias' list, can perhaps be understood as shorthand for the great variety of buildings dedicated to spectacle in ancient cities. I have already mentioned theatres and amphitheatres, circuses, stadia, and odea. We probably worry more about the differences between them than did the ancients, who adapted many structures to serve numerous functions. Gladiators fought at least once a year in the Theatre of Dionysus in Roman Athens, as they did in the Circus Maximus at Rome before the Colosseum was built. The Great Theatre of Ephesus was used for assemblies. Many Greek *bouleuteria* are difficult to distinguish from *odea*. During festivals all the public spaces and major streets of a city were liable to be co-opted for processions, sacrifices, and performances of different kinds. During the first centuries C.E. the commonest type of theatre built in Rome's northwest provinces was a kind of hybrid with a circular space that could be used for all sorts of entertainments instead of a stage, with seating just on one side, as in a theatre. This was an economical solution for communities that could only afford one building, although it was common enough to have an amphitheatre and a theatre and sometimes a stadium or circus as well. The last comprehensive catalogue of spectacle buildings documented more than six hundred examples.[38] That was in 1988, and every regional survey since then has added more.[39]

The final item Pausanias mentions is water supply. Civic fountains were another late addition to most cities. A few like Corinth, with the fountain of Peirene, had ancient springs within their walls. Many relied on cisterns to supplement river courses that ran shallow and brackish in the summer months. Hydraulic engineering and irrigation was developed independently in several places. Egypt and Babylonia had long histories of managing flood-water. Etruscan Italy developed sewers, storm drains, and gravity-fed water supply. Roman aqueducts grew from this tradition. Pergamum was one of the first eastern cities to have its own aqueduct. Cities in the east did not often rely on bringing water from a distance, perhaps because it made them vulnerable in time of siege, perhaps because the technical challenges and the cost were so high. All this changed with the Roman peace. Water was used in many ways in ancient cities. Running water might be used to wash out sewers and public latrines, to water gardens, and of course for drinking, although rainwater was preferred whenever possible, as it was cleaner. There were water features—artificial ponds—and natural springs were enhanced to make them more splendid. As use of Roman-style baths spread from the late first century B.C.E., more and more cities needed aqueducts to supply them.[40] During the second century C.E. a new style of urban monument became widespread: the monumental fountain. Often decorated with elaborate columns and statuary, these *nymphaea* represented extravagant displays of wealth and power. What greater display of generosity could the wealthy make than to provide limitless fresh water in the heat of a Mediterranean summer? At Aspendos a great series of arches carries the aqueduct across the valley from a distant hill onto the acropolis of the city, where the great *nymphaeum* was set up. A spectacular aqueduct and *nymphaeum* were provided for third-century C.E. Lepcis on the Libyan coast. Carthage had an aqueduct that was eventually 132 kilometres long. At Perge an open channel carried water down the centre of a long colonnaded street. This was an extravagance in the arid Mediterranean summer, a display of wealth just as impressive in its way as gold statues or marble temples.

All the City's a Stage

Pausanias' list of what was lacking from Panopeus shows us clearly what had changed in the physical appearance of cities between the archaic age and the Roman Empire. It was, in his day, a sort of living fossil, a community still living together around a temple, with a sense of their own past but not much else. Everything that in his eyes they lacked were in fact adornments that cities with access to patronage had acquired from the fourth century B.C.E. Panopeus was certainly not unusual and indeed perhaps the majority of cities were like this, even in the early Roman Empire. The world around had changed; they had not. Nor was Pausanias unusual, for the ideal of urbanism he holds up was perfectly conventional by the standards of his age and of his social class. A gulf had opened up between the experience of Mediterranean micro-cities and the dreams of civic magnificence. It was those dreams that were new. It was not always obvious that a city should contain much more than the homes of the gods and of their worshippers.

It is perfectly possible to account for these changes between the sixth century B.C.E. and the second C.E. in terms of economic growth, the concentration of wealth, and developments in design and technology. But this only tells us the how, not the why. What was the value of monumental cities, given that Mediterranean communities had done so well for so long without them? Nothing in the coagulating communities of the early first millennium predetermined that they would be expanded in the directions eventually chosen. Other things could have been done with those resources, and different social priorities might have brought forth other technologies. Notice the subjects on which Pausanias is silent: housing, infrastructure, manufacturing facilities, commercial premises, a means of delivering advances in health or well-being, or education aimed at the masses rather than solely at the young men in the gymnasium. Why did ancient cities grow up they way they did?

It is not unusual, among premodern urbanisms, for cities to develop into monumental forms. Not all do. Many European cities had little in the way of monuments in the Middle Ages beyond churches and castles. The Bronze Age cities of the Near East with their ziggurats, or the great royal cities of Assyria and Persia with vast palace courtiers, impressed observers. The capitals of Mexican and Andean states were spectacular. Early Chinese cities were perhaps less monumental than were the palaces of those who ruled them. Every kind of urbanization involves a concentration of power, and the complexity of urban societies is almost always reflected in steeper hierarchies of power. Cities were not the only places that the rulers of states could spend their wealth and display their power. They could bestow benefactions on sanctuaries, build rural palaces and great necropoleis like the tomb of the First Emperor of China, and they could spend on great roads and canals. Their cities could be inward-facing, restricting most of their population from penetrating far inside, or they could be built to gather up great crowds to observe spectacles and ceremonies. Monuments could be for display, to exercise control, or both.

The urban monumentality of the ancient Mediterranean was all about participation. Everything began from religious building, the great generation-long projects that brought communities together and then enabled them to fix their boundaries with their neighbours.[41] Sanctuaries were the original anchors of early Iron Age communities in Greece and in Italy, and perhaps in other areas too. They were places at which many more people than simply the immediate inhabitants would gather. Sacred precincts, sacred ways, and areas set aside for crowds of thousand to sit and spectate were all designed to increase the participation of wider groups.[42] Participating in a sacrifice and sharing in the meal that followed could only ever involve a handful of people directly. But there were also games held in honour of a god, or dramas performed within a festival, for which many more could be brought in. The monumentality of ancient Mediterranean cities, in other words, was geared to broad participation of city-state citizens in the running of the community. Greek urban architecture set the pace. Even Rome had no permanent monumental structures for drama, gladiatorial combats, or athletics before the last century B.C.E., relying instead on temporary arrangements in the forum and the valley of the circus Maximus. As Greek and Roman models of urban monumentality spread, so too did the characteristic architectural forms described at the start of the chapter.

One of the most obvious ways the monumental city was used was through processions.⁴³ Rome had its Sacred Way leading through the forum to the Capitol, and Athens had the Panathenaic route, which crossed the agora on the way to the entrance of the Acropolis. Evidence for processions comes from every period of antiquity. Athenian citizens processed through the city before the annual dramatic performances at the Greater Dionysia, and at the Panathenaic festival.⁴⁴ In Republican Rome aristocratic families would briefly take over the public spaces for their funerals. They began with processions in which actors wore masks of their most famous ancestors, and progressed to speeches and gladiatorial games in the forum. Then there was the procession of the triumph in Rome, in which a victorious general and his army marched through the streets from the Field of Mars to the Temple of Jupiter.⁴⁵ Later on Macedonian kings and Roman emperors organized their own processions through the streets of their capitals. Athenaeus recorded a procession organized in Alexandria by Ptolemy Philadelphus, probably in the first decades of the third century B.C.E.: there were apparently displays of exotic beasts, military parades, athletic and musical competitions and feasts, and the procession passed through the stadium to give as many people as possible a chance to see it.⁴⁶ A similar procession and display was organized by Antiochus IV of Seleucid Syria in the 160s B.C.E. A little later the arrival of a Roman emperor in a new city—his *adventus*—became a major event.⁴⁷ Crowds thronged the streets, special coins were minted, and the emperor dressed for the occasion in the most formal way possible. Salutaris' benefaction to Ephesus specified the route to be followed by his procession: it connected sanctuaries, urban squares, and the theatre.

Processions were an important way of extending participation in civic ritual; the same applied to theatres, stadia, and amphitheatres. Where we have detailed epigraphic accounts of how festivals should be performed, processions always form part of the preliminaries.⁴⁸ Only a few individuals could actually observe a victorious Roman general walk into the temple of Jupiter and put his robe on the statue of the god. But tens of thousands could watch him process through the city in triumph en route to that encounter with the deity.

Spectacles and games were popular, but even the most extravagant games lasted for only a few days. Monuments dedicated to spectacles extended the life of festivals, recalling past events and promising their recurrence. The law courts of Athens, the *dikasteria*, met in buildings whose scale reminded citizens that they all might participate in the huge juries of the democratic city. And because processions had to take place in a particular order, they also offered a way of expressing the rank and importance of the participants. That included the gods, for statues of the gods were often carried in the processions on their way to watch the games or attend banquets. The tiered ranks of seats in Roman theatres were also a means of sorting the audience into social and political classes. Eventually there would be imperial boxes at the grandest venues, like the imperial palace on the Palatine in Rome and the Hippodrome in Constantinople, and emperors and their family were as much part of the show as what happened on the race track or in the arena.

The monumentality of these cities demonstrates several things about ancient Mediterranean societies. It tells us that conscious efforts were made to involve urban populations even in periods when they were politically marginalized. It tells us that local consensuses had developed about civic values, including the value of living in a city. These tiny towns with their oversize theatres and piazzas also tell us about the power of ancient city-states to extract income from a wide area and spend it in a narrow one. Monumental cities celebrated exploitation and accumulation, provided a kind of support for the inequalities of the Mediterranean world, and were a focus for competition and rivalry that almost never became violent. Finally, the ruins of these spectacular buildings, for all they impress us for their permanence and their silence, attest to the energy of ancient civic societies and to their passions.

16

Founding New Cities

Classical Foundations

Communities can move, but relocating great monumental complexes is another matter. Once cities had grown their hard carapaces, they dug in. Monuments were one kind of investment that made it hard to move, but they were also a scaffolding for ceremony. Ceremonies, monuments, inscripions and statues provided reminders of their lengthening histories and growing bodies of myth. The urban network pushed it roots deeper and deeper into Mediterranean landscapes, and was more and more tightly entangled with shared senses of identity and political allegiance. Ancient cities thrived—most of them—but it was not a closed club. New cities were added, especially on the fringes of the network, until there were maybe two thousand cities across the Mediterranean and its nearer hinterlands.

Founding new cities was an ancient practice in the Near East. To begin with, it was closely associated with kings. The fourteenth-century Pharaoh Akhenaten founded a new city at Amana for the worship of the god Aten, to whom he was devoted. Assyrian kings of the New Kingdom boasted of their role as city founders in inscriptions.[1] The original capital of the Assyrians had been Assur, the city of their chief god, and it remained a religious centre, but it could not accommodate the imperial palaces of the expanding empire. In 879 B.C.E. King Ashurnasirpal II created a vast new capital for his empire at Kalhu (modern Nimrud) on the river Tigris. It covered an area of around 360 hectares and was surrounded with a wall 7.5 kilometres in length. Kalhu was linked to other centres by roads, the river, and a canal. People were brought from all over the empire to inhabit the city and work for it. There were temples, a military base, and a vast palace guarded by great images of winged bulls. Its population was over

50,000. Two other capitals were created in later years: Khorsabad, built by Sargon II in 706 B.C.E., and Nineveh, built just six years later by his successor, Sennacherib. These capitals and especially the palaces were decorated with great stone reliefs recording the warlike achievements of the king in pictures and in long cuneiform inscriptions. Other kings followed their example. Recent excavations at Sardis have shown the scale of building by Lydian kings as they created a great capital for themselves.[2]

Nineveh, the greatest of the Assyrians' imperial cities, astonished the ancient Near East. Nineveh was the vast city to which the God of the Hebrews sent Jonah to prophesy its destruction. When it did fall, in 612 B.C.E., the world was plunged into chaos.

What emerged from the chaos was the even greater empire of the Achaemenid Persian Kings. Nomads in origin, one of their first acts was to imitate their Assyrian predecessors and create a new capital for their new empire. The city was known to the Greeks as Persepolis, a literal translation of Parsa, or "Persian City." Its ruins include reliefs of their own—a new medium for Persians—showing the many peoples of their empire bringing tribute. Another new medium, writing, was put to use declaring that all they had achieved was due to the aid of their great god, Ahura Mazda. Alexander feasted in that palace, before it burned down in mysterious circumstances. Many of his successors had seen Persepolis in its prime, and perhaps their passion for city foundation owed something to that.

City foundation in the Mediterranean took different forms. Many new settlements appeared as populations rose in the archaic period, both in the Aegean world and beyond it, but there were no imperial powers to direct this. Greek writers of the fifth century and later did believe that some cities beyond the Aegean world had been founded by charismatic figures just a few centuries before, and some of those cities did have traditions (or even paid cult to) founders (termed *oikists*) like Battos of Cyrene. These foundation myths are highly formulaic, and like most oral traditions reveal more about the societies in which they were told than about the real past.[3] The reality, as I have described it already, was a rather messier and less planned series of collaborations and power plays in which local chieftains as well as various groups of incomers all played a part. Pithecusae—large, messy, polyglot, wealthy, and devoid of monuments, and, as far as we can tell, political institutions—represents one kind of starting point. Naucratis, created in Egypt by the pharaohs to contain and manage Greek-speaking merchants, and similar arrangements made between Phoenician traders and the rulers of Tartessos in southern Spain, provide other examples. There were episodes of conquest—the fortifications of Metapontum reveal this—and sometimes the conquerors were locals, as probably happened at Paestum. Fixing a single moment of foundation in these tangled narratives is pretty arbitrary.

It was not until the fifth century B.C.E. that planned city foundations really took off. The mobility of the archaic age arose from the weakness of early states, from their inability to control and contain their more dynamic elements. The foundations of the classical age were led by strong states like Corinth and Athens, but their start-up costs were high and so they were relatively rare. In 443–442 when Athens was at the height of its power, it set out to create a new city to be called Thurii on the gulf of Taranto. The aim was to provide a base en route to Sicily. The Athenians had been showing interest in Sicily from at least 458 when they made a treaty with the Elymians of Segesta. Sicily, like the Black Sea, was an important source of grain. By the 440s Athens controlled the Aegean, was recruiting Lycian cities in Persian Asia Minor to its league, and was sending expeditions to Cyprus, Syria, and Egypt. Thucydides was probably not the only one to think of it as a thalassocracy—a naval empire—to be compared to that of the mythical king Minos of Crete. The west was a natural area in which to expand. Unlike Sigeum or the Thracian Chersonese, Thurii was to be a proper polis from day one. Settlers were gathered from around the Greek world (so as not to reduce Athenian citizen manpower); it was given a constitution allegedly written by Herodotus, and a street plan designed by Hippodamus. It was also close to the site of the city of Sybaris—one of the rare cases of an ancient city that had been destroyed, in this case in 510 B.C.E., creating a rare and valuable gap in the exploitation of the landscape that could be exploited. Thurii was also close to another hegemonic city, Tarentum, a Doric-speaking community that claimed some sort of descent from Sparta. Tarentum and Thurii came into conflict almost immediately about control of the agricultural territory between the two, but the matter was resolved by the foundation of a joint colony between Thurii and Tarentum in 432 called Heraclea. Large-scale politics were at play. Tarentum would support Athens' expedition against its rival Syracuse, a Spartan ally. City foundations had become a new field of competition between hegemonic powers.

The two greatest city foundations of the fourth century were in mainland Greece, on the Peloponnese. Messene and Megalopolis were both created in the aftermath of the battle of Leuktra of 371 B.C.E., at which the Thebans and their allies shattered Spartan power. Although the Thebans were careful not to claim to be the founders, they were key instigators of both projects. It was their (brief) hegemony that ensured the two cities were built. Formally they had different backstories. The Messenians as a people had some sort of a collective memory that extended to before their effective enslavement by Sparta during the archaic period. How that identity was preserved during centuries of helotage—if it really was, and was not simply reinvented at a later date—is much debated.[4] But the creation of a city of Messene was represented as the restoration of a Messenian polis. It was splendidly resourced and built on the slopes of Mount Ithome, site of the greatest helot revolt against the Spartans.

Megalopolis was different. Its name literally meant "the great city," and it lived up to its name. Its circuit wall was 8.4 kilometres in circumference, so big it enclosed many areas that were never inhabited. Strabo called it the Great Desert. Pausanias claims the population came from more than forty villages. This resettlement programme was not entirely voluntary, even if five Arcadian poleis were named as sponsors or cofounders. Arcadia was one of those parts of the Greek world where the city-state had shallow roots. The Arcadians lived in the mountainous centre of the Peloponnese; they spoke their own ancient dialect of Greek that had its closest relative on Cyprus, and their cities were hardly states in the same sense as most Greek cities were. The new synoecism did not satisfy ancient or modern aspirations on the part of the Arcadians but was transparently a device (like Messene) to confine the Spartans within Laconia. It was controversial among some Arcadians, presumably because they understood it arose from hegemonic politics and not local needs. Megalopolis was a sign of things to come.

There were other synoecisms—forced mergers—but none were bottom-up creations. Local communities seem, on the whole, not to have wanted to pull up their roots and become part of something larger. The initiative seems always to have come from outside. By now this should surprise. Urbanism was safest and most resilient in the Mediterranean when it was practiced on a small scale: it generally took imperial interventions to create larger cities.

Royal Founders

The most energetic city founders over the next few centuries were the Macedonian kings, especially Alexander and those of his generals and their successors, who carved out kingdoms of his vast but short-lived empire.

Their concentrated military power, and the political influence it brought them, allowed them to seed cities from the Adriatic to Afghanistan and from the Crimea to Egypt. Some disappeared almost at once, but others had brilliant futures ahead of them.

City founding brought prestige across this vast area. It was associated with heroes among the Greeks and with mighty kings in Asia. Greeks had associated urban societies with civilized ones at least since Homer praised ancient cities in the *Iliad* and in the *Odyssey* described the Cyclopes, who did not live in cities, as monstrous. Some of their other subjects subscribed to ideas about the relationship of kingship and city-founding that went back long before the Persians and Assyrians to ancient Mesopotamian literature, like the Epic of Gilgamesh. The kings of Macedon—whose own Greek and civilized credentials were sometimes called into question—liked to represent themselves as civilizing agents, and promoting urbanism was one way they displayed this. Alexander's father Philip was even credited with civilizing the savage inhabitants of Upper Macedonia. Alexander dotted his conquests with new poleis, some of them called Alexandria. These new urban foundations were often built on solid Achaemenid-era foundations, but they all made Hellenism and Greek-style city life fundamental to the way they presented themselves.

Kings felt most free to meddle with the cities in the new conquered territories for the same reasons that the Sicilian tyrants of Sicily had found it easier to restructure the urban network of the island than anyone in the Aegean did. Cities that did not feature in ancient myths could be safely erased, moved, remodelled, and renamed in ways that Sparta, Argos, Delphi, Athens, and Corinth could not. Older cities might be "refounded." Ephesus recognized Lysimachus as its second founder, a mark of thanks for his contribution to restoring the urban fabric, but there were no huge movements of population or site. Athens did something of the same for Hadrian. Eventually the title "founder" became a conventional honour paid to the most generous benefactors.

Spear-won land was also felt to be fair game for resettlement. For the kings who ruled over former Persian territory this was an assertion of their ultimate right to dispose of property in their realms. There is a similarity here with European colonists in the age of expansion invoking the idea of *terra nullius*—a land over which no living person had legal title—as a convenient excuse for grabbing territory from indigenous peoples and reassigning it to colonists. Greeks and Macedonians overwrote the historical geographies of their new possessions. The landscapes of the Seleucid lands are dotted with place names brought from Macedonia, like Pieria and Pella. Cities restarted their calendars from the Seleucid Era, in which 312–311 B.C.E., the date of Seleucus I's reconquest of Babylon, was year zero. By the Roman period there were few genuine recollections of the world before Alexander.[5] Kings founded cities because they could.

Macedonian royal foundations often bore dynastic names such as Antioch, Seleuceia, Philippi, Philippopolis, Alexandria, Cassandreia, Laodicea, or Arsinoe.[6] Local rulers of non-Macedonian descent imitated them. When the Bithynian king Nicomedes rebuilt the Greek city of Astakos in the middle of the third century B.C.E. he renamed it Nicomedia. The city of Prusa was named after another Bithynian king, Prusias. Once Romans took over there were yet more names of this kind. Pompeiopolis in Paphlagonia was a foundation of the Roman general Pompey. Dozens of cities today incorporate the name Caesar and or Augustus, or its Greek equivalent, Sebaste. Zaragoza in Spain began life as Caesaraugusta, Cherchel in Algeria was once one of several Caesareas, Augst in Switzerland was once Augusta Raurica, Autun in Burgundy once Augustodunum, Aosta in Italy once Augusta Praetoria Salassorum, and so on. Cologne in Germany was once Colonia Claudia Ara Agrippinensium, the Claudian colony Altar of the Agrippiensians; the local tribe of the Ubii had changed their name in honour of a Roman princess born in the city.

Not all royal foundations were alike. Some were great capitals. Pella became Macedon's capital around the start of the fourth century, a generation before the creation of Megalopolis and Messene. It was originally a Greek port city, one of those linking Macedonia's interior to the Aegean seaways, and a defensible site as well. It was a logical place for the kings of Macedon to base themselves as they opened up Macedonia to the world. The city expanded very fast during the early fourth century. A great palace complex was built there, and a brilliant court that welcomed poets, dramatists, and eventually philosophers and artists too. Philip II and Alexander were both born there and it was their home whenever they were not on campaign.

As the Macedonian kingdoms multiplied after Alexander's death, so too did the capitals. Lysimachus created Lysimacheia in 309 as a capital for what turned out to be a rather short-lived kingdom on the Thracian Chersonese. Some were effectively refoundations. King Cassander of Macedon created a great naval base in 316 on the site of the city of Potidaea, and named it Cassandreia. Some of the dozen or more Alexandrias were also located on occupied sites, but Alexandria in Egypt was all new. Created early in the kingdom's history, it marked a fundamental reorientation of Ptolemaic Egypt in the direction of the Mediterranean. The previous capital had been at Memphis at the head of the Delta, near modern Cairo. Alexandria had vast palaces, temples, ceremonial quarters, entertainment buildings, and gymnasia as well as the temple of the Muses—the original Museum—and the library associated with it. It was also a major port, both military and commercial. Its wealth so eclipsed that of other cities in the province that after the Roman conquest the governors were known as the Prefects of Alexandria and Egypt.

The Seleucids had two capitals. Seleuceia, on the Tigris, was a vast city dominating southern Mesopotamia, its population supposedly greater than half a million, drawn in part from the populations of nearby cities, including Babylon. Those numbers seem very high and the site is no longer easier to work on given the decades of war and civil war that Iraq has suffered and continues to suffer, But aerial photography shows that the occupied area really was enormous. Together with Babylon, which still survived as a great religious centre and the last centre of Babylonian astronomy and cuneiform culture, it formed a unique cultural meeting point. Greek philosophy and rhetoric rubbed shoulders with Babylonian astrology and mathematics and a large Jewish population, for whom the Babylonian Talmud would eventually be written. When the Parthian Persian Empire took control of most of the eastern part of the Seleucid Empire they created another city right next to Seleuceia named Ctesiphon. This complex of super-cities appeared when one of the world's oldest and densest urban networks became the centre of successive empires. It was also the origin point of a religion created in the third century by the Persian prophet Mani, who combined elements of Zoroastrianism with Christianity and Buddhism. Manichaeism eventually was practiced from North Africa to China.

The Seleucids' other capital was Antioch, on the Orontes. Its site was near the modern Turkish Syrian border, at a key node in routes that led from the Mediterranean coast to the western terminal of trade routes to India and late China. It was a huge city, a major centre of diaspora Judaism (like Alexandria in Egypt) and of early Christianity too. It was also the site of a great sanctuary to Apollo in the suburb of Daphne. Like Alexandria it looked to the Mediterranean, and like Alexandria was situated on one of the larger rivers of the region and in one of the most productive agricultural regions of the

Mediterranean Basin. Alexandria, Antioch, and Seleuceia were all created at the turn of the fourth and third centuries B.C.E., new capitals for new kingdoms and products of their founders' intense rivalry.

Kings also founded a different king of city: military colonies. Their armies depended on Macedonian infantry, who fought in a modified version of the classical Greek phalanx with much longer lances, which allowed them to fight in much deeper formations. On the right ground the Macedonian phalanx was difficult to beat head-on, especially if its flanks were protected by armed troops with missile weapons and by cavalry. Ancient accounts present the Seleucid phalangites as supported by ethnic levies, most with their own special mode of fighting: Cretans with slings, Jewish archers, Thracian light troops with vicious bladed weapons called *falces* (pruning forks), light cavalrymen from Morocco, Gaul, or Spain. All were paid, but the Macedonian infantry were a professional army, not mercenaries.[7] Detachments were settled all over the Seleucid empire. Around thirty military colonies are known.

The Ptolemies also maintained an hereditary army, also composed of a range of units with ethnic military specialisms. These settlers often lived with civilian families, and were provided for by land allocated to them. They might farm these kleruchies themselves or let them out and live on the income. Like their Seleucid counterparts they were effectively an hereditary military force and liable to be called up at short notice. Although they mostly appear in historical accounts as national armies, these settlers were also armies of occupation. When the Ptolemies armed a proportion of their Egyptian subjects to fight in the Macedonian way they succeeded in inflicting a huge defeat on their Seleucid rivals at the battle of Raphia in 217 B.C.E., but the price was a generation of rebellions led by those same local levies.

Military colonies marked a new stage in the professionalization of ancient warfare. Before Alexander most hoplites had begun their careers in Greek citizen-armies. When campaigns were over, they simply went home. During the fourth century B.C.E. a number of long-standing mercenary armies are known. The most famous is the Ten Thousand, a hoplite force assembled by the Persian Prince Cyrus the Younger to support an attempted coup d'état against his elder brother. Xenophon took part in the expedition and his *Anabasis* narrates the long journey home, following Cyrus' death at Cunaxa near Babylon, over the Anatolian plateau to the Black Sea coast from which passage back to the Aegean was possible. Mercenaries like the Ten Thousand always expected to make money and then return home. But Alexander's army was also under arms for many years, and many of these soldiers—Greek mercenaries and Macedonian tribesmen alike—would never return home. When he stood down his great army of conquest he shared the spoils of victory, but then settled them in cities, some new, many old. Across the kingdoms into which Alexander's empire was divided their descendants became hereditary soldiers, part of an ethnically stratified class system.

Military colonies also represented a new stage in urbanism. For most of the last millennium B.C.E., Mediterranean cities had not been very specialized in economic terms. Most were very small, and most of the families within them farmed. Naturally some cities were also important ports, because of where they were located, and others benefited from local resources like the marble quarries of Paros and Naxos, or the timbered slopes of northwest Italy or Thrace. Creating a city in order to support a fragment of an army was a new departure. More complex states were producing a more differentiated urban network. Differences in functions also led to differences in prestige. Across the great hybrid kingdoms of Asia, these differences were often expressed in ethnic terms.

The privilege—the good fortune of being Greek or Macedonian—did not go unremarked. Indigenous cities had different fates under Macedonian and then Roman rule. Some thrived; others lost some of their population and lands to new foundations, and yet others began to transform themselves into something like Greek poleis. In Caria and Lydia, in Syria and Palestine, in Thrace and even southern France, populations began to use the Greek language in public inscriptions, made new images of their gods in ways that made use of Greek iconography, and borrowed Greek architecture for their temples, homes, and tombs. Greek institutions like the *ekklesia*, the *boule*, and the *gymnasion* began to appear. In some parts of coastal Asia Minor some of these changes were already underway from the fifth and fourth centuries B.C.E., well before Alexander's campaigns. In Anatolia and the Levant some cities that had been based around the temple of a powerful god began to repackage them with Greek iconographies and titles. Zeus Kasios, Jupiter Optimus Maximus Dolichenus, and Jupiter Heliopolitanus were products of this process. Their cities were not refounded but rather remodelled as Greek ones. Egyptians under Roman rule lobbied for their ancient nome capitals to be treated like Greek cities too, presumably because they observed the privileges enjoyed by foundations such as Alexandria and Antinoopolis.[8] Founding new cities did not just add more nodes to the network; in places it had a profound effect on other cities nearby.

Colonization Under the Roman Republic

The rise of Macedonian monarchies had promoted urban foundations in the east of the Mediterranean, but any hegemonic power that extended beyond the territory of a single city-state might have similar effects. Rome's expansion over Italy and in the western Mediterranean is the best example, but there were others, such as the creation of the Massiliot *comptoirs* along the Mediterranean coast of France, and Etruscan expansion within Italy.

By the fifth century B.C.E. the most fertile coastal plains of southern Italy and eastern Sicily were all occupied by Greek cities, meaning cities that looked like poleis, used Greek, and traced their ancestry back east. A group of other cities—on the Atlantic, in southern Spain, western Sicily, the Balearic Isles, and Sardinia—thought of themselves as Phoenician.[9] Even some indigenous communities had begun to make or assert connections to the east.[10] Etruscan urban networks had extended south of the Tiber and north of the Apennines, sometimes on new sites, often in the form of a more visible presence in old ones. This system had grown up slowly through tangled collaborations and shared projects, but very few of the cities were new foundations in the sense I have been using it.

Rome itself was a hybrid from the first. It began as a Latin-speaking syn-oecism of hilltop villages, perhaps already with some Sabines present in the mix. There were Greek traders and Greek gods almost from the start. By the sixth century Rome was ruled by an Etruscan dynasty, which brought new rituals and monumental styles. Rome's originality as an urbanizing power comes from its development of a new kind of city foundation, one in which what were created were not new city-states but semidetached fragments of Rome itself. The cities created by Greeks and Phoenicians and others, with varying levels of indigenous participation, were in principle new communities. Mother cities sometimes tried to assert their primacy, leaving a rich trace of legend and diplomacy.[11] But the distances involved, and the tiny populations at either end, made these links tenuous. Roman colonies, by contrast, were connected to Rome by land, by great trunk roads laid out across Italy, and by a common citizenship. *Coloniae* might be new cities, but they were not new city-states.

Map 8 Roman Colonization before 100 B.C.E.

The modern term "colony" comes from the Latin *colonia*. Etymologically it is connected with the Roman terms used for farming, and with cultivation and arable farming in particular. A *colonus* in Latin can mean a farmer or a member of a colony: a settler, in other words. *Coloniae* were settlements designed to give Roman citizens—and sometimes favoured allies—new land to farm. This, at any rate, was the way it was understood in the late Republic and early empire. As often with Roman history, we tend to see early periods through the eyes of later Latin writers. In this case the historians and orators we rely on lived long after the period they described. The earliest accounts of colonization as a phenomenon, including some lists of colonies, were mostly written down in the first and second centuries C.E. These authors apparently believed that colonies were a very ancient institution—almost as early as the city of Rome itself—and that *coloniae* were more or less the same in all periods. Some modern scholars took a similar view. Both were wrong.[12]

Let us start at the most mysterious point, the beginning. Rome could hardly have founded new cities before it was a city itself, so any story that a given colony was created in the eighth or seventh century must be a fantasy. Ostia, for example, at the mouth of the Tiber, was reputed to have been founded in the regal period. But the earliest archaeological trace is of a very small fortified camp from the late fourth century B.C.E. or even later. Why did early imperial writers get this wrong? One possibility it that we are dealing with a foundation myth designed to increase the status of the port—one story has Ostia founded in 620 B.C.E. by the third king of Rome Ancus Marcus, and this story was popularized (and perhaps invented) by the aristocratic house of the Marcii, who claimed descent from this king. It is possible too that there was confusion between different settlements around the shifting mouth of the Tiber. And in any case, Roman antiquarians did not really agree on a chronology of early Rome until the middle of the first century B.C.E.

It may also be that the early imperial writers were influenced by the politics of the late second century B.C.E., when the foundation of colonies had become a political hot potato.[13] To cut a long story short, part of the programme offered to the Roman people by the reforming tribunes Tiberius and Gaius Gracchus in the 130s and 120s B.C.E. was a fresh distribution of land. This would not have been easy, since the best land around the Mediterranean had long been claimed, and there were no longer wars of conquest in Italy likely to provide fresh supplies of spear-won territory. One idea was to reclaim land rented by Roman landowners, who did not have a secure right to it. Another was to found large new settlements, some in southern Italy and others overseas, including on the sites of recently demolished Carthage and Corinth. These schemes were very controversial. The wealthy naturally did not want to give up land they rented, nor did Italian-allied city-states, some of whose citizens were occupying it. Everyone feared that if distributions or colonization went ahead, the Gracchi would have a huge power base. There had been no new colonies for two generations, and the idea of sending some Roman citizens overseas permanently was hugely controversial. There was also a guilty conscience about the recent destruction of Corinth and Carthage: colonizing those sites might make this worse, or even be ill-omened. The arguments that raged about this programme—which contributed in the end to the murder of both Gracchi—created rival images of "the normal colony" that were ideological and anachronistic. The use of colonization in the aftermath of bouts of civil war as a means of settling and enriching soldiers from victorious armies kept the scheme controversial. Perhaps our early imperial sources retrojected some of this into Rome's deep past when trying to make sense of what the urban system looked like in their own day.

Modern accounts tend to be very cautious about what was going on in the fifth and early fourth centuries B.C.E. There is no archaeology to speak of, and it is clear that Roman writers of later periods were themselves unsure what to make of the traditions. The treaties with Carthage do seem to show that Romans had expansionist ambitions from an early date. There are statements by Greek historians about expeditions sent to Sardinia and Corsica in the early fourth century. Perhaps there were also garrisons in Etruria established not long after the destruction of Veii, traditionally 396 B.C.E., and the point at which Rome became the major power in central western Italy. But garrisons are not necessarily foundations for cities.

From the middle of the fourth century B.C.E. things become a little clearer. Around the time Messene and Megalopoleis were being founded to redraw the political landscape of the Peloponnese, the Romans were embarking on a long series of expeditions of conquest in the Apennines, known afterwards as the Samnite Wars. At the same time they were extending their power over Etruria to the north and Campania to the south. Over the next two hundred years or so around fifty colonies were formally founded by the Roman state. In theory this meant a decision by the senate and people to found a colony; identification of where it should be placed (often on spear-won land, sometimes into a conquered city); the identification of an aristocratic organizer (a *deductor*); the assembly of a core of citizen families each promised a portion of land; and then the creation, through ritual and surveying, of a brand-new urban kernel with territory attached.

The pace, however, was set by warfare. Plot the new colonies on a map, and the growing reach of Roman power emerges clearly. The supposedly fifth-century colonies are close to Rome, mostly within a day's march of the city. Those of the early fourth century were mostly in southern Etruria. By the 280s and 270s there were foundations in Etruria, down the west coast of Italy as far as Paestum and up and down the Appenines in the Samnite lands. Rome capitalized on its third-century successes against the Gallic tribes of Marché and over Pyrrhus to establish bases on the Adriatic, at Rimini in 264, Brindisi in 246, and in a few other places as well. As Rome's sphere of influence increased, so did the range of colonization. By the end of the third century there were foundations in the Po Valley. The foundation at Piacenza followed the defeat of the Gauls at Telamon in 225 B.C.E. The Second Punic War temporarily interrupted the conquest of the Po Valley, but after Hannibal was driven out of Italy and defeated the Romans returned to found a string of cities from Bologna to Aquileia. The 190s is also the period when colonies were planted on the toe of Italy.

Colonization eventually slowed down not because the Roman state grew weaker, but because the supply of land had run out. The wild mountaineers (who had never been quite as wild as Roman writers claimed) were themselves settling down.[14] Roman armies were now campaigning in Spain and north Italy, in Gaul, and occasionally in the Balkans and Asia Minor. Italian allies became partners, commercially and militarily if not yet politically, in running a Mediterranean empire. Snatching their land and imposing new settlements on them was less realistic.

Even during this slow conquest of Italy colonization was not a steady process. There were decades with no new foundations, and then bursts of activity. This partly reflected the rhythms of conquest but they were probably accentuated by competition within the elite. To complicate matters, some colonies were refounded several times. Sometime this was reinforcement, but often it was bolstering a failing settlement. Colonies failed for the same reasons other small towns failed: because they had been created on poor soils, or were in badly chosen locations, or because that initial group of a few hundred citizens could not sustain a sense of common purpose. The close connection to Rome did not always help. Migrants in the archaic

Mediterranean might have regretted their decision to move, but there was not much they could do about it. Reluctant Roman colonists could just walk home.

The distinguishing feature of what the Romans were doing is that they were founding cities—or camps, bases, outposts—without creating new city-states. Historians have argued endlessly about whether or not Republican Rome was a polis (the argument started in the first century B.C.), but there is no doubt that these Republican *coloniae* were not. They were fragments of a larger whole. Rome was experimenting, probably without quite realizing it, in creating a new kind of state, one that was united by kinship and cult, by law and by citizenship, yet was geographically dispersed. It was in a sense the opposite of a *synoecism*. The Roman state had not expanded by swallowing up its neighbours. There were cities still nominally independent within a day's march of Rome right up until the early first century B.C.E., and there were Romans who lived hundreds of miles from the city. Roman expansion, by war and alliance, had transformed Italy into a complex mosaic of territories.[15] From the fourth to the early second century B.C.E. the city of Rome was surrounded by other states with which it had a range of relationships from kinship (with the Latins) to the unequal treaties imposed on defeated neighbours that left them autonomous in their own territories, but without the freedom to choose their friends and enemies, and obliged to provide troops for Roman wars. And scattered across central Italy was an inland archipelago of Roman territory, *ager publicus*, made up of bigger and smaller chunks inserted between the lands of other peoples. Some of this spear-won land was organized around tiny urban centres (*coloniae*) whose inhabitants remained Roman citizens, were subject to the law and magistrates of Rome, and had the same rights obligations as other citizens. Other areas were simply farmed by tenants of the Roman state. The *coloniae* were mostly small by the standards of Mediterranean cities, just a few hundred families in many cases, but they were privileged. They benefited from Roman spending on public works, and some eventually acquired a full suite of civic monuments. And in disputes with their much more powerful neighbours, the colonists could always call in the might of Rome.

These political umbilicals to Rome were accompanied by physical ones. The conquest of the Apennines and of Italy was achieved not just by battles and settlement but also by a transformation of the landscape.[16] *Coloniae*, and other even smaller bases like Forum Novum (Newmarket in Latin) in the Sabine Hills, were founded along the great roads that connected

Rome to all the regions of Italy. Roman roads were tendrils reaching out into every part of Italy. The Appian Way was built in 312 from Rome to the Adriatic port (and colony) of Brindisi in the southeast. The Via Aurelia, built in 241, ran up the Tuscan coast to Pisa. The Via Flaminia, built in 220, led from Rome over the mountains to Rimini. After Hannibal's defeat the Via Aemilia connected Rimini to Piacenza. These were just the major routes. *Coloniae* were nodes on a network that moved citizen-soldiers, money, and information between the scattered parts of a national state growing up across the peninsula.

Typically *coloniae* of the fourth, third, and early second century numbered between three hundred and five hundred Roman citizens. Each colony accounted for between 1 and 2 per cent of the total citizen body, to judge from the census figures preserved by Livy. They were dotted at strategic passes and ports, rather as mediaeval castles were. They could provide advance notice of trouble, and be a base for the armies sent to deal with it. Later on there were other kinds of *coloniae*. Larger foundations were created in northern Italy, strung along roads that led from Genua to Aquileia in the aftermath of the defeat of the Gauls and then Hannibal. These were settlements of several thousand men, their populations recruited from Rome's Latin allies as well as from the citizenry and so-called Latin colonies. Their populations were ten or twenty times the size of those earlier Roman colonies; they governed themselves as far as domestic matters were concerned, and each colonist was allocated much more land. Their job was not to watch over the defeated locals, but to replace them. From the air it is still possible to make out the great grids into which the flat valley of the Po was divided so that the land might be more easily handed out to incomers.

The story of Roman Republican city foundation up and down the Italian peninsula is immensely complex. This is because in reality there was no one template always followed, and each situation might call for a slightly different solution. The simple division between Roman and Latin *coloniae* does not do justice to the wide variety of urban experiments the Roman state tried out as it struggled to create a huge system of control that was neither an empire nor a diaspora but a bit of both. There were *coloniae* imposed on existing cities, like Paestum, imposed on the city of Posidonia (Figure 27). There were *coloniae* built on greenfield sites, some so badly chosen they were abandoned within a decade. There were Roman *coloniae* as big as Latin ones, and there were many changes in the arrangements about citizenship. For a while Romans who joined Latin colonies

Figure 27 Paestum
vivids / Getty Images

had to give up their citizenship but could have it back if they returned to
Rome. Physically these cities often came to resemble each other, except
in size, and also to resemble the main cities of other Italian peoples, the
municipia. After the war fought between Rome and her Italian allies in
91–88 B.C.E. almost all free people in Italy became Roman citizens, and
the *municipia* and *coloniae* entered a new stage of cohabitation.[17] After the
murders of the Gracchi some of their ideas were nevertheless taken up. The
first *colonia* outside Italy was Narbonne in southern France, founded in 118
B.C.E. There were other urban experiments elsewhere in the west, cities
created by Roman generals in Spain and Gaul for populations who were
not quite Roman but closely connected to the Roman military, Carteia
and Gracchuris, Lugdunum Convenarum in France, and doubtless other
centres. Pompey even resettled pirates after his great command to eradicate
them in 67–66 B.C.E.

Coloniae found their final purpose during the civil wars of the end of the
Republic. At the end of the second century B.C.E. the link between a landed
citizenry and the legionary army had been broken. Desperate for troops
to wage larger and large-scale wars far from home, generals had begun to
recruit from the poorest sector of society. When the wars were over they

promised them land.[18] From the time of Sulla onwards great tracts of first Italian and then provincial land were confiscated and dispersed to veterans. Some took parcels of land, just as earlier some of those who moved into the newly conquered territories of the Po Valley did so as individuals.[19] But many veterans were imposed as groups on existing cities. That process gave the term *colonia* yet another meaning. Sulla took land from communities that had opposed him in the civil war of 83–80. Etruria and Campania suffered particularly from Sullan colonization.[20] A Sullan *colonia* was imposed on Pompeii, changing the culture of the Oscan city forever. Yet settling former soldiers in Italy was politically difficult. After the Social War most Italians were now Roman citizens. Both Pompey and Caesar founded some settlements in provincial land, but Italian towns bore the brunt of resettlement in the generation following the defeat of Pompey. It has been estimated that 130,000 veterans were given land in Italy between 47 and 14 B.C.E.[21] This is a staggering figure, the equivalent of creating a small city every year for a generation. In fact very few were settled in new cities, and the process was not gradual. A dozen or so were settled in 47–44 in the immediate aftermath of Caesar's victory over Pompey. The settlement programme after the defeat of Brutus and Cassius at Philippi was much more traumatic. After the Battle of Actium there were a few more, but the process more of less stopped in 14 B.C.E. Meanwhile colonies were being created on choice territories overseas, in Corsica and southern France, in Mediterranean Spain and North Africa, at strategic points around the Aegean—Corinth, Philippi, and Cnossos to names just a few—and in Asia Minor.[22] These new *coloniae* mostly had thousands of settlers, still Roman citizens although the link to Rome was stretched almost to the breaking point, and in an echo of their much smaller mid-Republican ancestors they were often made part of the machinery of control. Lyon was the hub of a great road system that connected Italy to the German frontier and later to Britain. Carthage was the seat of a governor and of a procurator who oversaw a large part of the supply of grain to Rome. The name of the remote colony of Antioch in Pisidiam translates not as Antioch *in* Pisidiam but Antioch *facing* Pisidia. Like other colonies in southern Turkey, it was part of the scaffolding of imperial rule.[23] The common theme running through all this activity was the control of people and of land.[24]

It makes some sense to distinguish between Mediterranean cities in terms of their origins. Most grew organically, meaning that any organization came from within the community, initial growth was slow, and an intimate link was former between city and territory. That link must often have been achieved by trial and error: we rarely see the traces of false starts, and in the ancient Mediterranean in particular it was the resilient cities that survived. Most survived at a scale not very different to the one they had reached early in their history. In other words, the reorganization of a community from village to city, and of a landscape from populated are to a state with boundaries, was often achieved well before historical records begin. Urban centres of a few thousand souls, with situations on the better soils and in locations where they could easily become nodes in wider systems, are present from the middle of the last millennium. What changed from the fourth century B.C.E. was the beginning of active engagement in city foundation by hegemonic cities and especially by kings. Not all of these experiments were successes. Megalopolis the Great Desert, and all those deserted Roman *coloniae* in southern Italy, remind us that state projects had no better track record in antiquity than they do today.[25] But in some cases, especially where infrastructure could be created to support new foundation or where political muscle ensured they would always receive at least their fair share of the resources, new foundations did make a major difference to the urban network of antiquity.

17

Ruling Through Cities

Mediterranean urbanism was never designed to be an instrument of state rule. Communities came together first of all in relation to local priorities, and then some were transformed—sometimes slowly, sometimes suddenly—into cities as population levels crept upward and international connections became more important. Specialists disagree about which point, between the eighth and sixth centuries, some of these cities became city-states: the problems are partly definitional, but mostly we just know too little about how most Mediterranean societies worked before the spread of public writing. Either way, the accent was always local until the end of the sixth century C.E. The rise of hegemonic cities and of kingdoms marked a major change. Persia, Athens, Syracuse, Marseilles, Rome, Macedon, and other powers all found in different ways that other people's cities could be conveniently co-opted into instruments of government. The loss of autonomy—literally, the right to live by their own laws—was bitterly resented everywhere. But the useful of city-states to their new rulers ensured the survival and in some cases the enrichment of ancient Mediterranean cities.

Garrison Cities

There were many ways to rule through cities. The simplest was to put soldiers in them. This was less of an option when most soldiers were also citizens, seasonal warriors taking up arms when required and usually when the agricultural year permitted it. But by the fifth century ways were being found around that.

Perhaps the idea came from Persia. The Achaemenids had often raised levies from one part of their empire and stationed them in a distant province for long periods. That is one of the origins of the Jewish diaspora in Egypt and Asia Minor and perhaps in the Persian Empire's eastern provinces, too. Some documents from a garrison at Elephantine, at the first cataract of the Nile, record the activities of a Jewish detachment posted there for a long period. The idea of using foreign levies as garrison troops, of course, was that they might be expected to be more loyal to the empire than sympathetic to locals. This tactic would be used again by the kings of the Macedonian states that succeeded Persia, and by Roman emperors. The difference between military colonies and garrisons was a matter of how long they served—not always obvious in advance to the soldiers posted there.

City-states had more difficulty creating long-term garrisons. During the sixth and fifth centuries there were Athenian kleruchs, groups of Athenians imposed on subject cities. Kleruchies ranged in size from a few hundred to a few thousand, and had plots of land allocated to them, but remained Athenian citizens and distinct from the populations of the poleis who compelled to host them. Perhaps they were more like colonists, although some at least remained closely attached to Athens. Kleruchies might operate as garrisons, protecting Athenian interests in strategic locations, and personally they gained at the expense of locals who had to give up their land. The system—which is still poorly understood—ended with Athens' defeat in the Peloponnesian War. The victors in that war, the Spartans, imposed their own garrisons in some cities, commanded by temporary governors, the hated *harmosts*, whose role was to keep allied or subjected city-states in line. But Sparta had manpower problems of its own, and could never have sustained long-term garrisons in many places. The system collapsed early in the fourth century and interstate politics reverted to a matter of treaties and alliances backed up by force.

Garrisoned cities came into their own with the rise of kingdoms and empires around the edges of the Mediterranean world. The Persians had already levied soldiers and ships from coastal cities in Phoenicia, Cyprus, and western Asia Minor. Greek mercenaries had served in all these areas for centuries, and in one sense the Persians were simply co-opting those energies and that biopower to serve their large aims. Macedon was the next to incorporate cities into their infrastructure of control. From 346 B.C.E. when Philip II forced a peace treaty of Athens, until the Roman destruction of the kingdom in 167 B.C.E., Macedon was the dominant land power in the Balkans. Reign upon reign, successive kings of Macedon led their armies south, down the east flank of mainland Greece, to engage with various alliances and leagues of Greek city-states. Part of that route lay through broad plains, those of Macedon itself, and of Thessaly and then Boeotia, but there were pinch points where the Balkan mountain ridges descended almost to the sea, where invading armies might meet resistance. The Persian Emperor Xerxes' army had been slowed at one of these in the summer of 480 B.C.E., at the pass of Thermopylae. A Roman army outmanoeuvred Antiochus III, the Seleucid ruler of Syria, on almost the same spot in 191 B.C.E. Securing the coastal route south was essential. So for much of the period of Macedonian domination garrisons were installed in a series of cities. Demetrias, founded in 294 B.C.E. on the Gulf of Pagardae, near modern Volos, was one. Eretreia, Oreus, and Chalkis on the island of Euboea opposite Thermopylae were others. Then there was the Acrocorinth above the ancient city of Corinth, a natural fortress that controlled the isthmus which connected the Peloponnese to the rest of the mainland. Constantly fought over, besieged, and exchanged in diplomatic negotiations, these cities came to be known as "the fetters of Greece." Macedonians and their enemies competed to establish garrisons in the cities, and to besiege them when they were in the hands of others. Similar tactics were used in the conquered territories of the former Persian Empire. Pergamon was a strategic point used by Persian vassals and a rebel satrap before it became a fortress used by Alexander's general Lysimachus. Many of the other "new" foundations of Alexander and the Seleucids were imposed on existing settlements that just happened to be in the right place for a group of mercenaries to be settled and based.

The label "fetters of Greece" shows that certain cities could acquire a symbolic importance based on their role in larger projects of enslavement. A much later example is provided by the revolt of the Iceni, led by their Queen Boudicca against Roman rule over southern Britain in 60 C.E. The island had been invaded by Claudius as recently as 43 C.E., and conquest was still very much a work in progress. London, as very recent finds of waterlogged documents have revealed, was already a growing commercial centre. Many parts of the south of the island were under direct rule, meaning tribes were being treated as if they were subject city-states of the kind that already existed in Gaul or Spain, but among these there were also territories ruled by tribal chiefs who had become Roman vassals, sometimes with honorary citizenship. Boudicca's husband had been one of these. The legions spent most summers campaigning farther north and west—they were in Wales when Boudicca rebelled—and across the emergent province tax collectors, imperial agents, and private lenders were all trying to make the most of the new possession. Boudicca's army did eventually attack and sack London, and also St Albans (Verulamium), which was the capital of the tribal city-state of the Catuvellauni, but their first target was the Roman colony at Colchester (Camulodunum), where the behaviour of veteran settlers and serving soldiers towards the evicted locals had apparently created huge resentment. This was also probably designated to be the centre of a provincial imperial cult, since the vast Temple of Claudius had been constructed there which seemed (in Tacitus' words) to be an *arx aeternae dominationis*, a citadel of everlasting dominion. If he had correctly captured local sentiments, then Colchester, like Demetrias and the Acrocorinth, had been identified as city made into an engine of oppression.

Tacitus might, of course, have been channelling one traditional Roman view of its own *coloniae*. Cicero sometimes referred to Roman colonies as *propugnacula imperii:* ramparts or forward posts of empire. This label does not apply to all of the many kinds of city and settlement given the title of *colonia* in the many centuries of its use, but it seems an accurate description of the small Roman colonies stationed in Apennine Italy at the end of a long Roman road, and also the ring of colonies set up in southern Asia Minor to control the plateau.[1] There were many kinds of garrison cities from military bases that seem minimally urban, to ancient cities like Corinth that found themselves in places of geopolitical importance when the economics of warfare changed to include standing armies. What was really happening was a partial mobilization of the urban networks of the ancient world to suit the security ends of new kinds of states.

Cities were useful garrison points for many reasons. Many were already walled. Most also provided a range of facilities useful to an army, among them shelter, water, and even food supplies. Many cities were also already placed at strategic nodes on transport systems. A road or best of all a port would allow troops to be moved in and out rapidly, and to be provisioned from a distance if they were besieged. During the fifth century B.C.E. several Greek cities built long walls that connected them to their ports. The greatest cities of southern Etruria each had nearby ports. At the mouth of the Tiber was Ostia, one of the first of Rome's maritime colonies. Syracuse and Carthage and Marseilles were all already port cities. When the Barcids created a Carthaginian dominion in Spain they ruled it from another port city, Cartagena (New Carthage). Making use of an existing city was usually cheaper and easier than creating a castle or a fortress from scratch, and then having to put all the infrastructure in place.

One of the best indications of how important garrison towns were to imperial conquerors is what the Romans did when there were no towns to garrison. From at least the early second century B.C.E., Roman armies on the march constructed elaborate purpose-built military camps. Polybius provides a very detailed description of how they did it at the time of the Hannibalic War, and excavations from the roughly contemporary site of Numancia in Spain largely confirm his account.[2] Those mid-Republican temporary camps sound—with their street grids, their gatehouses, and careful street planning—like pop-up cities. A century later on Julius Caesar's armies also built camps as they advanced through hostile territory in Gaul. When the campaigning season was over, generally in September or October but occasionally as late as November, his legions were dispersed into more permanent winter camps, *hibernae*, where they would be based until April or even May.[3] Their job was to keep an eye on the locals and prepare for their commander's return in the spring after a winter of political intriguing in Provence or south of the Alps. Surprisingly little is known about these winter bases—some at least were inside Iron Age hill forts—but if several thousand men were based in each for around half the year they would have needed to organize the provision of food, water, fuel, and waste disposal.[4]

In some ways ancient armies were cities on the move. Their ranks and units provided military analogues of the social classes and small communities out of which most ancient states were comprised. There are a few anecdotes from the historical writings of Thucydides and his successor Xenophon that present entire armies debating rival courses of action. This is hardly a surprise for democratic states like Athens, perhaps, since the soldiers on campaign were themselves citizens as well. They were accustomed to hearing rival speeches and to deciding between them, and some of the same people who were making those speeches in peacetime also led the armies in war. Rome had a more hierarchical society, and this too was mirrored in its armies. There was no quasi-democratic discussion, but Roman generals and their officers performed some of the functions of magistrates, giving rough justice and organizing collective worship just as priests and magistrates did at home. Roman generals addressed their men from the tribunal, just as they had learned to address citizen crowds at assemblies and less formal political assemblies (*contiones*) back home. Sometimes larger camps were even treated as if they were cities. When the Senate, prompted by the emperor Tiberius, decided to publish the results of its investigation into the death of the imperial prince Germanicus, it ordered that their decree be published in Rome, in the largest city of every province and in the winter quarters of every legion.

Great wars of conquest slowed during the reign of Augustus. The conquest of Europe had been a kind of distraction from the Augustan *coup d'état*, a demonstration that autocracy worked and that the new emperors were determined to make Rome great again. By the end of Augustus' reign there was less to prove, and fewer opponents left to prove it to. A few costly reverses had shown emperors that warfare could also be risky. Military camps began to be rebuilt in more permanent materials along the empire's northern frontier, like Hardknott Roman fort in Cumbria (Figure 28). Having a frontier was itself a novelty in some regions. The first roads all led outward towards enemy territory. By the end of the first century C.E. new roads were added parallel to the frontiers connecting legionary bases, forts, fortlets, and lookout posts along the broad limits of empire. Along the Rhine and the Danube there were river ports. If Republican *hibernae* were virtually cities, the permanent stone-built fortresses of the early empire certainly were. By

Figure 28 Hardknott Roman fort
David Lyons / Alamy Stock Photo

the end of the first century C.E. some legions were based in huge permanent bases, like those at Cologne and Mainz. Only a little later they were joined by major fortresses along the Danube. This new generation of legionary fortresses had internal road plans, industrial zones, bathhouses, temples, and even amphitheatres as well as parade grounds that doubled as military versions of the *forum*, and of course impressive walls and gatehouses. Recent studies of the material left in these forts has shown that their inhabitants led rather complex social lives. Among the soldiers there were potters, blacksmiths, doctors, clerks, and many other professions, just as in many small towns. Rather surprisingly there were also women and children living in the camps.[5] Finds of children's shoes and women's clothes dispel the old stereotype of tidy regimented camps for the legionaries and scruffy shanty towns (*canabae*) just down the road for common-law wives, illegitimate children, and bars and brothels. When soldiers of the second and third centuries listed their origins many now wrote *ex castris* (from the camps): they were second- or third-generation legionaries. These camps were in effect cities. The last generation of Roman *coloniae*, foundations like great veteran colony of Timgad in North Africa (see Figure 29), evoke military bases more than they do cities.

A few camps even became real civilian cities when the troops moved on. For a while the Roman frontier in Germany lay west of the Black Forest. When it advanced eastwards onto the Neckar Valley at the end of the first century C.E., a whole string of demobilized camps became the basis for new cities, some used as the administrative centres of new city-state units. The inscriptions and statues and religious offerings of towns like Ladenburg are very reminiscent of military camps, but the population was civilians.

Things were different in more urbanized parts of the empire. Where cities already existed, especially in the east, garrisons were often simply billetted on urban populations.[6] Sometimes one corner of the city was given over to the military. Nicopolis, on the outskirts of Alexandria, was a military base. The rich but tiny frontier town of Dura Europos on the Roman–Parthian frontier had a military garrison in one corner (see Figure 30). Documents preserved there show soldiers buying and selling property and interacting with the mixed urban population in other ways, too. So far so peaceful, but it is easy to imagine why commanders and municipal magistrates might agree that some degree of segregation was a good idea.

The military world was not always a world apart from that of ancient cities.[7] We see glimpses of soldiers in cities in many other documents from

Figure 29 Roman colony of Timgad, Algeria
Yann Arthus-Bertrand/Getty Images

the Roman east. The centurions and soldiers who play bit parts in the gospel narratives reflect this world too. Soldiers crop up in Pliny the Younger's Pontus-Bithynia letters, and in the fictionalized Greece of Apuleius' *Golden Ass*. Mostly we see them at ease, off-duty or on patrol, carrying messages or escorting tax-grain or prisoners or bullion, all-purpose errand boys rather than as an oppressive occupying army. Yet urban garrisons could be that as well. There were perhaps 40,000 soldiers of one kind or another in the city of Rome, and the Praetorian camp dominated the city in times of crisis.[8] There was an ugly incident in Alexandria in 216 C.E. when the emperor Caracalla turned his troops on the crowd. The emperors Theodosius sent his Gothic troops to attack the citizens of Thessalonica in 390 C.E. These events were rare, but the threat was omnipresent. The immediate trigger for the Jewish War was the behaviour of Roman soldiers in Jerusalem, which also had a fort within the walls. The monuments and epigraphy of the Roman Empire proclaim its stability. Most civic inscriptions celebrate good citizens, and portray a generally harmonious relation between emperors and subjects. The ubiquitous military presence even in the urban centres of interior

Figure 30 Dura Europus
Christine Osborne Pictures / Alamy Stock Photo

peaceful provinces reminds us that empire in the end rested on the threat of violence.

The Triumph of the Polis

When Alexander the Great died at Babylon in 323 B.C.E., his short and pyrotechnic reign nevertheless left much of the governmental structures of the Persian Empire intact. On his death it was handed it over to his generals. They fought over it, tore it to pieces, and then fought all over again with the pieces. The vast empire of Darius and Alexander was reduced to a chaos of successor states: some large, some small, some destined to last centuries, others gone in decades.

These fragments varied hugely in size and everything else. The Seleucids ruled (on a good day) from the Mediterranean coast to Afghanistan, but they had many bad days too when distant provinces went their own way, for a while or forever. In Egypt the Ptolemies re-established a kingdom that was even older than Persia, and grafted new features onto it. Some tiny kingdoms in Anatolia were probably wholly new, the creation of fierce local rulers sufficiently far from the larger centres of power. Then there were independent city-states, such as ancient Rhodes and the kingdom of the Maccabees, with their temple-city of Jerusalem. Dozens of tongues flourished across this vast world that had once been ruled through Persian and Aramaic, and where the language of powers was now Greek. Greek was the language of royal inscriptions, except for rare bi- and trilingual examples like the Rosetta Stone. It was the language of diplomacy, and the language borrowed by many new national literatures. Greek and the political conventions that came with it gave this huge region some sort of cultural unity, a stark contrast with its political fragmentation. It spilled out beyond the old borders of the empire of Xerxes to include other Balkan kingdoms like Pyrrhus' Epirus, the Greco-Scythian states on the northern Black Sea coast, and in some respects Sicily and southern Italy as well.[9] These changes, which seem so clear in retrospect, are obscured by some ancient texts which continued to speak of Greek cities as they had before, carried on speaking of Macedonian kings in the same way other Greeks had in the fourth century, or referred to the great kingdoms by geographical labels such as Egypt, Syria, and Macedon. For many subject peoples the empires of Persian, Macedonian, and Roman kings were temporary presences compared to their own antiquity deep rooted in myth and cult.[10] That was as ideological a claim as those based on royal descent or the support of the gods. From the outside—to us—the Mediterranean world had changed fundamentally from the middle of the last millennium when it was a mosaic of city-states, a few temporarily exercising hegemony over their neighbours. The cities were still there, but from now on they would always be dominated by empires.

Yet the Greek city-state thrived. Athens, Sparta, Rhodes, Ephesus, Miletus, and Smyrna all flourished under imperial rule. Visit their sites today and the most impressive buildings all date from these periods. The same was true of many other cities including, amazingly, a reborn Corinth. The greatest cities were wealthier than they had ever been, if more politically dependent. What we regard as democratic institutions withered away (where they had existed, for not all poleis were democratic) but their assemblies still met and their masses exercised some influence on the propertied classes that now ruled them.[11] Some smaller cities withered away as their populations moved to richer centres; a very few were abandoned altogether.[12]

Alongside these old cities in new clothing were some genuinely new foundations. The royal capitals were the most splendid: Alexandria in

Egypt, Antioch on the Orontes, Seleuceia on the Tigris, and Pergamum in northwest Asia Minor, as well as shorter-lived foundation like Lysimacheia on the Thracian Chersonesus and Cassandreia on the coast of Macedon. Macedonian soldiers, themselves only recent converts to urban life, provided populations for many cities, along with Greek mercenaries and populations transplanted from non-Greek settlements.

Not all the newer poleis were royal foundations. Some had existed since the early Iron Age or even the Bronze Age, but now reinvented themselves as Greek poleis for the cultural prestige this brought them. Some Lycian and Phoenician cities had begun to do this even under Achaemenid rule, so firmly had the Mediterranean become a Greek lake.[13] Now they were joined by cities that had once been Carian, Lydian, Hittite, and so on. Greek inscriptions replaced those in a dozen Anatolian languages. Local gods acquired new names, and magistrates new titles. By the second century C.E. diplomatic missions were despatched to ancient Greek cities to confirm bonds of kinship based on new myths of origin.[14] In Anatolia and in the Levant temple-states were repackaged as poleis but retained names like Hierapolis ("sacred city") or Doliche, the centre of the cult of Jupiter Dolichenus. The image of the gods and the architecture of their temples mixed Greek and local traditions. Other languages were used alongside Greek, and perhaps all sorts of local traditions too, but to their Macedonian and later their Roman rulers, they were just so many cities.

The last three centuries B.C.E. were not always an easy time for cities. Kings were more focused, for the most part, on the army and the court. The court was the focus of constant dynastic intrigue, revolving as in all monarchies around marriages, the succession, and the trustworthiness or not of the chief ministers. The army was the other power base that kings depended upon. Most spent much of their reign campaigning across disputed border territories, constantly trying to live up to the standard set by Philip and Alexander, and also trying to outdo their rivals.[15] When Antiochus III came to power in 222 B.C.E. he controlled little more than Syria and Mesopotamia. He at once fought a war with Ptolemaic Egypt to reassert his power in Syria and then crossed the Zagros Mountains to put down a rebellion in his eastern Iranian provinces. Meanwhile, his cousin Achaeus won over the army in Asia Minor and had himself crowned king. Fighting wars against Egypt, Achaeus, and eastern rebels including Parthian invaders occupied Antiochus more or less full time until 209 B.C.E. Unfortunately for him by the time he had re-established the Seleucid realm to what he considered its ancestral limits, he encountered Roman armies and diplomats operating for almost the first time in the Aegean world. Defeat by the Romans at Magnesia meant his hard-won prestige crumbled overnight and his reign ended in chaos, rather like that in which it had begun.

Cities were often caught up in the middle of these rivalries. At best they suffered from a tug of love as different dynasties competed to be their benefactors. The Antigonids of Macedonia and the Ptolemies of Egypt struggled to assert their influence in the Aegean world. But cities might also be fought over, compelled to pick sides, besieged or raided for manpower and wealth. Ptolemies and Seleucids clashed in Asia Minor, where many of the great cities wished to remain independent. Realistically the best they could hope for was benign neglect. Often they were so much collateral damage.

The entry of Rome into the eastern Mediterranean made things more difficult, at least to begin with. Historians still argue about the motors and mechanisms of Roman conquest: the greed and aggression of Rome's rulers is not in doubt, but how far they planned expansion, and how far they simply had to ride the tiger, is less clear.[16] It is the consequences for cities that matters here. Romans did not quite play by the local rules. On an early expedition into the northern Balkans they agreed with the Aetolians that they could have the cities, if Rome could have the movable plunder, including slaves. The Romans' appetite for loot was extraordinary, but at first they seemed reluctant to acquire new territory. Their active interest in any given region also fluctuated from year to year. Several Greek cities were caught out when Roman armies withdrew for decades, and they assumed they were free to develop independent policies. It could be terrifying when the Romans suddenly seemed to take an interest again, as their former ally Rhodes discovered. Eventually this style of sporadic imperialism proved unworkable. After a crisis in 146 C.E. a Roman province was created to replace the four republics into which the kingdom of Macedonia had been broken up two decades before. Not long afterwards another province replaced the Attalid kingdom of Pergamum, on the other side of the Aegean. Finally, the invasion of Asia and Greece by Mithridates King of Pontus forced Romans to try and formalize their hegemony. It would still be a century before the last great Macedonian monarchy, that of Egypt, was defeated and absorbed. Long before that it was clear that the cities had just passed over into the hands of new masters. They responded accordingly.

Cities had, of course, been dealing with kings for a very long time. There is a story in Herodotus about ambassadors from Athens and Argos bumping into each other at Susa when both had come to seek the support of the Persian king Artaxerxes.[17] This probably happened in the 440s B.C.E. Throughout the fourth century many cities sent ambassadors to Persian kings and satraps, and also to the court of Philip of Macedon. After Alexander, great energy was devoted to devising ways of managing rulers. Elaborate rhetorics of praise and persuasion were created; the rhetorical handbook attributed to Menander the Rhetor is very largely concerned with means of praising the powerful. The philosopher Dio of Prusa wrote a couple of treatises titled *On Kingship*. The same ideas appear in many other texts including Philodemus' *On the Good King according to Homer* and Seneca's *On Clemency*.[18] Honours were invented that might be offered to a king. Kings were hailed as saviours, as founders, as benefactors and in the case of barbarian kings, as Philhellenes. They were awarded portraits and statues and inscriptions were set up in their honour. As the Macedonian monarchies tumbled one by one this energy was redirected towards Rome.[19] Ruler-cult tribute was paid first to Rome and its generals and eventually to the emperors. Embassies that had once gone to royal courts now addressed Roman generals in the field, or else made the long journey to the Senate in Rome. As early as the reign of Augustus, embassies chased him all over the empire for a personal audience.

This was not a smooth transition. Even when Rome had defeated, humbled, and dismantled the major kingdoms—a messy process that took around two centuries—things were not immediately easier for the cities of the eastern Mediterranean. Many of the bloodiest campaigns in the civil wars that marked the birth pangs of the imperial monarchy were fought east of the Adriatic. Pompey was defeated at Pharsalus in Thessaly, Brutus and Cassius at Philippi in Macedonia, Antony and Cleopatra at Actium at he mouth of the Ambracian Gulf that opens onto the Adriatic south of Corfu. Romans slaughtered Romans where two hundred years before their ancestors had fought Macedonian monarchs and where Fulvius Nobilior had plundered Ambracia. During the Roman civil wars both cities and kings had to pick sides. Some cities—Sparta was one—turned out to be very good at spotting future winners, and profited accordingly. Others, including Athens, seems to have a knack for offending generals who would later win. Either way the cost of provisioning all those armies fell heavily on Roman allies, and heavier yet on her enemies.

Despite all this carnage, which has left a powerful trace in historical writing, the cities of Greece and Asia Minor emerged from the Roman civil wars in pretty good shape. From the reign of Augustus onwards a boom in public inscriptions records a growing dynamism in civic life. The wealthy had already contributed to the finances of their home cities in the third and second centuries B.C.E. and in some cases like Athens, even earlier. Under the early Roman Empire benefactions transformed the civic fabric.[20] Building in marble spread to more and more cities. Theatres, hippodromes, council houses, and gymnasia were built, and some were provided with lavish baths modelled on those of Roman Italy and supplied by new aqueducts. Great ceremonial ways were laid out, and fountains and markets. Some civic benefactors funded great festivals, which we often know about through the rich record of civic decrees that appears in this period.[21] Temples were rebuilt on a spectacular scale, dedicated to the gods of the city and often the emperors too.

Italian cities had a different, but parallel, history. They had never experienced Macedonian-style kingship. Yet they too were caught up first in wars of conquest and then in civil wars. Capua, Tarentum, and Syracuse all suffered for siding with Hannibal during his long years in Italy. The peninsula enjoyed more than a century of peace after Hannibal's defeat. Local elites prospered and some built wonderful houses for themselves; urban architecture in the south drew on eastern inspiration.[22] This was the age in which great mosaics began to be built, and elegant gardens decorated with marble statues from the east. Despite the growing tensions between Rome and her allies there was little fighting in Italy between the defeat of Hannibal and the 80s B.C.E. when first the Social War and then the civil war between Sulla and Marius led to brief peninsular-wide conflicts. The aftermath of the Social War was mostly benign. Rome won the battles but conceded the issue. Most Italians became Roman citizens, ushering in a long period in which their cities, the *municipia*, were both part of the Roman state and also in some way autonomous.[23] The civil wars were another matter. If you visit Pompeii you can still see the scars left on the city's walls by Sulla's artillery. Sulla also imposed resettlement programmes on some cities, and there were further impositions in the Triumviral period. Octavian's victory brought stability. As Augustus, he set about beautifying the city of Rome and as a consequence—partly in loyal imitation, and partly in a desire to avoid appearing to compete with him—the propertied classes of Italy began to beautify their own towns.[24] The first century C.E. saw *municipia* all over Italy equipped with theatres and amphitheatres, aqueducts and other civic monuments.

In the west as in the east, empire was in the end good for cities. One reason was the benefits that urban economies drew from peace, a peace that not only promoted agriculture, production, and trade but also relieved cities of the costs of warfare. But there was also a tacit recognition of the mutual reliance of imperial and local ruling classes.[25] In almost every part of the Roman Empire the propertied classes undertook to keep order, give justice, collect revenues, and do all the other things the emperors would otherwise have to organize for themselves. In return, local elites were given pretty much a free hand when it came to ruling over their fellow citizens. This was the hidden logic of Roman imperial rule. That collusion of interest was wrapped up in ideologies of honour and duty, education and the civilizing process, but it was fundamentally collaboration based on class solidarity. And for as long as the local propertied classes chose to live much of their lives in cities, and to administer their portion of the empire through civic institutions, the city-state thrived.

Government Without Cities

The Roman Empire, as it emerged from near disaster in the civil wars and as expansion slowed, found a stability that would last with rare interruptions for half a millennium. The foundations of its institutions, central and local, were urban. This might seem bizarre, given how late urbanism had come to the Mediterranean, given the ecological risks run by cities of any size beyond that of a large village, and given the success of military leaders since Alexander in subverting civic politics. Yet in the end the city-state, duly modified and repurposed, was the basic institution on which imperial rule rested. Civic elites mostly benefited, even if they were less free than before, and urban populations often enjoyed impressive amenities. All the same we might ask whether there were alternative routes Rome might have followed, and different building blocks on which she might have depended.

There have been many recent studies comparing different early empires, their economies and political structures, their ideologies and their internal dynamics.[26] In most respects the empires turn out to be very alike, vast culturally heterogenous domains unified by force and maintained by ideology, taking little of the surplus in tax or tribute and spending most of what they took on their rulers and their military forces. The Inca and Aztec, the Assyrians and Persians, the various empires in what is now China and

Iran, and the Maurya Empire in India all have a family likeness, as do the Macedonian kingdoms and Rome. But the use of city-states as organs of government is not one of these common features. Most ancient empires did rule over urban societies. With few if any exceptions they originated in aggressive states based on intensive agriculture, and cities were ubiquitous in societies of that kind. Cities are, after all, a key product of social complexity. But in only a few imperial systems were cities made essential parts of the apparatus of government. Why did the Romans come to rely on cities so heavily?

It helps to consider some of the alternatives. The Achaemenid Empire at its peak ruled over the kingdom of Egypt, over Greek and Phoenician city-states, the ancient kingdoms of the Lydians in Asia Minor, the Assyrians in northern Mesopotamia and the heavily urbanized region of Babylonia, and also over mountaineers in the Zagros and various nomads and semi-nomads in central Asia. Where they could, they tried to make connections with established power-brokers and recruit them to the imperial project. So Achaemenid Persian emperors patronized local temples in Egypt and Jerusalem, the Greek cities of Ionia and Cyprus, various elites in Babylon, and probably elsewhere too. The tablets found in the fortification walls at Persepolis show Babylonians, Greeks, and many others working in the palace.[27] There were moments of centralization—the reign of Darius for instance—when uniform coinage and governmental structures were rolled out and there was investment in communications. But mostly the Achaemenids made do with whatever was available in each area that might be put to work governing the empire. Their empire had, after all, been put together from a series of Iron Age kingdoms. Of these the Persians themselves had less relevant experience than almost any of their subjects to draw on. As a result they were quite dependent on what had gone before.

Egypt, for instance, had for millennia a highly centralized royal administration. The country was divided into forty-odd territorial districts called *nomes*, each with a governor who reported back to the royal court. There were some changes over time, of course. Sometimes Egypt was divided, and the southern boundary with Nubia moved up and down the Nile. The pharaohs' capital might be as far south as Luxor or as far north as the Delta. In some periods the priests of the most powerful temples achieved some independence from royal control. Yet the essential system of government by nome and governor (now called in Greek the *strategos*) survived numerous changes of dynasty including the periods of Persian, Macedonian, and

Roman rule. It was not until the third century C.E. that the main settlement in each in *nome*, now known as a metropolis, began to be treated like a city and the *nome* as a hole like a city-state. The Persians designated Egypt as one of the great provinces (*satrapies*) into which their empire was divided, appointed a governor (a *satrap*) with his Persian guard, and stationed garrisons at key points. Although the details were different from place to place, in most areas we can see how an imperial superstructure was built on top of local institutions in this way.

Herodotus provided an account of the Persian Empire at the time of Darius I, when there were around twenty satrapies.[28] Documents from later periods have slightly different lists, but the basic structure was unchanged. Each satrapy had a governor, a garrison, and a tax assessment, which varied from 170 to 1,000 talents. Babylonia and Egypt had the largest assessments, and areas populated mostly by nomadic peoples the smallest. That suggests a pragmatic assessment of their relative economic strength, although we do not know for certain of any census. Part of the tribute went back to the centre, and a part was allocated to provisioning the garrisons in each satrapy. Villages and pastoralists provided the governor with a portion of their produce.[29] Subject peoples also provided levies that together comprised the numerical bulk of the great armies of invasion raised by the early Achaemenid emperors. Some provided special tributes as well, horses from Cilicia, grain from Egypt, gold dust from India, and so on. City-states played little role in the system in most satrapies, because they had not played a major role in the kingdoms that Persia had absorbed.

Around the world early empires consistently drew on local institutions in this way. Where extended families and kinship groups had been important, as in much of the territory taken over by Qin and Han dynasties, these were the building blocks available to work with. The Mongols had to assemble their empire by engineering an alliance of nomad tribes. Even when imperial bureaucracies eventually became powerful, as in China and Rome, these grew up within structures assembled from pre-existing institutions.

The Roman emperors also had to make concessions to local circumstances: in much of the Mediterranean the only two institutions available were monarchies and city-states. The former Persian lands had been ruled for three centuries or so by Macedonian kings who left behind them hundreds of communities that thought of themselves as Greek poleis. The other key institutions of their empires—the army and the court—were casualties of Roman victory. In these lands the Romans either dealt with cities or they dealt with petty kingdoms, the last and weakest fragments of Achaemenid and Macedonian monarchy. Sometimes they chose one, sometimes the other. But by the end of the first century C.E. there is a clear trends away from ruling through friendly kings to ruling through territorial provinces managed by governors with all the work devolved to city-states. Why was it that in the end, city-states won out against all the alternatives?

The City and Its Advantages

One factor at least was familiarity.

Rome's earliest opponents in the Italian peninsula were mainly peoples like themselves, small-scale Italian societies urbanized to various degrees. Romans understood from their own experience how these communities worked, the nature of small-scale politics, the balances between masses and elite (or assemblies and councils), and how the formal distribution of role between magistrates who served for just a year or so worked alongside the long-lasting ties between propertied families. City-state politics was their comfort zone, and it is not very surprising that by the end of the millennium Italy was ruled more or less entirely by *municipia* of Roman citizens with just a few Italy-wide structures in place.[30]

The road had not been a smooth one. During the middle Republic, Romans were also fighting wars against mountaineers and the large tribes of Gallic Italy. For a long time none of these peoples were subject to tribute at all; lesser allies were simply required to provide troops for future wars. Roman leadership of Italy was quite minimalist as a result. The allies managed their own affairs—probably in wildly different ways—and so long as they obeyed the occasional command and provided troops when called upon to do so, Rome was content. Romans did profit materially from their campaigning. Apart from acquiring land and military labour, victorious generals also brought back booty that was shared between the gods, the general, and the soldiery. Some defeated powers—Carthage after 241 B.C.E., Macedon after 197 B.C.E., and the Aetolians in 189 B.C.E.—had to pay a "war indemnity," in effect tribute. That might be a single sum or an annual payment. Crucially, those paying remained notionally independent of Roman rule, although not immune to Roman interference.

Overseas expansion brought Rome into contact with other kinds of states. Syracuse and Carthage were superficially rather like Rome, hegemonic cities that ruled over larger areas in which smaller cities were subject to them. But their political economies were different. Both seemed to have levied tribute from subordinate states, and in the case of Carthage at least used part of this to fund a largely mercenary military. What other demands each hegemon put on their subjects is uncertain. The tax system of Sicily, at least, was more complex than that of Rome. Rome absorbed the *Lex Hieronica*—Hiero's system of taxation—after Syracuse was defeated in 212 B.C.E., and Roman governors dealt directly with the cities of Sicily. Rome did something similar with the tax systems of the kings of Pergamum when that kingdom was absorbed in 133 B.C.E. Royal prerogatives flowed to Rome, and after a disastrous experiment handing over the collection of taxes to companies of Roman tax-farmers, the cities were given responsibility for collecting imperial tax as well as their own local revenues. This was closer to ancestral Roman forms, although poleis were never identical to *municipia* in detail. There seems to have been no desire to homogenize these governmental forms.[31] So far, in other words, so Persian.

Rome only needed to become really creative when it took over regions that could not simply be recruited as subordinate allies (as in Italy) or left to manage with preconquest institutions. Something like the Italian unequal alliances were reproduced overseas in the Republican period. Some hegemonies were effectively broken up into tiny principalities or city-states. Macedon, after its defeat in 167 B.C.E., became four republics. After Carthage was destroyed in 146 B.C.E. the lesser kings of North Africa who had been Roman allies were each given part of her territory, while the core became a Roman province. When the last king of Pergamum bequeathed it (or his royal rights) to Rome in 133 B.C.E., Rome again retained just part of the kingdom as a province (and then dealt mainly with the cities within it), and gave other less desirable border areas to Anatolian kings. As late as the middle of the first century C.E. there were parts of Rome's territory still ruled by kings who served at the emperors' pleasure, in Thrace and Morocco, Britain and the Alps.[32] Some British chiefs used the Roman title Rex on their coinages, and at least one had Roman citizenship.[33] An Alpine chief of an earlier generation was both a king and a prefect.[34]

Petty kingdoms of a different kind survived in the east, especially among the ruins of the Ptolemaic and Seleucid realms. During the last generation of the Roman Republic kingdoms were absorbed and resuscitated, divided again and again and redistributed with bewildering frequency. Cyprus, Cyrenaica, Syria, and Judaea were all sliced and resliced several times. Pompey was responsible for much of this during his long campaigns in the east in the sixties, but Antony and Augustus did much the same. Commagene, on what is now the Turkish–Syrian border, remained independent until 72 C.E., as did the Nabataeans with their marvellous desert city of Petra into 106. Some of these dynasties, like the Herods in Judaea or the kings of Mauretania, became great city-builders, creating smaller versions of the Antiochs and Alexandrias built by greater monarchs. All in the end were, however, absorbed into provinces within which city-states were the main building blocks of government.

There remained some parts of the empire where there was no existing infrastructure that might be put to use. This was especially true in areas remote from the Mediterranean. The solution applied in most cases was to implant something like a city-state. There was probably no one single moment at which a clear plan to do this was formed. Rather, as local problems appeared—how to levy taxes, how to hand out justice, how to police brigands—the solutions Roman generals or the senate reached for were mostly familiar ones.

The first place we can observe this clearly was in the Iberian peninsula in the second century B.C.E. Spanish tribes in areas where Roman armies were stationed had been supporting them with irregular payments. As the temporary commands became more permanent, these payments were converted into a regular tribute called *stipendium*.[35] Again in the aftermath of the Social War, at the same time as Roman citizenship was being extended to citizens of allied cities in most of Italy, the area north of the river Po was reorganized. The communities that lived between and beyond the Roman colonies were mostly given the Latin right—a form of limited citizenship—and some of the Alpine tribes were attached (attributed) to communities down in the plain.[36] Those *attributi* remained excluded from Roman citizenship when the rest of the province was enfranchised by Caesar.

As Roman power extended east from Spain and west from Italy a broad swathe of southern France was brought under Roman control. The exact point when it became a regular province is not clear. There were wars in the lower Rhône Valley in the 120s and by 118 B.C.E. a *colonia* had been founded at Narbonne, one of the few legacies of the Gracchan plan for overseas colonization, and with it a major military road linking Italy and Spain. By Cicero's day there were some transit taxes imposed on the wine trade, and Caesar was able to use it as a base for his wars in the interior in the 50s. There are other signs too that the tribes of Mediterranean

France and the nearest neighbours inland were becoming embroiled in the Mediterranean economy and Roman politics. Wine was imported in great quantities from central Italy. Local currencies in the west began to converge on Roman weight standards.[37] Caesar and Octavian planted colonies over much of the area, potential models for imitation. Soon their neighbours included other cities whose populations had been gathered together from scattered villages.[38] When a regular tax system was rolled out over Gaul under Augustus, census allocations were made by tribe or city and increasingly each tribe was treated as a city-state and its chief settlement as a city. The Allobroges, who lived between the Rhône and Lake Geneva, made their capital at Vienne; the Volcae Arecomisci's was west of the Rhône at Nîmes; another group of Volcae established base at Toulouse, and so on. These centres soon closely resembled Italian municipia or Roman coloniae in terms of their monuments, largely because they had been designed by the same architects.[39]

Something similar was being done in some parts of the east at roughly the same time. When Pompey finally defeated Mithridates in 64 he did to Pontus what had been done to Macedon in 167—he abolished the kingdom and divided the new province into city-states, each based on an existing village. Each new city-state had responsibility for administering the surrounding territory, keeping order and ensuring the payment of tribute. Just a few years before Sulla had given similar responsibilities to the poleis of Asia Minor when the activities of the *publicani*—tax contractors—had provoked a major revolt against Rome. There is no sign that Roman generals or the Senate thought of their rule over the east as very different from their rule over the west; they applied similar solutions in each case. Around 87 B.C.E. two communities in the Ebro valley in Spain asked a Roman governor to arbitrate a dispute over water rights. His response was to formulate the exact issue that should be decided and then appoint a third community as a judge. Very similar procedures had been used by Quintus Mucius Scaevola, governor of Asia, less than a decade before for adjudicating between Greek cities.

Roman generals and emperors did not set out to fill the gaps between the urban networks of the ancient world, but the way they governed had that effect. The most familiar legal and institutional solutions were ones that had been developed for other purposes in Rome and in Roman Italy. On occasion they used other systems—ruling through client kings or handing over tax collection to public contractors—but when these failed they tended to revert to a city-state system of government.

City-states had several other advantages for the rulers. Unlike kingdoms, they were too small to be effective rebels. Urbanism was also associated with the kind of moral and culture values which Romans were beginning to use as one justification of their empire. Many cities already raised revenue of their own and were used to policing marginal areas, so they were well able to take on the burden. If municipal elites became richer as a result, and the rural and urban poor ended up more firmly under their control, that was a side effect with which the wealthy rulers of Rome could live.[40] Whether they realized it or not they show a strong bias in favour of social groups like themselves, and the kinds of political institution that ensured they dominated their communities. Chiefdoms, democracies, temple-states, and other exotic systems were less appealing than a community of citizens run by its richest and best-educated members.

Emperors and governors were prepared to encourage the development of those classes and the civic institutions they preferred. Money was occasionally provided to help give the new centres of these administrative tribal states—some of which were very large indeed—the kind of monuments that other cities in the empire enjoyed. Sometimes new sites were selected for the construction of capitals. The Aedui of Burgundy moved their capital from the hilltop of Mount Bibracte to the current site of Autun. Its Roman name was Augustodunum, a hybrid Roman-Celtic name meaning something like the fortified place of Augustus. Buildings for entertainments, schools, and temples were provided, as well as an impressive wall circuit. The few Latin and Greek texts that describe city-building of this kind tend to present it as a work of self improvement on the part of barbarians, perhaps encouraged and assisted a little by Roman governors. Probably locals did pay for the rebuilding in most cases, but in at least a few we can see Roman authorities being more active. Very recent excavations at the site of Waldgirmes in Hesse show the part-constructed but abandoned civic centre for one of the tribes that inhabited the territory east of the Rhine that Augustus was attempting to conquer, before a massive defeat at Kalkriese in 9 C.E. forced a retreat. Stone buildings had been laid out and a forum planned, but it remained a ghost town.

Government by city became in just a few generations the imperial norm. Local elites could not do everything. There remained some jobs for which public contractors (*publicani*) were preferred.[41] The tenants of imperial estates in North Africa paid their rent to contractors answering to the Roman officials in Carthage.[42] Tax farmers also had a role in the complex collection of transit duties from those going in and out of the Gallic provinces.[43] The military were entrusted with some duties too, escorting goods en route to Rome, providing staff for tax collection, and occasionally managing the affairs of tribes who had not yet been enticed into urbanism.

Mostly, however, the empire was ruled through cities. The local propertied classes formed councils, and annual magistrates took turns in shouldering responsibility. In many places the very richest citizens made great benefactions to their cities, paying for buildings, shows, and grain funds. A few chose to enter the imperial elite and might find themselves not only as equestrian procurators or senatorial governors, but also as patrons to their own hometowns as well. Their service was recognized by the emperors, who for nearly four centuries protected the rights and interests of cities, well aware how much this particular empire depended on them.[44]

18

The Ecology of Roman Urbanism

The Roman Urban Apogee

Urbanism is not easy to measure. For any place and time—the Mediterranean world under the Roman Empire for example—we could count the number of cities, or the proportion of the population that lived in cities, or we could look at their mean size, or even the size of the largest. Each of these indices tells us something about how urban a society is.

By most of these measures the ancient Mediterranean reached a peak of urbanism sometime between 150 and 250 C.E. This period, which more or less coincides with the greatest geographical extent of the Roman Empire and, more controversially, with a climatic optimum of a few centuries, is sometimes labelled the ancient urban apogee.[1] It is the period in which it is easiest to see the shape of ancient urban networks, how they operated, and their ecological rationale.

The urban apogee is a crude approximation. Things look much more complicated if we compare different parts of the Roman world. The new cities of temperate Europe, that part of the empire north of the Alps and furthest from the Mediterranean, probably stopped growing before 200 C.E. This has led many archaeologists to ask how deeply rooted urban economies ever were in this part of the empire.[2] It is hard to find any large urban monuments built in the north after that point. There were small wall circuits in some places, but these were often built rapidly in a crisis from stone taken from other monuments. The only exceptions were those cities that briefly housed imperial courts in the third and fourth centuries, cities such as Trier in Germany and Sirmium, just west of Belgrade. The cities founded north of the Danube in the early second century were largely abandoned before the end of the third, when Rome withdrew from Trajan's new Dacian provinces. Many North African cities thrived in the third century.[3] In a few of the cities of Asia Minor and Syria, spectacular building continued into the fourth century and their monuments were regularly used even later.[4] As a general rule, Roman cities flourished longest where they had the longest histories.

The populations of the very biggest cities fluctuated more than any others.[5] Rome in 200 C.E. may already have had fewer inhabitants than it did in Augustus' day. It was certainly a lot smaller in the early fourth century, when we have a catalogue of its buildings region by urban region. Around the same time, a New Rome had been created on the Bosporus by Constantine. Anywhere that an emperor stayed for long sprouted great monuments. The imperial baths and basilica at Trier and the huge palace at Split are still extraordinary. Less survives above ground of the late antique cityscapes of Antioch and Alexandria, but recent investigations have revealed the scale and splendour of each.[6] Occasional literary testimony contributes a sense of the dynamism of the greatest cities, their turbulent populations, their intellectual life, and their great ceremonies.[7]

These patterns only describe general trends. Look closer and there is the constant up and down of local urban histories. There were cities that grew as they found themselves at key points on road networks: Aosta on its high Alpine pass; Corinth with its two harbours, one opening to the Saronic Gulf and the Aegean, the other to the Gulf of Corinth and the Adriatic; or Amiens, suddenly finding itself at the road junction for a new highway to the channel after the conquest of Britain. Others shrank or were even abandoned as frontiers shifted, like that model city at Walgirmes in Hesse in anticipation of the creation of a new province that never came to be between the Rhine and the Elbe. Harbours silted up at various points. Some were dredged, but sometimes cities simply withered once the sea had abandoned them. Volcanoes and earthquakes shattered cities: Pompeii suffered from both in C.E. 62 and 79; the cities of Asia survived a catastrophic earthquake in the reign of Tiberius, Antioch another in C.E. 526. There were occasional tsunamis, including a particularly dreadful one in 365 C.E. One measure of the energy of early imperial urbanism is how resilient cities were, and how many recovered from natural catastrophes. Gripping accounts survive of sieges and the famines and plagues that went with them, from Athens in the fifth century B.C.E. to Antioch in the fifth century C.E.

Ancient writers were often more interested in the stories of individual cities.[8] Even those who wrote on a grand scale found the falls of Syracuse,

Marseilles, or Jerusalem irresistible subjects for a set-piece narration. Only with hindsight do the broader patterns become visible to us. Those patterns were never stable. All urban systems are in constant flux, if only because the economies and demographics on which they depend are also volatile.

An Unplanned Urban Civilization

The Roman Empire is a vantage point from which we can look back on a thousand years of urbanization. But every apogee is also a limit. Why did ancient urbanism peak then and there? Answers to those questions will only come from looking away from individual urban histories to the shape of grand patterns, and how they emerged.

The urban networks of the Roman world had not emerged through anyone's design. Nor was there any natural trend to urbanization. Humans might be preadapted for life in cities, but that is not the same as saying we are destined for it. Humans all over the planet have urban potential, but for most of our history that potential has not been realized. Looking back from the Roman urban apogee to the beginning of the last millennium B.C.E. in the Mediterranean world, it might seem tempting to tell a story of gradual and continuous growth, one in which the rise of cities intermeshes with economic growth and other signs of progress. Tempting, but that would be a mistake.

One of the main themes of this book has been that in each age different forces—selective pressures—operated on slow-growing human populations, offering new possibilities of where and how to live. Not every community exploited these possibilities in the same way, and usually we can only see the results of their deliberations. Concentrations of power appeared in several different places around the archaic Mediterranean—in Etruria, southern Spain, Sicily, and the Aegean world, to name the most important—and were connected to older centres in Anatolia, the Levant, and Egypt by mariners who had no interest in city-building. Cities arose in some areas out of trading posts, in others as by-products of state-building, occasionally (as in Egypt) because the local ecology compressed growing populations into such close proximity they were forced to develop more regimented ways of living together. It follows that the Egyptian route to urbanism was not the same as the Greek one, and so on.

During the middle of the last millennium B.C.E. a handful of hegemonic cities disseminated particular models of urban society. Generals, tyrants, and kings created a range of empires in the last centuries B.C.E. and in the course of this founded, destroyed, merged, and even moved some cities. The newly founded cities were not all alike. Roman *coloniae* were fragments of a territorial state that grew up like a parasite within the Italian peninsula. Greek poleis—often as much the creation of locals as incomers—provided a model for later foundations. Tiny units of soldiers were thrown back on the land to become part-time farmers who kept their swords sharp; others were imposed on existing urban societies. Then there were the new poleis of the east built by Carians, Lycians, Syrians, Jews, and others on the sites of older and slightly different foundations, and the *municipia* created in North Africa, Spain, Gaul, and Germany, sometimes on the site of or close to ancient hill forts. Romans invested few resources in enforcing uniformity. They tended to treat all subject cities in the same way, and had clear ideas about what constituted the best way to live. The result was a process of cultural convergence, as urban elites adopted Latin or Greek as languages of power, set up inscriptions in one or both in marble or bronze, imitated Roman or Greek institutions (law courts, athletics, banquets, councils, magistracies, gladiators, temples, and statues of the gods in the Greek tradition), and reaped the benefits of imperial approval by being made partners in the exploitation of the empire. The urban system of the Roman world emerged from all these different urban and quasi-urban experiments, pulled together first by conquest and then by the political economy of empire.

Classical literature cannot help us here, even if it sometimes seems to tell similar stories. The ancients did not grasp the complexity of these patterns and preferred simple narratives. Writers of the fifth century B.C.E. and later seem to have believed that most ancient Greek cities had been there from the Heroic Age, and that most new ones had been founded by Greek expeditions mounted in the face of either local opposition. It is only recently that we have understood how those stories were created and the ends they served.[9] Greeks had no clear understanding of the earliest stages of urbanization. The Heroic Age was remembered as a world of cities: the two great epic cycles concerned attacks on the cities of Thebes and Troy, with figures like Heracles and Theseus moving from city to city in their adventures. In this, as in much else, they resembled the heroes of Mesopotamian literature. Around the cities were less urban worlds. Odysseus, washed up on the shore of Scherie, described how he and his men had visited one such place:

From there grieving still at heart, we sailed on further along and reached the country of the lawless outrageous Cyclopes who, putting all their trust in the immortal gods, neither plow with their hands nor plant anything, but all grows for them without seed planting, without cultivations, wheat and barley and also the grapevines, which yield for them wine of strength, and it is Zeus' rain that waters it for them. These people have no institutions, no meetings for counsels; rather they make their habitations in caverns hollowed among the peaks of the high mountains, and each one is the law for his own wives and children, and cares nothing about the others.[10]

The idea that the familiar urban world was surrounded by wilderness inhab-ited by beasts and bestial humans also recalls Mesopotamian mythology, and in fact there are many other parallels. Homer stops short of sketching a civilizing process: there is no hint that one day the Cyclopes will be like the Greeks or the Phaeacians, nor that Greeks once lived as the Cyclopes did now. The first hint of that sort of theory of history comes at the start of history of Thucydides, written at the end of the fifth century B.C.E.

For instance, it is evident that the country now called Hellas had in ancient times no settled population; on the contrary, migrations were of frequent occurrence, the several tribes readily abandoning their homes under the pres-sure of superior numbers. Without commerce, without freedom of commu-nication either by land or sea, cultivating no more of their territory than the exigencies of life required, destitute of capital, never planting their land (for they could not tell when an invader might not come and take it all away, and when he did come they had no walls to stop him), thinking that the necessi-ties of daily sustenance could be supplied at one place as well as another, they cared little for shifting their habitation, and consequently neither built large cities nor attained to any other form of greatness.[11]

The idea that civilized societies had emerged from ancestral barbarism came to be widespread, perhaps already was when Thucydides made his sugges-tions about the deep past. That idea, and the association between cities and civilized life, seems implicit in the interest Macedonian kings showed in being celebrated as city-founders, and perhaps there are distant echoes of Gilgamesh King of Uruk here, too.

The apparent similarity of modern social evolutionary narratives to ancient myths of civilization can easily mislead us into buying into that story of gradual urbanization. What archaeological research and more crit-ical readings of ancient texts reveal, however, is the opposite. The Roman urban apogee was just the latest in a series of settlement systems and exchange systems separated by major discontinuities. Different pressures operated at different times. Generation after generation found new uses for urban places. Less visibly, many found no use for urban ways of life. The urban apogee might have been the high-water mark of classical cities, but it was not that high. We live in a world where just over half the population live in cities and where a small city has less than 500,000 inhabitants. There were a few places in the Roman Empire where maybe as many as 30 per cent of the population lived in cities, but in many regions the figure was closer to 5 per cent. Crucially, a small city in the ancient world had fewer than 5,000 inhabitants. Their urban experience was utterly unlike our own.

Urban Networks of the Roman World

The Roman urban system can be thought of as a series of distinct networks laid out over the same nodes.[12] The nodes were the cities, and the links or ties that connected them were roads, tracks, and seaways. Most roads and many boats carried travellers of all kinds, but some routes were more important for one purpose than another. Equally, some cities were central nodes in administrative networks but quite marginal when it came to commercial networks, or vice versa. This is why it makes sense to think of many networks rather than just one.

The most recent network to be constructed was the administrative network, the means by which the emperors used cities to harvest surplus and manage their subject peoples. Provinces did not have capitals in quite the way modern states do. The empire had no great bureaucracy and relied on governors being quite mobile, so there are no great buildings to compare with those built in New Delhi or Pretoria in the early twentieth century.[13] Yet in many places key functions were centralized in the cities where governors spent most of their time: Alexandria in Egypt, for example, or London in Britain. A second tier of cities were those that the governors visited on regular circuits, giving justice. Each was the centre of a *conventus* in the west or a *diocese* in the east, and cities sometimes competed for the privilege of being part of that group. Below these were the civic centres of each of the two thousand or so city-states (*civitates, reipublicae, municipia, coloniae,* poleis) through which most taxes were raised. Across the administrative network of the empire travellers brought requests and commands; taxes were transported; soldiers and imperial messengers carried information back and forth. Where communications were particularly vital hostels were established—at local expense of course—which those with permits from the emperor could use.[14]

A second network was generated by commerce. Some strands of this system were very ancient, shaped by the winds and currents or the sea. Most cities of any size had long depended on supply systems for some necessities, occasionally even for food. Regular sailing routes connected the greater cities of the Aegean bringing grain from the Black Sea, timber from Macedonia and Thrace, and slaves from all directions. Similar systems had evolved in the western Mediterranean to distribute the grain surpluses of North Africa and Sicily, the wine produced in central Italy, and the timber of the Apennines.

There were also more local networks that connected groups of islands with each other and the mainland, or simply joined up areas where maritime connections were easier than those across land. There are many parts of the Mediterranean where barren mountains come right down to the sea, and even in the nineteenth century many were easier to reach by boat than by road. Those local connections went back to the Neolithic in some cases, and some had barely been disrupted by the late Bronze Age collapse. Obsidian and salt, tin and copper, textiles and timber were ancient objects of trade. By the Roman period there were probably more vessels and more traffic, to judge from wrecks and the evidence of small ports dotted around the Mediterranean coast.

Then there were the connections made across ecological divides, linking complementary agricultural regimes. Vertical economies linked mountain pastures with nearby plains and coasts.[15] Short-range transhumance and the exchange of different fruits and grains made up part of this. In some areas, including Italy, peace and political unification probably made these exchanges easier. On a larger scale there was exchange between the north and south of the Mediterranean, and between the Mediterranean world and its continental hinterlands. Common tastes for food had developed that could not all be supplied locally. Olive oil was in demand everywhere but could be produced only in the Mediterranean world; wine also flowed north into lands that had previously only drunk beer. All the pepper consumed in the Roman world had come from India.

By the Roman period the appetite for rare commodities had grown. There was a profitable traffic in coloured marbles, silk, and incense. Other parts of the commercial network had been stimulated by imperial demands for taxation; some regions needed to increase their exports of food or manufactures to earn enough cash to pay their taxes.[16] Military roads and a well-paid army kicking its heels on the frontiers provided new opportunities too. The commercial system was a composite of many networks, each operating at its own scale. Precious metals were transported from one end of the empire to the other. Grain moved quite long distances, to the great cities and the major army camps; processed foods moved farther than fresh products, and so on. Every major city was hungry for food and water, for firewood and building materials, and for slaves. Cities flourished when they were well-placed to serve as hubs for these flows of goods.[17]

Alongside administrative and commercial networks were others that are less easier to measure. Religious networks are one example, such as the expanding circuit of places where athletic festivals took place, or the network of oracles that sometimes referred visitors to each other.[18] Healing shrines like those at Epidauros and Pergamum attracted visitors from far away as well as satisfying local needs. Some of the wealthy travelled long distances to be initiated at Eleusis. These journeys were prototypes of the great pilgrimage routes that would be so important in the Christian and Muslim Mediterraneans.[19] There were also kinship networks linking members of the empire's many diasporic peoples: Jews, Syrians, Africans, and Egyptians. There were networks linking places where population growth outstripped the supply or labour or land, and those giant cities and armies were hungry for more humans.[20] There were educational networks that led the most talented from small towns to major provincial cities and sometimes even to the imperial court.

Physically, all these networks used the same communications infrastructure. On land some great highways had mostly been built for the Roman legions, but they branched off into older local road systems.[21] Maritime networks were equally complex. Long-distance routes crossed deep water between the major ports. Some of the vessels that used these routes were so large they needed deep-water ports. A number of ports were built or expanded around the turn of the millennium to accommodate them and to help provision the largest of cities. Then there were medium-distance routes like those that crossed the Aegean or connected the major islands of the western Mediterranean to their respective hinterlands. Finally, there were (as there always had been) short-haul traffic up and down the coasts and from one island to another, routes run by tiny boats with crews of four or five men, never spending a night on the water. These short-haul routes originally moved local produce but had new roles distributing goods brought in on the much larger vessels that made the long-haul journeys.[22] The maritime network as a whole had grown, within the geographical constraints of the region, at the same time as cities had grown: as with roads, old networks had been joined up, new major routes added, and additional kinds of traffic were now carried.

Rivers provided a third component of the network along with some canals, on both of which a mixture of rafts, sail boats, and barges operated.[23] The largest rivers were important thoroughfares—the Rhine, the Mosel, and the Danube in Europe, and the Nile in Egypt. Figure 31 shows a vessel carrying wine barrels on the Mosel in Germany. But few Mediterranean rivers were navigable all year round for much of their courses (in contrast to today, when canalization and dredging has improved inland navigation).[24] Some would be suitable for moving goods downstream when the water was high. Moving large cargoes up stream was often impossible.

When we can document actual journeys—the travels of Paul, the route Pliny the Younger took to his province, the peregrinations of emperors—they often made use of all these means of transport for different legs of travel.[25] Cities provided some but not all the nodes in the network. Army

Figure 31 Burial monument in the form of a boat carrying wine
DEA / M. Borchi / Getty Images

camps—like cities in this respect as in many others—were strung along the highways in the north of the empire: many traders visited them simply because soldiers had a disposable income. Some routes led to major sites of rural production, such as the great pottery centres in the villages of central and northern Gaul, or the baking quarries of North Africa and the eastern desert of Egypt. A few imperial villas like that of Trajan at Centumcellae (modern Civitavecchia) or that of Hadrian at Tivoli had populations comparable to those of small towns, and many people needed to visit them. There were a few major sanctuaries like the oracle of Ammon in the Siwah Oasis that were remote from cities, although more often a world-famous sanctuary like that of Apollo at Grand in northern France or Glycon at Abonoteichus on the Black Sea coast of Turkey could put a small city on the map. The tangled infrastructures of empire are a good indication of how connected the Mediterranean and its hinterlands had become, and also of the limits of that connectivity.

Counting Cities

Urban networks reflect how societies work. Where towns are more or less alike and evenly scattered across the landscape we see a world that lives at a local scale, as self-sufficient as any small world could be. Where we can sort cities into many kinds, from market town to regional hub to national and international centre, we see a world that thrives on hierarchy. It might be necessary to travel a long way for some services—justice, higher education, shops where expensive foreign imports are sold—but this is a society that lives on complexity and power. Landscape shapes urban networks. During the Roman Empire cities lined the great rivers and thrived at the mouths of smaller ones, as did London on the Thames, Ephesus on the Cayster, and Amphipolis on the Strymon. The physical relief of the ancient world shaped the urban networks of antiquity at a the very large scale. Small islands could not sustain large cities, while larger plains or fertile river valleys could. Sometimes a sharp ecotone (between mountains and coast, forest and plain) created an opportunity. So did oases and mountain passes. No doubt there had been attempts to found cities in less suitable places back in the archaic era, but by the Roman period those early experiments had had centuries to fail or succeed. We might expect most cities that had survived to be relatively resilient, and relatively well suited to their immediate environments. A few new foundations faced less certain fortunes, but by the second century the great ages of city foundations had largely passed. The Roman urban system, as documented by the Peutinger Table (see Figure 32) was the product of a few centuries of selective pressures.

Different technologies shaped different networks in later periods. During the late nineteenth and early twentieth centuries the European imperial powers were connected to their distant possessions mainly by sea. As a result great port cities were built in southern Africa and India, many connected by rail and road to their hinterlands. Those cities and the networks that connected them were designed to facilitate the extraction of products and their export to distant markets. Once built, however, they shaped the development of colonial and postcolonial cities alike. Many former colonies today still show the traces of their imperial origin in the way road and rail networks are organized. Equally, the urban networks of North America still reflect the pattern of European colonization and of the subsequent westward expansion of the American frontier. Railways, canals, and cities have a certain inertia. They outlive their initial uses, and the connections they establish shape where people and businesses are located. The study of Roman road and urban networks in these terms has only just begun.[26]

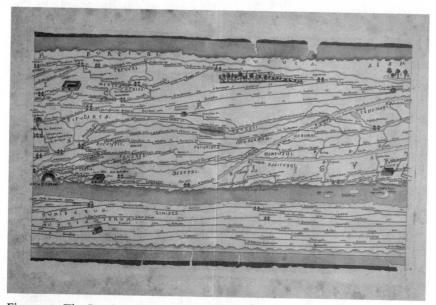

Figure 32 The Peutinger Table, a copy of a late antique map of the empire
The History Collection / Alamy Stock Photo

If we want to know what sort of urban networks characterized the Roman urban apogee, the first questions that needs to be answered are: How many cities were there, how big were they, and where were they located? A number of recent research projects have tried to answer these questions. The results will never be precise; we do not have data of the same quality as those used in recent UN surveys to quantify present-day urbanism.[27] But it is definitely possible to get a sense of the broad contours of urbanism in the Roman period.

As a baseline for comparison we can look back at the results of the *Inventory of Archaic and Classical Poleis* compiled by the Copenhagan Polis Centre, which focused on an earlier period of Mediterranean history.[28] By their estimate there were around 850 cities around the shores of the Mediterranean and Black Sea in the year 400 B.C.E., virtually all with populations in the low thousands. Only a couple of dozen had more than 10,000 people. Our question is how things had changed in the half-millennium or so that followed—an age of empires, of modest economic and demographic growth.

An urban system of this sort might have grown in several ways. In early modern Europe most cities grew in population at a fairly steady pace until the nineteenth century when power began to be concentrated in a few centres, the capitals of emerging nation-states, major commercial and then industrial centres.[29] Even today continental Europe has few really large cities compared with those of more centralized neighbours such as Turkey, Russia, and the United Kingdom. A different kind of growth happens when large cities grow and small ones shrink, or even reduce in number as their populations are drawn (or transported) to the new metropoles. The result is a steep hierarchy of cities, with smaller cities becoming dependent on larger ones. The *Inventory of Archaic and Classical Poleis* did find some evidence of the amalgamation of smaller cities—synoecism—as large ones grew. The creation of Megalopoleis and Messene, and the urban experiments of Sicilian tyrants, have already been mentioned. The new Roman provinces of northwestern Europe also underwent this sort of transformation, with just a few centres growing rapidly at the expense of others. The geographer Strabo described how populations living scattered in villages had been brought together when new towns were created in early Roman Gaul.[30] But these are local stories that can be explained by local circumstances. What about the larger patterns?

The most recent estimates suggest that between the period surveyed by the Copenhagen Polis Centre and the Roman urban apogee—a period of five or six hundred years—there was a modest growth in the number of cities, but in most cases there was little growth in the size of individual cities. There were some spectacular exceptions, cities like Rome and Alexandria, but most remained very small.

As far as numbers go, current estimates range from just under 1,400 to around 2,000 cities.[31] The differences in the count are mostly about where we fix the dividing line between the smallest cities and the largest villages. There is no dispute about the civic status of cities like Rome, Antioch, and Carthage, or even medium-sized cities like Pompeii or Philippi or Londinium. Deciding how many smaller centres really were cities is more difficult. The criteria we use—administrative role, monumentality, occupied area, economic activity, and so on—do not always coincide. Is everywhere that mints its own coinage a city? Do public monuments make the difference between villages and small cities? Should we rely on the official legal status of a settlement (although we do not always know what this was, especially in cases of small centres from which few written documents survive)? Some studies put most of their faith in texts from the Roman period, some in archaeological data. But we have very few texts, and many archaeological sites have not been extensively investigated. Even today there is no internationally accepted test of what makes a city: how much more difficult to decide for antiquity!

No official Roman lists survive, but they did exist once upon a time. The information was included in provincial censuses, the basis of tax collection. Governors, the tax officials known as procurators, and some others needed to know the list of cities in each province and the status of each, since there were sometimes legal disputes over whether or not a particular city had a right to its own laws, which cities the governor would visit to carry out the assizes, and so on. Lists of this kind lie behind some of the geographical books of Pliny the Elder's *Natural History* and also Ptolemy's *Geography*, written in the first and second centuries respectively but using older information.[32] Lists of Roman colonies survive in the history of Velleius Paterculus, written under the emperor Tiberius, and in the fourth-century *Book of Colonies*. Both used earlier material now lost to us. There are itineraries, too, and more descriptive geographies like those of Pomponius Mela and Strabo, which often mention the most important cities in each area (although again the smallest are treated less consistently). For some parts of the empire, enough public inscriptions survive for us to be fairly sure of which settlements were independent cities at the time they were set up.

These data refer to different periods within a four-hundred-year range, and we know that the status of some cities changed over time, some being promoted as a mark of imperial favour and some given autonomy when larger *civitates* were split up. Most sources of evidence are not equally good for all parts of the Roman Empire. Cities in the north and west put up fewer inscriptions (or at least fewer that have survived), and very few minted their own coins. Cities in Britain were unusual in that most had walls, which makes it easier to get some sense of their size compared to those in other provinces. Monumental assemblages varied wildly from one region to another; after all in some areas cities had been building theatres and stadia for longer than Rome had, while in others Roman colonies provided models of how to build cities. The mean distance between the cities Romans treated as capitals varied enormously. Where "*civitas*-capitals" were thin on the ground, other towns grew up as marketplaces and cult centres. One study of small towns in Roman Britain showed they were particularly likely to be located midway between two or more capitals.[33] The economic logic of urbanism was sometimes at odds with political geography.

With all these words of caution, there is a consensus among researchers that there were more cities in the Roman Empire than there had been in the classical Mediterranean, but not very many more. Given how much of the Mediterranean's continental hinterlands had been added to the Roman Empire, and how much bigger the empire was at its peak than the area considered by the Copenhagen Polis Centre, a modest increase in the number of cities is not that surprising. There is no doubt, by the way, that Rome was responsible for the northward extension of the urban network. The distribution of cities ends sharply at the northern frontier of the empire, right along its length from the Scottish border to the mouth of the Danube. The Sahara provided a different kind of limit to Roman urbanism, one based on the carrying capacity of the land rather than the rather arbitrary point at which the armies had stopped.

The Roman urban network was not an entirely closed system. The Nile Valley provided a corridor to Nubia, and there were also tenuous routes south from Roman North Africa across the Sahara to the Sahel. Neither region had much in the way of urbanism in that period. But routes through the Red Sea to India and East Africa also existed, and these did connect Roman cities to other urban systems. Exotica and luxury goods, spices and rare animals, and occasional travellers used these routes, just as they travelled the routes north to the Baltic and the Atlantic islands.[34] The main point where Roman cities connected to those in other jurisdictions was across the Empire's shifting eastern frontiers with Armenia and Persia. Any line drawn north to south across Anatolia, Syria, or Mesopotamia was arbitrary—one reason why this area was so often the scene of conflicts between various Roman and Persian imperial regimes between the last century B.C.E. and the seventh C.E. Cities were as valuable to one side as the other, and many, like Dura, changed hands several times.

The new cities that had appeared within the Roman Empire had various origins. The city foundations of Macedonian kings and the various colonization programmes of the Roman state had extended urbanism to some places which had never known cities before, many of them far from the sea. Yet many "new" foundations were actually located on the site of ancient cities. Settlements of former soldiers were imposed on existing communities, and temple complexes or royal centres were transformed into poleis.

More obviously new were the urban communities created in temperate Europe and on the Atlantic fringe of the empire from Morocco to Britain. In North Africa a landscape of defended villages, many located on hilltops, came to be supplemented by a few royal cities like that built by Juba at Cherchel or the spectacular site of Volubilis, a tribal centre that became by the end of the first century C.E. a Roman city. Some of the larger hill forts of central Europe were arguably also urban. Many were very large, and some had monuments, even if rather unfamiliar in kind to a classical eye, and complex internal organization. In other cases their ramparts also included large areas that were not settled, and the lives their inhabitants lived seem fairly similar to those of the inhabitants of contemporary villages.[35] However we classify them, Roman conquest brought major changes. Some were converted into Roman-style cities, as happened at Silchester in southern Britain. At Nîmes in Provence, a pre-Roman settlement became a Roman colony and gathered to it the populations of many other pre-Roman centres. Quite often new cities were created on greenfield sites, usually at a lower elevation. The trade-off between accessibility and defence had been changed by the Roman peace, and in any case it was easier to lay out street grids, a forum, and all the other amenities of a Roman town on a relatively flat site like Autun than on the mountaintop site of Mont Beuvray, which it replaced as capital of the Aedui, who inhabited much of what is now Burgundy. A long-term oscillation between defensible sites on the hills and more connectable ones on the plains is common in many part of the empire. The Swiss valleys are full of lakeside cities on the slopes below prehistoric hill forts. Often in late antiquity the town retreated back to those same hilltops, and cathedrals were built on the ruins of those hill forts. Many Mediterranean islands still have an old city inland—such as the many Greek villages called Kastro or Palaiokastro, or the city of Mdina on Malta—along with lively but more exposed ports. Everywhere some settlements were abandoned, a few flourished, and others became small towns, sidelined by the new roads and maritime routes that together formed the nervous and circulatory system of the empire.

Urban Scale

Modest expansion of the urban network between 400 B.C.E. and C.E. 200 is not so surprising given the expansion of the Roman Empire in the same period and the long slow rise in the Mediterranean population. Two other changes tell us a bit more about Roman urbanism. One is the spectacular physical transformation of so many of them. The other is the fact that most cities remained quite small.

The physical transformation of cities was the subject of an earlier chapter, but it is worth sketching the general pattern again. The spread of a new style of urban monuments from the fourth century B.C.E. carried on until the early Roman period. With regional variations, the temples and fortifications which had been the most impressive features of archaic cities came to be supplemented with all sorts of buildings for public use. The irregular open spaces used for political meetings came to have a more and more regular form and areas were separated out for markets, others for games and festivals, yet others for political meetings. The new cities created in the first centuries C.E. were usually supplied with most of this from the start. In parts of Spain, Gaul, Britain, and Germany this often took the form of a regular planned forum with basilicas, temples, and other buildings framing it. Older cities, if they had wealthy benefactors, often accumulated some of the more specialized civic buildings such as a macellum (a retail market for perishable foodstuffs), an odeon, a library, or a nymphaeum fed by an aqueduct. The *scale* of public buildings increased too, made possible by economic growth and advances in construction techniques. Concrete that set underwater made possible more elaborate harbours, bathhouses, and fishponds. Construction in brick—much lighter and less expensive than stone—allowed much larger structures to be created. Palaces, basilicas, and warehouses were all built at larger and larger scales. Paved roads, bridges, arches, and aqueducts were the less glamorous but essential underpinnings of urban development.

Not all Roman cities enjoyed all these features, of course. If we want to see a complete set of urban amenities it is necessary to visit middle-sized cities like Athens or Lepcis Magna, or the imperial capitals. But some monument types were widespread. Around 200 amphitheatres are known, and given few cities had more than one, this would suggest that about one in ten cities were provided with this especially expensive category of monument.[36] I mentioned already that a survey of amphitheatres, theatres, and circuses conducted in the 1980s catalogued just over 650 monuments, and that this total is now certainly an underestimate.[37] A recent survey reckoned there were between 380 and 470 entertainment structures in Italy alone.[38] The most common monuments were theatres, some of which were designed so that they could be venues for beast hunts and gladiatorial combats within an arena as well as for performances on a stage. This sort of structure was much cheaper to build than an amphitheatre—many were built into hillsides, like Greek theatres—and examples are known from military camps and secondary towns as well as urban centres. Many seem to have been designed to accommodate more than the population of the settlement itself: sometimes this was for ambition and display, but we know that people from nearby towns would come and attend games, and also that rural populations might visit for an annual festival or one that took place once every four years. Most towns that had amphitheatres also had theatres; many others had theatres or hybrid buildings that could serve many functions.

Monumental urbanization reflected new aesthetic values and new technologies, new notions of a political community, new ethics of aristocratic generosity, and intense competition for prestige between cities and between benefactors. The dissemination of monuments across the Roman urban system reveals the spread of those ideals as well as of the skills and techniques needed to realize them. The pace of building in the late first and early second centuries C.E. is also extraordinary when we think of the cost. Modern building booms are often clearly linked to economic and demographic growth. Most historians believe the Roman world experienced modest economic growth, but we cannot explain the physical transformation of ancient cities in terms of growth alone. The inescapable conclusion is that the monumentalization of ancient cities derived from an increase in inequality. Ostensibly monuments were paid for by the rich, but the rich were much wealthier in the second century C.E. than they had been in the fourth century B.C.E. The spectacular monuments of Roman cities can only be explained in terms of increased exploitation of the masses, and most of whom still lived in the countryside.

That conclusion also depends on calculating the size of the urban population, which in the end comes down to reckoning the total population of the two thousand or so cities. Calculating the size of ancient urban populations is, in the end, almost always a matter for archaeology. Few ancient records of population figures survive, and when we have them we can rarely guess how accurate ancient headcounts were. Often we are not sure exactly who was included (just males or the heads of families? all permanent residents? just the free population? some nearby country-dwellers as well?). Calculations have been attempted on the basis of water supply, but this is difficult to get right and in the end tells us maximum carrying capacity rather than actual use, and how can we be sure of water demands for cities with great public baths and fountains? The size of theatres or circuses tells us about urban ambitions, and for many games and other festivals the crowds were swelled by country-dwellers or even the inhabitants of neighbouring towns.

If we want comparable figures from a large number of cities we need to begin by looking at occupied areas.[39] This can be problematic. Some new cities were planned on an extravagant scale, and we cannot be sure all the blocks were actually developed: that is particularly the case in the new cities of the Roman west, where street grids were often laid out at a very early stage in a city's development. Then there is the question of population density. Most Roman cities had areas of less than 50 hectares in size, so none were very low-density compared to examples from other early societies.[40] Yet there were gardens and even vineyards inside some Roman cities, and it would be a mistake to imagine continuous conurbation.[41] Many ancient cities certainly thinned out at their edges, with market-gardens and other productive activities located in the suburbia, alongside tombs.[42]

All this is worth bearing in mind when we ask just how big most Roman cities and their populations were. One estimate reckons there were 1,856 cities in the Roman Empire, but that 1,500 of them had populations of less than 5,000 people.[43] Only six had populations over 100,000, less than sixty over 30,000. A more recent calculation from the same project offered a total of 1,388 cities.[44] On the basis of evidence for occupied area in 885 of these cities, it is argued that about two-thirds had populations of 5,000 or less.

It seems likely the proportion was even higher, since smaller cities are less likely to produce good evidence for their size than larger ones, and since the original 1,388 is at the lower end of the estimates for the number of cities in the empire. It seems most likely that 80 per cent or so of Roman cities had populations in the low thousands. The Copenhagen Polis Centre estimated around 85 per cent of cities had populations under 5,000 in 400 B.C.E. In this respect, at least, surprisingly little had changed in half a millennium.

This is the really remarkable fact about the Roman urban apogee: most cities remained small. The populations of most Roman cities remained still lower than those of some Neolithic villages in ancient Anatolia and the Near East. More significantly, most of the older cities had not grown in size since the fifth century B.C.E., despite a general population growth across the Mediterranean region estimated at 0.1 to 0.15 per cent per annum.[45] This is a stark reminder that urban systems do not all grow in the same way. European urbanization proceeded by growth across the system: small, middle, and larger cities all expanded. That was not the case in antiquity, where a fraction of cities seem to have broken from the pack and grown extraordinarily fast. Rapid urbanization is known from other periods of history. There is the state-managed kind, as when Assyrians transplanted large numbers of their vassals to North Assyria to build, inhabit, and provide for great royal cities like Nineveh. That did not happen in the Roman case. There are also periods of rapid urbanization stimulated by European empires, or the Industrial Revolution. Again, there are no real parallels to Rome. The ancient Mediterranean urban boom seems to have been produced by a combination of economic growth and ancient imperialism, and structured by the unforgiving ecology of the region. Even where local rulers had become rich enough to endow their home towns with every kind of spectacular public monument, the spectres of hunger and thirst kept resident populations low.

The Contours of Roman Urbanism

These sort of calculations can only be carried out on the very large scale. That is necessary if we want to answer questions such as: What proportion of the population lived in cities? (The answer is somewhere between 10 and 20 per cent, according to most estimates.) But numbers like these do not tell us much about what actual ancient cities were like because they conceal huge differences between various parts of the empire.

The urban network of the Roman Empire was largely formed of earlier networks that have been connected up by the forces unleashed by trade and empire. Those earlier networks—and their urban components—retained some of their original features, many of which were adaptive ones that took into account the ecological diversity of the empire's many landscapes.

The region with the longest tradition of continuous urbanism was the Nile Valley.[46] Bronze Age urbanism here was shaped by the dense concentration of cultivable lands along the valley and the sharp ecological boundaries with the terrain on either side. The sharpening of these ecotones set the scene for both state-building and urbanism, compressing populations into narrower and narrower spaces. Organizing these populations to get the most out of the alluvial soils had been achieved in part by creating cities wherever feasible. By the Roman period, after more than thirty dynasties of Pharaonic rule and the experience of being incorporated into a variety of empires throughout the last millennium B.C.E., Egypt remained one of the most urbanized areas of the empire.[47] Alexandria, the capital built by the Macedonian Ptolemies to replace Pharaonic Memphis, probably had a population of around half a million. Ptolemais and Memphis had perhaps 100,000 inhabitants each, and the Roman foundation of Antinoopolis under Hadrian was also very large. The balance between these centres changed over the centuries. There were also more than forty nomes, each with a metropolis that from the start of the Roman period was treated more and more like a Greek city, at least administratively. These centres varied enormously in size. Some were in effect sacred cities, with an architecture and structure that was highly traditional. Others were more or less Greek in architecture. The size of many can be estimated, and it is very likely that a number had populations in the tens of thousands. Egypt also contained a number of large villages and some, especially those in the Fayum, had civic monuments and populations of several thousand. By ancient standards the density of cities and their size was extraordinary. Perhaps 30 or 40 per cent of the population lived in cities, and most must have been closely involved in urban life.[48]

Asia Minor (more or less equivalent to modern Asiatic Turkey) comprised several urban hot-spots, and we know a good deal about them from public inscriptions and texts written in the Roman period.[49] The central Anatolian plateau itself was never densely urbanized, and had quite a distinctive history in antiquity.[50] Much of it is around 1,000 metres above sea level and compared to the Mediterranean world, it has very cold winters and old summers. Rings of mountains made many parts difficult to access before the modern period, and there were few major centres none of which were large. On its western and southern flanks, however, water and sediment descending from the plateau had created agriculturally rich areas. Aegean Turkey was the richest part of Anatolia, benefiting from the relatively high rainfall of a west-facing coast and the bounty of the plateau. A string of major cities expanded in the river valleys and coastal gulfs. The Maeander Valley alone nourished Miletus, Priene, Magnesia, Tralles, and the sanctuary at Didyma.[51] Farther up the coast Ephesus, Smyrna, and Pergamum each grew to be major centres under the Roman peace.[52] On the southern coast of Asia Minor the cities of Lycia, now thoroughly Greek in language and architecture, tended to be much smaller. The plain of Pamphylia to the east still has some of the most spectacular ruins of Roman cities anywhere: Aspendus, with its great theatre and an acropolis provided with water by a valley-crossing aqueduct; and Perge, with its long colonnaded street down which a torrent of water ran from a fountain at the top. It would be easy to describe other small urban systems around the edge of the Anatolia massif: the former Carian cities of the southwest, a cluster surrounding the sea of Marmara in the northwest, the Roman foundations (or promotions) of Pontic villages.

There were also parts of the empire where cities were small and far apart. Perhaps less than 10 per cent of the population of Roman Britain or non-Mediterranean Gaul lived in cities, and very few can have had more than 10,000 inhabitants.[53] These were regions where the civitas capitals were hundreds of kilometres apart, meaning that great swathes of the landscape had to look elsewhere for market and other functions. There is, in fact, good archaeological evidence for secondary centres that grew up to satisfy demand the cities could not provide.[54] Often the capital of a tribal state was simply the largest of five or six smaller centres. Monuments are thin on the ground in these regions, even though they were relatively prosperous and in ecological terms much less precarious than many parts of the Mediterranean world. Money and skills lavished on sanctuaries and especially on grand rural villas shows that it would have been perfectly possible to fund and build rather grander cities north of the Alps. Perhaps local aristocrats had never quite been persuaded of the virtues of urbanism, even though in other respects they were happy to spend money on the same

kinds of things as their counterparts elsewhere, such as baths, mosaics, wine
and oil, and gladiatorial games.

There were many other local systems. These included the densely packed
small cities of the North African interior; the great trading centres along
the valleys of the Rhône and the Guadalquivir; the thin lines of military,
ex-military, and paramilitary settlements along the Rhine; the Neckar and
the Danube valleys; the coastal urban systems of the Adriatic and the Black
Sea; the dense mesh of cities in Campania; the temple-states and caravan
cities of the Levant and Syria. It would be easy to go on. But the point has
been made. Roman urbanism was a loose coordination of many regional
systems: some ancient, some very recent, and others that had been evolving
and changing over the last millennium B.C.E. and in its imperial centuries.

Ecology and Urbanism

The Mediterranean world was an inhospitable place for cities. During the
centuries in which Rome first conquered and then held the coasts, peninsulas, and islands of the Middle Sea, urbanism reached its ancient limits.
Even so most cities remained small, because big cities put such a strain on
the resources of this arid region with its thin soils and bare mountainsides.
It seems very likely that most expanded until they reached the limits of how
many people could be sustained by their territory, and then stopped. Those
limits could not have been known in advance, of course, but once they were
reached the solution was obvious. The extent of mobility in ancient times
can be overestimated, but if there was ever a period when it was easy to
relocate to another region, to move to a larger city or to join the military, it
was the early Roman Empire.[55]

It also seems likely that ecological constraints impacted on the creation
of new cities from the middle of the last millennium B.C.E. One sign of a
scarcity of territory is provide by the rapidity with which cities that had
been destroyed—such as Sybaris, Corinth, and Carthage—were replaced.
Another is that colonies created in the last century B.C.E. were so often
implanted on existing cities rather than on greenfield sites (unless they were
founded in continental Europe or like Timgad, in upland Algeria). New
foundations within the Mediterranean Basin typically relied on royal or
imperial support in order to thrive. The dynastic foundations of Demetrias
and Cassandreia did not flourish under Rome, even though the latter was

"refreshed" as a Roman colony. Numerous Roman *coloniae* failed to take. Livy describes second-century colonies in southern Italy abandoned by their settlers, and there were triumviral ones in France that never fulfilled their promise.

The Roman apogee, in other words, was likely the maximum level of urbanization that could be sustained in the region, given the technology of the day, and even then it was dependent on imperial support for the larger cities, and the incidental benefits of peace and consequent economic growth brought by political unification. Some would add a favourable moment in terms of climate, one that increased agricultural productivity and the amount of land available to cultivation. But mapping ancient climate and connecting it to historical events is still in its infancy, and as yet no consensus has been reached.[56]

Small cities remained more sustainable and resilient. Sustainability meant the capacity to securing enough food, fuel, water, and timber for their populations on a regular basis, and in some areas during frequent bad years. If this could not be achieved by commerce or imperial support, a large population was not viable. Resilience meant the capacity to recover from irregular disasters and from catastrophes. The catastrophes most noticed by ancient writers were dramatic and sudden: the sack of a city, its destruction by earthquake or other natural disaster, a devastating plague or food crisis. There were slow-moving catastrophes too, such as the silting up of a harbour, the erosion of soils, and the deforestation that often caused it. Almost all these disasters were much more serious for bigger cities than smaller ones. Staying small was a survival strategy for ancient cities: a mitigation of risk, an adaption to a harsh and unpredictable environment.

So much for the big picture. The Mediterranean Basin is not uniform of course, and some cities were much less precarious than others. Over the last decades researchers have come to appreciate more and more the significance of its fragmentation into micro-regions.[57] The fact that shortages and disasters tended to be local rather than uniform gave a big advantage to cities that were well connected, at least after the necessary maritime transport was available. But the scale of connectivity can be exaggerated. Ancient transport could not move populations quickly, so help had to come to them. The seas were effectively closed for large vessels for half the year, so emergency rations and profiteering traders were equally out of the question. News spread slowly in antiquity.[58] Ideally those with food surpluses would have quickly redirected them to areas struck by food shortages, but communication was often not good enough to make that possible. Dearth must have led to death and malnutrition more often than to migration or profit.

Looking at the contours of Roman urbanism, we can see that things were not so bad everywhere. There were places where things were generally good. The Mediterranean is not watered by many large rivers, but cities in the lower valleys of the Rhône and the Po were nurtured by Alpine meltwater. The dense urbanism of Egypt and to a lesser extent the valleys of Syrian Orontes and the Maeander were well-protected from food crises. The cluster of middling to large cities that we can identify around the empire almost always occurred in areas with rich soils and plenty of water, areas like Campania or the Beqaa Valley in Syria. If there were additional sources of wealth—marble or fisheries, timber or slaves, olive oil or eastern trade goods—so much the better. Fundamentally, however, the contours of Roman urbanism reflect the varied productivity of the land. The only exceptions to this rule were those few cities created and sustained by imperial power, the megalopoleis that could feed upon the world.

PART IV

De-Urbanization

19

The Megalopoleis

Cypresses Among Willows

During the last two centuries B.C.E. the population of the city of Rome doubled in size roughly every fifty years.[1] Towards the end of this process, around 40 B.C.E., the Roman poet Virgil imagined two shepherds discussing the city. One, Tityrus, begins as follows:

> Meliboeus, stupidly I used to think that the City they call Rome
> was just like this town of ours here, the place we shepherds often
> bring the tender young lambs of our flocks.
> Just as puppies are like dogs, and kids are like mother goats,
> so I used to compare the great with the small.
> But Rome has lifted her head as high among other cities,
> as cypress trees tower among the weeping willows.[2]

Obviously this is not innocent reportage. As so often in history a period of intense urban growth stimulated a kind of romantic nostalgia for the supposedly simpler life of the countryside. Virgil's immediate models were pastoral poems created in some of the largest cities of the Mediterranean world, Syracuse and Alexandria. His implausibly well educated shepherd-poets (depicted in a mediaeval manuscript in Figure 33) were customized to entertain readers and audiences enmeshed in urban life, offering an imaginary rural viewpoint from which to admire it.[3]

Pastoral signals a sense of rapid social change that was rare in antiquity. Today we take technological progress for granted. Many of us can remember a world with no mobile phones, no Internet, and no cheap air travel. If we look at a movie made thirty years ago we see an utterly different material world, one in which clothes, cars, and houses are all different to those we know today. Most ancient populations were much less aware of this kind of change. It was possible to imagine a mythical time when gods walked the

Figure 33 Meliboeus and Tityrus discuss Rome, in a mediaeval manuscript
The History Collection / Alamy Stock Photo

earth and heroes fought monsters. Myth and epic described that world very
well, and were the foundations of an education for those lucky enough to
have one. Virgil did something more complex in his masterpiece the *Aeneid*,
a new foundation poem for Augustan Rome that juxtaposes the heroic age,
Roman history, and the modernity of Virgil's own age. Aeneas, the hero
of the poem, is the son of a goddess, and his story begins with an escape
from burning Troy; he moves west, is present at the founding of Carthage,
comes to Italy, is given visions of Rome's rise to glory, and even visits the
future site of Rome, where he hears the story of Hercules fighting with
the giant Cacus, and experiences a different kind of pastoral counterpart to
the city Augustus was rebuilding in marble as Virgil wrote. Virgil's poetics
depends again and again on the rubbing of contemporary politics against a
mythic past.

When it came to historical time, however, most ancient writers tended to
think of the past as very much like the present, and they imagined the future
as more of the same. The archaic city-states summoned up by Herodotus

or Livy are in most respects very like those of their own day. Thucydides and Aristotle explicitly wrote for the benefit of future generations, whom they imagined would live in city-states like the ones they knew. Tacitus and Marcus Aurelius both saw the future as a continuing alternation of good and bad emperors. Moments like the Augustan Age—when a widespread consensus emerged that the world had changed forever—are quite rare. It has been written that the Battle of Actium, the naval battle that ended the last Republican Civil War about a decade after Virgil wrote his *Eclogues*, came to seem a sort of "secular miracle."[4] The miracle was not positive for everyone, of course, but the end of chaotic war and the stability and prosperity that followed really did change the classical world irreversibly, just as Alexander's conquests had done.

No one who lived in or near Rome during the last decades B.C.E. could have failed to be aware of the rapid expansion of the city, the rebuilding of ancient monuments on an unprecedented scale, the generalization of an architecture in marble, the laying out of new public spaces, and the provision of new amenities from subsidized grain to a fire bridge.[5] This transformation had started slow and gathered pace. Victorious generals had for centuries built new temples or restored old ones, funded from the spoils of conquest, often to satisfy vows made on the battlefield to one god or another. As the scale of conquest increased, so did the size of the monuments.

From the fifties B.C.E. the competition between rival generals transformed entire precincts. The field of Mars, the open space enclosed within the curve of the Tiber that more or less corresponds to today's *centro storico*, offered large expanses for extravagant constructions. Pompey built Rome's first permanent theatre with a great precinct attached in which there were displays of Greek sculpture and great gardens. His rival Caesar created a multipurpose complex replacing "voting pens" used in elections, again lavish in imported marble and on a grand scale. Octavian's ally Agrippa laid out gardens and a public bathhouse in the same area, with a monumental basis supplied by aqueduct. Among Augustus' many architectural gifts to the city was a vast *horologium*—a meridian line set into a paved area with one of the obelisks he had brought back from Egypt to cast the shadow. Nearby was the Altar of Peace, vowed by the Senate in honour of Augustus, an elaborate structure that echoed the famous altar built at Pergamum. By the Tiber a monumental tomb was constructed by Augustus for himself and his family, a mausoleum that would outdo the Tomb of Alexander he had visited in Alexandria after the defeat of Antony and the death of Cleopatra.

Elsewhere in the city the ancient forum was remodelled and received new monuments, while great temples, each with their own forum precincts, were added by Julius Caesar and Augustus. Augustus rebuilt temples on the Capitol, on the Palatine, and at other locations, again on a fabulous scale.[6] The city had three theatres at his death. Caesar had already transformed the Circus Maximus, a long valley terraced and flattened for chariot-racing and other events, into a great multifunctional complex unsurpassed before the building of the Colosseum a century later by the Flavian dynasty. The imperial city had public gardens as well as public baths, and more and more amenities were added throughout the first, second, and early third centuries C.E. Many of these projects required new infrastructure improvements: harbour facilities, new roads, aqueducts. All this building provided casual labour for many and swelled the city's population. The best estimates are that it peaked around one million under Augustus and stayed nearly that large for almost three hundred years.

From our longer perspective it is easy to see precedents for the rise of giant cities in the last centuries B.C.E.[7] Athens and Syracuse, Corinth and Carthage, and Rome were already much larger than the Mediterranean norm in the fourth century B.C.E. Their great size was in each case sustained by a mixture of political influence and commercial power.[8] By commercial power I do not mean that those city-states ran huge centralized enterprises, or even that they licensed companies comparable to the joint-stock companies that dominated European mercantile expansion from the seventeenth century onwards. Simply, large cities located on or near the sea became hubs that offered opportunities to domestic producers and overseas merchants alike; military power also offered opportunities. Athenian kleruchs based in allied cities, Carthaginian exploitation of the mines at Cartagena, the Roman use of public contracts to supply armies abroad and manage the building programmes paid for by booty and indemnities all provide examples of the ancient nexus between war, commerce, and urbanization.

Empire made possible even greater cities. The conquest of the Persian Empire by Alexander suddenly raised the limit on the size of populations that could be sustained even by hegemonic cities like Athens and Syracuse, which had maybe had as many as 50,000 inhabitants.[9] The capacity of kings to tax globally and spend locally, to concentrate wealth in one place on earth, was unprecedented. Diverting tribute by members of the Delian League to build a few temples in Athens was nothing in comparison. Messene and Megalopolis and the forced synoecisms of Sicily were easily overtaken in scale. A Ptolemy or an Antiochus could create a giant city in just a few years. Empires could supply capitals that could never have been supported by their hinterlands, and this changed the urban network completely. What had been loose and mainly regional networks of cities, often framed by a region like central Italy or the Aegean, were now coordinated on a much larger scale. At their centre were new, giant cities, the megalopoleis.[10]

This style of urban foundation was only new in the Mediterranean world. Assyrian, Babylonian, and Persian kings had built giant cities: Khorsabad and Nineveh, Babylon and Persepolis were the most spectacular. Cities like Egyptian Alexandria, Antioch on the Orontes, Roman Carthage and Rome itself, each with populations of over 100,000 people, were the first truly enormous cities of the Mediterranean Basin proper. Antinoopolis, Athens, Corinth, Cyrene, Ephesus, Memphis, Miletus, Ptolemais, Smyrna, Syracuse, and perhaps a few others were just behind them.[11] Seleuceia on the Tigris and Ctesiphon together formed another huge conurbation in Babylonia, just beyond the Roman frontier. Other early empires had their giant cities too. What makes the existence of Mediterranean megalopoleis extraordinary is the ecological dimension. If most urban populations in the ancient Mediterranean peaked in the thousands, what made a city of several hundreds of thousands possible? That question can be divided into three parts. How were megalopoleis created? What made them sustainable? What new challenges did they impose on their inhabitants and rulers?

The Growth of Cities

Most large cities in history owe their growth to the interplay of many factors. Location, and the opportunities it offered, was perhaps the most important factor determining if a new foundation thrived or not. This was as true of antiquity as it has been of later periods.

London is a good example. It was not a prominent centre in the late pre-Roman Iron Age, apparently lying on the borders of two of the major preconquest kingdoms. It was not initially chosen to be a key place in the administration of the province conquered by Claudius' invasion force in C.E. 43. Colchester, a veteran colony which was placed on the site of a major preconquest centre, was chosen for the provincial ruler-cult. Within just a few years of conquest there was a community based in what is now the City of London. Its exact origins are uncertain, but from the earliest the population included Gauls, Britons, and Romans (using Latin, as the very recent finds of writing tablets from the Bloomberg excavations show), and mostly involved in trade. After both London and Colchester were sacked by Boudicaa of the Iceni, within twenty years after the conquest London emerged as the new centre of the province's administration. It was now a major city with a garrison and soldiers on detachment to assist the governor and the procurator, a wall circuit, a massive forum, and an amphitheatre. Location was key. Like so many provincial metropoleis after it, London was well-situated in terms of maritime connections. It was positioned at a point where sea-going vessels could be docked and where the river could still be bridged. The same factors that made it a good base for cross-channel traders made it a good place from which to rule Britain. Organic growth attracted the administrative centre and once there, the presence of Roman soldiers made it even more attractive to traders. Once the provincial administration was gone, and links with the continent withered away, in the fifth century, so did London. For centuries London's Roman walls enclosed an area sparsely inhabited and the site of London was as marginal to the new Anglo-Saxon kingdoms as it had been in the Iron Age. But with the growth of the Anglo-Saxon and Anglo-Norman state, its locational advantages were again apparent. A cathedral and a palace were built at Westminster before the Norman conquest, traders gathered again on the site of the Roman city, and in the thirteenth century it became once again a centre of government. Over the centuries that followed Westminster and London grew together, and London became more and more of cultural capital and mercantile hub, eventually a megalopoleis and an imperial capital. Similar stories could be told of other great cities of today's world: Rome and Istanbul, Alexandria, Athens, and Lisbon. The combination of a good location and accumulated traditions of greatness have allowed many cities to be reinvented century after century.

For antiquity Corinth would be another good case with its two ports, the natural fortress offered by the Acrocorinth, its potential to control the land route between the Peloponnese and the rest of Greece (as one of the "fetters of Greece"), its major sanctuaries and the Isthmian Games that took place at one of them every four years, its tyrants, and its maritime connections in the archaic period that evolved into naval power in the fifth century B.C.E. Like London, its location was vital for its success. Corinth was in principle abandoned for a century between Mummius' sack and the Caesarian refoundation, but it is difficult to imagine the population moved far away, and there are signs of cultic and architectural continuities from the Greek polis to the Roman *colonia*. The city grew rapidly after its refoundation; Roman governors of Achaea spent considerable time there, and its imperial monuments are spectacular.[12] Corinth became a major Christian centre in late antiquity and continued to be prominent until the general collapse of urbanism in the sixth century C.E.

Locational factors explain why some cities grew to greater size than others. They also help explain why some of them grew a little larger in the Roman period. Those cities that were well-positioned as regional centres of communications often became important in new empire-wide networks. Once road systems and sailing routes had become anchored on particular cities they benefited from any new kinds of traffic, such as pilgrimages in the fourth century C.E. and after. The Roman habit of using cities to rule its empire, along with the economic growth promoted by Roman peace and Roman taxation, fed growth in the greatest cities of the empire. Often they clearly grew at the expense of their nearest neighbours.[13] The situation varied from region to region but in general, the urban networks of the empire were more hierarchical than what had gone before.[14] Yet that handful of really enormous cities—those I have been calling megalopoleis—needed more than this, more than a climate generally favourable to the growth of urban hubs. They demanded imperial will.

Building Megalopoleis

Perhaps the most spectacular example is a megalopolis not yet mentioned: the new Rome that Constantine, the first Christian emperor, founded on the Bosporos. The city was built on the site of the Greek polis of Byzantium, a city dating to the seventh century B.C.E. which for its first one thousand years of its history had played a relatively minor role in the historical dramas of each age. It was ruled by the Persians, allied with the Athenians, and besieged by Philip of Macedon. During the early Roman Empire it profited from its location on the European side of the southern mouth of the Black Sea. The region had two great natural resources, the marble that gave the Sea of Marmara its name, and the annual migrations of fish from the Black Sea to the Mediterranean. Fed by the nutrients washed down by the Russian rivers, several species of large fish spawned in the northern Black Sea and migrated each year into Mediterranean waters following the strong

surface current that flows from one sea to the other.[15] Like the Phoenician
and Spanish settlements on either side of the straits of Gibraltar, the other
mouth of the Mediterranean, the Greek cities of the sea of Marmara grew
rich on fishing and from the sale and export of preserved fish products.
Byzantium was also famous for its wall that made a fortress of the triangular
promontory on which it stood. That strategic position and the city's multiple harbours meant it also grew rich on tolls. It picked the wrong side in
a Roman civil war at the end of the second century C.E. and was sacked by
the victor Septimius Severus, but was immediately rebuilt on an even larger
scale. A century later it was chosen by Constantine as the site for his new
capital, known variously as New Rome, Constantinople, and today, Istanbul.

Location explains Constantine's choice. By the end of the third century
the empire was under increased military pressure on two fronts. Beginning
in the middle of the second century C.E. migrations from central Europe
and from the steppe created a string of conflicts along the northern frontier
which more or less corresponded to the line of the Rhine and the Danube
rivers. From around the same time there was a long series of wars with
the Persian Empire with which Rome fought for control of Mesopotamia
and Syria and which threatened Rome's control of Anatolia. Together these
created what we now call the third-century military crisis, which among
other things exposed the financial inflexibility of the empire when faced
with more than one crisis at a time, and its difficulty in coordinating war on
multiple fronts. The situation was recovered through changes to the tax system, a move to more mobile armies combined with fortified strong-points,
and the development of an imperial college in which several emperors (not
all equal of course) shared the burden of leadership. These emperors distributed themselves in a series of temporary capitals nearer the stress points.
Tetrarchic capitals, each equipped with all that an imperial court desired,
appeared along the northern and eastern frontier of the empire. Emperors
were based for longer or shorter period in York in Britain, Trier in Germany,
in Milan and eventually Ravenna in northern Italy, via several bases in the
Balkans (Split and Sirmium being the most famous) to Nicomedia in northwest Anatolia, Antioch in Syria, and occasionally Alexandria. Byzantium was
more or less at the centre of this band of territory, at one terminal of the
via Egnatia, the great Roman highway to the east, and midway between
threats from Goths and others beyond the Danube and threats from Persians
beyond the Euphrates.

Rome had proved a hopeless centre for coordinating wars on the frontiers: it was simply too far from the action and in an age of slow communications, this was crucial. From the second century many emperors spent years away from the city, with unforeseen consequences for the elite of the city. Embassies now went to the camps, not the city; imperial edicts now took precedence over decrees of the senate, and yet conversely in the absence of the emperors some senators were able to become more prominent. The office of urban prefect became more and more prominent and a political gulf opened up between the aristocracy and the court.[16] A barbarian raid came quite close to sacking Rome in C.E. 270 and over the five years that followed the emperor Aurelian built a 19- kilometre circuit wall, much of which survives today. It was hastily built in concrete faced with brick rather than stone, and to economize on time and cost it incorporated several existing buildings into the circuit. Rome was safe—for the time being—but was never an important imperial capital again.

Byzantium, by contrast, was excellently positioned for communications and for defence. It simply needed a strong wall on the land side and naval protections. The one weakness of the city was the shortage of water. Recent excavations have traced the course of the aqueduct systems that supplied it, but these would be no good in a siege. Vast cisterns still lie under the city. Constantine turned the city from a provincial polis into an imperial capital. Severus, when he rebuilt it, had already more or less doubled its size, and it was strong enough in 324 for Constantine's enemy Licinius to shelter there, but Constantine seems to have started almost from scratch, destroying the walls and rebuilding the land defences 3 kilometres west of where they had been. The result was a city five times the area of the one built by Severus, and ten times the size of the city Severus had sacked. The city had a new plan, one that gestured to Old Rome with a list of seven hills (the city of Istanbul is much flatter than that of Rome), fourteen regions, a new Capitolium and Senate House, a forum, public baths, and more. Socially it was utterly different. Constantinople had a senate, but it never had the entrenched power of great aristocratic families like those that had in some periods dominated the senate of Rome. The worship of the old gods was perhaps not wholly banished, but Christian basilicae were central in Constantinople. In Rome, Constantine's basilical churches were located around the edge of the ancient city, not exactly marginalized as they were physically impressive monuments greeting those arriving from most directions, but still cohabiting the city with other gods. The contrast between the two cities remains a productive field of research.[17]

Constantine's urban makeover was so extensive that it is now almost impossible to reconstruct the plans of the Roman and Greek cities that lay beneath his capital. A great palace was linked to the hippodrome—just as the Severan palace on the Palatine in Rome had been linked to the Circus Maximus (see Figure 34). This was where emperors and people met, where they watched circus games and especially chariot races together, where crowds rioted, and where emperors (no longer gods nor priests) would display themselves in splendid ceremonial. Art works were imported to adorn the city, and a Christian religious topography was incorporated into the city from the first. The cost of building Constantinople was extraordinary. Yet it was built very quickly. Work started in 324 and the city was inaugurated six years later. Work continued until Constantine's death in 337 and more slowly thereafter, but there was never any question that it would be supplanted in the way that other temporary capitals of the tetrarchic period had been. Constantinople remained the capital of the Roman Empire until the fifteenth century, and the spiritual capital of the Greek people for even longer.

Figure 34 Imperial Palace from Circus Maximus, Rome
Andrea Sanzo / EyeEm / Getty Images

Only emperors could command the quantities of materials, food, and labour to make these megalopolitan dreams a reality. Constantine arranged for a permanent grain supply from Egypt sufficient for 80,000 people, so he was clearly already thinking of his city as joining that dozen or so largest centres in an empire of two thousand cities. The population soon grew beyond that expectation. Sometime in the late fourth or early fifth century Constantinople became the largest city in the empire. Meanwhile the population of Rome itself was in rapid decline.[18] The urban population of Rome by the late fourth century was probably already reduced to around half a million, maybe even less. By the early sixth century it may have been as small as 60,000. Over the same period Constantinople grew, its population peaking perhaps around 500,000. Exactly when it reached this point is uncertain, but the construction of a new land wall by Theodosius, two kilometres to the west of Constantine's, in the early fifth century may suggest expansion was already an issue within a century of the city's foundation. The number of granaries was increased. The harbour facilities were improved around the same time. Both are good indications of a rising population. Hadrian had provided one aqueduct, Constantine another, and yet another was completed in 368 during the reign of the emperor Valens. A major drought led Theodosius to built yet another in the last decades of the fourth century. Major building programmes continued in the fifth and sixth centuries. Some of this was new work and some necessitated by devastating fires, another consequence of the poor water supply.

Procopius wrote an account of Justinian's building programmes in the early sixth century, but they marked the peak of urban development. It was in Justinian's reign that the city suffered one of the most devastating plagues recorded for antiquity. On some estimates the population was halved after 545.[19] Building activity ceased around 600. Political disasters followed. Egypt was lost first to the Persians in 618 and again in 628, and then definitively to the Arab invasion of 640. Egyptian grain, conveyed to Constantinople by the fleet based in Alexandria, had been essential for sustaining the population of the capital. The emperor Heraclius ended the supply of free grain in 618 and the population plummeted, to between 40,000 and 70,000.[20] During the so-called Byzantine Dark Ages (roughly the seventh and eighth centuries) the population was in the tens of thousands, no new building took place, three of its four harbours went out of use, and most civic amenities collapsed. The city survived sieges, earthquakes, and plague, but it was no longer a megalopolis. The last of the cypresses had fallen, and only willows were left. Constantinople's rapid expansion in the fourth and fifth centuries and even more rapid collapse in the early seventh shows more clearly than anything that its status as a megalopolis was utterly dependent on imperial support. In this its history echoes that of some of the Near Eastern royal cities, founded at the command of a king and withering away when resources were allocated elsewhere.

Not all megalopoleis had the same trajectory, but all depended on imperial largesse. It is conventional to treat the rise of Rome as a steadier rise to greatness. This is certainly the way Romans liked to think of it. They created a whole series of mythical origins (Hercules, Aeneas, and Romulus and Remus, to name just the most famous) and a national narrative in which the early kings were culture heros and the leaders of the free republic were distinguished by their virtue and community-mindedness. Imperial domination was explained largely in terms of divine favour rewarding piety and moral probity. The history of the city and that of the empire were mysteriously conflated, with the result that no real explanation for urban growth was ever provided in ancient sources. Modern writers have too often followed this lead.

Rome's urban growth is to be explained by a combination of factors. Already by around 500 B.C.E. it was one of that small group of larger and more complex cities that also included Athens, Corinth, Miletus, and Syracuse.[21] How this happened is beyond the reach of historical sources, but we can make some good guesses. Its location was very favourable, close to the sea on a navigable river with easy access to the timber and other resources of Umbria and the Apennines and to salt production sites on the coast. Western central Italy was, and remains, one of the more agriculturally rich micro-regions of the Mediterranean, well-watered with deep soils enriched in places by recent volcanism. Less obviously, Rome probably benefited from not being part of a cluster of Etruscan or Greek cities but marginal to both. The first treaty with Carthage shows that in the middle of the last millennium it was already a power in Italy and overseas. During the fourth and third centuries it grew in size partly by allowing citizens of other Latin states to migrate to Rome and partly through converting freed slaves into citizens. Manpower was essential for the Roman pattern of expansion, through frequent wars and occasional settlements. The population probably did not reach 100,000 until the second century B.C.E., the point at which it became effective capital of the Mediterranean with Carthage humbled and destroyed and the

Macedonian-ruled kingdoms of the east cowed. The spoils of Carthage largely paid for the Aqua Marcia, one of the longest of the city's aqueducts built between 144 and 140 B.C.E. Shortly afterwards subsidized grain began to be distributed in generous quantities to many of the citizens.[22] Free grain followed in the first century and was continued by the emperors, eventually with other food distributions added, until the fifth century C.E. Most researchers think the population peaked around one million in the reign of Augustus, and remained around that size until its accelerating decline from the fourth century C.E.

The population histories of the other Mediterranean megalopoleis are more difficult to make out. Alexandria in Egypt was founded either by Alexander the Great or by his immediate successors; either way it experienced a very rapid period of growth in the late fourth and early third centuries.[23] Estimates for the Ptolemaic period and for the early Roman Empire place the population around 250,000 to 300,000. Antioch on the Orontes, founded around the same time, was on the same scale. Both cities were capitals of major empires, and both became key cities in Roman provincial and military systems; both remained important up until the Arab conquests in the seventh century, and both remained major centres well into the Middle Ages and beyond. Their later prominence means there is little to see now of the buildings of the Roman period but the ruins of the Roman period theatre in Alexandria (see Figure 35) still survive. Both Alexandria and Antioch were gateway cities, key nodes on routes connecting the Mediterranean world to continental hinterlands. Alexandria offered not only access to the Nile Valley and Sudan beyond but also to the Indian Ocean trade. Antioch, also sited in a rich agricultural valley, was one starting point for routes heading east via Syria to Mesopotamia and central Asia. Antioch in the sixth century was a major point of contention between the Roman and Persian Empires. Each wished to possess it rather than destroy it, but in the process much damage was done both to the physical structure and to the population, part of whom were deported to Persia after the sack of C.E. 540. Add to this fire, earthquake, and plague, and the resilience of the city was severely tested. Alexandria had its own history of riots and attempted coups, but was less exposed to any rival powers.

Carthage, destroyed along with Corinth in 146 B.C.E., was (again like Corinth) refounded as a Roman colony a century or so later. Planned by Caesar, the new city was dedicated in 29 B.C.E. By the second and third

Figure 35 Roman Theatre in Alexandria
Les Stocker / Getty Images

centuries C.E. it covered an area of 340 hectares. Great campaigns of monumental building can be dated to the Antonine and Severan periods; that is, to the second half of the second century C.E. and the beginning of the third. A huge forum complex, spectacular public baths, a theatre, amphitheatre, odeon, and circus are all known, as well as great harbour installations, private housing, and a street grid anchored on the hilltop acropolis known as the Byrsa. Estimates of the population of Roman Carthage range from 70,000 to 300,000.[24] More recent work has tried to uncover the Augustan colony underneath the second-century structures, and it is becoming clear that Roman Carthage was from the start planned on a grand scale.[25] A street plan was laid out that reflected that of the Punic city, but extended it much farther. The hilltop of the Byrsa was decapitated, lowering it by 9 metres or so to form a platform of around 30,000 square metres for the forum. Great vaulted substructures were built to support terracing around it. Great cisterns were constructed and linked to springs to provide a water supply well before the provision of an aqueduct. There are traces of private housing for the wealthy, and a spectacular sea front. The refoundation of Carthage was clearly a prestige project, so perhaps its origins were more like those of Alexandria or Constantinople than Rome. Whether its population was from the start enormous—and if so we wonder where they came from, since only 3,000 colonists are recorded—or whether it took a century or more to fill the city is difficult to say.[26]

Building a megalopolis had to be an imperial act. Who but an emperor had the power to make such momentous decisions? Whether the chosen site was a ruin or an existing city, each new foundation was an act of expropriation and of erasure. A new year zero was established. The costs were formidable in terms of labour, in materials, and in the skills or surveyors, architects and craftsmen of which no empire ever had enough. Workforces needed to be fed as they built, and before any great new city could be built, a temporary city of workers had to be established. Some materials had to be brought from afar. Rome was fortunate that the Tiber Valley clays were at hand to be turned into bricks. The brickmaking industry was vast. Marbles were more unevenly distributed around the Mediterranean Basin, and even after the quarries at Luni were opened up, coloured marbles and granites had to be brought from sites in the Aegean, North Africa, and the eastern desert of Egypt. For the largest buildings timbers had to be fetched from the few forests of great trees around the Mediterranean, from Lebanon, from Macedonia, a few from the wooded Apennines above Genoa.

Most of the skills involved in city-building were not new. The Greeks had been planning and laying out entire city grids from at least the eighth century B.C.E. The construction of Roman colonies in Italy during the third and second century B.C.E. were dependent on skills in surveying, architecture, and hydraulics. Some of the logistical and technical expertise was similar to that required in a military campaign. Older cities did not often provide opportunities for large-scale planning until kings or generals intervened, as Hadrian did at Athens or Constantine at Byzantium. The constraints on urbanism were political and economic rather than technical, and emperors changed this. Control of manpower on this sort of scale had been a prerequisite for the construction of pyramids in Egypt and ziggurats in Babylonia. What Macedonian kings and Roman emperors brought was the power to focus the resources of the vast domains on a single place. Alexandria, Roman Carthage, and Constantinople show the potential of focused imperial power.

Sustaining the Megalopolis

Foundation was one thing. But what mechanisms were used to sustain these giant cities? There were some things that every ancient city needed. Fundamentally it needed people, food, and water. If a city ran out of any of these, even for a short period of time, it would collapse. In the longer term a city also needed building materials: stone, timber, metal, bricks, and tiles. It needed fuel for light and heat. It needed tools and clothes, and it needed metals.[27]

No city was ever self-sufficient. Occasionally ancient writers imagined ideal communities in the past or the future that could satisfy all their needs from their own territory. Archaeologists know the importance of long-distance trade in metals from the Bronze Age, and of other materials such as obsidian, even earlier. All the same, the problems of supply were much more tractable for villagers or the inhabitants of small towns than for those who lived in megalopoleis. In towns of just a few thousand people—like most ancient cities in other words—many of the population grew their own food in nearby fields and in gardens just outside it, or even inside the city limits. Cisterns and wells supplied the water needs of small populations even when the city was not located on a river (as many or most were). In many parts of the Mediterranean Basin there were frequent food shortages, years of low rainfall, or years when bad weather or crop disease interrupted the growing season at a vulnerable point. During the thousands of years when the Mediterranean world was a world of villages and most of its inhabitants were farmers, various remedies had been devised.[28] Peasants diversified their risk, growing different crops in case one failed, or farming lots of small plots. They relied on storage of different kinds. They stored grain, learned to preserve milk as cheese, to dry meat, and they built cisterns to store water. They invested in "social storage," the building of relationships with others who would help them out when they needed it in return for help in the future. All of this carried on into the classical era, with more crops with which to diversify, wider networks of friends, and more sophisticated storage systems.[29] Small cities, many of which were not much bigger than villages, could mostly rely on new versions of these old habits to sustain themselves.

The larger the city, however, the more difficult all this became. Larger populations faced two linked problems: greater demand and greater risk. Larger cities had a much greater footprint every single year. Risk was a different matter, since it was about cities surviving in bad years. Small cities were quite successful at risk-buffering. Large ones simply could not store enough of the necessities to cope with a prolonged shortage.

Demand is the easier issue to tackle. Beyond a certain size no city could supply its needs without significant imports from elsewhere. Water was (and remains) a particularly scarce commodity in the region.[30] There is plenty of Roman period evidence, including quite a large amount of law, for communities and individual landlords fighting over water rights.[31] The only way to bring water from far away was by aqueducts. Most were quite short and brought water from higher ground (intercepting rivers, harnessing springs, tapping aquifers) to urban consumers. Long aqueduct systems were really only worth constructing in times of peace, because otherwise they made cities too vulnerable. Rome's first large-scale aqueduct was the Aqua Appia built in 312 B.C.E., and was a modest 16 kilometres long. The Aqua Marcia, paid for from booty after the destruction of Carthage and Corinth, was about 90 kilometres long. More were added up until the Aqua Traiana in the early second century C.E.. These were not all designed just to bring drinking water: water was also used in public fountains, in public and private gardens, in a vast range of industrial processes from textile production to mining, and especially in bath complexes. Aqueduct water was used in some areas to flush drains and make (cleaner) rainwater available for drinking. Carthage had cisterns and in the second century an aqueduct from Zaghouan, 90 kilometres away. The aqueducts of Constantinople have already been mentioned. Many aqueducts probably remain to be found and mapped.

Feeding urban populations posed a problem for large cities from at least the fifth century B.C.E., when Athens was regularly importing grain from the Black Sea and from Egypt. This reflects not just the growth of Athens as an imperial city, but also the peculiarly arid environment of Attica and much of the Aegean. Things were easier in the western Mediterranean, where Rome expanded within a range of fertile and well-watered landscapes south of the Apennines and north of the Mezzogiorno. Supplying the city involved getting access to grain surpluses from Campania and Etruria, but especially from Sicily and Sardinia and ultimately from North Africa and Egypt as well. Rome's demand for food (and other goods) transformed the economy of central Italy. By land, river, and sea the imperial metropolis drew goods to it. Its hinterland was vast and increasingly focused on the city.[32] Most of the large cities of the Roman Empire were located in fertile river valleys, locations where waters and grain were generally in good supply. This was true of Antioch on the Orontes, Alexandria in Egypt, Memphis, Ptolemais, Seleuceia on the Tigris, and the cities of the Maeander Valley. Carthage was located by the mouth of the Medjerda river, which made the uplands of what are now Tunisia and Algeria into major grain-producing regions. Milan was in the heart of the Po Valley. The second-tier cities were mostly coastal, making them easier to provision in bad years. Ephesus, Marseilles, Athens, Corinth, Lepcis, and Cyrene all had impressive harbours. They were a source of profit in good years, but also essential for provisioning the population.

Imperial powers used their muscle to ensure preferential access to the main grain-producing areas within the region. Rome took a tithe of grain from the Sicilian cities. Tax incentives were offered to traders with large enough ships willing to use them to bring grain to Rome. Larger cities established grain funds, and granaries were set up to try to even out the effects of fluctuations in supply. Piracy was suppressed—repeatedly—and grain from imperial estates shipped first to Rome and then to Constantinople. Price controls were replaced by grain distributions, and complex means devised to make sure the grain went to the politically important sections of the populace, with imperial officials placed in charge.[33] Ancient cities never engaged in charity as such, but the effect of free and cheap grain must have made things easier for almost everyone, even if handouts went on the basis of high social status rather than need. It was political muscle too that ensured the megalopoleis could cope with risk. Not all were situated in areas very susceptible to local crop failures. One Roman oration, Pliny's *Panegyric to Trajan*, makes a huge deal out of the freak situation in which Egypt needed to import grain. But some cities, including both Rome and Constantinople, were protected by imperial funding, by vast storage facilities, and by preferential access to tax grain and the grain grown on the emperors' expanding estates.

The last necessity for a megalopoleis was a population. Near Eastern kings had simply transported subject populations to new lands when they created royal cities, some to inhabit the cities and others to farm the surrounding land.[34] There was some forced synoecism in antiquity at the foundation of Arcadian Megalopolis and probably in some Sicilian cases too, but Romans seem not to have done this on a large scale.[35] Some cities in the western provinces, such as Nîmes and Vienne and perhaps Saintes, seem to have been originally populated by drawing together inhabitants from a number of smaller settlements, but this was to create cities of a few thousand at most.[36] Megalopoleis were of another order. However we imagine the original peopling of Carthage and Alexandria, Antioch and Constantinople—and there is very little information about this—the question of how they were sustained is even more difficult. People might migrate to a major city in its early stages in search of opportunities, but that can hardly explain how a city remained large. It is widely accepted that large preindustrial cities had death rates far in excess of their birth rates. Poor sanitation, coupled with malnutrition and undernutrition, made the poorest inhabitants of ancient cities vulnerable to a range of endemic diseases. Rome was particularly vulnerable to malaria, the Nile Valley to leprosy, and other airborne diseases thrived given how close populations were.[37] Fire and poor building practices all impacted the experience of the masses. Infant mortality must have been high. The "urban graveyard effect," as it has been called, meant that large cities only stayed large if they were sustained by constant immigration.

Some of these migrants must have come from the countryside or from smaller towns. Egyptians flowed to Alexandria, Africans to Carthage, and everyone to Rome and then later to Constantinople. But the voluntary migration of freeborn individuals cannot have satisfied the demands of the megalopoleis. The transport infrastructure did not exist to move so many people each year to Rome, and there is no sign of small towns shrinking as the megalopoleis swallowed up their population. For Italy, in fact, we can document very closely the *growth* of municipia and increases in public spending there precisely while Rome was at its peak.[38] Repeatedly scholars have concluded that the population of Rome and perhaps other large cities was topped up by migrants in chains. Slaves entered the city through purchase by the great houses, the emperors, and those who wanted to use them in manufacture. As expensive commodities, many received better food and accommodation than many of the freeborn masses, but they were also subject to all sorts of abuse. A proportion, perhaps quite small, was eventually freed, although they and their property did not completely escape their masters' control and they were replaced by new generations of slaves. The grubby secret of ancient megalopoleis was that they were not inhabited by a privileged and cosmopolitan citizenry, but were largely cities of slaves and former slaves.

Food, water, and fresh bodies were just the start. Rare stone, marbles, timber, wine, oil, preserved foods, and rarer goods like pepper, incense, and spices all found their way to the great lockup warehouses of the megalopoleis and their ports. These were supplied by merchants, partly by land and river and largely by sea. It followed that emperors and kings had to invest in great harbour facilities and roads. Alexandria had its Pharos, the lighthouse that guided vessels coming across the open sea, and two great sea harbours protected by a combination of islands, promontories, and harbour moles. South of the city another harbour opened onto Lake Maerotis. Networks of canals and ports had made the Delta navigable at least since the seventh century B.C.E. Great harbours were built by Herod the Great at Caesarea Maritima in the last two decades B.C.E., using the relatively new invention of concrete that would set underwater. The great port of Ephesus—today silted up and 8 or 9 kilometres from the sea—did not just serve the city itself. Road networks led north to Smyrna, up the Maeander Valley, and east into southern Anatolia. Roman governors of the province of Asia had standing orders to make landfall there, a special honour for the city but also a sign of its pre-eminence as the maritime gateway to Asia. Over the last few years the huge and elaborate port of Rome has been mapped, explored, and in part excavated. Caesar, Claudius, and eventually Trajan improved it by providing shelter for vessels, a lighthouse and warehouses, and creating canal connections to the Tiber. Great cities were always attractive market-places: the aggregate demand of their populations, especially the wealthier citizens, was a big draw but they were also places people came to from else-where in search of rare and exotic goods, and also necessities.

Urban Risk

Satisfying the vast and regular demand of the megalopoleis was one thing. Protecting a major city from risk was another. Large cities faced many of the same threats as small ones—poor harvests, drought, flood, fire, disease, war, earthquakes—but were often more seriously impacted. Population densities were often greater in the megalopoleis, and a smaller proportion of their inhabitants were involved in food production. It would have been difficult to evacuate megalopoleis as Pompeii and Herculaneum were partly evacu-ated in 79 C.E. Civil unrest was also more of a threat when urban mobs were larger and more anonymous. Their rulers knew this and made what prepa-rations they could to regulate threats, such as food crises, floods, and fires.

Risk, first of all. Hunger was a constant threat, and brought with it other consequences. In the long term the malnourished became weak and vul-nerable to disease; in the short term when the price of food rose, urban populations rioted. There is documentation of riots in Rome, Alexandria, and Constantinople that led to emergency responses, such as opening up imperial granaries. The mob might turn on those it suspected of speculating in grain, on the magistrates, or on the emperor himself. Warehouses, grain funds, and laws against speculation were all used to try to stop the cycle of rising prices, hoarding, and violence. On occasion there were attempts to expel "useless mouths" or to ration food. The wealthy could usually evade difficult situations but the larger the urban mob, the more concerned authorities were to restore the food supply.

Large cities were also more vulnerable to fire, which spread more quickly when buildings were packed close together. The philosopher Seneca wrote a homily on what could be learned from the destruction of the city of Lyon by fire sometime in the middle of the first century C.E.[39] His answer was that all things pass, including all cities, and we should be glad to live among inevitable decay. There were many fires in Rome, and what the Caesars learned from them was the importance of building regulations and the use of a fire brigade. Adequate spacing between buildings, construction in safe materials, and clear access routes all helped, but Rome burned and burned. The great fire of Nero's reign is the most famous—many blamed him, he blamed the Christians—but Rome was reborn on a yet more splendid scale. It never escaped the threat of fires. Just a few years ago a manuscript was found in a Greek monastery including a treatise written by the doctor Galen, titled *On the Avoidance of Grief.* One of his examples is his own loss of much of his personal library when warehouses along the via sacra caught fire in 192 C.E. Measures were also undertaken to protect some cities from floods. Rome—much of it built on the Tiber flood plain—was particularly vulnerable, and floods brought health threats of their own since Roman drains doubled as sewers.[40]

Hunger, fire, and flood were joined by plague. Ancient cities were unhealthy places at the best of times: their death rate was so high because of a combination of mal- and undernourishment, poor waste disposal, general insanitary conditions, and the density of population. Weak bodies packed close together are an easy target for many pathogens, both those communicated from person to person and those carried by pests of various kinds. A range of diseases were endemic in many cities, including malaria and tuberculosis. The larger the city, the more vulnerable the population. In a very general way there is agreement that population growth, and especially the growth of cities and long-distance trade across Eurasia, made it easier for epidemics to move from one urbanized region to another.[41] It is more difficult to determine exactly which plague it was that struck Athens near the beginning of the Peloponnesian War, when a large part of the population of Attica sheltered within the long walls; which plague swept the Roman world in the Antonine Age, moving so fast that an emperor and his entourage set to outrun it on horseback; and exactly what was responsible for the devastating mortality of Justinian's reign. Long-standing attempts to use descriptions in ancient texts to identify the pathogens behind particular epidemics have been inconclusive, partly because ancient writers did not described symptoms in the way modern medical specialists do. But a more and more, a precise picture of ancient disease history is about to emerge from investigations based on ancient DNA. So far only provisional accounts can be written, and it is still unclear how dramatic the mortality events were and how long-lasting their consequences.[42]

One final category of natural disaster was earthquake. This at least was even-handed, striking small cities as well as large. Some of the most populous areas of the Mediterranean were (and still are) especially at risk: the western coast of what is now Turkey suffered a devastating quake in 19 C.E. early in the reign of Tiberius, so serious that the emperor remitted five years of imperial taxes so that the money could be reallocated to reconstruction. Another vulnerable zone was the isthmus of Corinth, where the local cult of Poseidon the Earthshaker did not save his sanctuaries. Syrian Antioch suffered a devastating earthquake in C.E. 526, with massive fatalities and a series of fires that followed. Then there was central Italy, especially the bay of Naples. Great cities were only vulnerable if they had been built up, and built up in the form of shaky apartment buildings known as insulae. In some earthquake-prone areas it looks very as if this form of building was deliberately avoided.

Megalopolitan Societies

Shifts in scale have a dramatic effect on the social order. A city of a few thousand is not a face-to-face society, and no one person could have known the names of all of his or her fellow citizens. Yet the social networks inside small communities are densely tangled. Friends of friends comprise a very large group, kinsmen quite a broad set, and strangers are easy to spot. Communal habits form easily and are policed almost without anyone being aware of it. Charisma works powerfully in a small world. These tightly bounded social universes had been co-opted in the classical city for experiments in direct democracy, to summon up an occasional army, and to take part in collective religious activities. Some of this still made cities of a few thousand work.

Multiply this one hundred-fold, however, and the social pattern is completely broken. The urban societies of the megalopoleis were unlike anything that had come before. It is very tempting to use modern experiences of giant cities an analogies, but it many ways ancient megalopoleis were quite different. Most large modern cities have grown up organically, while most ancient megalopoleis were the creation of empires. Communication across our cities is easy, with the result that some people live far from where they live, and local communities of immigrant groups form with their own shops, temples, and social networks. This can rarely have been possible in ancient megalopoleis. Their social networks much have been much more local, and the cities must have been full of new arrivals. Integrating a megalopolis was a real challenge to ancient authorities, who sometime found that methods of ruling smaller cities could not easily be scaled up.

There were certainly attempt to do just that. Ceremonial and its accompanying monumentality provide good examples. This is visible in the great colonnaded boulevards that the greatest Syrian, Asian, and North African cities began to build from the second and third centuries C.E. Those streets were built with processions in mind, and were often anchored on a spectacular view. At Ephesus the Arcadian Way led from the harbour right up to the Great Theatre. At Lepcis the colonnaded street led up from the harbour to the new forum and a spectacular fountain. These great public roads connected great public spaces. Agorai and fora were bigger than ever, their limits now clearly delimited by grand buildings, temples, basilicas, stoas, or law courts. The other great public gathering spaces were the theatres, amphitheatres, and circuses or hippodromes. These often served several purposes, with assemblies meeting in theatres, or temple steps turned over to drama, for example. Together spaces and routes—both adorned with statues, arches, and inscriptions—shaped the way people moved around the city and the views it presented to them. On its many festival days each of these great cities provided the stage for civic pageantry and political theatre.

Yet the soft matter that clothed these shining skeletons is more difficult to see. It is certain that not all these great cities were alike. The contrasts between Rome and Constantinople have already been pointed out. One ancient, its monuments wrapped in myth, its structures accumulated over centuries, its society dominated by an aristocracy that thought it had a title to rule; the other new, largely Christian from the start, focused on the court and the bishops rather than on ancient houses. Alexandria and Antioch had their own pre-Roman traditions. In Syria cities still dated events by the Seleucid era. Alexandria had rich citizens, but until the early third century they were not allowed to have a senate to match that of Rome. What difference did it make to the way the wealthiest Alexandrines interacted with each other, or with the masses, that they never met publicly to discuss political affairs? Antioch is even more mysterious in socially terms. We see the presence of the wealthy in the gorgeous mosaics of villas that surround the city. Our best vision of the city is in the fourth century, when it was a complicated mix of military base, imperial capital, and Greek super-polis with the rhetorical culture that went with it. It was also a zone of religious conflict with key roles being taken by the bishop, the pagan emperor, and a populace torn between the ancient sanctuary at Daphne and the cult of new martyrs. The elites of the different megalopoleis varied considerably in their culture, their collective identity, their political engagement, and probably too in how rich they were.

Nor were the masses the same in each megalopolis, despite the similarity of the facilities provided for their entertainment. Rome was, as I have said, probably restocked each generation by slaves. Alexandria may have been different, perhaps drawing population from the densely packed villages and cities of the Nile Valley. A few cities—but not Rome—seem genuinely cosmopolitan, and this emerges most clearly in religious practice and language. There is a story near the beginning of the *Acts the Apostles* of Jews and proselytes (converts or partial converts to Judaism) gathered in Jerusalem to celebrate Pentecost, having come from diasporic communities located in much of the Persian and Roman empires. It immediately reminds a modern reader of all the nationalities and languages gathered at Mecca to perform the Hajj. It is striking how many of the emergent religions of Roman antiquity were formed in great cities. Antioch, it was said, was the first place where the followers of Christ were called Christians. The Parthian capital of Ctesiphon next to Seleucia was the supposedly the place where Manichaeism was created, drawing on Zoroastrian, Christian, and many other traditions. Mithras was quite likely created in Ostia or Rome by hybridizing Persian, Greek, and Roman elements. In most respects, however, these cities were neither salad bowls nor melting pots. No middle classes patronized a dozen varieties of national restaurants, statuary and the visual arts mostly conformed to local rules, and the vast majority of tomb-stones were in Latin in the west, Greek in the east.

One thing the megalopoleis did share was the power to stun. The real-life counterparts of Virgil's shepherd must have been astonished when they made the journey from their tiny market towns and arrived at the spectac-ular gates or ports of a megalopolis. Ammianus describes barbarian envoys visiting late antique Rome who marvelled as Jonah did at Nineveh. Orators sang the praises of the cities they visited. We still have texts of speeches celebrating Rome, Corinth, and Athens, traces of praise poetry directed at Roman Carthage, and a great mass of poetry on the merits of differ-ent cities. Although few could have afforded to imitate them, these cities must have established some sort of ideal notion of what cities could be. The painted harbour frontages on Pompeian walls, the elaborate illustra-tions of walled cities on some late antique books, and the birds-eye view of Jerusalem on the Madaba map all pick out monuments most cities could only have dreamt of.

The megalopoleis stand out as extraordinary urban projects against the background of the very small-scale cities that were the norm in the Mediterranean world. Most modern urban networks in the Global North are more gradated, with small, medium, large, and perhaps some quite large cities in them. There were not so many medium-ranked cities in antiquity, and megalopoleis did not emerge gradually from their ranks or recede back into them gracefully. Only imperial power could create and sustain the giants cities, and if imperial power failed, their collapse would be as quick as their rise.

20

Postclassical

The Network Changes

The Roman urban apogee was located sometime in the early third century C.E., with due allowances for variation from one area to another. At this point there were more cities than ever before in the Mediterranean and its continental hinterlands; there were bigger cities than there had ever been in the region; and the proportion of the population that lived in cities, if low by modern standards, was also greater than ever before. The sheer number of urban residents was a continual stimulation for commodity trade. All this, together with massive investment in monumental building and lavish civic ceremonial, has convinced most historians that this was the period of maximum economic prosperity. For what it is worth Greenland ice cores suggest that the level of metallurgical production in this period would not be rivalled before the Industrial Revolution. It was also the period of peak connectivity.

We must not exaggerate. The period of peak urbanism was still a world of tiny cities: perhaps three-quarters had only a few thousand inhabitants each. But there were a number of cities of more than ten or even fifty thousand, and a handful of giant cities—what I have called megalopoleis—with populations in the hundreds of thousands. The larger cities were greedy consumers in the hungry and thirsty landscapes of the ancient Mediterranean where 80 per cent of the population, free or slave, laboured in the fields. More ships than ever before crossed the waves. A few were larger than had ever been used on the Mediterranean. But peak connectivity did not mean everyone moved all the time. Perhaps one in a thousand people made a long-distance journey every year. Most lived their lives within small worlds.

What happened to cities after the urban apogee has been a major focus of research in recent years.[1] Historians of late antiquity—roughly the fourth through seventh centuries C.E.—more often write now of transformation than of decline. There is certainly some point in getting away from the tragic and moral undercurrents of decline and fall. But the debate between "bad change" and "just change" still smuggles in the assumption that it is change that needs to be explained. Change is in fact the norm in all ecological systems. The ideas of an ecological balance or harmony is simply romantic, or else the product of looking at a system for a very short time. Some systems last longer than others and change proceeds at different rates, but in principle stability is just as much a problem to be explained as is alteration. The ancient world was not a stable system by most measures. The great multispecies society of the ancient Mediterranean was in constant flux, and cities reflected this as much as did any other indicator.

Once again it helps to think of the network as a whole rather than of individual cities. The fates and fortunes of individual cities were always subject to local factors. Trier on the Mosel, capital of one of the most northerly German tribes, was transformed by a few years of an emperor's presence. Its Roman period monuments today have few rivals north of the Alps. Amiens, farther west, shrank dramatically in size until by the end of the fourth century C.E. a city with a planned area of more than 100 hectares, that had expanded when it became a stage on the route to Britain, had collapsed down to a tiny settlement of just a few hectares around a central fortress. Neither is typical of "the" late antique city, since there was no such thing. But behind the noise of individual cities growing and shrinking, a few more general patterns are visible.

One clear pattern is dramatic shrinkage in the megalopoleis. This was not a smooth process. Rome began to shrink early in the fourth century, just as Constantinople was expanding rapidly, and Rome continued to decline until its aqueducts were cut during the Gothic Wars of the sixth century. By then its population had dropped to perhaps 10,000 from an Augustan peak of around a million. Constantinople rose and fell on a different timescale. Perhaps it already had a population of 100,000 by Constantine's death, and its peak in the fifth and sixth centuries was 500,000: by the early seventh century when the distribution of grain was discontinued it plummeted to a few tens of thousands. The rate of decline in Alexandria and Antioch is difficult to gauge. Both remained important centres before and after the

Arab conquests of the seventh century, but that does not mean their populations remained high. The collapse of imperial power, as military pressure increased costs and loss of territory reduced revenues, meant that later
Roman emperors were less and less able to sustain megalopoleis. It was only
their great wealth that had raised them up and kept them prosperous. By the
end of the seventh century C.E. the largest cities in the Mediterranean were
probably not much bigger than they had been in the fourth century B.C.E.

A second clear trend is the reduction of the geographical area covered
by the Roman urban network. Cities disappeared from some of the regions
abandoned by the Roman state from the late third century on, but it was
not a sudden process. The first area to be abandoned was Dacia, conquered
in 117 C.E. by Trajan and abandoned by Aurelian in 271. The cities there were
not immediately evacuated, but what life was like in them in the centuries
that followed is very unclear. Garrisons were also withdrawn in the late
third century from the inland parts of Mauretania Tingitana, Rome's distant
province in Atlantic North Africa. Volubilis was one of the cities abandoned,
but it was then occupied by Berber tribes and was still functioning as a city
when the Arab invaders arrived in the first decade of the eighth century. It
may be relevant that the city predated the Roman takeover of the region.
The most extreme example is provided by Britain, abandoned during the
fifth century C.E.[2] The province had had around one hundred walled settlements under Roman rule, about a fifth of them the capitals of tribal
states, but most were tiny and monuments were few and unimpressive. Life
continued for a while after the troops were withdrawn, but then there was
a catastrophic loss of technology and production took place on a much
more local scale, and the monetary economy disappeared.[3] When sites like
Winchester and Canterbury and London became cities again in the early
Middle Ages, only the wall circuits of the Roman cities remained to be
repurposed and repopulated with different kind of urbanism.

Contractions of the Roman urban network on its peripheries are dramatic, but they mask a third pattern of change: that in much of the Roman
north new public building had stopped even before the Roman urban apogee.[4] The civic monuments of cities in non-Mediterranean Gaul, in Britain,
and in Germany were mostly built between the first decades C.E. and the
middle of the second century. Fora, temples, theatres, and amphitheatres,
where they existed as separate structures, were often planned early on in
a town's history. Some were certainly paid for by powerful benefactors,
as was common in the Mediterranean world. There is a small dossier of

inscriptions marking the generosity of local aristocrats, although it does not compare to those from Italy or Africa, let alone those in the east.[5] Many buildings were funded either by the emperors or from public funds.[6] Neither the relatively low level of investment in monuments nor the fact that monument-building had largely ended before 200 C.E. reflects poverty. Many northern cities had vast territories compared to those of the average Mediterranean city-state. Agricultural yields were generally greater and also more dependable, thanks to more abundant rainfall and deeper soils. The scale of third- and fourth-century villa-building was also impressive. The most obvious interpretation is that although most northern cities continued to serve economic functions as market towns and had some administrative role, the aesthetics and ideals of urbanism as they had been elaborated in the Mediterranean world did not hold the imagination of northern elites. Something similar happened, to a lesser degree and generally a little later, in other areas of the Roman west.[7] Cities remained important in the cultural imagination, but few were prepared to pay for traditional forms of monument.

Some support for this is provided by a new form of monumentality that appeared more than a century after the end of the construction of more traditional civic monuments. This was the construction of large churches, beginning in the reign of Constantine and becoming widespread by the early fifth century. There are strong regional variations in the timing of this activity, perhaps reflecting regional variations in the pace of conversions to Christianity, perhaps reflecting economic differences as well. It is fairly clear, however, that this was rarely a case of transferring spending from one project to another, since in most cases there was a long gap between the last theatre, bathhouse, or forum complexes and the first really substantial churches. Often, especially in the west, this took place first on the outskirts of cities, either to avoid conflict with non-Christians over central sites or more likely in order to be closer to the tombs of the martyrs, usually located in the graveyards that lined major approaches to the city. By the fifth and sixth centuries churches, with their associated approach roads and ancillary buildings, were beginning to restructure urban topography. In a some cases temples were appropriated as churches and often, as in Lisbon and Seville and Damascus, churches were constructed on the sites of major civic shrines. Changing priorities are also revealed by a diminishing attention to maintaining the public spaces that had been the centre of early imperial cities. Open fora and agorai received less attention and were even left out of new fortified inner circuits, as happened at Ephesus.[8] At Athens the agora was bisected by the new inner wall (see Figure 36). The great colonnaded streets of the second and third century were overtaken by shops, until they became the prototype of souks. Waterfronts were allowed to encroach into rivers.[9] Civic authorities all over the empire did less to preserve these spaces.

A fourth pattern is the shrinking of urban populations. This is where it is really important to think of the network as a whole, rather than of individual cities. There were a few cities—most obviously the tetrarchic capitals and Constantinople above all, but a few others such as Ostia, the port of Rome—where the second-century population figures were sustained or even surpassed in this period. But in terms of the total urban population, there is no doubt that there was a major reduction. Almost every large city we know in detail contracted in size over the late third and fourth centuries. A common feature of late antique cities was an inner fortified circuit, often constructed from dismantled monuments and incorporating sections of existing ones such as theatres and amphitheatres. This appears in western cities such as London, Amiens, and Périgueux and eastern ones such as Athens, Corinth, and Side. The Aurelian walls too, although much grander and not built out of dismembered monuments, represent an inner

Figure 36 Inner circuit wall built across Athenian Agora
Martin Garnham / Alamy Stock Photo

circuit built rapidly in the context of military insecurity. It is also clear that many suburban areas and even some central ones went out of use, and that in places the outskirts of town were given over to farming. No systematic survey exists of late Roman population sizes to be compared with those carried out for the fourth century B.C.E. or the early empire, but the conclusion from individual city and regional studies is inescapable. The total population living in towns had plummeted, and the larger cities in particular were dramatically effected.

The collapse in the aggregate urban population has several implications. For a start, this meant a collapse in the demand for long-distance trade in commodities, especially in foodstuffs. Smaller cities had always been more able to support themselves from their immediate hinterlands, and presumably that remained the case. Rome and Constantinople at their peak had to be supplied from North Africa and Egypt with grain, and even imperial Athens had consumed grain from Egypt and the Black Sea. As larger cities became smaller and smaller in terms of population, their aggregate demand grew less. The impact of a collapse in demand on primary producers and merchants is easy to imagine. If the total population of the empire was also shrinking, then the profitability of agriculture may not have been so seriously hit. But merchants went of business, and farmers probably produced smaller surpluses. The great vessels plying their way across the open sea from one deep water harbour to another became a thing of the past. The long-distance trade in luxuries never entirely disappeared: it existed in the archaic age and would survive through the early Middle Ages, carrying papyrus, spices, metalwork, and other low-bulk/high-value goods for the elite. But everything that depended on mass consumption was affected. So were other economic activities, such as stone quarrying and brick production. Many late antique buildings reused material from early monuments in any case. Whether this was by necessity or for economy is uncertain.

These changes in the economy as a consequence of diminishing urban demand interacted with another trend that had been evidence for some time: the localization of production closer and closer to sites of consumption. The peak period of long-distance trade, to judge from the evidence of shipwrecks, had been the last century B.C.E. and first C.E. New styles and tastes spread across an unprecedented geographical range as everyone wanted Greek and Italian wine, Spanish olive oil, and marble from Asia Minor. This coincided with the great expansion of the urban network of antiquity, although demand was not only found in the cities. The expense of

course was ruinous, and during the first century C.E. most provincial societies tried to supply these tastes locally. Quarries were opened up near growing cities.[10] Vines were grown farther and farther from the Mediterranean.
Provincial industries emerged in the production of anything that could be
transported in amphorae or barrels. Local potters learned to make high-
quality ceramics and also bricks and tiles close to where they were consumed. Long-distance trade was already being replaced by regional trading
systems in the late first and early second centuries C.E.

When this trend interacted with the shrinking of urban populations,
the impact on long-distance exchange was dramatic. Local styles emerged
in pottery, wall painting, and domestic architecture, visibly related to one
another by descent but interacting less than in the past. The trade patterns
we can detect in late antiquity are more regional than global. Western
Mediterranean ports like Marseilles, Pisa, Ostia, and Carthage remained
important but they now served largely regional exchanges. Constantinople
and Alexandria in the east became the most important axis for commodity
trade until the seventh century.

These economic changes also indicate a fifth pattern of change and the
final one I want to emphasize: the development of regionalism. The growth
of a Mediterranean urban network in the last centuries B.C.E. and the first
C.E. had tended towards a wider integration of local economies and societies
across the Mediterranean world, one that has appropriately been compared
to modern globalization processes.[11] The urban network in the second century C.E. had been broader than ever before; had carried more traffic, especially in terms of goods; and its nodes had been more hierarchically ordered.
One way to summarize the direction of change in the period 200–700 C.E.
is that these trends were reversed. There was less hierarchy in the system, less
traffic moved across it, and it was less integrated at the largest scale. Instead
we see a resurgence of regional networks linking cities that were much
more alike to each other in size and function.

Explaining Change

Every urban system in history has been the product of many forces operating at the same time. Like a weather system, there is never one single factor
that explains its configuration at any given moment, nor its degree of stability. Nor do these factors all operate in the same time scale. Fernand Braudel,

in his epic account of the Mediterranean in the age of Philip II, distinguished different periodicities of change, of which the two most famous are the long term (physical geography, geomorphology, climate) and the short term of the history of events.[12] Today we are more aware today of the impermanence of even the most fundamental features of the Mediterranean world.[13] Mediterranean flora are in fact still in a process of recolonizing the region after the last glacial period.[14] Sea levels have fluctuated considerably in the last few thousand years, drowning cities in the bay of Naples and in the Delta of the Nile, while silting up of rivers has left other port cities like Pisa and Ephesus far from the sea. The history of Mediterranean forests is in the course of being rewritten, as is the disease history of the region.[15] Human activity is a part of these histories, but as this book has argued, it is too simple to treat the lands, fauna, and flora of the region as a stable system on which human beings impacted.

Traditionally historians of late antiquity often preferred catastrophic explanations located in the shortest term possible, the history of events. So changes to the urban networks have been ascribed to the conversion of Constantine, various German invasions, the collapse of the western Roman Empire over the fifth century C.E., or the Arab conquests of the seventh. One reason for this was because historians took the stability of the early imperial system for granted and believed that only a great shock could have disrupted it. Another was that they overvalued ancient testimony. This book cites few ancient witnesses, not because their views were not valid, but because very few ancient observers had enough information or a broad enough perspective to see what was happening to urbanism as a whole, rather than what was happening to their own city. From our better-informed perspective the urban system as a whole looks less stable now, but some of these so-called catastrophes have turned out on examination not to be real watersheds in the history of cities. The trade of Carthage with Rome continued after the Vandal conquests. The Visigothic rulers in Spain were in fact one of the last ancient regimes to create new urban foundations. The Mediterranean was not bisected either economically or culturally by the Arab conquests.[16]

Currently two sets of factors seem the most likely to be important in explaining how the processes of network-building and urbanization went into reverse between the second and third centuries C.E. Both may be involved, but one set is much less certain than the other, at least for the moment.

The area of most uncertainty concerns the role played by climate change and epidemics. It has been noticed for some time that during the last century B.C.E. and the first two C.E. centuries, conditions were a few degrees warmer than before or after, and that in this period the climate was also relatively stable. This has become known as the Roman climatic optimum, and obviously coincides chronologically with the period of urbanization leading up to the Roman urban apogee. Establishing the details of this required contributions from a mass of different disciplines, including glaciology and dendrochronology; the study of ice cores, stalagmites, pollen from lake beds, and much else; but a great deal of progress has been made in recent years.[17] The more difficult task is to work out how these large-scale trends were transmitted to local conditions, and then how they impacted human experience. Changes in crop yields, in sea levels, and in the carrying capacity of different landscapes are all likely. Turning all this into history is more tricky. Temperature rises do not correspond necessarily to economic prosperity, and it is perfectly possible to explain urbanization without recourse to climate change. At the moment we have a correlation and some possible links, but not much more than that. Disease history is equally complex. The difficulty of identifying the particular pathogens responsible for attested epidemics has already been noted. Again, their impact on human populations and on demographic trends is uncertain. Some scholars see major events like the Antonine plague or the Justinianic pandemic as leading to huge increases in mortality which were not recovered for generations. That is not impossible, but alternative views are also plausible based on more recent epidemics. Mass mortality might hurt an economy severely that relied, as the Roman one did, mainly on human labour. But there are attested cases where mortality has been quite variable, such as in reducing the numbers of the old and sick much more than the young and healthy and thereby giving agricultural societies a short-term boost. The economic consequences in that case would be different, perhaps even positive in the short term. For late antiquity we would also like to know whether epidemics effected town-dwellers more or less than rural populations, incomers like the Germans (who crossed into the Mediterranean world on several occasions during this period) more or less than those who were there already, and so on. More knowledge of the pathogens involved may eventually help here, since some are much more dependent than others for transmission in dense populations like those of cities. It is certainly possible to hypothesize scenarios in which global cooling or the arrival of epidemic diseases undermined the economic and demographic regimes on which ancient cities depended with long-term consequences for the network as a whole, but at the moment there remains room for doubt or at least alternative reconstructions.[18]

We are on much firmer ground with a second set of explanations which relate changes in urban networks to the collapse, by stages, of the imperial Roman state. The impact on first Rome and then Constantinople of emperors scaling back what they provided has already been mentioned. The megalopoleis had been created by imperial fiat. When emperors could not—or would not—sustain them, they became much more vulnerable. A great part of the population of the city of Rome was sustained directly or indirectly by imperial spending. Building projects, the various supply networks, and the purchasing power of those paid by the palace all operated as ways through which imperial wealth was passed on to the Roman masses. When this spending slowed down from the third century, it grew harder to live in Rome. When the loss of Egypt prompted the emperors to drastically reduce what was given to the masses in Constantinople, similar effects were felt. The fact that megalopoleis were sustained by constant immigration means that we do not need to explain where the population went: it was simply no longer replaced.

Other cities were also partly sustained by their role in imperial administration. City-states had been made instruments of government from the last century B.C.E. onwards; indeed this was the rationale for the creation of new city-states all over the Latin west and also in some eastern areas like Pontus. From the fourth century C.E. cities had been partly replaced in the administration as the later Roman Empire generated more of a bureaucracy. But cities and civic elites remained essential complements to central government, especially in the collection of taxes. When the western empire collapsed in the fifth century and was replaced by a series of kingdoms ruled by Visigoths, Ostrogoths, Burgundians, Vandals, and others, the cities of southern France, Spain, and Africa survived, at least for a while. One reason was that the new rulers more or less annexed the tax systems of their Roman predecessors.[19] Only when the monetized tax systems of the Roman model were replaced by other systems of extraction, did cities shrink.

Empire arguably also created an environment favourable to cities. Economically cities have always faced in two directions. They function as a point of coordination for their immediate territories, providing a central place for functions ranging from the provision of justice to the organization of markets. Yet they are also nodes in much wider networks, places where local economic activities connected to the wider world. Neither function depends on the existence of political structures overarching the world of independent city-states, but empire casually facilitated many of the outward-facing activities of cities. Political unification provided some minimal institutions that made trade easier, such as common currencies, weights and measures, and legal systems. Empire created and sustained much infrastructure for its own mainly military purposes that were also useful to cities: roads, harbours, bridges, and warehouses. Most importantly, empire provided some measure of security, preventing intercity warfare and limiting piracy and banditry.

From the middle of the third century empire was much less good at providing almost all of this. There are several anecdotes of cities deep inside the empire from Tarraco to Athens and Ephesus where local citizens had to take security into their own hands when barbarian raids penetrated deep behind the frontiers.[20] Inflation and a collapse of the currency was repaired in the late third century, but the tax burden became heavier in the fourth. The new system of a college of emperors acting in concert helped a little with managing war on more than one frontier, but from the late fourth century the western provinces began to collapse as large groups moved in from the north of the Danube and east of the Rhine. By the middle of the fifth century Roman control in the west was in effect limited to the Mediterranean regions, and by 500 C.E. it was parcelled up among kingdoms ruled by German kings with the assistance of armies based on their retinue and administrations staffed by former Roman subjects. Cities retained some role in government for the first few generations, and some, especially port cities on the Mediterranean, continued to participate in international exchange. The general trend, however, was for their local functions to become more important as the political landscape fragmented.

Political fragmentation, combined with the trends toward local self-sufficiency already mentioned, means that it is more and more difficult to write about a single urban system. Most recent histories have stressed the differences between the urban histories of different regions.[21] Italian cities had various fates. Shifts in the political gravity brought late antique imperial courts first to Milan, and then more defensively to Ravenna. In some parts of the peninsula urban shrinkage was profound, but in many northern cities the transformation into the Middle Ages was so gradual and organic that Roman street planning may still be detected in the plans of the old towns.[22]

North Africa had a small urban boom in the fourth century, a century or more after public building had stopped in the north.[23] Some African cities were still thriving in the fifth century and when Justinian's armies recaptured much of it from the Vandals, there were still cities functioning along the coasts. Some Greek cities in Asia Minor and the Near East thrived into the sixth century, fought over by Roman and Persian emperors right up to the eve of the Arab conquests.[24] Jerusalem, sacked in the Jewish War of C.E. 70 and again by Trajan, had been rebuilt and refounded as a Roman colony by Hadrian in the 130s. After the conversion of Constantine it flourished as a pilgrimage centre until it was sacked in 614 C.E. by the Persians, who carried off much of the population along with the booty.

Resilience and Legacy

One other way to think about what happened to cities after the Roman urban apogee is in terms of their resilience.

Resilience is a measure of how successfully and quickly a complex system is able to recover from a severe shock. The concept was originally developed in ecology as a way to describe how likely entire ecosystems were to recover from stresses. Resilient systems are those that self regulate effectively or spring back rapidly.[25] More fragile systems are more liable to complete collapse. Typically, systems are resilient if they are interconnected in ways that mean no one element is essential to all the others. Biodiversity is sometimes thought to enhance the resilience of an ecological system. The idea has been extended to many other kinds of systems including human societies, climatic systems, and cities.[26] A city entirely dependent on one industry or on state subsidy is less resilient than one with many sources of support. The capacity to rebalance within a system is also usually thought important. Predicting resilience is difficult, of course, and in historical cases we often only detect a lack of resilience at the moment a system collapses.[27]

Seneca, in the letter mentioned in the last chapter, wrote that although many cities had recovered from fire and earthquake, Lyon was finished. He was wrong, of course. Elsewhere in his letter he quotes the anti-Roman historian Timagenes, who had been a hostage in the city in the late Republic and early empire. Timagenes claimed the only thing that upset him when he saw Roman buildings burning was the knowledge they would be rebuilt on an even grander scale. This was closer to the mark. Ancient cities were in fact very resilient. This is evident from the enormous life-spans of the most famous ones. Athens is around 3,500 years old; Rome, Syracuse, Marseilles, Istanbul, and many others have been major centres for more than 2,500 years. If we included cities succeeded by other ones on roughly the same site, such as Carthage and Tunis, it is clear that most cities that were prominent in antiquity remain important today.

Resilience is demonstrated most of all by rapid recovery from disaster. Most ancient cities that we know to have suffered terrible food crises, fires, earthquakes, or floods recovered within a generation. Not much short of a volcano could kill an ancient city; Pompeii and Herculaneum are the key cases here. This tells us something about the importance of cities to ancient populations: rulers, the wealthy, and the poor all came to the rescue when a city suffered a catastrophe. It maybe also tells us something about the importance of particular locations in the urban network. By the turn of the millennium many cities were locked into sets of relations so powerful that if a city was broken it was generally replaced in more or less the same spot.

The effects of the most common category of man-made disaster illustrates this. Most of the major ancient cities underwent terrifying sieges and sacks at least once in their very long histories. Athens was sacked by the Roman general Sulla, and then three hundred years later by the Heruli from the Black Sea; Syracuse and Carthage and Corinth and Tarentum were all sacked by the Romans; Ephesus by Mithridates in 88 B.C.E., then by Sulla, then by the Goths in the third century; Alexandria and Marseilles were both besieged by Caesar; Byzantium by Severus; Rome by Sulla and others during the Republican civil wars and again in the struggle over who would replace Nero, and at the end of antiquity by the Vandals and the Goths. Yet for most of this period, cities bounced back. The devastating fire of Lyon has left no certain archaeological traces, so complete was its recovery.

There are, however, some signs of reduced resilience at the end of the period. The Justinianic plague seems to have cast a longer shadow than its Antonine predecessor. Was it a more virulent pathogen? This is certainly possible, especially if it was a new variety of bubonic plague brought from India. Or are we looking at a decrease in resilience, in the capacity to recover after the initial shock? The earthquake of Antioch reputedly killed hundreds of thousands, wrecked the greatest monuments, pagan and Christian alike, and damaged the port. Soon afterwards it was captured by the Persians and its population taken into exile. Despite strenuous efforts to rebuild, Antioch never recovered. By contrast, the cities of Asia that suffered a devastating earthquake in the reign of Tiberius made a very rapid recovery: their late first- and early second-century monuments and epigraphy are as impressive as for any area of the empire. It seems at least worth considering whether late antique cities were less resistant than their early imperial predecessors.

An erosion of resilience is difficult to detect. If a given city escaped siege or some other disaster, life might continue for centuries in much the same physical spaces and manner as before without any danger signs showing. Yet there is reason to think some of the safety networks had become threadbare. Disaster-struck cities in the past had relied on imperial support, the resources of private individuals, and the strong economic networks in which they were enmeshed to help recovery. None of these were as well placed to offer help in late antiquity as they had been earlier. Imperial support for cities was occasionally available in the early fourth century C.E.;[28] it seems less forthcoming in the centuries that followed. Disasters, of course, continued. A devastating tsunami in 365 C.E. wreaked havoc from southern Greece to Alexandria, and there is no hint here of major disaster relief.[29] The imperial court was caught up in a usurpation at the time and religious controversy as well. Economic connections were less strong towards the end of the period and cities came to rely mostly on the efforts of their richest citizens, whose civic obligations were insisted on by emperors until the end of the fourth century.[30] Some cities were more fortunate in this respect than were others. Ephesus and Athens both weathered barbarian raids in the third century and remained important in the following centuries. Ephesus suffered earthquakes and sacks in the seventh century but up until then seems to have maintained a lively civic life. Athens was an important centre for education in the late fourth century when Libanius studied there, and probably until Justinian closed the philosophical schools of Athens in C.E. 526. A few cities in this period could also count on support from bishops, but few of these commanded sufficient economic resources to remedy major disasters. Rome in the sixth century was one exception and Gregory the Great, pope from 590 to 604, did organize charitable relief in the city and for refugees there. More generally, however, there is an impression that cities of any size were less resilient in the sixth century than they had been in the fourth. For some it was a matter of waiting until disaster fell.

There was an alternative, of course, and one that most cities in the end took, if only by default. This was to contract in size. The disasters we hear of affected larger rather than smaller cities, and that is only partly a function of their greater prominence in the historical record and the greater visibility of their archaelogical remains. Cities of a few thousand had always been better suited to deal with the regular catastrophes of Mediterranean life— with food shortage, drought, floods, and fire. The very large cities had been raised up against the ecological odds by the intervention of political powers. The political fragmentation of the Mediterranean Basin between 400 and 700 meant no such projects could be realized again, and few earlier ones supported. The resilient city of the sixth and seventh century had just a few thousand inhabitants and although it was well connected to other places, it was not dependent on them for food or the other necessities of life.

Afterword

Mediterranean Antiquity, an Urban Episode

It is always difficult to know where to start a story and where to finish it. The heart of this story was the labourious processes through which cities were planted around the Mediterranean Sea in the last millennium B.C.E. and the first centuries C.E. We have inherited a myth of classical antiquity as a world of cities. Because we have also inherited the idea that city-dwelling is in some way associated with that bundle of values we call civilization, ancient cities (or more often the Ancient City[1]) have assumed an exaggerated place in the way we imagine antiquity. One object of this book has been to present the results of more recent investigations. Cities came late to the Mediterranean world; they were mostly very small, and most people did not live in them. And most cities were created by accident, not as part of a civilizing process planned from the start and then promoted until the early Middle Ages. These revelations have come from thinking harder about the environmental constraints on ancient populations, about how fragmented landscapes and an unreliable climate set limits on living together that only imperial states could (briefly) transcend. Politically, mythologically, and architecturally, many of these tiny communities acted out their urban dreams. Economically, demographically, and agriculturally, it was dangerous to take those dreams too seriously.

Why then did they dream of cities? Would it not have been simpler to remain in the more sustainable hamlets and villages that could weather the occasional crisis? My answer has been twofold. First, I have pointed out the cluster of human features that have led so many societies into experimenting with towns since early in the Holocene period. Our social brains, our omnivory, our mobility, our restless propensity to seek solutions in migration and in nesting, creating tight bands of solidarity, have combined to make us urbanizable. We are not the only urban species, just as we are not the only social one. But it is a social evolutionary path along which we are easily led, as an accidental consequence of other kinds of evolution. My second answer has been that once these farmer communities—each settled in their tiny territories—had emerged, connections between them provided channels through which ideas, technologies, and people spread, beginning processes of competition that led to state-formation, wide urban networks, and a tiny scatter of megacities, all sustained by empire, until it no longer was.

Plato once compared the peoples of the Mediterranean to frogs sitting around a pond, and went on to imagine other ponds elsewhere on the earth, with other kinds of frogs sitting around them. Parallels between his cosmology and our own understanding of the last fifteen thousand years of global history soon break down. But it is correct that the millennium and a half of urban experiment this book has documented has its parallels elsewhere on the planet. There were urban moments that started a good deal earlier in the Near East and China, urban moments that started later in Africa and in the Americas, and in some places, Europe and India for example, there were several urban moments interspersed with periods in which writing was lost and the descendents of city-dwellers went back to living in villages.

The big picture is of a species that since the ice last retreated has repeatedly begun to build more elaborate nests and networks of nests, almost all of which have collapsed or become simplified. The ancient Mediterranean is not very special in this perspective. It is certainly not the model of a civilization others should follow. Perhaps it is better documented than most and has been investigated for longer, partly because of the accident of what was done with its remains afterwards. We are often tempted by a bigger picture: one in which we lived until recently like animals, and then once we learned to farm were drawn almost automatically into village life, cities and civilization. At first glance the pace of urbanization over the last eight thousand years seems to confirm this story of human progress. A closer inspection shows that complex social systems have often collapsed, and they have certainly often become decentralized and more fragmented. There is absolutely no guarantee that our current rate of globalization will be continued until we are maximally connected and uniformly urbanized. If the study of ancient cities teaches us anything it is that there have been many urban moments, but few that lasted more than a few centuries.

Urban systems rarely disappear without trace. Their relics are a resource for those who come after. Roman city walls in southern Britain provided shells within which Anglo-Saxons built different kinds of nests a few centuries later. The early Islamic rulers of what is now Tunisia gathered slender columns taken from Roman-period temples to create a forest of pillars within the great mosque of Kairouan. The palaces and cathedrals of mediaeval Europe were also inspired in part by Roman remains, as well as by those Romans who remained very much alive on the Bosporos in Constantine's megalopolis. Traces of urban life carried on in northern Italy and in Syria, and in a few other places where there was no sudden rupture between antiquity and the Middle Ages.[2]

Civilization is a value often given by the powerful to what they withhold from others. Even when they conceive of themselves as chosen to disseminate that value, that sense of mission only signals the inequality further. But not all urban projects were generated by that mindset. City life, I have argued, is not the same as an urban destiny. Groups of people created cities for all sorts of reasons in antiquity, and then found new uses for them. Urbanization was neither a fall from grace nor the first steps to a refined humanity. Cities seem like solutions to many kinds of problems, and are neither good nor bad in themselves. An expression of one dimension of what it is to be human, they are also completely natural, like termite hills and coral reefs. This book has drawn at times on human biology, ecology, economics, and climatology to tell its story but the materials that make the ancient Mediterranean urban moment so brilliant are human creations: art, texts, statues, and buildings, all of them as natural as their creators.

Further Reading

Scholars have been debating ancient cities for over a century now.

Social scientists often begin from Max Weber's *The City* (1922), which was originally part of his monumental work *Economy and Society*.[1] This is one of the foundational works of sociology, and in it Weber tried to describe through a series of types the ways in which the economic roles played by cities changed over time. Weber thought ancient cities (by which he mainly meant those of Greece and Rome) worked quite differently from mediaeval European and modern cities. A string of books, articles, and collections have challenged, refined, and built on his ideas since then.[2]

For archaeologists there has been another inspiration: the work of V. Gordon Childe, who coined the term "urban revolution" in his book *Man Makes Himself*. He argued that along with the preceding "Neolithic Revolution," the birth of cities was one of the fundamental watersheds in our social evolution.[3] He based his thought about cities (and definitions of them) on the results of excavations in the Fertile Crescent. Unsurprisingly, they fit the ancient societies of the Bronze Age Near East better than some other examples of early urbanism.

Since the time when Weber and Childe wrote we have all become much more aware of how different early urban traditions were from each other. Today's cities are actually much more like each other than their predecessors were, as architectural styles and technologies have spread around the globe. There is a distant echo here of the processes by which ancient Mediterranean cities converged on a common material style even if they had started life as Iron Age hill forts, Syrian temple-states, or tiny Greek poleis clinging to the barren rocks of the Aegean world.

The great mass of new information gathered by archaeologists and historians (and helped by geographers, sociologists, economists, and many others) is too much for any one person to master. Our solution has been to meet regularly to exchange news of different ancient urban civilizations, and just occasionally to try and see what ancient cities had in common, as well as the many ways in which they were different. Some of the meetings have produced valuable edited books that record the state of our knowledge at different times.[4] I have found some of these collections fantastically use-ful when writing the early parts of this book, especially Storey's collection *Urbanism in the Preindustrial World* and Marcus and Sabloff's *The Ancient City*.[5] A new collection came out, just as I was writing, as part of the *Cambridge World History*, and that too helped me try and get some sense of the first five thousand years of urbanism.[6] Monica L. Smith's *Cities the First 6000 years* appeared too late for me to make use of it, but it is bold and exciting explo-ration of urbanism on a truly global scale.[7] Occasionally a particularly brave scholar tries to pull the threads together and suggest some broad patterns. Michael E. Smith in many articles and a blog has done more than most to develop the comparative study of urbanism.[8] Other polymaths point out that some of the patterns we take for granted are not quite as obviously true as they seem. Among the iconoclastic studies I recommend Norman Yoffee's *Myths of the Archaic State* and David Wengrow's *What Makes Civilization?*[9]

The cities of the ancient Mediterranean have their own literature, one that sometimes intersects with these wider debates. Max Weber's ideas about ancient cities are best known to specialists on Greece and Rome through the work of Moses Finley and his use of Weber's idea of a "consumer city," a city that exploited the surrounding countryside without providing anything very useful in return in the way of manufactures or services. This was a cen-trepiece of his book *The Ancient Economy*, and has remained controversial ever since.[10] There have also been several collections on the ancient cities of the Mediterranean world.[11] An excellent introduction to all this is provided by Arjun Zuiderhoek's *The Ancient City*.[12] Gordon Childe's ideas have been influential on archaeologists and historians investigating the first stages of urbanism in the archaic period. Robin Osborne and Barry Cunliffe's edited collection *Mediterranean Urbanization 800–600 B.C.* provides an impressive reassessment.[13] So too does the more recent *Cambridge Prehistory of the Bronze and Iron Age Mediterranean*.[14] Alongside these great projects of synthesis there have been a few books that challenge our assumptions and make new argu-ments about the importance of ancient cities, or indeed their unimportance. The book owes a huge amount to the new ideas produced in *The Corrupting Sea* and in *The Making of the Middle Sea*.[15]

Writing this book I have become more and more conscious how fast the picture is changing. More data is always welcome, and especially more kinds of data. It is still quite early to write a history of urbanism that takes into account the history of animals and plants, or that views cities as part of networks, as points in a wider landscape or as nodes organizing the mobility of people and goods. The history of disease and climate change is now firmly on the agenda, and those histories will have to be bound together with the history of cities. Some historians believe cities will become less central to our study of the past. I doubt it, because so much was invested by Mediterranean populations in the traditions, monuments, and upkeep of cities. But there is no doubt in my mind that in thirty years' time the natural history of urbanism will look quite different. And that is a good thing.

Timeline

A World Without Cities

2.5 million years B.P. (Before Present) to 12,000 B.P., the Pleistocene Era: Genus *homo* appears near the start and various species of early humans move around Africa and Eurasia, expanding their range in interglacial periods, retreating into warmer places whenever the glaciers expanded.

About 300, 000 B.P.: First evidence for *homo sapiens* (modern humans).

70,000–20,000 B.P.: Modern humans move out of Africa and rapidly spread east into Asia and Australia and west to the Atlantic, keeping south of the ice sheets, encountering and replacing other groups of early humans en route.

About 27,000 B.P.: The last glacial maximum.

About 15,000 B.P.: The first humans enter the Americas and settle most of North and South America in a few thousand years.

Before 12,000 B.P.: Modern humans occupy most land masses except the most remote Pacific and Atlantic islands and Antarctica. Most are fishers, gatherers, and hunters and most live in small mobile groups. *Homo sapiens* are now the only species of human on earth.

11,500–7,000 B.P., the early Holocene Era: Global temperatures rose, glaciers retreated, sea levels rose rapidly.

10,000–5000 B.P.: Farming invented independently in many locations across the globe. Many species of plants and animals are domesticated. Villages of farmers appear around the world and populations settle and begin to grow. First experiments in metallurgy.

Early Urbanisms

Almost every episode of urban origins was preceded by centuries of slow growth. Start dates often simply signal a sudden change in the scale of the monuments and perhaps rapid growth in populations. Many of these dates will probably be revised by future research.

4000 B.C.E., (Before the Common Era): Cities appear in northern and southern Mesopotamia (Tell Brak and Uruk).

3500 B.C.E.: Hierakonopolis, the earliest Egyptian city known to date.

2800–1900 B.C.E.: Harappan urbanism in valley of the Indus.

1900–1350 B.C.E.: Erlitou urbanism in the Yellow River Valley, China.

1700–1425 B.C.E.: Minoan Crete (Neopalatial period).

500 B.C.E.–900 C.E.: Maya low-density urbanism in central America.

100 B.C.E.–200 C.E.: Monte Albán, a major urban centre in Mexico.

400–900 C.E.: Cities appear in Wari Empire of Peru.

500–900 C.E.: Jenne-jeno and Timbuktu among first Niger Valley cities.

1200–1400 C.E.: Mound complex at Cahokia, in present-day US state of Illinois.

1300–1500 C.E.: Low-density urbanism in Upper Xingu Basin, Amazonia.

The Last and First Millennia in the Mediterranean and Ancient Near East

1200–1150 B.C.E.: Late Bronze Age Collapse; destruction of palaces in Crete and southern Greece, population displacements, the destruction of Ugarit in the Levant, of Enkomi on Cyprus, the end of the Hittite Empire, and of the Egyptian New Kingdom.

911–609 B.C.E.: Assyrian New Kingdom dominates Near East with major royal cities at Kalhu (Nimrud), Dur-Sharrukin (Khorsabad), and Nineveh (Mosul)

900–800 B.C.E.: Phoenicians from Tyre regularly visiting Spanish centres around the Straits of Gibraltar.

Middle of eighth century B.C.E.: Etruscan cities and states emerge from Villanovan culture of central western Italy.

About 750–700 B.C.E.: Pithecusae in the Bay of Naples a major point on contact between Euboean Greeks, indigenous Italian peoples, and perhaps others.

Between 735 and 580 B.C.E.: A number of Greek cities created on the island of Sicily and also in south and central Italy.

Seventh and sixth centuries B.C.E.: Greek outposts and cities appear around the Black Sea, the Adriatic, and in Mediterranean France and northeast Spain.

550 B.C.E.: Conquest of Lydia brings Persian Empire into direct contact with Greek world; Darius I (522–486 B.C.E.) founds royal centres of Persepolis and Susa.

538–516 B.C.E.: Temple rebuilt in Jerusalem.

509 B.C.E.: Traditional date for the overthow of the last kings of Rome and the foundation of the Republic.

479–403 B.C.E.: Athens is dominant naval power in the Aegean, following defeat of two Persian expeditions.

370–367 B.C.E.: Foundation of Messene and Megalopoleis.

Between 338 and 177 B.C.E.: Rome settles communities of citizens in *coloniae* on conquered territory throughout Italy.

334–323 B.C.E.: Alexander of Macedon conquers the Persian Empire, founds numerous cities including Alexandria in Egypt.

300 B.C.E.: Foundation of Antioch in Syria.

211 B.C.E.: Syracuse captured by Rome after a long siege; Sicily becomes Rome's first overseas territory.

146 B.C.E.: Rome destroys Carthage at end of Third Punic War, and in the same year the Greek city of Corinth; both refounded a century later.

60 B.C.E.–60C.E.: Roman expansion accelerates resulting in control of the entire Mediterranean Basin, half of Europe, Egypt, and much of the Near East.

31 B.C.E.–14 C.E.: Reign of Augustus, Rome's first emperor; numerous cities founded in Mediterranean provinces to accommodate civil war veterans and to organize conquered territory in Europe and Asia Minor; city of Rome now largest city in Mediterranean world with around 1 million inhabitants.

70 C.E.: Jerusalem sacked by and temple destroyed.

98–117 C.E.: Trajan's reign takes empire to maximum extent with incorporation of much of Romania (Dacia) and briefly also Mesopotamia.

117–138 C.E.: Reign of Hadrian, who sponsors and encourages building in Athens, founds the city of Antinoopolis in Egypt, and refounds Jerusalem as Colonia Aelia Capitolina.

About 150–200 C.E.: Ancient urban apogee; size and number of ancient cities and the extent of the ancient urban network reach a peak in this period.

165–180 C.E.: Antonine plague.

235–284 C.E.: Military crisis of third century; Rome recovers but withdraws from territory north of Danube and from Atlantic Mauretania.

324 C.E.: Constantine founds Constantinople on the site of Byzantium.

378 C.E.: Roman armies defeated at Adrianople and various groups enter the empire, leading to sack of Rome by the Goths in 410 C.E. and the Vandals in 455 C.E.; last western emperor deposed in 476 C.E.

379–395 C.E.: Reign of Theodosius, last emperor to reign in west and east.

527–65 C.E.: Reign of Justinian; Roman (Byzantine) reconquest of North Africa and parts of Italy and Spain; major building projects in Constantinople, Jerusalem, and other eastern cities.

541–543 C.E.: Arrival of Justinianic plague.

636–697 C.E.: Arab conquests of Roman Near East, Persian Empire, and North Africa.

661 C.E.: Umayyad Caliphate founded in Damascus.

Notes

CHAPTER 1

1. Worldometers, n.d., "Current World Population," accessed 16th December 2019, http://www.worldometers.info/world-population/.
2. United Nations, n.d., "World Urbanization Prospects 2018," accessed 16th December 2019 https://esa.un.org/unpd/wup/.
3. See Smith (2002, 2009) on complexity as a criterion for urbanism. See too Smith (2012).
4. Flannery and Marcus (2012) trace the history of accumulation and inequality even further back before agriculture.
5. A thrilling account is given by Frankopan (2015).
6. Woolf (2012), Edwards (1999).
7. An excellent introduction to current thought is Zuiderhoek (2016).
8. Scobie (1990), Quartermaine (1995).
9. Pocock (1999–2005), Boletsi and Moser (2015), Sheehan (1980).

CHAPTER 2

1. There are many collections comparing ancient cities. Some of the best are Ucko, Tringham, and Dimbleby (1972), Storey (2006), Marcus and Sabloff (2008), and Abrams and Wrigley (1978). There have been some useful journal surveys too including Cowgill (2004), Yoffee (2009), and Smith (2002). A wonderful place to keep track of new developments is Michael E. Smith's blog "Wide Urban World," at http://wideurban-world.blogspot.com/.
2. Mithen (2003) offers an impressive global history of the Holocene.
3. Gamble (2013).
4. A strong theme of Diamond (1997).
5. MacCormack (2007).
6. Abu-Lughod (1989).
7. See Parker (2008), and on a related theme Vasunia (2013).

8. Stringer (2011) and Gamble (2013) both offer lucid accounts of various stages of this story, but new discoveries already make some of their accounts out of date.

9. See Crawford and Campbell (2012) for an intriguing discussion of our difference from other apes. For a lucid up-to-date account of the expansion of early humans see Bellwood (2013) and the first volume of Ness (2013), edited by Bellwood.

10. O'Brien and Johnson (2005).

11. Stringer (2011), Gamble (2010).

12. Taylor (2010), Hodder (2018).

13. Mithen (1996).

14. Wells and Stock (2012).

15. See Colinvaux (1978) for the idea of a leap down the food chain.

16. Sahlins (1974).

17. Wilson (2012).

18. Dunbar (1998), Dunbar, Gamble, and Gowlett (2010).

19. Aureli et al. (2008). For a brilliant application see Graeber and Wengrow (2018).

20. Trautmann, Feeley-Harnik, and Mitani (2011).

21. Hodder (2012).

CHAPTER 3

1. A vast literature is devoted to this change. Good guides include Barker (2006) and Bellwood (2001, 2005). Interesting dimensions explored in Diamond and Bellwood (2003), Zeder (2008), and Price and Bar-Yosef (2011).

2. Colinvaux (1978).

3. Bellwood (2005).

4. Diamond (1997).

5. Crosby (1972, 1986).

6. Mintz (1985).

7. Diamond and Bellwood (2003).

8. A wonderful, and elegaic, case study is Elvin (2004).

9. Sahlins (1974).

10. Hodder (1990).

11. Hodder (2010).

12. Dunbar (1993, 1998).

13. Sherratt (1990).
14. Schmidt (2010), Banning (2011).
15. Sherratt (2007).
16. Sherratt (1983), Greenfield (2010), Halstead and Isaakidou (2011).

CHAPTER 4

1. The most accessible translation is George (2000). For more detail see George (2003).
2. On Sumer and the Mesopotamian Bronze Age see Postgate (1992a), Van De Mieroop (1997), and Crawford (2004).
3. For cuneiform and its origins, uses, and history see Radner and Robson (2011).
4. Brown (2008).
5. See Adams (1981) and for a clear recent account McMahon (2013). The rise of cities is located within in much larger scale patterns of change by Wilkinson et al. (2014).
6. Oates et al. (2007).
7. Postgate (1992a).
8. A classic formulation is that of Childe (1950). Modern commentaries on this narrative include Smith (2009), Yoffee (2005), and Wengrow (2010).
9. Clarke (1979).

CHAPTER 5

1. For this kaleidoscopic chapter I have drawn heavily on the essays gathered in Renfrew and Bahn (2014).
2. Scott (1998).
3. Adams (1981).
4. Kohl (2007), Wilkinson, Sherratt, and Bennet (2011), Wilkinson et al. (2014).
5. Wengrow (2006).
6. Allchin (1995), Kenoyer (2008), Wright (2010).
7. Zadneprovsky (1995).
8. Chang (1974, 1986), von Falkenhausen (2008). On early China in general see Feng (2013).
9. Adams (1966), Hirth (2008), Manzanilla (2014).
10. Isendahl and Smith (2013).

11. Makowski (2008).
12. Among a large number of comparative studies of the origin of urbanism are Childe (1950) with Smith (2009); Adams (1966), Smith (1989), Yoffee (2005). A few conferences have produced good collections of essays about different early urbanisms: Nichols and Charlton (1997), Smith (2003), Storey (2006), Marcus and Sabloff (2008), Creekmore and Fisher (2014), Yoffee (2015). Thought-provoking challenges to the orthodoxy are offered by Clarke (1979), Yoffee (2009), and Graeber and Wengrow (2018).
13. Smith (2009, 2012), Yoffee (2005).
14. Childe (1942).
15. Renfrew (1979), Yoffee and Cowgill (1988), Tainter (1988), Diamond (2005), Middleton (2017).
16. Fletcher (2012).
17. Leighton (1999, 155–157).
18. Blake (2008).
19. Fourchard (2011).
20. Kusimba (2008), Kusimba, Kusimba, and Agbaje-Williams (2006).
21. Clarke (1979).
22. Sherratt (1990).

CHAPTER 6

1. Purcell (2016).
2. On premodern globalizations see Kohl (2007), Jennings (2011), Pitts and Versluys (2015), Boivin and Fraschetti (2018).
3. Anthony (2007).
4. Wengrow (2014).
5. Wilkinson et al. (2014).
6. Schneider (1977), Rowlands, Larsen, and Kristiansen (1987), Sherratt (1993).
7. Trigger (2003).
8. Woods (2010), Houston (2004).
9. Bryce (2005).
10. Kristiansen and Suchowska-Ducke (2015).
11. Sherratt (1981, 1983), Greenfield (2010), Halstead and Isaakidou (2011).
12. Fagan (2015).
13. Clutton-Brook (1992).
14. Anthony (2007, 2013).

15. Szuchmann (2009).
16. Harmanşah (2013), Bryce (2013).
17. Bryce (2005).
18. Harding and Coles (1979).
19. Kristiansen and Larsson (2005).
20. Cherry (1990), Broodbank (2006).
21. Broodbank (2013). For the connection with developments in the Ancient Near East see Sherratt and Sherratt (1991).
22. Broodbank (2010).
23. Pulak (1998), Wachsmann (2000).

CHAPTER 7

1. Fundamental studies include Broodbank (2013) on prehistory and Horden and Purcell (2000) on the historical period. See also Grove and Rackham (2001, Abulafia (2003), Harris (2005), Malkin (2005), Blake and Knapp (2005), Horden and Kinoshita (2014). This chapter and the next also draw heavily on Knapp and van Dommelen (2015).
2. King (1999).
3. On wetlands, see Purcell (1996b), Marzano (2013), Blouin (2014). On upland resources see Garnsey (1988b).
4. A theme of Horden and Purcell (2000).
5. Garnsey (1988a), Halstead and O'Shea (1989).
6. Thonemann (2011).
7. Osborne and Cunliffe (2005) considers the Iron Age, but some essays have wider application, e.g., Purcell (2005b).
8. Garnsey (1988a, 1999).
9. Cherry (1990), Dawson (2011).
10. See Malone (2015) for a clear account.
11. Halstead and O'Shea (1982).
12. On maritime transport see Bass (1972), Casson (1974), André and Baslez (1993), Pomey (1997), Robinson and Wilson (2011), Harris and Iara (2011).
13. Finley (1964), Grethlein (2010).
14. Knapp (2008) is the best guide to Cyprus in prehistory.
15. For discussion of the various ways to interpret this see Knapp (1990).
16. Manning et al. (2014).
17. Cline and Harris-Cline (1998).
18. Broodbank (2000).

19. Dickinson (1994), Bennet (2007). A classic study with much still of value is Renfrew (1972). For a short synoptic account see Dickinson (2014), and for collections of recent work see Shelmerdine (2008), Cline (2010).

20. Letesson and Knappett (2017).

21. Whitelaw (2017).

22. Bevan (2010), Bevan and Wilson (2013), Whitelaw (2017).

23. Whitelaw (2000).

24. Manning (2008).

25. Chadwick (1976).

26. Kelder (2006).

27. Blake (2008).

28. Sandars (1978).

29. Michel (2008).

30. Rossel et al. (2008).

31. Edens and Kohl (1993).

32. Sherratt (1993).

CHAPTER 8

1. Murray (2017).

2. Snodgrass (1971), Whitley (1991), Morgan (2009), Morris (2000).

3. Morris (2007).

4. Iacovou (2008, 2012), Knapp (2008), Janes (2010).

5. Sherratt (2003).

6. See Snodgrass (1989) on the complexities of the transition. More widely, see Wertime and Muhly (1980), Sørensen and Thomas (1989).

7. For the wider picture, see Wertime and Muhly (1980), Sørensen and Thomas (1989).

8. On the tenth century and after see the general account in Whitley (2001), and also discussion in Morris (2000), Morgan (2009), and Papadopolous (2015). Still useful are Snodgrass (1971, 1980) and many of the papers now republished in Snodgrass (2006).

9. Popham, Touloupa, and Sackett (1982). The site has generated a huge bibliography alongside the fieldwork publications in the British School of Athens supplements series. For various interpretations see Morris (2000), Whitley (2001), Osborne (2009).

10. For parallels to the structure lying under the mound see Marzarakis Ainian (1997).

11. Morgan (2003), chapter 3.
12. Wees (1992), Bowden (1993), Brown (1984).
13. Blake (2008).
14. Kelder (2006).
15. Janes (2010), Iacovou (2012).
16. Aubet (2001, 2008), Sagona (2008), González de Canales, Serrano, and Llompart (2006).
17. On identity issues see Crawley Quinn and Vella (2014), Quinn (2017).
18. Radner (2010).
19. On the Near eastern background see Aubet (2013).
20. Negbi (1992), Shaw (1989).
21. Curtin (1984), Bentley (1993).
22. Polanyi, Arensberg, and Pearson (1957).
23. On ports-of-trade see Polanyi, Arensberg, and Pearson (1957); on Naukratis see Möller (2000).
24. Aubet (2008). For the link to Assyrian expansion see Frankenstein (1979).
25. Wachsmann (2000).
26. Harris and Iara (2011), Robinson and Wilson (2011).
27. Neville (2007), Sherratt and Sherratt (1993).
28. For the calculations see Scheidel (2007), Frier (2000).
29. Bresson (2005).
30. The have been attempts to give the language of colonization new meanings more appropriate to antiquity, but the modern resonances are so strong it seems better to do without it. On the debate see Osborne (1998b), Boardman (2001), Hurst and Owen (2005), Purcell (2005a), Bradley and Wilson (2006). Naturally there is a great deal of importance in studies that do use this analogy, e.g., Boardman (1964), Graham (1982), Descoeudres (1990), Tsetskhladze and De Angelis (1994), Boardman (1999).
31. Quite apart from the lack of evidence for a difference in their activities, some early characterizations of Phoenicians have uncomfortable anti-semitic resonances.
32. A vivid account is included in Cunliffe (2001).
33. Dietler and López-Ruiz (2009).
34. Blake (1998), van Dommelen (1998, 2002), Hayne (2010).
35. Van Dommelen (2005), Hodos (2006), Bietti Sestieri (2015).
36. On early Iron Age Italian societies see Ridgway and Ridgway (1979), Smith (1996, 2005), Bradley, Isayev, and Riva (2007).

CHAPTER 9

1. Clarke (1979) says it as well as any. See also Smith (1989, 2002).
2. See Osborne and Cunliffe (2005) for an overview.
3. Riva (2005).
4. On the Etruscans and their ancestry see Barker and Rasmussen (1998), Spivey and Stoddart (1990). On the first cities see Riva (2010).
5. For the big picture see Sherratt and Sherratt (1993).
6. See Riva and Vella (2006) for discussion of the term. Also see Riva (2010), chapter 3.
7. On the global culture of the symposia see Murray (1990), Murray and Tecusan (1995).
8. Frey (1969), Zaghetto (2007). And for north of the Alps see Bouloumié (1988).
9. Izzet (2007).
10. Stoddart and Whitley (1988).
11. Barker and Rasmussen (1998).
12. Hansen (2000, 2002). See also Mohlo, Raaflaub, and Emlen (1991), Nichols and Charlton (1997).
13. For an example from Greece see Millett (1993).
14. Harris (1971).
15. Renfrew and Cherry (1986), Snodgrass (1986).
16. Smith (1996). For wider contexts see Bradley, Isayev, and Riva (2007), Harding and Coles (1979).
17. A good account is included in Cornell (1995).
18. Dietler (1989).
19. Riva (2015).
20. Blake (2015).
21. Hodos (2009, 2006), van Dommelen (2012).
22. Among other guides to this period see Snodgrass (1980), Fisher and van Wees (1998), Osborne and Cunliffe (2005), Osborne (2009), Raaflaub and van Wees (2009), Riva (2010), Hall (2014).
23. Jeffrey and Johnson (1990), Powell (1991).
24. Finley (1964). See also Morris (2000), Grethlein (2010).
25. Vansina (1985). For an application to Greek history see Hall (2008).
26. Morris (1986).
27. See Feeney (2016) on the great exception, Rome.
28. Bickerman (1952), Dougherty (1993b), Wiseman (1995), Malkin (1998), Erskine (2001), Calame (2003), Gruen (2005), Hall (2008), Woolf (2011), and many others.

29. Erskine (2001).
30. See Hornblower and Morgan (2007) for some historical context.
31. Hall (1989).
32. Hall (2002). See also Hall (2004).
33. Van Dommelen (2005), Purcell (2005b).
34. On the demographics of Greek expansion see Scheidel (2003b).
35. Ridgway (1992), Snodgrass (1994), Ridgway (1994).
36. Graham (1982), Boardman (1999).
37. Purcell (2005b).

CHAPTER 10

1. See Malkin (2011) for a compelling account.
2. Snodgrass (1971, 2006). See also Morris (1987), Whitley (1991), de Polignac (1995). For a clear up-to-date account see Morgan (2009).
3. Morris (1991).
4. Fletcher (2012).
5. For the wider story see Mithen (2012).
6. Garnsey (1988a).
7. West (2003), Austin (1970).
8. See Herodotus *Histories* 7.102, with discussion in Thomas (2000, 103–113).
9. Morris (2004), Ober (2010).
10. Scully (1990).
11. Morris (1986).
12. Snodgrass (1980), Burkert (1992).
13. Osborne (1998a).
14. Osborne (1998b).
15. Snodgrass (1994).
16. Osborne (2009).
17. See Ridgway (1992), and for Sicily see de Angelis (2016).
18. Möller (2000), Villing and Schlotzhauer (2006).
19. Braun (1982), Brown (1984).
20. Scheidel (2003b).
21. Harris (1989), Adams, Janse, and Swain (2002). For the wider picture see Mullen and James (2012).
22. Cartledge (1993), Skinner (2012).
23. On the ideology of mother and daughter cities see Graham (1964), with Shepherd (2009).
24. Malkin (2011). See also Hall (2002, 2004).

25. Zugtriegel (2017).
26. Hall (1989).
27. Woolf (1994).
28. Dietler and López-Ruiz (2009).
29. Scheidel (2003b).
30. Hansen and Nielsen (2004).
31. Osborne (2009, 110–124), Tsetskhladze (2006a, b).
32. Calame (2003), Dougherty (1993b), Hall (2008), Hornblower (2004).

CHAPTER 11

1. Frederiksen (1984).
2. The phrase is that of Lane Fox (2008).
3. Erskine (2001).
4. Malkin (1994).
5. Purcell (1990b).
6. Morgan (1990).
7. Luraghi (2006).
8. Granovetter (1973).
9. Herman (1987).
10. Murray (1990), Bouloumié (1988).
11. Snodgrass (1986), Renfrew and Cherry (1986).
12. Bowden (1993).
13. D'Agostino (1990).
14. Salmon (1984).
15. Shipley (1984).
16. Scheidel (2003b) and also Morris (1987).
17. Scheidel (2007).
18. Osborne (1987).
19. Wees (1992).

CHAPTER 12

1. See Herodotus 1.163–167 for the story.
2. Finley (1964), Grethlein (2010).
3. Thomas (1989).
4. Hansen (2000, 2002).
5. Morris (1987), Riva (2010).

6. See de Polignac (1995), with elaboration in Alcock and Osborne (1994), Morgan (2003).
7. Yoffee (2005).
8. Cartledge (2009).
9. Herodotus *Histories*, 3.80–82.
10. Morgan (2003), Dench (1995).
11. Lewis (2006).
12. Osborne (1995).
13. Eisenstadt (1963), Morris and Scheidel (2009), Alcock et al. (2001), Arnason and Raaflaub (2011), Bang and Bayly (2011).
14. Lewis (1994), Mairs (2011). On material aspects of the satrapal system see now Khatchadourian (2016).
15. Kuhrt (2001).
16. Hansen and Nielsen (2004).
17. Jones (1999), Price (2005).
18. Aubet (2001), Crawley Quinn and Vella (2014), Quinn (2017).

CHAPTER 13

1. Abulafia (2003, 2011), Horden and Kinoshita (2014).
2. Horden and Purcell (2000).
3. Horden and Purcell (2000), Broodbank (2013), Malkin (2011).
4. Halstead and O'Shea (1982).
5. Shaw (2004).
6. Harrison (2000).
7. Khatchadourian (2016), Briant (1982).
8. Postgate (1992b), Radner (2012), Bedford (2009).
9. Kuhrt (1987, 2001).
10. Sherwin-White and Kuhrt (1993), Millar (1993).
11. Alcock et al. (2001), Bang and Bayly (2011, 2003).
12. Briant (2012).
13. Woolf (2012, 19–23).
14. Calame (2003), Hall (2005), Dougherty (1993b).
15. Woolf (2017).
16. Lavan (2013).
17. Cartledge (2002).
18. Malkin (1994).
19. Morris (2009).

20. Nixon and Price (1990).
21. See Scheidel (2007) and for a slightly higher figure Frier (2000).
22. Garnsey (1988a).
23. Terrenato (2019).
24. Polybius *Histories*, 3.22.

CHAPTER 14

1. Fernández-Götz, Wendling, and Winger (2014), Fernández-Götz and Krausse (2017), Buchsenschutz (2015).
2. Isayev (2007), Bradley, Isayev, and Riva (2007).
3. Zanker (1976), Terrenato (2019).
4. Dench (1995).
5. Williams (2001).
6. Williams (2001).
7. Champion (1980, 2013), Nachtergael (1977).
8. Frankenstein and Rowlands (1978).
9. Sherratt and Sherratt (1993), Sherratt and Sherratt (1991).
10. Harris (1999a, 1980), Nash Briggs (2003), Scheidel (1997), Nash (1985, 1987), Taylor (2001).
11. Sherratt (1995).
12. Arrian, *Alexander's Expedition* 7.9.2.
13. Briant (2002).
14. Gruen (1984).
15. Austin (1986).
16. Sherwin-White and Kuhrt (1993).
17. Whittaker (1978).
18. Gabba (1976).
19. De Ste. Croix (1981).

CHAPTER 15

1. Kennedy (1985).
2. On the recovery of the classical past see Schnapp (1997).
3. Lepelley (1979–1981).
4. Greenhalgh (2012).
5. MacDonald (1986).
6. Lane Fox (1986).

7. Rogers (1991).
8. Spawforth and Walker (1986), Jones (1999).
9. Spawforth (1994), Nachtergael (1977).
10. Newby (2005), Oliver (1968).
11. Swain (1996, 284–297).
12. Burrell (2004).
13. Oliver (1970), Tobin (1997).
14. Whitmarsh (2010).
15. Howgego, Heuchert, and Burnett (2005).
16. Clarke (2008), Price (2005).
17. Harding (2008).
18. Veyne (1976), Zuiderhoek (2009), Gauthier (1985), Nutton (1978).
19. Van Bremen (1996), Hemelrijk (2015).
20. Garnsey (1991).
21. Zuiderhoek (2009).
22. Morris (1992), Davidson (1997).
23. Loraux (1981).
24. Mattingly (1997).
25. Stewart (2004).
26. Ferrary (1988).
27. Oliver (1970, 1983).
28. Dodge and Ward-Perkins (1992).
29. Meiggs (1980, 1982), Harris (2017).
30. Steinby (1993).
31. Oleson (2008).
32. Nielsen (1990), Delaine (1997).
33. Pausanias 10.4.1, discussed helpfully by Prezler (2007, 90–93).
34. Elsner (1992).
35. Yegul (1992).
36. König (2005), van Nijf (2001).
37. Caldelli (1993, 1997).
38. Golvin (1988).
39. Rossetto and Sartorio (1994), Tosi (2003), Laurence, Esmonde Cleary, and Sears (2011).
40. Yegul (1992).
41. De Polignac (1995).
42. Burkert (1987).

43. Östenberg, Malmberg, and Bjørnebye (2015).
44. Goldhill (1987), Parker (1996).
45. Flower (2004), Beard (2007).
46. Rice (1983).
47. Rice (1983), Price (1987), McCormick (1986).
48. Rogers (1991), Wörrle (1988), Graf (2015).

CHAPTER 16

1. Harmanşah (2012).
2. Greenwalt (1995), Cahill (2008).
3. Dougherty (1993b, 1993a).
4. Alcock (2002), Luraghi (2008), Luraghi and Alcock (2003).
5. Millar (1993).
6. Woolf (2017), Radner (2012).
7. Bar-Kochva (1979).
8. Bowman and Rathbone (1992).
9. Crawley Quinn and Vella (2014), Quinn (2017), van Dommelen (1998, 2002, 2005).
10. Erskine (2001), Woolf (2011), Jiménez Díez (2015).
11. Graham (1964).
12. For the traditional position on Roman colonies see Vittinghof (1952), Salmon (1969). For recent challenges see Patterson (2006a), Bispham (2006), Sweetman (2011), Pelgrom and Stek (2014).
13. Bispham (2006).
14. Dench (1995).
15. Terrenato (2019), van Dommelen and Terrenato (2007).
16. Purcell (1990a).
17. Bispham (2007), a story continued in Patterson (2006b).
18. Rosenstein (2004), Hopkins (1978a), Broadhead (2007), Brunt (1962), Keppie (1983).
19. Broadhead (2000, 2007).
20. Salmon (1969, 128–132).
21. Keppie (1983).
22. Sweetman (2011).
23. Levick (1967).
24. De Ligt and Northwood (2008).
25. Scott (1998).

CHAPTER 17

1. Levick (1967).
2. Polybius VI.27–42.
3. Raaflaub and Ramsey (2017).
4. Erdkamp (1998).
5. Allison (2013), van Driel-Murray (1995).
6. Isaac (1990).
7. MacMullen (1963).
8. Coulston (2000), Bingham (2013).
9. See Shipley (2000), Prag and Crawley Quinn (2013) for recent re-evaluations.
10. Millar (1969), de Lange (1978), Ma (1999).
11. Gauthier (1985).
12. Alcock (1993).
13. Millar (1983b).
14. Spawforth and Walker (1986), Jones (1999).
15. Austin (1986), Ma (2003).
16. Harris (1979), Gruen (1984), Eckstein (2007, 2006).
17. Herodotus 7.151.
18. Murray (1965), Swain (1996).
19. Small (1996), Price (1984).
20. Veyne (1976), Zuiderhoek (2009).
21. Wörrle (1988), Mitchell (1990).
22. Cébeillac-Gervason (1981).
23. Bispham (2007).
24. Eck (1984).
25. Brunt (1976).
26. See Eisenstadt (1963), Hardt and Negri (2000) on empires in general. On early empires see Alcock et al. (2001), Bang and Kolodziejczyz (2012), Arnason and Raaflaub (2011). For their dynamics, see Lavan, Payne, and Weisweiler (2016), Morris and Scheidel (2009).
27. Lewis (1994).
28. Herodotos *Histories* 3.89–97.
29. Briant (1982, 2017).
30. Eck (1979).
31. Brunt (1981), Cottier et al. (2008).
32. Braund (1982).

33. Creighton (2000) and *RIB* 91.
34. Cornwell (2015).
35. Richardson (1976).
36. Chilver (1941, 7–8).
37. Tchernia (1983), Crawford (1985), Hermon (1993).
38. Woolf (1998, 2000).
39. Ward-Perkins (1970).
40. De Ste. Croix (1981).
41. Brunt (1990).
42. Kehoe (1988).
43. France (2001).
44. Millar (1983a).

CHAPTER 18

1. See McCormick et al. (2012) for the Roman warm period. For views of the whole of Roman urbanism see Hopkins (1978b), Gros and Torelli (2007).
2. Reece (1988), Jones (1987); compare with Laurence, Esmonde Cleary, and Sears (2011).
3. Lepelley (1979–1981).
4. Foss (1979), Kennedy (1985), Roueché and Reynolds (1989).
5. Nicolet, Ilibert, and Depaule (2000).
6. Kondoleon (2000), McKenzie (2007).
7. Haas (1997), Liebeschuetz (1972), Sandwell (2007).
8. Clarke (2008).
9. Dougherty (1993b), Malkin (1994, 2011).
10. Homer *Odyssey*, 9.105–115 (trans. Lattimore).
11. Thucydides *History*, 1.2.1-2 (trans. Crawley).
12. Morley (1997).
13. Haensch (1997).
14. Mitchell (1976), Kolb (2001).
15. Garnsey (1988b).
16. Hopkins (1980, 1995–1996).
17. See Morley (1996, 1997), Rathbone (2009) on the impact of Rome on existing networks.
18. Rutherford (2007, 2013), van Nijf and Williamson (2015), Collar (2013).
19. Elsner and Rutherford (2005).

20. Woolf (2016).

21. Adams (2007), Alcock, Bodel, and Talbert (2012), Laurence (1999), Chevallier (1976).

22. Schäfer (2016), Harris and Iara (2011).

23. Campbell (2012), Malmberg (2015), Purcell (2012).

24. Leveau (1999), Patterson and Coarelli (2008).

25. Adams and Laurence (2001), Adams (2007), Casson (1974).

26. Laurence (1999), Adams and Laurence (2001), Alcock, Bodel, and Talbert (2012).

27. The 2018 report on *World Urbanization Prospects* can be read at United Nations, n.d., "World Urbanization Prospects 2018," accessed 16th December 2019 https://esa.un.org/unpd/wup/.

28. Hansen and Nielsen (2004).

29. De Vries (1984).

30. Woolf (2000).

31. See Universiteit Leiden, n.d., "An empire of two thousand cities", accessed 16th December 2019 https://www.universiteitleiden.nl/en/research/research-projects/humanities/an-empire-of-2000-cities-urban-networks-and-economic-integration-in-the-roman-empire (2,000 cities); Bowman and Wilson (2011); especially Wilson (2011) (1,856 cities). Most recently see Hanson (2016) (1,388 cities).

32. Shaw (1981).

33. Hodder and Hassall (1971).

34. Purcell (2016).

35. Woolf (1993), Pitts (2010), Fernández-Götz (2014), Fernández-Götz and Krausse (2013, 2017), Fernández-Götz, Wendling, and Winger (2014).

36. See https://github.com/sfsheath/roman-amphitheaters. See also Laurence, Esmonde Cleary, and Sears (2011, chapter 10).

37. Golvin (1988).

38. Tosi (2003).

39. Wilson (2011), Hanson (2016).

40. Kusimba (2008), Fletcher (2012), Isendahl and Smith (2013).

41. Jashemski (1979–1993).

42. Purcell (1988), Goodman (2007), Esmonde Cleary (1987).

43. Wilson (2011).

44. Hanson (2016).

45. Scheidel (2007), Frier (2000).

46. Wengrow (2006).
47. Bowman (2000) and for villages, see Rathbone (1990).
48. Bagnall and Frier (1994).
49. Jones (1937, 1940).
50. Mitchell (1993), Thonemann (2013).
51. Thonemann (2011).
52. Ma (1999).
53. Millett (1990), Woolf (1998), Laurence, Esmonde Cleary, and Sears (2011).
54. Burnham and Wacher (1990), Petit and Mangan (1994).
55. On mobility in the Roman period see de Ligt and Tacoma (2016), Lo Cascio, Giardina, and Tacoma (2017), Tacoma (2016), Woolf (2016), Moatti (2004, 2006, 2013, 2014).
56. Harper (2017), McCormick et al. (2012), Scheidel (2018).
57. Halstead and O'Shea (1989), Garnsey (1988a), Horden and Purcell (2000).
58. Lewis (1996), Kolb (2000).

CHAPTER 19

1. See Brunt (1971) for an early estimate. See also Hopkins (1978a, 1978b), Storey (1997).
2. Virgil *Eclogue*, 11.19–25.
3. For some views of the Roman cultural context see Habinek and Schiesaro (1997), Wallace-Hadrill (2008), Edwards (1996).
4. Zanker (1988).
5. Purcell (1996a), Haselberger (2002), Favro (2005), Haselberger (2007).
6. Gros (1976).
7. This chapter owes a good deal to Nicolet, Ilibert, and Depaule (2000), the fruit of a project summarized by Virlouvet (2011).
8. Morris (2006).
9. Morris (2006), Gutiérrez, Terrenato, and Otto (2015).
10. Nicolet, Ilibert, and Depaule (2000).
11. For recent estimates of the largest cities of the Roman Mediterranean see Woolf (1997), Wilson (2011), Hanson (2016, 51–56, 66–74). Wilson estimated five cities of over 100,000, Woolf and Hanson around ten cities. These totals are highly approximate.
12. Romano (2000), König (2001).

13. Alcock (1993).

14. Morley (1997), Schäfer (2016), Woolf (1997), Pitts and Versluys (2015).

15. Bekker-Nielsen (2005).

16. Matthews (1975), Harris (1999b).

17. Krautheimer (1983), Van Dam (2010), Grig and Kelly (2012), and on Rome in this period see Curran (2000).

18. Purcell (1999).

19. For these estimage see the entry for Constantinople in Khazhdan (1991).

20. Wickham (2009).

21. Purcell (2010).

22. Garnsey (1988a).

23. Scheidel (2004a).

24. Hanson (2016, 54).

25. Rakob (2000); see also the description in Strabo *Geography*, 17.3.15.

26. Hanson (2016) calculates a peak population of 150,000 on the basis of occupied area; Rakob (2000) cites Hurst's calculation of an Augustan population of up to 30,000, rising to a peak of 70,000–100,000 in the second century.

27. Garnsey (1988a), Ravitaillement (1994), Erdkamp (2005), Papi (2007), Alston and van Nijf (2008).

28. Forbes and Foxhall (1982), Garnsey (1988a), Halstead and O'Shea (1989).

29. Van Oyen (2015).

30. Mithen (2012).

31. Richardson (1983), Bannon (2009).

32. Morley (1996), Garnsey (1988a), Ravitaillement (1994), Jongman (2007).

33. Pavis d'Escurac (1976), Virlouvet (1995).

34. Radner (2012).

35. Woolf (2017).

36. Woolf (2000).

37. Scheidel (2003a, 2001, 2005, 2004b). For different views see Hin (2013), Lo Cascio (2006).

38. Patterson (2006b).

39. Seneca *Epistles*, 91.

40. Aldrete (2007).

41. McNeill (1976).

42. Little (2007). For a recent survey see Harper (2017), but see also Haldon et al. (2018).

CHAPTER 20

1. For overviews see Whittow (1990), Loseby (2009). Key studies and collections include Rich (1992), Christie and Loseby (1996), Lavan (2001), Liebeschuetz (2001), Krause and Witschel (2006).
2. Esmonde Cleary (1989, 2013).
3. Ward-Perkins (2005).
4. Laurence, Esmonde Cleary, and Sears (2011).
5. De Kisch (1979), Woolf (2000).
6. Blagg (1990), Hörster (2001).
7. Février et al. (1980), Kulikowski (2004), Esmonde Cleary (2013), Underwood (2019).
8. Loseby (2009).
9. Kennedy (1985).
10. Russell (2013, 2012).
11. Pitts and Versluys (2015), Belich et al. (2016), Witcher (2000), Sweetman (2007), Hingley (2005).
12. Braudel (1949).
13. Horden and Kinoshita (2014).
14. Sallares (1991).
15. Grove and Rackham (2001), Harris (2013), Hope and Marshall (2000).
16. See Pirenne (1937) for the original thesis of a seventh-century watershed. See Hodges and Whitehouse (1983) and for and interesting re-evaluation see Squatriti (2002).
17. McCormick et al. (2012), Scheidel (2018).
18. See Harper (2017) for the best scenario of this kind to date. For doubts see Haldon et al. (2018).
19. Wickham (1984).
20. Millar (1969).
21. Wickham (2005), especially chapter 10.
22. Ward-Perkins (1984).
23. Lepelley (1979–1981).
24. Foss (1979), Liebeschuetz (1972), Sandwell (2007).
25. Holling (1973).
26. Redman and Kinzig (2003); see also McAnany and Yoffee (2010) with critical comments by Bollig (2014), White and O'Hare (2014).
27. McAnany and Yoffee (2010).
28. Lenski (2016).

29. Kelly (2004).
30. Millar (1983a).

AFTERWORD

1. Fustel de Coulanges (1864), Finley (1977), Jones (1940), Murray and Price (1990).
2. Wickham (2005).

FURTHER READING

1. Weber (1958).
2. Wirth (1938), Sjoberg (1960), Finley (1977), Abrams and Wrigley (1978).
3. Childe (1939, 1950), nicely discussed by Smith (2009).
4. Ucko, Tringham, and Dimbleby (1972), Abrams and Wrigley (1978). This second collection was intended to include an essay that has been very influential in this book, Clarke (1979), but his early death meant it was published later with his collected papers.
5. Storey (2006), Marcus and Sabloff (2008). Despite the titles there is also interesting material on urbanism in Nichols and Charlton (1997).
6. Yoffee (2015).
7. Smith (2019)
8. Smith (2002, 2009, 2010, 2012), and see The Wide Urban World (n.d.) consulted on 16th December 2019 http://wideurbanworld.blogspot.com/.
9. See Yoffee (2005) and also his paper (2009); Wengrow (2010) and also Graeber and Wengrow (2018).
10. See Finley (1973, 1977), with responses by Leveau (1983, 1985), Parkins (1997), Mattingly and Salmon (2001), Purcell (2010), Osborne and Wallace-Hadrill (2013).
11. Rich and Wallace-Hadrill (1991).
12. Zuiderhoek (2016).
13. Osborne and Cunliffe (2005).
14. Knapp and van Dommelen (2015).
15. Horden and Purcell (2000), Broodbank (2013).

Bibliography

Abrams, Philip, and E. A. Wrigley, eds. 1978. *Towns in Societies: Essays in Economic History and Historical Sociology, Past and Present Publications.* Cambridge: Cambridge University Press.

Abu-Lughod, Janet. 1989. *Before European Hegemony: The World System, A.D. 1250–1350.* Oxford: Oxford University Press.

Abulafia, David, ed. 2003. *The Mediterranean in History* London: Thames and Hudson.

Abulafia, David. 2011. *The Great Sea: A Human History of the Mediterranean.* London: Allen Lane.

Adams, Colin. 2007. *Land Transport in Roman Egypt: A Study of Economics and Administration in a Roman Province.* Oxford: Oxford University Press.

Adams, Colin, and Ray Laurence, eds. 2001. *Travel and Geography in the Roman Empire.* London: Routledge.

Adams, J. N., Mark Janse, and Simon Swain, eds. 2002. *Bilingualism in Ancient Society; Language Contact and the Written Text.* Oxford: Oxford University Press.

Adams, Robert McC. 1966. *The Evolution of Urban Society: Early Mesopotamia and Prehispanic Mexico.* London: Weidenfield and Nicolson.

Adams, Robert McC. 1981. *Heartland of Cities: Surveys of Ancient Settlement and Land Use on the Central Floodplain of the Euphrates.* Chicago: University of Chicago Press.

Alcock, Susan E. 1993. *Graecia Capta: The Landscapes of Roman Greece.* Cambridge: Cambridge University Press.

Alcock, Susan E. 2002. *Archaeologies of the Greek Past: Landscape, Monuments and Memories.* Cambridge: Cambridge University Press.

Alcock, Susan E., John Bodel, and Richard J. A. Talbert, eds. 2012. *Highways, Byways, and Road Systems in the Pre-Modern World.* Malden: Wiley-Blackwell.

Alcock, Susan E., T. D'Altroy, K. D. Morrison, and C. M. Sinopoli, eds. 2001. *Empires: Perspectives from Archaeology and History.* New York: Cambridge University Press.

Alcock, Susan E., and Robin Osborne, eds. 1994. *Placing the Gods: Sanctuaries and Sacred Space in Ancient Greece.* Cambridge: Cambridge University Press.

Aldrete, Gregory S. 2007. *Floods of the Tiber in Ancient Rome.* Baltimore: Johns Hopkins University Press.

Allchin, F. Raymond. 1995. *The Archaeology of Early Historic South Asia: The Emergence of Cities and States.* Cambridge: Cambridge University Press.

Allison, Penelope M. 2013. *People and Spaces in Roman Military Bases.* Cambridge: Cambridge University Press.

Alston, Richard, and Onno van Nijf, eds. 2008. *Feeding the Ancient Greek City*. Louvain-la-Neuve, Belgium: Peeters.

André, Jean-Marie, and Marie-Françoise Baslez. 1993. *Voyager dans l'Antiquité*. Paris: Fayard.

Anthony, David W. 2007. *The Horse, the Wheel and Language: How Bronze Age Riders from the Eurasian Steppes Shaped the Modern World*. Princeton, NJ: Princeton University Press.

Anthony, David W. 2013. "Horses, Ancient Near East and Pharaonic Egypt." In *The Encyclopaedia of Ancient History*, edited by Roger Bagnall, 3311–3314. Malden, MA: Blackwell.

Arnason, Johann P., and Kurt Raaflaub, eds. 2011. *The Roman Empire in Context: Historical and ComparativePperspectives*. Malden, MA: Wiley-Blackwell.

Aubet, Maria Eugenia. 2001. *The Phoenicians and the West: Politics, Colonies and Trade*, 2nd ed. Cambridge: Cambridge University Press.

Aubet, Maria Eugenia. 2008. "Political and Economic Implications of the New Phoenician Chronologies." In *Beyond the Homeland: Markers in Phoenician Chronology*, edited by Claudia Sagona, 179–191. Leuven: Peeters Publishing.

Aubet, Maria Eugenia. 2013. *Commerce and Colonization in the Ancient Near East*. Cambridge: Cambridge University Press.

Aureli, Filipo, Filippo Aureli, Colleen M. Schaffner, Christophe Boesch, Simon K. Bearder, Josep Call, Colin A. Chapman, Richard Connor, Anthony Di Fiore, Robin I. M. Dunbar, S. Peter Henzi, Kay Holekamp, Amanda H.Korstjens, Robert Layton, Phyllis Lee, Julia Lehmann, Joseph H.Manson, Gabriel Ramos-Fernandez, Karen B. Strier, and Carel P. van Schaik 2008. "Fission-Fusion Dynamics." *Current Anthropology* 49 (4): 627–654.

Austin, Michel. 1970. *Greece and Egypt in the Archaic Age: Proceedings of the Cambridge Philological Society Supplements*. Cambridge: Cambridge Philological Society.

Austin, Michel. 1986. "Hellenistic Kings, War and the Economy." *Classical Quarterly* 36 (2): 450–466.

Bagnall, Roger, and Bruce W. Frier. 1994. *The Demography of Roman Egypt*. Cambridge: Cambridge University Press.

Bang, Peter Fibiger, and Christopher A. Bayly. 2003. "Tributary Empires in History: Comparative Perspectives from Antiquity to the Late Mediaeval," special issue of *The Mediaeval History Journal* 6 (2).

Bang, Peter Fibiger, and Christopher A. Bayly, eds. 2011. *Tributary Empires in Global History*. Basingstoke: Palgrave MacMillan.

Bang, Peter Fibiger, and Dariusz Kolodziejczyz, eds. 2012. *Universal Empire: A Comparative Approach to Imperial Culture and Representation in Eurasian History*. Cambridge: Cambridge University Press.

Banning, E. B. 2011. "So Fair a House: Göbekli Tepe and the Identification of Temples in the Pre-Pottery Neolithic of the Near East." *Current Anthropology* 52 (5): 619–660.

Bannon, Cynthia. 2009. *Gardens and Neighbours: Private Water Rights in Roman Italy.* Ann Arbor: University of Michigan Press.

Bar-Kochva, Bezalel. 1979. *The Seleucid Army: Organization and Tactics in the Great Campaigns.* Cambridge: Cambridge University Press.

Barker, Graeme. 2006. *The Agricultural Revolution in Prehistory: Why Did Foragers Become Farmers?* Oxford: Oxford University Press.

Barker, Graeme, and Tom Rasmussen. 1998. *The Etruscans.* Malden, MA: Blackwell.

Bass, George, ed. 1972. *History of Seafaring.* London: Thames and Hudson.

Beard, Mary. 2007. *The Roman Triumph.* Cambridge, MA: Harvard University Press.

Bedford, Peter R. 2009. "The Neo-Assyrian Empire." In *The Dynamics of Ancient Empires: State Power from Assyria to Byzantium,* edited by Ian Morris and Walter Scheidel, 30–65. New York: Oxford University Press.

Bekker-Nielsen, Tønnes, ed. 2005. *Ancient Fishing and Fish Processing in the Black Sea Region.* Aarhus: Aarhus University Press.

Belich, James, John Darwin, Margret Frenz, and Chris Wickham, eds. 2016. *The Prospect of Global History.* Oxford: Oxford University Press.

Bellwood, Peter. 2001. "Early Agriculturalist Population Diasporas? Farming, Languages, and Genes." *Annual Review of Anthropology* 30: 181–207.

Bellwood, Peter. 2005. *First Farmers: The Origins of Agricultural Societies.* Malden, MA: Blackwell.

Bellwood, Peter. 2013. *First Migrants: Ancient Migration in Global Perspective.* Malden, MA: Blackwell.

Bennet, John. 2007. "The Aegean Bronze Age." In *Cambridge Economic History of the Greco-Roman World,* edited by Walter Scheidel, Ian Morris, and Richard P. Saller, 175–210. Cambridge: Cambridge University Press.

Bentley, Jerry H. 1993. *Old World Encounters: Cross-Cultural Contacts and Exchanges in Pre-Modern Times.* Oxford: Oxford University Press.

Bevan, Andrew. 2010. "Political Geography and Palatial Crete." *Journal of Mediterranean Archaeology* 23 (1): 27–54.

Bevan, Andrew, and Alan G. Wilson. 2013. "Models of Settlement Hierarchy Based on Partial Evidence." *Journal of Archaeological Science* 40 (5): 2415–2427.

Bickerman, Elias. 1952. "Origines Gentium." *Classical Philology* 47 (2): 65–81.

Bietti Sestieri, Anna Maria. 2015. "Sicily in Mediterranean History in the Second Millennium B.C." In *Cambridge Prehistory of the Bronze and Iron Age Mediterranean,* edited by A. Bernard Knapp and Peter van Dommelen, 74–95. New York: Cambridge University Press.

Bingham, Sandra. 2013. *The Praetorian Guard: A History of Rome's Elite Special Forces.* London: I. B. Tauris.

Bispham, Edward. 2006. "Coloniam Deducere: How Roman Was Roman Colonization during the Middle Republic." In *Greek and Roman Colonization: Origins, Ideologies and Interactions,* edited by Guy Bradley and John-Paul Wilson, 73–160. Swansea: Classical Press of Wales.

Bispham, Edward. 2007. *From Asculum to Actium: The Municipalization of Italy from the Social War to Augustus.* Oxford: Oxford University Press.

Blagg, Tom. 1990. "Architectural Munificence in Britain. The Evidence of Inscriptions." *Britannia* 21: 13–31.

Blake, Emma. 1998. "Sardinia's Nuraghi: Four Millennia of Becoming." *World Archaeology* 30 (1): 59–71.

Blake, Emma. 2008. "The Mycenaeans in Italy. A Minimalist Position." *Papers of the British School at Rome* 76: 1–34.

Blake, Emma. 2015. "Late Bronze Age Sardinia: acephalous cohesion." In *Cambridge Prehistory of the Bronze and Iron Age Mediterranean*, edited by A. Bernard Knapp and Peter van Dommelen, 96–108. New York: Cambridge University Press.

Blake, Emma, and A. Bernard Knapp, eds. 2005. *The Archaeology of Mediterranean Prehistory.* Malden, MA: Blackwell.

Blouin, Katherine. 2014. *Triangular Landscapes: Environment, Society, and the State in the Nile Delta under Roman Rule.* Oxford: Oxford University Press.

Boardman, John. 1964. *The Greeks Overseas.* London: Penguin Books.

Boardman, John. 1999. *The Greeks Overseas: Their Early Colonies and Trade,* 4th ed. London: Thames and Hudson.

Boardman, John. 2001. "Aspects of 'Colonization'." *Bulletin of the American Schools of Oriental Research* 322 (May 2001): 33–42.

Boivin, Nicole, and Michael Fraschetti, eds. 2018. *Globalization in Prehistory: Contact, Exchange, and the "People Without History."* Cambridge: Cambridge University Press.

Boletsi, Maria, and Christian Moser, eds. 2015. *Barbarism Revisited: New Perspectives on an Old Concept.* Leiden: Brill.

Bollig, Michael. 2014. "Resilience—Analytical Tool, Bridging Concept or Developmental Goal? Anthropological Perspectives on the Use of a Border Object." *Zeitschrift für Ethnologie* 139 (2): 253–279.

Bouloumié, Bernard. 1988. "Le symposion gréco-étrusque et l'aristocratie celtique." In *Les Princes Celtes et la Méditerranée*, edited by Jean-Pierre Mohen, Alain Duval, and Christian Eluère, 343–383. Paris: Documentation Française.

Bowden, Hugh. 1993. "Hoplites and Homer: Warfare, Hero Cult and the Ideology of the Polis." In *War and Society in the Roman World*, edited by John Rich and Graham Shipley, 45–63. London: Routledge.

Bowman, Alan. 2000. "Urbanization in Roman Egypt." In *Romanization and the City: Creations, Transformations and Failures*, edited by Elizabeth Fentress, 173–187. Portsmouth, RI: Journal of Roman Archaeology.

Bowman, Alan K., and Dominic Rathbone. 1992. "Cities and Administration in Roman Egypt." *Journal of Roman Studies* (82): 107–127.

Bowman, Alan, and Andrew Wilson, eds. 2011. *Settlement, Urbanization, and Population.* Oxford: Oxford University Press.

Bradley, Guy, Elena Isayev, and Corinna Riva, eds. 2007. *Ancient Italy: Regions Without Boundaries.* Exeter: University of Exeter Press.

Bradley, Guy, and John-Paul Wilson, eds. 2006. *Greek and Roman Colonization: Origins, Ideologies and Interactions*. Swansea: Classical Press of Wales.

Braudel, Fernand. 1949. *La Mediterranee et le Monde mediterraneen, a l'epoque de Philippe II*. Paris: A. Colin.

Braun, T. F. R. G. 1982. "The Greeks in the Near East." In *Cambridge Ancient History III: The Expansion of the Greek World, Eighth to Sixth Centuries B.C.*, edited by John Boardman and N. G. L. Hammond, 1–31. Cambridge: Cambridge University Press.

Braund, David. 1982. *Rome and the Friendly King: The Character of the Client Kingship*. London: Croom Helm.

Bresson, Alain. 2005. "Ecology and Beyond. The Mediterranean Paradigm." In *Rethinking the Mediterranean*, edited by William Vernon Harris, 94–114. Oxford: Oxford University Press.

Briant, Pierre. 1982. *Rois, Tributs et Paysans: Études sur les formations tributaires du Moyen-Orient ancien*. Paris: Les Belles Lettres.

Briant, Pierre. 2002. *From Cyrus to Alexander: A History of the Persian Empire*, translated by Peter T. Daniels. Winona Lake: Eisenbraun.

Briant, Pierre. 2012. "From the Indus to the Mediterranean: The Administrative Organization and Logistics of the Great Roads of the Achaemenid Empire." In *Highways, Byways, and Road Systems in the Pre-Modern World*, edited by Susan E. Alcock, John Bodel, and Richard J. A. Talbert, 184–201. Malden, MA: Wiley-Blackwell.

Briant, Pierre. 2017. *Kings, Countries, Peoples: Selected Studies on the Achaemenid Empire*. Translated by Amélie Kuhrt, Stuttgart: Franz Steiner Verlag.

Broadhead, William. 2000. "Migration and Transformation in Northern Italy in the 3rd–1st Centuries B.C." *Bulletin of the Institute of Classical Studies* (44): 145–166.

Broadhead, William. 2007. "Colonization, Land Distribution and Veteran Settlement." In *Companion to the Roman Army*, edited by Paul Erdkamp, 148–163. Malden, MA: Wiley-Blackwell.

Broodbank, Cyprian. 2000. *An Island Archaeology of the Early Cyclades*. Cambridge: Cambridge University Press.

Broodbank, Cyprian. 2006. "The Origins and Early Development of Mediterranean Maritime Activity." *Journal of Mediterranean Archaeology* 19 (2): 199–230.

Broodbank, Cyprian. 2010. "'Ships A-sail from Over the Rim of the Sea': Voyaging, Sailing and the Making of Mediterranean Societies c. 3500–800 B.C." In *The Global Origins and Development of Seafaring*, edited by Atholl J. Anderson, James H. Barrett, and Katherine V. Boyle, 249–264. Cambridge: McDonald Institute for Archaeological Research.

Broodbank, Cyprian. 2013. *The Making of the Middle Sea: A History of the Mediterranean from the Beginning to the Emergence of the Classical World*. New York: Oxford University Press.

Brown, David. 2008. "Increasingly Redundant: The Growing Obsolescence of the Cuneiform Script in Babylonia from 539 B.C." In *The Disappearance of Writing*

Systems: Perspectives on Literacy and Communication, edited by John Baines, John Bennet, and Stephen Houston, 73–101. London: Equinox.

Brown, Richard B. 1984. "Greeks in Assyria: Some Overlooked Evidence." *Classical World* 77 (5): 300–303.

Brunt, P. A. 1962. "The Army and the Land in the Roman Revolution." *Journal of Roman Studies* 52: 69–86.

Brunt, P. A. 1971. *Italian Manpower 225 B.C.–A.D. 14*. Oxford: Oxford University Press.

Brunt, P. A. 1976. "The Romanization of the Local Ruling Classes in the Roman Empire." In *Assimilation et résistance à la culture gréco-romaine dans le monde ancien: Travaux du VIe Congrès international d'études classiques (Madrid, septembre 1974)*, edited by D. M. Pippidi, 161–173. Bucharest and Paris: Editura Academiei and Les Belles Lettres.

Brunt, P. A. 1981. "The Revenues of Rome." *Journal of Roman Studies* 71: 161–172.

Brunt, P. A. 1990. "Publicans in the Principate." In *Roman Imperial Themes*, 354–432. Oxford: Clarendon Press.

Bryce, Trevor. 2005. *The Kingdom of the Hittites. New Edition*. Oxford: Oxford University Press.

Bryce, Trevor. 2013. "Anatolian States." In *The Oxford Handbook of the State in the Ancient Near East and Mediterranean*, edited by Peter Fibiger Bang and Walter Scheidel, 161–179. New York: Oxford University Press.

Buchsenschutz, Olivier, ed. 2015. *L'Europe celtique à l'âge du Fer (VIIIe-Ier siècles), Nouvelle Clio, l'histories et ses problèmes*. Paris: Presses Universitaires de France.

Burkert, Walter. 1987. "Die antike Stadte als Festgemeinschaft." In *Stadt und Fest: Zu Geschichte und Gegenwart europäischer Festkultur*, edited by Paul Hugger, Walter Burkert, and Ernst Lichtenhahn, 25–44. Unträgeri: W&H Verlags.

Burkert, Walter. 1992. *The Orientalizing Revolution: Near Eastern Influence on Greek Culture in the Early Archaic Age*. Cambridge, MA: Harvard University Press.

Burnham, B. C., and John Wacher. 1990. *The Small Towns of Roman Britain*. Berkeley: University of California Press.

Burrell, Barbara. 2004. *Neokoroi: Greek Cities and Roman Emperors*. Leiden: Brill.

Cahill, Nicholas, ed. 2008. *Love for Lydia: A Sardis Anniversary Volume Presented to Crawford H. Greenewalt, Jr., Archaeological Exploration of Sardis*. Cambridge, MA: Archaeological Exploration of Sardis.

Calame, Claude. 2003. *Myth and History in Ancient Greece: The Symbolic Creation of a Colony*. Princeton, NJ: Princeton University Press.

Caldelli, Maria L. 1993. *L'agon Capitolinus: Storia et protagonistici dall'istituzione domiziana al IV secolo, Studi pubblicati dall'Istituto italiano per la storia antica*. Rome: Istituto italiano per la storia antica.

Caldelli, Maria L. 1997. "Gli agoni nelle regioni occidentali dell'impero: La Gallia Narbonensis." *Memorie delle Accademia Nazionale dei Lincei, Classe de Scienze morali, storiche e filologische* ser IX t. 9 (4): 387–481.

Campbell, Brian. 2012. *Rivers and the Power of Ancient Rome, Studies in the history of Greece and Rome*. Chapel Hill: University of North Carolina Press.

Cartledge, Paul. 1993. *The Greeks: A Portrait of Self and Others*. Oxford: Oxford University Press.

Cartledge, Paul. 2002. *Sparta and Laconia: A Regional History 1300–362*. 2nd ed. London: Routledge.

Cartledge, Paul. 2009. *Ancient Greek Political Thought in Practice*. Cambridge: Cambridge University Press.

Casson, Lionel. 1974. *Travel in the Ancient World*. Baltimore: Johns Hopkins University Press.

Cébeillac-Gervason, M., ed. 1981. *Les bourgeoisies municipales italiennes aux IIe et Ier siècles av. J-C*. Centre Jean Berard, Institut Français de Naples: Éditions du CNRS & Bibliothèque de l'Institut Français de Naples,

Chadwick, John. 1976. *The Mycenaean World*. Cambridge: Cambridge University Press.

Champion, T. C. 1980. "Mass Migration in Later Prehistoric Europe." In *Transport Technology and Social Change: Papers Delivered at Tekniska Museet Symposium No 2, Stockholm, 1979*, edited by Per Sörbom, 33–42. Stockholm: Tekniska Museet.

Champion, T. C. 2013. "Protohistoric European Migrations." In *Encyclopaedia of Global Human Migration*, edited by Immanuel Ness, 2463–2468. Malden, MA: Wiley-Blackwell.

Chang, K. C. 1974. "Urbanism and the King in Ancient China." *World Archaeology* 6 (1): 1–14.

Chang, K. C. 1986. *The Archaeology of Ancient China*. 4th enlarged and revised ed. New Haven, CT: Yale University Press.

Cherry, John F. 1990. "The First Colonization of the Mediterranean Islands: A Review of Recent Research." *Journal of Mediterranean Archaeology* 3 (1): 145–221.

Chevallier, Raymond. 1976. *Roman Roads*. London: Batsford.

Childe, V. Gordon. 1939. *Man Makes Himself*. London: Watts & Co.

Childe, V. Gordon. 1942. *What Happened in History*. Harmondsworth: Penguin Books.

Childe, V. Gordon. 1950. "The Urban Revolution." *Town Planning Review* 21 (1): 3–17.

Chilver, G. E. F. 1941. *Cisalpine Gaul: Social and Economic History from 49 BC to the Death of Trajan*. Oxford: Clarendon.

Christie, Neil, and S. T. Loseby, eds. 1996. *Towns in Transition: Urban Evolution in Late Antiquity and the Early Middle Ages*. Aldershot: Scolar.

Clarke, David L. 1979. "Towns in the Development of Early Civilization." In *Analytical Archaeologist: Collected Papers of David L. Clarke Edited By His Colleagues*, edited by N. G. L. Hammond, 435–443. London: Academic Press.

Clarke, Katherine. 2008. *Making Time for the Past: Local History and the Polis*. Oxford: Oxford University Press.

Cline, E. H., ed. 2010. *Oxford Handbook of the Bronze Age Aegean*. Oxford: Oxford University Press.

Cline, E. H., and D. Harris-Cline, eds. 1998. *The Aegean and the Orient in the Second Millennium: Proceedings of the 50th Anniversary Symposium, University of Cincinnati, 18–20 April 1997, Aegaeum*. Liège: University de Liège.

Clutton-Brook, Juliet. 1992. *Horse Power: A History of the Horse and the Donkey in Human Societies*. Cambridge, MA: Harvard University Press.

Colinvaux, Paul A. 1978. *Why Big Fierce Animals Are Rare: An Ecologist's Perspective*. Princeton, NJ: Princeton University Press.

Collar, Anna. 2013. *Religious Networks in the Roman Empire: The Spread of New Ideas*. Cambridge: Cambridge University Press.

Cornell, Tim. 1995. *The Beginnings of Rome: Italy and Rome from the Bronze Age to the Punic Wars (c. 1000–264 BC)*. London: Routledge.

Cornwell, Hannah. 2015. "The King Who Would Be Prefect: Authority and Identity in the Cottian Alps." *Journal of Roman Studies* 105: 41–72.

Cottier, Michel, Michael H. Crawford, C. V. Crowther, Jean-Louis Ferrary, Barbara Levick, and Michael Wörrle, eds. 2008. *The Customs Law of Asia*. Oxford: Oxford University Press.

Coulston, J. C. N. 2000. "Armed and Belted Men: The Soldiery in Imperial Rome." In *Ancient Rome: The Archaeology of the Eternal City*, edited by J. C. N. Coulston and Hazel Dodge, 76–118. Oxford: Oxford University School of Archaeology.

Cowgill, George. 2004. "Origins and Development of Urbanism: Archaeological Perspectives." *Annual Review of Anthropology* (33): 525–549.

Crawford, Harriet E. W. 2004. *Sumer and the Sumerians*. 2nd ed. Cambridge: Cambridge University Press.

Crawford, Michael H. 1985. *Coinage and Money under the Roman Republic: Italy and the Mediterranean Economy*. London: Methuen.

Crawford, Michael H., and Benjamin C. Campbell, eds. 2012. *Causes and Consequences of Human Migration: An Evolutionary Perspective*. New York: Cambridge University Press.

Crawley Quinn, Josephine, and Nicholas C. Vella, eds. 2014. *The Punic Mediterranean: Identities and identification from Phoenician Settlement to Roman Rule*. Cambridge: Cambridge University Press.

Creekmore, Andrew T., and Kevin D. Fisher, eds. 2014. *Making Ancient Cities: Space and Place in Early Urban Societies*. New York: Cambridge University Press.

Creighton, John. 2000. *Coins and Power in Late Iron Age Britain*. Cambridge: Cambridge University Press.

Crosby, Alfred W. 1972. *The Colombian Exchange: Biological and Cultural Consequences of 1492*. Westport, CT: Greenwood.

Crosby, Alfred W. 1986. *Ecological Imperialism: The Biological Expansion of Europe, 900–1900*. Cambridge: Cambridge University Press.

Cunliffe, Barry. 2001. *Facing the Ocean: The Atlantic and Its Peoples, 8000 BC–1500 AD*. Oxford: Oxford University Press.

Curran, John. 2000. *Pagan City and Christian Capital: Rome in the Fourth Century*. Oxford: Clarendon Press.

Curtin, Philip. 1984. *Cross-Cultural Trade in World History*. Cambridge: Cambridge University Press.

D'Agostino, Bruno. 1990. "Military Organization and Social Structure in Archaic Etruria." In *The Greek City from Homer to Alexander*, edited by Oswyn Murray and S .R. F. Price, 59–84. Oxford: Oxford University Press.

Davidson, James. 1997. *Courtesans and Fishcakes: The Consuming Passions of Classical Athens*. London: Harper Collins.

Dawson, Helen. 2011. "Island Colonization: Settling the Neolithic Question." In *Islands in the Neolithic: IInitial Occupation and Survival Strategies in the Mediterranean*, edited by Nellie Phoca-Cosmetatou, 31–53. Oxford: University of Oxford School of Archaeology.

de Angelis, Franco. 2016. *Archaic and Classical Greek Sicily: A Social and Economic History*. New York: Oxford University Press.

De Kisch, Yves. 1979. "Tarifs de donation en Gaule romaine d'après des inscriptions." *Ktema* 4: 259–280.

de Lange, N. R. M. 1978. "Jewish Attitudes to the Roman Empire." In *Imperialism in the Ancient World*, edited by Peter Garnsey and C. R. Whittaker, 255–281. Cambridge: Cambridge University Press.

de Ligt, Luuk, and Simon Northwood, eds. 2008. *People, Land and Politics: Demographic Developments and the Transformation of Roman Italy 300 BC–AD 14*. Leiden: Brill.

de Ligt, Luuk, and Laurens E. Tacoma, eds. 2016. *Migration and Mobility in the Early Roman Empire*. Leiden: Brill.

de Polignac, F. 1984. *La naissance de la cité greque: Cultes, espaces et société VIII-VI siécle av. J. C.* Paris, Éditions la Découverte.

de Polignac, François. 1995. *Cults, Territory, and the Origins of the Greek City-State*. Translated by Janet Lloyd. Chicago: University of Chicago Press.

de Ste. Croix, G. E. M. 1981. *The Class Struggle in the Ancient Greek World: From the Archaic Age to the Arab Conquests*. London: Duckworth.

de Vries, Jan. 1984. *European Urbanization 1500–1800*. London: Methuen.

Delaine, Janet. 1997. *The Baths of Caracalla: A Study in the Design, Construction, and Economics of Large-Scale Building Projects in Imperial Rome*. Portsmouth, RI: Journal of Roman Archaeology.

Dench, Emma. 1995. *From Barbarians to New Men: Greek, Roman and Modern Perceptions of Peoples of the Central Apennines*. Oxford: Oxford University Press.

Descoeudres, Jean-Paul, ed. 1990. *Greek Colonists and Native Populations: Proceedings of the First Australian Congress of Classical Archaeology Held in Honour of Emeritus Professor A. D. Trendall, Sydney, 9–14 July 1985*. Oxford: Clarendon Press.

Diamond, Jared. 1997. *Guns, Germs and Steel: A Short History of Everybody for the Last 13,000 Years*. London: Jonathon Cape.

Diamond, Jared M. 2005. *Collapse: How Societies Choose to Fail or Survive*. London: Allen Lane.

Diamond, Jared, and Peter Bellwood. 2003. "Farmers and Their Languages: The First Expansions." *Science* 300: 597–603.

Dickinson, Oliver. 1994. *The Aegean Bronze Age*. Cambridge: Cambridge University Press.

Dickinson, Oliver. 2014. "The Aegean." In *Cambridge World Prehistory*, edited by Colin Renfrew and Paul Bahn, 1860–1884. New York: Cambridge University Press.

Dietler, Michael. 1989. "Greeks, Etruscans and Thirsty Barbarians: Early Iron Age Interaction in the Rhône Basin of France." In *Centre and Periphery: Comparative Studies in Archaeology*, edited by Tim Champion, 127–141. London: Unwin Hyman.

Dietler, Michael, and Caroline López-Ruiz, eds. 2009. *Colonial Encounters in Ancient Iberia: Phoenician, Greek and Indigenous Relations*. Chicago: Chicago University Press.

Dodge, Hazel, and Bryan Ward-Perkins, eds. 1992. *Marble in Antiquity: Collected Papers of J. B. Ward-Perkins*. London: British School at Rome.

Dougherty, Carol. 1993a. "It's Murder to Found a Colony." In *Cultural Poetics in Archaic Greece: Cult, Performance, Politics*, edited by Carol Dougherty and Leslie Kurke, 178–198. Cambridge: Cambridge University Press.

Dougherty, Carol. 1993b. *The Poetics of Colonization: From City to Text in Archaic Greece*. New York: Oxford University Press.

Dunbar, Robin. 1993. "Coevolution of Neocortical Size, Group Size and Language in Humans." *Behavioral and Brain Sciences* 16: 681–735.

Dunbar, Robin. 1998. "The Social Brain Hypothesis." *Evolutionary Biology* 6 (5): 178–190.

Dunbar, Robin, Clive Gamble, and John Gowlett, eds. 2010. *Social Brain, Distributed Mind: Proceedings of the British Academy*. Oxford: Oxford University Press.

Eck, Werner. 1979. *Die staatliche Organisation Italiens in der hohen Kaiserzeit, Vestigia*. Munich: Beck.

Eck, Werner. 1984. "Senatorial Self-Representation: Developments in the Augustan period." In *Caesar Augustus: Seven Aspects*, edited by Fergus Millar and Erich Segal, 129–167. Oxford: Oxford University Press.

Eckstein, Arthur M. 2006. *Mediterranean Anarchy, Interstate War and the Rise of Rome: Hellenistic Culture and Society*. Berkeley: University of California Press.

Eckstein, Arthur M. 2007. *Rome Enters the Greek East: From Anarchy to Hierarchy in the Hellenistic Mediterranean 230–170 BC*. Oxford: Blackwell Publishers.

Edens, C. M., and Philip L. Kohl. 1993. "Trade and World Systems in Early Bronze Age West Asia." In *Trade and Exchange in Prehistoric Europe*, edited by Chris Scarre and Frances Healy, 17–34. Oxford: Oxbow Books.

Edwards, Catharine. 1996. *Writing Rome: Textual Approaches to the City*. Cambridge: Cambridge University Press.

Edwards, Catharine, ed. 1999. *Roman Presences: Receptions of Rome in European Culture, 1789–1945*. Cambridge: Cambridge University Press.

Eisenstadt, Shmuel. 1963. *The Political Systems of Empires: The Rise and Fall of the Historical Bureaucratic Societies*. London: Free Press of Glencoe.

Elsner, Jas. 1992. "Pausanias: A Greek Pilgrim in the Roman World." *Past and Present* 135: 3–29.

Elsner, Jas, and Ian Rutherford, eds. 2005. *Pilgrimage in Graeco-Roman and Early Christian Antiquity: Seeing the Gods*. Oxford: Oxford University Press.

Elvin, Mark. 2004. *The Retreat of the Elephants: An Environmental History of China*. New Haven, CT: Yale University Press.

Erdkamp, Paul. 1998. *Hunger and the Sword: Warfare and Food Supply in Roman Republican Wars (264–30 B.C.)*. Amsterdam: J. C. Gieben.

Erdkamp, Paul. 2005. *The Grain Market in the Roman Empire: A Social, Political and Economic Study*. Cambridge: Cambridge University Press.

Erskine, Andrew. 2001. *Troy Between Greece and Rome: Local Tradition and Imperial Power*. Oxford: Oxford University Press.

Esmonde Cleary, Simon. 1987. *Extra-Mural Areas of Romano-British Towns*. Oxford: British Archaeological Reports.

Esmonde Cleary, Simon. 1989. *The Ending of Roman Britain*. London: Batsford.

Esmonde Cleary, Simon. 2013. *The Roman West, AD 200–500: An Archaeological Study*. Cambridge: Cambridge University Press.

Fagan, Brian. 2015. *The Intimate Bond: How Animals Shaped Human History*. New York: Bloomsbury.

Favro, Diane. 2005. "Making Rome a World City." In *The Cambridge Companion to the Age of Augustus*, edited by Karl Galinsky, 234–263. New York: Cambridge University Press.

Feeney, Denis. 2016. *Beyond Greek: The Beginnings of Latin Literature*. Cambridge, MA: Harvard University Press.

Feng, Li. 2013. *Early China: A Social and Cultural History*. Cambridge: Cambridge University Press.

Fernández-Götz, Manuel. 2014. "Reassessing the Oppida: The Role of Power and Religion." *Oxford Journal of Archaeology* 33 (4): 379–394.

Fernández-Götz, Manuel, and Dirk Krausse. 2013. "Rethinking Early Iron Age Urbanisation in Central Europe: The Heuneburg Site and Its Archaeological Environment." *Antiquity* 87 (336): 473–487.

Fernández-Götz, Manuel, and Dirk Krausse, eds. 2017. *Eurasia at the Dawn of History: Urbanization and Social Change*. Cambridge: Cambridge University Press.

Fernández-Götz, Manuel, Holger Wendling, and Katja Winger, eds. 2014. *Paths to Complexity: Centralisation and Urbanisation in Iron Age Europe*. Oxford: Oxbow Books.

Ferrary, Jean-Louis. 1988. *Philhellénisme et impérialisme: aspects idéologiques de la conquête romaine du monde hellénistique, de la Seconde Guerre de Macédoine à la Guerre contre Mithridate, Bibliothèque des Ecoles Françaises d'Athènes et de Rome*. Rome: Ecole Française de Rome.

Février, P. A., M. Fixot, C. Goudineau, and V Kruta. 1980. *Histoire de la France Urbaine: I. La ville antique*. Paris: Seuil.

Finley, M. I. 1964. "Myth, Memory and History." *History and Theory* 4 (3): 281–302.

Finley, M. I. 1973. *The Ancient Economy*. Berkeley: University of California Press.

Finley, M. I. 1977. "The Ancient City: From Fustel de Coulanges to Max Weber and beyond." *Comparative Studies in Society and History* 19 (3): 305–327.

Fisher, Nick, and Hans van Wees, eds. 1998. *Archaic Greece: New Approaches and New Evidence*. Swansea: Classical Press of Wales.

Flannery, Kent, and Joyce Marcus. 2012. *The Creation of Inequality: How Our Prehistoric Ancestors Set the Stage for Monarchy, Slavery and Empire*. Cambridge, MA: Harvard University Press.

Fletcher, Roland. 2012. "Low Density, Agrarian Based Urbanism: Scale, Power and Ecology." In *The Comparative Archaeology of Complex Societies*, edited by Michael E. Smith, 285–320. New York: Cambridge University Press.

Flower, Harriet. 2004. "Spectacle and Political Culture in the Roman Republic." In *Cambridge Companion to the Roman Republic*, edited by Harriet Flower, 322–343. New York: Cambridge University Press.

Foss, Clive. 1979. *Ephesus After Antiquity: A Late Antique, Byzantine and Turkish City*. Cambridge: Cambridge University Press.

Fourchard, Laurent 2011. "Between World History and State Formation: New Perspectives on Africa's Cities." *Journal of African History* 52 (2): 223–248.

Foxhall, Lin and Forbes, Hamish A., 1982. "Sitometreia: The Role of Grain as a Staple Food in Classical Antiquity." *Chiron* 12: 41–90.

France, Jérôme. 2001. *Quadragesima Galliarum: L'organisation douanière des provinces alpestres, gauloises et germaniques de l'Empire romain, 1er siècle avant J.-C. - 3er siècle après J.-C.*, Collections de l'École française à Rome. Rome.

Frankenstein, Susan. 1979. "The Phoenicians in the Far West: A Function of Neo-Assyrian Imperialism." In *Power and Propaganda: A Symposium on Ancient Empires*, edited by Møgens Trolle Larsen, 263–294. Copenhagen: Akademisk Forlag.

Frankenstein, Susan, and Michael Rowlands. 1978. "The Internal Structure and Regional Context of Early Iron Age Society in South-Western Germany." *Bulletin of the Institute of Archaeology of the University of London* 15: 73–112.

Frankopan, Peter. 2015. *The Silk Roads: A New History of the World*. London: Bloomsbury.

Frederiksen, M. 1984. *Campania*. London: British School at Rome.

Frey, Otto-Herman. 1969. *Die Entstehung der Situlenkunst: Studien zur figürlich verzierten Toreutik von Este, Römisch-germanische Forschungen*. Berlin: De Gruyter.

Frier, Bruce W. 2000. "Demography." In *Cambridge Ancient History, Volume XI: The High Empire, A.D. 70–192*, edited by Alan Bowman, Peter Garnsey, and Dominic Rathbone, 787–816. Cambridge: Cambridge University Press.

Fustel de Coulanges, Numa Denis. 1864. *La cité antique: Étude sur le culte, le droit, les institutions de la Grèce et de Rome*. Paris: Hachette.

Gabba, Emilio. 1976. *Republican Rome: The Army and the Allies*. Oxford: Blackwell Publishers.

Gamble, Clive. 2010. "Technologies of Separation and the Evolution of Social Extension." In *Social Brain, Distributed Mind*, edited by Robin Dunbar, Clive Gamble, and John Gowlett, 17–42. Oxford: Oxford University Press.

Gamble, Clive. 2013. *Settling the Earth: The Archaeology of Deep Human History*. Cambridge: Cambridge University Press.

Garnsey, Peter. 1988a. *Famine and Food Supply in the Greco-Roman World: Responses to Risk and Crisis*. Cambridge: Cambridge University Press.

Garnsey, Peter. 1988b. "Mountain Economies in Southern Europe." In *Pastoral Economies in Classical Antiquity*, edited by C. R. Whittaker, 196–209. Cambridge: Cambridge Philological Society.

Garnsey, Peter. 1991. "Review Article: The Generosity of Veyne." *Journal of Roman Studies* 81: 164–168.

Garnsey, Peter. 1999. *Food and Society in Classical Antiquity*. Cambridge: Cambridge University Press.

Gauthier, Philippe. 1985. *Les cités grecques et leurs bienfaiteurs Bulletin de correspondance hellénique, suppléments*. Athens: École française d'Athènes.

George, Andrew. 2000. *The Epic of Gilgamesh*. London: Penguin Books.

George, Andrew. 2003. *The Babylonian Gilgamesh Epic: Introduction, Critical Edition and Cuneiform Texts*. Oxford: Oxford University Press.

Goldhill, Simon. 1987. "The Greater Dionysia and Civic Ideology." *Journal of Hellenic Studies* 107: 58–76.

Golvin, Jean-Claude. 1988. *L'amphithéâtre romain: Essai sur la théorisation de sa forme et de ses fonctions*. 2 vols, *Publications du Centre Pierre Paris (UA 991)*. Paris: De Boccard.

González de Canales, F., L. Serrano, and J. Llompart. 2006. "The Pre-Colonial Phoenician Emporium of Huelva ca 900–770 BC." *Babesch* 81: 13–29.

Goodman, Penny. 2007. *The Roman City and Its Periphery: From Rome to Gaul*. London: Routledge.

Graeber, and David Wengrow. 2018. "How To Change the Course of Human History (at Least, the Part That Has Happened Already)." *Eurozine* March 2, 2018. Consulted on December 17, 2019 https://www.eurozine.com/change-course-human-history/

Graf, Fritz. 2015. *Roman Festivals in the Greek East: From the Early Empire to the Middle Byzantine Era*. Cambridge: Cambridge University Press.

Graham, A. J. 1964. *Colony and Mother City in Ancient Greece*. Manchester: Manchester University Press.

Graham, A. J. 1982. "The Colonial Expansion of Greece." In *Cambridge Ancient History III.3: The Expansion of the Greek World, Eighth to Sixth Centuries B.C.*, edited by John Boardman and N. G. L. Hammond, 83–162. Cambridge: Cambridge University Press.

Granovetter, Mark S. 1973. "The Strength of Weak Ties." *American Journal of Sociology* 78 (6): 1360–1380.

Greenfield, Haskel J. 2010. "The Secondary Products Revolution: The Past, the Present and the Future." *World Archaeology* 42 (1): 29–54.

Greenhalgh, Michael. 2012. *From Constantinople to Córduba: Dismantling Ancient Architecture in the East, North Africa and Islamic Spain*. Leiden: Brill.

Greenwalt, Crawford H. 1995. "Sardis in the Age of Xenophon." *Pallas* 43: 125–145.

Grethlein, Jonas. 2010. *The Greeks and their Past: Poetry, Oratory and History in the Fifth Century BCE*. Cambridge: Cambridge University Press.

Grig, Lucy, and Gavin Kelly, eds. 2012. *Two Romes: Rome and Constantinople in Late Antiquity*. Oxford: Oxford University Press.

Gros, Pierre. 1976. *Aurea Templa: Recherches sur l'architecture religieuse de Rome à l'époque d'Auguste, Bibliothèque des écoles françaises d'Athènes et de Rome*. Rome: École française de Rome.

Gros, Pierre, and Mario Torelli. 2007. *Storia dell'urbanistica: Il mondo romano*. 3rd ed. Rome: La Terza.

Grove, A. T., and Oliver Rackham. 2001. *The Nature of Mediterranean Europe: An Ecological History*. New Haven, CT: Yale University Press.

Gruen, Erich. 1984. *The Hellenistic World and the Coming of Rome*. 2 vols. Berkeley: University of California Press.

Gruen, Erich, ed. 2005. *Cultural Borrowings and Ethnic Appropriations in Antiquity*. Stuttgart: Franz Steiner Verlag.

Gutiérrez, Geraldo, Nicola Terrenato, and Adelheid Otto. 2015. "Imperial Cities." In *The Cambridge World History III: Early Cities in Comparative Perspective 4000 BCE–1200 CE*, edited by Norman Yoffee, 532–545. Cambridge: Cambridge University Press.

Haas, Christopher. 1997. *Alexandria in Late Antiquity: Topography and Social Conflict*. Baltimore: Johns Hopkins University Press.

Habinek, Thomas, and Alessandro Schiesaro, eds. 1997. *The Roman Cultural Revolution*. Cambridge: Cambridge University Press.

Haensch, Rudolf. 1997. *Capita Provinciarum: Statthaltersitze und Provinzialverwaltung in der römischen Kaiserzeit, Kölner Forschungen*. Mainz: von Zabern.

Haldon, John F., Hugh Elton, Sabine R. Huebner, Adam Izdebski, Lee Mordechai, and Timothy P. Newfield. 2018. "Plagues, Climate Change, and the End of an Empire: A Response to Kyle Harper's The Fate of Rome. Part 1 Climate," *History Compass* (e12508;).

Haldon, John F., Hugh Elton, Sabine R. Huebner, Adam Izdebski, Lee Mordechai, and Timothy P. Newfield. 2018. "Plagues, Climate Change, and the End of an Empire: A Response to Kyle Harper's The Fate of Rome. Part 2 Plagues and a Crisis of Empire." *History Compass* (e12506).

Haldon, John F., Hugh Elton, Sabine R. Huebner, Adam Izdebski, Lee Mordechai, and Timothy P. Newfield. 2018. "Plagues, Climate Change, and the End of an Empire: A Response to Kyle Harper's The Fate of Rome. Part 3 Disease, Agency and Collapse." *History Compass* (e12507).

Hall, Edith. 1989. *Inventing the Barbarian: Greek Self-Definition Through Tragedy*. Oxford: Oxford University Press.

Hall, Jonathan M. 2002. *Hellenicity: Between Ethnicity and Culture*. Chicago: Chicago University Press.

Hall, Jonathan M. 2004. "How 'Greek' Were The Early Western Greeks?" In *Greek Identity in the Western Mediterranean: Papers in Honour of Brian Shefton*, edited by Kathryn Lomas, 35–54. Leiden: Brill.

Hall, Jonathan M. 2005. "*Arcades His Oris:* Greek Projection on the Italian Ethnoscape?" In *Cultural Borrowings and Ethnic Appropriations in Antiquity*, edited by Erich Gruen, 259–284. Stuttgart: Franz Steiner Verlag.

Hall, Jonathan M. 2008. "Foundation Stories." In *Greek Colonisation: An Account of Greek Colonies and Other Settlements Overseas*, edited by Gocha R Tsetskhladze, 383–426. Leiden: Brill.

Hall, Jonathan M. 2014. *A History of the Archaic Greek World, ca. 1200–479 BCE.* 2nd ed. Chichester: Wiley-Blackwell.

Halstead, Paul, and Valasia Isaakidou. 2011. "Revolutionary Secondary Products: the Development and Significance of Milking, Animal-Traction and Wool-Gathering in Later Prehistoric Europe and the Near East." In *Interweaving Worlds: Systemic Interaction in Eurasia 7th to 1st Millennia BC*, edited by Toby C. Wilkinson, Susan Sherratt, and John Bennet, 61–76. Oxford: Oxbow.

Halstead, Paul, and John O'Shea. 1982. "A Friend in Need is a Friend Indeed: Social Storage and the Origins of Social Ranking." In *Ranking, Resources and Exchange: Aspects of the Archaeology of Early European Society*, edited by Colin Renfrew and Stephen Shennan, 92–99. Cambridge: Cambridge University Press.

Halstead, Paul, and John O'Shea, eds. 1989. *Bad Year Economics: Cultural Responses to Risk and Uncertainty*. Cambridge: Cambridge University Press.

Hansen, Mogens Herman, ed. 2000. *A Comparative Study of Thirty City-State Cultures: An Investigation Conducted by the Copenhagen Polis Centre, Historisk-filosofiske Skrifter*. Copenhagen: Det Kongelige Dansk Videnskabernes Selskab.

Hansen, Mogens Herman, ed. 2002. *A Comparative Study of Six City-State Cultures: An Investigation Conducted by the Copenhagen Polis Centre, Historisk-filosofiske Skrifter*. Copenhagen: Det Kongelige Dansk Videnskabernes Selskab.

Hansen, Møgens Hermann, and Thomas Heine Nielsen. 2004. *An Inventory of Archaic and Classical Poleis: An Investigation Conducted by the Copenhagen Polis Centre for the Danish National Research Foundation*. Oxford: Oxford University Press.

Hanson, J. S. 2016. *An Urban Geography of the Roman World: 100 BC–AD 300*. Oxford: Archeopress.

Harding, Anthony F., and John M. Coles. 1979. *The Bronze Age in Europe: An Introduction to the Prehistory of Europe c. 2000–700*. London: Methuen.

Harding, Phillip. 2008. *The Story of Athens: The Fragments of the Local Chronicles of Attika*. London: Routledge.

Hardt, M., and A Negri. 2000. *Empire*. Cambridge, MA: Harvard University Press.

Harmanşah, Ömür. 2012. "Beyond Aššur: New Cities and the Assyrian Politics of Landscape." *Bulletin of the American Schools of Oriental Research* 365: 53–77.

Harmanşah, Ömür. 2013. *Cities and the Shaping of Memory in the Ancient Near East*. Cambridge: Cambridge University Press.

Harper, Kyle. 2017. *The Fate of Rome: Climate, Disease and the End of an Empire*. Princeton, NJ: Princeton University Press.

Harris, William Vernon. 1971. *Rome in Etruria and Umbria*. Oxford: Clarendon Press.

Harris, William Vernon. 1979. *War and Imperialism in Republican Rome, 327–70 B.C.* Oxford: Clarendon Press.

Harris, William Vernon. 1980. "Towards a Study of the Roman Slave Trade." In *The Seaborne Commerce of Ancient Rome*, edited by John H. D'Arms and E. C. Kopff, 117–140. Rome: American Academy in Rome.

Harris, William Vernon. 1989. *Ancient Literacy*. Cambridge, MA: Harvard University Press.

Harris, William Vernon. 1999a. "Demography, Geography and the Sources of Roman Slaves." *Journal of Roman Studies* 89: 62–75.

Harris, William Vernon, ed. 1999b. *The Transformations of Urbs Roma in Late Antiquity, Journal of Roman Archaeology Supplements*. Portsmouth, RI: Journal of Roman Archaeology.

Harris, William Vernon, ed. 2005. *Rethinking the Mediterranean*. Oxford: Oxford University Press.

Harris, William Vernon. 2013. "Defining and Detecting Mediterranean Deforestation 800 BCE–700 CE." In *The Ancient Mediterranean Environment between Science and History*, edited by William Vernon Harris, 173–194. Leiden: Brill.

Harris, William Vernon. 2017. "The Indispensable Commodity: Notes on the Economy of Wood in the Roman Mediterranean." In *Trade, Commerce, and the State in the Roman World*, edited by Alan Bowman and Andrew Wilson, 211–236. Oxford: Oxford University Press.

Harris, William Vernon, and K. Iara, eds. 2011. *Maritime Technology in the Ancient Economy: Ship-Design and Navigation*. Portsmouth, RI: Journal of Roman Archaeology.

Harrison, Thomas. 2000. *The Emptiness of Asia: Aeschylus' Persians and the History of the Fifth Century*. London: Duckworth.

Haselberger, Lothar, ed. 2002. *Mapping Augustan Rome*. Portsmouth, RI: Journal of Roman Archaeology.

Haselberger, Lothar. 2007. *Urbem Ornare: Die Stadt Rom und ihre Gestaltumwandlung unter Augustus. Rome's urban metamorphosis under Augustus*. Portsmouth, RI: Journal of Roman Archaeology.

Hayne, Jeremy. 2010. "Entangled Identities on Iron Age Sardinia?" In *Material Connections in the Ancient Mediterranean: Mobility, Materiality and Identity*, edited by Peter van Dommelen and A. Bernard Knapp, 147–169. London: Routledge.

Hemelrijk, Emily A. 2015. *Hidden Lives, Public Personae: Women and Civic Life in the Roman West*. Oxford: Oxford University Press.

Herman, Gabriel. 1987. *Ritualized Friendship and the Greek City*. Cambridge: Cambridge University Press.

Hermon, Ella. 1993. *Rome et la Gaule Transalpine avant César (125–59 av. J.-C.), Diáphora*. Quebec: Presses de l'Université Laval.

Hin, Saskia. 2013. *The Demography of Roman Italy: Population Dynamics in an Ancient Conquest Society 201 BCE–14 CE*. Cambridge: Cambridge University Press.

Hingley, Richard. 2005. *Globalizing Roman Culture: Unity, Diversity and Empire*. London: Routledge.

Hirth, Kenneth G. 2008. "Incidental Urbanism: The Structure of the Prehispanic City in Central Mexico." In *The Ancient City: New Perspectives on Urbanism in the Old and New World*, edited by Joyce Marcus and Jeremy A. Sabloff, 273–297. Santa Fe: School for Advance Research Press.

Hodder, Ian. 1990. *The Domestication of Europe*. Oxford: Blackwell.

Hodder, Ian, ed. 2010. *Religion in the Emergence of Civilization: Çatalhöyük as a Case Study*. Cambridge: Cambridge University Press.

Hodder, Ian. 2012. *Entanglement: An Archaeology of the Relationships Between Objects and Things*. Malden, MA: Wiley-Blackwell.

Hodder, Ian. 2018. *Where Are We Heading? The Evolution of Humans and Things*. New Haven, CT: Yale University Press.

Hodder, Ian, and Mark Hassall. 1971. "The Non-Random Spacing of Romano-British Walled Towns." *Man* 6 (3): 391–407.

Hodges, Richard, and David Whitehouse. 1983. *Mohammed, Charlemagne, and the Origins of Europe: Archaeology and the Pirenne Thesis*. London: Duckworth.

Hodos, Tamar. 2006. *Local Responses to Colonization in the Iron Age Mediterranean*. Abingdon: Routledge.

Hodos, Tamar. 2009. "Colonial Engagements in the Global Mediterranean Iron Age." *Cambridge Archaeological Journal* 19 (2): 221–241.

Holling, C. S. 1973. "Resilience and Stability of Ecological Systems." *Annual Review of Ecology and Systematics* 4: 1–28.

Hope, Valerie M., and Eireann Marshall, eds. 2000. *Death and Disease in the Ancient City*. London: Routledge.

Hopkins, Keith. 1978a. *Conquerors and Slaves: Sociological Studies in Roman History I*. Cambridge: Cambridge University Press.

Hopkins, Keith. 1978b. "Economic Growth and Towns in Classical Antiquity." In *Towns in Societies: Essays in Economic History and Historical Sociology*, edited by Philip Abrams and E. A Wrigley, 35–77. Cambridge: Cambridge University Press.

Hopkins, Keith. 1980. "Taxes and Trade in the Roman empire, 200 BC–AD 200." *Journal of Roman Studies* 70: 101–125.

Hopkins, Keith. 1995–1996. "Rome, Taxes, Rents and Trade." *Kodai* 6/7: 41–75.

Horden, Peregrine, and Sharon Kinoshita, eds. 2014. *A Companion to Mediterranean History*. Chichester: John Wiley and Sons.

Horden, Peregrine, and Nicholas Purcell. 2000. *The Corrupting Sea: A Study of Mediterranean History*. Oxford: Blackwell Publishers.

Hornblower, Simon. 2004. *Thucydides and Pindar: Historical Narrative and the World of Epinikian Poetry*. Oxford: Oxford University Press.

Hornblower, Simon, and Catherine Morgan, eds. 2007. *Pindar's Poetry, Patrons, and Festivals, from Archaic Greece to the Roman Empire*. Oxford: Oxford University Press.

Hörster, Marietta. 2001. *Bauinschriften römischer Kaiser: Untersuchung zur Inschriftenpraxis und Bautätigkeit in den Städten des westlichen Imperium Romanum in der Zeit des Prinzipats*. Stuttgart: Franz Steiner.

Houston, Stephen, ed. 2004. *The First Writing: Script Invention as History and Process.* Cambridge: Cambridge University Press.

Howgego, Christopher, Volker Heuchert, and Andrew Burnett, eds. 2005. *Coinage and Identity in the Roman Provinces.* Oxford: Oxford University Press.

Hurst, Henry, and Sara Owen, eds. 2005. *Ancient Colonizations: Analogy, Similarity and Difference.* London: Duckworth.

Iacovou, Maria. 2008. "Cultural and Political Configurations in Iron Age Cyprus: The Sequel to a Protohistoric Episode." *American Journal of Archaeology* 112 (4): 625–657.

Iacovou, Maria, ed. 2012. *Cyprus and the Aegean in the Early Iron Age: The Legacy of Nicolas Coldstream.* Nicosia: Bank of Cyprus Cultural Foundation.

Isaac, Benjamin. 1990. *The Limits of Empire: The Roman Army in the East.* Oxford: Clarendon Press.

Isayev, Elena. 2007. *Inside Ancient Lucania: Dialogues in History and Archaeology.* London: Institute of Classical Studies.

Isendahl, Christian, and Michael E. Smith. 2013. "Sustainable Agrarian Urbanism: The Low-Density Cities of the Mayas and the Aztecs." *Cities.* 31: 132–143.

Izzet, Vedia. 2007. *The Archaeology of Etruscan Society.* Cambridge: Cambridge University Press.

Janes, Sarah. 2010. "Negotiating Island Interactions: Cyprus, the Aegean and the Levant in the Late Bronze to Early Iron Ages." In *Material Connections in the Ancient Mediterranean: Mobility, Materiality and Identity*, edited by Peter van Dommelen and A. Bernard Knapp, 126–146. London: Routledge.

Jashemski, Wilhelmina F. 1979–1993. *The Gardens of Pompeii, Herculaneum and the Villas Destroyed by Vesuvius.* 2 vols. New Rochelle, NY: A. D. Caratzas.

Jeffrey, L. H., and A. W. Johnson. 1990. *The Local Scripts of Archaic Greece: A Study of the Origin of the Greek Alphabet and Its Development from the Eighth to the Fifth Centuries B.C.* 2nd revised ed. Oxford: Clarendon Press.

Jennings, Justin. 2011. *Globalizations and the Ancient World.* New York: Cambridge University Press.

Jiménez Díez, Alicia. 2015. "The Western Empire and the "People without History". A Case Study from Southern Iberia." In *Cultural Memories in the Roman Empire*, edited by Karl Galinsky and Kenneth Lapatin, 170–190. Los Angeles: Getty Publications.

Jones, A. H. M. 1937. *The Cities of the Eastern Roman Provinces.* 2nd ed. Oxford: Clarendon Press.

Jones, A. H. M. 1940. *The Greek City from Alexander to Justinian.* Oxford: Oxford University Press.

Jones, Christopher P. 1999. *Kinship Diplomacy in the Ancient World.* Cambridge, MA: Harvard University Press.

Jones, R. F. J. 1987. "A False Start? The Roman Urbanisation of Western Europe." *World Archaeology* 19 (1): 47–58.

Jongman, Willem M. 2007. "The Early Roman Empire: Consumption." In *Cambridge Economic History of the Greco-Roman World*, edited by Walter Scheidel, Ian Morris, and Richard P. Saller, 592–618. Cambridge: Cambridge University Press.

Kehoe, Dennis P. 1988. *The Economics of Agriculture on Roman Imperial Estates in North Africa, Hypomnemeta*. Göttingen: Vandenhoeck and Ruprecht.

Kelder, Jorrit M. 2006. "Mycenaeans in Western Anatolia." *Talanta* 36–37 (2004–2005): 49–86.

Kelly, Gavin. 2004. "Ammianus and the Great Tsunami." *Journal of Roman Studies* 94: 141–167.

Kennedy, Hugh. 1985. "From Polis to Madina: Urban Change in Late Antique and Early Islamic Syria." *Past and Present* 106 (1): 3–27.

Kenoyer, Jonathan Mark. 2008. "Indus Urbanism: New Perspectives on Its Origins and Culture." In *The Ancient City: New Perspectives on Urbanism in the Old and New World*, edited by Joyce Marcus and Jeremy A. Sabloff, 183–208. Santa Fe: School for Advance Research Press.

Keppie, Lawrence J. F. 1983. *Colonisation and Veteran Settlement in Italy 47–14 BC*. London: British School at Rome.

Khatchadourian, Lori. 2016. *Imperial Matter: Ancient Persia and the Archaeology of Empires*. Oakland, CA: University of California Press.

Khazhdan, Alexander P. 1991. *The Oxford Dictionary of Byzantium*. 3 vols. Oxford: Oxford University Press.

King, Anthony C. 1999. "Diet in the Roman World: A Regional Inter-Site Comparison of the Mammal Bones." *Journal of Roman Archaeology* 12 (1): 168–202.

Knapp, A. Bernard. 1990. "Production, Location, and Integration in Bronze Age Cyprus." *Current Anthropology* 31 (2): 147–176.

Knapp, A. Bernard. 2008. *Prehistoric and Protohistoric Cyprus: Identity, Insularity, and Connectivity*. New York: Oxford University Press.

Knapp, A. Bernard, and Peter van Dommelen, eds. 2015. *Cambridge Prehistory of the Bronze and Iron Age Mediterranean*. New York: Cambridge University Press.

Kohl, Philip L. 2007. *The Making of Bronze Age Eurasia*. New York: Cambridge University Press.

Kolb, Anne. 2000. *Transport und Nachrichtentransfer im Römischen Reich, Klio: Beiträge zur alten Geschichte. Beihefte, neue Folge*. Berlin: Akademie Verlag.

Kolb, Anne. 2001. "Transport and Communication in the Roman State: The Cursus Publicus." In *Travel and Geography in the Roman Empire*, edited by Colin Adams and Ray Laurence, 95–105. London: Routledge.

Kondoleon, Christine, ed. 2000. *Antioch the Lost Ancient City*. Princeton, NJ: Princeton University Press.

König, Jason. 2001. "Favorinus' *Corinthian Oration* in its Corinthian Context." *Proceedings of the Cambridge Philological Society* 47: 141–171.

König, Jason. 2005. *Athletics and Literature in the Roman Empire*. Cambridge: Cambridge University Press.

Krause, Jens-Uwe, and Christian Witschel, eds. 2006. *Die Stadt in der Spätantike--Niedergang oder Wandel? Akten des internationalen Kolloquiums in München am 30. und 31. Mai 2003.* Vol. 190, *Historia Einzelschriften* Stuttgart: Steiner.

Krautheimer, Richard. 1983. *Three Christian Capitals: Topography and Politics.* Berkeley: University of California Press.

Kristiansen, Kristian, and Thomas B. Larsson. 2005. *The Rise of Bronze Age Society: Travels, Transmissions and Transformations.* Cambridge: Cambridge University Press.

Kristiansen, Kristian, and Paulina Suchowska-Ducke. 2015. "Connected Histories: the Dynamics of Bronze Age. Interaction and Trade 1500–1100 BC." *Proceedings of the Prehistoric Society* 81: 361–392.

Kuhrt, Amélie. 1987. "Usurpation, Conquest and Ceremonial: From Babylon to Persia." In *Rituals of Royalty: Power and Ceremonial in Traditional Societies*, edited by David Cannadine and Simon Price, 20–55. Cambridge: Cambridge University Press.

Kuhrt, Amélie. 2001. "The Achaemenid Persian Empire (c. 550–c. 330 BCE): Continuities, Adaptations, Transformations." In *Empires: Perspectives from Archaeology and History*, edited by Susan E. Alcock, T. D'Altroy, K. D. Morrison, and C. M. Sinopoli, 93–123. New York: Cambridge University Press.

Kulikowski, Michael. 2004. *Late Roman Spain and Its Cities.* Baltimore: Johns Hopkins University Press.

Kusimba, Chapurukha M. 2008. "Early African Cities: Their Role in the Shaping of Urban and Rural Interaction Spheres." In *The Ancient City: New Perspectives on Urbanism in the Old and New World*, edited by Joyce Marcus and Jeremy A. Sabloff, 229–246. Santa Fe: School for Advance Research Press.

Kusimba, Chapurukha M., Sibel Barut Kusimba, and Babatunde Agbaje-Williams. 2006. "Precolonial African Cities: Size and Density." In *Urbanism in the Preindustrial World: Cross-Cultural Approaches*, edited by Glenn R. Storey, 145–158. Tuscaloosa: University of Alabama Press.

Lane Fox, Robin. 1986. *Pagans and Christians in the Mediterranean World from the Second Century A.D. to the Conversion of Constantine.* Harmondsworth: Viking.

Lane Fox, Robin. 2008. *Travelling Heroes: Greeks and Their Myths in the Epic Age of Homer.* London: Allen Lane.

Laurence, Ray. 1999. *The Roads of Roman Italy: Mobility and Cultural Change.* London: Routledge.

Laurence, Ray, Simon Esmonde Cleary, and Gareth Sears. 2011. *The City in the Roman West c 250 BC–AD 250.* Cambridge: Cambridge University Press.

Lavan, Luke, ed. 2001. *Recent Research in Late-Antique Urbanism.* Portsmouth, RI: Journal of Roman Archaeology.

Lavan, Myles. 2013. *Slaves to Rome: Paradigms of Empire in Roman Culture.* Cambridge: Cambridge University Press.

Lavan, Myles, Richard E. Payne, and John Weisweiler, eds. 2016. *Cosmopolitanism and Empire: Universal Rulers, Local Elites, and Cultural Integration in the Ancient Near East and Mediterranean.* Cambridge: Cambridge University Press.

Leighton, Robert. 1999. *Sicily Before History: An Archaeological Survey from the Paleolithic to the Iron Age.* London: Duckworth.

Lenski, Noel. 2016. *Constantine and the Cities: Imperial Authority and Civic Politics. Empire and after.* Philadelphia PA: University of Pennsylvania Press.

Lepelley, Claude. 1979–1981. *Les Cités de l'Afrique romaine au Bas-Empire.* 2 vols. Paris: Études Augustiniennes.

Letesson, Quentin, and Carl Knappett, eds. 2017. *Minoan Architecture and Urbanism: New Perspectives on an Ancient Built Environment.* Oxford: Oxford University Press.

Leveau, Philippe. 1983. "La ville antique, 'ville de consommation' (Parasitisme social et économie antique)?" *Études rurales* 89–91: 275–289.

Leveau, Philippe, ed. 1985. *L'origine des richesses dépensées dans la ville antique: Actes du colloque organisé à Aix-en-Provence (11–12 mai 1984).* Aix-en-Provence: Centre Camille Jullian.

Leveau, Philippe. 1999. "Le Rhône romain: Dynamiques fluviales, dynamiques sociales." *Gallia* 56: 1–175.

Levick, Barbara. 1967. *Roman Colonies in Southern Asia Minor.* Oxford: Clarendon.

Lewis, D. M. 1994. "The Persepolis Tablets: Speech, Seal and Script." In *Literacy and Power in the Ancient World,* edited by Alan K. Bowman and Greg Woolf, 17–32. Cambridge: Cambridge University Press.

Lewis, Sian. 1996. *News and Society in the Greek Polis.* London: Duckworth.

Lewis, Sian, ed. 2006. *Ancient Tyranny.* Edinburgh: Edinburgh University Press.

Liebeschuetz, W. 1972. *Antioch: City and Imperial Administration in the Later Roman Empire.* Oxford: Clarendon Press.

Liebeschuetz, W. 2001. *The Decline and Fall of the Roman City.* Oxford: Oxford University Press.

Little, Lester K., ed. 2007. *Plague and the End of Antiquity: The Pandemic of 541–750.* Cambridge: Cambridge University Press and The American Academy in Rome.

Lo Cascio, Elio. 2006. "Did the Population of Imperial Rome Reproduce Itself?" In *Urbanism in the Preindustrial World: Cross-Cultural Approaches,* edited by Glenn R. Storey, 52–68. Tuscaloosa: University of Alabama Press.

Lo Cascio, Elio, Andrea Giardina, and Laurens E. Tacoma, eds. 2017. *The Impact of Mobility and Migration in the Early Roman Empire: Impact of Empire.* Leiden: Brill.

Loraux, Nicole. 1981. *L'invention d'Athènes: Histoire de l'oraison funèbre dans la 'cité classique', Civilisations et sociétés.* Paris: Mouton.

Loseby, S. T. 2009. "Mediterranean Cities." In *A Companion to Late Antiquity,* edited by Philippe Rousseau, 139–155. Malden, MA: Wiley-Blackwell.

Luraghi, Nino. 2006. "Traders, Pirates, Warriors: The Proto-History of Greek Mercenary Soldiers in the Eastern Mediterranean." *Phoenix* 60 (1/2): 21–47.

Luraghi, Nino. 2008. *The Ancient Messenians: Constructions of Ethnicity and Memory.* Cambridge: Cambridge University Press.

Luraghi, Nino, and Susan E. Alcock, eds. 2003. *Helots and their Masters in Laconia and Messenia: Histories, Ideologies, Structures*. Washington, DC and Cambridge, MA: Centre for Hellenic Studies and Harvard University Press.

Ma, John. 1999. *Antiochos III and the Cities of Western Asia Minor*. Oxford: Oxford University Press.

Ma, John. 2003. "Peer Polity Interaction in the Hellenistic Age." *Past and Present* 180: 9–39.

MacCormack, Sabine. 2007. *On the Wings of Time: Rome, the Incas, Spain, and Peru*. Princeton, NJ: Princeton University Press.

MacDonald, William L. 1986. *The Architecture of the Roman Empire II: An Urban Appraisal*. New Haven, CT: Yale University Press.

MacMullen, Ramsay. 1963. *Soldier and Civilian in the Later Roman Empire*. Cambridge, MA: Harvard University Press.

Mairs, Rachel. 2011. *The Archaeology of the Hellenistic Far East*. Oxford: Archaeopress.

Makowski, Krzysztof. 2008. "Andean Urbanism." In *Handbook of South American Archaeology*, edited by Helaine Silverman and William H. Isbell, 633–657.

Malkin, Irad. 1994. *Myth and Territory in the Spartan Mediterranean*. Cambridge: Cambridge University Press.

Malkin, Irad. 1998. *The Returns of Odysseus: Colonization and Ethnicity*. Berkeley: University of California Press.

Malkin, Irad, ed. 2005. *Mediterranean Paradigms and Classical Antiquity*. London: Routledge.

Malkin, Irad. 2011. *A Small Greek World: Networks in the Ancient Mediterranean*. New York: Oxford University Press.

Malmberg, Simon. 2015. "'Ships are Seen Gliding Swiftly along the Sacred Tiber': The River as an Artery of Urban Movement and Development." In *The Moving City. Processions, Passages and Promenades in Ancient Rome*, edited by Ida Östenberg, Simon Malmberg, and Jonas Bjørnebye, 187–201. London: Bloomsbury.

Malone, Caroline. 2015. "The Neolithic in Mediterranean Europe." In *The Oxford Handbook of Mediterranean Europe*, edited by Chris Fowler, Jan Harding, and Daniela Hofmann, 175–194. Oxford: Oxford University Press.

Manning, Sturt W. 2008. "Formation of the Palaces." In *Cambridge Companion to the Aegean Bronze Age*, edited by Cynthia W. Shelmerdine, 105–120. Cambridge: Cambridge University Press.

Manning, Sturt W., Andreou, Georgia-Marina, Fisher, Kevin D., Gerard-Little, Peregrine, Kearns, Catherine, Leon, Jeffrey F., Sewell, David A. and Urban, Thomas M. 2014. "Becoming Urban: Investigating the Anatomy of the Late Bronze Age Complex, Maroni, Cyprus." *Journal of Mediterranean Archaeology* 27 (1): 3–32.

Manzanilla, Linda R. 2014. "The Basin of Mexico." In *The Cambridge World Prehistory*, edited by Colin Renfrew and Paul Bahn, 986–104. New York: Cambridge University Press.

Marcus, Joyce, and Jeremy A. Sabloff, eds. 2008. *The Ancient City: New Perspectives on Urbanism in the Old and New World*. Santa Fe: School for Advanced Research Press.

Marzano, Annalisa. 2013. *Harvesting the Sea: The Exploitation of Marine Resources in the Roman Mediterranean*. Oxford: Oxford University Press.

Marzarakis Ainian, Alexander. 1997. *From Rulers' Dwellings to Temples: Architecure Religion and Society in Early Iron Age Greece (1100–700 B.C.)*. Jonsered: Paul Åströms Förlag.

Matthews, John F. 1975. *Western Aristocracies and Imperial Court, A.D. 364–425*. Oxford: Clarendon Press.

Mattingly, David, and John Salmon, eds. 2001. *Economies Beyond Agriculture in the Classical World*. New York: Routledge.

Mattingly, H. 1997. "Athens Between Rome and the Kings 229/8–129 BC." In *Hellenistic Constructs: Essays in Culture, History and Historiography*, edited by Paul Cartledge, Peter Garnsey, and Erich Gruen, 120–144. Berkeley: University of California Press.

McAnany, Patricia, and Norman Yoffee, eds. 2010. *Questioning Collapse: Human Resilience, Ecological Vulnerability, and the Aftermath of Empire*. Cambridge: Cambridge University Press.

McCormick, Michael. 1986. *Eternal Victory: Triumphal Rulership in Late Antiquity, Byzantium and the Early Medieval West*. Cambridge: Cambridge University Press.

McCormick, Michael, Büntgen, Ulf, Cane, Mark A., Cook, Edward R., Harper, Kyle, Huybers, Peter, Litt, Thomas, Manning, Sturt W., Mayewski, Paul Andrew, More, Alexander F. M., Nicolussi, Kurt, Tegel. Willy 2012. "Climate Change During and After the Roman Empire: Reconstructing the Past from Scientific and Historical Evidence." *Journal of Interdisciplinary History* 43 (2): 169–220.

McKenzie, Judith. 2007. *The Architecture of Alexandria and Egypt, 300 BC to AD 700*. New Haven, CT: Yale University Press.

McMahon, Augusta. 2013. "Mesopotamia." In *The Oxford Handbook of Cities in World History*, edited by Peter Clark, 31–48. Oxford: Oxford University Press.

McNeill, William H. 1976. *Plagues and Peoples*. Garden City, NY: Anchor Press/ Doubleday.

Meiggs, Russell. 1980. "Seaborne Timber Supplies to Rome." In *The Seaborne Commerce of Ancient Rome*, edited by John H. D'Arms and E. C. Kopff, 185–196. Rome: American Academy in Rome.

Meiggs, Russell. 1982. *Trees and Timber in the Ancient Mediterranean World*. Oxford: Oxford University Press.

Michel, Cécile. 2008. "The Old Assyrian Trade in the Light of Recent Kültepe Archives." *Journal of the Canadian Society for Mesopotamian Studies*: 71–82.

Middleton, Guy. 2017. *Understanding Collapse: Ancient History and Modern Myths*. Cambridge: Cambridge University Press.

Millar, Fergus. 1969. "P. Herennius Dexippus: The Greek World and the Third-Century Invasions." *Journal of Roman Studies* 59: 12–29.

Millar, Fergus. 1983a. "Empire and City, Augustus to Julian: Obligations, Excuses and Statuses." *Journal of Roman Studies* 73: 76–96.

Millar, Fergus. 1983b. "The Phoenician Cities: A Case Study in Hellenization." *Proceedings of the Cambridge Philological Society* 29: 54–71.

Millar, Fergus. 1993. *The Roman Near East, 31 BC–AD 337.* Cambridge, MA: Harvard University Press.

Millett, Martin. 1990. *The Romanization of Britain: An Archaeological Essay.* Cambridge: Cambridge University Press.

Millett, Paul. 1993. "Warfare, Economy, and Democracy in Classical Athens." In *War and Society in the Greek World*, edited by John Rich and Graham Shipley, 177–196. London: Routledge.

Mintz, Sidney. 1985. *Sweetness and Power: The Place of Sugar in Modern History.* New York: Viking.

Mitchell, Stephen. 1976. "Requisitioned Transport in the Roman Empire: A New Inscription from Pisidia." *Journal of Roman Studies* 66: 106–131.

Mitchell, Stephen. 1990. "Festivals, Games and Civic Life in Roman Asia Minor." *Journal of Roman Studies* 80: 183–193.

Mitchell, Stephen. 1993. *Anatolia: Land, Men and Gods in Asia Minor, Volume I: The Celts and the Impact of Roman Rule.* Oxford: Oxford University Press.

Mithen, Steven. 1996. *The Prehistory of the Mind: The Cognitive Origins of Art, Religion and Science.* London: Thames and Hudson.

Mithen, Steven. 2003. *After the Ice: A Global Human History, 20,000–5000 B.C.* London: Weidenfield and Nicolson.

Mithen, Steven. 2012. *Thirst: Water and Power in the Ancient World.* Cambridge, MA: Harvard University Press.

Moatti, Claudia, ed. 2004. *La mobilité des personnes en Méditerranée de l'antiquité à l'époque modern: Procédures de contrôle et documents d'identification, Collection de l'Ecole française de Rome.* Rome: École française de Rome.

Moatti, Claudia. 2006. "Translation, Migration, and Communication in the Roman Empire: Three Aspects of Movement in history." *Classical Antiquity* 25 (1): 109–140.

Moatti, Claudia. 2013. "Immigration and Cosmopolitanization." In *Cambridge Companion to Ancient Rome*, edited by Paul Erdkamp, 77–92. Cambridge: Cambridge University Press.

Moatti, Claudia. 2014. "Mobility and Identity Between the Second and the Fourth Centuries: The 'Cosmopolitization' of the Roman Empire." In *The City in the Classical and Post-Classical world: Changing Contexts of Power and Identity*, edited by Claudia Rapp and H. A. Drake, 130–152. Cambridge: Cambridge University Press.

Mohlo, Anthony, Kurt Raaflaub, and Julia Emlen, eds. 1991. *City States in Classical Antiquity and Mediaeval Italy: Athens and Rome, Florence and Venice.* Stuttgart: Franz Steiner Verlag.

Möller, Astrid. 2000. *Naukratis: Trade in Archaic Greece.* Oxford: Oxford University Press.

Morgan, Catherine. 1990. *Athletes and Oracles: The Transformation of Olympia and Delphi in the Eighth Century BC.* Cambridge: Cambridge University Press.

Morgan, Catherine. 2003. *Early Greek States Beyond the Polis*. London: Routledge.

Morgan, Catherine. 2009. "The Early Iron Age." In *A Companion to Archaic Greece*, edited by Kurt Raaflaub and Hans van Wees, 43–63. Malden, MA: Wiley-Blackwell.

Morley, Neville. 1996. *Metropolis and Hinterland: The City of Rome and the Italian Economy 200 B.C.–A.D.200*. Cambridge: Cambridge University Press.

Morley, Neville. 1997. "Cities in Context: Urban Systems in Roman Italy." In *Roman Urbanism. Beyond the Consumer City*, edited by Helen Parkins, 42–58. London: Routledge.

Morris, Ian. 1986. "The Use and Abuse of Homer." *Classical Antiquity* 5 (1): 81–138.

Morris, Ian. 1987. *Burial and Ancient Society: The Rise of the Greek City-State*. Cambridge: Cambridge University Press.

Morris, Ian. 1991. "The Early Polis as City and State." In *City and Country in the Ancient World*, edited by John Rich and Andrew Wallace-Hadrill, 25–57. London: Routledge.

Morris, Ian. 1992. *Death Ritual and Social Structure in Classical Antiquity*. Cambridge: Cambridge University Press.

Morris, Ian. 2000. *Archaeology as Cultural History: Words and Things in Iron Age Greece*. Malden, MA: Blackwell.

Morris, Ian. 2004. "Economic Growth in Ancient Greece." *Journal of Institutional and Theoretical Economics / Zeitschrift für die gesamte Staatswissenschaft* 160 (4): 709–742.

Morris, Ian. 2006. "The Growth of Greek Cities in the First Millennium BC." In *Urbanism in the Preindustrial World: Cross-Cultural Approaches*, edited by Glenn R. Storey, 27–51. Tuscaloosa: University of Alabama Press.

Morris, Ian. 2007. "Early Iron Age Greece." In *Cambridge Economic History of the Greco-Roman World*, edited by Walter Scheidel, Ian Morris, and Richard P. Saller, 211–241. Cambridge: Cambridge University Press.

Morris, Ian. 2009. "The Greater Athenian State." In *The Dynamics of Ancient Empires: State Power from Assyria to Byzantium*, edited by Ian Morris and Walter Scheidel, 99–177. New York: Oxford University Press.

Morris, Ian, and Walter Scheidel, eds. 2009. *The Dynamics of Early Empires: State Power from Assyria to Byzantium*. Oxford: Oxford University Press.

Mullen, Alex, and Patrick James, eds. 2012. *Multilingualism in the Graeco-Roman World*. Cambridge: Cambridge University Press.

Murray, Oswyn. 1965. "Philodemus on the Good King According to Homer." *Journal of Roman Studies* 55 (1/2): 161–182.

Murray, Oswyn, ed. 1990. *Sympotica: A Symposium on the Symposion*. Oxford: Clarendon.

Murray, Oswyn, and Simon Price, eds. 1990. *The Greek City from Homer to Alexander*. Oxford: Oxford University Press.

Murray, Oswyn, and Manuela Tecusan, eds. 1995. *In Vino Veritas*. London: British School at Rome.

Murray, Sarah C. 2017. *The Collapse of the Mycenaean Economy: Imports, Trade, and Institutions, 1300–700 BCE*. New York: Cambridge University Press.

Nachtergael, G. 1977. *Les Galates en Grèce et les Sôteria de Delphes: Recherches d'Histoire et d'Épigraphie Hellénistiques, Mémoires de la Classe de Lettres.* Bruxelles: Académie Royale de Belgique.

Nash Briggs, Daphne. 2003. "Metals, Salt and Slaves: Economic Links Between Gaul and Italy from the Eighth to the Last Sixth Centuries BC." *Oxford Journal of Archaeology* 22 (3): 243–259.

Nash, Daphne. 1985. "Celtic Territorial Expansion and the Mediterranean World." In *Settlement and Society: Aspects of West European Prehistory in the First Century B.C,* edited by T. C. Champion and J. V. S. Megaw, 45–67. Leicester: Leicester University Press.

Nash, Daphne. 1987. "Imperial Expansion under the Roman Republic." In *Centre and Periphery in the Ancient World,* edited by Michael Rowlands, Møgens Trolle Larsen, and Kristian Kristiansen, 87–103. Cambridge: Cambridge University Press.

Negbi, Ora. 1992. "Early Phoenician Presence in the Mediterranean Islands: A Reappraisal." *American Journal of Archaeology* 96 (4): 599–615.

Ness, Immanuel, ed. 2013. *Encyclopaedia of Global Human Migration.* Malden, MA: Wiley-Blackwell.

Neville, Ann. 2007. *Mountains of Silver, Rivers of Gold: The Phoenicians in Iberia.* Oxford: Oxbow Books.

Newby, Zahra. 2005. *Greek Athletics in the Roman World: Victory and Virtue.* New York: Oxford University Press.

Nichols, Deborah L., and Thomas H. Charlton, eds. 1997. *The Archaeology of City States: Cross-Cultural Approaches.* Washington, DC: Smithsonian Institution Press.

Nicolet, Claude, Robert Ilibert, and Jean-Charles Depaule, eds. 2000. *Mégapoles Méditerranéennes: Géographie urbaine rétrospective, Collection de l'école française de Rome.* Rome: École française de Rome.

Nielsen, I. 1990. *Thermae et Balnea: The Architecture and Cultural History of Roman Baths.* 2 vols. Aarhus: Aarhus University Press.

Nixon, Lucia, and Simon Price. 1990. "The Size and Resources of Greek Cities." In *The Greek City from Homer to Alexander,* edited by Oswyn Murray and Simon Price, 137–170. Oxford: Oxford University Press.

Nutton, Vivian. 1978. "The Beneficial Ideology." In *Imperialism in the Ancient World,* edited by Peter Garnsey and C. R. Whittaker, 209–221. Cambridge: Cambridge University Press.

O'Brien, Stephen J., and Warren E. Johnson. 2005. "Big Cat Genomics." *Annual Review of Genomics and Human Genetics* 6: 407–429.

Oates, Joan, Augusta McMahon, Philip Karsgaard, and Jason Ur. 2007. "Early Mesopotamian Urbanism: A New View from the North." *Antiquity* 81: 585–600.

Ober, Josiah. 2010. "Wealthy Hellas." *Transactions and Proceedings of the American Philological Association* 140 (2): 241–286.

Oleson, John Peter, ed. 2008. *The Oxford Handbook of Engineering and Technology in the Classical World.* Oxford: Oxford University Press.

Oliver, James H. 1968. *The Civilizing Power: A Study of the Panathenaic Discourse of Aelius Aristides Against the Background of Literature and Cultural Conflict, with Text, Translation, and Commentary.* Philadelphia: American Philosophical Society.

Oliver, James H. 1970. *Marcus Aurelius: Aspects of Civic and Cultural Policy in the East, Hesperia Supplements.* Princeton, NJ: American School of Classical Studies in Athens.

Oliver, James H. 1983. *The Civic Tradition and Roman Athens.* Baltimore: Johns Hopkins University Press.

Osborne, Robin. 1987. *Classical Landscape with Figures: The Ancient Greek City and Its Countryside.* London: G. Philip.

Osborne, Robin. 1995. *Demos: The Discovery of Classical Attika* Cambridge: Cambridge University Press.

Osborne, Robin. 1998a. *Archaic and Classical Greek Art.* Oxford: Oxford University Press.

Osborne, Robin. 1998b. "Early Greek Colonisation? The Nature of Greek Settlement in the West." In *Archaic Greece: New Approaches and New Evidence*, edited by Nick Fisher and Hans van Wees, 251–270. Swansea: Classical Press of Wales.

Osborne, Robin. 2009. *Greece in the Making 1200–479 BC.* 2nd ed. London: Routledge.

Osborne, Robin, and Barry Cunliffe, eds. 2005. *Mediterranean Urbanization 800–600 BC: Proceedings of the British Academy.* Oxford: Oxford University Press.

Osborne, Robin, and Andrew Wallace-Hadrill. 2013. "Cities of the Ancient Mediterranean." In *The Oxford Handbook of Cities in World History*, edited by Peter Clark, 49–65. Oxford: Oxford University Press.

Östenberg, Ida, Simon Malmberg, and Jonas Bjørnebye, eds. 2015. *The Moving City: Processions, Passages and Promenades in Ancient Rome.* London: Bloomsbury.

Papadopolous, John K. 2015. "Greece in the Early Iron Age: Mobility, Commodities, Polities and Literacy." In *Cambridge Prehistory of the Bronze and Iron Age Mediterranean*, edited by A. Bernard Knapp and Peter van Dommelen, 178–195. Cambridge: Cambridge University Press.

Papi, Emanuele, ed. 2007. *Supplying Rome and the Empire.* Portsmouth, RI: Journal of Roman Archaeology.

Parker, Grant. 2008. *The Making of Roman India: Greek Culture in the Roman World.* Cambridge: Cambridge University Press.

Parker, Robert. 1996. *Athenian Religion: A History.* Oxford: Oxford University Press.

Parkins, Helen M., ed. 1997. *Roman Urbanism: Beyond the Consumer City.* London: Routledge.

Patterson, Helen, and Filippo Coarelli, eds. 2008. *Mercator Placidissimus: The Tiber Valley in Antiquity: New Research in the Upper and Middle River Valley, Rome 27–28 February 2004, Quaderni di Eutopia.* Rome: Edizioni Quasar.

Patterson, John R. 2006a. "Colonization and Historiography: The Roman Republic." In *Greek and Roman Colonization: Origins, Ideologies and Interactions*, edited by Guy Bradley and John-Paul Wilson, 189–212. Swansea: Classical Press of Wales.

Patterson, John R. 2006b. *Landscapes and Cities: Rural Settlement and Civic Transformation in Early Imperial Italy*. Oxford: Oxford University Press.

Pavis d'Escurac, Henriette. 1976. *La préfecture de l'annone: Service administratif impérial d'Auguste à Constantin*. Vol. 226, *Bibliothèque des écoles françaises d'Athènes et de Rome* Rome: École française de Rome.

Pelgrom, Jeromia, and Tessa Stek, eds. 2014. *Roman Republican Colonization: New Perspectives from Archaeology and Ancient History, Papers of the Royal Dutch Institute in Rome*. Rome: Palombi Editori.

Petit, Jean-Paul, and Michel Mangan, eds. 1994. *Les agglomérations secondaires: La Gaule Belgique, les Germanies et l'Occident romain*. Paris: Errance.

Pirenne, Henri. 1937. *Mahomet et Charlemagne*. Paris: F. Alcan.

Pitts, Martin. 2010. "Re-Thinking the Southern British Oppida: Networks, Kingdoms and Material Culture." *European Journal of Archaeology* 13 (1): 32–63.

Pitts, Martin, and Miguel John Versluys, eds. 2015. *Globalisation and the Roman World: World History, Connectivity and Material Culture*. New York: Cambridge University Press.

Pocock, J. G. A. 1999–2005. *Barbarism and Religion*. Cambridge: Cambridge University Press.

Polanyi, Karl, Conrad Maynadier Arensberg, and Harry W. Pearson, eds. 1957. *Trade and Market in the Early Empires: Economies in History and Theory*. Glencoe, IL: Free Press.

Pomey, Patrice, ed. 1997. *La navigation dans l'antiquité*. Aix-en-Provence: Édisud.

Popham, M. E., E. Touloupa, and L. H. Sackett. 1982. "The Hero of Lefkandi." *Antiquity* 56 (218): 169–174.

Postgate, J. N. 1992a. *Early Mesopotamia: Society and Economy at the Dawn of History*. London: Routledge.

Postgate, J. N. 1992b. "The Land of Assur and the Yoke of Assur." *World Archaeology* 23 (3): 247–263.

Powell, Barry B. 1991. *Homer and the Origin of the Greek Alphabet*. Cambridge: Cambridge University Press.

Prag, Jonathan R. W., and Josephine Crawley Quinn, eds. 2013. *The Hellenistic West: Rethinking the Ancient Mediterranean*. Cambridge: Cambridge University Press.

Prezler, Maria. 2007. *Pausanias: Travel Writing in Ancient Greece*. London: Duckworth.

Price, Simon. 1984. *Rituals and Power: The Roman Imperial Cult in Roman Asia Minor*. Cambridge: Cambridge University Press.

Price, Simon. 1987. "From Noble Funerals to Divine Cult: The Consecration of Roman Emperors." In *Rituals of Royalty: Power and Ceremonial in Traditional Societies*, edited by David Cannadine and Simon Price, 56–105. Cambridge: Cambridge University Press.

Price, Simon. 2005. "Local Mythologies in the Greek East." In *Coinage and Identity in the Roman Provinces*, edited by Christopher Howgego, Volker Heuchert, and Andrew Burnett, 115–124. Oxford: Oxford University Press.

Price, T. Douglas, and Ofer Bar-Yosef, eds. 2011. *The Origins of Agriculture: New Data, New Ideas*. Chicago: University of Chicago Press.

Pulak, Cemal. 1998. "The Uluburun Shipwreck: An Overview." *International Journal of Nautical Archaeology* 27 (3): 188–224.

Purcell, Nicholas. 1988. "Town in Country and Country in Town." In *The Ancient Roman Villa Garden*, edited by E. MacDougall, 185–203. Washington, DC: Dumbarton Oaks.

Purcell, Nicholas. 1990a. "The Creation of Provincial Landscape: The Roman Impact on Cisalpine Gaul." In *The Early Roman Empire in the West*, edited by Tom Blagg and M. Millett, 7–29. Oxford: Oxbow Books.

Purcell, Nicholas. 1990b. "Mobility and the Polis." In *The Greek City from Homer to Alexander*, edited by Oswyn Murray and Simon Price, 29–58. Oxford: Oxford University Press.

Purcell, Nicholas. 1996a. "Rome and Its Development Under Augustus and His Successors." In *Cambridge Ancient History, Volume X: The Augustan Empire 43 B.C.–A.D. 69*, edited by Alan Bowman, Edward Champlin, and Andrew Lintott, 782–811. Cambridge: Cambridge University Press.

Purcell, Nicholas. 1996b. "Rome and the Management of Water: Environment, Culture and Power." In *Human Landscapes in Classical Antiquity: Environment and Culture*, edited by Graham Shipley and John Salmon, 180–212. New York: Routledge.

Purcell, Nicholas. 1999. "The Populace of Rome in Late Antiquity: Problems of Classification and Historical Description." In *The Transformations of Urbs Roma in Late Antiquity*, edited by William Vernon Harris, 135–161. Portsmouth, RI: Journal of Roman Archaeology.

Purcell, Nicholas. 2005a. "Colonization and Mediterranean History." In *Ancient Colonizations: Analogy, Similarity and Difference*, edited by Henry Hurst and Sara Owen, 115–139. London: Duckworth.

Purcell, Nicholas. 2005b. "Statics and Dynamics: Ancient Mediterranean Urbanism." In *Mediterranean Urbanization 800–600 BC*, edited by Robin Osborne and Barry Cunliffe, 249–272. Oxford: Oxford University Press.

Purcell, Nicholas. 2010. "Urbanism." In *The Oxford Handbook of Roman Studies*, edited by Alessandro Barchiesi and Walter Scheidel, 579–592. Oxford: Oxford University Press.

Purcell, Nicholas. 2012. "Rivers and the Geography of Power." *Pallas* 90: 373–387.

Purcell, Nicholas. 2016. "Unnecessary Dependences: Illustrating Circulation in Pre-Modern Large-Scale History." In *The Prospect of Global History*, edited by James Belich, John Darwin, Margret Frenz, and Chris Wickham, 65–79. Oxford: Oxford University Press.

Quartermaine, Luisa. 1995. "'Slouching Towards Rome'. Mussolini's Imperial Vision." In *Urban Society in Roman Itay*, edited by Tim Cornell and Kathryn Lomas, 203–215. London: University College London Press.

Quinn, Josephine. 2017. *In Search of the Phoenicians*. Princeton, NJ: Princeton University Press.

Raaflaub, Kurt, and John T. Ramsey. 2017. "Reconstructing the Chronology of Caesar's Gallic Wars." *Histos* 11: 1–74.

Raaflaub, Kurt, and Hans van Wees, eds. 2009. *A Companion to Archaic Greece*. Malden, MA: Blackwell.

Radner, Karen. 2010. "The Stele of Sargon II of Assyria at Kiton: A Focus for an Emerging Cypriot Identity?" In *Interkulturalität in der Alten Welt: Vorderasien, Hellas, Ägypten und die vielfältigen Ebenen des Kontakts*, edited by Robert Rollinger, Birgit Gufler, Martin Lang, and Irene Madreiter, 429–449. Wiesbaden: Harrassowitz Verlag.

Radner, Karen. 2012. "Mass Deportation: The Assyrian Resettlement Policy." University College London. N.d. consulted on 17th December 2019 http://www.ucl.ac.uk/sargon/essentials/governors/massdeportation/.

Radner, Karen, and Eleanor Robson, eds. 2011. *The Oxford Handbook to Cuneiform Culture*. Oxford: Oxford University Press.

Rakob, Friedrich. 2000. "The Making of Augustan Carthage." In *Romanization and the City: Creations, Transformations and Failures*, edited by Elizabeth Fentress, 72–82. Portsmouth, RI: Journal of Roman Archaeology.

Rathbone, Dominic. 1990. "Villages, Land and Population in Graeco-Roman Egypt." *Proceedings of the Cambridge Philological Society* 36: 103–142.

Rathbone, Dominic. 2009. "Merchant Networks in the Greek World: The Impact of Rome." In *Greek and Roman Networks in the Mediterranean*, edited by Irad Malkin, Christy Constantakopoulou, and Katerina Panagopoulou, 299–310. London: Routledge.

Ravitaillement. 1994. *Le ravitaillement en blé de Rome et des centres urbains des débuts de la République jusqu'au Haut Empire: actes du colloque international organisé par le Centre Jean Bérard et l'URA 994 du CNRS, Naples, 14–16 février 1991., Collection de l'École française de Rome*. Rome: École française de Rome.

Redman, Charles L, and Ann P Kinzig. 2003. "Resilience of Past Landscapes: Resilience Theory, Society, and the Longue Durée." *Conservation Ecology* 7 (1). Article 14

Reece, Richard. 1988. *My Roman Britain*. Cirencester: Cotswold Studies.

Renfrew, Colin. 1972. *The Emergence of Civilization: The Cyclades and the Aegean in the Third Millennium BC*. London: Methuen.

Renfrew, Colin. 1979. "Systems Collapse as Social Transformation: Catastrophe and Anastrophe in Early State Societies." In *Transformations: Mathematical Approaches to Culture Change*, edited by Colin Renfrew and K. L. Cooke, 481–506. New York: Academic Press.

Renfrew, Colin, and Paul Bahn, eds. 2014. *Cambridge World Prehistory*. 3 vols. New York: Cambridge University Press.

Renfrew, Colin, and John F. Cherry, eds. 1986. *Peer Polity Interaction and Socio-Political Change*. Cambridge: Cambridge University Press.

Rice, E. E. 1983. *The Grand Procession of Ptolemy Philadelphus*. Oxford: Oxford University Press.

Rich, John, ed. 1992. *The City in Late Antiquity*. London: Routledge.

Rich, John, and Andrew Wallace-Hadrill, eds. 1991. *City and Country in the Ancient World*. London: Routledge.

Richardson, John S. 1976. "The Spanish Mines and the Development of Provincial Taxation in the Second Century B.C." *Journal of Roman Studies* 66: 139–152.

Richardson, John S. 1983. "The Tabula Contrebiensis: Roman Law in Spain in the Early First Century BC." *Journal of Roman Studies* 73: 33–41.

Ridgway, David. 1992. *The First Western Greeks*. Cambridge: Cambridge University Press.

Ridgway, David. 1994. "Phoenicians and Greeks in the West: A View from Pithekoussai." In *The Archaeology of Greek Colonization: Essays Dedicated to Sir John Boardman*, edited by Gocha R Tsetskhladze and Franco De Angelis, 35–46. Oxford: Oxford Committee for Archaeology.

Ridgway, David, and Francesca R. Ridgway, eds. 1979. *Italy Before the Romans: The Iron Age, Orientalizing, and Etruscan Periods*. New York: Academic Press.

Riva, Corinna. 2005. "The Culture of Urbanization in the Mediterranean c. 800–600." In *Mediterranean Urbanization 800–600 BC*, edited by Robin Osborne and Barry Cunliffe, 203–232. Oxford: Oxford University Press.

Riva, Corinna. 2010. *The Urbanization of Etruria: Funerary Practices and Social Change 700–600 BC*. Cambridge: Cambridge University Press.

Riva, Corinna. 2015. "Connectivity Beyond the Urban Community in Central Italy." In *Cambridge Prehistory of the Bronze and Iron Age Mediterranean*, edited by A. Bernard Knapp and Peter van Dommelen, 437–453. Cambridge: Cambridge University Press.

Riva, Corinna, and Nicholas C. Vella, eds. 2006. *Debating Orientalization: Multidisc iplinary Approaches to Change in the Ancient Mediterranean*. Oakville, CT: Equinox.

Robinson, Damian, and Andrew Wilson, eds. 2011. *Maritime Archaeology and Ancient Trade in the Mediterranean*. Oxford: Oxford Centre for Maritime Archaeology.

Rogers, Guy M. 1991. *The Sacred Identity of Ephesos: Foundation Myths of a Roman city*. London: Routledge.

Romano, David. 2000. "A Tale of Two Cities: Roman Colonies at Corinth." In *Romanization and the City: Creations, Transformations and Failures*, edited by Elizabeth Fentress, 83–104. Portsmouth, RI: Journal of Roman Archaeology.

Rosenstein, Nathan Stewart. 2004. *Rome at War: Farms, Families and Death in the Middle Republic*. Chapel Hill: University of North Carolina Press.

Rossel, Stine, Marshall, Fiona, Peters, Joris, Pilgram, Tom, Adams, Matthew D. and O'Connor, David. 2008. "Domestication of the Donkey: Timing, Processes, and Indicators." *Proceedings of the National Academy of Sciences* 105 (10): 3715–3720.

Rossetto, Paola Ciancio, and Giuseppina Pisani Sartorio, eds. 1994. *Teatri greci e romani alle origini del linguaggio rappresentato: Censimento analitico.* 3 vols. Rome: Edizioni SEAT.

Roueché, Charlotte, and Joyce Reynolds. 1989. *Aphrodisias in Late Antiquity: The Late Roman and Byzantine Inscriptions Including Texts from the Excavations at Aphrodisias Conducted by Kenan T. Erim.* London: Society of Roman Studies.

Rowlands, Michael, Møgens Trolle Larsen, and Kristian Kristiansen, eds. 1987. *Centre and Periphery in the Ancient World.* Cambridge: Cambridge University Press.

Russell, Ben. 2012. "Shipwrecks and Stone Cargoes: Some Observations." In *Interdisciplinary Studies on Ancient Stone*, edited by A. Gutierez, P. Lapuente, and I. Roda, 533–539. Tarragona: ICAC.

Russell, Ben. 2013. *The Economics of the Roman Stone Trade.* Oxford: Oxford University Press.

Rutherford, Ian. 2007. "Network Theory and Theoric Networks." *Mediterranean Historical Review* 22 (1): 23–37.

Rutherford, Ian. 2013. *State Pilgrims and Sacred Observers in Ancient Greece: A Study of Theôriâ and Theôroi.* Cambridge: Cambridge University Press.

Sagona, Claudia, ed. 2008. *Beyond the Homeland: Markers in Phoenician Chronology.* Leuven: Peeters Publishing.

Sahlins, Marshall. 1974. *Stone Age Economics.* London: Routledge.

Sallares, Robert. 1991. *The Ecology of the Ancient Greek World.* London: Duckworth.

Salmon, Edward Togo. 1969. *Roman Colonization under the Republic.* London: Thames and Hudson.

Salmon, John. 1984. *Wealthy Corinth: A History of the City to 338 BC.* Oxford: Clarendon.

Sandars, N. K. 1978. *The Sea Peoples: Warriors of the Ancient Mediterranean, 1250–1150 BC.* London: Thames and Hudson.

Sandwell, Isabella. 2007. *Religious Identity in Late Antiquity: Greeks, Jews, and Christians in Antioch.* Cambridge: Cambridge University Press.

Schäfer, Christoph, ed. 2016. *Connecting the Ancient World: Mediterranean Shipping, Maritime Networks and Their Impact, Pharos.* Rahden /Westf.: Verlag Marie Leidorf, Rahden.

Scheidel, Walter. 1997. "Quantifying the Sources of Slaves in the Early Roman Empire." *Journal of Roman Studies* 87: 156–169.

Scheidel, Walter. 2001. *Death on the Nile: Disease and the Demography of Roman Egypt, Mnemosyne Supplements.* Leiden: Brill.

Scheidel, Walter. 2003a. "Germs for Rome." In *Rome the Cosmopolis*, edited by Catharine Edwards and Greg Woolf, 158–176. Cambridge: Cambridge University Press.

Scheidel, Walter. 2003b. "The Greek Demographic Expansion: Models and Comparisons." *Journal of Hellenic Studies* (123): 120–140.

Scheidel, Walter. 2004a. "Creating a Metropolis: A Comparative Demographic Perspective." In *Ancient Alexandria Between Egypt and Greece*, edited by William Vernon Harris and Giovanni Ruffini. Leiden: Brill.

Scheidel, Walter. 2004b. "Human Mobility in Roman Italy, I: The Free Population." *Journal of Roman Studies* 94: 1–26.

Scheidel, Walter. 2005. "Human Mobility in Roman Italy, II: The Slave Population." *Journal of Roman Studies* 95: 64–79.

Scheidel, Walter. 2007. "Demography." In *Cambridge Economic History of the Greco-Roman World*, edited by Walter Scheidel, Ian Morris, and Richard P. Saller, 38–86. Cambridge: Cambridge University Press.

Scheidel, Walter, ed. 2018. *The Science of Roman History: Biology, Climate, and the Future of the Past*. Princeton, NJ: Princeton University Press.

Schmidt, Klaus. 2010. "Göbekli Tepe—The Stone Age Sanctuaries: New Results of Ongoing Excavations with a Special Focus on Sculptures and High Reliefs." *Documenta Praehistorica* 37: 239–256.

Schnapp, Alain. 1997. *The Discovery of the Past*. New York: Harry N. Abrams.

Schneider, Jane. 1977. "Was There a Pre-Capitalist World-System?" *Peasant Studies* 6 (1): 20–29.

Scobie, Alexander. 1990. *Hitler's State Architecture: The Impact of Classical Antiquity*. University Park: Pennsylvania State University Press.

Scott, James C. 1998. *Seeing Like a State: How Certain Schemes to Improve the Human Condition Have Failed*. New Haven, CT: Yale University Press.

Scully, Stephen. 1990. *Homer and the Sacred City*. Ithaca, NY: Cornell University Press.

Shaw, Brent D. 1981. "The Elder Pliny's African Geography." *Historia: Zeitschrift für Alte Geschichte* 30 (4): 421–471.

Shaw, Brent D. 2004. "A Peculiar Island: Maghrib and Mediterranean." *Mediterranean Historical Review* 18 (2): 93–125.

Shaw, Joseph W. 1989. "Phoenicians in Southern Crete." *American Journal of Archaeology* 93 (2): 165–183.

Sheehan, Barry. 1980. *Savagism and Civility: Indians and Englishmen in Colonial Virginia*. Cambridge: Cambridge University Press.

Shelmerdine, Cynthia W., ed. 2008. *Cambridge Companion to the Aegean Bronze Age*. Cambridge: Cambridge University Press.

Shepherd, Gillian. 2009. "Greek 'Colonisation' in Sicily and the West: Some Problems of Evidence and Interpretation Twenty-Five Years On." *Pallas* 79: 15–25.

Sherratt, Andrew. 1981. "Plough and Pastoralism: Aspects of the Secondary Products Revolution." In *Pattern of the Past: Studies in Honour of David Clarke*, edited by Ian Hodder, Glynn Isaac, and Norman Hammond, 261–305. Cambridge: Cambridge University Press.

Sherratt, Andrew. 1983. "The Secondary Exploitation of Animals in the Old World." *World Archaeology* 15 (1): 90–104.

Sherratt, Andrew. 1990. "The Genesis of Megaliths: Monumentality, Ethnicity and Social Complexity in Neolithic North-West Europe." *World Archaeology* 22 (2): 147–167.

Sherratt, Andrew. 1993. "What Would a Bronze-Age World System Look Like? Relations Between Temperate Europe and the Mediterranean in Later Prehistory." *Journal of European Archaeology* 1 (2): 1–57.

Sherratt, Andrew. 1995. "Fata Morgana: Illusion and Reality in 'Greco-Barbarian Relations'." *Cambridge Archaeological Journal* 5 (1): 139–156.

Sherratt, Andrew. 2007. "Alcohol and Its Alternatives: Symbol and Substance in Pre-Industrial Cultures." In *Consuming Habits: Global and Historical Perspectives on How Cultures Define Drugs*, edited by Jordan Goodman, Paul E. Lovejoy, and Andrew Sherratt, 11–45. London: Routledge.

Sherratt, Andrew, and Susan Sherratt. 1991. "From Luxuries to Commodities: The Nature of Mediterranean Bronze Age Trading Systems." In *Bronze Age Trade in the Mediterranean: Papers Presented at the Conference Held at Rewley House, Oxford in December 1989*, edited by N. H. Gale, 351–386. Jonsered: Paul Åströms Verlag.

Sherratt, Susan. 2003. "Visible Writing: Questions of Script and Identity in Early Iron Age Greece and Cyprus." *Oxford Journal of Archaeology* 22 (3): 225–242.

Sherratt, Susan, and Andrew Sherratt. 1993. "The Growth of the Mediterranean Economy in the Early First Millennium BC." *World Archaeology* 24 (3): 361–378.

Sherwin-White, Susan, and Amélie Kuhrt. 1993. *From Samarkhand to Sardis: A New Approach to the Seleucid Empire*. London: Duckworth.

Shipley, Graham. 1984. *A History of Samos, 800–188 BC*. Oxford: Clarendon.

Shipley, Graham. 2000. *The Greek World After Alexander, 323–30 B.C.* London: Routledge.

Sjoberg, Gideon. 1960. *The Preindustrial City: Past and Present*. Glencoe, IL: The Free Press.

Skinner, Joseph. 2012. *The Invention of Greek Ethnography: From Homer to Herodotus* Oxford: Oxford University Press.

Small, Alistair, ed. 1996. *Subject and Ruler: The Cult of the Ruling Power in Classical Antiquity: Papers Presented at a Conference Held in the University of Alberta on April 13–15, 1994 to Celebrate the 65th Anniversary of Duncan Fishwick*. Ann Arbor MI: Journal of Roman Archaeology.

Smith, Christopher. 1996. *Early Rome and Latium: Economy and Society c. 1000 - 500 BC*. Oxford: Oxford University Press.

Smith, Christopher. 2005. "The Beginnings of Urbanization in Rome." In *Mediterranean Urbanization 800–600 BC*, edited by Robin Osborne and Barry Cunliffe, 91–111. Oxford: Oxford University Press.

Smith, Michael E. 1989. "Cities, Towns and Urbanism: Comment on Sanders and Webster." *American Anthropologist* 91 (2): 454–460.

Smith, Michael E. 2002. "The Earliest Cities." In *Urban Life: Readings in the Anthropology of the City*, edited by George Gmelch and Walter P. Zenner, 3–19. Prospect Heights, IL: Waveland Press.

Smith, Michael E. 2009. "V. Gordon Childe and the Urban Revolution: A Historical Perspective on a Revolution in Urban Studies." *Town Planning Review* 80 (1): 3–29.

Smith, Michael E. 2010. "The Archaeological Study of Neighborhoods and Districts in Ancient Cities." *Journal of Anthropological Archaeology* 29: 137–154.

Smith, Michael E., ed. 2012. *The Comparative Archaeology of Complex Societies.* New York: Cambridge University Press.

Smith, Monica L., ed. 2003. *The Social Construction of Ancient Cities.* Washington, DC: Smithsonian Institution Press.

Smith, Monica L. 2019. *Cities. The first 6000 years.* London: Simon and Schuster UK.

Snodgrass, A. M. 1971. *The Dark Age of Greece: An Archaeological Survey of the Eleventh to the Eighth Centuries B.C.* Edinburgh: Edinburgh University Press.

Snodgrass, A. M. 1986. "Interaction By Design: The Greek City State." In *Peer Polity Interaction and Socio-Political Change*, edited by Colin Renfrew and John F. Cherry, 47–58. Cambridge: Cambridge University Press.

Snodgrass, A. M. 1989. "The Coming of the Iron Age in Greece: Europe's earliest Bronze / Iron Transition." In *The Bronze Age-Iron Age Transition in Europe: Aspects of Continuity and Change in European Societies c. 1200 to 500 B.C.*, edited by Marie-Louise Sørensen and Roger Thomas, 22–35. Oxford: British Archaeological Reports.

Snodgrass, A. M. 1994. "The Growth and Standing of the Early Western Colonies." In *The Archaeology of Greek Colonization: Essays Dedicated to Sir John Boardman*, edited by Gocha R Tsetskhladze and Franco De Angelis, 1–10. Oxford: Oxford Committee for Archaeology.

Snodgrass, A. M. 2006. *Archaeology and the Emergence of Greece* New York: Cornell University Press.

Snodgrass, Anthony. 1980. *Archaic Greece: The Age of Experiment.* London: J. M. Dent.

Sørensen, Marie-Louise, and Roger Thomas, eds. 1989. *The Bronze Age-Iron Age Transition in Europe: Aspects of Continuity and Change in European Societies c. 1200 to 500 B.C.* 2 vols. Oxford: British Archaeological Reports.

Spawforth, A. J. S., and Susan Walker. 1986. "The World of the Panhellenion. II: Three Dorian Cities." *Journal of Roman Studies* 76: 88–105.

Spawforth, Antony. 1994. "Symbol of Unity? The Persian-Wars Tradition in the Roman Empire." In *Greek Historiography*, edited by Simon Hornblower, 233–2247. Oxford: Clarendon.

Spivey, Nigel, and Simon Stoddart. 1990. *Etruscan Italy.* London: Batsford.

Squatriti, Paulo. 2002. "Review Article: Mohammed, the Early Medieval Mediterranean, and Charlemagne." *Early Medieval Europe* 11 (3): 263–279.

Steinby, Margareta. 1993. "L'organizzazione produttiva dei laterizi: un modello interpretativo per l'*instrumentum* in genere?" In *The Inscribed Economy: Production and Distribution in the Roman Empire in the Light of Instrumentum Domesticum,* edited by William Vernon Harris, 139–143. Portsmouth, RI: Journal of Roman Archaeology.

Stewart, Andrew F. 2004. *Attalos, Athens, and the Akropolis: The Pergamene "Little Barbarians" and their Roman and Renaissance Legacy.* Cambridge: Cambridge University Press.

Stoddart, Simon, and James Whitley. 1988. "The Social Context of Literacy in Archaic Greece and Etruria." *Antiquity* 62: 761–772.

Storey, Glenn R. 1997. "The Population of Ancient Rome." *Antiquity* 71 (274): 966–978.

Storey, Glenn R., ed. 2006. *Urbanism in the Preindustrial World: Cross-Cultural Approaches.* Tuscaloosa: University of Alabama Press.

Stringer, Chris. 2011. *The Origin of Our Species.* London: Penguin.

Swain, Simon. 1996. *Hellenism and Empire: Language, Classicism and Power in the Greek World, AD 50–250.* Oxford: Clarendon Press.

Sweetman, Rebecca J. 2007. "Roman Knossos: The Nature of a Globalized City." *American Journal of Archaeology* 111 (1): 61–81.

Sweetman, Rebecca J., ed. 2011. *Roman Colonies in the First Century of Their Foundation.* Oxford: Oxbow Books.

Szuchmann, Jeffrey, ed. 2009. *Nomads, Tribes, and the State in the Ancient Near East: A Cross-Disciplinary Perspective.* Chicago: Oriental Institute of the University of Chicago.

Tacoma, Laurens E. 2016. *Moving Romans: Migration to Rome in the Principate.* Oxford: Oxford University Press.

Tainter, Joseph A. 1988. *The Collapse of Complex Societies.* Cambridge: Cambridge University Press.

Taylor, Timothy. 2001. "Believing the Ancients: Quantitative and Qualitative Dimensions of Slavery and the Slave Trade in Later Prehistoric Eurasia." *World Archaeology* 33 (1): 27–43.

Taylor, Timothy. 2010. *The Artificial Ape: How Technology Changed the Course of Human Evolution.* Basingstoke: MacMillan.

Tchernia, André. 1983. "Italian Wine in Gaul at the end of the Republic." In *Trade in the Ancient Economy,* edited by Peter Garnsey, Keith Hopkins, and C. R. Whittaker, 87–104. London.

Terrenato, Nicola. 2019. *The Early Roman Expansion into Italy.* Cambridge: Cambridge University Press.

Thomas, Rosalind. 1989. *Oral Tradition and Written Record in Classical Athens.* Cambridge: Cambridge University Press.

Thomas, Rosalind. 2000. *Herodotus in Context: Ethnography, Science and the Art of Persuasion.* Cambridge: Cambridge University Press.

Thonemann, Peter. 2011. *The Maeander Valley: A Historical Geography from Antiquity to Byzantium.* Cambridge: Cambridge University Press.

Thonemann, Peter, ed. 2013. *Roman Phrygia: Culture and Society.* Cambridge: Cambridge University Press.

Tobin, Jennifer. 1997. *Herodes Attikos and the City of Athens: Patronage and Conflict under the Antonines.* Amsterdam: Gieben.

Tosi, Giovanna, ed. 2003. *Gli edifici per spettacoli nell'Italia romana.* 2 vols. Rome: Quasar.

Trautmann, Thomas R., Gillian Feeley-Harnik, and C. Mitani. 2011. "Deep Kinship." In *Deep History: The Architecture of Past and Present,* edited by Andrew Shryock and Daniel Lord Smail, 160–188. Berkeley: University of California Press.

Trigger, Bruce G. 2003. *Understanding Early Civilizations.* New York: Cambridge University Press.

Tsetskhladze, Gocha R. 2006a. *Greek Colonisation: An Account of Greek Colonies and Other Settlements Overseas.* Vol. 1, *Mnemosyne Supplements.* Leiden: Brill.

Tsetskhladze, Gocha R. 2006b. "Introduction: Revisiting Greek Colonisation." In *Greek Colonisation: An Account of Greek Colonies and Other Settlements Overseas,* edited by Gocha R Tsetskhladze, xxiii–lxxx. Leiden: Brill.

Tsetskhladze, Gocha R., and Franco De Angelis, eds. 1994. *The Archaeology of Greek Colonization: Essays Dedicated to Sir John Boardman.* Oxford: Oxford Committee for Archaeology.

Ucko, Peter, Ruth Tringham, and G. W. Dimbleby, eds. 1972. *Man: Settlement and Urbanism.* London: Duckworth.

Underwood, Douglas. 2019. *(Re)using Ruins: Public Building in the Cities of the Late Antique West, A.D. 300–600.* Leiden: Brill.

van Bremen, Riet. 1996. *The Limits of Participation: Women and Civic Life in the Greek East in the Hellenistic and Roman Periods.* Amsterdam: J. C. Gieben.

Van Dam, Raymond. 2010. *Rome and Constantinople: Rewriting Roman History During Late Antiquity.* Waco TX: Baylor University Press.

Van De Mieroop, Marc. 1997. *The Ancient Mesopotamian City.* Oxford: Oxford University Press.

van Dommelen, Peter. 1998. *On Colonial Grounds: A Comparative Study of Colonialism and Rural Settlement in First Millennium BC West Central Sardinia.* Leiden: Faculty of Archaeology, Leiden University.

van Dommelen, Peter. 2002. "Ambiguous Matters: Colonialism and Local Identities in Punic Sardinia." In *The Archaeology of Colonialism,* edited by Claire L Lyons and John K. Papadopolous, 121–147. Los Angeles: Getty Research Institute.

van Dommelen, Peter. 2005. "Urban Foundations? Colonial Settlement and Urbanization in the Western Mediterranean." In *Mediterranean Urbanization 800–600 BC,* edited by Robin Osborne and Barry Cunliffe, 143–167. Oxford: Oxford University Press.

van Dommelen, Peter. 2012. "Colonialism and Migration in the Ancient Mediterranean." *Annual Review of Anthropology* 41 (1): 393–409.

van Dommelen, Peter, and Nicola Terrenato, eds. 2007. *Articulating Local Cultures: Power and Identity Under the Expanding Roman Republic.* Portsmouth, RI: Journal of Roman Archaeology.

van Driel-Murray, Carol. 1995. "Gender in Question." In *TRAC 1992: Theoretical Roman Archaeology: Second Conference Proceedings*, edited by Peter Rush, 3–21. Avebury: Aldershot.

van Nijf, Onno. 2001. "Local Heroes: Athletics, Festivals and Elite Self-Fashioning in the Roman East." In *Being Greek Under Rome: Cultural Identity, the Second Sophistic and the Development of Empire*, edited by Simon Goldhill, 309–334. Cambridge: Cambridge University Press.

van Nijf, Onno M., and Christina G. Williamson. 2015. "Re-Inventing Traditions: Connecting Contests in the Hellenistic and Roman World." In *Reinventing 'The Invention of Tradition'? Indigenous Pasts and the Roman Present. Conference Cologne 14–15 November 2013*, edited by Dietrich Boschung, Alexandra W. Busch, and Miguel John Versluys, 95–111. Paderborn: Wilhelm Fink.

Van Oyen, Astrid. 2015. "The Moral Architecture of Villa Storage in Italy in the 1st Century BC." *Journal of Roman Archaeology* 28 (1): 97–123.

Vansina, Jan. 1985. *Oral Tradition as History*. London: James Curry.

Vasunia, Phiroze. 2013. *The Classics and Colonial India*. Oxford: Oxford University Press.

Veyne, Paul. 1976. *Le pain et le cirque: Sociologie historique d'un pluralisme politique*. Paris: Seuil.

Villing, Alexandra, and Udo Schlotzhauer, eds. 2006. *Naukratis: Greek Diversity in Egypt*. London: British Museum Press.

Virlouvet, Catherine. 1995. *Tessera frumentaria: Les procedures de distribution du blé public a Rome a la fin de la republique et au debut de l'empire*. Vol. 286, *Bibliothèque des écoles françaises d'Athènes et de Rome* Rome: École française de Rome.

Virlouvet, Catherine. 2011. "Claude Nicolet et les Mégapoles méditerranéennes." *Cahiers du Centre Gustave Glotz* 22: 135–140.

Vittinghof, Friederch. 1952. *Römische Kolonisation und Bürgerrechtspolitik unter Caesar und Augustus*. Mainz: Verlag der Akademie der Wissenschaften und der Literatur.

von Falkenhausen, Lothar. 2008. "Stages in the Development of 'Cities' in Pre-Imperial China." In *The Ancient City: New Perspectives on Urbanism in the Old and New World*, edited by Joyce Marcus and Jeremy A. Sabloff, 209–228. Santa Fe: School for Advance Research Press.

Wachsmann, Shelley. 2000. "Some Notes on Mediterranean Seafaring in the Second Millennium BC." In *The Wall Paintings of Thera: Proceedings of the first International Symposium*, edited by Susan Sherratt, 803–824. Athens: Thera Foundation.

Wallace-Hadrill, Andrew. 2008. *Rome's Cultural Revolution*. New York: Cambridge University Press.

Ward-Perkins, Bryan. 1984. *From Classical Antiquity to the Middle Ages: Urban Public Building in Northern and Central Italy AD 300–850*. Oxford: Oxford University Press.

Ward-Perkins, Bryan. 2005. *The Fall of Rome and the End of Civilization*. Oxford: Oxford University Press.

Ward-Perkins, J. B. 1970. "From Republic to Empire: Reflections on the Early Provincial Architecture of the Roman West." *Journal of Roman Studies* 60: 1–19.

Weber, Max. 1958. *The City*. New York: The Free Press.

Wees, Hans van. 1992. *Status Warriors: War, Violence and Society in Homer and History*. Amsterdam: J. C. Gieben.

Wells, Jonathon C. K., and Jay T. Stock. 2012. "The Biology of Human Migration: The Ape That Won't Commit?" In *Causes and Consequences of Human Migration: An Evolutionary Perspective*, edited by Michael H. Crawford and Benjamin C. Campbell, 45–64. New York: Cambridge University Press.

Wengrow, David. 2006. *The Archaeology of Early Egypt: Social Transformations in North-East Africa, 10,000 to 2650 BC*. Cambridge: Cambridge University Press.

Wengrow, David. 2010. *What Makes Civilization? The Ancient Near East and the Future of the West*. Oxford: Oxford University Press.

Wengrow, David. 2014. *The Origins of Monsters: Image and Cognition in the First Age of Mechanical Reproduction*. Princeton, NJ: Princeton University Press.

Wertime, Theodore A., and James D. Muhly, eds. 1980. *The Coming of the Age of Iron*. New Haven, CT: Yale University Press.

West, Stephanie. 2003. "'The Most Marvellous of All Seas': The Greek Encounter with the Euxine." *Greece & Rome* 50 (2): 151–167.

White, Iain, and Paul O'Hare. 2014. "From Rhetoric to Reality: Which Resilience, Why Resilience, and Whose Resilience In Spatial Planning?" *Environment and Planning C: Government and Policy* 32 (5): 934–950.

Whitelaw, Todd. 2000. "Beyond the Palace: A Century of Excavation in Europe's Oldest City." *Bulletin of the Institute of Classical Studies* 44 (22): 223–226.

Whitelaw, Todd. 2017. "The Development and Character of Urban Communities in Prehistoric Crete in their Regional Context: A Preliminary Study." In *Minoan Architecture and Urbanism: New Perspectives on an Ancient Built Environment*, edited by Quentin Letesson and Carl Knappett, 114–180. Oxford: Oxford University Press.

Whitley, James. 1991. *Style and Society in Dark Age Greece: The Changing Face of a Pre-Literate Society, 1100–700 BC*. Cambridge: Cambridge University Press.

Whitley, James. 2001. *The Archaeology of Ancient Greece*. Cambridge: Cambridge University Press.

Whitmarsh, Tim, ed. 2010. *Local Knowledge and Microidentities in the Imperial Greek World*. Cambridge: Cambridge University Press.

Whittaker, C. R. 1978. "Carthaginian Imperialism in the Fifth and Fourth Centuries." In *Imperialism in the Ancient World*, edited by Peter Garnsey and C. R. Whittaker, 59–90. Cambridge: Cambridge University Press.

Whittow, Mark. 1990. "Ruling the Late Roman and Early Byzantine City: A Continuous History." *Past and Present* 129: 3–29.

Wickham, Chris. 1984. "The Other Transition: From the Ancient World to Feudalism." *Past and Present* 103: 3–36.

Wickham, Chris. 2005. *Framing the Early Middle Ages: Europe and the Mediterranean, 400–800*. Oxford: Oxford University Press.

Wickham, Chris. 2009. *The Inheritance of Rome: A History of Europe from 400 to 1000*. London: Allen Lane.

Wilkinson, Toby C., Philip, Graham, Bradbury, J., Dunford, R., Donoghue, D., Galiatsatos, N., Lawrence, D., Ricci, A., and Smith, S.L. 2014. "Contextualizing Early Urbanization: Settlement Cores, Early States and Agro-Pastoral Strategies in the Fertile Crescent During the Fourth and Third Millennia BC." *Journal of World Prehistory* 27: 43–109.

Wilkinson, Toby C., Susan Sherratt, and John Bennet, eds. 2011. *Interweaving Worlds: Systemic Interactions in Eurasia, 7th to the 1st Millennia BC.* Oxford: Oxbow Books.

Williams, Jonathan H. C. 2001. *Beyond the Rubicon: Romans and Gauls in Northern Italy.* Oxford: Oxford University Press.

Wilson, Andrew. 2011. "City Sizes and Urbanization in the Roman Empire." In *Settlement, Urbanization, and Population*, edited by Alan Bowman and Andrew Wilson, 161–195. Oxford: Oxford University Press.

Wilson, Edward O. 2012. *The Social Conquest of Earth.* New York: Liveright Publishing Corporation.

Wirth, Louis. 1938. "Urbanism as a Way of Life." *American Journal of Sociology* 44 (1): 1–24.

Wiseman, T. Peter. 1995. *Remus: A Roman Myth.* Cambridge: Cambridge University Press.

Witcher, Robert. 2000. "Globalisation and Roman Imperialism: Perspectives on Identities in Roman Italy." In *The Emergence of State Identities in Italy in the First Millennium B.C.*, edited by Edward Herring and Kathryn Lomas, 213–225. London: Accordia Research Institute.

Woods, Christopher, ed. 2010. *Visible Language: Inventions of Writing in the Ancient Middle East and Beyond.* Chicago: Oriental Institute of the University of Chicago.

Woolf, Greg. 1993. "Rethinking the Oppida." *Oxford Journal of Archaeology* 12 (2): 223–234.

Woolf, Greg. 1994. "Power and the Spread of Writing in the West." In *Literacy and Power in the Ancient World*, edited by Alan Bowman and Greg Woolf, 84–98. Cambridge: Cambridge University Press.

Woolf, Greg. 1997. "The Roman Urbanization of the East." In *The Early Roman Empire in the East*, edited by Susan E Alcock, 1–14. Oxford: Oxbow Books.

Woolf, Greg. 1998. *Becoming Roman: The Origins of Provincial Civilization in Gaul.* Cambridge: Cambridge University Press.

Woolf, Greg. 2000. "Urbanization and Its Discontents in Early Roman Gaul." In *Romanization and the City: Creations, Transformations and Failures*, edited by Elizabeth Fentress, 115–132. Portsmouth, RI: Journal of Roman Archaeology.

Woolf, Greg. 2011. *Tales of the Barbarians: Ethnography and Empire in the Roman West.* Malden, MA: Wiley-Blackwell.

Woolf, Greg. 2012. *Rome: An Empire's Story.* New York: Oxford University Press.

Woolf, Greg. 2016. "Movers and Stayers." In *Migration and Mobility in the Early Roman Empire*, edited by Luuk de Ligt and Laurens E. Tacoma, 440–463. Leiden: Brill.

Woolf, Greg. 2017. "Moving Peoples in the Early Roman Empire." In *The Impact of Mobility and Migration in the Roman Empire*, edited by Elio Lo Cascio, Laurens E. Tacoma, and Miriam J. Groen-Vallinga, 25–41. Leiden: Brill.

Wörrle, Michael. 1988. *Stadt und Fest in kaiserzeitlichen Kleinasien: Studien zu einer agonistischen Stiftung aus Oinoanda, Vestigia*. Munich: C. H. Beck.

Wright, Rita P. 2010. *The Ancient Indus: Urbanism, Economy, and Society*. New York: Cambridge University Press.

Yegul, Fikret K. 1992. *Baths and Bathing in the Roman World*. Cambridge, MA: MIT Press.

Yoffee, Norman. 2005. *Myths of the Archaic State: Evolution of the Earliest Cities, States, and Civilizations*. Cambridge: Cambridge University Press.

Yoffee, Norman. 2009. "Making Ancient Cities Plausible." *Reviews in Anthropology* 38: 264–289.

Yoffee, Norman, ed. 2015. *The Cambridge World History III: Early Cities in Comparative Perspective 4000 BCE–1200 CE*. Cambridge: Cambridge University Press.

Yoffee, Norman, and George L. Cowgill, eds. 1988. *The Collapse of Ancient States and Civilizations*. Tucson: University of Arizona Press.

Zadneprovsky, Y. A. 1995. "Early Urban Developments in Central Asia." *Iran* 33: 155–159.

Zaghetto, Luca. 2007. "Iconography and Language: The Missing Link." In *Literacy and the State in the Ancient Mediterranean*, edited by Kathryn Lomas, R. D. Whitehouse, and J. B. Wilkins, 171–181. London: Accordia Research Institute.

Zanker, Paul, ed. 1976. *Hellenismus in Mittelitalien*. 2 vols. Göttingen.

Zanker, Paul. 1988. *The Power of Images in the Age of Augustus*. Ann Arbor: University of Michigan Press.

Zeder, Melinda A. 2008. "Domestication and Early Agriculture in the Mediterranean Basin: Origins, Diffusion, and Impact." *Proceedings of the National Academy of Sciences of the United States of America* 105 (33): 11587–11604.

Zugtriegel, Gabriel. 2017. *Colonization and Subalternity in Classical Greece: Experience of the Nonelite Population*. Cambridge: Cambridge University Press.

Zuiderhoek, Arjan. 2009. *The Politics of Munificence in the Roman Empire: Citizens, Elites and Benefactors in Asia Minor*. Cambridge: Cambridge University Press.

Zuiderhoek, Arjan. 2016. *The Ancient City: Key Themes in Ancient History*. Cambridge: Cambridge University Press.

Index

For the benefit of digital users, indexed terms that span two pages (e.g., 52–53) may, on occasion, appear on only one of those pages.